The Way of Life

The Rediscovered Teachings of the Twelve Jewish Apostles to the Gentiles

The Didache
Copyright © 2017 by Vine of David, a publishing ministry of
First Fruits of Zion, Inc.

Design, editing, and compiling: Jerusalem, Israel
Translation: Vine of David
Printing and distribution: USA

Comments and questions may be sent to: feedback@vineofdavid.org

Vine of David is an imprint of the ministry of First Fruits of Zion dedicated to providing liturgical resources for the Messianic Jewish movement and to resurrecting the voices of Messianic pioneers and luminaries. If you would like to assist in the publication of these voices from the past, you can sponsor the and publication of their important works by visiting www.vineofdavid.org for needs and opportunities.

The Bram Center for Messianic Jewish Learning is in the heart of Jerusalem. Short term learning, day tours, or to visit The Bram Center please write to: info@thebramcenter.org.

First Fruits of Zion
Israel / United States

US Distribution: PO Box 649, Marshfield, Missouri 65706-0649 USA
Phone: (417) 468-2741   Web: www.ffoz.org

ISBN: 978-1-941534-24-3 : Hardcover
ISBN: 978-1-941534-92-2 : Softcover

Also available from Vine of David:
The Sabbath Table
The Concealed Light
The Everlasting Jew
Window on Mount Zion
The Siege of Jerusalem
Testimony to Israel
The Delitzch Hebrew Gospels
Vine of David Haggadah
Meal of Messiah
Love and the Messianic Age

First Fruits of Zion: www.ffoz.org
Vine of David: www.vineofdavid.org

The Way of Life

The Rediscovered Teachings of the Twelve Jewish Apostles to the Gentiles

Didache: A New Translation and Messianic Jewish Commentary

TOBY JANICKI

Table of Contents

Preface	vii
Layout and Features	ix
Foreword	xi
Introduction	1

THE DIDACHE
Greek and English Text	25

COMMENTARY ON THE TEXT OF THE DIDACHE
Chapter One	51
Chapter Two	87
Chapter Three	129
Chapter Four	169
Chapter Five	207
Chapter Six	235
Chapter Seven	257
Chapter Eight	293
Chapter Nine	329
Chapter Ten	365
Chapter Eleven	393
Chapter Twelve	427
Chapter Thirteen	443
Chapter Fourteen	469
Chapter Fifteen	493
Chapter Sixteen	519
Conclusion	555
Appendices	557

Preface

The first time I read through the Didache was in 2006. I had previously heard about the book in Bible College, and occasionally I came across quotes and citations of the Didache in various books and Bible commentaries, but the document never struck me as being particularly significant. It was not until I was about to go on a trip to Israel that I decided to print out a I had found online and read it on the long flight. My colleague Daniel Lancaster had been talking to me about the importance of the work and his desire to see it examined through a Messianic Jewish lens. This book would turn out to be one of the most pivotal reads of my life.

As I read through the Didache, I felt as if I was traveling back in time. I felt as though I was sitting at the feet of the earliest Jewish disciples of Yeshua as they taught me what daily Torah life should look like for Gentile believers in Messiah. I found it to be an incredible work—thoroughly Jewish and thoroughly Messianic. Over time the Didache would have a major impact on my practice as a Messianic Gentile. I began to wonder why it is that more people in the Messianic Jewish movement don't study this document.

Then I realized the problem. As I began studying commentaries on the Didache, reading a plethora of books and articles, I discovered two things. First, on a popular level, most Didache studies were dominated by denominational church interpretations, which were not seeking to put the Didache back into its Jewish context. Second, those who were studying it from a Jewish perspective were doing so primarily on an academic level, which largely left laymen in the dust. I recognized the need for a fresh of the Didache with a commentary from a Messianic Jewish perspective.

The goal of this book is to take the best scholarship on the Didache and unpack it for the Messianic Jewish and Gentile world. That's not to say that I have adopted a purely popular tone. The nature of the material makes an academic reading and discussion necessary. At the same time, I tried to add a devotional element that helps the reader apply the words of the Didache for spiritual instruction and growth.

We chose to publish this work under our Vine of David imprint in keeping with the objectives of this sister ministry of First Fruits of Zion. Vine of David was created, in part, to resurrect Messianic Jewish voices from the past and present them to the modern Messianic movement. The Didache is such a work, written by devout Messianic Jews who sought to bring the message of the kingdom of

heaven to the nations. The Didache will assist both Messianic Jews and Gentiles in their life of discipleship and Torah.

I would like to thank Boaz Michael for assigning this project to me, for believing in this work, and for giving me his full support and commitment. Without him, this book would remain an unrealized dream. I would also like to thank my colleague Daniel Lancaster for initially suggesting that I read the Didache and for his countless hours spent reviewing the material and helping me sharpen the message of the book. I am also indebted to Aaron Eby for his work on the and checking the Hebrew throughout. Additionally, thanks to Sheldon Wilson, Jeremiah Michael, and Ronald Gilden for reviewing each chapter and offering many helpful suggestions and corrections. I would also like to thank Henri Goulet for his check of the Greek text. Thank you as well to the rest of the First Fruits of Zion staff for all your various roles in the many stages of production of this book. Last, but not least, I want to thank my wife, Shannon, and my four children, Aharon, Hannah, Isaac, and Abigail, for your support as I often spent many late hours working on the manuscript. Whether you know it or not, my conversations with each of you about the developing material influenced the work, and many of your ideas are represented within.

The Didache can help Gentile believers navigate their way through the obligations of discipleship and Torah life while maintaining their unique identity alongside the Jewish people. My prayer is that this book is helpful not only to Messianic Gentiles but to Messianic Jews as well. Although the apostles created the original Didache as an initiation for new Gentile disciples of Messiah, there is much here for Jewish believers as well. As our title suggests, the Didache presents the Way of Life and urges us to make choices every day that keep us on that path. May this work be fruitful in helping all of us choose life.

Toby Janicki
10 SHEVAT 5777

Toby Janicki is the director of the 12-21 Messianic Youth Initiative of First Fruits of Zion. He also contributes regularly to *Messiah Journal*, and has written several books and articles including *God-Fearers: Gentiles and the God of Israel*. Toby has a bachelor's degree in Practical Theology from Christ for the Nations Institute in Dallas, Texas.

Layout and Features

The commentary for each chapter is divided into two parts. Each chapter begins with an overview discussing the main theme of the chapter, and fleshes out certain topics that need to be understood in some detail to get the full context of the text. The second section is that of the commentary proper. This section will go verse by verse, and builds upon the overview, getting into more specific detail within the text.

Overview

Commentary

Practical Application

Chapters 7 through 15 contain a section in the overview entitled "Practical Application." While the immediate application of chapters 1 through 6 can be ascertained from the commentary and chapter 16 is an apocalypse, the other chapters can be slightly challenging when it comes to applying the instructions within for everyday application today. In an effort to aid with that process the Practical Application section has been added to those chapters.

Foreword

Ever since the Didache's rediscovery and publication, scholars have debated its origin, its province, its authorship, its readership, its significance, and ultimately, its meaning. Is it an authentic first-century document or a later redaction of one transmitting authentic strands of apostolic tradition? Or is it a Jewish document retrofitted for use by early Christians? Or is it a Christian ecclesiastical document intended to clarify points of church order? Theories abound, and interpretations vary widely.

Toby Janicki's commentary interacts with earlier Didache scholarship, but it starts with a unique set of assumptions. Janicki approaches the Didache assuming that it is simultaneously the work of first-century Judaism and an apostolic document transmitting teaching from the early Jewish Yeshua-followers to Gentile communities of Yeshua-disciples. From this perspective, we could compare the Didache with Pauline instruction to Gentile communities of disciples in the Diaspora. The advantage of this approach is that it dispels the argument about the document's origins, Christian or Jewish, by assuming both. In other words, Janicki reads the Didache as a work of first-century Messianic Judaism.

Today the term Messianic Judaism refers to the religion of Jewish disciples of Yeshua who accept the teachings of Yeshua of Nazareth but nonetheless retain their Jewish identity and religious practice. Messianic Judaism has been defined by Boaz Michael of First Fruits of Zion as the practice of Judaism in light of the revelation of the New Testament. Messianic Jewish teachers maintain that neither Yeshua nor his first followers envisioned a separate and distinct faith movement outside of or disconnected from Judaism. They never broke with Judaism or started a new religion but rather understood themselves as a sect within the Jewish people of their day, or to say it another way, as one of the many Judaisms of the first century. This perspective sees the first Christians as neither fish nor fowl, but rather, as devout Jews, faithful to the Torah and Jewish tradition, loyal to Yeshua the Nazarene (whom they believed to be both the Messiah and raised from the dead), and proclaiming his message of repentance and the coming kingdom announced by the prophets. They believed Yeshua to be the promised Messiah, yet they remained faithful Jews within the covenant of Torah. Their writings and perspectives, including all the texts comprising the New Testament, must be read within that paradigm.

Within that context, the Didache fits quite naturally as a solution to the "Gentile Problem," i.e., what to do with the large numbers of Gentiles in the Roman world who were abandoning the gods and adopting Jewish monotheism in the name of Yeshua of Nazareth. According to Paul's writings and Acts 15, such Gentiles were neither Jewish nor were they idolaters—neither fish nor fowl. A third category had emerged: Gentiles living in Jewish theological space. Paul's writings attempt to address that third category. A Messianic Jewish commentary is one that accepts this paradigm of continuity between Judaism and Yeshua-faith and interprets the text accordingly.

Janicki's commentary displays an acute understanding of the Jewish environment of the Gospels and how that understanding must, in turn, shape our interpretation of the Didache. I am reminded of a graduate seminar I attended many years ago in which we translated sections of the Didache and several other first-century Greek texts relevant to our study of the Gospels and the book of Acts. Remarkably, at no point in the discussion did even the possibility of the Didache's Jewish orientation arise. I regret to say that I witnessed this seminar produce yet another generation of Bible teachers who believed the Didache bears witness to the New Testament's alleged anti-Judaism.

Janicki's commentary moves in a refreshingly different direction. Aligning himself with a growing cadre of scholars, Janicki believes the teaching of the apostles to be Torah-centric and firmly anchored in the world of first-century Judaism. The apostles' teaching about ethical behavior was not based on a set of transcendent and ethereal truths taught by Yeshua—far from it. Rather, their teachings were based upon Yeshua's authoritative interpretation of the Torah. Janicki is thus very much on the mark when he argues that the Didache is "a thoroughly Jewish work authored by a Jewish believer" and in turn that the Didache functioned as "Halachah for Gentiles."

While Gentile believers were not expected to keep the Torah in precisely the same way as their Jewish brothers and sisters, they did need to know how to follow the law on a practical level *as it applied to them*. Citing the work of William Telfer, Janicki is again on the mark when he writes, "The Didache could be looked at as 'an expansion of' the Great Commission." In other words, the Didache is a concrete fulfillment of Yeshua's command to make disciples of all the nations, "teaching them to observe everything I commanded you" (Matthew 28:20).

Biblical scholars have on the one hand emphasized the importance of this command while on the other they have leached away its potency by denying that

Yeshua is here instructing his disciples to teach the nations to obey his interpretation of the Torah. While acknowledging the Jewish foundation upon which the early community of believers was built, they have failed to take that community's connection to first-century Judaism seriously. Janicki avoids these interpretive missteps and asserts the Didache to be an instruction manual for Gentiles entering the world of Judaism.

Because of these facts—recognizing the centrality of Torah in the teaching of Yeshua and the apostles and displaying a sensitivity to the Didache's inherent Jewishness and organic connection to Judaism—Janicki has produced a volume that provides us with invaluable insights about this important document. The limitations of space prevent me from enumerating those contributions here, so I am content to point the reader to one simple but very important example.

Consider Janicki's exposition of Didache 11.2, which discusses the community's reception of visiting teachers. The Didache, according to Janicki, asserts that visiting teachers who support and uphold the Torah "should be received as from the Lord." He buttresses this claim on one side with an appeal to Yeshua's programmatic statement in Matthew 5:17–20, in which the Messiah affirms that he came to fulfill the law and asserts that his followers must pursue a righteousness that exceeds the righteousness of the Pharisees. He supports this assertion on the other side with an appeal to mishnaic texts such as m.*Avot* 4:9 and m.*Horayot* 1:3, which affirm the importance of not abolishing any of the Torah's commandments.

The community that produced the Didache took Yeshua's command literally and sought to help Gentile converts in their midst grow in faith by helping them discover how they, too, were supposed to obey the Torah. Janicki's exposition of passages like Didache 11.2 will no doubt discomfort those who believe Yeshua's inauguration of the new covenant rendered the Law of Moses obsolete. Similarly, it will make some cringe to suggest that the early church (*ekklesia*) embraced Torah obedience as the benchmark of ethical behavior. Nevertheless, we must allow these texts to speak for themselves and wrestle with the evidence, whatever the outcome.

Up until now, most commentaries on the Didache have focused on the parting of ways between Christianity and Judaism, using the Didache as forensic evidence of that rupture. By definition, such an approach emphasizes the disjuncture between the two religions, and, as a result, the Didache is understood in antithesis to early Judaism. A Messianic Jewish approach to the text works in the opposite direction, emphasizing the commonalities and placing the Didache into context as a Jewish work consistent with first-century Judaism's universal values and teachings.

Toby Janicki has undertaken an enormous task in creating such a commentary on the Didache. He is not an academic, but his work stands on its own merit rather than his credentials. He demonstrates his autodidactic mastery of the field by deftly drawing on all the relevant sources: Jewish, Christian, and Roman. As a Gentile practicing Messianic Judaism, Janicki not only has a personal stake in the Didache, he also has a familiarity with Jewish sources and halachic issues as they relate to Gentiles—a primary concern of the Didache's instructions. That familiarity sheds light on otherwise obscure and arcane topics under discussion in the Didache.

I am grateful to First Fruits of Zion for taking the time and expending the effort necessary to produce this enormous contribution to the study of first-century Judaism, early Christianity, and the practice of Messianic Judaism. The Didache may have originally been intended as a guide and catechism for Gentile believers in Yeshua, but, as a Messianic Jew, I can attest that the Didache has just as much to say to me as it does to my Gentile brothers and sisters in Messiah.

Noel Rabinowitz, Ph.D.
PROFESSOR OF BIBLICAL STUDIES, THE ISRAEL STUDY CENTER
RISHON LEZION, ISRAEL

Prior to this post, Dr. Rabinowitz served as Associate Professor of New Testament Studies at the King's College in New York City.

Introduction

Since its recent discovery the Didache has become an increasingly popular book for both laymen and academics alike. It has drawn the attention of Jewish, Protestant, and Catholic scholars, and it is steadily gaining broad appeal to the average Christian reader as well. Despite the fact that the book itself is quite short, no longer than the canonical book of Galatians, a surprisingly vast number of articles and books have been written in attempts to decipher its content and origin. The book's decidedly Jewish content coupled with its early date make it an authentic window into the life of the earliest believing community during a time when that community was still firmly planted within Judaism.

The title Didache (Διδαχή) means "teaching" and is taken from the first word of the book. The work is also known by the longer title *The Teaching of the Twelve Apostles*[1] or the still longer *The Teaching of the Lord to the Gentiles through the Twelve Apostles*,[2] which is the complete first line of the book. The Didache consists of sixteen chapters. Although we will treat the entire work as one homogeneous unit, the academic community often refers to chapters 1–6 as a separate unit called the "Two Ways," which, quite probably, existed in some form before it was incorporated into the Didache. It appears that some early church writers referred to the entire Didache by this title as well.

History

The Didache enjoyed popularity among the early believers. Early church writers mentioned it and quoted from it frequently. Clement of Alexandria (second century), who is the earliest to mention the Didache, seemed to regard it as Scripture

---

1 Διδαχὴ τῶν δώδεκα ἀποστόλων. "The 'instructions of the apostles' was a household word already in the New Testament. In Acts the tradition is quoted that the first congregation 'persevered in *the instructions of the apostles* [διδαχῇ τῶν ἀποστόλων]' (Acts 2:42). Consistently, instruction, alongside preaching and healing, is an important activity of the apostles (Acts 4:2, 18, 5:21, 25, 42). "This is the threefold summary of the mission of Jesus and his representatives" (Peter J. Tomson, *'If This Be from Heaven ...' Jesus and the New Testament Authors in Their Relationship to Judaism* [Sheffield, England: Sheffield Academic, 2001], 381).

2 Διδαχὴ κυρίου διὰ τῶν δώδεκα ἀποστόλων τοῖς ἔθνεσιν, which is also found in the Latin *Doctrina*.

when he quoted from it in the *Stromata*.[3] Origen (early to mid-third century) treated it as Scripture in his *First Principles* while living in Alexandria,[4] but it appears that he changed his position after he moved to Caesarea, where the book was not viewed as canonical.[5]

Eusebius (third century) mentioned it by name, along with Revelation, as one of the books that some accept as canonical and others reject.[6] Athanasius (third century) listed the *Teaching of the Twelve Apostles* as one of the books "not indeed included in the Canon, but appointed by the Fathers to be read by those who newly join us, and who wish for instruction in the word of godliness."[7]

In the late fourth century, Rufinus of Aquileia described the Two Ways as "read in the churches but not brought forward for the confirmation of doctrine."[8] Didymus the Blind (fourth century) mentioned it by the title *The Teaching of the Apostolic Catechesis* in his commentary on the Psalms and Ecclesiastes.

The Didache also appears in a reworked form in the late fourth-century Apostolic Constitutions,[9] which accounts for the confusion of the two books in later church literature. However, by the fifth century, the Didache fell out of popularity and was thereafter referenced much less. The *Catalogue of the Sixty Canonical Books* (600 CE) mentions *The Travels and Teachings of the Apostles*, which is believed to be the Didache.[10] The *Stichometry* of Nicephorus (850 CE) listed it as a "rejected book," that is, apocryphal. The last known reference to the Didache was by John Zonaras in the twelfth century and Matthgens Blastares in the fourteenth

---

3   Clement of Alexandria, *Stromata* 1.20 quoting Didache 3.5. Also in his *Quis Dives Salvetur* 29, "He it is that poured wine on our wounded souls the blood of David's vine" seems to be a quote of a more developed version of "for the holy vine of your servant David" (Didache 9.2). See Daniel Nessim, "Didache, Torah, Gentile and Jew: A Paradigm of Unity and Distinction," (PhD diss., University of Exeter, forthcoming), 22.
4   Origen, *First Principles* 3.2.7: "And therefore Holy Scripture teaches us to receive all that happens as sent by God, knowing that without him no event occurs." The later part appears to be a quote of Didache 3.10: "Knowing that nothing happens apart from God."
5   Robert A. Kraft, *Barnabas and the Didache* (vol. 3 of *The Apostolic Fathers: A New and Commentary*; ed. Robert M. Grant; New York, NY: Thomas Nelson, 1965), 171.
6   Eusebius, *Ecclesiastical History* 3.25.4.
7   Athanasius, *Festal Letters* 39.
8   Rufinus of Aquileia, *On the Creed* 38.
9   Apostolic Constitutions 7.
10 Huub van de Sandt and David Flusser, *The Didache: Its Jewish Sources and Its Place in Early Judaism and Christianity* (Minneapolis, MN: Fortress, 2002), 3.

century,[11] but both mentioned it in such a way as to appear to indicate that they did not have access to an actual copy.

The Two Ways section of the Didache shows up separately in several early church documents. It appears along with contents similar to Didache 16, in the early second-century apocryphal Epistle of Barnabas,[12] placing it in competition with Clement of Alexandria's *Stromata* for the earliest patristic references to Didache material.[13] The Two Ways is found as well in the Latin *Doctrina Apostolorum* (second century), another important early textual witness to the Didache.[14] It is also found quoted or reworked throughout early church literature in documents such as the *Apostolic Church-Ordinance* (300 CE), the *Arabic Life of Shenoute* (fifth century), the *Rule of the Master* (sixth century) and the Chinese *Sutra of Hearing the Messiah* (seventh century).

Why did the Didache fall out of use? Scholars speculate that the "'primitive' concern of itinerant apostles, prophets, and teachers" coupled with its "meager ethical, ritual, and ecclesiastical provisions were too archaic to be reconciled with contemporary practice."[15] In other words, instead of answering why contemporary church practice did not reflect the instructions in the Didache, the church discarded the book as antiquated. The organizational structure of the church had moved far beyond the simple communities and concerns reflected in the document. As we shall see, the Didache was meant to introduce new Gentile initiates into the world of Jewish monotheism, Torah life, and Judaism—objectives that made the document no longer applicable to fully developed Christianity. Over time it fell into obscurity and oblivion.

Additionally, the Didache functioned as a primitive Church Order, and so was continually updated to keep it relevant for the communities that used it. For example, the Apostolic Constitutions (likewise, the Ethiopic Church Order) utilized the Didache, updated what they wanted to keep and discarded what was no longer

---

11 Roswell D. Hitchcock and Francis Brown, *Teaching of the Twelve Apostles: Recently Discovered and Published by Philotheos Bryennios, Metropolitan of Nicomedia* (Santa Clara, CA: Church History Publishing, 2001), xxxii.
12 Barnabas 18.1–21.1.
13 *Stromata* 1.20. See commentary on Didache 3.5.
14 For an English of the *Doctrina*, see Edgar J. Goodspeed, *The Apostolic Fathers: An American* (London, England: Independent, 1950), 5–7. Wherever the *Doctrina* is quoted in the commentary, we have based it on Goodspeed's. Goodspeed suggests that the *Doctrina* was a Latin of the Greek source used by the Didache for its Two Ways section. See "The Didache, Barnabas, and the Doctrina," *American Theological Review* 27 [1945]: 228–247.
15 Van de Sandt and Flusser, *The Didache*, 3.

relevant. Elements of the Apostolic Constitutions and other Church Orders can be seen in modern catechisms. This means that some of the teachings in the Didache—or minimally its function as a primitive Church Order—laid the groundwork for what became modern Church Orders. So while the Didache itself was lost, some of its teaching can still be found in some church documents even today.

Amazing Rediscovery

In 1873, Greek Orthodox archbishop Philotheos Bryennios was rummaging around in the monastery library of the Greek Covenant of the Holy Sepulchre in Istanbul when he discovered an ancient collection of Christian manuscripts bound in a single volume. Unbeknownst to him at the time, sandwiched between two longer works was the long-lost Greek text of the Didache. Years later Bryennios realized the treasure that he had found. The collection that Bryennios found was not actually published until 1883. The manuscript is dated by "Leon the scribe and sinner" to June 11, 1056, and it now resides in the Orthodox patriarchate in Jerusalem cataloged as *Codex Hierosolymitanus 54*.

Although Bryennios' manuscript includes the only complete version of the Didache found to date, other older fragments of the Didache have been discovered since then. In 1922, two Greek fragments containing sections of the Didache were discovered in Oxyrhynchus, Egypt.[16] The nature of the texts (now cataloged as *Oxyrhynchus Papyrus* 1782) was very close to the version found by Bryennios, thus helping to solidify the accuracy of *Codex Hierosolymitanus*. These fragments date back to the late fourth century, making them the oldest Didache manuscripts found to date and some 650 years older than *Codex Hierosolymitanus*.

A Coptic fragment from Cairo, Egypt was published in 1924. It dates back to the fifth century CE and is therefore the oldest textual witness for sections 10.3b through 12.2a.[17] It also includes some textual variants that deviate from *Codex Hierosolymitanus*, in particular an "ointment" prayer in chapter 10 after verse 7.

---

16 Didache 1.3b–4a, 2.7b– 3.2a. For the Greek text, see Kurt Niederwimmer, *The Didache: Hermeneia—A Critical and Historical Commentary on the Bible* (Minneapolis, MN: Fortress, 1998), 22. Also Bernard P. Grenfell and Arthur S. Hunt, *The Oxyrhynchus Papyri: Part XV*, (London, England: Oxford University, 1922) 12–15.

17 For an English , see G. Horner, "A New Papyrus Fragment of the 'Didache' in Coptic," *Journal of Theological Studies* 25 (1924): 225–231; F. Stanley Jones and Paul A. Mirecki, "Considerations on the Coptic Papyrus of the Didache," in *The Didache in Context: Essays on Its Text, History & Transmission* (ed. Clayton N. Jefford; Leiden, Holland: Brill, 1995), 47–87.

The next-to-last page of the Didache from the *Codex Hierosolymitanus*. The codex is housed in the Library of the Church of the Holy Sepulchre in Jerusalem. (Photo courtesy Murray Smith, Christ College, Sydney)

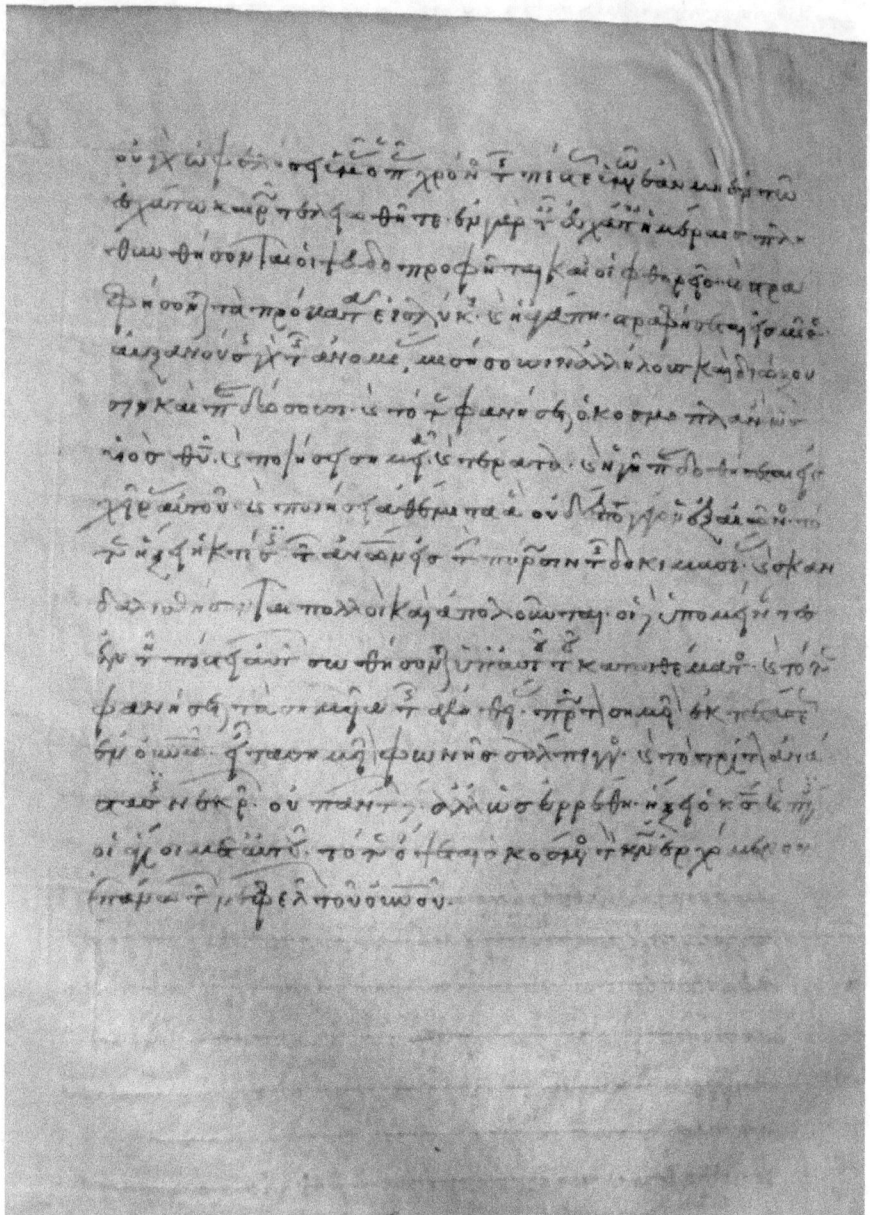

The last page of the Didache from the *Codex Hierosolymitanus*. The codex is housed in the Library of the Church of the Holy Sepulchre in Jerusalem. (Photo courtesy Murray Smith, Christ College, Sydney)

Additional fragments were inserted into and therefore preserved in The Ethiopic Church Order.[18] This indicates that at one point a complete version of the Didache appears to have circulated in the Ethiopic dialect.

A nearly complete Georgian version of the Didache, lacking only sections 1.5–6 and 13.5–7, was found in Constantinople in 1923 and copied by Simon Pheikrishvili.[19] One notable variation was the addition of the words "written in the year 90 or 100 after the Lord Christ" in the title. Although the original Georgian manuscript was never published, various copies of it have been made available in several works. Nevertheless, the original manuscript has since been lost, and most scholars feel that the work itself is a modern of *Codex Hierosolymitanus*.[20] While it still is an important work for Didache studies, "in light of its late and dubious tradition, the Georgian version is not to be regarded as an equal witness."[21]

Therefore, despite the fact that other manuscripts of the Didache have been found, *Codex Hierosolymitanus* remains the most complete and reliable version found to date. In turn, we will draw primarily from this manuscript in the commentary, but we will also mention significant variant readings where applicable.

Controversy

Even though the Didache itself is quite brief, there has been no shortage of controversy and debate surrounding its content and origin. Christian scholars were initially excited at the discovery of a long-lost early church text, but it was not long before some discomfort about the manuscript ensued. Roman Catholics appreciated the regulations on fasting and prayer but were dismayed that these so-called Eucharistic texts were missing some of the most important language of canonical Christian liturgy. On the other hand, Protestants were excited about the Eucharist omissions, but they were puzzled by the rigid disciplines such as fasting twice a week that seemed to betray a "works-based righteousness" suspiciously

---

18   Didache 11.3–13.7, 8.1–2a; and possibly a version of 6.2–3. For an English , see G. Horner, *The Statutes of the Apostles or Canones Ecclesiastici* (London, England: Williams & Norgate, 1904), 193–194.
19   Grigol Peradse collated the Georgian version with the Greek text, and today his work is all that remains of the Georgian version of the Didache. See Grigol Peradse, "Die Lehre der zwölf Apostel aus der georgischen Überlieferung" *Zeitschrift für die neutestamentliche Wissenschaft und die Kunde der älteren Kirche* 31 (1932): 111–116.
20   "It now appears, however, that the Georgian was actually a modern of the Didache, not an independent witness to its text" (Bart D. Erhman, ed., *Loeb Classical Library: The Apostolic Fathers Volume* 1 [trans. Bart D. Ehrman; London, England: Harvard University, 2005], 412–413).
21   Niederwimmer, *The Didache: Hermeneia*, 27.

reminiscent of the asceticism and spiritual disciplines of Roman Catholicism and Orthodoxy. Both sides attempted various interpretations and dating schemes to help place the Didache into their denominational paradigm.

Thomas O'Loughlin states, "The more any group bases their current practice on the assertion that they are doing/preaching what was done by either Jesus or the apostles, the more they will be antagonized by the Didache."[22] The key to appreciating the Didache is simply to let it speak for itself. While it is often tempting to try to find personal justification in the Didache, people of all denominations need to learn to approach the Didache on its own terms and not try to place it into their own theological box or religious practice.

Academic scholars have also engaged in a series of debates about the Didache. They disagree over the dating of the document: Does it indeed go back to the apostles, or is it a late composition from the fourth century? Others argue that parts of the Didache (in particular the Two Ways section) are not original but are rather adapted from earlier Jewish documents that circulated during the late Second Temple Period. Still others suggest that the Didache depends on the canonical Gospel of Matthew and on the book of James. Most scholars understand the document as pieced together from several different sources and not as one coherent unit.

For our purposes, we will take a conservative approach with the Didache, accepting the tradition that it was written by Jewish believers during or just after the Apostolic Era, viewing it as a single cohesive document (albeit comprised of earlier sources like the "Two Ways" and the teachings of Yeshua) that is firmly rooted within the Judaism of its day.

Composition Date

Most scholars generally agree that the Didache was probably written either in Egypt or, more likely, Syria or even Judea sometime between the late first to early second century.[23] Some speculate that it (or at least early portions of it) may have been written as early as 50 CE. This would mean that the Didache contains material that

---

[22] Thomas O'Loughlin, *The Didache: A Window on the Earliest Christians* (Grand Rapids, MI: Baker, 2010), 8.

[23] Joan Hazelden Walker writes, "I appreciate that just as this document went from Antioch eastwards at a very early date, so too, it could have travelled southwards, and that its original home may well have been in Jerusalem or thereabouts" (Walker, "A Pre-Marcan Dating for the Didache: Further Thoughts of a Liturgist," *Studia Biblica* 3 [1978]: 404).

is actually older than the canonical Gospels and was written during the generation after the Master's death.[24] As with the Gospels and the rabbinic law, the contents of the document probably circulated orally before landing in the Didache. In fact, its very structure suggests mnemonic devices lingering beneath the surface, "residual oral-aural clues in the manuscript."[25] While the Didache contains sayings of the Master, it appears that it preserves a strand of oral tradition independent of the earliest oral traditions of the canonical Gospels.[26]

One of the aspects of the document that betrays an early composition date is the fact that "the style and substance bear the mark of archaic simplicity."[27] The contents are devoid of the type of fanciful and Gnostic musings we find in other non-canonical material of the second century. Instead, the Didache is a halachic work containing practical instruction for everyday living. The Didache is also silent on the issue of persecution and devoid of the doctrinal and theological teachings that permeate the Pauline epistles. Even the relationship between Messiah and

---

24 Aaron Milavec, *The Didache: Text, , Analysis, and Commentary* (Collegeville, MN: Liturgical, 2003), ix.
25 Ibid., 57.
26 Ibid., xiii. Alan Garrow suspects that the gospel tradition in the Didache was used by Matthew in the composition of his gospel. He feels that the Didache might be a candidate for what scholars refer to as Q, the long-lost source used by both Matthew and Luke. See Alan J.P. Garrow, *The Gospel of Matthew's Dependence on the Didache* (New York, NY: Bloomsbury, 2012), and "An Extant Instance of 'Q,'" *New Testament Studies* 62 no. 3 (July, 2016): 398–417. Cf. Walker, "A Pre-Marcan Dating for the Didache," 403–411. Alternatively, the authors of the Didache may have had access to Q or to a Semitic version of something like it, and the Didache's Yeshua sayings represent their .
27 George Cantrell Allen, *The Didache: Or, the Teaching of the Twelve Apostles* (London, England: Astolat, 1903), xv.

the Father is expressed in primitive terminology. The Didache itself is free from any kind of creed:[28]

> The entire system of the Didache displays little taste for negotiating, defining, and defending the exalted titles and functions of Jesus. Rather, the Didache is taken up with the business of passing on the Way of Life revealed to its authors by the Father through his servant Jesus.[29]

This has caused some to question whether or not the Didache was written before Paul's letters or at the very least written without knowledge of them. Others speculate that Paul himself knew of the Didache and referred to it as the "teaching" in Romans 6:17 and Titus 1:9.[30] Some even suspect that Paul used its text in his writings, in particular the opening chapters referred to as the Two Ways.[31]

Even the vocabulary of the Didache has caused scholars to point to an early date. The Greek text uses language similar to the biblical text. It is written in Koine

---

28 "Their Christology can hardly be reconstructed on the basis of the Didache alone, but they evidently regarded Jesus Christ as the 'servant/child' (Gr. παῖς: 9:2–3, 10:2–3) of God, as the Son of God the Father (7:1, 3) and as 'the Lord' (8:2, 10:5, etc.). The organic unity between Christ and the church is underlined by the metaphor 'The holy vine of your servant David' (9:1) ... In the prayers for the eucharistic meal in chs. 9 and 10, considerable stress is put on giving thanks for the experienced bestowal of revelation, life and knowledge, and on the fact that 'spiritual food and drink and eternal life' have been granted through Jesus." See Oskar Skarsaune and Reidar Hvalvik, eds., *Jewish Believers in Jesus: The Early Centuries* (Peabody, MA: Hendrickson, 2007), 645–646. Cf. "The christological perspective of the Didache seems rooted, then, in an understanding of the relationship between Jesus' activity and God's reign (= God's presence, arrival) ... As Lars Hartman has suggested, early Jewish-Christian believers saw in Jesus' activity a signal that God's reign is arriving in words and works. In the struggle of Jesus with evil powers, God fights them and makes the divine power known. Thus, Jesus' acts of preaching and healing, with their radical challenge to *metanonia*, announce the advent of God's royal reign and the eschatological exercise of God's royal power. The appropriate response is conversion and *faith*, that is, the life-changing recognition that in Jesus' ministry the reign of God over sin and evil can be definitively seen and experienced. Jesus' way of receiving sinners into the reign of God is thus to enact and pronounce *forgiveness*." See Nathan Mitchell, "Baptism in the Didache," in *The Didache in Context: Essays on Its Text, History & Transmission* (ed. Clayton N. Jefford; Leiden, Holland: Brill, 1995), 233. See also Daniel F.J. Nessim, "Didache and Trinity: Proto-Trinitarianism in an Early Christian Community" (paper presented at the annual meeting of the ETS, San Antonio, TX, 16 November 2006).
29 Milavec, *The Didache: Text, , Analysis, and Commentary*, 40.
30 Allen, *The Didache*, xiv. Alan Garrow feels that Paul is drawing upon Didache 16 in 1 Thessalonians 4:15–17. He argues that the "word from the Lord" (4:15) was "the tradition preserved in Didache 16." See Garrow, "The Eschatological Tradition behind 1 Thessalonians: Didache 16," *Journal for the Study of the New Testament* 32, no. 2 (2009): 191–215. Far more likely, both Paul and the Didache shared a common eschatological tradition derived from the early transmission of the words of Yeshua.
31 Gedaliah Alon, "The Halacha in the Teaching of the Twelve Apostles," in *The Didache in Modern Research* (ed. Jonathan A. Draper; Leiden, Holland: Brill, 1996), 166.

Greek using 552 different words, of which 504 are found in the New Testament and 497 in the Septuagint.[32]

Authorship

When we examine the material of the Didache, "there is nothing to identify the Didachist as anything other than a Messianic Jew."[33] The longest title of the Didache, *The Teaching of the Lord to the Gentiles by the Twelve Apostles*, would have us believe that the Didache contains instructions that were transmitted by the apostles through the halachic authority that was invested in them by the Master himself.[34] While scholars debate which, if any, of the book's several titles were attached to its original composition, this raises the question of whether or not the Didache actually goes back to the original twelve apostles. Did the teaching in the Didache emerge from the oral traditions and legal rulings of the Jerusalem Council? The suggested early date of composition coupled with the character of the contents makes that seem possible. Jonathan Draper writes: "The earlier the date for this text is pushed, the more likely it was associated from the beginning with, or even originated from, the twelve apostles in Jerusalem, as its title states."[35] As we will discuss, the Didache was the natural outgrowth of the Jerusalem Council's rulings regarding Gentiles in Acts 15. It seems reasonable to suggest that the Didache represents the teachings, traditions, and legal decisions authored by the early heads

---

32 Milavec, *The Didache: Text, , Analysis, and Commentary*, xii–xiii.
33 Jefford, "Authority and Perspective in the Didache," in *The Didache: A Missing Piece of the Puzzle in Early Jewish Christianity* (eds. Draper and Jefford; Atlanta, GA: Society of Biblical Literature, 2015), 57.
34 The later reworked version of the Didache that appears in the third-century *Apostolic Church-Ordinance* presents the material in such a way that it is as if the apostles are delivering the material orally. Sections are introduced with "John said," "Peter said," "Andrew said," "Philip said," "Simon said," "James said," "Nathanael said," "Thomas said," "Cephas said," and "Bartholomew said." Although this is artificial and should not be taken as authentic, it does give further evidence of an early tradition connecting the material to the apostles. Evidence suggests that the *Apostolic Church-Ordinance* did not make this up but it can be attributed to an earlier source. See Alistair Stewart (-Sykes), *On the Two Ways: Life or Death, Light or Darkness: Foundational Texts in the Tradition* (Yonkers, NY: St. Vladimir's Seminary Press, 2011), 98. Also curious is the opening of *The Directions Through Clement and the Canons of the Holy Apostles* (also third century): "Greetings, sons and daughters, in the name of the Master Yeshua the Messiah. John and Matthew and Peter and Andrew and Philip and Simon and James and Nathanael and Thomas and Kephas and Bartholomew and Jude the son of James" (ibid., 106).
35 Draper, "The Holy Vine of David Made Known to the Gentiles through God's Servant Jesus: 'Christian Judaism' in the Didache," in *Jewish Christianity Reconsidered: Rethinking Ancient Groups and Texts* (ed. Matt Jackson-McCabe; Minneapolis, MN: Fortress, 2007), 281.

of the Jerusalem assembly, such as James the brother of the Master (30–62 CE) or Simeon son of Clopas (62–117 CE).[36]

Another curious title for the Didache circulated in the church early on. The fourth-century church theologian Rufinus of Aquileia gives it the secondary title *Judgment of Peter*.[37] Other church writers mention the *Judgment of Peter* but do not specifically connect that title to the Didache. The fourth-century bishop Optatus the African quotes a passage in a letter that he says is from Peter's epistle. While the passage is not found in any of the canonical Petrine literature, it bears striking resemblance to a saying in the Didache.[38] Furthermore, both 2 Peter and sections of the pseudepigraphical Clementine Homilies (which are attributed to Clement, Peter's disciple) contain teachings very similar to the Two Ways section of the Didache.[39] Some connection between Peter, chief among the apostles, and the Didache might be possible.

Alternatively, we might connect the Didache with the Apostle Barnabas, Paul's original traveling companion. The Two Ways section from the Didache is associated with the apocryphal Epistle of Barnabas, and it is possible that the Epistle of Barnabas was wrongly attributed to the Apostle Barnabas because it included

---

36   Some have suggested that Simeon son of Clopas was the actual author of the Didache. He was the successor of James the Just as *nasi* of the Jerusalem Messianic community and would have been about the right age to have written the work. See William Varner, *The Way of the Didache: The First Christian Handbook* (New York, NY: University Press of America, 2007), 82–83. It is interesting that both Simeon son of Clopas as well as Simon Peter have been suggested as authors of the Didache. Both have also been suggested as candidates for the elusive Simon HaQalpho(s)ni of rabbinic literature who is said to be "a leader of poets" and "composed a great many hymns for Israel." If these rabbinic legends are true then it is fitting that the beautiful liturgical prayers of chapters 9 and 10 be attributed to either Simeon son of Clopas or Simon Peter. See Toby Janicki, "Remembering Yeshua's Chief Disciple: The Apostle Peter in Rabbinic Literature," *Messiah Journal* 112 (Winter 2013): 37–44; Aaron Eby, "I Will Give Praise: A Poem Ascribed to Simon Peter," *Messiah Journal* 112 (Winter 2013): 45–50; D. Thomas Lancaster, "Simeon, Son of Clopas," *Messiah Journal* 112 (Winter 2013): 51–52.

37   *Commentary on the Apostles' Creed 38.*

38   "In the letter, Optatus states that the apostle Peter says in his epistle, 'Do not judge your brothers with partiality.' This quotation is not found in either of the two canonical Petrine epistles, nor is it attributed to Peter elsewhere in the New Testament. Adolf Harnack speculates that this quotation may be a combination of James 2:1 and 4:11, 43 wrongly attributed by Optatus to Peter. Other commentators have noted the 1 Peter parallels in the verses immediately preceding 4:11 as the possible reason for Optatus' (supposed) error. In fact, the Two Ways states 'Do not accuse with partiality anyone of a wrongdoing' (*Barnabas* 19:4) and 'Judge justly; do not accuse with partiality [anyone] of a wrongdoing' (Didache 4.3). This is undoubtedly the source of Optatus' quotation-despite minor differences in wording. Optatus is not loose in this quotation in the usual manner of ancient writers, but purposely alters its wording to suit his needs in making certain points to the Donatists" (Robert E. Aldridge, "Peter and the 'Two Ways,'" *Vigiliae Christianae* 53, no. 3 [August 1999]: 245–246).

39   E.g., 2 Peter 2:1–2, 15; Pseudo-Clementine Homilies 7.7–8, 10.2.

some of his material. In reality, the Two Ways section is artlessly tacked onto the end of that epistle. Moreover, the traditional association with Barnabas is derived from the title *Epistle of Barnabas*, which appears only in some manuscripts and only at the end of the Two Ways section.[40]

The Barnabas theory involves speculation about the origin and development of the Didache. Before Paul was ordained as the apostle to the Gentiles, Barnabas had that commission. The apostles in Jerusalem had sent Barnabas to Antioch to investigate claims about Gentiles becoming disciples of Yeshua. Barnabas might have penned a basic catechism and primer in ethical monotheism for the new Gentile believers: the Two Ways section of the Didache. Later development of the document would have naturally included sayings of the Master and other community rules and standards that the apostles had generated for the early Gentile communities.

Whether or not the Didache actually goes back to Peter, Barnabas, or another of the apostolic authorities in Jerusalem cannot be ascertained with any confidence. At the same time, when one compares the teachings of the Didache to the New Testament, it seems certain that the essential thrust of the book follows the same path as the teachings of the apostles and breathes the spirit of our Master Yeshua.

Inherent Jewishness

One of the most compelling reasons to view the Didache as a first-century document that could be linked back to the teachings of the apostles is the inherent Jewish nature of the text. This is a quality lacking in most other early non-canonical works. The Didache represents a community that was still "living within the ambit of Torah"[41] in which "a high degree of continuity with the mother religion is preserved."[42] The Didache preserves a time when believers in Messiah were still within the fold of Judaism.

The contents of the Didache divide up nicely into four tractates. The first is the Two Ways section (chapters 1–6), the second is on liturgy (7–10), the third is on congregational order and halachah (11–15), and the last section offers a short

---

40 See Bart D. Erhman, ed., *Loeb Classical Library: The Apostolic Fathers Volume* II (trans. Bart D. Ehrman; London, England: Harvard University, 2005), 83.
41 Mitchell, "Baptism in the Didache," 231.
42 Anders Ekenberg, "Evidence for Jewish Believers in 'Church Orders' and Liturgical Texts," in *Jewish Believers in Jesus: The Early Centuries* (ed. Oskar Skarsaune and Reidar Hvalvik; Peabody, MA: Hendrickson, 2007), 643.

apocalyptic teaching (16).[43] The Didache can be classified as a type of "ancient Mishnah" that contains "Judaeo-Christian halachot."[44] Joseph Mueller writes that "the Didache treats the same content areas as the Mishnah and comes up with its prescriptions by using the same sources or methods as does Jewish halakhah."[45] It presents numerous injunctions on ethics as well as instructions in ceremonial commandments such as immersion, prayer, dietary laws, and priestly dues. In essence, it contains a "brief manifesto of the fundamentals of life according to Judaism."[46]

Scholars have noted the Jewish nature of the opening Two Ways section in particular. This has caused some to speculate that chapters 1–6 were borrowed from an already existing Jewish document or oral tradition. It is far more probable to assume that the writers of the Didache were Jewish and thus tapping into the same ethical and apodictic streams as the writers of later Jewish literature rather than copying their works. The writer of the Didache was "following in a very long train of thought and expression":[47]

> [The introduction to the Didache proposes] a paradigm for the principles of religion which are based, in the main, on *Torat hamidot* ["the ethics of the law"], which devolved from Scripture and which permeates the tannaitic Mishnah, the Apocrypha, and the books written by the scholars of Israel in Greek.[48]

---

43 Matthew Larsen and Michael Svigel note the parallel between this type of structure and the "basic teaching" mentioned in Hebrews 6 with four elements: 1. Repentance from dead works and faith toward God, (Two Ways); 2. Instruction about baptisms (Immersion and surrounding relevant liturgy); 3. Laying on of hands, (Leadership, congregational order); 4. Resurrection of the dead, and eternal judgment. (Short apocalypse). Larsen and Svigel don't argue that the author of Hebrews knew the Didache as we have it, but more likely some kind of training manual for believers very similar to the Didache (Larsen and Svigel, "The First Century Two Ways Catechesis and Hebrews 6:1–6" in *The Didache: A Missing Piece of the Puzzle in Early Jewish Christianity* [eds. Draper and Jefford; Atlanta, GA: Society of Biblical Literature, 2015], 477–496).
44 Alon, "The Halacha in the Teaching of the Twelve Apostles," 165; Frédéric Manns, *Le Judéochristianisme, mémoire ou prophétie* (Paris, France: Beauchesne, 2000), 337. A similar argument has been made for the *Didascalia* in Charlotte Fonrobert, "The Didascalia Apostolorum: A Mishnah for the Disciples of Jesus," *Journal of Early Christian Studies* 9, no. 4 (Winter 2011): 483–509.
45 Joseph Mueller, "The Ancient Church Order Literature: Genre or Tradition?" *Journal of Early Christian Studies* 15, no. 3 (2007): 357, n. 60.
46 Alon, "The Halacha in the Teaching of the Twelve Apostles," 167.
47 Varner, *The Way of the Didache*, 57.
48 Alon, "The Halacha in the Teaching of the Twelve Apostles," 166.

Scholars who object to the authenticity of the Didache on the basis of its inherent Jewishness betray their own ignorance of the inherent Jewishness of first-century Christianity. We do find many similarities between the Two Ways section and other Jewish literature, but those similarities should point to the Didache's authenticity as early Messianic Jewish literature rather than to adopted or borrowed material.

Even the so-called golden rule or vocabulary such as "saints" and "those whom the Spirit has prepared"[49] found within the Didache, terms that at first glance might sound more Christian than Jewish, find their roots in the Judaism of the first century. The phrase "Do not do to another what you would not want done to you" is actually phrased in the opposite form to what we find in the Gospels—"Whatever you wish that others would do to you, do also to them"[50]—and is closer to the version attributed to the first-century sage Hillel: "What is hateful to you, do not to your neighbor."[51] "Saints" (*hagioi*, ἅγιοι) corresponds to the Hebrew *tzaddikim* ("righteous ones," צדיקים), which we have translated as "righteous," and the phrase "those whom the Spirit has prepared" is similar to Hebrew terms such as *kedoshim* ("set-apart ones," קדושים) and *bechirim* ("chosen ones," בחירים). These are all attested to in Jewish literature from the period.[52] As we pointed out, the vocabulary of the Didache is very biblical where 504 of its 552 different words are found in the New Testament and 497 in the Septuagint.[53] Obviously, both the New Testament and the Septuagint are inherently Jewish documents and the Didache betrays a Semitic background.

Some argue that the very fact that the Didache contains Eucharistic texts clearly puts it within a period of time that represents an established Christian liturgy distinct from Judaism. Yet again, as will be explained in the commentary, the language of these blessings and prayers find its direct parallel and counterpart in the Judaism of the first few centuries CE. In fact, many scholars speculate that these table blessings do not represent a Eucharistic or sacramental communion service because they lack any mention of Messiah's blood or body or even his words "Do this in remembrance of me" (Luke 22:19), which are staples of established Eucharist

---

49   Didache 1.2, 4.2, 10.
50   Matthew 7:12.
51   b.*Shabbat* 31a.
52   Alon, "The Halacha in the Teaching of the Twelve Apostles," 166; e.g., 1 Enoch 48:1; 2 Baruch 66:2; b.*Yevamot* 19a.
53   Milavec, *The Didache: Text, , Analysis, and Commentary*, xii–xiii.

prayers.[54] It seems more probable that they simply parallel the blessings for common (and sacred) meals found in Jewish liturgical tradition.

Some sections of the Didache appear to prescribe legal rulings that contradict the normative Judaism of the day such as alternate fasting days to distinguish from the practice of the "hypocrites." These disputes should all be viewed as intra-Jewish in much the same way that our Master debated with the Pharisees. Marcello del Verme elaborates:

> There is no reason to state that in the Didache there is a trace of an irreversible "parting of the ways" between Christian community or communities and the Jews, namely of an already accomplished separation or distinction between Early Christianity and the Synagogue.[55]

Draper adds that he sees "nothing to indicate the emergence of Didache ... on the one side and the rabbis on the other as two different symbolic universes constructed in opposition to each other."[56] The Didache preserves the believing community in its infancy when it was still well grounded within Judaism. Some suggest that it may also be one of the last voices of authentic apostolic faith—what Géza Vermes called "the last flowering of Judeo-Christianity."[57]

Halachah for Gentiles

Now that we have established the Didache as a thoroughly Jewish work authored by an early Jewish believer, if not by the apostles themselves, we must now answer the question of who the intended audience of the Didache was. The longer title of the document, *The Teaching of the Lord to the Gentiles through the Twelve Apostles*, suggests that this work was understood to have been penned for non-Jewish believers, and in turn, most scholars concur with this opinion:

---

54   Hans Lietzmann, *Mass and the Lord's Supper* (Leiden, Holland: Brill, 1979), 188–194; Draper, "The Holy Vine of David Made Known to the Gentiles through God's Servant Jesus," 269–273.
55   Marcello del Verme, *Didache and Judaism: Jewish Roots of an Ancient Christian-Jewish Work* (New York, NY: T&T Clark, 2004), 87.
56   Draper, "Do the Didache and Matthew Reflect an 'Irrevocable Parting of the Ways' with Judaism?" in *Matthew and the Didache: Two Documents from the Same Jewish-Christian Milieu?* (ed. Van de Sandt; Minneapolis, MN: Fortress, 2005), 240.
57   Géza Vermes, "From Jewish to Gentile: How the Jesus Movement became Christianity," *Biblical Archeology Review* 38, no. 6 (November/December 2012): 78.

It apparently was intended as a prescriptive code principally for gentiles rather than for Jews who, as a result of their education, grasped what God required of them. When it came to gentiles, however, who had grown up in households in which pagan gods and pagan standards of morality abounded, the line of former beliefs and conduct had to be changed.[58]

The focus of the Didache was upon training Gentiles to live the Way of Life revealed by the Father through his servant Jesus with the expectation that they would be included in the final gathering of Israel into God's kingdom on earth.[59]

The basic function of the Didache in the early church was as a "catechetical handbook" designed for those who were joining the Christian family from among the Gentiles.[60]

The contents of the Didache mark it as an instruction booklet of sorts for new Gentile believers. It may be considered "catechetical instruction" for Gentiles to prepare them for immersion into the faith and entrance into Yeshua's school of disciples.[61]

At the Jerusalem Council the apostles made a legal decision that Gentiles who came to faith in Messiah should not be compelled to legally convert to Judaism and become responsible for the full yoke of the Torah as Jews.[62] Instead, the apostles obligated the God-fearing Gentile believers to the rules and prohibitions that governed the stranger sojourning with Israel.[63] They explicitly stated four initial prohibitions: sexual immorality, food sacrificed to idols, things strangled, and blood. However, the brevity of the ruling left a vacuum. What else should be required of the Gentiles as they progressed in their faith? While they would not

---

58   Van de Sandt and Flusser, *The Didache*, 31–32.
59   Milavec, "Gentile Identity in the Didache Communities as Early Signs of the Parting of the Ways" (paper presented at the annual meeting of the Society of Biblical Literature, San Antonio, TX, 23 November 2004), 2.
60   Varner, *The Way of the Didache*, 3.
61   D. Thomas Lancaster, *Elementary Principles: Six Foundational Principles of Ancient Jewish Christianity* (Marshfield, MO: First Fruits of Zion, 2014), 66–70. See also Larsen and Svigel, "The First Century Two Ways Catechesis and Hebrews 6:1–6."
62   Acts 15.
63   See Toby Janicki, "The Ger Toshav Residing within Israel," *Messiah Journal* (Summer 2015): 15–22, and Richard Bauckham, "James and the Jerusalem Council Decision," *Introduction to Messianic Judaism* (ed. David Rudolph and Joel Willitts; Grand Rapids, MI: Zondervan, 2013), 178–186.

be required to follow Torah in the same manner as a Jewish believer, they would certainly need practical guidance for everyday life and community. What should fellowship look like? How would they apply priestly dues in the Diaspora? When should they pray? All these questions are answered in the Didache with such simplicity and Jewishness that one can almost feel the heartbeat of the apostles beneath its instructions.[64] This adds to the probability that at least some key contents of the Didache do indeed go back to oral traditions and legal rulings of the apostles.

The Didache could be looked at "as an expansion of" the Great Commission:[65]

> Go therefore and make disciples of all nations, baptizing them in the name of the Father and of the Son and of the Holy Spirit, teaching them to observe all that I have commanded you. And behold, I am with you always, to the end of the age. (Matthew 28:19–20)

Perhaps it might even represent some of the instructions that the Master delivered to the Twelve during the forty days prior to his ascension.[66] In that time he could have been giving legal rulings on some of the fundamentals of the faith as they related to the "repentance and forgiveness of sins" that was now to be "proclaimed in his name to all nations" (Luke 24:47).[67]

Even the order of the contents of the Didache itself adds further evidence that the work was intended for new Gentile believers entering into the world of Judaism:

> The organizational thread is this: the Didache unfolds the comprehensive, step by step program used for the formation of a gentile convert. By following the order of the Didache, mentors training novices were assured of following the progressive, ordered, and psychologically sound path that master trainers had effectively culled from their own successful practice in apprenticing novices.[68]

---

64 William Telfer theorizes, "The Didachist conceived his book as an encyclical under the hand of St. Peter, addressed to the Gentile brethren of Antioch, Syria, and Cilicia, parallel with and superseding the Jerusalem encyclical of Acts 15" (Telfer, "The *Didache* and the Apostolic Synod of Antioch," *Journal of Theological Studies* 40 [1939]: 133–146, 258–271). While his theory is not widely accepted, it is interesting that he sees the Didache as the result of a second "Jerusalem Council."
65 Sherman Elbridge Johnson, "A Subsidiary Motive for the Writing of the Didache," in *Munera Studiosa* (eds. Massey Hamilton Shepherd, Jr. and Johnson; Cambridge, MA: Episcopal Theological School, 1946), 122.
66 Acts 1:3; Johnson, "A Subsidiary Motive for the Writing of the Didache," 113.
67 Cf. Acts 1:8.
68 Milavec, *The Didache: Text, , Analysis, and Commentary*, x–xi.

These new Gentile believers, while not becoming legally Jewish, were taking on "a *kind* of Jewish identity," while remaining ethnically as non-Jews.[69]

Rabbinic and apocryphal sources indicate precedence for issuing such instructions to non-Jews in the Judaism of the period.[70] Early midrashic texts mention "halachah of proselytes."[71] We find in the Talmud that potential proselytes were "given instruction in some of the minor and some of the major commandments."[72] One such document that has been preserved is the minor tractate of the Talmud titled *Gerim*. It bears content similar to that of the Didache, giving instructions for both the convert (*ger tzedek*, גר צדק) and the resident alien (*ger toshav*, גר תושב).[73] Pseudo-Phocylides, which was written around the beginning of the first century CE, appears to be a Jewish work intended to introduce the Greek world to the basic tenets of Jewish ethics and morality. Therefore, the Didache falls into the same genre of writing as the instructions given to the resident alien and the God-fearer, both of which were categories of righteous Gentiles who, while not going so far as to convert to become Jewish, practiced many aspects of Judaism.[74] In this way the Didache is a Mishnah for Gentile believers. It addresses key halachic issues of everyday life and community.

Oral and Written Tradition

If the Didache is a type of apostolic Mishnah for new Gentile believers, we should not be surprised to find some similarities between it and the Mishnah. Both documents first circulated orally. The Mishnah contains material transmitted orally for hundreds of years before it was compiled into a written volume around 200 CE. Therefore, it is sprinkled with vocabulary that indicates an oral history: "Rabbi

---

69 Stephen Filan, "Identity in the Didache Community," in *The Didache: A Missing Piece of the Puzzle in Early Jewish Christianity* (eds. Draper and Jefford; Atlanta, GA: Society of Biblical Literature, 2015), 22.
70 Solomon Schechter and Kaufmann Kohler, "Didache," *Jewish Encyclopedia* 4:585–588.
71 *Ecclesiastes Rabbah* 5:7; *Ruth Rabbah* 2:12, 22.
72 b.*Yevamot* 47a.
73 "It is remarkable that there is such detailed agreement between what is (in later texts, of course) recorded of Jewish practice with proselytes and the second person singular section of the Didache. It makes it inherently likely that Jewish influence is strong in this stratum of the text and that it is the same stratum" (Draper, "A Continuing Enigma: the 'Yoke of the Lord' in Didache 6.2–3 and Early Jewish-Christian Relations," in *The Image of the Judaeo-Christians in Ancient Jewish and Christian Literature* [ed. Peter J. Tomson and Doris Lambers-Petry; Tübingen, Germany: Mohr Siebeck, 2003], 118–120).
74 "There are righteous individuals among the nations of the world who do have a share in the world to come" (t.*Sanhedrin* 13:1). "Said Rav Yehudah: These are the thirty righteous men among the nations of the world by whose virtue the nations of the world continue to exist" (b.*Chullin* 92a). Cf. b.*Sanhedrin* 105a.

so and so says," "truly they say," "others have said," "he taught," etc. We find the same tendencies in the Didache: "who speaks the word of God to you" (4.1), "at the words you have heard" (3.8), "the Lord even said" (9.5), "having first said all these things" (7.1).[75] The Mishnah and the Didache both represent literary forms derived from a rich oral tradition.

In rabbinic literature the Mishnah functions as the nucleus of the oral law, yet variant oral traditions circulated that were not recorded in the Mishnah. Some were eventually folded into a work known as the *Tosefta* (300 CE). Other variant oral traditions known as *baraitot* were not recorded until the Talmud was compiled in 400 CE. The Talmud itself consists of the Mishnah and commentary upon the Mishnah known as the Gemara. The Gemara attempts to find proofs and scriptural support for the Mishnah's rulings. A similar history of oral and written tradition exists with the Didache.

Rabbinic Literature	Apostolic Literature
Mishnah	Didache
Gemara	Apostolic Constitutions
Tosefta	Epistle of Barnabas *Doctrina Apostolorum*

If we compare the Didache to the Mishnah, then the Two Ways section of the Epistle of Barnabas can be compared to the *Tosefta*. Epistle of Barnabas contains a section of the Didache that is very similar to the Two Ways section in Didache 1–6.[76] The places where the Epistle of Barnabas material deviates from the Didache version suggest that a Jewish hand was behind the Two Ways section of Epistle of Barnabas; the differences are too Jewish and too early for us to consider them to be the result of a reworking of the Didache by a Gentile Christian copyist. Instead, the tone of the Two Ways section in Epistle of Barnabas seems to suggest that it derives from an alternate version of the tradition that circulated among the

---

75 Milavec, "The Distress Signals of Didache Research," in *The Didache: A Missing Piece of the Puzzle in Early Jewish Christianity* (eds. Draper and Jefford; Atlanta, GA: Society of Biblical Literature, 2015), 62–64.

76 James N. Rhodes suggests that the Two Ways theme is found not just in chapters 18–20 but throughout the work. See "The Two Ways Tradition in the Epistle of Barnabas: Revisiting an Old Question," *The Catholic Biblical Quarterly* 73 (2011): 797–816.

early believers. It is significant that a complete version of the Epistle of Barnabas is found in *Codex Sinaiticus* (fourth century), where it appears as an appendix to the New Testament, indicating that it was considered a very important work at an early date. In a few places the Epistle of Barnabas version puts a kind of spiritual, mystical spin on the Didache material in a style of exegesis similar to the way the modern Chasidic movement allegorizes the Torah and halachic texts. The Epistle of Barnabas therefore remains an important document in Didache research and is referenced where applicable throughout this commentary.

Another *Tosefta*-like source is the *Doctrina Apostolorum*, which contains a Latin version of the Two Ways. While some scholars feel that the *Doctrina* is a copy of the Didache, others have argued convincingly that it, like the Epistle of Barnabas, represents a separate strain of tradition. The Latin version we possess today seems to have been created in the third century, but the Greek version from which it was translated goes back to the end of the first century.[77] The Greek version must have been derived from oral and/or written traditions that go back even earlier. Therefore, it is another important textual witness for Didache studies. Like the Epistle of Barnabas, the *Doctrina* is much too Jewish to be the work of a late Christian copyist. This is true even in places where it deviates from the Didache. One significant way in which the *Doctrina* differs from the Epistle of Barnabas is its usage of sayings of the Master. Unlike the Epistle of Barnabas, which does not appear to incorporate any teachings of Yeshua, the *Doctrina* alludes to and sometimes directly quotes Yeshua's sayings. Additionally, while the Epistle of Barnabas at times seems to disregard the order of content in its source, the *Doctrina* is much more organized and follows the flow of the Didache. For these reasons, variants from the *Doctrina* play into the first six chapters of this commentary.

The Didache also appears in the Apostolic Constitutions (fourth century).[78] Some of the wording changed as the Didache material entered the Apostolic Constitutions, and, most interestingly, the new version added scriptural citations from both the Hebrew Scriptures and the New Testament to augment and validate the Didache's teachings. A parallel evolution and expansion occurred in Talmudic literature as the compilers of the Gemara provided proof texts to validate the

---

77 Goodspeed, *The Apostolic Fathers*, 1–3; Van de Sandt and Flusser, *The Didache*, 61–63, 113–120.
78 Apostolic Constitutions 7.

Mishnah.[79] Did the compiler of Apostolic Constitutions provide the expansions to the Didache, or do these represent the hand of an earlier editor familiar with Jewish exegesis? Perhaps the text of Apostolic Constitutions draws from a version of the Didache that had been amplified by an earlier community of Jewish believers. In essence, then, this section of the Apostolic Constitutions is a kind of apostolic Talmud.[80] It may even contain Didache-like traditions that were not recorded either in the Didache or the Epistle of Barnabas that would be akin to the talmudic *baraitot*.[81] For that reason, as with the Epistle of Barnabas and the *Doctrina*, we also include the Apostolic Constitutions version as much as possible in the commentary of the Didache.

Discipleship for All

Some scholars believe that the Didache was originally intended to be studied by believers in pairs. Didache historian Aaron Milavec explains that the wording throughout the Didache itself suggests that it was to be studied one-on-one with an expert (one seasoned in the faith):

> The Didache offers evidence suggesting that each novice was paired off with a single spiritual master. The principle clue for this is the fact that the entire training program (save for Didache 1.3) addresses a single novice using the second-person singular.[82]

The new initiate into the community would have been paired with a teacher in the model of discipleship. It reminds us of the Master's words: "Whoever receives

---

[79] The rabbis employed a talmudic hermeneutic, *asmachta* ("support," אסמכתא), in which a biblical verse was cited as support for a legal ruling. See Rabbi Adin Steinsaltz, *The Talmud Steinsaltz Edition: A Reference Guide* (New York, NY: Random, 1989), 149. Joseph Mueller also notes the similarity with the way "the Apostolic Constitutions reworks the *Didascalia* and the Talmud develops further the Mishnah" (Mueller, "The Ancient Church Order Literature," 352).

[80] "Evan M. Synek (1997; 1998) has described the Apostolic Constitutions, which contain a redacted form of the Didache in Book VII, as a 'Christian Talmud'" (Jonathan A. Draper, "Pure Sacrifice in Didache 14 as Jewish Christian Exegesis," *Neotestamentica* 42, no. 2 (2008): 255).

[81] Edgar J. Goodspeed proposes: "The history of the four texts would thus appear to be that a short Greek Didache was composed early in the second century (now lost but represented by the in *De Doctrina*); that a Greek *Barnabas* was written about AD 130, and appears reflected in the Latin version of ch. 1–17; that with the aid of this short form of Barnabas, the primitive Didache was expanded soon after AD 150 into the Greek Didache published by Bryennius; and that with the aid of the primitive Didache expanded into the Greek Barnabas" ("The Didache, Barnabas, and the Doctrina," 228). Although he proposes later dates than we are suggesting in this commentary, his history of the four texts seems plausible.

[82] Milavec, *The Didache: Text,, Analysis, and Commentary*, 48.

you receives me, and whoever receives me receives him who sent me."[83] The layout of the Didache allows the new disciple to progress slowly from introductory material into the more complex rituals of daily living and community.

This is similar to the rabbinic concept of *chavruta* (חברותא), which is the method of studying in pairs. The student studies sometimes with a partner on the same level of learning and at other times with a more advanced student. Both partnerships help the student learn in a unique way. Today this takes place in Jewish educational settings such as in a yeshiva, but rabbinic texts such as the Mishnah indicate that this study method existed already in the first few centuries CE:

> Joshua ben Perachiah would say: "Procure for yourself a teacher [*rav*], and acquire for yourself a colleague [*chaver*]." (m.*Avot* 1:6)

> Rabbi Nehorai said: "Uproot yourself to live in a community where Torah is studied; say not that the Torah will come to you. Only with your colleagues [*chaverim*] can your studies become established. Do not lean upon your own understanding." (m.*Avot* 4:14)

Both the rabbinic community and the Didache emphasize learning with a teacher. One was not to attempt to rely upon his or her own understanding but instead to seek out the guidance of teachers and colleagues.

Milavec also points out that the Didache, unlike many documents in the ancient world, seems to have been written with both male and female disciples in mind. Evidence that the teachings were "intended for both men and women" are found in the facts that the Didache addresses female-specific issues such as abortion (2.2), the term "my child" is used throughout instead of the popular "my son," and the instruction given in 4.9 about discipline for both a son and a daughter indicates address to both men and women, since in the ancient world the training of a daughter was typically the responsibility of the mother.[84]

Yeshua had several female disciples. In Luke 10:39, we read of Mary, who "sat at the Lord's feet and listened to his teaching," which is an idiom for discipleship.[85] Also, in Luke 8:1-3, we read of several women who followed the Master. Women continued to play an integral role in the Acts community and Paul's epistles. Therefore, it should be no surprise that the Didache addresses both male and female disciples of the Master.

---

83   Matthew 10:40.
84   Milavec, *The Didache: Text, , Analysis, and Commentary*, 77–78.
85   cf. m.*Avot* 1:4.

Conclusion

Despite all the religious and academic argumentation over the Didache, a sweet simplicity pervades the document and makes it intriguing to read and study. The very fact that it represents not a collection of lofty theology and doctrine but rather something that "is everyday and ordinary" gives it an air of authority and authenticity.[86] The text compels us to read on as we get glimpses of the life and practice of the early Jewish and Gentile believers in Messiah. It represents a time when Christianity as a religion separate from Judaism had not even been fathomed. Milavec summarizes:

> The Didache represents a bridge to the past. In the Didache, the centrality of Jesus is affirmed, but so are the election of Israel and the promises made to David. In the Didache one finds the first steps of a Jewish movement to define itself at the boundaries of Judaism as a legitimate expression of true religion bent on the inclusion of gentiles in the promises made to Israel ... Thus, the Didache represents a Christianity free of anti-Judaism, and for that reason, it bears an importance in our times to aid Christians to arrive at self-definition that allows them to acknowledge that "Jews remain very dear to God, for the sake of the patriarchs, since God does not take back the gifts he bestowed or the choice he made [of Israel]" (Vatican II, *Nostra Aetate* sec. 4).[87]

For students of the Bible and followers of Messiah, the Didache is, as Tony Jones calls it, "the most important book you've never heard of."[88] Because of its early date and inherent grounding in Judaism, it gives us a view unparalleled in any other non-canonical literature of what being a disciple of the Master was all about. It most certainly deserves to be treated as one of the greatest Torah works of the early Messianic community and should be studied by all followers of Messiah—both Jews and non-Jews. May the Lord of Legions be pleased to bless us through the holy vine of his servant David that he made known to us through his servant Yeshua as we study the wellspring of the Didache. To him be the glory forever.

---

86 Tony Jones, *The Teaching of the Twelve: Believing & Practicing the Primitive Christianity of the Ancient Didache Community* (Brewster, MA: Paraclete, 2009), 10.
87 Milavec, *The Didache: Faith, Hope, & Life of the Earliest Christian Communities, 50–70 C.E.*, 562.
88 Jones, *The Teaching of the Twelve*, 1.

The Didache

GREEK AND ENGLISH TEXT

Διδαχὴ τῶν δώδεκα ἀποστόλων

Διδαχὴ κυρίου διὰ τῶν
δώδεκα ἀποστόλων τοῖς ἔθνεσιν

Chapter 1

1.1 Ὁδοὶ δύο εἰσί, μία τῆς ζωῆς καὶ μία τοῦ θανάτου, διαφορὰ δὲ πολλὴ μεταξὺ τῶν δύο ὁδῶν.

1.2 Ἡ μὲν οὖν ὁδὸς τῆς ζωῆς ἐστὶν αὕτη· πρῶτον ἀγαπήσεις τὸν θεὸν τὸν ποιήσαντά σε· δεύτερον τὸν πλησίον σου ὡς σεαυτόν· πάντα δὲ ὅσα ἐὰν θελήσῃς μὴ γίνεσθαί σοι, καὶ σὺ ἄλλῳ μὴ ποίει.

1.3 τούτων δέ τῶν λόγων ἡ διδαχή ἐστιν αὕτη·
Εὐλογεῖτε τοὺς καταρωμένους ὑμῖν καὶ προσεύχεσθε ὑπὲρ τῶν ἐχθρῶν ὑμῶν, νηστεύετε δὲ ὑπὲρ τῶν διωκόντων ὑμᾶς, ποία γὰρ χάρις ἐὰν ἀγαπᾶτε τοὺς ἀγαπῶντας ὑμᾶς; οὐχὶ καὶ τὰ ἔθνη τὸ αὐτὸ ποιοῦσιν; ὑμεῖς δὲ ἀγαπᾶτε τοὺς μισοῦντας ὑμᾶς καὶ οὐχ ἕξετε ἐχθρόν.

1.4 ἀπέχου τῶν σαρκικῶν καὶ σωματικῶν ἐπιθυμιῶν· ἐάν τίς σοι δῷ ῥάπισμα εἰς τὴν δεξιὰν σιαγόνα, στρέψον αὐτῷ καὶ τὴν ἄλλην, καὶ ἔσῃ τέλειος· ἐὰν ἀγγαρεύσῃ σέ τις μίλιον ἕν, ὕπαγε μετ' αὐτοῦ δύο· ἐὰν ἄρῃ τις τὸ ἱμάτιόν σου, δὸς αὐτῷ καὶ τὸν χιτῶνα· ἐὰν λάβῃ τις ἀπὸ σοῦ τὸ σόν, μὴ ἀπαίτει· οὐδὲ γὰρ δύνασαι.

1.5 παντὶ τῷ αἰτοῦντί σε δίδου καὶ μὴ ἀπαίτει· πᾶσι γὰρ θέλει δίδοσθαι ὁ πατὴρ ἐκ τῶν ἰδίων χαρισμάτων. μακάριος ὁ διδοὺς κατὰ τὴν ἐντολήν, ἀθῷος γάρ ἐστιν. οὐαὶ τῷ λαμβάνοντι· εἰ μὲν γὰρ χρείαν ἔχων λαμβάνει τις, ἀθῷος ἔσται· ὁ δὲ μὴ χρείαν ἔχων δώσει δίκην, ἵνα τί ἔλαβε καὶ εἰς τί· ἐν συνοχῇ δὲ γενόμενος ἐξετασθήσεται περὶ ὧν

The Teaching of the Twelve Apostles

The Teaching of the Lord to the Gentiles through the Twelve Apostles

Chapter 1

1.1 There are two ways: one of life and one of death; however, there is a great difference between the two ways.

1.2 Now the Way of Life is this: First, you shall love God who made you; second, you shall love your fellow as yourself. Whatever you do not want to happen to you, do not do to one another.

1.3 This is the teaching about these matters:
Speak well of those who speak ill of you, and pray for your enemies; fast for those who persecute you, for what special favor do you merit if you love those who love you? Do not even the Gentiles do the same? However, you are to love those who hate you, and you will not have any enemies.

1.4 Restrain yourself from natural and physical inclinations: if someone strikes you on the right cheek, turn the other to him, and you will be complete. If someone forces you to go one mile, go with him two. If someone takes away your cloak, give him your tunic also. If someone takes away what is yours, do not demand it back, for you are not even able to get it back.

1.5 Give to whoever asks, and do not demand it back, for the Father wants to give of his own gifts to everyone. Contentment awaits one who gives according to the commandment, for he is blameless. How terrible for one who takes! For anyone who has a need and takes will be blameless; but one who does not have a need will give an account as to why he took it and for what purpose. And when he is put into prison, he will be questioned

ἔπραξε καὶ οὐκ ἐξελεύσεται ἐκεῖθεν, μέχρις οὗ ἀποδῷ τὸν ἔσχατον κοδράντην.

1.6 ἀλλὰ καὶ περὶ τούτου δὲ εἴρηται· Ἱδρωσάτω ἡ ἐλεημοσύνη σου εἰς τὰς χεῖράς σου, μέχρις ἂν γνῷς τίνι δῷς.

Chapter 2

2.1 Δευτέρα δὲ ἐντολὴ τῆς διδαχῆς·

2.2 οὐ φονεύσεις, οὐ μοιχεύσεις, οὐ παιδοφθορήσεις, οὐ πορνεύσεις, οὐ κλέψεις, οὐ μαγεύσεις, οὐ φαρμακεύσεις, οὐ φονεύσεις τέκνον ἐν φθορᾷ οὐδὲ γεννηθὲν ἀποκτενεῖς. οὐκ ἐπιθυμήσεις τὰ τοῦ πλησίον.

2.3 οὐκ ἐπιορκήσεις, οὐ ψευδομαρτυρήσεις, οὐ κακολογήσεις, οὐ μνησικακήσεις.

2.4 οὐκ ἔσῃ διγνώμων οὐδὲ δίγλωσσος· παγὶς γὰρ θανάτου ἡ διγλωσσία.

2.5 οὐκ ἔσται ὁ λόγος σου ψευδής οὐ κενός, ἀλλὰ μεμεστωμένος πράξει.

2.6 οὐκ ἔσῃ πλεονέκτης οὐδὲ ἅρπαξ οὐδὲ ὑποκριτὴς οὐδὲ κακοήθης οὐδὲ ὑπερήφανος. οὐ λήψῃ βουλὴν πονηρὰν κατὰ τοῦ πλησίον σου.

2.7 οὐ μισήσεις πάντα ἄνθρωπον, ἀλλὰ οὓς μὲν ἐλέγξεις, περὶ δὲ ὧν προσεύξῃ, οὓς δὲ ἀγαπήσεις ὑπὲρ τὴν ψυχήν σου.

Chapter 3

3.1 Τέκνον μου, φεῦγε ἀπὸ παντὸς πονηροῦ καὶ ἀπὸ παντὸς ὁμοίου αὐτοῦ.

3.2 μὴ γίνου ὀργίλος· ὁδηγεῖ γὰρ ἡ ὀργὴ πρὸς τὸν φόνον· μηδὲ ζηλωτὴς μηδὲ ἐριστικὸς μηδὲ θυμικός· ἐκ γὰρ τούτων ἁπάντων φόνοι γεννῶνται.

3.3 τέκνον μου, μὴ γίνου ἐπιθυμητής· ὁδηγεῖ γὰρ ἡ ἐπιθυμία πρὸς τὴν πορνείαν· μηδὲ αἰσχρολόγος μηδὲ ὑψηλόφθαλμος· ἐκ γὰρ τούτων ἁπάντων μοιχεῖαι γεννῶνται.

3.4 τέκνον μου, μὴ γίνου οἰωνοσκόπος· ἐπειδὴ ὁδηγεῖ εἰς τὴν εἰδωλολατρίαν· μηδὲ ἐπαοιδὸς μηδὲ μαθηματικὸς μηδὲ περικαθαίρων

thoroughly about what he has done, and he will not get out from there until he has paid the last penny.

1.6 But regarding this it has also been said, "Let your donation sweat in your hands until you know to whom to give it."

Chapter 2

2.1 And the second commandment of the teaching is:

2.2 Do not murder. Do not commit adultery. Do not practice pederasty. Do not commit sexual immorality. Do not steal. Do not practice magic. Do not use potions. Do not murder children through abortion nor kill them after they have been born. Do not covet the things that belong to your fellow.

2.3 Do not swear falsely. Do not bear false witness. Do not slander anyone. Do not hold grudges.

2.4 Do not be double-minded or double-tongued, for a double tongue is a deadly trap.

2.5 Do not let your word be false or empty, but let it be fulfilled in action.

2.6 Do not be greedy, or predatory, or hypocritical, or malicious, or arrogant. Do not plot evil against your fellow.

2.7 Do not hate any human being; but some you are to rebuke, and some you are to pray for, yet some you are to love even more than your own life.

Chapter 3

3.1 My child, flee from all evil and everything like it.

3.2 Do not be an angry person, for anger leads to murder; nor be envious, nor adversarial, nor hot-tempered, for from all these things murder results.

3.3 My child, do not be a lustful person, for lust leads to sexual immorality; nor be foul-mouthed, nor one who looks up at women, for from all these things adultery results.

3.4 My child, do not be a diviner, because this leads to idolatry; nor be one who casts spells, nor one who studies astrology, nor one who performs

μηδὲ θέλε αὐτὰ βλέπειν· ἐκ γὰρ τούτων ἁπάντων εἰδωλολατρία γεννᾶται.

3.5 τέκνον μου, μὴ γίνου ψεύστης· ἐπειδὴ ὁδηγεῖ τὸ ψεῦσμα εἰς τὴν κλοπήν· μηδὲ φιλάργυρος μηδὲ κενόδοξος· ἐκ γὰρ τούτων ἁπάντων κλοπαὶ γεννῶνται.

3.6 τέκνον μου, μὴ γίνου γόγγυσος· ἐπειδὴ ὁδηγεῖ εἰς τὴν βλασφημίαν· μηδὲ αὐθάδης μηδὲ πονηρόφρων· ἐκ γὰρ τούτων ἁπάντων βλασφημίαι γεννῶνται.

3.7 ἴσθι δὲ πραΰς· ἐπεὶ οἱ πραεῖς κληρονομήσουσι τὴν γῆν.

3.8 γίνου μακρόθυμος καὶ ἐλεήμων καὶ ἄκακος καὶ ἡσύχιος καὶ ἀγαθὸς καὶ τρέμων τοὺς λόγους διὰ παντός, οὓς ἤκουσας.

3.9 οὐχ ὑψώσεις σεαυτὸν οὐδὲ δώσεις τῇ ψυχῇ σου θράσος. οὐ κολληθήσεται ἡ ψυχή σου μετὰ ὑψηλῶν, ἀλλὰ μετὰ δικαίων καὶ ταπεινῶν ἀναστραφήσῃ.

3.10 τὰ συμβαίνοντά σοι ἐνεργήματα ὡς ἀγαθὰ προσδέξῃ, εἰδὼς ὅτι ἄτερ θεοῦ οὐδὲν γίνεται.

Chapter 4

4.1 Τέκνον μου, τοῦ λαλοῦντός σοι τὸν λόγον τοῦ θεοῦ μνησθήσῃ νυκτὸς καὶ ἡμέρας· τιμήσεις δὲ αὐτὸν ὡς κύριον· ὅθεν γὰρ ἡ κυριότης λαλεῖται, ἐκεῖ κύριος ἐστιν.

4.2 ἐκζητήσεις δὲ καθ᾽ ἡμέραν τὰ πρόσωπα τῶν ἁγίων, ἵνα ἐπαναπαῇς τοῖς λόγοις αὐτῶν.

4.3 οὐ ποθήσεις σχίσμα, εἰρηνεύσεις δὲ μαχομένους. κρινεῖς δικαίως, οὐ λήψῃ πρόσωπον ἐλέγξαι ἐπὶ παραπτώμασιν.

4.4 οὐ διψυχήσεις, πότερον ἔσται ἢ οὔ.

4.5 Μὴ γίνου πρὸς μὲν τὸ λαβεῖν ἐκτείνων τὰς χεῖρας, πρὸς δὲ τὸ δοῦναι συσπῶν.

4.6 ἐὰν ἔχῃς διὰ τῶν χειρῶν σου, δώσεις λύτρωσιν ἁμαρτιῶν σου.

4.7 οὐ διστάσεις δοῦναι οὐδὲ διδοὺς γογγύσεις· γνώσῃ γὰρ τίς ἐστιν ὁ τοῦ μισθοῦ καλὸς ἀνταποδότης.

purification rites. Do not even desire to see these things, for from all these things idolatry results.

3.5 My child, do not be a liar, because lying leads to theft; nor be one who loves money, nor be glory-seeking, for from all these things theft results.

3.6 My child, do not be a complainer, because this leads to blasphemy; nor be egocentric, nor malevolent, for from all these things blasphemy results.

3.7 Rather, be humble, because the humble will inherit the earth.

3.8 Be patient, merciful, gentle, quiet, and good-natured, always trembling at the words that you have heard.

3.9 Do not aggrandize yourself nor give overconfidence to yourself. Do not connect yourself with the lofty, but rather associate with the righteous and lowly.

3.10 Accept the things that happen to you as being for the good, knowing that nothing happens apart from God.

Chapter 4

4.1 My child, remember night and day the teacher who speaks the word of God to you, and esteem him as the Lord, for where lordship is spoken of, there the Lord is.

4.2 And every day seek the presence of the righteous so that you may lean upon their words.

4.3 Do not crave conflict, but bring those who are quarrelling to peaceful reconciliation. Judge righteously; do not show partiality when rebuking transgressions.

4.4 Do not be indecisive as to whether or not your judgment is correct.

4.5 Do not be one who stretches out his hands to receive but then pulls them back in regard to giving.

4.6 If you have the means, give a ransom for your sins.

4.7 Do not hesitate to give, and do not complain when giving, for you will find out who is the good payer of wages.

4.8 οὐκ ἀποστραφήσῃ τὸν ἐνδεόμενον, συγκοινωνήσεις δὲ πάντα τῷ ἀδελφῷ σου καὶ οὐκ ἐρεῖς ἴδια εἶναι· εἰ γὰρ ἐν τῷ ἀθανάτῳ κοινωνοί ἐστε, πόσῳ μᾶλλον ἐν τοῖς θνητοῖς.

4.9 Οὐκ ἀρεῖς τὴν χεῖρά σου ἀπὸ τοῦ υἱοῦ σου ἢ ἀπὸ τῆς θυγατρός σου, ἀλλὰ ἀπὸ νεότητος διδάξεις τὸν φόβον τοῦ θεοῦ.

4.10 οὐκ ἐπιτάξεις δούλῳ σου ἢ παιδίσκῃ, τοῖς ἐπὶ τὸν αὐτὸν θεὸν ἐλπίζουσιν ἐν πικρίᾳ σου, μήποτε οὐ μὴ φοβηθήσονται τὸν ἐπ' ἀμφοτέροις θεόν· οὐ γὰρ ἔρχεται κατὰ πρόσωπον καλέσαι, ἀλλ' ἐφ' οὓς τὸ πνεῦμα ἡτοίμασεν.

4.11 ὑμεῖς δὲ οἱ δοῦλοι ὑποταγήσεσθε τοῖς κυρίοις ὑμῶν ὡς τύπῳ θεοῦ ἐν αἰσχύνῃ καὶ φόβῳ.

4.12 Μισήσεις πᾶσαν ὑπόκρισιν καὶ πᾶν ὃ μὴ ἀρεστὸν τῷ κυρίῳ.

4.13 οὐ μὴ ἐγκαταλίπῃς ἐντολὰς κυρίου, φυλάξεις δὲ ἃ παρέλαβες, μήτε προστιθεὶς μήτε ἀφαιρῶν.

4.14 ἐν ἐκκλησίᾳ ἐξομολογήσῃ τὰ παραπτώματά σου, καὶ οὐ προσελεύσῃ ἐπὶ προσευχήν σου ἐν συνειδήσει πονηρᾷ. αὕτη ἐστὶν ἡ ὁδὸς τῆς ζωῆς.

Chapter 5

5.1 Ἡ δὲ τοῦ θανάτου ὁδός ἐστιν αὕτη· πρῶτον πάντων πονηρά ἐστι καὶ κατάρας μεστή· φόνοι, μοιχεῖαι, ἐπιθυμίαι, πορνεῖαι, κλοπαί, εἰδωλολατρίαι, μαγεῖαι, φαρμακίαι, ἁρπαγαί, ψευδομαρτυρίαι, ὑποκρίσεις, διπλοκαρδία, δόλος, ὑπερηφανία, κακία, αὐθάδεια, πλεονεξία, αἰσχρολογία, ζηλοτυπία, θρασύτης, ὕψος, ἀλαζονεία·

5.2 διῶκται ἀγαθῶν, μισοῦντες ἀλήθειαν, ἀγαπῶντες ψεῦδος, οὐ γινώσκοντες μισθὸν δικαιοσύνης, οὐ κολλώμενοι ἀγαθῷ οὐδὲ κρίσει δικαίᾳ, ἀγρυπνοῦντες οὐκ εἰς τὸ ἀγαθόν, ἀλλ' εἰς τὸ πονηρόν· ὧν μακρὰν πραΰτης καὶ ὑπομονή, μάταια ἀγαπῶντες, διώκοντες ἀνταπόδομα, οὐκ ἐλεοῦντες πτωχόν, οὐ πονοῦντες ἐπὶ καταπονουμένῳ, οὐ γινώσκοντες τὸν ποιήσαντα αὐτούς, φονεῖς

4.8 Do not turn away someone who is in need; rather, share all things in common with your brother. Do not claim ownership, for if you are common partners in what is immortal, how much more so in what is mortal!

4.9 Do not withhold your hand from your son or daughter, but teach them the fear of God from their youth.

4.10 Do not harshly give orders to your servant or maid who put their hope in the same God, or else they might lose their fear of God, who is over both of you. For God does not intend to call anyone according to status; rather, he calls those whom the Spirit has prepared.

4.11 And as for you servants, submit yourselves to your masters in humility and fear, as they are an example of the authority of God.

4.12 You shall hate every form of hypocrisy and everything that does not please the Lord.

4.13 Do not forsake the commandments of the Lord, but keep what you have received, neither adding to nor subtracting from it.

4.14 Confess your transgressions in the assembly, and you will not draw near in prayer with a guilty conscience. This is the Way of Life.

Chapter 5

5.1 But this is the Way of Death, which is first of all evil and full of curses: murder, adultery, lust, sexual immorality, theft, idolatry, magic, use of potions, robbery, false witness, hypocrisy, duplicity, deceit, arrogance, malice, egocentrism, greed, foul speech, jealousy, overconfidence, loftiness, and pretension.

5.2 It is the way of those who persecute good; those who hate truth; those who love falsehood; those who are ignorant of the wages of righteousness; those who do not cling to what is good or to righteous judgment; those who keep watch not for good but for wickedness; those who are far from being considerate and persevering; those who love frivolous things; those who seek repayment; those who are merciless to the poor; those who do not trouble themselves for the oppressed; those who do not recognize the

τέκνων, φθορεῖς πλάσματος θεοῦ, ἀποστρεφόμενοι τὸν ἐνδεόμενον, καταπονοῦντες τὸν θλιβόμενον, πλουσίων παράκλητοι, πενήτων ἄνομοι κριταί, πανθαμάρτητοι· ῥυσθείητε, τέκνα, ἀπὸ τούτων ἁπάντων.

Chapter 6

6.1 Ὅρα μὴ τίς σε πλανήσῃ ἀπὸ ταύτης τῆς ὁδοῦ τῆς διδαχῆς, ἐπεὶ παρεκτὸς θεοῦ σε διδάσκει.

6.2 εἰ μὲν γὰρ δύνασαι βαστάσαι ὅλον τὸν ζυγὸν τοῦ κυρίου, τέλειος ἔσῃ· εἰ δ᾽ οὐ δύνασαι, ὃ δύνῃ τοῦτο ποίει.

6.3 Περὶ δὲ τῆς βρώσεως, ὃ δύνασαι βάστασον· ἀπὸ δὲ τοῦ εἰδωλοθύτου λίαν πρόσεχε· λατρεία γάρ ἐστι θεῶν νεκρῶν.

Chapter 7

7.1 Περὶ δὲ τοῦ βαπτίσματος, οὕτω βαπτίσατε· ταῦτα πάντα προειπόντες, βαπτίσατε εἰς τὸ ὄνομα τοῦ πατρὸς καὶ τοῦ υἱοῦ καὶ τοῦ ἁγίου πνεύματος ἐν ὕδατι ζῶντι.

7.2 ἐὰν δὲ μὴ ἔχῃς ὕδωρ ζῶν, εἰς ἄλλο ὕδωρ βάπτισον· εἰ δ᾽ οὐ δύνασαι ἐν ψυχρῷ, ἐν θερμῷ.

7.3 ἐὰν δὲ ἀμφότερα μὴ ἔχῃς, ἔκχεον εἰς τὴν κεφαλὴν τρὶς ὕδωρ εἰς ὄνομα πατρὸς καὶ υἱοῦ καὶ ἁγίου πνεύματος.

7.4 πρὸ δὲ τοῦ βαπτίσματος προνηστευσάτω ὁ βαπτίζων καὶ ὁ βαπτιζόμενος καὶ εἴ τινες ἄλλοι δύνανται. κελεύεις δὲ νηστεῦσαι τὸν βαπτιζόμενον πρὸ μιᾶς ἢ δύο.

Chapter 8

8.1 Αἱ δὲ νηστεῖαι ὑμῶν μὴ ἔστωσαν μετὰ τῶν ὑποκριτῶν· νηστεύουσι γὰρ δευτέρᾳ σαββάτων καὶ πέμπτῃ· ὑμεῖς δὲ νηστεύσατε τετράδα καὶ παρασκευήν.

one who made them; those who murder children; those who corrupt what God has formed; those who turn away the needy; those who oppress the greatly distressed; those who are advocates of the wealthy; and those who are lawless judges of the poor—those who are utterly sinful. Children, may you be rescued from all of these!

Chapter 6

6.1 See that no one leads you astray from this way of teaching, because he does not teach you according to God.

6.2 If you can bear the whole yoke of the Lord, you will be complete; but if you cannot, then do what you can.

6.3 Concerning food, bear what you can, but scrupulously guard yourself from what has been offered to idols, because it is the worship of dead gods.

Chapter 7

7.1 Concerning immersion, immerse in this way:
Having first said all these things, immerse in the name of the Father and the Son and the Holy Spirit in living water.

7.2 But if you do not have living water, immerse in other water; and if you cannot immerse in cold water, then immerse in warm water.

7.3 But if you do not have either in sufficient quantity to immerse, pour water on the head three times in the name of the Father and the Son and the Holy Spirit.

7.4 Prior to the immersion, the one performing the immersion and the one being immersed should fast beforehand, and also any others if they can. Require the one being immersed to fast one or two days prior to the immersion.

Chapter 8

8.1 Your fast days should not coincide with those of the hypocrites, for they fast on the second day of the week and on the fifth day. But you are to fast on the fourth day and on the preparation day.

8.2 μηδὲ προσεύχεσθε ὡς οἱ ὑποκριταί, ἀλλ᾿ ὡς ἐκέλευσεν ὁ κύριος ἐν τῷ εὐαγγελίῳ αὐτοῦ,
οὕτως προσεύχεσθε·
> Πάτερ ἡμῶν ὁ ἐν τῷ οὐρανῷ,
> ἁγιασθήτω τὸ ὄνομά σου,
> ἐλθέτω ἡ βασιλεία σου,
> γενηθήτω τὸ θέλημά σου
> ὡς ἐν οὐρανῷ καὶ ἐπὶ γῆς·
> τὸν ἄρτον ἡμῶν τὸν ἐπιούσιον δὸς ἡμῖν σήμερον,
> καὶ ἄφες ἡμῖν τὴν ὀφειλὴν ἡμῶν
> ὡς καὶ ἡμεῖς ἀφίεμεν τοῖς ὀφειλέταις ἡμῶν,
> καὶ μὴ εἰσενέγκῃς ἡμᾶς εἰς πειρασμόν,
> ἀλλὰ ῥῦσαι ἡμᾶς ἀπὸ τοῦ πονηροῦ·
> ὅτι σοῦ ἐστιν ἡ δύναμις καὶ ἡ δόξα εἰς τοὺς αἰῶνας.

8.3 τρὶς τῆς ἡμέρας οὕτω προσεύχεσθε.

Chapter 9

9.1 Περὶ δὲ τῆς εὐχαριστίας, οὕτως εὐχαριστήσατε·

9.2 πρῶτον περὶ τοῦ ποτηρίου·
> Εὐχαριστοῦμέν σοι, πάτερ ἡμῶν, ὑπὲρ τῆς ἁγίας ἀμπέλου Δαυεὶδ τοῦ παιδός σου, ἧς ἐγνώρισας ἡμῖν διὰ Ἰησοῦ τοῦ παιδός σου· σοὶ ἡ δόξα εἰς τοὺς αἰῶνας.

9.3 Περὶ δὲ τοῦ κλάσματος·
> Εὐχαριστοῦμέν σοι, πάτερ ἡμῶν, ὑπὲρ τῆς ζωῆς καὶ γνώσεως, ἧς ἐγνώρισας ἡμῖν διὰ Ἰησοῦ τοῦ παιδός σου· σοὶ ἡ δόξα εἰς τοὺς αἰῶνας.

9.4 ὥσπερ ἦν τοῦτο τὸ κλάσμα διεσκορπισμένον ἐπάνω τῶν ὀρέων καὶ συναχθὲν ἐγένετο ἕν, οὕτω συναχθήτω σου ἡ ἐκκλησία ἀπὸ τῶν περάτων τῆς γῆς εἰς τὴν σὴν βασιλείαν· ὅτι σοῦ ἐστιν ἡ δόξα καὶ ἡ δύναμις διὰ Ἰησοῦ Χριστοῦ εἰς τοὺς αἰῶνας.

8.2 Nor should you pray like the hypocrites but just as the Lord commanded in his good news.

This is what you should pray:

    Our Father, who is in heaven,
    Let your name be sanctified.
    Let your kingdom come;
    Let your will be done—as in heaven, so on earth.
    Our bread of tomorrow, immediately give us today,
    And pardon us our debt,
    As we also pardon those indebted to us.
    And do not bring us into testing,
    But rescue us from what is evil.
    For yours is the power and the glory, forever and ever.

8.3 This is what you should pray three times a day.

Chapter 9

9.1 Now concerning the giving of thanks, give thanks in this way:

9.2 First, concerning the cup:

We thank you, our Father, for the holy vine of your servant David that you made known to us through your servant Yeshua. Yours is the glory forever.

9.3 Next, concerning the piece of bread:

We thank you, our Father, for the life and the knowledge that you made known to us through your servant Yeshua. Yours is the glory forever.

9.4 Just as this piece of bread was scattered over the mountains and gathered together, so may your assembly be gathered from the ends of the earth into your kingdom. For yours is the glory and the power through Yeshua the Messiah forever.

9.5 μηδεὶς δὲ φαγέτω μηδὲ πιέτω ἀπὸ τῆς εὐχαριστίας ὑμῶν, ἀλλ᾽ οἱ βαπτισθέντες εἰς ὄνομα κυρίου, καὶ γὰρ περὶ τούτου εἴρηκεν ὁ κύριος· Μὴ δῶτε τὸ ἅγιον τοῖς κυσί.

Chapter 10

10.1 Μετὰ δὲ τὸ ἐμπλησθῆναι οὕτως εὐχαριστήσατε·

10.2 Εὐχαριστοῦμέν σοι, πάτερ ἅγιε, ὑπὲρ τοῦ ἁγίου ὀνόματός σου, οὗ κατεσκήνωσας ἐν ταῖς καρδίαις ἡμῶν, καὶ ὑπὲρ τῆς γνώσεως καὶ πίστεως καὶ ἀθανασίας, ἧς ἐγνώρισας ἡμῖν διὰ Ἰησοῦ τοῦ παιδός σου· σοὶ ἡ δόξα εἰς τοὺς αἰῶνας.

10.3 σύ, δέσποτα παντοκράτορ, ἔκτισας τὰ πάντα ἕνεκεν τοῦ ὀνόματός σου, τροφήν τε καὶ ποτὸν ἔδωκας τοῖς ἀνθρώποις εἰς ἀπόλαυσιν, ἵνα σοι εὐχαριστήσωσιν· ἡμῖν δὲ ἐχαρίσω πνευματικὴν τροφὴν καὶ ποτὸν καὶ ζωὴν αἰώνιον διὰ τοῦ παιδός σου.

10.4 πρὸ πάντων εὐχαριστοῦμέν σοι ὅτι δυνατὸς εἶ σύ· σοὶ ἡ δόξα εἰς τοὺς αἰῶνας.

10.5 μνήσθητι, κύριε, τῆς ἐκκλησίας σου, τοῦ ῥύσασθαι αὐτὴν ἀπὸ παντὸς πονηροῦ καὶ τελειῶσαι αὐτὴν ἐν τῇ ἀγάπῃ σου, καὶ σύναξον αὐτὴν ἀπὸ τῶν τεσσάρων ἀνέμων τὴν ἁγιασθεῖσαν εἰς τὴν σὴν βασιλείαν, ἣν ἡτοίμασας αὐτῇ· ὅτι σοῦ ἐστὶν ἡ δύναμις καὶ ἡ δόξα εἰς τοὺς αἰῶνας.

10.6 ἐλθέτω χάρις καὶ παρελθέτω ὁ κόσμος οὗτος. Ὡσαννὰ τῷ θεῷ Δαυείδ. εἴ τις ἅγιός ἐστιν, ἐρχέσθω· εἴ τις οὐκ ἐστί, μετανοείτω· μαρὰν ἀθά. ἀμήν.

10.7 τοῖς δὲ προφήταις ἐπιτρέπετε εὐχαριστεῖν ὅσα θέλουσιν.

Chapter 11

11.1 Ὃς ἂν οὖν ἐλθὼν διδάξῃ ὑμᾶς ταῦτα πάντα τὰ προειρημένα, δέξασθε αὐτόν·

9.5 But do not let anyone eat or drink by means of your giving of thanks except those immersed in the name of the Lord, for the Lord even said concerning this, "Do not give what is holy to the dogs."

Chapter 10

10.1 After you have been satisfied, give thanks in this way:

10.2 We thank you, our holy Father, for your holy name that you have caused to dwell in our hearts; and for the knowledge, faithfulness, and eternal life that you have made known to us through your servant Yeshua. Yours is the glory forever.

10.3 You, O Lord of Legions, created all things for the sake of your name; you gave nourishment and drink for human beings to enjoy in order that they would give thanks to you. You also bestowed upon us spiritual nourishment and drink and eternal life through your servant.

10.4 And for all things we thank you because you are powerful. Yours is the glory forever.

10.5 Remember, O Lord, your congregation, to rescue her from all evil and to make her complete in your love. Gather her, the sanctified, from the four winds to your kingdom that you have prepared for her. For yours is the power and the glory forever.

10.6 May grace come, and may this world pass away. *Hoshana* to the God of David! Everyone who is holy, let him come. Everyone who is not, let him repent. *Maran etha*! Amen.

10.7 Permit the prophets to lead the giving of thanks as much as they desire.

Chapter 11

11.1 Now receive whoever comes to teach you in all that has just been said.

11.2 ἐὰν δὲ αὐτὸς ὁ διδάσκων στραφεὶς διδάσκῃ ἄλλην διδαχὴν εἰς τὸ καταλῦσαι, μὴ αὐτοῦ ἀκούσητε· εἰς δὲ τὸ προσθεῖναι δικαιοσύνην καὶ γνῶσιν κυρίου, δέξασθε αὐτὸν ὡς κύριον.

11.3 Περὶ δὲ τῶν ἀποστόλων καὶ προφητῶν, κατὰ τὸ δόγμα τοῦ εὐαγγελίου οὕτως ποιήσατε·

11.4 πᾶς δὲ ἀπόστολος ἐρχόμενος πρὸς ὑμᾶς δεχθήτω ὡς κύριος.

11.5 οὐ μενεῖ δὲ εἰ μὴ ἡμέραν μίαν· ἐὰν δὲ ᾖ χρεία, καὶ τὴν ἄλλην· τρεῖς δὲ ἐὰν μείνῃ, ψευδοπροφήτης ἐστίν.

11.6 ἐξερχόμενος δὲ ὁ ἀπόστολος μηδὲν λαμβανέτω εἰ μὴ ἄρτον ἕως οὗ αὐλισθῇ· ἐὰν δὲ ἀργύριον αἰτῇ, ψευδοπροφήτης ἐστί.

11.7 καὶ πάντα προφήτην λαλοῦντα ἐν πνεύματι οὐ πειράσετε οὐδὲ διακρινεῖτε· πᾶσα γὰρ ἁμαρτία ἀφεθήσεται, αὕτη δὲ ἡ ἁμαρτία οὐκ ἀφεθήσεται.

11.8 οὐ πᾶς δὲ ὁ λαλῶν ἐν πνεύματι προφήτης ἐστίν, ἀλλ᾽ ἐὰν ἔχῃ τοὺς τρόπους κυρίου· ἀπὸ οὖν τῶν τρόπων γνωσθήσεται ὁ ψευδοπροφήτης καὶ ὁ προφήτης.

11.9 καὶ πᾶς προφήτης ὁρίζων τράπεζαν ἐν πνεύματι οὐ φάγεται ἀπ᾽ αὐτῆς· εἰ δὲ μήγε, ψευδοπροφήτης ἐστί.

11.10 πᾶς δὲ προφήτης διδάσκων τὴν ἀλήθειαν εἰ ἃ διδάσκει οὐ ποιεῖ, ψευδοπροφήτης ἐστίν.

11.11 πᾶς δὲ προφήτης δεδοκιμασμένος ἀληθινός ποιῶν εἰς μυστήριον κοσμικὸν ἐκκλησίας, μὴ διδάσκων δὲ ποιεῖν ὅσα αὐτὸς ποιεῖ, οὐ κριθήσεται ἐφ᾽ ὑμῶν· μετὰ θεοῦ γὰρ ἔχει τὴν κρίσιν· ὡσαύτως γὰρ ἐποίησαν καὶ οἱ ἀρχαῖοι προφῆται.

11.12 ὃς δ᾽ ἂν εἴπῃ ἐν πνεύματι· Δός μοι ἀργύρια, ἢ ἕτερά τινα, οὐκ ἀκούσεσθε αὐτοῦ· ἐὰν δὲ περὶ ἄλλων ὑστερούντων εἴπῃ δοῦναι, μηδεὶς αὐτὸν κρινέτω.

11.2 But if this teacher, having turned aside, were to teach a different kind of teaching to undermine this teaching, do not obey him. However, if his teaching serves to promote righteousness and knowledge of the Lord, receive him as the Lord.

11.3 Concerning the emissaries and prophets, according to the ordinance of the good news, this is what you should do:

11.4 Let every emissary who comes to you be received as the Lord.

11.5 He shall stay only one day, but if it is absolutely necessary, he may stay another day. However, if he stays three days, he is a false prophet.

11.6 And when the emissary leaves, let him take nothing except bread to sustain him until he finds a new place to stay. But if he asks for money, he is a false prophet.

11.7 Do not put to the test nor pass judgment on any prophet who speaks in the Spirit, for every sin will be forgiven, but this sin will not be forgiven.

11.8 Yet not everyone who speaks in the Spirit is a prophet; rather, only if he has the conduct of the Lord. Therefore, the false prophet and the true prophet should be recognized by this conduct.

11.9 Any prophet who orders in the Spirit that a dining table be set may not eat from it; otherwise, he is a false prophet.

11.10 If any prophet who teaches the truth does not do what he instructs, he is a false prophet.

11.11 Any prophet who, after having been proven to be true, acts in accordance with the earthly mystery of the assembly but does not instruct you to do what he himself does, shall not be liable to judgment before you, because his judgment remains with God, for all the ancient prophets did so as well.

11.12 But whoever might say in the Spirit, "Give me money," or something else, do not obey him. However, if he should say to give on behalf of others who are poor and in need, let no one judge him.

Chapter 12

12.1   Πᾶς δὲ ὁ ἐρχόμενος ἐν ὀνόματι κυρίου δεχθήτω· ἔπειτα δὲ δοκιμάσαντες αὐτὸν γνώσεσθε, σύνεσιν γὰρ ἕξετε δεξιὰν καὶ ἀριστεράν.

12.2   εἰ μὲν παρόδιός ἐστιν ὁ ἐρχόμενος, βοηθεῖτε αὐτῷ ὅσον δύνασθε· οὐ μενεῖ δὲ πρὸς ὑμᾶς εἰ μὴ δύο ἢ τρεῖς ἡμέρας, ἐὰν ᾖ ἀνάγκη.

12.3   εἰ δὲ θέλει πρὸς ὑμᾶς καθῆσθαι, τεχνίτης ὤν, ἐργαζέσθω καὶ φαγέτω.

12.4   εἰ δὲ οὐκ ἔχει τέχνην, κατὰ τὴν σύνεσιν ὑμῶν προνοήσατε πῶς μὴ ἀργὸς μεθ᾽ ὑμῶν ζήσεται Χριστιανός.

12.5   εἰ δ᾽ οὐ θέλει οὕτω ποιεῖν, χριστέμπορός ἐστιν· προσέχετε ἀπὸ τῶν τοιούτων.

Chapter 13

13.1   Πᾶς δὲ προφήτης ἀληθινὸς θέλων καθῆσθαι πρὸς ὑμᾶς ἄξιός ἐστιν τῆς τροφῆς αὐτοῦ.

13.2   ὡσαύτως διδάσκαλος ἀληθινός ἐστιν ἄξιος καὶ αὐτός, ὥσπερ ὁ ἐργάτης τῆς τροφῆς αὐτοῦ.

13.3   πᾶσαν οὖν ἀπαρχὴν γεννημάτων ληνοῦ καὶ ἅλωνος, βοῶν τε καὶ προβάτων, λαβὼν δώσεις τὴν ἀπαρχὴν τοῖς προφήταις· αὐτοὶ γάρ εἰσιν οἱ ἀρχιερεῖς ὑμῶν.

13.4   ἐὰν δὲ μὴ ἔχητε προφήτην, δότε τοῖς πτωχοῖς.

13.5   ἐὰν σιτίαν ποιῇς, τὴν ἀπαρχὴν λαβὼν δὸς κατὰ τὴν ἐντολήν.

13.6   ὡσαύτως κεράμιον οἴνου ἢ ἐλαίου ἀνοίξας, τὴν ἀπαρχὴν λαβὼν δὸς τοῖς προφήταις.

13.7   ἀργυρίου δὲ καὶ ἱματισμοῦ καὶ παντὸς κτήματος λαβὼν τὴν ἀπαρχήν, ὡς ἄν σοι δόξῃ δὸς κατὰ τὴν ἐντολήν.

Chapter 12

12.1 Let anyone who comes in the name of the Lord be received, but then after you have scrutinized him, you will know if he is true, because you will be able to discern between right and wrong.

12.2 If the one who comes is a traveler, help him as much as you can, but he may not stay with you more than two, or if necessary three, days.

12.3 But if he wants to live among you and is a craftsman, let him work and eat.

12.4 If he does not have a skill, according to your discernment take into consideration how he will avoid living idly among you as a follower of the Messiah.

12.5 But if he is not willing to do so, he is a Messiah peddler. Guard yourselves from people like this!

Chapter 13

13.1 Every true prophet who wants to live among you is entitled to his sustenance.

13.2 Likewise, a true teacher is also entitled, just as the worker is entitled to his sustenance.

13.3 Therefore, you shall take every first part of the produce of the wine press and threshing floor, and of both cattle and sheep, and give it to the prophets, because they are your high priests.

13.4 But if you do not have a prophet, give it to the poor.

13.5 When you make a batch of bread dough, take the first part and give it according to the commandment.

13.6 Likewise, when you open a vessel of wine or oil, take the first part and give it to the prophets.

13.7 Also of money and clothing and any other possession, take the first part as it seems fitting to you, and give it according to the commandment.

Chapter 14

14.1 Κατὰ κυριακὴν δὲ κυρίου συναχθέντες κλάσατε ἄρτον καὶ εὐχαριστήσατε, προεξομολογησάμενοι τὰ παραπτώματα ὑμῶν, ὅπως καθαρὰ ἡ θυσία ὑμῶν ᾖ.

14.2 πᾶς δὲ ἔχων τὴν ἀμφιβολίαν μετὰ τοῦ ἑταίρου αὐτοῦ μὴ συνελθέτω ὑμῖν, ἕως οὗ διαλλαγῶσιν, ἵνα μὴ κοινωθῇ ἡ θυσία ὑμῶν.

14.3 αὕτη γάρ ἐστιν ἡ ῥηθεῖσα ὑπὸ κυρίου· Ἐν παντὶ τόπῳ καὶ χρόνῳ προσφέρειν μοι θυσίαν καθαράν· ὅτι βασιλεὺς μέγας εἰμί, λέγει κύριος, καὶ τὸ ὄνομά μου θαυμαστὸν ἐν τοῖς ἔθνεσι.

Chapter 15

15.1 Χειροτονήσατε οὖν ἑαυτοῖς ἐπισκόπους καὶ διακόνους ἀξίους τοῦ κυρίου, ἄνδρας πραεῖς καὶ ἀφιλαργύρους καὶ ἀληθεῖς καὶ δεδοκιμασμένους· ὑμῖν γὰρ λειτουργοῦσι καὶ αὐτοὶ τὴν λειτουργίαν τῶν προφητῶν καὶ διδασκάλων.

15.2 μὴ οὖν ὑπερίδητε αὐτούς· αὐτοὶ γάρ εἰσιν οἱ τετιμημένοι ὑμῶν μετὰ τῶν προφητῶν καὶ διδασκάλων.

15.3 Ἐλέγχετε δὲ ἀλλήλους μὴ ἐν ὀργῇ, ἀλλ' ἐν εἰρήνῃ, ὡς ἔχετε ἐν τῷ εὐαγγελίῳ· καὶ παντὶ ἀστοχοῦντι κατὰ τοῦ ἑτέρου μηδεὶς λαλείτω μηδὲ παρ' ὑμῶν ἀκουέτω, ἕως οὗ μετανοήσῃ.

15.4 τὰς δὲ εὐχὰς ὑμῶν καὶ τὰς ἐλεημοσύνας καὶ πάσας τὰς πράξεις οὕτως ποιήσατε, ὡς ἔχετε ἐν τῷ εὐαγγελίῳ τοῦ κυρίου ἡμῶν.

Chapter 16

16.1 Γρηγορεῖτε ὑπὲρ τῆς ζωῆς ὑμῶν· οἱ λύχνοι ὑμῶν μὴ σβεσθήτωσαν, καὶ αἱ ὀσφύες ὑμῶν μὴ ἐκλυέσθωσαν, ἀλλὰ γίνεσθε ἕτοιμοι· οὐ γὰρ οἴδατε τὴν ὥραν, ἐν ᾗ ὁ κύριος ἡμῶν ἔρχεται.

16.2 πυκνῶς δὲ συναχθήσεσθε ζητοῦντες τὰ ἀνήκοντα ταῖς ψυχαῖς ὑμῶν· οὐ γὰρ ὠφελήσει ὑμᾶς ὁ πᾶς χρόνος τῆς πίστεως ὑμῶν, ἐὰν μὴ ἐν τῷ ἐσχάτῳ καιρῷ τελειωθῆτε.

Chapter 14

14.1 On the day of the Lord, being gathered together, break bread and give thanks after having confessed your transgressions, so that your sacrifice may be pure.

14.2 But do not let anyone who has a quarrel with his fellow come together with you until they have reconciled, so that your sacrifice may not be impure.

14.3 For this is what was spoken by the Lord: "'In every place and time, offer me a pure sacrifice ... because I am a great king,' says the Lord, 'and my name is awesome among the Gentiles.'"

Chapter 15

15.1 Therefore, designate for yourselves overseers and administrators worthy of the Lord—humble men and not lovers of money, and truthful and proven—because they also perform the service of the prophets and teachers.

15.2 Do not then look down on them, for they are your honored ones along with the prophets and teachers.

15.3 Do not rebuke one another in anger but rather in peace, just as you have been taught in the good news. And if anyone has wronged another person, let no one speak to him nor let him hear from you until he repents.

15.4 Carry out your prayers and donations and all your good deeds just as you have been taught in the good news of our Lord.

Chapter 16

16.1 Be vigilant for your life—do not let your lamps be snuffed out, and do not let your loins be ungirded—but be ready, for you do not know the hour in which our Lord is coming.

16.2 Gather together often, seeking what is appropriate for your lives, because your entire time of faithfulness will be of no benefit to you if you will not have been made complete at the end of time.

16.3 ἐν γὰρ ταῖς ἐσχάταις ἡμέραις πληθυνθήσονται οἱ ψευδοπροφῆται καὶ οἱ φθορεῖς, καὶ στραφήσονται τὰ πρόβατα εἰς λύκους, καὶ ἡ ἀγάπη στραφήσεται εἰς μῖσος.

16.4 αὐξανούσης γὰρ τῆς ἀνομίας μισήσουσιν ἀλλήλους καὶ διώξουσιν καὶ παραδώσουσι. καὶ τότε φανήσεται ὁ κοσμοπλανὴς ὡς υἱὸς θεοῦ καὶ ποιήσει σημεῖα καὶ τέρατα, καὶ ἡ γῆ παραδοθήσεται εἰς χεῖρας αὐτοῦ, καὶ ποιήσει ἀθέμιτα, ἃ οὐδέποτε γέγονεν ἐξ αἰῶνος.

16.5 τότε ἥξει ἡ κτίσις τῶν ἀνθρώπων εἰς τὴν πύρωσιν τῆς δοκιμασίας, καὶ σκανδαλισθήσονται πολλοὶ καὶ ἀπολοῦνται· οἱ δὲ ὑπομείναντες ἐν τῇ πίστει αὐτῶν σωθήσονται ὑπ' αὐτοῦ τοῦ καταθέματος.

16.6 καὶ τότε φανήσεται τὰ σημεῖα τῆς ἀληθείας· πρῶτον σημεῖον ἐκπετάσεως ἐν οὐρανῷ, εἶτα σημεῖον φωνῆς σάλπιγγος, καὶ τὸ τρίτον ἀνάστασις νεκρῶν·

16.7 οὐ πάντων δέ, ἀλλ' ὡς ἐρρέθη·

Ἥξει ὁ κύριος καὶ πάντες οἱ ἅγιοι μετ' αὐτοῦ.

16.8 τότε ὄψεται ὁ κόσμος τὸν κύριον ἐρχόμενον ἐπάνω τῶν νεφελῶν τοῦ οὐρανοῦ.

16.3 For in the end of days, false prophets and those who cause corruption will increase in number, and the sheep will be changed into wolves, and love will be changed into hate.

16.4 Because of the increase of lawlessness, those who have fallen away will hate one another; they will also persecute one another, and they will even betray one another. And then the deceiver of the world will appear as a son of God, and he will perform signs and wonders, and the earth will be delivered into his power, and he will commit disgusting acts such as have never taken place since the beginning of time.

16.5 Then the entire human race will enter the trial by fire, and many will be caused to stumble and will perish, but those who endure in their faithfulness will be saved by the very one who is cursed.

16.6 And then the signs of the truth will appear: the first sign, an expansion in the heavens; next, the sign of the sound of the trumpet; and the third sign, the resurrection of the dead.

16.7 However, not the resurrection of everyone but rather as it is said:
    "The Lord will come, and all the righteous along with him."

16.8 Then the world will behold the Lord coming upon the clouds of heaven.

Commentary

ON THE TEXT OF THE DIDACHE

Chapter One

DIDACHE 1

1.1 There are two ways: one of life and one of death;[1] however, there is a great difference between the two ways.

1.2 Now the Way of Life is this: First, you shall love God[2] who made you; second, you shall love your fellow as yourself.[3] Whatever you do not want to happen to you, do not do to one another.[4]

1.3 This is the teaching about these matters:
Speak well of those who speak ill of you,[5] and pray for your enemies;[6] fast for those who persecute you, for what special favor do you merit if you love those who love you?[7] Do not even the Gentiles do the same?[8] However, you are to love those who hate you,[9] and you will not have any enemies.

1.4 Restrain yourself from natural and physical inclinations:[10] if someone strikes you on the right cheek, turn the other to him,[11] and you will be complete.[12] If someone forces you to go one mile, go with him two.[13] If someone takes away your cloak, give him your tunic also.[14] If someone

---

1 Deuteronomy 30:15; Jeremiah 21:8; Matthew 7:13–14.
2 Deuteronomy 6:5, 11:1; Matthew 22:37; Mark 12:30.
3 Leviticus 19:18; Matthew 5:43, 19:19, 22:39; Mark 12:31; Luke 10:27; Romans 13:9; Galatians 5:14; James 2:8.
4 Matthew 7:12; Luke 6:31.
5 Luke 6:28.
6 Matthew 5:44; Luke 6:28.
7 Matthew 5:46; Luke 6:32.
8 Matthew 5:47.
9 Matthew 5:44; Luke 6:27.
10 Colossians 3:5–8; 1 Thessalonians 4:3–5, 7; 2 Timothy 2:22; Titus 2:12; 1 Peter 2:11; 1 John 2:15–16.
11 Matthew 5:39; Luke 6:29.
12 Matthew 5:48.
13 Matthew 5:41.
14 Matthew 5:40; Luke 6:29.

takes away what is yours, do not demand it back,[15] for you are not even able to get it back.

1.5 Give to whoever asks, and do not demand it back,[16] for the Father wants to give of his own gifts to everyone. Contentment awaits one who gives according to the commandment, for he is blameless. How terrible for one who takes! For anyone who has a need and takes will be blameless; but one who does not have a need will give an account as to why he took it and for what purpose. And when he is put into prison, he will be questioned thoroughly about what he has done, and he will not get out from there until he has paid the last penny.[17]

1.6 But regarding this it has also been said, "Let your donation sweat in your hands until you know to whom to give it."

---

15 Luke 6:30.
16 Matthew 5:42; Luke 6:30.
17 Matthew 5:26; Luke 12:59.

Overview

The Didache opens with a choice: the Way of Life or the Way of Death. We see this distinctly in chapter 1, which begins a section commonly called the "Two Ways" (chapters 1–6). In the biblical and the Jewish worldview, life is about choices—and the path that one chooses on a daily basis will ultimately decide one's destiny.

Not only is life full of choices, it is also a progressive journey that never stops. Biblical metaphors that speak of life as a way, a path, a road, or a journey imply movement, the progress of time, and the daily freedom to choose.[18] The Didache is a manual to aid the new Gentile in Messiah in making correct choices on his new path of discipleship—his journey through life.

Ethics versus Theology

The Didache, a brief and to-the-point work, focuses not on what one must believe but rather on how one must live. Its anonymous author presupposes that his readers have already made a commitment to follow the Master. They have had their life-altering epiphany and recognized Yeshua of Nazareth as the Savior not just of the Jewish people but of the entire world. They must now be instructed as to how to walk in the Way of Life. Thomas O'Loughlin aptly comments that "the Didache can start with a set of rules because these presuppose a relationship: the rules show the parameters of the relationship one is choosing."[19] The entire Didache is about navigating correctly the path that the new believer has just chosen. Therefore, it begins with ethical instruction, not theology.

The notion of choosing the correct path, or way, through life was so intrinsic to the early believing community that one of the first names that they applied to themselves was "The Way."[20] In Hebrew this would be the familiar expression *HaDerech* (הדרך), and it may have been an abbreviation for "the way of salvation"

---

18   Thomas O'Loughlin, *The Didache: A Window on the Earliest Christians* (Grand Rapids, MI: Baker, 2010), 28.
19   Ibid., 31.
20   Acts 19:9, 23; 22:4; 24:14, 22. The other names that appear in the book of Acts are "Christian"/Messianist (11:26) and "sect of the Nazarenes" (24:5).

or "the way of God," which was certainly paralleled in the Didache's Way of Life.[21] Milavec writes that "the Didache focuses on orthopraxis in much the same way as does the Manual of Discipline or the Mishnah."[22] Believing in the Master calls for walking daily in the instructions of the Way of Life.

The Two Ways

Some scholars are inclined to view the Two Ways section of the Didache as a reworking of an earlier Jewish work due to its thoroughly Jewish flavor and context. The assumption is unwarranted. An earlier Jewish Two Ways document has never been found. Instead, it makes sense that a first-century "Christian" document would sound thoroughly Jewish simply because it had been written by Jews immersed in Judaism. The apostles and early Jewish believers considered themselves a messianic reformation sect within Judaism, not outside the Jewish people and religion.

Gentiles coming to faith in the God of Israel would have been familiar with the "Two Ways" concept from their own cultural background. Similar ideas are found in Greek works such as Xenophon's *Socrates' Memorabilia* and Plato's *Chariot Allegory*.[23] In fact, the metaphor of choosing between two distinct paths in life "was commonplace in ancient (and not only ancient) moral philosophy."[24] Yet, none of this compares to the plethora of examples and prominence that the two-choices teaching played in Judaism.

In the last book of the Torah, just before Israel was about to advance into the promised land, the LORD set a choice before the children of Israel and told them to decide between two separate paths:

---

21   Cf. Acts 16:17 and Geza Vermes, "From Jewish to Gentile: How the Jesus Movement became Christianity," *Biblical Archeology Review* 38, no. 6 (November/December 2012): 54. It is interesting that it is written of Noah, the quintessential righteous Gentile: "Noah was a righteous man, blameless in his generation. Noah walked with God ... he did all that God commanded him" (Genesis 6:9, 22). Hence a possible connection between the Way of Life, walking with God, and walking out the commandments in righteousness.
22   Aaron Milavec, "The Distress Signals of Didache Research," in *The Didache: A Missing Piece of the Puzzle in Early Jewish Christianity* (eds. Jonathan A. Draper and Clayton N. Jefford; Atlanta, GA: Society of Biblical Literature, 2015), 68.
23   Xenophon, *Memorabilia* 2.1.21–34; Plato, *Chariot Allegory* throughout. Cf. Hesiod, *Opera et Dies* 287–292.
24   Kurt Niederwimmer, *The Didache: A Commentary* (Minneapolis, MN: Fortress Press, 1998), 59. The Qur'an speaks of two paths: "the right path, the path of those whom you have blessed" and the one "of those who have evoked your anger and ... go astray" (Qur'an 1:6–7). Parallel traditions even exist in Buddhist thought with its teachings on the "noble eightfold path." (*Nagara Sutta*).

> I am setting before you today a blessing and a curse: the blessing, if you obey the commandments of the LORD your God, which I command you today, and the curse, if you do not obey the commandments of the LORD your God. (Deuteronomy 11:26–28)

The people had been given the Torah, God's righteous instruction for their lives, and now they needed to choose whether to obey or disobey:

> I have set before you today life and good, death and evil. If you obey the commandments of the LORD your God that I command you today ... then you shall live and multiply ... But if your heart turns away ... you shall surely perish. (Deuteronomy 30:15–18)

The book of Psalms contrasts the "the way of the righteous" with the "way of the wicked."[25] Proverbs admonishes its readers to avoid "the path of the wicked" and "the way of the evil" and instead to tread on the "path of the righteous."[26] The Prophet Jeremiah called the Jewish people to repent before the onset of exile, warning them that there were two paths ahead of them: "Thus says the LORD: Behold, I set before you the way of life and the way of death" (Jeremiah 21:8).

The theme of choosing between two ways continued in the intertestamental period.[27] One of the most important examples of this is from the Dead Sea Scrolls, in which scholars find a strain of tradition similar to the Didache:

> Those born of truth spring from a fountain of light, but those born of falsehood spring from a source of darkness. All the children of righteousness are ruled by the Prince of Light and walk in the ways of light, but all the children of falsehood are ruled by the Angel of Darkness and walk in the way of darkness. (Community Rule [1QS] iii, 19–21)[28]

Rabbinic literature is also replete with examples of the two-ways thinking. Rabbi Yochanan questioned his disciples about what constituted "the good way" and what constituted "the evil way."[29] The sages state that "the words of the Torah

---

25 Psalm 1:6.
26 Proverbs 4:14–19.
27 1 Enoch 94:1–5; 2 Enoch 30:13–15; Testament of Asher 1:3–5. Cf. Philo, *On the Special Laws* 4.108.
28 For the full context of the Two Ways in the Community Rule (1QS), see III, 17–IV, 26.
29 m.*Avot* 2:9. Cf. 2:1.

direct those who study them from the paths of death to the paths of life."[30] Rabbi Joshua tells the following parable describing the two paths of life:

> It can be compared to a king who constructed two paths, one full of thorns, briars, and thistles, and one with spices. The blind walk on the evil road, so that the thorns add wound upon wound, but those who see walk on the good road, with the result that both they and the clothes they wear become scented. God, likewise, constructed two roads, one for the righteous and one for the wicked; he who has no eyes walks in the way of the wicked and stumbles ... The righteous, however, who walk in their integrity, acquire [a blessing] and so do their children after them. (*Genesis Rabbah* 30:20)

Therefore, the concept of the two ways in life was firmly rooted within Judaism and filled the pages of its literature. The Jewish disciples of the Master naturally tapped into that rich Jewish tradition when they penned the Didache.

Freedom of Destiny

Implied in the two-ways theology was freedom of choice. This made Judaism attractive to the pagan world. In most non-Jewish religions, the stars or the gods ultimately determined a person's destiny; the ordinary person supposed that he could do little to control the outcome of his own life. Commenting on Deuteronomy 30:14–18 and the Didache, O'Loughlin writes:

> There is no place here for cosmic fatalism such as the notion that our destiny was written in the stars. In this vision our destiny is in our own hands: we must positively choose good and deliberately avoid evil ... The notion of a religion that gave full scope of moral action (think of alternatives such as a religion that is a series of attempts to placate an angry deity) was one of the attractive features of Judaism around the time of Jesus and an important reason why it was attracting converts who were known as "proselytes" or "fearers of God" or "worshippers of God."[31]

---

30 b.*Chaggigah* 3a.
31 O'Loughlin, *The Didache*, 30.

Many of the Gentiles who had found the God of Israel and his son Yeshua the Messiah were drawn by the idea that this new faith gave them a choice about the direction of their lives. It is perhaps in light of this that the Didache opens with the Jewish teaching of the two ways. With this newfound freedom of choice, however, came grave responsibility and consequence. These new Gentile believers would need to be careful to continually choose the Way of Life over the Way of Death.

The difference between the two paths is seen not only in what they contain but also in how the Didache presents them: "The 'don'ts' are a list of actions to avoid, but the Way of Life is presented [in the Didache] in a far more all-embracing way: here are the underlying attitudes that must inform particular actions."[32] This presentation of the Way of Life is in keeping with the teachings of the Master, which emphasized an internalization of the Torah's ethical principles—not merely rote compliance with God's commands but also the heart attitude behind one's behavior. When a righteous heart lines up with righteous actions, a person is truly free to choose the path that leads to life.

Love of God and Love of Neighbor

The basis for the Way of Life in contrast to the Way of Death is twofold: Disciples of the Master are required to love God, and they are required to love their fellow (that is, their neighbor). The pairing of these two commandments comes directly from the teachings of the Master. In response to a question about which was the greatest of all the commandments, our Master Yeshua answered:

> You shall love the Lord your God with all your heart and with all your soul and with all your mind. This is the great and first commandment. And a second is like it: You shall love your neighbor as yourself. (Matthew 22:37–39)

The Master did not randomly draw these verses together but used a common rabbinic interpretative method called *gezerah shavah* (גזירה שוה), a hermeneutical principle in which two verses are combined based on a common word found in both. Leviticus 19:18 and Deuteronomy 6:5 both contain the Hebrew word *v'ahavta* (ואהבת), "you shall love." This form of the verb *ahav* (אהב) appears only three times in the Torah, and Yeshua cites two of those uses here. The third instance is the

---

32 Ibid., 30.

commandment to "love [the stranger] as yourself" (Leviticus 19:34), which may form the basis for Luke's version of the parable of the good Samaritan.[33]

These two injunctions, love of God and love of neighbor, permeate the New Testament, and both had a deep impact upon the early Messianic community. The Apostle John urges his readers, "If anyone says, 'I love God,' and hates his brother, he is a liar; for he who does not love his brother whom he has seen cannot love God whom he has not seen" (1 John 4:20). Samuel Lachs points out that it is "reasonable to assume the combination was commonplace in rabbinic teachings."[34] Although the Master had his own unique way of combining these two commandments, the pairing is firmly grounded in Jewish thought and interpretation.

The Didache seems either to paraphrase the Master's teachings on these two commandments or to quote an alternate (oral or written) gospel tradition that we no longer possess. The Didache takes the two commandments seriously and, following its early mention of them, dedicates the rest of the work to expounding upon them:

> It's no exaggeration to say that everything else in the Didache flows from this headwater ... As with the command to love God, the exhortation to love one's neighbor as oneself can really be seen as the fount from which the rest of the Didache's teachings flow.[35]

The Didache, then, is truly an exposition of the two great commandments of loving God and loving one's fellow. These two commandments are the essence of Torah life and Judaism. It was imperative for new Gentile believers, and it is imperative for us as Yeshua's disciples today, to write on our hearts these two great commandments and learn what it means to abound and walk in this Messianic community of love.

---

[33] Luke 10:30–37. For a full discussion of this passage, see D. Thomas Lancaster, *Torah Club: Chronicles of the Messiah* (6 vols.; Marshfield, MO: First Fruits of Zion, 2014), 3:890–893.

[34] Samuel Tobias Lachs, *A Rabbinic Commentary on the New Testament: The Gospels of Matthew, Mark and Luke* (Jersey City, NJ: KTAV, 1987), 281; Testament of Issachar 5; Testament of Dan 5. Cf. Sirach 7:30; Philo, *On the Special Laws* 2.63; m.*Avot* 3:18. This pairing of love of HaShem and of fellow is also found in mystical Chasidic thought: "The Alter Rebbe repeated what the Mezritcher Maggid said quoting the Baal Shem Tov: 'Love your fellow like yourself' is an interpretation of and commentary on 'Love HaShem your God.' He who loves his fellow Jew loves God, because the Jew has within himself a 'part of God Above.' Therefore, when one loves the Jew—i.e., his inner essence—one loves God" (Rebbe Menachem Mendel Schneerson, *HaYom Yom: From Day to Day* [Brooklyn, NY: Otzar Hachassidim Lubavitch, 2006], 78).

[35] Tony Jones, *The Teaching of the Twelve: Believing & Practicing the Primitive Christianity of the Ancient Didache Community* (Brewster, MA: Paraclete, 2009), 59.

Lost Gospel Tradition?

Many scholars believe that a great deal of the first chapter of the Didache, in particular verses 1.3–5, (known as the "evangelical section" or "evangelical addition") represents material drawn from non-canonical collections of gospel sayings. Tony Jones writes, "While they are not attributed to Jesus, it seems clear from the context and from the parallels ... that we should read them as the catechumens of the Didache community read them: teachings directly from Jesus."[36] The sayings may be from no longer extant written or oral traditions. They most probably represent a line of tradition that is either independent of the Synoptic Gospels or was source material from which both the Synoptic Gospels and the Didache drew.[37]

The teachings of Didache 1 are similar to many of the sayings in the Sermon on the Mount. Even when it seems that the teachings divert from those we find in Matthew 5–7, parallels in vocabulary and theme, such as that seen in the triad of almsgiving, prayer, and fasting, as well as references to the term "Gentiles" point to close connection between the first chapter of the Didache and the canonical words of our Master Yeshua.[38]

These passages, like the canonical Gospels themselves, paint a picture of the Master as totally faithful to the Torah of Moses:

---

36 Jones, *The Teaching of the Twelve*, 63.
37 It is of note that the Didache never quotes a gospel by name (or for that matter any New Testament book) and that no Didache quotations appear to be of the Johannine tradition. However, throughout the work there does appear to be an "unequivocal connection between the Didache and Matthew, but it is just as clear that this could not involve the final text of Matthew" (Peter J. Tomson, *'If This Be from Heaven ...': Jesus and the New Testament Authors in Their Relationship to Judaism* [Sheffield, England: Sheffield Academic, 2001], 386). Alan J.P. Garrow suspects that the gospel tradition in the Didache was utilized by Matthew in the composition of his gospel. He feels that the Didache might be a candidate for what scholars refer to as Q, the long-lost source utilized by both Matthew and Luke: "Didache 1.2–5a preserves extensive parallels to a Low DT passage (Luke 6:27–36; Matthew 5:38–48) and so deserves attention as a potential candidate for the role of 'Q'" (Alan Garrow, "An Extant Instance of 'Q,'" *New Testament Studies* 62, no. 3 [July 2016]: 398–417). See also Garrow, *The Gospel of Matthew's Dependence on the Didache* (New York, NY: Bloomsbury, 2012) and Joan Hazelden Walker, "A Pre-Marcan Dating for the Didache: Further Thoughts of a Liturgist," *Studia Biblica* 3 (1978): 403–411. Alternatively, the authors of the Didache may have had access to Q or to a Semitic version of something like it, and the Didache's Yeshua sayings may represent their .
38 Clayton N. Jefford, *The Sayings of Jesus in the Teaching of the Twelve Apostles* (New York, NY: Brill, 1989), 43–48. For fasting, praying, and almsgiving, see Matthew 6:2–6, 16–18, and for use of the term "Gentiles," see Matthew 5:47, 6:7, 32. "The most characteristic trait of the Didache as a gospel commentary is that it attempts to put the sayings of Jesus on a rational, 'common sense,' basis as much as possible. They prick the conscience of those who face them squarely, and call forth heroic response" (Sherman Elbridge Johnson, "A Subsidiary Motive for the Writing of the Didache," in *Munera Studiosa* [ed. Massey Hamilton Shepherd, Jr., and Sherman Eldridge Johnson; Cambridge, MA: Episcopal Theological School, 1946], 115).

These sayings are never represented as new, or different, ethical standards. Rather, they are assumed to be in continuity with the Mosaic Law.[39]

This points to the greater context of the Didache, a document written by a community of believers still rooted within the Judaism of their day, faithful to Torah and the traditions of the Jewish people. Like Paul in Acts they could truly say that they had not transgressed "against the Torah of the Jews, nor against the Temple" or "against [their] people or the customs of [their] fathers."[40] The Didache's reliance on sayings of the Master and, for that matter, its plethora of quotes from the Scriptures (in particular the Torah and the Prophets) show us that the writer of the Didache is not asking us to rely on his authority but rather, as he does, on the authority of the Master's teachings and on the words of Scripture.

---

[39] Jonathan Reed, "The Hebrew Epic and the *Didache*," in *The Didache in Context: Essays on Its Text, History & Transmission* (ed. Clayton N. Jefford; New York, NY: Brill, 1995), 217–219.
[40] Acts 25:8, 28:17.

Commentary

🕪 *There are two ways: one of life and one of death;
however, there is a great difference between the two ways.*
(DIDACHE 1.1)

The Didache contains no formal introduction and instead cuts to the chase by immediately introducing and explaining the two ways: the Way of Life and the Way of Death. These words appear to be based on a tradition going back to the Master's instructions:

> Enter by the narrow gate. For the gate is wide and the way is easy that leads to destruction, and those who enter by it are many. For the gate is narrow and the way is hard that leads to life, and those who find it are few. (Matthew 7:13–14)[41]

Later works such as the Epistle of Barnabas spiritualize the two-ways teaching:

> Now let us transition to yet another kind of knowledge and teaching. There are two ways of teaching and authority: one of light and one of darkness; however, there is a great difference between the two ways. For over the one are assigned illuminating angels of God, but over the other are assigned angels of the Adversary. Likewise, the one way is that of

---

41 Some manuscripts of Matthew contain only the first mention of "gate" and speak solely of the "way" thereafter: "The way is wide and easy that leads to destruction ... Narrow and hard is the way that leads to life."

[1.1]
There are two ways: one of life and one of death; however, there is a great difference between the two ways.

the Lord who is from everlasting and forever, but the other way is that of the prince of this present time of evil. (Barnabas 18.1–2)[42]

The Testament of Asher states, "There are two ways of good and evil, and with these are the two inclinations."[43] These interpretations of the two ways are consistent with rabbinic teachings about the two impulses that drive a human being: the evil inclination (*yetzer hara*, יצר הרע) and the good inclination (*yetzer hatov*, יצר הטוב). In both of these examples, the style of exegesis is similar to the way in which the modern Chasidic movement allegorizes the Torah and ancient rabbinic texts.

The Apostolic Constitutions amplifies the Didache's words with citations from Scripture: "I have set before you life and death … Choose life, that you … may live" (Deuteronomy 30:19); "How long will you go limping between two different opinions? If the LORD is God, follow him" (1 Kings 18:21); "No one can serve two

---

42   "Adversary" is literally "satan" (שטן) in the Greek (*satanas*, σατανᾶς). This spiritualization is also found in *Doctrina* 1.1: "There are two ways in the world, that of life and that of death, of light and of darkness. Over them are set two angels, one of right, the other of wrong." The big difference between the Epistle of Barnabas and the *Doctrina* is that the former makes reference to multiple angels whereas the latter mentions only the two. A similar strain of tradition is found in the Dead Sea Scrolls: "Those born of truth spring from a fountain of light, but those born of falsehood spring from a source of darkness. All the children of righteousness are ruled by the Prince of Light and walk in the ways of light, but all the children of falsehood are ruled by the Angel of Darkness and walk in the way of darkness" (Community Rule [1QS] III, 19–21). We also find two angels in the talmudic tradition of angels, one good and one evil, that accompany one on his way home from the synagogue on the eve of the Sabbath (b.*Shabbat* 119b). The language about "the Way of Light" and "the Way of Darkness" in the Epistle of Barnabas and the *Doctrina* sounds similar to Johannine light and dark metaphors. For example, "The light is among you for a little while longer. Walk while you have the light, lest darkness overtake you. The one who walks in the darkness does not know where he is going. While you have the light, believe in the light, that you may become sons of light" (John 12:35–36). *Doctrina* adds "in this world," which is also found in the Two Ways material of the Community Rule (1QS) III, 17–IV, 26.

43   Testament of Asher 1:5–8.

masters, for either he will hate the one and love the other, or he will be devoted to the one and despise the other" (Matthew 6:24).⁴⁴

We find two striking parallels to this two-ways material in the Talmud: "There are two ways before me, one leading to Paradise and the other to Gehinnom" (b.*Brachot* 28b); "The words of the Torah direct those who study them from the paths of death to the paths of life" (b.*Chagigah* 3b).

> [1.1]
> *There are two ways: one of life and one of death; however, there is a great difference between the two ways.*

⚜ Now the Way of Life is this: First, you shall love God who made you. (DIDACHE 1.2)

This verse paraphrases the words of the *Shma*: "You shall love the LORD your God" (Deuteronomy 6:5, 11:1). The Master prioritized this injunction as one of two commandments on which "depend all the Torah and the Prophets."⁴⁵ The version of the Didache preserved in the Apostolic Constitutions strengthens the work's connection with the *Shma* by adding to the command: "Love the Lord God with all your mind, and with all your soul, who is the one and only God, besides whom there is no other."⁴⁶ "You shall love the God who made you" is similar to Sirach's "With all your strength love your Maker."⁴⁷

Although the commandment obviously derives from Deuteronomy 6:4–5, the Didache does not include the words, "Hear, O Israel: The LORD our God, the LORD

---

44 Apostolic Constitutions 7.2. The full passage reads: "The lawgiver Moses said to the Israelites: 'Behold, I have set before your face the way of life and the way of death,' and added, 'Choose life that you may live' [Deuteronomy 30:19]. Elijah the prophet also said to the people: 'How long will you halt with both your legs? If the Lord be God, follow him' [1 Kings 18:21]. The Master Yeshua also said justly: 'No one can serve two masters, for he will either hate the one, and love the other, or he will be devoted to the one and despise the other' [Matthew 6:24]. We also, following our teacher Messiah, 'who is the Savior of all men, especially of those who believe' [1 Timothy 4:10], are obliged to say that there are two ways: one of life and one of death; which have no comparison one with another, for they are very different, or rather entirely separate; and the way of life is that of nature, but that of death was afterwards introduced—it not being according to the mind of God, but from the snares of the adversary." The Apostolic Constitutions utilizes a hermeneutic known in rabbinic exegesis as *asmachta* ("support," אסמכתא), by which a biblical verse is cited as support for legal rulings. As was pointed out in the introduction, this may be evidence that certain sections of the Apostolic Constitutions draw from a version of the Didache that was amplified by an earlier community of Jewish believers.
45 Matthew 22:40.
46 Apostolic Constitutions 7.2. Justin Martyr quotes a similar saying from non-canonical gospel material: "That we should worship God alone, he therefore persuaded us: 'The greatest commandment is: "You shall worship the Lord your God, and him only shall you serve, with all your heart, and with all your strength, the Lord God that made you"'" (Justin, *First Apology* 16).
47 Sirach 7:30.

[1.2]
Now the Way of Life is this: First, you shall love God who made you.

is one." Moreover, instead of stating that one is to love "the LORD your God," it substitutes "God who made you."[48] This broader, more universal language about God may indicate that the words were tailored for broader application than within the narrow confines of Jewish covenantal language.[49] Aaron Milavec writes that this is fitting, "because Gentiles meet the Lord of Israel not as the God 'who brought you out of the land of Egypt' (Exodus 20:2), but as 'the God who made you.'"[50]

The subsequent commandment in Didache 2, "you shall love your fellow as yourself," receives immediate elucidation in the earliest chapters of the Two Ways section, but the commandment "you shall love God who made you" is not addressed at all—at least not until the Didache's later chapters (in the sections on idol food, fasting, praying, and tithing). Although this inversion appears to be contrary to the order in which the Didache initially presents the two injunctions, this type of A, B, B, A chiastic structure also appears in rabbinic literature (this is where two topics are introduced in the order A, B and then expounded upon in reverse order B, A).[51] It may also be that the Didache has in mind the principle of the Master that one reconcile with one's neighbor first before approaching God: "First be reconciled to your brother, and then come and offer your gift" (Matthew 5:24). As HaShem spoke to Cain, "If you do well, will you not be accepted?" (Genesis 4:7).

The Epistle of Barnabas expands the Didache's words with a more mystical treatment, albeit in a Jewish manner:

> The Way of Light is this: If anyone intends to journey to the appointed place, he must hurry to arrive there through his deeds. Therefore, the

---

48 Both the Epistle of Barnabas (19.2) and the *Apostolic Church Order* (4) add, "You shall give glory to the One who ransomed you from death." The *Apostolic Church Order* additionally inserting the phrase from the *Shma* "with all your heart" (Deuteronomy 6:5): "You shall love the God who made you with all your heart".

49 "The God who made you" is reminiscent of the blessing recited by women during the morning blessings section of Shacharit: "Blessed are You, O LORD ... who made me according to His will." Although the latter was not created until sometime in the Middle Ages (it first appears in the medieval law code *Arba'ah Turim* by Jacob ben Asher), the themes are similar.

50 Aaron Milavec, *The Didache: Faith, Hope, & Life of the Earliest Christian Communities, 50–70 C.E.* (New York, NY: Newman, 2003), 122. The exodus would become part of the Gentile believers' spiritual heritage. Paul, writing to a mixed congregation in Corinth, states, "I want you to know, brothers, that *our fathers* were all under the cloud, and all passed through the sea, and all were baptized into Moses in the cloud and in the sea, and all ate the same spiritual food, and all drank the same spiritual drink" (1 Corinthians 10:1–4, emphasis added).

51 E.g., "The Tanna commences with the evening [*Shma*], and proceeds then to the morning [*Shma*]. While dealing with the morning [*Shma*], he expounds all the matters relating to it, and then he returns again to the matters relating to the evening [*Shma*]" (b.*Brachot* 2a). Also m.*Avot* 5:7: "Seven things are in a boor, and seven in a wise man. The wise man ... and their opposites are in the clod."

knowledge given us in which to walk is this: You shall love the One[52] who made you. You shall revere the One who formed you.[53] You shall give glory to the One who ransomed you from death. (Barnabas 19.1–2)[54]

⊯ *Second, you shall love your fellow as yourself.* (DIDACHE 1.2)

In the Didache's rendering of the second of the "greatest commandments," the Torah's injunction from Leviticus 19:18 is not paraphrased at all.[55] Jewish law defines "fellow," or "neighbor" (*rea*, רע), as one's fellow Jew. This is not to say that traditional Judaism promotes unloving behavior to outsiders, but Jewish interpretation limits the definition of "your fellow" to "your fellow Jew."[56] The Master addressed this interpretation with the parable of the Good Samaritan (Luke 10:29–37) and broadened the definition of one's fellow as one's fellow human being, regardless of a person's ethnic or religious background.

Some rabbis over the years have agreed with Yeshua's definition of "fellow," if not legally at least homiletically. For example, we read in an early commentary on Leviticus 19:18, "'You shall love your fellow as yourself.' Rabbi Akiba said: 'This is the greatest principle of the Torah.' Ben Azzai states: '"This is the book of the descendants of Adam" (Genesis 5:1). This is an even greater principle.'"[57] Ben Azzai argues that the overarching principle of the Torah is that we are all related to one

---

52 The sages also used the title one (*echad*, אחד) to refer to God. E.g., "[Rabbi Ishmael] used to say: 'Judge not alone, for none may judge alone except One'" (m.*Avot* 4:8). See Rabbi A. Marmorstein, *The Old Rabbinic Doctrine of God* (New York, NY: KTAV Publishing, 1968), 65.
53 Cf. Jeremiah 1:5; Psalm 139:13–16. The Epistle of Barnabas combines both the fear and love of God as comprising the way of light. Judaism stresses that one must have both of these traits in his service of God and his walk of Torah. To cite a much later example of the same concept, the Alter Rebbe of Chabad Lubavitch, Schneur Zalman, described fear and love as the "two wings" of a bird that enable one to serve God properly and allow one's study and practice of "Torah and commandments to soar on high" (*Tanya, Likkutei Amarim* 41).
54 This expansion is not found in the *Doctrina*: "The way of life is this: first, you shall love the eternal (*aeternum*) God who made you" (1.2). "Eternal God" most likely goes back to the common title for *Elohei Olam* (אלהי עולם).
55 The Greek text matches exactly with the Septuagint.
56 However, Rabbi Aaron of Worms (1754–1836) taught that "each time *re'a* appears in biblical texts, its intended referent is humanity at large" (*Kan Tahor* 10b–11b as paraphrased in Jay R. Berkovitz, "Changing Conceptions of Gentiles at the Threshold of Modernity," in *Formulating Responses in an Egalitarian Age* [ed. Marc D. Stern; New York, NY: Rowman & Littlefield, 2005], 148).
57 *Sifra* on Leviticus 19:18.

[1.2]
Second, you shall love your fellow as yourself.

man, that is, to Adam. Hillel declares, "Love your fellow creatures and bring them close to Torah."[58] Rabbi Chayim Vital exhorts, "Love all people, even gentiles."[59]

The Hebrew text of Leviticus 19:18 can be literally translated, "Love to your fellow as yourself."[60] In the Gospels, Yeshua paraphrases the mandate, "Whatever you wish that others would do to you, do also to them, for this is the Law and the Prophets" (Matthew 7:12). His interpretation makes the commandment about action, not feelings. The Apostle Paul also identified this commandment as the summary of all the commandments and taught that the whole Torah is summarized in this one injunction.[61] James the brother of the Master declared it to be the "royal law."[62] The Epistle of Barnabas states, "You shall love your fellow even more than your own life."[63]

◈ *Whatever you do not want to happen to you, do not do to one another.* (DIDACHE 1.2)

This is usually referred to as the negative form of the Golden Rule, the positive form being, as stated above, "Whatever you wish that others would do to you, do also to them." We find the negative form in the words of Hillel: "What is hateful to

---

58   m.*Avot* 1:12. Cf. m.*Avot* 3:14: [Rabbi Akiva] used to say, "Beloved is man in that he was created in the image [of God]," to which *Tosefot Yom Tov* comments, "Rabbi Akiva is speaking about the value of all people … He wished to benefit all peoples including Noachides … Rabbi Akiva seeks to elevate all the inhabitants of the world."

59   Rabbi Chayim Vital, *Sha'arei Kedusha* 1:6. Cf. "The trait of openheartedness—to include the whole world, all of humanity—belongs to Abraham. When it comes from recognition of the special stand of the nation of Israel, and from that flows a love of all people, that is praiseworthy, like Abraham, the father of many nations" (Rabbi Kook, *Orot*, 169). So also Rabbi Moshe Cordovaero: "One should accustom himself to love his fellow men in his heart—even the wicked as if they were his brothers. Moreover, [he should pursue this quality] until love for all peoples is fixed in his heart" (*Tomer Devorah* 3 [from Rabbi Moshe Cordovaero, *Sefer Tomer Devorah* (trans. Rabbi Dov Fink and Rabbi Shimon Finkelman; Jerusalem, Israel: Tomer, 2005), 41]). Also Messianic luminary Rabbi Isaac Lichtenstein, basing himself on *Tanna Eliyahu Rabbah* 109, writes, "The universal character of Jewish charity finds a still more extended expression in the following sentence: 'Your neighbor is your brother; hence the command to love your neighbor embraces the heathen also'" (*The Everlasting Jew: Selected Writings of Rabbi Isaac Lichtenstein* [ed. Jordan Gayle Levy and D. Thomas Lancaster; Marshfield, MO, Vine of David, 2013], 73).

60   See Avigdor Bonchek, *Studying the Torah: A Guide to In-Depth Interpretation* (Northvale, NJ: Jason Aronson, 1997), 106–107.

61   Romans 13:9; Galatians 5:14.

62   James 2:8.

63   Barnabas 19.5. Cf. Didache 2.7.

you, do not to your neighbor."⁶⁴ Despite the fact that the Synoptic Gospels record the Master as saying only the positive form of the Golden Rule,⁶⁵ there is no reason to believe that Yeshua could not have uttered the negative form on other occasions as well. The negative form of the Golden Rule appears more frequently in ancient Jewish literature than does the positive formulation. Textual variants to Acts 15:29 contain it as an additional injunction to the Apostolic Decree: "What you do not wish to be done to yourselves, do not do to another."⁶⁶

> [1.2]
> *Whatever you do not want to happen to you, do not do to one another.*

Judaism links the Golden Rule midrashically to the interpretation of "as yourself" (*kamochah*, כמוך) from Leviticus 19:18.⁶⁷ How do you love your fellow "as yourself"? By doing to him what you want done to you and vice versa. Targum Pseudo-Jonathan paraphrases Leviticus 19:18 this way: "You shall love your fellow, so what is hateful to you, do not do to him."⁶⁸

In Jewish ethical teaching, this rule is directly connected to the character quality of righteousness (*tzedek*, צדק). Truly righteous behavior is exemplified in showing love to others. The eighteenth-century Jewish ethical work *Cheshbon HaNefesh* comments, "To 'love your neighbor as yourself,' [is] an obligation which our Sages characterize as being the foundation of the Torah."⁶⁹

The negative formulation of the Golden Rule is expanded upon in chapter 2 of the Didache as "the second commandment." In this way the Didache organizes legislation into categories of positive commandments and negative commandments. The positive commandments (in chapter 1) fall under the category of "you shall love your neighbor as yourself," and the negative commandments (in chapter 2)

---

64 b.*Shabbat* 31a. Cf. Tobit 4:15; Romans 13:10.
65 Matthew 7:12; Luke 6:31.
66 It is possible that the Two Ways injunction influenced this textual variant on Acts 15:29.
67 In Sirach 28:3–4 we find, "One man bears hatred against another, and does he seek pardon from the Lord? He shows no mercy to a man, *which is like himself*: and does he ask forgiveness of his own sins?" (emphasis added). Similarly, "If you hate your fellow man whose deeds are evil *like your own*, I the Lord am judge to punish that same man, and if you love your fellow man whose deeds are proper *like your own*, I the Lord am faithful and merciful toward you" (*Avot DeRabbi Natan* 26 [B], emphasis added).
68 The appearance of both the positive and negative commandment form of the injunction to love one's fellow is similar to the rabbinic concept of *aseh v'lo ta'aseh* ("a positive and a negative commandment," עשה ולא תעשה), where this occurs in the Torah. In the Torah, "the fact that a commandment is stated both positively and negatively has Halakhic significance: although the performance of a positive commandment supersedes a negative commandment, this rule does not apply if the negative commandment is itself reinforced by a positive commandment" (Rabbi Adin Steinsaltz, *The Talmud Steinsaltz Edition: A Reference Guide* [New York, NY: Random, 1989], 243).
69 Rabbi Menachem Mendel Levin, *Cheshbon HaNefesh: A Guide to Self-Improvement and Character Refinement* (trans. Rabbi Shraga Silverstein; New York, NY: Feldheim, 1995), 149. The Golden rule is connected back to the idea of freedom of choice and the rabbinic principles of "measure for measure." Your destiny is controlled not by fate but by what you do to others, for so that will be done back to you.

fall under the category of "Whatever you do not want to happen to you, do not do to one another."

⚜ *This is the teaching about these matters.* (DIDACHE 1.3)

The Didache now explains and interprets what it means to love one's fellow, listing commandments that fall under the category of "you shall love your neighbor as yourself."[70] This begins a section that extends through the rest of the chapter and weaves together sayings of the Master. Because a similar parallel section is not found in either the Epistle of Barnabas or the *Doctrina Apostolorum*, many scholars believe that this section was not a part of the original version of the Didache or the Two Ways (which is believed to already have existed when the Didache was written).[71] Scholars refer to this section (1.3b–2.1) as the "evangelical section" or "evangelical addition." Several scholars assume the section was added to the already existing Jewish Two Ways document in order to Christianize it, but there might be a better explanation.

The pattern of moving from the general to specific is reminiscent of rabbinic literature, in particular of the Gemara, which expounds upon the Mishnah. If we hold to our theory that the original version of the Didache was composed by Jewish believers—perhaps even the apostles—it is possible that this section was added during the Apostolic Era. It could have functioned as a way to help new Gentile believers learn the words of the Master while, at the same time, creating a kind of Gemara-style explanation on the core commandment of loving one's neighbor.

This rabbinic method of exegesis is called *perush* (פרוש), which means "commentary" or "interpretation."[72] The Greek word used in verse 3 for "teaching"

---

[70] The Epistle of Barnabas reads, "Therefore, the knowledge given us in which to walk is this" (19.1), and the *Doctrina* states, "And the explanation (*interpretatio*) of these words is this" (1.3).

[71] However, 1.3c–1.4 is found in the *Oxyrhynchus Papyrus* fragments of the Didache, which are the oldest Didache manuscripts found to date, and the Georgian version is missing only 1.5–6. Christopher M. Tuckett points out when comparing *Codex Hierosolymitanus* (H) to the *Oxyrhynchus Papyrus* fragments (P): "Of particular importance for the present discussion are a couple of places where the Didache's text seems to be clearly parallel to material appearing in Matthew/Luke; in both instances the H readings are closer to the gospel texts than the P readings. Thus, it is possible that the text of H has, in the course of transmission, been assimilated to the (more familiar) NT wording in parallel passages" ("The Didache and the Writings That Later Formed the New Testament" in *The Reception of the New Testament in the Apostolic Fathers* (ed. Andrew F. Gregory and Christopher M. Tuckett; New York, NY: Oxford University Press, 2005), 85.

[72] Eliyahu Krupnick, *The Gateway to Learning: A Systematic Introduction to the Study of Talmud* (New York, NY: Feldheim, 1998), 25–27.

(*didache*, διδαχή) in this context may be read in step with *perush*. Hillel uses the word *perush* in his famous summary of the Torah: "What is hateful to you, do not to your fellow. The rest is commentary [*perush*]. Go and learn" (b.*Shabbat* 31a). Huub van de Sandt and David Flusser note that "the similarity is striking" between Hillel's order and the Didache's, both of which give the golden rule and then offer commentary upon it.[73] This may point to a common tradition from which both are drawing.[74]

[1.3]
This is the teaching about these matters.

The Didache treats the injunction to love one's fellow as comprising two distinct commandments. The first commandment involves positive actions to be performed ("you shall love your fellow as yourself"), which will be expounded upon for the rest of chapter 1. "The second commandment" (2.1) involves negative actions to be avoided ("Whatever you do not want to happen to you, do not do to one another"), and this will be expounded upon in chapter 2.

⁌ Speak well of those who speak ill of you. (DIDACHE 1.3)

The content of this saying sounds similar to the Master's words in Luke 6:28, "Bless those who curse you," but it is different enough to indicate an independent source. Paul enjoins the believing community in Rome, "Bless those who persecute you; bless and do not curse them" (Romans 12:14). The sages of Israel praise those "who are insulted but do not insult others in revenge" and "who hear themselves reproached without replying."[75] Disciples of our Master Yeshua are not to retaliate verbally against those who curse and slander them. Instead they are commanded to defy human nature and the selfish desire to retaliate and instead to speak well of their abusers. In the words of *Derech Eretz Zuta*, "Do not seek to wrong him who wronged you."[76]

The rest of chapter 1 expounds upon the details of loving one's neighbor with a specific emphasis on the Master's injunction, "Love your enemies."[77] In his parable

---

73   Huub van de Sandt and David Flusser, *The Didache: Its Jewish Sources and Its Place in Early Judaism and Christianity* (Minneapolis, MN: Fortress, 2002), 132.
74   "Deuteronomy 6, the Golden Rule, and the Decalogue form essential parts of the bedrock for the prescriptions of the whole Didache ... But the similarities between these three first-century texts help to illustrate the idea that the author of the Didache believed its 1.3–5 to form part of interpretation of the Old Testament law proper to the messianic age" (Joseph G. Mueller, "The Ancient Church Order Literature: Genre or Tradition?" *Journal of Early Christian Studies* 15 no. 3 [Fall 2007]: 361).
75   b.*Yoma* 23a.
76   *Derek Eretz Zuta* 2:5 (58a).
77   Matthew 5:44; Luke 6:27.

[1.3] *Speak well of those who speak ill of you.*

of the Good Samaritan, Yeshua included not only Gentiles but also enemies in the Torah's definition of "fellow." After all, we do not need to be commanded to show love to those who are kind to us. Rather, true Torah life demands acts of love for one's enemies. It seems the Didache is drawing upon the way the Torah couples the commandment to "Love your fellow as yourself" with the commandment "You shall not take vengeance or bear a grudge against the sons of your own people" (Leviticus 19:18). Instead of retaliating and holding a grudge against our enemies, we are to show them love and view them as our fellow.

In the context of the Gospels, the enemies of the Master's Jewish disciples would have been primarily Roman idolaters, Jewish apostates, and sectarians, such as the Sadducees. In the context of the Didache, the enemies of the Gentile disciples would more likely have been the Roman authorities and perhaps even family members or friends who did not accept the Gentile believer's "new religious convictions."[78] The new Gentile believers in Messiah dealt with the consequences of accepting a monotheistic faith in a completely polytheistic, idolatrous world. It was not easy for them to break with paganism, and they paid in social consequences and outright persecution. The Didache urges them not to become bitter but instead to walk in sacrificial love. Anger and retaliation would not end the persecution nor bring others to Messiah; however, acting completely opposite to expectation would testify to God's love.

And pray for your enemies. (DIDACHE 1.3)

This saying is reminiscent of the Master's words, "Pray for those who persecute you" (Matthew 5:44),[79] and, "Pray for those who abuse you" (Luke 6:28). A direct parallel appears in the non-canonical gospel fragment *Oxyrhynchus* 1224: "Pray for your enemies. For the one who is not against you is for you. The one who is far away today, tomorrow will be near you."

The Talmud tells the story of Rabbi Meir as he lived near bandits who constantly troubled him. In desperation he prayed that they would die. His wife, Beruria, said to him, "What makes you think a prayer like that is permissible? ... Instead

---

78 Milavec, *The Didache: Faith, Hope, and Life of the Earliest Christian Communities, 50–70 C.E.*, 99.
79 The Greek of the Apostolic Constitutions (7.2) renders this line from the Didache as a midrashic combination of these two Gospel verses: "Pray for those who abuse you."

you should pray for them that they will repent, and then there will be no more wicked."⁸⁰ So Rabbi Meir prayed for them, and they repented.

[1.3]
And pray for your enemies.

Acts of kindness toward our enemies bend our hearts toward them. Praying for our enemies brings the individual into our minds and hearts and draws the persecutor toward the persecuted. As disciples of the Master, we must first and foremost look at everyone as created in the image of God and as fellow human beings. Praying for our enemies helps remove our anger and negative emotions and at the same time helps us focus on the perpetrator as the one truly in need.

❙❙▸ *Fast for those who persecute you.* (DIDACHE 1.3)

Although this saying in verse 3 is not found in the canonical Gospels, it is almost identical to "Pray for those who persecute you" (Matthew 5:44); it simply replaces "pray" with "fast." The version of this saying in the Didache likely reflects an authentic oral tradition of Yeshua's words not found in the Synoptic Gospels.⁸¹ Note that the Sermon on the Mount also connects the discipline of fasting with that of prayer (Matthew 6:5–18).

Throughout the Bible and in Jewish tradition, prayer is closely associated with fasting. For example, in 2 Samuel 12, David fasts and petitions God for his child to be saved from death. In the book of Esther, the Jews fast and pray for their deliverance.⁸² Fast days in Jewish tradition have always been accompanied by extra prayer, and on the great fast day of Yom Kippur, prayer services are conducted throughout the day. In his letter to the Philippians, Polycarp urges the believers to be "constant in fasting and entreating the all-seeing God."⁸³

Fasting is also connected to justice. Isaiah describes the acceptable fast that the Lord chooses: "To let the oppressed go free, and to break every yoke … to share your bread with the hungry and bring the homeless poor into your house; when you see the naked, to cover him" (Isaiah 58:6–7). This has a strong connection to fasting for one's enemies. Jones comments, "A sacrificial act on behalf of the persecutor may, in fact, fulfill every kind of justice hoped for by Isaiah: seeing the persecutor in need of grace. Seen through this Isaiahic lens, the persecutor

---

80   b.*Brachot* 10a.
81   Canon Spence, *The Teaching of the Twelve Apostles* (London, England: James Nisbet and Co., 1885), 10.
82   Esther 4:16. While prayer is not explicitly mentioned, it is implied. Cf. *Esther Rabbah* 8:7.
83   Polycarp, *To the Philippians* 7.2.

[1.3]
And pray for your enemies.

is one with the oppressed, hungry, and naked."[84] Fasting for our enemies causes the one being wronged to take a compassionate look at the perpetrator and to see their broken soul.

> *For what special favor do you merit if you love those who love you? Do not even the Gentiles do the same?*
> (DIDACHE 1.3)

This is a shorter version of the Master's words in Matthew 5:46–47: "If you love those who love you, what reward do you have? Do not even the tax collectors do the same? And if you greet only your brothers, what more are you doing than others? Do not even the Gentiles do the same?"[85] There is no merit in loving those who do likewise to us; their reciprocal kindness is our reward. The Didache points out that the true challenge in this command is extending ourselves to those who will never return our gestures of kindness. That is true selfless love.

The rabbis refer to obtaining merit or favor with God as *zechut* (זכות). An act of *zechut* is an exceptionally selfless deed that tips the scales of judgment in a person's favor. *Zechut* is defined as a favorable judgment, an acquittal, or merit, but in rabbinic literature "it came to be applied to the protecting influence of freely chosen good conduct over and above what was required by the Law."[86] The Master asked his disciples to go beyond the letter of the Torah and to perform acts of *zechut* in line with the spirit of the Torah. It is important to note that *zechut* is not the same as earning one's salvation by good works. Rather, acts of loving-kindness express true repentance and therefore accrue *zechut*.

This concept is deeply embedded in the gospel message. John the Baptist began his ministry by giving instructions in *zechut* to those wanting to repent: "Whoever has two tunics is to share with him who has none, and whoever has food is to do likewise" (Luke 3:11). Zacchaeus performed an act of *zechut* by going above and beyond what the Torah required for restitution, and in turn the Master told him, "Today salvation has come to this house."[87] Cornelius merited the visitation of an

---

84 Jones, *The Teaching of the Twelve*, 72.
85 Cf. Luke 6:32–33. The Apostolic Constitutions (7.2) renders it, "Love your enemies. For what special favor do you merit if you love those who love you? Do not even the Gentiles do the same?" (Matthew 5:44, 46–47; Luke 6:32). The *Oxyrhynchus Papyrus* fragments has "Do not even the Gentiles do this?"
86 Joan Taylor, *The Immerser: John the Baptist within Second Temple Judaism* (Grand Rapids, MI: Eerdmans, 1997), 124. E.g., m.*Sanhedrin* 4:1, 5:4–5, 6:1.
87 Luke 19:9.

angel, who told him, "Your prayers and your alms have ascended as a memorial before God" (Acts 10:4). His alms and prayers were an act of *zechut* before the Lord. The Apostle Peter writes, "What credit [*zechut*] is it if, when you sin and are beaten for it, you endure? But if when you do good and suffer for it you endure, this is a gracious thing in the sight of God" (1 Peter 2:20).

In the original context of the Master's saying, Yeshua used the term "Gentiles" in antithesis to his Jewish disciples. In the same way, when the word appears in the context of Didache 1.3, it must be understood to refer to idolaters who have not yet accepted the God of Israel. In the New Testament we find the Greek term *ethnos* (ἔθνος), usually translated "Gentiles," used both as a designation for heathens and as a term for non-Jews who have come to know Messiah.[88] This dual usage is in keeping with the Hebrew word *goy* (גוי), which can refer to a crowd, a nation, a people, or even a pagan. The Didache's point in its use of the word is that even idolaters are kind to their friends; true piety calls for a higher standard.

> [1.3]
> *For what special favor do you merit if you love those who love you? Do not even the Gentiles do the same?*

⁍ *However, you are to love those who hate you, and you will not have any enemies.* (DIDACHE 1.3)

The first part of this saying is similar to our Master Yeshua's injunction, "Love your enemies" (Matthew 5:44; Luke 6:27).[89]

The Apostolic Constitutions provides scriptural support for this: "He says, 'Do not hate any man; not an Egyptian, nor an Edomite' [Deuteronomy 23:7], for they are all the workmanship of God."[90] Both the Edomites and the Egyptians were enemy nations to the nation of Israel. Nevertheless, the Torah commands the Jewish people to love them and not to treat them wrongly, despite what they

---

88 For "Gentile" as "heathen," see 1 Thessalonians 4:5; 1 Peter 4:3; for "Gentile" as "non-Jewish disciple," see Acts 15:23; Ephesians 3:1, 6. See also Toby Janicki, *God-Fearers: Gentiles & the God of Israel* (Marshfield, MO: First Fruits of Zion, 2012), 15–25. In Matthew's version the Greek word is *ethnikoi* (ἐθνικοί), which is slightly different than *ethnos*, and Lachs suggests that it refers to the rabbinic term *ammei ha'aretz* ("people of the land," עמי הארץ), i.e., the Jewish population who were generally ignorant of the Torah (Lachs, *A Rabbinic Commentary on the New Testament*, 109–110).

89 It has been suggested that the Master found the injunction to love one's enemies through a midrashic reading of "You shall love your fellow" using the rabbinic method of *al tikrei* (אל תקרי), by which "your fellow" (*re'acha*, רעך) is read as "your enemy" (*ra'acha*, רעך). The *Oxyrhynchus Papyrus* fragments render this as "However, you are to feel brotherly affection for those who hate you, and you will not have any enemies." It then adds the clarifying transitional statement: "Hear what you need to do to save your spirit. First of all ..." Interestingly, the exact text τί σε δεῖ ("what you need") appears in Acts 9:6.

90 Apostolic Constitutions 7.2. It then adds, "Avoid not the persons but the sentiments of the wicked."

[1.3]
However, you are to love those who hate you, and you will not have any enemies.

did to Israel. The book of Proverbs instructs us, "Do not rejoice when your enemy falls, and let not your heart be glad when he stumbles."[91] Exodus 23:4–5 enjoins us, if we see the animal of our enemy or one who hates us lost or fallen, that we must assist in its rescue, despite the fact that our instinct is to refrain from helping. The *Sifrei* cites a similar injunction in Deuteronomy 22:4, but notes that in that passage it speaks of "your brother." It asks "Why does it [Deuteronomy] say 'your brother?' This teaches us that the Torah speaks against man's evil inclination." In other words, it says "your enemy" in one place and "your brother" in the other because they are really one and the same.

The Didache states here in verse 3 that if we love our haters, we will not have any enemies. In Hebrew this saying may have had a different connotation. The conjunction "and" in Hebrew (*vav*, ו) can have the connotation of "in order to," giving the saying this sense: "You are to love those who hate you, *in order to* not have any enemies."[92] In this vein the Apostle Paul writes, "'If your enemy is hungry, feed him; if he is thirsty, give him something to drink; for by so doing you will heap burning coals on his head.' Do not be overcome by evil, but overcome evil with good" (Romans 12:20–21, quoting Proverbs 25:21).[93] The sages say, "Who is the greatest hero of all? The one who turns an enemy into a friend."[94]

Niederwimmer has summed this up nicely: "Those who persist in loving their enemies will ultimately paralyze their aggression. Love destroys enemies."[95] We are to strive to be like our Master, who found "favor with God and man."[96]

◈ Restrain yourself from natural and physical inclinations.
(DIDACHE 1.4)

While verse 4 is not a direct quotation from the Gospels or Epistles, similar themes to that found here abound in the New Testament.[97] For example the Apostle Peter writes: "Beloved, I urge you as sojourners and exiles to abstain from the passions

---

91 Proverbs 24:17.
92 David Bivin, "'And' or 'In order to' Remarry," *Jerusalem Perspective* 50 (January–March 1996):10–17, 35–38.
93 Cf. Testament of Gad 6.1–4.
94 *Avot DeRabbi Natan* 23 (A).
95 Niederwimmer, *The Didache*, 75.
96 Luke 2:52. Cf. m.*Avot* 3:13.
97 One of the *Oxyrhynchus Papyrus* fragments of the Didache (Folio 1r) simply reads, "Keep away from natural inclinations."

of the flesh, which wage war against your soul" (1 Peter 2:11). The Master calls us to take up our cross daily, and in the same light Paul urges us to daily present our "bodies as a living sacrifice," which requires dying to self.⁹⁸ Paul writes in Titus 2:12, "Renounce ungodliness and worldly passions, and … live self-controlled, upright, and godly lives."⁹⁹ Disciples of the Master are exhorted to die to their own desires and earthly passions and instead to seek to serve God alone. In this context the battle is with the ego; it is indeed a struggle to love one's enemies and suppress revenge and anger.

[1.4]
Restrain yourself from natural and physical inclinations.

Jewish teaching, as we have noted, divides human motivations into two categories: the evil inclination (*yetzer hara*) and the good inclination (*yetzer hatov*). The evil inclination may be what the Master had in mind when he taught us to pray, "Deliver us from evil."¹⁰⁰ Judaism also speaks of two distinct souls that comprise a human being. Man contains a divine soul (*neshamah*, נשמה), which is that preexistent aspect of the soul—the "breath" of God that he breathes into human beings—and an animal soul (*nefesh*, נפש), which, although not intrinsically evil, is inclined toward the carnal and material. Paul's discussions about the dichotomy between flesh and spirit reflect the concept of the dual animal/spiritual nature of human beings. Both the evil inclination and the animal soul must be battled and channeled into righteousness.

The character quality of humility (*anavah*, ענוה) is at the heart of the instructions of Didache 1.3–5. It is only when we nullify our own egos and lower our esteem of ourselves that we will be able to overlook the wrongs that have been done to us and turn the other cheek. If we are in constant demand of personal justice and the full measure of our rights, we will be unable to meet the standard to which the Master is calling us. Rabbi Moshe Cordovaero writes that "humility" is the true key to loving one's fellow, and "thus, when insults are meted out to him, he will rejoice in them, and contrary [to the typical reaction], he will desire them."¹⁰¹

---

98   Luke 9:23; Romans 12:1.
99   Cf. Colossians 3:5–8; 1 Thessalonians 4:3–5; 2 Timothy 2:22; 1 John 2:15–16. Cf. Romans 1:24–31; Galatians 5:19–21; Ephesians 2:3.
100 Matthew 6:13.
101 *Tomer Devorah* 3 (from Rabbi Cordovaero, *Sefer Tomer Devorah*, 39–41).

> *If someone strikes you on the right cheek, turn the other to him and you will be complete.* (DIDACHE 1.4)

We come now to the first of four sayings dealing with the specifics of showing love to an enemy. Each of them illustrates the rabbinic concept of "beyond the letter of the law" (*lifnim mishurat hadin*, לפנים משורת הדין), which refers to the practice of doing more than what is minimally required by the Torah. The following four cases in the Didache involve setting aside one's rights and showing magnanimous behavior toward an enemy. The Apostolic Constitutions adds, "Not that revenge is evil, but that patience is more honorable. For David says, 'If I have repaid those that repaid me with evil' (Psalm 7:4)."[102]

The first part of this saying finds a parallel in Luke 6:29, but it is most closely aligned with Matthew 5:39: "If anyone slaps you on the right cheek, turn to him the other also."[103] Since most people are right-handed, the most common way to hit someone on the right cheek would be with a backhanded slap. When the sages were defining compensation for bodily injury, they ruled that a backhanded slap was to be compensated twice as much as a regular one,[104] since the backhanded slap was meant not only to cause bodily harm but to humiliate.[105]

It should be noted that Yeshua himself did not literally turn the other cheek when he was struck by an officer of the high priest but instead demanded justification from his strikers.[106] It seems best to read "turn the other cheek" passages as hyperbolic sayings about not seeking revenge when one has been wronged.[107] When disciples take on a posture of non-retaliation, they directly imitate Messiah: "I gave my back to those who strike, and my cheeks to those who pull out the beard; I hid not my face from disgrace and spitting" (Isaiah 50:6). The Apostle Peter describes the Master's submission: "When he was reviled, he did not revile in return; when he suffered, he did not threaten, but continued entrusting himself to him who judges justly" (1 Peter 2:23).

---

102 Apostolic Constitutions 7.2.
103 The first part of the Greek of this saying in the Apostolic Constitutions' version (7:2) is almost identical to Matthew 5:44.
104 m.*Bava Kama* 8:6.
105 Walter Wink, *Engaging the Powers: Discernment and Resistance in a World of Domination* (Minneapolis, MN: Fortress, 1992), 196.
106 John 18:23.
107 Exaggeration and hyperbole were not uncommon in rabbinic hermeneutics. The sages used a teaching method called *guzma* ("exaggeration," גוזמא). See also Rabbi Steinsaltz, *The Talmud Steinsaltz Edition: A Reference Guide*, 92.

Despite being persecuted and abused, the disciple of the Master is not to seek revenge. Proverbs teaches, "Do not say, 'I will repay evil'; wait for the LORD, and he will deliver you" (Proverbs 20:22), and Paul urges, "Beloved, never avenge yourselves, but leave it to the wrath of God" (Romans 12:19). We are to rely on our Father in heaven to defend us. The writers of the Dead Sea Scrolls shared this perspective: "I will pay to no man the reward of evil. I will pursue him with goodness, for judgment of all the living is with God, and it is he who will render to man his reward."[108]

[1.4]
If someone strikes you on the right cheek, turn the other to him and you will be complete.

After the Didache exhorts us not to seek revenge, it states, "and you will be complete." This is parallel to the way the Master closes out the "love your enemies" section of the Sermon on the Mount with, "You therefore must be perfect" (Matthew 5:48). In both the Gospels and the Didache, the original Hebrew word behind the Greek word translated into English as "perfect" (*teleios*, τέλειος) would most likely be *tamim* (תמים). *Tamim* can be understood as "perfect," but it also has the connotation of "complete," "balanced," "innocent," or "unblemished." For example, the Torah instructs Israel, "You shall be blameless [*tamim*] before the LORD your God" (Deuteronomy 18:13). In the context of the Didache and Matthew 5:48 a better might say, "You will thus be impartial." The exhortation is for us to be impartial and equitable in all our dealings with people; when we do so, we are blameless before God. In our quest to become perfect, we become more like our Master, who is perfect.

⚜ *If someone forces you to go one mile, go with him two.*
(DIDACHE 1.4)

This is an identical parallel to Matthew 5:41. Under the tyranny of Roman occupation, Roman soldiers could force a man without Roman citizenship to carry a load for them. Few things would have been more hateful for Jewish people and non-Roman citizens than to be forced to serve the Romans like pack animals. The Greek Stoic philosopher Epictetus similarly writes, "If there be a press, and a soldier should lay hold of [your donkey], let it go, do not resist, nor murmur; if you do, you will receive blows, and nevertheless you will also lose the donkey."[109]

Our Master Yeshua instructed his disciples to disarm their opponents by going an extra mile. Instead of complaining, a follower of the Master was to acquiesce

---

108 Community Rule (1QS) x, 17–20.
109 Epictetus, *Dissertations* 4.1.79.

[1.4] *If someone forces you to go one mile, go with him two.*

without protest and perform even more than was expected. This act of total love and submission would send a tremendous message about the character of the God of Israel. Additionally, "The first mile renders to Caesar the things that are Caesar's, the second mile, by meeting oppression with kindness, renders to God the things that are God's."[110]

> *If someone takes away your cloak, give him your tunic also.* (DIDACHE 1.4)

This statement is similar to the canonical saying, "If anyone would sue you and take your tunic, let him have your cloak as well" (Matthew 5:40), and this is how it is rendered in the Apostolic Constitutions.[111] The "tunic" (*chiton*, χιτών) was a plain undergarment usually made of linen, whereas the "cloak" (*himation*, ἱμάτιον) was a heavier outer garment generally made of wool. In the Jewish context of Matthew, the tunic would correspond to the *chaluk* (חלוק) and the cloak to the *tallit* (טלית).[112]

Based upon Matthew's and the Apostolic Constitutions' rendering "if anyone would sue you," the context of this saying is that of litigation. In a court of law, a creditor could quite literally demand the shirt off a debtor's back. Rather than resist the litigation, Yeshua advised his disciple to go further and give the creditor his cloak as well. The Torah forbids creditors from seizing a man's cloak, and Amos chastises those who transgress this prohibition.[113] The Didache instructs us to demonstrate our good faith by voluntarily setting aside our rights. This would surely merit favor with God, for the sages say that "the Holy One, blessed be He, loves the one who does not insist on his full rights" (b.*Pesachim* 113b).

Furthermore, the Master taught his disciples to avoid going to court altogether and instead to attempt to settle with their accusers before a case went to court.[114] While our Master Yeshua was speaking to disciples within the Jewish community, the Apostle Paul told the mixed Jewish/Gentile community of Corinth the same thing: They should avoid going to court and instead settle their disputes within the body of believers and before a court of congregational elders.[115]

---

110   T.W. Manson, *The Sayings of Jesus* (London, England: SCM, 1971), 160.
111   Apostolic Constitutions 7.2. Cf. Luke 6:29.
112   David Bivin, "The Hem of His Garment," *Jerusalem Perspective* 7 (1988): 2.
113   Exodus 22:26–27; Deuteronomy 24:13; Amos 2:8.
114   Matthew 5:25; Luke 12:58.
115   1 Corinthians 6:1–6.

> *If someone takes away what is yours, do not demand it back, for you are not even able to get it back.* (DIDACHE 1.4)

A close parallel to this command is found in the Master's words, "From one who takes away your goods do not demand them back" (Luke 6:30).[116] Such behavior is reminiscent of m.*Avot* 5:3: "One who says: 'What's mine is yours and what's yours is yours' is pious."

The litigation context from the previous saying should be assumed here as well. Historical circumstances from around the time of the writing of the Didache may help shed light on the meaning of this saying. At that time the Roman emperor Domitian was strictly enforcing the *Fiscus Judaicus* (Jewish tax), which had been introduced by his father Vespasian.[117] Every Jewish person in the Roman Empire was required to pay an annual poll tax of two drachmas. Although Roman law required only Jews to pay the tax, the authorities did not distinguish between those who were legally Jewish and people who merely practiced aspects of Judaism. That ambiguity sometimes made God-fearing Gentile believers liable for the tax as well. If a court convicted someone of being Jewish and of having failed to pay the required tax, that person might face imprisonment, the confiscation of his property, or even execution.

The Roman historian Suetonius writes about the arrest and prosecution of Gentiles "who did not publicly acknowledge the Jewish faith but lived as Jews."[118] The God-fearing Gentile believers did not publicly acknowledge their faith, because they feared arrest and persecution, and they did not pay the *Fiscus Judaicus*, because they were not Jewish. Gentiles in the Didache community may have faced the same dilemma and, after having been accused of skirting the *Fiscus Judaicus*, would have had their property forcibly taken from them by the Roman government.

The Didache admonishes its readers to accept these chastisements and not to retaliate. After all, they were "not even able" (not able to), fight against the Roman government. Instead, once again, they were to rely on their Father in heaven who would "plead their cause and rob of life those who rob them" (Proverbs 22:23). Neiderwimmer gets to the heart of the Didache:

---

116   This is how it is rendered in the Apostolic Constitutions (7.2) as well.
117   This section draws from the more detailed discussion found in D. Thomas Lancaster, *Torah Club: Chronicles of the Apostles* (6 vols.; Marshfield, MO: First Fruits of Zion, 2016), 4:1203–1204.
118   Suetonius, *Domitianus* 12.2.

> [1.4]
> *If someone takes away what is yours, do not demand it back, for you are not even able to get it back.*

In renunciation of a violent enforcement of one's own right the law of a higher, although paradoxical, order becomes visible: the law of the reign of God. At the same time the attitude of those who are insulted, oppressed, and robbed … reveals the peculiar powerlessness of aggression. Those who live according to the precepts have removed themselves from the ordinary norms and rules of society and set themselves on a road that (as far as *this* world is concerned) leads to the discipleship of the cross and (in light of what is *to come*) to the reign of God.[119]

In other words, refraining from retaliation is part of the way of discipleship to the Master and reflects the order of the Messianic Era. Hence, the Georgian version of the Didache states: "You are not able to do this, and for the sake of your faith."

⁕ Give to whoever asks and do not demand it back.
(DIDACHE 1.5)

We find parallels to this statement in both Matthew 5:42, "Give to the one who [asks] from you, and do not refuse the one who would borrow from you,"[120] and Luke 6:30, "Give to everyone who [asks] from you, and from one who takes away your goods do not demand them back." The Apostolic Constitutions (7.2) cites Matthew 5:42 and also Psalm 112:5: "It is well with the man who deals generously and lends."

At first glance it appears that the Didache enjoins us to give anything to anyone who asks us for it. However, the Greek word for "asks" is *aiteo* (αἰτέω), which is the equivalent in the Septuagint to the Hebrew word *sha'al* (שאל). In Mishnaic Hebrew *sha'al* can be used in the sense of borrowing.[121] The passage may be referring to someone who wants to borrow something rather than take it. This makes sense

---

119 Neiderwimmer, *The Didache*, 79.
120 The Apostolic Constitutions (7.2) renders this verse from the Didache with a passage almost identical to Matthew 5:42 but with slightly different wording in Greek.
121 E.g., m.*Shabbat* 23:1; m.*Taanit* 4:8.

in light of the instructions not to ask for the item back; if it had been given, one would not expect it to be returned.¹²²

The Torah commands, "If you lend money to any of my people with you who is poor, you shall not be like a moneylender to him, and you shall not exact interest from him" (Exodus 22:25). The sages interpreted this injunction to mean that when we lend to the poor among God's people, we cannot hound them for repayment the way that a creditor might. Our Master Yeshua says, "Love your enemies, and do good, and lend, expecting nothing in return, and your reward will be great, and you will be sons of the Most High, for he is kind to the ungrateful and the evil" (Luke 6:35).

The Master's saying in the Gospels likely pertains to lending money just before the Sabbatical Year. People often refused to give out loans just before the Sabbatical Year because all loans would be canceled in that year.¹²³ In the Didache, however, the context is not the Sabbatical Year because the Sabbatical restrictions do not apply to non-Jews living in the Diaspora. Instead it should be read in the general sense that one should not hold back from lending due to a fear of not having an item returned or paid back.

The Didache's attitude toward lending is echoed by Sirach: "Today he lends, tomorrow he will demand it back; hateful is such a one" (20.15). When we freely lend something, we should not hound someone as would a creditor who is waiting for the loaned item to be returned. Furthermore, the context here should remain within the scope of loving one's enemies. One should not hold back from lending someone something as a way of exacting revenge on that person.

[1.5]
Give to whoever asks and do not demand it back.

---

122 The version of the saying from Matthew 5:42 is couched in Hebrew poetry. "Give to the one who [asks]" is parallel to "not refuse ... borrow." The Greek word for "borrow" here is *danizo* (δανίζω) and corresponds in the Septuagint to the Hebrew word *lavah* (לוה). Why two Hebrew words for "borrow"? *Sha'al* refers to borrowing an item that is returned, such as a lawn mower, and *lavah* refers to borrowing something like money, when the same money is not returned but rather an equal amount. See David Bivin and Roy Blizzard, Jr., *Understanding the Difficult Words of Jesus: New Insights from a Hebraic Perspective* (Shippensburg, PA: Destiny Image, 1994), 73–75.

123 Deuteronomy 15:1–3. This was such a major issue during that time that the poor were unable to obtain credit. Hillel the Elder instituted a legal loophole called the *prosbul* that allowed people to loan money without having the debt canceled (m.*Shevi'it* 10:3). If that was the context, Yeshua was urging people to loan money without concern for whether it was paid back or not. He says in the Lukan version, "If you lend to those from whom you expect to receive, what credit is that to you? Even sinners lend to sinners, to get back the same amount" (Luke 6:34).

◈ *For the Father wants to give of his own gifts to everyone.*
   (DIDACHE 1.5)

The rest of chapter 1 has no close canonical or non-canonical Gospel parallels, but it seems clear that these sayings should also be viewed as words of the Master. The Apostolic Constitutions brings in the Master's words: "For the Father wants to give to everyone, 'for he makes his sun rise on the evil and on the good, and sends rain on the just and on the unjust'" (Matthew 5:45).[124]

In Jewish thought God's material blessings are meant to be shared by all mankind: not only are the needy entitled to alms, but the wealthy are obligated to give.[125] The Torah instructs, "As the LORD your God has blessed you, you shall give to him" (Deuteronomy 15:14). The universal Pseudo-Phocylides teaches, "What God has given to you, give of it to the needy."

When we give charity, we are in reality giving of what does not belong to us. Rather, we are giving of "that which is his."[126] That is one of the main reasons we should give: to share God's bounty with all his creatures. In the act of giving, the disciple of the Master becomes "a servant of the lender" (Proverbs 22:7)—that is, a manager of the divine gifts.[127]

In essence, the Didache asks us to imitate God: Just as he has given freely to us, so we should freely give to others.

◈ *Contentment awaits one who gives according to the commandment, for he is blameless.* (DIDACHE 1.5)

This saying in verse 5 is a beatitude, a common form of Jewish wisdom sayings. It follows the typical beatitude formula such as those found in Matthew 5:3–11. It forms a couplet in antithesis with an ensuing "woe" statement: "How terrible for the one who takes." Yeshua used the same mirror symmetry to contrast beatitudes against woe statements in Luke 6:20–26. In this instance "Contentment awaits one who gives" is balanced in the next part of verse 5 by, "How terrible for the one who takes!" The closest canonical saying of the Master to this is the one reported

---

124 Apostolic Constitutions 7.2.
125 Neiderwimmer, *The Didache*, 82.
126 m.*Avot* 2:7.
127 *Leviticus Rabbah* 34:2.

by Paul in Acts 20:35: "It is more blessed to give than to receive."[128] The Apostolic Constitutions renders this, "It is therefore reasonable to give to all out of your own labors; for he says, 'Honor the Lord out of your righteous labors' (Proverbs 3:9)."[129]

The Didache makes reference to the commandment of charity. The sages of Israel derived two commandments pertaining to charity from the text of the Torah in Deuteronomy 15:7–8: "If there is a poor man with you ... you shall not harden your heart, nor close your hand from your poor brother; but you shall freely open your hand to him." "You shall open your hand to him" was taken as the positive commandment to give charity, whereas "you shall not harden your heart or shut your hand against your poor brother" was interpreted as the negative commandment not to ignore a person in need.

It can be inferred that when the Didache speaks about giving "according to the commandment," it not only has the Torah's injunctions in mind but also the Master's halachah. In the parable of the widow's gift, we learn that our giving should not merely be out of our surplus; we should give sacrificially. Our Master Yeshua further instructed, "When you give to the needy, sound no trumpet before you ... But when you give to the needy, do not let your left hand know what your right hand is doing, so that your giving may be in secret" (Matthew 6:2–4). When we give in this manner, our Father in heaven promises to reward us.

This Didache passage teaches that when we give in accordance with the Torah's commandments on charity, we will be "blameless." The Greek word here for "blameless" is *athoos* (ἀθῷος) which corresponds in the Septuagint to the Hebrew word *nakah* (נקה). *Nakah* means "to be clear," and it is used in rabbinic literature in both a judicial and a heavenly sense.[130] The disciple who gives is blameless in regard to his stewardship over his resources, because he gives according to the commandment.

[1.5]
Contentment awaits one who gives according to the commandment, for he is blameless.

---

128 Cf. "He then that gives is guiltless; for as he received from the Lord the ministration to perform it, he has performed it in sincerity, by making no distinction to whom to give or not to give" (Shepherd of Hermas, Mandate 2.6 [27.6]). Also 1 Clement 2.1.
129 Apostolic Constitutions 7.2.
130 Marcus Jastrow, "נקי, נקה" in *A Dictionary of the Targumim, the Talmud Babli and Yerushalmi, and the Midrashic Literature* (2 vols.; New York, NY, Pardes, 1950), 2:932.

> ◈ *How terrible for one who takes!*
> *For anyone who has a need and takes will be blameless;*
> *but one who does not have a need will give an account as to*
> *why he took it and for what purpose. And when he is put into*
> *prison, he will be questioned thoroughly about what he*
> *has done, and he will not get out from there until*
> *he has paid the last penny.* (DIDACHE (1.5))

Again, there are no direct parallels to this saying in the canonical Gospels. Matthew 5:25–26 seems to correspond to it but has a completely different context: "Come to terms quickly with your accuser … lest your accuser hand you over to the judge, and the judge to the guard, and you be put in prison … You will never get out until you have paid the last penny."[131]

In the context of the Didache, verse 5 is saying that the one who receives should be warned about taking charity if he does not truly need it. If he receives in need, he shall not be judged; however, if he receives when he does not need, he shall pay a penalty. Once this is made clear, the Didache then gives halachic instruction for both the giver and the receiver. The rich are to give according to the commandment, and the poor are to receive only when necessary. When someone receives alms under false pretenses, he will be punished as a debtor who has defaulted on a loan—thrown into a Roman debtor's prison and not released until he has paid the debt. The Greek word *kodrantes* (κοδράντης) "is the smallest denomination of coin and indicates that the debt will be paid to the last balance."[132]

The sages believed that one who received charity but did not need it would be punished by actually becoming needy:

> Our Rabbis taught: If a man pretends to have a blind eye, a swollen belly or a shrunken leg, he will not pass out from this world before actually coming into such a condition. If a man accepts charity and is not in

---

[131] Cf. Luke 12:58–59. The section also bears slight resemblance to the Beatitudes section in Luke 6:20–26 with its opposing "blessed are you … woe to you" phrases. Cf. "He who is liable to confiscation of goods falls ill and is not healed until he pays all that is decreed against him. When he has paid his money penalty he is healed and goes out from his prison, and therefore it is fitting that one should assist him to pay his fine and be released" (*Zohar* III, 299b).

[132] Philip Schaff, *The Oldest Church Manual Called the Teaching of the Twelve Apostles* (Edinburgh, Scotland: T&T Clark, 1885), 166. In Hebrew *kodrantes* would refer to a *prutah* (פרוטה), which was the smallest denomination of currency in Jewish law that could be paid for legal purposes.

need of it his end [will be that] he will not pass out of the world before he comes to such a condition.¹³³

Both Matthew 5:26 and the Didache speak of such an individual not getting out of prison until the last penny is paid. Rabbi Yechiel Tzvi Lichtenstein comments on the Matthew version: "The allusion, of course, is to Geihinnom. Christian scholars have not understood this because, in their opinion, those who enter Geihinnom never come out for eternity."¹³⁴ Rabbi Lichtenstein sees this language about prison and repayment as alluding to the amount of time that one will have to spend in Geihinnom in order to purge his sin. In Jewish theology a person can enter Geihinnom, suffer for his transgressions, and later be released.

[1.5]
How terrible for one who takes! For anyone who has a need and takes will be blameless; but one who does not have a need will give an account as to why he took it and for what purpose. And when he is put into prison, he will be questioned thoroughly about what he has done, and he will not get out from there until he has paid the last penny.

> *But regarding this it has also been said, "Let your donation sweat in your hands until you know to whom to give it."* (DIDACHE 1.6)

There are no parallels to this saying in the canonical Gospels or in apocryphal material attributed to Yeshua. This statement may have been a saying of the Master, but the Didache appears to be quoting what it considers a scriptural source.¹³⁵

The common Hebrew expression "it has been said" (*shene'emar*, שנאמר) was used in rabbinic literature to introduce a quotation from the Hebrew Scriptures.¹³⁶ Yet the exact source of this quotation remains a mystery. Some scholars suggest that the quotation is from a now extinct apocryphal source.¹³⁷ The proverb seems to have been popular in the early believing community.¹³⁸

---

133   b.*Ketubot* 68a.
134   Yechiel Tzvi Lichtenstein, *Commentary on the New Testament* (trans. Aaron Eby and Robert Morris; Marshfield, MO: Vine of David, unpublished) on Matthew 5:26; trans. of *Bi'ur Lesifrei Brit HaChadashah* (8 vols.; Leipzig, Germany: Professor G. Dahlman, 1891–1904).
135   The style here is similar to the talmudic hermeneutic *asmachta* ("support," אסמכתא), in which a biblical verse is cited as support for a halachah. See Rabbi Steinsaltz, *The Talmud Steinsaltz Edition: A Reference Guide*, 149.
136   Bruce M. Metzger, "The Formulas Introducing Quotations of Scripture in the NT and the Mishnah," *Journal of Biblical Literature* 70, no. 4 (December 1951): 297–307. See also Rabbi Steinsaltz, *The Talmud Steinsaltz Edition: A Reference Guide*, 96. This is the same phrase that is used to introduce the scriptural quotation of Zechariah 14:5 in Didache 16.7.
137   Others suggest a combination of several texts. For example, "By the sweat of your face you shall eat bread" (Genesis 3:19); "Let him labor, doing honest work with his own hands, so that he may have something to share with anyone in need" (Ephesians 4:28); and, "If you do a kindness, know to whom you do it, and you will be thanked for your good deeds" (Sirach 12:1).
138   An almost direct parallel is found in Augustine's commentary on Psalm 147:13.

[1.6] *But regarding this it has also been said, "Let your donation sweat in your hands until you know to whom to give it."*

"Let your donation sweat in your hands" seems to indicate an eagerness to give. It may be similar to the modern English expression "burning a hole in your pocket." It's sweating because one is so anxious to give it to someone as soon as possible and they don't want it in their hands any more.

At the same time, the Didache challenges the giver to use some discernment regarding to whom he gives money. The Apostolic Constitutions adds, "So that the holy be preferred," which implies that the needs of the community should be considered first.[139] A disciple of the Master should hold on to his money until he finds a worthy cause to which to give it. We are not to give hastily. While in the earlier passage the receiver is warned of the consequences of receiving charity when not in need, here the giver is told to "know to whom to give it." Indeed, blessed is the one who freely gives charity, but at the same time the Didache teaches that he should do so wisely, using caution, prudence, and common sense.

---

139 Apostolic Constitutions 7.2, perhaps quoting or alluding to Galatians 6:10.

Chapter Two

DIDACHE 2

2.1 And the second commandment of the teaching is:

2.2 Do not murder.[1] Do not commit adultery.[2] Do not practice pederasty. Do not commit sexual immorality.[3] Do not steal.[4] Do not practice magic.[5] Do not use potions. Do not murder children through abortion nor kill them after they have been born. Do not covet the things that belong to your fellow.[6]

2.3 Do not swear falsely.[7] Do not bear false witness.[8] Do not slander anyone.[9] Do not hold grudges.[10]

2.4 Do not be double-minded[11] or double-tongued,[12] for a double tongue is a deadly trap.

2.5 Do not let your word be false or empty, but let it be fulfilled in action.[13]

---

1 Exodus 20:13; Deuteronomy 5:17; Matthew 5:21, 19:18; Mark 10:19; Luke 18:20; Romans 13:9; James 2:11.
2 Exodus 20:14; Deuteronomy 5:18; Matthew 5:27, 19:18; Mark 10:19; Luke 18:20; Romans 2:22, 13:9; James 2:11.
3 Acts 15:20, 29, 21:25; 1 Corinthians 6:13, 18, 10:8; 1 Thessalonians 4:3; Hebrews 12:16.
4 Exodus 20:15; Leviticus 19:11; Deuteronomy 5:19; Matthew 19:18; Romans 13:9.
5 Exodus 22:18; Leviticus 19:26, 31; Deuteronomy 18:10–11.
6 Exodus 20:17; Deuteronomy 5:21; Romans 7:7, 13:9; Ephesians 5:3.
7 Leviticus 19:12; Matthew 5:33.
8 Exodus 20:16; Deuteronomy 5:20; Matthew 19:18; Mark 10:19; Luke 18:20.
9 1 Peter 2:1.
10 Leviticus 19:18.
11 James 1:7–8.
12 1 Timothy 3:8.
13 Numbers 30:2; Deuteronomy 23:23.

2.6 Do not be greedy,[14] or predatory, or hypocritical,[15] or malicious, or arrogant.[16] Do not plot evil against your fellow.[17]

2.7 Do not hate any human being; but some you are to rebuke,[18] and some you are to pray for, yet some you are to love even more than your own life.

---

14 Luke 12:15; Ephesians 5:3; Colossians 3:5.
15 1 Peter 2:1.
16 Romans 12:3.
17 Proverbs 3:29; Zechariah 8:17.
18 Leviticus 19:17.

Overview

Chapter 2 opens by introducing us to the "second commandment of the teaching" of the Didache. One might naturally assume that the words "second commandment" refer to "Love your fellow as yourself," distinguishing it from the first commandment, "You shall love God who made you" (1.2). On the contrary, the term "second commandment of the teaching" refers to a distinction between the positive and negative forms of the Golden Rule. The first two chapters of the Didache, as was explained in chapter 1 of this work, are organized under the following scheme:

- FIRST COMMANDMENT OF THE TEACHING: *You shall love your fellow as yourself.*
    - Positive Commandments
    - Didache 1.3–6
- SECOND COMMANDMENT OF THE TEACHING: *Whatever you do not want to happen to you, do not do to one another.*
    - Negative Commandments
    - Didache 2.1–7

While chapter 1 expounds the first commandment "Love your fellow as yourself," this chapter expands upon the commandment "Whatever you do not want to happen to you, do not do to one another" (1.2). It includes prohibitions ranging from abortion to slander. At first glance it may appear that this list is a mishmash of restrictions with no particular method of organization, but upon closer examination, we see that the writer of the Didache has a clear method of teaching and a specific purpose for each negative commandment that he lists.

The inventory of prohibitions in chapter 2 contains "downright distasteful" sins, "cataloguing some of the most heinous acts that humans can perpetuate upon one another."[19] Few transgressions are more despicable than murder, adultery, and the exposure and molestation of children, yet the very fact that these prohibitions had to be listed is evidence that those reading the Didache had struggled

---

19   Tony Jones, *The Teaching of the Twelve: Believing & Practicing the Primitive Christianity of the Ancient Didache Community* (Brewster, MA: Paraclete, 2009), 73.

with these very sins before coming to faith in Messiah. This list is the evidence of God's grace upon their former lives and transgressions. God loved them enough to forgive them. In this light the list of heinous sins is actually "the heart of God on paper."[20] But this collection of prohibitions is also a call, as the Apostle Peter wrote, to walk "as obedient children": "Do not be conformed to the passions of your former ignorance, but as he who called you is holy, you also be holy in all your conduct" (1 Peter 1:14–15).

The Centrality of the Decalogue

The first list of prohibitions, found in verse 2, centers around the Decalogue, in particular the second tablet—the last five commandments. While in modern times it seems that the Ten Commandments play a more prominent role in Christianity than they do in Judaism, in the first century this set of instructions was central to the Jewish faith.

In Second-Temple times the Ten Commandments were recited in conjunction with the morning *Shma* in the Temple liturgy.[21] They are even found in some of the tefillin parchments from Qumran, where the Dead Sea Scrolls were discovered.[22]

The Decalogue was also viewed as a summary of the entire Torah: the first five commandments dealing with love for God and the second five dealing with love for one's fellow. Each commandment of the Torah can be placed into one of the Ten Commandments. Philo writes, "The ten commandments are the heads of all the particular and special laws which are recorded throughout all the history of the giving of the law related in the sacred scriptures."[23] It is therefore clear that the Decalogue played a key role in Judaism at the time of the writing of the Didache.

As the words of the Master in Didache 1 assert the authority of Yeshua, so the presence of the Ten Commandments in the work affirms the Didache's commitment to the Torah of Moses. Contrary to many Hellenistic Jewish texts of the day, the Didache "does not argue *to* the Torah but *from* it, taking [the Torah's] authority as self-evident"; furthermore, it "avoids any contrast between the Mosaic law and the

---

20 Ibid., 73.
21 m. *Tamid* 5:1. However, the Talmud says that this practice stopped because certain "heretics" began to say that only the Decalogue was given at Sinai; this may be a reference to the early believers reciting it on a daily basis. See b. *Brachot* 12a.
22 Yigael Yadin, *Tefillin from Qumran (XQ Phyl 1–4)* (Jerusalem, Israel: Israel Exploration Society, 1969), 9. The church father Jerome also reports that a pair of tefillin that he saw contained the Decalogue (*Commentary on Matthew* 23:6).
23 Philo, *On the Decalogue* 154.

dominical teaching."[24] The inclusion of the Decalogue shows that the writers of the Didache, in addition to expounding the teachings of Yeshua, were on a mission to teach the fundamentals of Judaism to the nations.[25] The contents do not present a new religion but rather a continuation of what was already contained in Judaism.

The Decalogue and the Shma

The Decalogue is thought to be not only a summary of the Torah but also "the very essence of the *Shma*."[26] This explains its pairing with the *Shma* in the morning liturgy of the Second Temple Period and in tefillin from Qumran. One of the oldest Hebrew manuscripts, the *Nash Papyrus* (165–137 BCE), contains only the *Shma* and the Decalogue.[27] Early on a clear bond could be seen between the two.[28]

This is important for the purposes of the Didache, because as we saw, while not overtly evoking Deuteronomy 6:5 ("You shall love the LORD your God with all your heart and with all your soul and with all your might"), the opening lines of the Didache ("You shall love God who made you") clearly have the backdrop of the *Shma* in mind. Even the idea of two choices, "one of life and one of death" (1.1), can be found in Deuteronomy 11:13–21 (the second paragraph of the *Shma*), where we see that obedience equals blessing, and disobedience equals cursing. Therefore, when the writer of the Didache clearly draws on the Decalogue here in 2.2 and does so in a *Shma* context, he is in step with the Judaism of his day, which often paired the Ten Commandments and the *Shma* together.

---

24 Kari Syreeni, "The Sermon on the Mount and the Two Ways Teaching of the Didache," in *Matthew and the Didache: Two Documents from the Same Jewish-Christian Milieu?* (ed. Huub van de Sandt; Assen, Netherlands: Fortress, 2005), 95–96.
25 Huub van de Sandt and David Flusser, *The Didache: Its Jewish Sources and Its Place in Early Judaism and Christianity* (Minneapolis, MN: Fortress, 2002), 162.
26 y.*Brachot* 1:5.
27 James R. Adair, Jr., "Nash Papyrus," *Eerdmans Dictionary of the Bible* (ed. David Noel Freedman; Grand Rapids, MI: Eerdmans, 2000), 948; W.F. Albright, "A Biblical Fragment from the Maccabaean Age: The Nash Papyrus," *Journal of Biblical Literature* 56 no. 3 (1937): 145–176.
28 It's worth noting that the Didache follows the Community Rule in practice by opening with something akin to the *Shma* and then a series of commandments. This would imply that these types of Jewish community "charters" commonly opened with (at least) the *Shma*. See Community Rule (1QS) I, 1–11.

The Decalogue in the Didache

While Didache 2.2 makes use of the Decalogue, it primarily focuses on the last five of the Ten Commandments. This is very much in line with other writings of the period that were specifically designed for non-Jews:

> Neither commit adultery, nor arouse male passions. Neither plot treachery, nor defile your hands with blood. Do not become rich unjustly, but from holy means live. Be content with what is yours and abstain from the things of others. Do not speak lies, but the truth always speak. First honor God, and then your parents. (Pseudo-Phocylides 3–8)[29]

Although Pseudo-Phocylides adds honor of parents (which is the last of the first five of the Ten Commandments), it otherwise ignores the first tablet, or the first five commandments, when speaking to non-Jews about the Decalogue. We find a similar pattern in the Clementine Homilies, which was written by Jewish followers of Yeshua:

> As the God-fearing Jews have heard, do you also hear ... Let each man be minded to do to his neighbor those good things he wishes for himself. And you may all find out what is good, by holding some such conversation as the following with yourselves: You would not like to be murdered; do not murder another man: you would not like your wife to be seduced by another; do not commit adultery: you would not like any of your things to be stolen from you; steal nothing from another. (Pseudo-Clementine Homilies 7.4)[30]

The Clementine Homilies connects the last five commandments with the Golden Rule, that is, the commandment to love one's neighbor as oneself.[31] Therefore, an important connection exists between the last five commandments of the Decalogue and the injunction to love one's neighbor. Based upon the expression "as the God-fearing Jews have heard," there seems to have been a midrashic tradition

---

29   Cf. Jubilees 7:20–28. It is significant that in the rabbinic legend about the Torah being given first to the seventy nations of the world before Israel, the commandments that are mentioned are all from the last five: murder, adultery, and theft *(Sifrei,* Deuteronomy 343).
30   Cf. Pseudo-Clementine Homilies 8.23.
31   "The idea that all of the commandments of Torah are embedded in the Ten Commandments probably resulted in the notion that the last five of these commandments, dealing with the relations between man and his fellow man, are concentrated in the command to love one's neighbor" (Van de Sandt and Flusser, *The Didache,* 165).

that circulated in Jewish circles of the day connecting these two commands.³² This is exactly what happens in the Didache—chapter 1 begins with the injunction to "love your fellow as yourself," and the Golden Rule then leads into the Decalogue in chapter 2.

Indeed, we find further examples of this connection in the New Testament. When the Master is asked a question about obtaining eternal life, he brings the two together:

> You shall not murder, You shall not commit adultery, You shall not steal, You shall not bear false witness, Honor your father and mother, and, You shall love your neighbor as yourself. (Matthew 19:18–19)³³

Paul, writing to Gentile believers in Rome, states,

> The commandments, "You shall not commit adultery, You shall not murder, You shall not steal, You shall not covet," and any other commandment, are summed up in this word: "You shall love your neighbor as yourself." (Romans 13:9)³⁴

Both the Master and Paul combine injunctions from the last five of the Ten Commandments with Leviticus 19:18 ("Love your neighbor as yourself"). The Didache's pairing of the last five commandments of the Decalogue with the Golden Rule finds its precedence in the Judaism of the day, including the world of the Master and the apostles. It is likely that this combination was popular among the early Jewish believers.

Structure of the Didache Decalogue

The reordering of the Decalogue and the expounding of its prohibitions, which we find here in Didache 2.2, are completely in line with other Jewish sources from the

---

32   Ibid. It could be that Hillel's second rule of interpretation "general and particular" (*kelal uferat*, כלל ופרט) is being used here, in which the general commandment (loving one's neighbor) is illustrated in the particular (the last five commandments of the Decalogue).
33   Cf. Mark 10:18–19.
34   Ellis argues that Paul in Romans 13:9 is using logic similar to Hillel's second rule of interpretation "general and particular," in which "the particular commandments are apparently regarded as illustrative examples of the general [i.e., 'love your neighbor as yourself']" (E. Earle Ellis, *The Old Testament in Early Christianity: Canon and Interpretation in the Light of Modern Research* [Grand Rapids, MI: Baker, 1991], 90).

same time period. In its version of the Decalogue, the Didache preserves the tenfold repetition of "Do not," which retains the linguistic structure of the Decalogue:[35]

	The Didache	The Decalogue
1	Do not murder.	Exodus 20:13; Deuteronomy 5:17
2	Do not commit adultery.	Exodus 20:14; Deuteronomy 5:18
3	Do not practice pederasty.	N/A
4	Do not commit sexual immorality.	N/A
5	Do not steal.	Exodus 20:15; Deuteronomy 5:19
6	Do not practice magic.	N/A
7	Do not use potions.	N/A
8	Do not murder children through abortion.	N/A
9	[Do not] kill [children] after they have been born.	N/A
10	Do not covet the things that belong to your neighbor.	Exodus 20:17; Deuteronomy 5:21

Prohibited Speech and Action

The rest of chapter 2 (2.3–7) is split into three sub-sections: first, verses 3–5 detail five prohibitions of speech; then verse 6 lists five evil character traits; and finally, verse 7 contains summary points that divide people into three basic categories.

---

35 Aaron Milavec, *The Didache: Faith, Hope, & Life of the Earliest Christian Communities, 50–70 C.E.* (New York, NY: Newman, 2003), 117.

Prohibited Speech		Evil Character Traits	
2.3	Swearing falsely	2.6	Envy
	Bearing false witness		Predation
	Slandering anyone		Hypocrisy
	Holding grudges		Malice
2.4–5	Using double-minded, double-tongued, false, or empty words		Arrogance

Final Summary Points Dividing People into Three Categories	
2.7	Those we are to rebuke
	Those we are to pray for
	Those we are to love more than our own life

In this section the Didache, in a similar manner to the book of James, combines the theme of Leviticus 19:18 ("You shall love your neighbor") with material from the Holiness Code (Leviticus 17–26) to form an "ethical concentration of the Torah."[36] Other such lists appear in the New Testament:

> What comes out of a person is what defiles him. For from within, out of the heart of man, come evil thoughts, sexual immorality, theft, murder, adultery, coveting, wickedness, deceit, sensuality, envy, slander, pride, foolishness. All these evil things come from within, and they defile a person. (Mark 7:20–23)

> They were filled with all manner of unrighteousness, evil, covetousness, malice. They are full of envy, murder, strife, deceit, maliciousness. They are gossips, slanderers, haters of God, insolent, haughty, boastful, inventors of evil, disobedient to parents, foolish, faithless, heartless, ruthless. (Romans 1:29–31)

---

36 Syreeni, "The Sermon on the Mount and the Two Ways Teaching of the Didache," 95.

It was important to address proper speech and character traits up front for the new Gentile believers. The focus, once again, is on actions and not doctrine or a list of what to believe. As James, the brother of the Master says, "A person is justified by works and not by faith alone" (James 2:24). To demonstrate our repentance and faith in Messiah Yeshua, we need to display a lifestyle that is consistent with Torah and the Way of Life.

Commentary

⦿ And the second commandment of the teaching is ...
(DIDACHE 2.1)

Chapter 2 begins with an introductory statement on "the second commandment," which was first introduced in chapter 1: "Whatever you do not want to happen to you, do not do to one another" (1.2).

As was pointed out in chapter 1, the Didache treats the injunction to love one's fellow as comprising two distinct commandments. The first commandment involves positive actions to be performed ("You shall love your fellow as yourself"), which were expounded on in 1.3–5. "The second commandment" involves negative actions to be avoided in light of the negative form of the Golden Rule (1.2), which are expounded on here in chapter 2.

The second chapter of the Didache focuses on the application of the commandment "Whatever you do not want to happen to you, do not do to one another" as expressed in the Decalogue. The Didache here also brings ethical injunctions on word and deed specifically tailored for its Gentile audience and the issues that non-Jewish believers faced in their Greco-Roman pagan cultural context.

⦿ Do not murder. (DIDACHE 2.2)

The Didache here begins its list from the Decalogue with the sixth commandment (the first command of the second tablet).[37] Murder, along with adultery, was considered one of the classic prohibitions of Judaism. As does the Didache, Yeshua dealt with these two injunctions side by side in the Sermon on the Mount, and James, the brother of the Master, cited murder in connection with adultery as transgressions of the Torah.[38]

Rashbam points out that in the Torah the Hebrew verb *ratzach* ("to murder," רצח) refers only to unlawful killing; the Bible does not use this word in the context of war or justifiable killings. Therefore, this prohibition should not be viewed as

---

37 The Greek text matches exactly with the Septuagint for Exodus 20:13 and Deuteronomy 5:17.
38 Matthew 5:21, 27; James 2:11.

[2.2] *Do not murder.* forbidding killing in cases of self-defense, wartime, or the administration of capital punishment. The Apostolic Constitutions aptly expands this section of the Didache:

> "Do not murder;" that is, do not destroy a man like yourself: for you dissolve what was well made. Not as if all killing were wicked, but only that of the innocent: but the killing which is just is reserved to the magistrates alone. (Apostolic Constitutions 7.2)

The penalty for murder in the Torah is death. This is a universal rule, as it was established even before the Torah was given: "Whoever sheds the blood of man, by man shall his blood be shed" (Genesis 9:6); and murder is prohibited because "God made man in his own image":[39]

> This teaches that each person in some sense contains a reflection of God, and therefore possesses a dimension of holiness. Taking a human life diminishes a measure of the Divine image that is present in the world, and without God's permission it is strictly forbidden. At the same time, murder is an act of rebellion against God himself, who blessed mankind, "to be fruitful and multiply" (Genesis 1:28) and "He did not create it for emptiness; he fashioned it to be inhabited" (Isaiah 45:18).[40]

In turn, the prohibition of murder is included in the Noachide Laws, and Paul, in his letter to the Romans, cites this commandment explicitly: "You shall not murder."[41] Based on a literal reading of Genesis 9:5, "your blood for your souls I will require," the sages interpreted the prohibition to include suicide.[42]

The Master, using the rabbinic method of *guzma* ("exaggeration," גוזמא), interpreted not just the physical act of killing someone but anger itself as a transgression of the prohibition of murder.[43] The sages made the same connection: "He who

---

39 Cf. Jubilees 7:28.
40 Rabbi Moshe Weiner, *The Divine Code* (ed. Dr. Michael Schulman; 2d ed.; Pittsburgh, PA: Ask Noah International, 2011), 370.
41 b.*Sanhedrin* 56a; Romans 13:9. Cf. Pseudo-Phocylides 4.
42 *Genesis Rabbah* 34:13.
43 Matthew 5:21–22.

publically shames his neighbor, it is as though he shed his blood."[44] As disciples of the Master, we are not to commit murder, literally or figuratively.

[2.2]
Do not commit adultery.

◁ Do not commit adultery. (DIDACHE 2.2)

The prohibition of adultery is the seventh commandment of the Decalogue.[45] In the Torah adultery was a capital crime punishable by stoning.[46] As with murder, adultery was considered by the sages of Israel to be a universal prohibition and is cited in Paul's letter to the Romans.[47]

To commit adultery (*na'af*, נאף) in the biblical context specifically refers to voluntary sexual relations between a married (or betrothed) woman and a man who is not her husband. The definition does not include a married man's extra-marital relations with single women.[48] A married man who had sexual relations with an unmarried woman was considered guilty of sexual immorality but not adultery.

However, our Master Yeshua broadened the definition of adultery to include the marital unfaithfulness of the husband. According to Yeshua, the man who illegitimately divorces his wife and then "marries another commits adultery"; that is, he "commits adultery against" his first wife.[49] This means that the Master made adultery equally applicable to both men and women. In the Master's interpretation of the Torah, husbands are held to the same standard of marital fidelity to which the Torah holds married women. Yeshua's ruling does not contradict the Torah's

---

44 b.*Bava Metzia* 58a. Rabbi Moshe Weiner goes so far as to say it should at least be permitted for a person to allow himself to be put to death rather than publicly humiliate someone "because of the dictum, 'Is your blood redder than that of your fellow?' This can be seen as a fortiori from Tamar (Genesis 38:25), who submitted herself to be executed rather than embarrass Judah (since publicly embarrassing a person is likened to murder). However, it is unclear whether a person is *obligated* to give up his life to avoid injuring or raping another" (*The Divine Code*, 402).
45 The Greek text matches exactly the Septuagint for Exodus 20:14 and Deuteronomy 5:18.
46 Deuteronomy 22:24.
47 b.*Sanhedrin* 56a; Pseudo-Phocylides 3; Romans 13:9. The sages themselves debated the exact details of this prohibition as it relates to Gentiles: "'Any prohibited sexual intercourse for which an Israelite court would inflict the death penalty, is prohibited for the Noachide, but any prohibited sexual intercourse for which an Israelite court would not inflict the death penalty is not prohibited for Noachides,' said Rabbi Meir. But the sages say, 'There are many examples of prohibited sexual intercourse for which an Israelite court would not inflict the death penalty but which is prohibited for the Noachide'" (t.*Avodah Zarah* 8:4).
48 Jeffrey Tigay, *JPS Torah Commentary: Deuteronomy* (Philadelphia, PA: Jewish Publication Society, 1996), 71.
49 Mark 10:11 and Matthew 19:9.

[2.2]
Do not commit adultery.

definition of adultery; instead, it augments it based upon the monogamy/fidelity principle that Yeshua derived from Genesis.[50]

The Apostolic Constitutions expounds on the Didache in light of the Master's halachah:

> Do not commit adultery: for you divide one flesh into two. "The two shall be one flesh" [Genesis 2:24]: for the husband and wife are one in nature, in consent, in union, in disposition, and the conduct of life; but they are separated in sex and number. (Apostolic Constitutions 7.2)

The Master also homiletically (again using the rabbinic method of *guzma*) likened adultery of the heart to the actual sin itself: "I say to you that everyone who looks at a woman with lustful intent has already committed adultery with her in his heart" (Matthew 5:28). The Talmud echoes his sentiments: "Unchaste imagination is more injurious than the sin itself."[51] As with murder, we must be vigilant against all forms of adultery, constantly guarding our eyes and hearts.

In a rabbinic manner of teaching, the next two prohibitions move from the general (adultery) to the specific (child molestation and fornication).[52] Both issues needed to be specifically addressed to Gentiles from the Greco-Roman world who were entering the believing community. These two injunctions constitute the first of three pairs of commandments added to the Decalogue in Didache 2.2.

◆ *Do not practice pederasty.* (DIDACHE 2.2)

The Greek word here for "practice pederasty" (*paidophthoriseis*, παιδοφθορήσεις) is related to the modern English word "pedophilia." The corruption is specifically sexual in nature, as can be deduced from the prohibition's placement between adultery and fornication.[53]

---

50 Mark 10:6–9, citing Genesis 1:27; 2:24. This section has been drawn from the longer discussion found in D. Thomas Lancaster, *Torah Club: Chronicles of the Messiah* (6 vols.; Marshfield, MO: First Fruits of Zion, 2011), 3:959.

51 b.*Yoma* 29a.

52 This is similar to Hillel's second rule of interpretation "general and particular" (*kelal uferat*, כלל ופרט). See Rabbi Adin Steinsaltz, *The Talmud Steinsaltz Edition: A Reference Guide* (New York, NY: Random, 1989), 152–153.

53 The Epistle of Barnabas (10.6) midrashically derives the prohibition on corrupting boys from Leviticus 11:6.

Pedophilia was so obviously wrong in the Jewish culture that it does not even receive mention in the Torah.⁵⁴ In the Greco-Roman world, on the other hand, homosexual relations between "young men, an older and younger partner" were completely socially acceptable.⁵⁵ Culturally acceptable pedophilia in the Greco-Roman world began "in honorable means whereby upper-class parents entrusted their son to an older, respected male for the purposes of advancing his imitation into manhood."⁵⁶ For the first twelve years of their lives, boys were solely under the care of women (nurses and mothers), but when boys turned twelve, they were initiated into values and virtues from a masculine perspective, which often included sexual experiences.

[2.2]
Do not practice pederasty.

In Jewish texts of the ancient world, homosexuality and adultery are often paired together under the category of prohibited sexual unions.⁵⁷ In the Jewish mind the Gentile culture's corruption of young boys by older males invoked the Torah's prohibition on homosexuality. In mentioning pedophilia immediately following the prohibition of adultery, the Didache alludes to the Torah's prohibition on homosexuality—at least this is how the Apostolic Constitutions interprets it:

> Do not practice pederasty for this wickedness is contrary to nature, and arose from Sodom, which was therefore entirely consumed with fire sent from God. Let such a one be accursed: and all the people shall say, "So be it." (Apostolic Constitutions 7.2)⁵⁸

---

54   We find this prohibition mentioned in later Jewish literature. The Testament of Levi (17:11) speaks against "corrupters of children and beasts," and Philo mentions those who have a "love of boys" and how this leads to changing "their manly character into an effeminate one" (*On the Special Laws* 3.37. Cf. *On the Contemplative Life* 52, 57–61). Also, the universal Jewish work Pseudo-Phocylides urges, "Protect the youthful good looks of a young body, for many lust for mingling with a male" (213–214).
55   Robin Lane Fox, *Pagans and Christians* (New York, NY: Knopf, 1987), 342.
56   Milavec, *The Didache: Faith, Hope, and Life of the Earliest Christian Communites, 50–70 C.E*, 132.
57   P.W. van der Horst, ed., *The Sentences of Pseudo-Phocylides* (Leiden, The Netherlands: Brill, 1978), 111. "This is also the case in non-Jewish texts ... Though in general homosexuality was more accepted (and even defended) in the Greek world than among the Jews."
58   Cf. Deuteronomy 27:20–23. Homosexuality was rampant in Hellenistic society, so this prohibition would certainly need to be addressed in a document written to new believers. The Torah calls homosexuality an "abomination" (*to'evah*, תועבה) and punishable by death (Leviticus 18:22, 20:13) and the New Testament forbids homosexuality for both Jews and Gentiles as well (Romans 1:27; 1 Corinthians 6:9; 1 Timothy 1:10). Judaism considers the prohibition incumbent upon Gentiles as well, and Rabbi Menachem Azaria de Fano states in his *Asarah Ma'amaros* that Noachides should not even create marriage contracts for homosexuals. See b.*Chullin* 92a and Rabbi Shmuel ben Hofni, Gaon's list of the thirty commandments incumbent upon Noachides from the Cairo Genizah. While the Torah specifically prohibits male homosexuality, the sages extended it to lesbianism (*Sifra* on Leviticus 18:3. Cf. Pseudo-Phocylides 192). Paul also mentions the prohibition against lesbianism in his epistles to non-Jewish believers (Romans 1:26–27).

[2.2]
Do not practice pederasty.

Most believers today do not need a commandment to warn them against pedophilia. However, we do need reminders about the importance of protecting young children against the dangers of this world. The Master teaches us, "Whoever causes one of these little ones who believe in me to sin, it would be better for him if a great millstone were hung around his neck and he were thrown into the sea" (Mark 9:42).[59] Not only do we as parents and elders need to be careful in the example we set for the younger generation, but we need to guard children against those influences and people who would entice them into spiritual and physical pederasty.

Do not commit sexual immorality. (DIDACHE 2.2)

Like the prohibition on pedophilia, so too, the prohibition on sexual immorality is an expansion of the one on adultery. The Greek term *porneuo* (πορνεύω) is often translated "fornication." The word refers to more than just adultery; it refers to "unnatural sexual acts of all kinds."[60] Under the definitions of Jewish law, it includes all forms of sexual intimacy outside marriage—and even some forms within marriage. The Apostolic Constitutions (7.2) connects the broad prohibition on sexual immorality to the Septuagint's rendering of Deuteronomy 23:17: "There shall not be a sexually immoral person among the sons of Israel." The Jerusalem Council of Acts 15 imposed the same prohibition upon new Gentile believers.

The Apostle Paul deals extensively with sexual immorality in 1 Corinthians. He states that the "sexually immoral" shall "not inherit the kingdom of God" and that believers should not even "associate with sexually immoral people."[61] Instead, disciples of the Master are to "flee from sexual immorality," as "the body is not meant for sexual immorality, but for the Lord, and the Lord for the body."[62] Paul uses the incident in the wilderness when Israel "began to whore with the daughters of Moab"[63] as a scriptural proof: "We must not indulge in sexual immorality as some of them did, and twenty-three thousand fell in a single day" (1 Corinthians 10:8).

This injunction against sexual immorality is based on Leviticus 18 and 20, in which a plethora of commandments regarding sexual relations is given. It includes

---

59   Matthew 18:6; Luke 17:2.
60   Kurt Niederwimmer, *The Didache: Hermeneia—A Critical and Historical Commentary on the Bible* (Minneapolis, MN: Fortress, 1998), 89.
61   1 Corinthians 5:9–11, 6:9. Cf. Hebrews 12:16; Jude 7; Revelation 2:21, 21:8, 22:15.
62   1 Corinthians 6:13, 18. Cf. Galatians 5:19; Colossians 3:5; 1 Thessalonians 4:3–5.
63   Numbers 25:1.

both moral and ritual aspects of sexual purity.[64] According to these two chapters of Leviticus, improper relations include bestiality, homosexuality, and incest. This would also encompass instructions about the period of separation imposed upon a husband and wife during her menstruation period (*niddah,* נידה).[65] The Clementine Homilies even extends the injunction to ritually wash after sexual relations upon believers from the nations.[66]

[2.2]
Do not commit sexual immorality.

Based on Leviticus 18:6—"None of you shall approach any one of his close relatives to uncover nakedness"—Judaism enforces safeguards that prevent even the hint of sexual immorality.[67] The sages reason that if one should be this careful with one's blood relatives (that is, one's family), how much more so with non-relatives. Practices such as *shomer negi'ah* ("guarding touch," שומר נגיעה), which limits touch between a man and woman who are neither married nor related, and *yichud* ("seclusion," יחוד), which direct that an unmarried man and woman take care not to be secluded alone, help to guard against even the appearance of evil. Also included in this command is the injunction of undertaking marriage through a proper ceremony, because the prohibitions of improper sexual relations make sense only if the institution of marriage exists through a proper Torah-ordained

---

64 For a good overview of an argument for the ritual aspect of sexual purity in the decision of the Jerusalem Council in Acts 15:20, 29, see Marcel Simon, "The Apostolic Decree and Its Setting in the Ancient Church," *Bulletin John Rylands Library* 52, no. 2 (1970): 437–460.

65 Milavec, *The Didache: Faith, Hope, and Life of the Earliest Christian Communities, 50–70 C.E*, 135. Cf. "The women on their part should keep the law of purification" (Pseudo-Clementine Homilies 7.8); "When the natural purgations do appear in the wives, let not their husbands approach them, out of regard to the children to be begotten; for the law has forbidden it, for it says: 'Do not come near your wife when she is in her separation' (Leviticus 18:19)" (Apostolic Constitutions 6.28).

66 "Not to live any longer impurely; to wash after intercourse; that the women on their part should keep the law of purification" (Pseudo-Clementine Homilies 7.8). For an argument on this being an authentic interpretation of *porneia* (fornication) in Acts 15:20, 29, see Simon, "The Apostolic Decree and Its Setting in the Ancient Church." Cf. Augustine's questions to Pope Gregory the Great about Christians observing the Levitical purity laws in Britain in the sixth century (Bede, *Ecclesiastical History of the English People* 1.27).

67 The Hebrew word translated "nakedness" is *ervah* (ערוה) and actually has a much wider connotation of immodest behavior in general.

[2.2] Do not commit sexual immorality.

ceremony.[68] Along with that comes the Scripture's prohibitions on promiscuity and prostitution.[69]

The Apostle Paul reiterates many of these prohibitions surrounding sexual immorality throughout his letters.[70] One simple injunction, refraining from sexual immorality, is an umbrella commandment that includes dozens of further detailed commandments from the Torah. It is clear from the perspective of both the apostles and the Didache that the Torah's twenty-five-plus commandments prohibiting sexual transgressions are binding upon Gentile believers, as all are included in the prohibition of sexual immorality. For disciples of the Master, it is incumbent upon us to thoroughly study these Torah laws and the traditional halachah surrounding them. As the Apostle Paul tells us, "Sexual immorality ... must not even be named among you, as is proper among saints" (Ephesians 5:3).

◈ *Do not steal.* (DIDACHE 2.2)

This is the eighth commandment of the Decalogue.[71] The Hebrew word for "steal" (*ganav*, גנב) can refer either to theft of goods or to kidnapping.[72]

The Apostolic Constitutions expands on this command, citing numerous examples of those who were punished severely for stealing:

> Achan, when he had stolen in Israel at Jericho, was stoned to death [Joshua 7]; and Gehazi, who stole, and told a lie, inherited the leprosy of Naaman [2 Kings 5]; and Judas, who stole the poor's money [John 12:6], betrayed the Lord of glory to the Jews, and repented, and hanged

---

68   The sages derive this from the verse, "When a man takes a wife and marries her" (Deuteronomy 24:1). Rabbi Shmuel ben Holfni points out that Genesis 34:12—"Ask me for as great a bride price and gift as you will, and I will give whatever you say to me. Only give me the young woman to be my wife"—is evidence that commandment of formal marriage existed before Sinai and is incumbent upon all peoples. The Apostle Paul makes several references to the institution of marriage in his various epistles to Gentile congregations, including the injunction, "Each man should have his own wife and each woman her own husband" (1 Corinthians 7:2. Cf. 7:10–40; Romans 7:2–3).

69   Both of these fall under the single Hebrew word *zenut* (זנות). The Torah's use of the word is not limited to acts of sex for hire; it includes any and all extramarital sexual contact. E.g., Genesis 34:31, 38:24; Leviticus 19:29, 21:7, 9, 14; Numbers 25:1; Deuteronomy 22:21.

70   E.g., Romans 1:26–27; 1 Corinthians 5:1, 6:15–16. Cf. Jubilees 7:20.

71   The Greek text matches exactly with the Septuagint for Exodus 20:15 and Deuteronomy 5:19.

72   Nahum Sarna, *JPS Torah Commentary: Exodus* (Philadelphia, PA: Jewish Publication Society, 1991), 114. Because all nine other injunctions of the Ten Commandments were capital crimes, the sages interpreted the prohibition of stealing in the Decalogue as referring to kidnapping.

himself, and burst asunder in the midst, and all his bowels gushed out [Matthew 27:5; Acts 1:18]; and Ananias, and Sapphira his wife, who stole their own goods, and tempted the Spirit of the Lord, were immediately, at the sentence of Peter our fellow-apostle, struck dead [Acts 5].[73]

[2.2]
Do not steal.

In the Torah "You shall not steal" is stated as a general commandment and afterward broken down into more specific commandments. For example, we find the prohibition on robbing in secret (Leviticus 19:11) and another on robbing openly with force (Leviticus 19:13). By extension there are also commandments against overcharging (Leviticus 25:14) and using false weights and measures (Deuteronomy 25:13–15) as well as the positive commandment to return that which has been stolen (Leviticus 6:4). Rabbi Aaron Lichtenstein finds sixteen such injunctions under the prohibition to steal that are applicable to non-Jews.[74] As with sexual immorality, in order to fully obey the commandment not to steal, we must study and become familiar with all the command's sub-laws and applications.

The Apostle Paul recognized that former thieves were entering into the Messianic movement, and he thus urged, "Let the thief no longer steal, but rather let him labor, doing honest work with his own hands, so that he may have something to share with anyone in need" (Ephesians 4:28).[75]

⚜ *Do not practice magic.* (DIDACHE 2.2)

This prohibition begins a new section dealing specifically with occult arts. The prohibition on the practice of magic functions as a general prohibition, and the ones that follow are more specific components. The four injunctions on this matter make up the second and third pairs of commandments that are added to the Decalogue in Didache 2.2.

The negative commandment against magic is often paired with adultery and was another of the quintessential prohibitions of the Judaism of the day.[76] The practice of magic was prevalent in Hellenistic societies "as a result of Greek contact with

---

73   Apostolic Constitutions 7.2.
74   Rabbi Aaron Lichtenstein, *The Seven Laws of Noah* (3rd Edition; New York, NY: Rabbi Jacob Joseph School, 1995), 20–27. Cf. b.*Sanhedrin* 56a; Pseudo-Phocylides 5–6.
75   This commandment is explicitly given to Gentile believers in Romans 13:9.
76   "Both vices, taken together, are especially abhorrent when practiced by Gentiles" (Niederwimmer, *The Didache*, 89).

[2.2]
Do not practice magic.

Near Eastern magical practices, especially those prevalent in Egypt."[77] Magic was used both for personal gain and true spiritual aspirations. In turn, the prohibition of magic is sometimes explicitly included in the Noachide Laws.[78]

That is not to say that magic was not a problem for the Jewish community as well. Indeed, "there was much Jewish magic in antiquity."[79] This is why, perhaps, a plethora of commandments in the Torah speak of sorcery and fortune-telling having the same connotation as magic. Not only were these activities prohibited, but the penalty for participating in them was death.[80] God urges Israel, "Do not turn to mediums or necromancers; do not seek them out, and so make yourselves unclean by them: I am the LORD your God" (Leviticus 19:31). These prohibitions are even echoed in the Mishnah.[81] Despite this fact, we find Jewish magicians mentioned in the book of Acts.[82]

◆ *Do not use potions.* (DIDACHE 2.2)

This prohibition is a more specific component of the previous one on magic, and these two are often found mentioned together in both Jewish and Christian works of the period.[83] In this context the Greek word *pharmakeuseis* (φαρμακεύσεις) refers to one who makes or compounds poisons or drugs for use in the occult, which could include "using incantations to ensure their supernatural efficacy."[84] However, it is sometimes just translated "sorcery."

As with magic, this practice was widespread in the Greco-Roman world. Yet even there it was not considered a respectable religious practice but rather "the illegal insider dealing of people who were overambitious to achieve personal end."[85]

---

77   Milavec, *The Didache: Faith, Hope, and Life of the Earliest Christian Communities, 50–70 C.E*, 132.
78   b.*Sanhedrin* 56b; t.*Avodah Zarah* 8:6. Cf. Pseudo-Phocylides 149.
79   Van der Horst, *The Sentences of Pseudo-Phocylides*, 213.
80   Exodus 22:18; Leviticus 19:26; Deuteronomy 18:9–14.
81   E.g., m.*Sanhedrin* 7:7, 11, 10:1.
82   Acts 8:9, 13:8.
83   Van der Horst, *The Sentences of Pseudo-Phocylides*, 212. For example, "Make no potions; keep away from magical books" (149). Philo mentions "men polluted both in hands and mind" who were "sorcerers and poisoners" (*On the Special Laws* 3.93); we also find in Didache 5.1 that the Way of Death includes "use of potions" and "magic" (cf. Barnabas 20.1; *Doctrina* 5.1). The Apostolic Constitutions (7.3) connects both of these to Exodus 22:18.
84   Milavec, *The Didache: Faith, Hope, and Life of the Earliest Christian Communities, 50–70 C.E*, 138. In the Septuagint *pharmakeuein* is related to the Hebrew word *kashaf* ("sorcerer," כשף).
85   Fox, *Pagans and Christians*, 37.

The Apostolic Constitutions connects this prohibition directly to the Torah commandment: "You shall not permit a sorceress to live" (Exodus 22:18).[86] According to the Torah, a sorcerer should not even be found in Israel's midst (Deuteronomy 18:10).

It is apparent from the writings of the apostles that sorcery was an issue in the early believing communities.[87] Paul counts "sorcery" as one of "the works of the flesh."[88] The book of Revelation recounts how Babylon had deceived the nations by its sorcery and how by the end of the age, many remained unrepentant for "their sorceries."[89]

[2.2] *Do not use potions.*

◆ *Do not murder children through abortion.* (DIDACHE 2.2)

The Didache now addresses two issues having to do with the murder of children. Some scholars believe that these two should be taken as specific commandments under the general category of magic. A link between abortion and sorcery most certainly exists, because at the time the Didache was written, most abortions were induced with poisons or potions. The Greek historian Plutarch writes about "licentious women who employ drugs and instruments to produce abortion for the sake of the enjoyment of conceiving again."[90] Jewish legend taught that in the days of the flood women would use charms, spells, and potions in order to induce abortions.[91]

While this prohibition of abortion is the oldest reference to this issue by believers in Messiah, "it is certain that from the beginning [that] Christians, following Old Testament and Jewish custom, rejected abortion."[92] In fact, some historians conclude that the believers' rejection of abortion contributed to the early growth of the Messianic movement—fewer women died due to botched abortions, and more babies were born to believers than to those in pagan society.[93]

While the Torah contains no specific mention of abortion, the prohibition of this act may be derived from several of its texts. For example, the Apostolic

---

86   Apostolic Constitutions 7.3. Cf. Josephus, *Antiquities of the Jews* 4:179/viii.34.
87   Cf. Shepherd of Hermas, Vision 3.9 (17.7–8).
88   Galatians 5:19–20.
89   Revelation 9:21, 18:23. Cf. Sibylline Oracles 5:165.
90   *De Tuenda Sanitate Praecepta*, 22. Cf. Euripides, *Andromache* 355–360.
91   1 Enoch 7:1; *Genesis Rabbah* 23:2.
92   Niederwimmer, *The Didache*, 90.
93   Milavec, *The Didache: Faith, Hope, and Life of the Earliest Christian Communities, 50–70 C.E*, 140.

[2.2] *Do not murder children through abortion.*

Constitutions provides scriptural support for the Didache's prohibition on abortion from Exodus:

> When men strive together and hit a pregnant woman, so that her children come out, but there is no harm, the one who hit her shall surely be fined, as the woman's husband shall impose on him, and he shall pay as the judges determine. But if there is harm, then you shall pay life for life (Exodus 21:22–23).[94]

While early rabbinic writings interpret the damage here as referring to the mother,[95] the Septuagint interprets this as referring to the fetus: "But if it be perfectly formed, he shall give life for life." Notice that the stage of the fetus is a determining factor. It is from this text that Philo derives the prohibitions on abortion and exposure.[96] Some commentators also derive this prohibition metaphorically from Leviticus 18:21: "You shall not give any of your children to offer them to Molech."[97] Rabbi Ishmael derived the prohibition from a hyper-literal reading of Genesis 9:6: "Because it is written, 'Whoever sheds the blood of man within [another] man, shall his blood be shed.' What is a 'man within [another] man'?—An embryo in his mother's womb."[98]

In early rabbinic writings abortion, while strictly forbidden, was not considered murder, because the viability of the child before it was born could not be proven. Perhaps an aborted child would not have survived the full term of the pregnancy.[99] However, once a baby was born, killing it was considered murder.[100] The sages "deduced the prohibition against abortion by an *a fortiori* argument from the laws concerning abstention from procreation, or onanism, or having sexual relations with one's wife when it is likely to harm the fetus in the womb—the perpetrator

---

94 Apostolic Constitutions 7.3.
95 b.*Bava Kama* 56a.
96 Philo, *On the Special Laws* 3.108–119. Philo also writes about the prohibition of sacrificing pregnant animals (Philo, *On the Virtues* 137).
97 Cf. Leviticus 20:2–5. The sages ruled that the prohibition of offering children to Molech was incumbent upon Gentiles as well as Jews, as it would be contained under the prohibition of idolatry. See Rabbi Menachem Azariah of Fano's *Asarah Maamarot* and Rabbi Shmuel ben Hofni Gaon's list of thirty commandments incumbent on Noachides from the Cairo Genizah.
98 b.*Sanhedrin* 57b. Based on this logic Rabbi Ishmael advocated for the death penalty for abortion, but his opinion was not accepted by the majority and never carried out in practice.
99 b.*Chullin* 33a. However, most modern rabbinic authorities hold that abortion is considered a form of murder.
100 m.*Niddah* 5:3; b.*Niddah* 44b.

being regarded as a 'shedder of blood.'"¹⁰¹ In the *Zohar* it is taught that one who aborts a baby "destroys the King's workmanship and so causes the Holy One to depart from the world."¹⁰² However, the sages did allow abortions in cases in which the mother's life was in danger, "for her life takes precedence over its life."¹⁰³ In modern day Jewish law, opinions are divided as to whether abortion constitutes murder and under what circumstances abortion should be permitted.

[2.2]
Do not murder children through abortion.

In the Greco-Roman world, abortion was in broad use. Both abortion and infanticide were viewed in Hellenistic society as normal modes of family planning:¹⁰⁴

> Does a man hate the members of his own body when he uses the knife upon them? There is no anger there, but the pitying desire to heal. Mad dogs we knock on the head; the fierce and savage ox we slay; sickly sheep we put to the knife to keep them from infecting the flock; unnatural progeny we destroy; we drown even children who at birth are weakly and abnormal. Yet it is not anger but reason that separates the harmful from the sound. (Seneca, *On Anger* 1.15.2)

Because of this we find the prohibitions against such actions greatly emphasized in Jewish sources meant for non-Jewish instruction. For example, in Pseudo-Phocylides: "Do not let a woman destroy the unborn infant in her belly, nor after its birth throw it before the dogs and the vultures as prey."¹⁰⁵ Abortion was also included in the Noachide prohibitions.¹⁰⁶

⁂ *Nor kill them after they have been born.* (DIDACHE 2.2)

This prohibition on infanticide should be seen, like the one on abortion, as fitting under the head prohibition of magic.¹⁰⁷ Coupling the prohibition of infanticide with abortion was common in Jewish literature.¹⁰⁸ The Apostolic Constitutions

---

101 Menachem Elon, "Abortion," *Encyclopedia Judaica* 1:271.
102 *Zohar* II, 3b.
103 m.*Oholot* 7:6.
104 Milavec, *The Didache: Faith, Hope, and Life of the Earliest Christian Communities, 50–70 C.E*, 139.
105 Pseudo-Phocylides 184–185.
106 b.*Sanhedrin* 57b.
107 There is a manuscript discrepancy regarding the word γεννηθὲν ("been born") in *Codex Hierosolymitanus* which appears as γεννηθέντα in other ancient manuscripts. Regardless, the "after they have been born" is not affected.
108 E.g., Pseudo-Phocylides 184–185; Josephus, *Against Apion* 2:202/xxv.

[2.2] *Nor kill them after they have been born.* derives this prohibition along with abortion from the Septuagint's rendering of Exodus 21:23:

> Do not murder children through abortion, nor kill them after they have been born; for "everything that is shaped, and has received a soul from God, if it be slain, shall be avenged, as being unjustly destroyed."[109]

Despite its absolutely abhorrent nature, infanticide, like abortion, was regularly used in the Hellenistic world as a method of birth control. This practice was especially rampant when famine stalked the land.[110]

Indeed, Philo records that "some of them slay them with their own hands, and stifle the first breath of their children ... others throw them into the depths of a river, or of a sea ... Others, again, carry them out into a desert place to expose them there."[111]

The second-century Roman historian Tacitus marveled that Jews considered infanticide immoral: "It is a crime among them to kill any newly-born infant!"[112] He considered this evidence for what he believed to be the superstitious nature of the Jewish religion.

The spirit of both abortion and infanticide are completely contrary to the Torah's view of children. In Judaism the commandment in Genesis to "be fruitful

---

109 Apostolic Constitutions 7.3. While not citing an explicit passage Tertullian states: "Indeed the Law of Moses punishes with appropriate penalties the man who shall cause abortion" (*On the Soul* 37).
110 Peter J. Tomson, *'If this be from Heaven ...' Jesus and the New Testament Authors in Their Relationship to Judaism* (Sheffield, England: Sheffield Academic Press, 2001), 382.
111 Philo, *On the Special Laws* 3.114–115. Cf. Philo, *On the Virtues* 131–132; Sibylline Oracles 3.765–766.
112 Tacitus, *Histories* 5.

and multiply" is viewed as an injunction to procreate.[113] The Scriptures are full of exhortations on the blessings of children: "Behold, children are a heritage from the LORD, the fruit of the womb a reward. Like arrows in the hand of a warrior are the children of one's youth. Blessed is the man who fills his quiver with them!" (Psalm 127:3–5). The early church writers stressed that one of the main purposes of marital relations was the procreation of children.[114] It is important that disciples of the Master not only grasp Scripture's abhorrence of the unnecessary destruction of life but also understand the centrality of children and family in Torah life.

[2.2] *Nor kill them after they have been born.*

◈ *Nor shall you covet the things that belong to your neighbor.*
(DIDACHE 2.2)

The Didache now quotes the tenth commandment, thus concluding its version of the Decalogue.[115] The Apostolic Constitutions connects this statement to Exodus 20:17 and Deuteronomy 5:21 by rendering the prohibition, "Do not covet the things that belong to your neighbor, as his wife, or his servant, or his ox, or his field."[116]

---

113   Genesis 1:28. Also Genesis 8:17, 9:1, 7. "A man shall not abstain from the performance of the duty of the propagation of the race unless he already has children. [As to the number]: Beit Shammai ruled, 'two males,' and Beit Hillel ruled, 'male and a female,' for it is stated in scripture, 'male and female created he them'" (m.*Yevamot* 6:6). The majority opinion in Judaism is that this commandment was originally given to all nations but was then at Sinai restricted to only the Jewish people (b.*Sanhedrin* 59a) as it was one of the commandments "not repeated." For a full discussion, see David Neustadter, "The Universal Nature of *Pru Urvu* and an Analysis of its Implications," *Tradition* 40, no. 4 (2007): 50–67. A few rabbinic authorities, however, do feel that this commandment still applies to Gentiles, e.g., Rabbi Achai Gaon, *Sheiltot*, *Sheilta* 165; the commentary upon this work by Rabbi Naftali Zvi Yehuda Berlin, *Ha'mek She'eila*, in which he argues for an alternative interpretation of b.*Sanhedrin* 59a that does not remove the obligation of *p'ru urvu* from Gentiles; and Rabbi Menachem Azariah of Fano, who includes the commandments to be fruitful and multiply in his list of the thirty commandments incumbent on Gentiles in *Asarah Maamarot*. However, even the Talmud agrees that Gentiles are included in Isaiah 45:18—"The LORD, who created the heavens (he is God!), who formed the earth and made it (he established it; he did not create it empty, he formed it to be inhabited!)"—which is another verse cited as a source for the injunction to bear children (b.*Bechorot* 47a). According to Rabbi Moshe Weiner, "The practical difference is that if Gentiles were expressly commanded to procreate, then they would be obligated to do so even if it would cause them discomfort or trouble ... An individual Gentile is thus exempt if he would experience any serious discomfort as a result of fulfilling it" (*The Divine Code*, 510).
114   See David W. Bercot, ed., *A Dictionary of Early Christian Beliefs: A Reference Guide to More Than 700 Topics Discussed by the Early Church Fathers* (Peabody, MA: Hendrickson, 1998), 536–538.
115   The wording is slightly different than the Septuagint.
116   Apostolic Constitutions 7.3.

[2.2]
Nor shall you covet the things that belong to your neighbor.

This command is included in Jewish writings meant for non-Jews and is also found in Paul's letter to the Romans.[117]

Scholars and sages alike have debated the meaning of this commandment. The Hebrew word *chamad* ("covet," חמד) can describe merely inappropriate desire for what belongs to another, but at times it can also refer to a longing that moves beyond a passive mental state and into an active pursuit of the object.[118] Ibn Ezra argues that this commandment is simply God's directive that a person should control his thoughts and desires to such an extent that the thought of coveting other people's property would be abhorrent. On the other hand, the *Mechilta* teaches that one is guilty of transgressing this injunction only if desire leads to action.[119]

When we covet the possessions of others, we show that we are not happy with what God has given us. Ibn Ezra continues, "Everyone should rejoice in their lot and try not to covet something that is not theirs because coveting demonstrates a lack of faith in God … Everyone must trust that their Creator will sustain them."[120] His comment connects coveting to worrying. In a similar manner, our Master instructs us, "Do not be anxious about your life, what you will eat or what you will drink, nor about your body, what you will put on … Your heavenly Father knows that you need them all" (Matthew 6:25, 32). While our heavenly Father will not always give us what we want, he will always provide us with what we need, and we are commanded to be content with that.

Do not swear falsely. (DIDACHE 2.3)

Verse 3 begins a new section (2.3–5) that focuses on five restrictions on speech. It opens with a prohibition from Leviticus 19:12: "You shall not swear by my name falsely, and so profane the name of your God: I am the LORD."[121] The Torah states that when a false oath is taken up in God's name, it is *chillul HaShem* ("profanation of the Name," חילול השם) because it makes God out to be a liar. The Didache's omission of "by my name" universalizes this commandment, making it applicable to all oaths, not just those made in God's name. Rabbi Moshe Weiner writes: "We find

---

117 Pseudo-Phocylides 6; Romans 7:7.
118 Tigay, *JPS Torah Commentary: Deuteronomy*, 72.
119 *Mechilta*, BaChodesh 8, Exodus 20:14.
120 Rabbi A.J. Rosenberg, *Shemoth: A New English* (2 vols.; New York, NY: Judaica, 1995), 1:318.
121 The wording is slightly different from the Septuagint, but the content is the same.

in the Torah that from the earliest times the concept of an oath was regarded as a sacred obligation by Gentiles as well (See for example Genesis 21:22ff, 26:28ff)."[122]

[2.3] *Do not swear falsely.*

According to the Mishnah and the *Sifra*, "swearing falsely" is a parallel to the third commandment of the Decalogue: "You shall not take the name of the LORD your God in vain, for the LORD will not hold him guiltless who takes his name in vain" (Exodus 20:7).[123] Philo interprets this commandment as a demand to tell the truth at all times, whether one is under oath or not, and the Talmud even extends this to an injunction against making unnecessary blessings.[124] The Torah forbids both making false oaths and vows as well as breaking oaths: "If you make a vow to the LORD your God, you shall not delay fulfilling it" (Deuteronomy 23:21).[125]

The Apostolic Constitutions connects this to the Master's words:

> Do not swear falsely; for it is said, "Do not take an oath at all" [Matthew 5:34]. But if that cannot be avoided, you shall swear truly; for, "Every one that swears by Him shall be commended'" [Psalm 63:11].[126]

Whether one is vowing or not, one's word should be binding. As the sages say, "Let your 'no' and 'yes' both be righteous."[127]

This injunction, as was mentioned above, begins a series of five commandments related to sins of the tongue.[128] Some scholars feel that the prohibition on swearing falsely should be viewed as a general commandment and the following four commandments as sub-categories. Proper speech is a foundation principle in Judaism and is dealt with extensively in the laws of evil speech (*lashon hara*, לשון הרע). In fact, the *Doctrina* version of the prohibition on swearing falsely simply says,

---

122   Rabbi Weiner, *The Divine Code*, 261.
123   Baruch A. Levine, *JPS Torah Commentary: Leviticus* (New York, NY: Jewish Publication Society, 1989), 127. Cf. Deuteronomy 5:11. The Epistle of Barnabas includes "Do not take the Lord's name in vain" (19.5) in its parallel section to the Didache's Decalogue.
124   Philo, *On the Decalogue* 84; b.*Brachot* 33a.
125   The verse goes on to tell us that it is the Lord himself who will punish the offender. The Prophet Zechariah instructs Israel to "love no false oath," for this is one of the things that the Lord hates (Zechariah 8:17). This prohibition is included in Jewish writings meant for non-Jews and is also found in Paul's epistle to Timothy (1 Timothy 1:10; Pseudo-Phocylides 16.).
126   Apostolic Constitutions 7.3.
127   b.*Bava Metzia* 49a.
128   Jonathan Draper feels that these are all based on direct quotations or paraphrases from the Holiness Section (Leviticus 18–19), thus providing a link between 2.2 and 2.3–5, and that all are centered around the commandment to love one's neighbor (Leviticus 19:18): swearing falsely (Leviticus 19:12), bearing false witness (Leviticus 19:16), speaking badly (Leviticus 19:14), holding grudges (Leviticus 19:18), and double-minded/tongued (Leviticus 19:16). See Draper, "A Commentary on the Didache in Light of the Dead Sea Scrolls and Related Documents" (PhD diss., St. John's College, 1983), 56–59.

[2.3]
Do not swear falsely.

"Do not speak evil" (2.3). James tells us that "if anyone thinks he is religious and does not bridle his tongue but deceives his heart, this person's religion is worthless" (James 1:26), while the Master teaches, "What comes out of a person is what defiles him" (Mark 7:20). It is not surprising then that the Didache seeks to instruct in proper speech so early on in the new Gentile believer's training.

◆ Do not bear false witness. (DIDACHE 2.3)

The second commandment of proper speech comes from the ninth commandment of the Decalogue.[129] The prohibition on false witness refers to testimony in a court of law.

Witnesses in court cases were one of the most important factors in the biblical judicial system. Evidence needed to be established upon the testimony of "two witnesses or of three witnesses,"[130] and those who bore false witness were punished in kind: "If the witness is a false witness and has accused his brother falsely, then you shall do to him as he had meant to do to his brother" (Deuteronomy 19:18–19).

Proverbs states that "a man who bears false witness against his neighbor is like a war club, or a sword, or a sharp arrow" and also says that "a false witness will perish."[131] The Apostolic Constitutions includes a Greek version of Proverbs 14:31: "He that falsely accuses the needy provokes to anger him that made him."[132] For the non-Jewish audience of the Didache, the commandment not to bear false witness was a reminder to tell the complete truth, even in the secular courts of the Hellenistic world.

This prohibition, however, has been hermeneutically expanded to include deceitful speech in general. As disciples of the Master, we should speak the truth, whether in a court setting or not. The Torah commands, "You shall not deal falsely; you shall not lie to one another" (Leviticus 19:11). A sub-prohibition of not bearing false witness is found in Leviticus 19:16: "You shall not go around as a slanderer among your people." This is one of the main texts upon which Judaism bases the

---

129   The Greek text matches the Septuagint for both Exodus 20:16 and Deuteronomy 5:20.
130   Deuteronomy 17:6, 19:15.
131   Proverbs 25:18, 21:28.
132   Apostolic Constitutions 7.3. This Greek version is different than the Septuagint and might have been chosen because it evokes language similar to that of Didache 1.2: "You shall love the God who made you."

principles of evil speech. Yeshua connects "false witness" and "slander" in his list of evil things that come out of the heart.[133]

[2.3] Do not bear false witness.

ⵙ *Do not slander anyone.* (DIDACHE 2.3)

The Greek word for "slander," *kakologeo* (κακολογέω), has the connotation of "speaking evil." The Apostolic Constitutions renders this, "Do not slander anyone; for says he, 'Love not to slander, lest you be taken away' [Proverbs 20:13 Septuagint]."[134] The Apostle Peter echoes this injunction when he writes, "Put away all malice and all deceit and hypocrisy and envy and all slander" (1 Peter 2:1).

In the Septuagint *kakologeo* corresponds to the verbal root *k-l-l* (קלל), which has the much stronger connotation of "to curse." This is the sense in which it should be interpreted here in the Didache. In the Hebrew Scriptures *k-l-l* is the complete opposite of *b-r-k* (ברך), which means "to bless." Sarna defines *k-l-l* as "treating with contempt and humiliating."[135]

The Torah is filled with commandments against cursing (*k-l-l*). Leviticus 20:9 instructs, "Anyone who curses his father or his mother shall surely be put to death; he has cursed his father or his mother; his blood is upon him," and in Exodus 22:28, "You shall not revile God, nor curse a ruler of your people." Although the Torah prohibits the most grievous forms of cursing (those against parents and rulers), the Didache through midrashic exegesis expands these prohibitions to "anyone." Rabbi Moshe Weiner writes: "A Gentile must likewise respect God's creatures, and thus one is not to curse or harm humans for they are created by God 'in his image and likeness' as it were."[136]

The slander the Didache prohibits is the most vicious and hateful kind. No disciple of Yeshua was permitted to spew such venom toward anyone. In Judaism "slander" is known as *motzi shem ra* (מוציא שם רע) and is considered the worst form of gossip one can commit. Whereas the other forms, *rechilut* (minor gossip about the details of someone's life, רכילות) and *lashon hara* (negative but true gossip, לשון הרע), are based on actual fact, *motzi shem ra* is full of purposeful lies and falsehoods and is in turn tantamount to murdering an individual.

---

133   Matthew 15:19.
134   Apostolic Constitutions 7.4.
135   Sarna, *JPS Torah Commentary: Exodus*, 123.
136   Rabbi Weiner, *The Divine Code*, 261.

[2.3]
Do not slander anyone.

The rabbis interpret "You shall not wrong one another" (Leviticus 25:17) as referring to sinful words (*ona'at devarim*, אונאת דברים) that cause another person pain, embarrassment, anger, or fear. Hurtful words are worse than causing another person monetary loss, because "for the former restoration is possible, but not for the latter."[137] It is very difficult to fully repair the damage done through evil speech. The Master tells us, "Whoever insults his brother will be liable to the council; and whoever says, 'You fool!' will be liable to the hell of fire" (Matthew 5:22).

The opposite of "slander" is positive and uplifting speech (*lashon tov*, לשון טוב). Just as our words have the power to tear someone down, causing grave sin, so they also have "the power to lift a heart, put a light in the eyes and make their world suddenly appear a kinder, more welcoming place."[138] The *Zohar* teaches that if one has an opportunity to speak positive words, it is forbidden not to do so.[139] As disciples of the Master, we should not only avoid slander but should seek opportunities to speak positive words to everyone with whom we come in contact, bringing repair to the world (*tikkun olam*, תיקון עולם).

Do not hold grudges. (DIDACHE 2.3)

Disciples of the Master are forbidden to be of an unforgiving and irreconcilable mind-set.[140] Many of the new Gentile believers would experience persecution and abuse from their family and friends for their newfound faith. They were not permitted to hold on to these evils and let them fester inside. Instead they were to turn the other cheek (1.4) and love their enemies (1.3), exercising the utmost humility (1.4).

While not specifically a verbal sin, holding grudges can indeed be brought on by speaking or listening to evil speech. Additionally, grudges can lead someone to slander the one with whom he is angry. In this way the prohibition of holding grudges fits into the larger category of proper speech.

The Torah instructs in the Holiness Code, "You shall not take vengeance or bear a grudge against the sons of your own people, but you shall love your neighbor as yourself" (Leviticus 19:18). The Prophet Zechariah commanded during the time of

---

137   b.*Bava Metzia* 58b.
138   Chana Nestlebaum, *Positive Word Power: Building a Better World with the Words You Speak* (ed. Shaindy Appelbaum; Brooklyn, NY: Mesorah, 2009), 13.
139   Ibid., 12.
140   Niederwimmer, *The Didache*, 91. the Epistle of Barnabas adds "against your brother" to this verse (19.4).

Israel's oppression by foreign rulers, "Let none of you devise evil against another in your heart."[141] The Apostolic Constitutions cites the Septuagint's rendering of Proverbs 12:28: "The ways of those that remember injuries lead to death."

[2.3] *Do not hold grudges.*

Likewise, in his letter to the Romans, Paul lists "maliciousness" under the character traits of those who do not acknowledge God, and the Apostle Peter instructs believers to put away "malice."[142] Clement, a disciple of Peter, continues along this theme: "You ought to please the Almighty God in righteousness and truth and long-suffering with holiness, laying aside malice and pursuing concord in love and peace, being instant in gentleness."[143] To follow Messiah, we must suffer insult and affliction, as he did, without harboring thoughts of unforgiveness and revenge. Instead may we too have the strength to say, "Father, forgive them, for they know not what they do" (Luke 23:34).

◆ *Do not be double-minded or double-tongued, for a double tongue is a deadly trap.* (DIDACHE 2.4)

This verse and the next together comprise the fifth and final rule of proper speech. The Didache exhorts us to not be as one who is unstable in word and thought. The prohibition on the double mind warns against disingenuousness. The double-minded person does not keep his word or follow through with his resolutions and good intentions. The prohibition on the double tongue warns against duplicity, such as when one flatters a person to his face and speaks ill of him behind his back. The double-tongued man speaks in such and such a way to please one person but changes his words or alters his sentiments when speaking to another party.

Sirach similarly admonishes, "Do not winnow with every wind, nor follow every path: the double-tongued sinner does that," and the Sibylline Oracles warns against "ungodly, false, double-tongued, immoral men."[144] The Apostolic Constitutions cites two passages from the Septuagint to bolster the Didache's injunction: "A man's own lips are a strong snare to him" (Proverbs 6:2), and, "A talkative person shall not be prospered upon earth" (Psalm 140:11).[145]

---

141 Zechariah 7:10.
142 Romans 1:29; 1 Peter 2:1.
143 1 Clement 62.2. Cf. 2.5.
144 Sirach 5:9; Sibylline Oracles 3.45.
145 Apostolic Constitutions 7.4.

[2.4]
Do not be double-minded or double-tongued, for a double tongue is a deadly trap.

Although not a direct quotation, the style and content of the Didache command here are similar to many passages in the Hebrew Scriptures. For example, "I hate the double-minded, but I love your law" (Psalm 119:113), and, "You are snared in the words of your mouth, caught in the words of your mouth" (Proverbs 6:2). Proverbs contrasts those who have a double tongue with those who are righteous: "An evil man is ensnared by the transgression of his lips, but the righteous escapes from trouble" (Proverbs 12:13). The phrase "snare of death" is found several times in the book of Proverbs.[146]

The apostles also speak against being double-tongued and double-minded. Paul requires all deacons to be "dignified, not double-tongued."[147] James, the brother of the Master writes, "Purify your hearts, you double-minded," and he speaks in detail about the dangers of the tongue as he laments the fact that from "the same mouth come blessing and cursing."[148] He speaks of the one who doubts and lacks faith in God as "a double-minded man, unstable in all his ways" (James 1:8).

Do not let your word be false or empty, but let it be fulfilled in action. (DIDACHE 2.5)

This is a continuation of 2.4 and of the fifth speech prohibition.[149] When one's word is false, it is untrue, and when one's word is empty, it is unfulfilled. Both describe a case in which one's words do not match up with his actions. The Didache exhorts us as disciples of our Master Yeshua to match our words with deeds.

The Torah has several prohibitions against empty speech. The Apostolic Constitutions connects this passage in the Didache with "You shall not deal falsely" (Leviticus 19:11).[150] The sages interpreted the injunction of Numbers 30:2 ("If a man vows a vow to the LORD, or swears an oath to bind himself by a pledge, he shall not break his word. He shall do according to all that proceeds out of his mouth") as a prohibition forbidding the breaking not only of vows and oaths but of any word that comes out of one's mouth. This is echoed in the verse, "You shall be careful

---

146 Proverbs 13:14, 14:27, 21:6.
147 1 Timothy 3:8.
148 James 4:8, 3:1–12.
149 *Doctrina* has the inverse: "empty or false."
150 Apostolic Constitutions 7.4. In the Apostolic Constitutions, Leviticus 19:11 and Matthew 12:36 are midrashically combined together as: "You shall give an account for every idle word."

to do what has passed your lips" (Deuteronomy 23:23). In other words, we should be careful to fulfill every verbal commitment that we make.¹⁵¹

[2.5]
Do not let your word be false or empty, but let it be fulfilled in action.

The Apostolic Constitutions also cites the Master's words: "People will give account for every careless word they speak" (Matthew 12:36).¹⁵² The apostles also stress that our words are to be backed up with action: "Little children, let us not love in word or talk but in deed and in truth" (1 John 3:18). Clement states that in such a manner our wisdom is displayed and urges, "Let the wise display his wisdom, not in words, but in good works";¹⁵³ and indeed, this should be the disciple's relationship to the Torah: "Be doers of the word, and not hearers only, deceiving yourselves" (James 1:22).

False speech is a most grievous sin, as the person who utters such cannot be trusted. When followers of the Master, who bear the name of God, display such behavior, it is all the more heinous, as it becomes a false reflection of the character of Messiah and of the Lord himself.

The Epistle of Barnabas parallels this section with a completely different admonition. Rather than a warning on false speech, the Epistle of Barnabas' version prohibits teaching Torah to the uninitiated: "The word of God must not depart from you among those in impurity" (Barnabas 19.4).¹⁵⁴

⁍ *Do not be greedy.* (DIDACHE 2.6)

Verse 6 contains a section in which five evil character traits are detailed.¹⁵⁵ It begins with an injunction against being "greedy," which comes from the Greek word *pleonektes* (πλεονέκτης) and can mean "greed" or "covetousness." This injunction is similar to the prohibition at the end of 2.2 and is most certainly based upon the

---

151 "The Noachide laws include the prohibition on swearing falsely and violating an oath under the categorical prohibition on blasphemy" (D. Thomas Lancaster, *Torah Club: Depths of the Torah* [6 vols.; Marshfield, MO: First Fruits of Zion, 2017], 4.1475).
152 Apostolic Constitutions 7.4. Cf. "Even the superfluous conversation between a man and his wife is declared to a person in the hour of his death" (b.*Chagigah* 5b). Also 2 Peter 2:1–3; Ephesians 5:6.
153 1 Clement 38.2.
154 This parallels the Master's words, "Do not give dogs what is holy, and do not throw your pearls before pigs, lest they trample them underfoot and turn to attack you" (Matthew 7:6), which is quoted by the Didache in 9.5. The sages had a similar view about teaching Torah to idolaters (cf. b.*Chagigah* 13a; *Exodus Rabbah* 47:1).
155 The Epistle of Barnabas simply lists the first trait, "Do not be greedy" (19.6), while the *Doctrina* includes six traits: "Do not be lustful (*cupidus*) or predatory, or rapacious or an idolater, or contentious or ill-humored" (2.6).

[2.6]
Do not be greedy.

tenth commandment of the Decalogue, "You shall not covet."[156] "Greedy" also appears in the vice list of 5.1. The Master lists "coveting" as one of the evils that come "from within, out of the heart of man" that "defile a person."[157] The Apostolic Constitutions cites the Septuagint version of Habakkuk 2:9: "Woe to him that covets an evil covetousness to his house."[158]

The Apostle Paul's letters often admonish against envy and greed. Paul lists these among the characteristics of those who "did not see fit to acknowledge God," and he warns his readers that greed "must not even be named among you," because greedy individuals have "no inheritance in the kingdom of Messiah and God."[159] Instead Paul tells the Colossians: "Put to death therefore what is earthly in you: … covetousness, which is idolatry" (Colossians 3:5).[160] We are to be happy and content with what the Lord has given to us.

Greed is considered one of the most grievous sins in Jewish ethical teaching. A constant striving for material and social gain can only adversely affect our spiritual life and put us in danger. This is why the Master urges, "Take care, and be on your guard against all [greed], for one's life does not consist in the abundance of his possessions" (Luke 12:15).

A connection exists between greed and the ensuing prohibition on false words in 2 Peter 2:3: "In their greed they will exploit you with false words." Additionally, Kurt Niederwimmer points out that Didache 2.6 "begins with prohibitions recalling the ninth and tenth commandments of the Decalogue but then moves to phraseology opposing offenses against love of neighbor."[161] These can be divided into the five injurious dispositions, or "sins of attitude,"[162] that we see listed in verse 6. The first two relate to goods and the last two to ego. The middle prohibition of hypocrisy can relate to both groups.

---

156   Exodus 20:17; Deuteronomy 5:21.
157   Mark 7:21–23.
158   Apostolic Constitutions 7.4.
159   Romans 1:28–29; Ephesians 5:3–5. Cf. 1 Thessalonians 2:5; 2 Peter 2:14.
160   Cf. 1 Clement 35.5. Cf. Apocalypse of Moses 19:3; Pseudo-Clementine Recognitions 4.31.
161   Niederwimmer, *The Didache*, 92.
162   William Varner, *The Way of the Didache: The First Christian Handbook* (New York, NY: University Press of America, 2007), 63.

⁌ *Or predatory.* (DIDACHE 2.6)

The Greek word for "predatory" *arpax* (ἅρπαξ) can be translated "greedy," "robber," "extortioner," or "swindler." Yet it refers not just to one who is greedy in attitude but whose lust for materialism spews over into action. Yeshua uses this word to describe false prophets when he calls them "ravenous wolves."[163] The word describes someone who seeks forcefully to obtain that which he desires. In this way "predatory" is akin to the prohibition against stealing in 2.2. Theft is later listed as a vice in 5.1.

The Apostle Paul includes this level of greed with other major sins as he urges the Corinthians "not to associate with anyone who bears the name of brother if he is guilty of sexual immorality or greed, or is an idolater, reviler, drunkard, or swindler—not even to eat with such a one" (1 Corinthians 5:11). He tells them that "swindlers" will not "inherit the kingdom of God."[164] As disciples of the Master, we are to avoid not only predatory greed but also any association at all with those who display such character traits.

Predatory behavior is dangerous and sinful, and it defies biblical sensibilities. Material possessions are fleeting and only temporary. Our Master Yeshua instructs, "Take care, and be on your guard against all covetousness, for one's life does not consist in the abundance of his possessions" (Luke 12:15). He then tells his disciples a parable about a rich man who greedily stores all his possessions for himself. After he dies suddenly, God tells him, "Fool! This night your soul is required of you, and the things you have prepared, whose will they be?" (Luke 12:20). The Master summarizes, "So is the one who lays up treasure for himself and is not rich toward God" (Luke 12:21). Rather, we should strive to store up our treasures with our heavenly Father.[165]

⁌ *Or hypocritical.* (DIDACHE 2.6)

The term "hypocrite" appears in the Didache several times.[166] The Apostolic Constitutions midrashically alludes to Matthew 24:51 when it states, "Do not be a hypocrite, lest your portion be with them" (7.5).

---

163 Matthew 7:15.
164 1 Corinthians 6:10.
165 Matthew 6:20.
166 Didache 4.12, 5.1, 8.1–2.

[2.6] Or hypocritical.

Most commentators are inclined to define "hypocrite" as someone who behaves in a disingenuous manner, creates a façade of piety, or says one thing and does another. In particular this is usually directly linked to the Pharisees. This is primarily based upon the Master's criticism: "The scribes and the Pharisees sit on Moses' seat, so practice and observe whatever they tell you—but not what they do. For they preach, but do not practice" (Matthew 23:2–3). Yet, the word hypocrite is not found in the immediate context but only appears later in verse 23. Additionally, while the Master does call some Pharisees hypocrites,[167] the term is not solely used to describe the members of the Pharisaic party.[168]

The Greek word for "hypocrite" is *hupokrites* (ὑποκριτής), which refers to a "stage performer" or an "actor."[169] In turn, it is better to define "hypocrite" in the context of the Didache and the New Testament as someone who puts on a show of godliness and performs a religious obligation in an ostentatious way to attract attention, to be seen by others, and recognized as pious. The Master used the word to describe people who enjoy attention and praise for their righteous acts such as charity, prayer, and fasting:

> Thus, when you give to the needy, sound no trumpet before you, as the hypocrites do in the synagogues and in the streets, that they may be praised by others. Truly, I say to you, they have received their reward. (Matthew 6:2)

> And when you pray, you must not be like the hypocrites. For they love to stand and pray in the synagogues and at the street corners, that they may be seen by others. Truly, I say to you, they have received their reward. (Matthew 6:5)

> And when you fast, do not look gloomy like the hypocrites, for they disfigure their faces that their fasting may be seen by others. Truly, I say to you, they have received their reward. (Matthew 6:16)

The hypocrite performs the good deed for the sake of his appearance in the eyes of men; he is more concerned with glorifying himself than with bringing glory to his Father in heaven. By taking reward in the present in the form of accolades and respect, he loses his reward in the kingdom.

---

167 Matthew 15:7, 22:18, 23:1–29; Mark 7:6; Luke 12:1.
168 Matthew 7:5, 24:48–51; Luke 6:42, 12:56.
169 It is also related to the Hebrew *chanaf* (חָנֵף), which has the broader connotation of "godless."

By commending us not to be "hypocritical," the Didache warns us not to perform good deeds for the sake of receiving praise from men. Rather, we should observe the commandments because they are God's will and through their performance we bring godliness into this world and honor to his name. As our Master teaches: "Let your light shine before others, so that they may see your good works and give glory to your Father who is in heaven" (Matthew 5:16).

[2.6]
Or hypocritical.

🔊 *Or malicious.* (DIDACHE 2.6)

Though the Greek word here can be translated as "ill-mannered," this term does not refer only to those who lack social breeding. *Kakoethes* (κακοήθης), meaning "malignant," "malevolent," or "immoral," describes someone who is characterized by an overall disposition of maliciousness and spitefulness. The Apostolic Constitutions combines ill manners with the Didache's following injunction against pride: "Do not be malicious nor arrogant: 'for God resists the arrogant' [Proverbs 3:34 Septuagint]."[170] The Apostle Paul lists "malice" among the sins of those who are given over to a debased mind.[171] This type of behavior was unacceptable within the believing community.

On the contrary, disciples of the Master were expected to be courteous and to live a life of good manners. In the Mishnah we read, "Good is the study of Torah with *derech eretz*, as involvement with both makes one forget sin."[172] *Derech eretz* (literally "way of the land," ארץ דרך) in this context is interpreted as referring to proper social behavior. Good manners are so highly regarded in Judaism that the sages say that "*derech eretz* comes before Torah."[173]

Paul likewise urges disciples of Messiah to walk in a "manner of life" that is "worthy of the gospel of [Messiah]."[174] The Scriptures are filled with injunctions about proper social conduct. For example, Leviticus teaches us to stand up before the elderly,[175] and the Master teaches about proper etiquette at banquets: "When

---

170 Apostolic Constitutions 7.5.
171 Romans 1:28–29. The Sibylline Oracles (3.45) likewise exhorts against "ungodly ... false, double-tongued, immoral men, adulterous, idolatrous, designing fraud, an evil madness raving in their hearts, for themselves plundering, having shameless soul," and Clement teaches that we should cast off "from ourselves all unrighteousness and iniquity, covetousness, strife, malignity, and deceit" (1 Clement 35.5).
172 m.*Avot* 2:2.
173 *Leviticus Rabbah* 9:3.
174 Philippians 1:27.
175 Leviticus 19:32.

[2.6]
Or malicious.

you are invited, go and sit in the lowest place, so that when your host comes he may say to you, 'Friend, move up higher.' Then you will be honored in the presence of all who sit at table with you" (Luke 14:10). Good manners encompass more than being polite or having good social etiquette; they are to be a hallmark in the life of a disciple.

⚜ *Or arrogant.* (DIDACHE 2.6)

In Jewish thought the character trait of pride (*ga'avah*, גאוה) is considered one of the most grievous character traits. We read in Proverbs: "Everyone who is arrogant in heart is an abomination to the LORD; be assured, he will not go unpunished" (16:5), to which the sages comment, "Anyone who is arrogant before his Creator, will not be cleansed from the judgment of Gehinnom."[176] The Talmud goes so far as to say that HaShem and the proud man "cannot both dwell in the world."[177]

In Jewish tradition pride is even likened to idolatry.[178] The arrogant person thinks of himself as more important than anyone else, even more so than God. This attitude, like idolatry, puts something else in the place of God.

While not specifically a commandment in the Torah, the sages derive the prohibition on haughtiness from several passages.[179] For example, "Hear and give ear; be not proud, for the LORD has spoken" (Jeremiah 13:15). Israel is warned: "Take care lest ... your heart be lifted up, and you forget the LORD your God" (Deuteronomy 8:14); it is "the proud man who forgets his Creator."[180] The Master tells us that arrogance is one of the things that truly defiles a man.[181]

In his famous chapter on love, the Apostle Paul writes that love "is not arrogant," and he also writes of those who are prideful, that we should "avoid such people."[182] The Apostolic Constitutions, along with the Apostles Peter and James,

---

176   *Proverbs Rabbah* 13:3.
177   b.*Sotah* 5a. Cf. Isaiah 13:11; Luke 1:51.
178   "Haughtiness is equivalent to idolatry, as it is written [Deuteronomy 7:26]: 'And you shall not bring an abomination with your house;' and it is also written [Proverbs 16:5]: 'An abomination of the Lord is every one that is proud of heart.' Since the abomination mentioned in Deuteronomy is idolatry, and the same expression is used in Proverbs, hence we learn that haughtiness is equivalent to idolatry" (*Derech Eretz Rabbah* 11).
179   b.*Sotah* 5a.
180   Rabbi Gavriel Zaloshinsky, *The Ways of the Tzaddikim* (trans. Rabbi Shraga Silverstein; 2 vols.; New York, NY: Feldheim, 1996), 1:27.
181   Mark 7:20–23.
182   1 Corinthians 13:4; 2 Timothy 3:5. Cf. Romans 1:29–31; Titus 1:7.

quotes Proverbs 3:34: "God opposes the proud, but gives grace to the humble," to which Peter adds, "Clothe yourselves, all of you, with humility toward one another" (1 Peter 5:5).[183] Additionally, the Apostle Paul warns Gentile believers, "Do not be arrogant toward the branches [the Jewish people]. If you are, remember it is not you who support the root, but the root that supports you" (Romans 11:18).[184]

[2.6]
Or arrogant.

◐ *Do not plot evil against your fellow.* (DIDACHE 2.6)

This fifth and final evil trait listed in verse 6 forbids malevolent and antagonistic planning against one's neighbor.[185] It is not a new prohibition. Along with the subsequent statement in 2.7, it summarizes the principles taught in chapter 2. The basic premise of all the commandments taught thus far is not to do evil unto one's fellow.

The Apostolic Constitutions (7.5) seems to connect this to Deuteronomy 1:17, "Do not accept persons in judgment; for the judgment is the Lord's." In other words, it sees the evil being plotted here as a form of revenge. Instead, a disciple of Yeshua is to rely on the justice of his Father in heaven.

What is particularly heinous about plotting evil is that it is done in secret without the victim even knowing what is being planned. It is a betrayal of one's neighbor, "who dwells trustingly beside" him.[186] Such trust and love between neighbors is a foundational principle of the Didache's vision for community.

The biblical wisdom books have much to say about those who plot evil: "Deceit is in the heart of those who devise evil"; one should rather "plan peace" that they may "have joy" (Proverbs 12:20). The man who plots evil is called "worthless," and his words are like "scorching fire."[187] David prays to the Lord that he will defend him against "those who treacherously plot evil."[188] The wicked man "plots trouble while on his bed; he sets himself in a way that is not good; he does not reject evil" (Psalm 36:4).

The Prophet Zechariah urges us not to even entertain evil thoughts in our minds: "Do not devise evil in your hearts against one another" (Zechariah 8:17). In turn, the Epistle of Barnabas links evil plots with arrogance: "Do not plot evil against

---

183 James 4:6. Cf. 1 Clement 30.2.
184 Cf. 1 Clement 16.2, 30.1, 35.5, 49.5, 57.2, 59.3.
185 Niederwimmer, *The Didache*, 92.
186 Proverbs 3:29.
187 Proverbs 16:27.
188 Psalm 59:5. Cf. 140:8.

[2.6]
Do not plot evil against your fellow.

your fellow. Do not give overconfidence to yourself."[189] It is the "arrogant" (just mentioned) who have the audacity to carry out such plotting. Rather, we are to seek to do good to those around us, showing them the kindness of our heavenly Father.

> *Do not hate any human being; but some you are to rebuke, and some you are to pray for, yet some you are to love even more than your own life.* (DIDACHE 2.7)

Verse 7, the summary verse of chapter 2, could actually be said to be the "cornerstone verse of the entire Didache."[190] It is reminiscent of a passage by Jude, our Master's brother: "Have mercy on those who doubt; save others by snatching them out of the fire; to others show mercy with fear, hating even the garment stained by the flesh" (Jude 22–23). The verse reflects the message of love that our Master Yeshua taught: a love that results in challenging some, praying for others, and giving up our lives for still others.[191] The Apostolic Constitutions cites two proof texts:

> Do not hate any human being; you are to rebuke "your brother," and not "incur sin because of him" [Leviticus 19:17]; and "Reprove a wise man, and he will love you" [Proverbs 9:8].[192]

This Didache passage sets forth three different types of people: First are those we should rebuke for their transgressions. This section is constructed largely upon Leviticus 19:17, although one notable difference is that the biblical "brother" is replaced by the universal "any human being," emphasizing once again the non-Jewish

---

189 Barnabas 19.3. "Do not give overconfidence to yourself" is found word for word in Didache 3.9.
190 Jones, *The Teaching of the Twelve*, 75.
191 This verse is almost completely missing from the Epistle of Barnabas, which simply states, "You shall love your fellow more than your own life," and the *Doctrina*, which reads, "Do not hate anybody. Some you are to love more than your own soul (*animam*)" (2.7). It is possible, since the Epistle of Barnabas and the *Doctrina* also lack the non-canonical gospel material of 1.3–5, that this saying, too, is linked to no-longer extant sayings of the Master. It is found in one of the *Oxyrhynchus Papyrus* fragments of the Didache (Folio 1r). Curiously, the *Oxyrhynchus Papyrus* fragments of the Didache contain only sections of 1.3–4, 2.7, and 3.1–2, all of which could be linked back to non-canonical sayings of the Master.
192 Apostolic Constitutions 7.5. Cf. "However, you are to love those who hate you, and you will not have any enemies" (Didache 1.3). Note that the Apostolic Constitutions paraphrases Leviticus 19:7, and just as in the Didache, it uses "any human being" in place of the biblical "brother."

audience of the Didache.¹⁹³ Although, it appears while the Apostolic Constitutions opens up not hating anyone to "any human being," it limits rebuke and reproof to only those within the community, i.e., "your brother." In rabbinic exegesis this passage from Leviticus represents the positive commandment to rebuke one's fellow when he is in sin.¹⁹⁴ In turn, not to rebuke someone when one is able to become an accomplice in that person's sin. The Master expounds on Leviticus 19:17, explaining the proper steps for rebuking in Matthew 18:15–18.

The second group, those we "are to pray for," seems to indicate people who have not confessed their sins yet cannot be reprimanded for one reason or another. Rabbi Steinsaltz writes that in rebuking "one should only reprimand someone who will accept the reprimand, and one must not reprimand someone who has vehemently expressed unwillingness to be reprimanded."¹⁹⁵ In such cases the Didache instructs us to pray for a person rather than rebuke him. Through our prayers we hope to bring the person to repentance.

Finally, for the third group, the Didache instructs, "Yet some you are to love even more than your own life," which most commentaries see as applying to members of one's own community—those who have repented and are walking in the Way of Life. The commandment to love applies to all mankind, of course, but different measures apply for each of the three groups of people. For some—those in this third group—we need to be willing to make the ultimate sacrifice. The Master himself tells us, "Greater love has no one than this, that someone lay down his life for his friends" (John 15:13), and in a non-canonical saying that echoes the Didache's language, Yeshua says, "Love your brother like your soul, guard him like the pupil of your eye."¹⁹⁶

[2.7]
Do not hate any human being; but some you are to rebuke, and some you are to pray for, yet some you are to love even more than your own life.

---

193 Additionally, while we would expect in Greek "no one," the Didache has "any human being," literally "any man" (*kal adam*, כל אדם), which is "a common Hebraism [and] an indication of the Hebrew origin of the writer." See Philip Schaff, *The Oldest Church Manual Called the Teaching of the Twelve Apostles* (Edinburgh, Scotland: T&T Clark, 1885), 170.
194 In Jewish halachah, some even included Noachides in this commandment: "Rabbi Judah the Pious observes: 'When one sees a Noachide sinning, if one can correct him, one should, since God sent Jonah to Nineveh to return them to his path'" (*Sefer HaChasidim* 1124 as quoted in Michael J. Broyde, "Jewish Law and American Public Policy," in *Formulating Responses in an Egalitarian Society* [ed. Marc Stern; New York, NY: Rowman & Littlefield, 2005], 115).
195 Rabbi Steinsaltz, *The Talmud Steinsaltz Edition: A Reference Guide*, 271.
196 Gospel of Thomas 25. The New Testament mentions Epaphroditus, who "nearly died for the work of Messiah, risking his life to complete what was lacking" (Philippians 2:30), and in Revelation we read of martyrs who "loved not their lives even unto death" (Revelation 12:11).

[2.7]
Do not hate any human being; but some you are to rebuke, and some you are to pray for, yet some you are to love even more than your own life.

The Greek word *psuche* ("life," ψυχή) corresponds in the Septuagint primarily to the Hebrew word *nefesh* ("soul," נפש). This then connects to "You shall love the LORD … with all your soul" (Deuteronomy 6:5), and naturally so, because in the Didache and in the teachings of the Master, our love for God is displayed in our love for our fellow.[197] Indeed, the sages interpret "with all your soul" as a willingness to give up our life.[198] In the Epistle of Barnabas this line is conflated with Leviticus 19:18: "You shall love your fellow more than your own life."[199] In the Didache "Love your neighbor as yourself" becomes "Love your neighbor more than yourself."

---

197   Interestingly, the Georgian version reads, "All these things you shall do but you shall love the Lord more than your own soul."
198   m.*Brachot* 9:5.
199   Barnabas 19.5.

Chapter Three

DIDACHE 3

3.1 My child, flee from all evil and everything like it.

3.2 Do not be an angry person, for anger leads to murder; nor be envious, nor adversarial, nor hot-tempered, for from all these things murder results.[1]

3.3 My child, do not be a lustful person,[2] for lust leads to sexual immorality; nor be foul-mouthed,[3] nor one who looks up at women, for from all these things adultery results.[4]

3.4 My child, do not be a diviner,[5] because this leads to idolatry; nor be one who casts spells,[6] nor one who studies astrology,[7] nor one who performs purification rites.[8] Do not even desire to see these things, for from all these things idolatry results.

3.5 My child, do not be a liar,[9] because lying leads to theft; nor be one who loves money,[10] nor be glory-seeking, for from all these things theft results.

3.6 My child, do not be a complainer,[11] because this leads to blasphemy; nor be egocentric,[12] nor malevolent, for from all these things blasphemy results.

3.7 Rather, be humble, because the humble will inherit the earth.[13]

---

1 Matthew 5:21–22.
2 1 Thessalonians 4:5.
3 Proverbs 4:24; Ephesians 4:29, 5:4; Colossians 3:8.
4 Matthew 5:27–28.
5 Leviticus 19:26; Deuteronomy 18:10.
6 Deuteronomy 18:10–11.
7 Deuteronomy 4:19; Jeremiah 10:2.
8 Deuteronomy 18:10.
9 Leviticus 19:11; Colossians 3:9.
10 Hebrews 13:5.
11 1 Corinthians 10:10.
12 Titus 1:7.
13 Psalm 37:11; Matthew 5:5.

3.8 Be patient,[14] merciful, innocent, quiet,[15] and good-natured, always trembling at the words that you have heard.[16]

3.9 Do not aggrandize yourself nor give overconfidence to yourself. Do not connect yourself with the lofty, but rather associate with the righteous and lowly.[17]

3.10 Accept the things that happen to you as being for the good,[18] knowing that nothing happens apart from God.

---

14 1 Thessalonians 5:14; James 5:7–8.
15 1 Timothy 2:2; 1 Thessalonians 4:11; 2 Thessalonians 3:12; 1 Peter 3:4.
16 Isaiah 66:2, 5.
17 Leviticus 19:15; Romans 12:16.
18 Romans 8:28.

Overview

Chapter 3 of the Didache continues on the theme of the Decalogue. Like chapter 2, chapter 3 can be divided into two parts. It opens with admonitions regarding minor sins that can lead to major sins (3.1–6), and it closes with a list of positive Messiah-like traits that its audience is urged to adopt (3.7–10). Both sections exhort us to a life of righteous conduct and to be on guard against all forms of sin.

Put Off and Put On

The two parts go hand in hand. The negative traits listed in the first section are replaced by the five positive qualities of the latter section. This kind of pattern was common in the literature of the day. We find an example of this in Ephesians 4:22–24, where Paul writes:

> Put off your old self, which belongs to your former manner of life and is corrupt through deceitful desires, and ... be renewed in the spirit of your minds, and ... put on the new self, created after the likeness of God in true righteousness and holiness.

James, the brother of the Master, also urges, "Put away all filthiness and rampant wickedness and receive with meekness the implanted word, which is able to save your souls" (James 1:21).

The Didache was to be a manual for new believers in Messiah who were entering into the Messianic community. Its instruction begins with negative behaviors that one should remove and only then enters into the righteous behaviors required for holy living. In the words of Paul, one must "put off" before one can "put on."

First Section: Discipleship

The opening verse of chapter 3 addresses the audience as "my child" for the first time in the book. The same address appears five times in this chapter and once in chapter 4, with the plural "children" appearing later, in chapter 5.[19] The frequent

---

[19] Didache 3.3, 4, 5, 6, 4.1, 5.2.

use of "my child" in verses 1–6 of chapter 3 has led scholars to label this the "*teknon* section," *teknon* (τέκνον) being the Greek word for "child."[20]

The use of "my child" indicates that a teacher-disciple relationship is occurring within the text in which the teacher is the "father," and the disciple is the "son." In the Hebrew Scriptures we see Elisha, the disciple of Elijah the prophet, calling Elijah "my father."[21] In rabbinic literature the sage at the head of an academy of Torah is referred to as the father, and his disciples are called his family; hence terms such as the "House of Hillel" (*Beit Hillel*) and the "House of Shammai" (*Beit Shammai*).[22] We read in the Talmud,

> Resh Lakish said: "He who teaches Torah to his neighbor's son is regarded by Scripture as though he had fashioned him [i.e., fathered him]." (b.*Sanhedrin* 99b)

The Master alluded to this relationship when he said to the Pharisees, "By whom do your sons [i.e., "your disciples"] cast them out?"[23] The collected words of the early Torah masters are even called *Pirkei Avot* ("Sayings of the Fathers").

Therefore, when the Didache uses the expressions "my child" and "my children," it taps into the rich culture of discipleship within Jewish tradition. Although the Master urged his followers not to call anyone "rabbi" or "father" in the sense of ascribing complete authority to another person,[24] the Didache emphasizes the teacher-disciple relationship and, in a roundabout way, encourages its readers to find their own teachers to help instruct them in the Way of Life.[25]

Minor to Major

In the *teknon* section (3.1–6) the Didache instructs its audience to be careful of minor sins lest they lead to grave sins.[26] "My child, flee from all evil and everything

---

20 Jewish wisdom literature more commonly uses the expression "my son" (*beni*, בני), as seen, for example, throughout the books of Proverbs and Sirach. Yet we find the term "my children" in the New Testament. E.g., Galatians 4:19; 1 John 2:1; 3 John 1:4. *Teknon* ("my child") probably represents a Greek rendering of the Hebrew term *beni* ("my son").
21 2 Kings 2:12.
22 Cf. b.*Bava Batra* 10b.
23 Luke 11:19.
24 Matthew 23:8–9.
25 Cf. m.*Avot* 1:6.
26 Similarly, in rabbinic tradition non-Jews wishing to convert to Judaism were "given instruction in some of the minor and some of the major commandments" (b.*Yevamot* 47a).

like it" (3.1). Like chapter 2, chapter 3 is structured around the Ten Commandments; it could be said to contain "as it were a second Decalogue against more refined sins and passions of the heart which lead to the grosser sins of deed."[27] These commandments are the five precepts of the ten that the sages interpreted as universally applicable: blasphemy, idolatry, adultery, bloodshed, and robbery.[28] The sages considered these five commandments to constitute universal rule (alluded to in Leviticus 18:4 as "my rules"), because they could have been deduced by human reason if they had not been written.[29] All this is evidence that the Didache did not randomly choose these prohibitions but rather drew upon the didactic models of Jewish tradition, in which these five are considered among the gravest transgressions and, as has been mentioned, universally applicable.

Didache 3.1 introduces a general principle which is followed by five specific cases (3.2–6). The *teknon* section can be organized as follows:[30]

---

27 Philip Schaff, *The Oldest Church Manual Called the Teaching of the Twelve Apostles* (Edinburgh, Scotland: T&T Clark, 1885), 170–171.
28 This excepts social laws and the prohibition of flesh from a living animal. See *Sifra* on Leviticus 18:4; b.*Sanhedrin* 56a; b.*Yoma* 67b. David Flusser writes that this section of the Didache "reflect[s] the trespasses against the common or 'natural' ethical law." See Flusser, *Judaism and the Origins of Christianity* (Jerusalem, Israel: Magnes, 1988), 508.
29 b.*Yoma* 67b.
30 Kurt Niederwimmer (*The Didache: Hermeneia—A Critical and Historical Commentary on the Bible* [Minneapolis, MN: Fortress, 1998], 96) has further pointed out that each of these five prohibitions follow the same structural pattern. Using the example of 3.1–2, he divides each saying like this:

My child,	Address
Do not be an angry person,	First warning
for anger leads to murder;	First reason
nor be envious, nor adversarial, nor hot-tempered,	Second warning
for from all of these things murder results.	Second reason

General Principle	
3.1	Flee from evil and everything like it

Specifics of General Principle	
3.2	Anger leads to murder
3.3	Lust leads to sexual immorality
3.4	Divination leads to idolatry
3.5	Lying leads to theft
3.6	Complaining leads to blasphemy

The main crux of the teaching in this section is that the transgression of so-called light prohibitions will lead to the transgression of heavy commandments. William Varner writes that "the structure of the passage is fraught with features that would be familiar to Jewish readers."[31] Examples from Jewish literature can be cited:

> My children, the love of money leads to idolatry; because, when led astray through money, men name as gods those who are not gods, and it causes him who hath it to fall into madness. (Testament of Judah 19:1)[32]

> The commencement of making vows is the door to foolishness. Ritual uncleanness leads to idolatry. Frivolity with women is the beginning of adultery. (*Derech Eretz Zuta* 3:6 [58b])[33]

> If a person transgresses a minor commandment, he will eventually transgress a major commandment. If he transgresses, "you shall love your fellow as yourself" [Leviticus 19:18], he will eventually transgress,

---

31 William Varner, *The Way of the Didache: The First Christian Handbook* (New York, NY: University Press of America, 2007), 64. Huub van de Sandt and David Flusser elaborate by adding that in rabbinic literature "the evaluation of a light sin as 'leading (המביא) to transgression' of a weighty one is formulated in grammatical terms by the causitive *hif'il* of the verb בוא," and this is the same pattern we see in the Greek text of the Didache. "The stylistic pattern of these single phrases with the repeated stereotyped formula ὁδηγεῖ γὰρ … πρὸς may be traced back to rabbinic literature and, especially, in the *Testaments of the Twelve Patriarchs*." See Van de Sandt and Flusser, *The Didache: Its Jewish Sources and Its Place in Early Judaism and Christianity* (Minneapolis, MN: Fortress, 2002), 171–172.

32 Cf. Testament of Judah 14:1; Testament of Rueben 2:8–9.

33 Cf. *Derech Eretz Zuta* 1:15 [58a], 5:4 58b.

"you shall not take vengeance or bear a grudge" [Leviticus 19:18], "you shall not hate your brother" [Leviticus 19:17], and "that your brother may live beside you" [Leviticus 25:36], until he ends up shedding blood. Therefore it is written, "If anyone hates his fellow and lies in wait for him and attacks him and strikes him fatally so that he dies, and he flees into one of these cities ..." (*Sifrei*, Deuteronomy 186)[34]

We find this same reasoning and structure in the New Testament:

> They have eyes full of adultery, insatiable for sin. They entice unsteady souls. They have hearts trained in greed. Accursed children! (2 Peter 2:14)

> You desire and do not have, so you murder. You covet and cannot obtain, so you fight and quarrel. You do not have, because you do not ask. (James 4:2)[35]

Fences

The exegetical method used by the Didache in this section is, at its core, "the very essence of the Pharisaic interpretation of the Law."[36] According to the Mishnah, the Men of the Great Synagogue commanded their disciples to "make a fence around the Torah."[37] The sages felt that in order to prevent the Torah from being transgressed, they needed to set up protections around the commandments. For example: "Tithes form a fence to wealth [greed], vows form a fence to self-restraint; a fence to wisdom is silence."[38] *Avot DeRabbi Natan* says that Adam was the first to construct a fence around the Torah in that he said, "We should not touch it" (Genesis 3:3), whereas the LORD originally had only commanded, "You shall not

---

34 Cf. m.*Avot* 4:2.
35 Cf. James 1:14–15.
36 Solomon Schechter and Kaufman Kohler, "Didache," in *Jewish Encyclopedia* (New York, NY: KTAV, 1906) 4:585–588. Some have suggested that when the Didache makes the progression from minor transgressions to major ones, it is employing the rabbinic method of *kal vachomer* ("light and heavy," קל וחומר), which is used to say, "If [A] is true, then how much more so [B]." See Huub van de Sandt, "Law and Ethics in Matthew's Antitheses and James's Letter: A Reorientation of Halakah in Line with the Jewish Two Ways 3:1–6," in *Matthew, James, and Didache: Three Related Documents in Their Jewish and Christian Settings* (ed. Huub van de Sandt and Jürgen K. Zangenberg; Atlanta, GA: Society of Biblical Literature, 2008), 330. But when the Didache instructs its audience, "Do not get angry, for anger leads to murder" (3.2) or, "My child, do not be lustful, for lust leads to fornication" (3.3), it seems more probable that it is accessing the rabbinic method of "fences."
37 m.*Avot* 1:1.
38 m.*Avot* 3:13.

eat" (Genesis 2:17).[39] Even in the Decalogue the tenth commandment ("You shall not covet") acts as a fence to transgressing the sixth, seventh, eighth, and ninth commandments ("You shall not murder," "commit adultery," "steal," or "bear false witness").[40]

Yeshua took a similar attitude in the Sermon on the Mount. In Matthew 5:20 he told his disciples, "Unless your righteousness exceeds that of the scribes and Pharisees, you will never enter the kingdom of heaven." How was it to exceed the scribes and Pharisees? By setting up fences around the weightier matters of the Torah.[41] The Master taught that if the commandment states that we should not murder, a fence to committing murder would be to prohibit harboring anger in one's heart. The commandment states that one may not commit adultery; therefore, a fence to committing adultery would be to prohibit lust with the eyes. The commandment states that one may not break a vow; therefore, a fence to breaking vows would be to prohibit vowing at all.

The Didache follows this rabbinic method of fencing in 3.1–6. One should not be "lustful," because lust leads to "sexual immorality"; in other words, not lusting is a fence to the prohibition of fornication. One should not be involved in "divination," because it leads to "idolatry"; that is, the prohibition on divination is a fence to the prohibition of idolatry. One should not be a "liar," because lying leads to "theft"; so the prohibition on dishonesty is a fence to the prohibition of theft. In turn, the Didache establishes fences that prevent minor sins from turning into major sins.

Unlike rabbinic literature, the teachings of the Master and the Didache offer no fences regarding halachic issues but instead focus on the moral or weightier precepts of the Torah. This focus is in line with ancient Chasidim of the Tannaitic Period, who believed that "the fulfillment of halachic duty did not exhaust moral responsibility." In like manner, the Didache presents "high ethical rules that appeal to universal morality."[42]

---

39   *Avot DeRabbi Natan* 1 (B).
40   George Cantrell Allen, *The Didache: Or, the Teaching of the Twelve Apostles* (London, England: Astolat, 1903), 12.
41   Matthew 5:21–48.
42   Van de Sandt, "Law and Ethics in Matthew's Antitheses and James's Letter," in *Matthew, James, and Didache* (ed. Van de Sandt and Zangenberg), 322.

Guarding Thoughts

Many of the minor infractions the Didache mentions begin with the thoughts of the heart. The Torah warns us "not to follow after your own heart."[43] Our Master Yeshua teaches, "Out of the heart come evil thoughts, murder, adultery, sexual immorality, theft, false witness, slander" (Matthew 15:19). Paul also warned the Corinthians that their thoughts had the power to lead them "astray from a sincere and pure devotion to Messiah."[44]

Jewish teaching on ethics stresses that control of one's thoughts is the key to righteous living. It is stated in *Cheshbon HaNefesh*:

> As concerns being careful and guarding one's thoughts, it is fitting that you not ignore guarding your thoughts, ideas and the musings of your heart, for the greater part of imperfection and rectification of one's actions is only through them.[45]

We must constantly guard not only what we are doing but also what we are thinking. After all, our thoughts lead us to action, for better or for worse. By managing the thoughts of our hearts, we can prevent ourselves from committing a great many sins.

Second Section: Injunctions on Humility

After listing character traits in the first section that we are to "put off," the Didache goes into a series of behavior traits that we should "put on." This new section (3.7–10) is largely centered on the trait of humility: "Rather, be humble because

---

43 Numbers 15:39.
44 2 Corinthians 11:3.
45 Rabbi Menachem Mendel Levin, *Cheshbon HaNefesh: A Guide to Self-Improvement and Character Refinement* (trans. Rabbi Shraga Silverstein; New York, NY: Feldheim, 1995), 3–5. Rebbe Nachman of Breslov taught: "Guard your thoughts carefully, for thought can literally create a living thing. The higher a faculty, the further it can reach. You can kick something with your foot, but throw it higher with your hand. You can reach still farther with your voice, calling to a person very far away. Hearing reaches yet further, for you can hear sounds like gunfire from a very great distance. Your sight reaches even further, seeing things in the sky. Highest of all is the mind, which can penetrate the loftiest heights. You must therefore safeguard your mind above all else" (Rabbi Nathan of Nemirov, *Rebbe Nachman's Wisdom* [trans. Rabbi Aryeh Kaplan; Monsey, NY: Breslov Research Institute, 1973], 150).

the humble will inherit the earth" (3.7).⁴⁶ Much of this section (especially verses 8–10) finds parallels in chapter 4 of the Didache.

The contents of this section find thematic parallels in the New Testament. Didache 3.7 appears to draw from Matthew 5:5 ("Blessed are the meek, for they shall inherit the earth"). Of the six dispositions mentioned in 3.8, "patience" in its Greek derivative is used a total of twelve times in the New Testament, "good-natured" seventy-seven times, and the other four twice each.⁴⁷ We also find in this section similar vocabulary to that found in the work of the Apostle Peter's disciple Clement:

> Let us therefore be humble, brethren, laying aside all arrogance and conceit and folly and anger, and let us do that which is written … For Messiah Yeshua spoke, teaching forbearance and long-suffering … that we may walk in obedience to his hallowed words, with lowliness of mind. (1 Clement 13.1–3)

Parallel themes can be found in other Jewish works of the period as well.⁴⁸ Significantly, a similar list appears in the Two Ways material in the Qumran scrolls:

---

46 Many scholars have labeled this section "the *anavim* ["humble ones," עֲנָוִים] sayings," sometimes even extending it to all the other material of chapter 4 as well. Verse 7 is quoting Psalm 37:11, and there the word in Hebrew is *anavim*, but in the Tanach the *anavim* refers not to the meek and mild but rather to the powerless, the downtrodden, the subjugated, and the victimized. They would take on simplicity, with the posture of humility, while living out a faithful Torah life.

The material of 3.7–10 seems to reflect these character traits and have thus led scholars to associate this section with the *anavim*: "In these admonitions the ideal of the group is sketched in a few strokes: it is not the condition of the wealthy and influential but of the poor and exploited, if, and to the extent that, their condition is associated with an attitude of submission to God. Then is given to these, and especially to these, the great promise: the inheritance of the land. Submission and hope are founded on the unimpeachable certainty that fate is governed by God, and therefore it can only serve to benefit the pious" (Niederwimmer, *The Didache*, 102).

Others feel that this material reflects instead those well versed in the technicalities of Torah and Jewish exegesis. John Kloppenborg argues that this material rather reflects sophisticated rabbinic type teaching: "The immediately preceding section, Didache 3.1–6, is concerned to articulate an aetiology and genealogy of vices, arguing that there is a direct and necessary connection between lesser vices such as anger not expressly proscribed by the Torah, and murder, part of the Decalogue. This kind of discourse, which seeks to establish family resemblances among certain behaviors, and operates from and seeks to illustrate the theoretical unity of the Torah, belongs to a sophisticated moral speculation, hardly consistent with addressees far down the social ladder" (John S. Kloppenborg, "Poverty and Piety in Matthew, James, and the Didache," in *Matthew, James, and Didache: Three Related documents in Their Jewish and Christian Settings* (ed. Huub van de Sandt and Jurgen K. Zangenberg; Atlanta, GA: Society of Biblical Literature, 2008), 219).

47 Aaron Milavec, *The Didache: Faith, Hope, & Life of the Earliest Christian Communities, 50–70 C.E.* (New York, NY: Newman, 2003), 157.

48 Cf. Testament of Dan 6:9.

These are their ways in the world for the enlightenment of the heart of man ... a spirit of humility, patience, abundant charity, unending goodness, understanding, and intelligence. (Community Rule [1QS] IV, 2–3)

THE WORDS OF THE MASTER

The Didache, throughout the work, seems to access non-canonical, oral or written sayings of the Master. The *teknon* section (3.1–6) appears to draw from material parallel to the Sermon on the Mount, in particular from Matthew 5:21–48.[49] As we have pointed out above, both the Didache and Yeshua use the rabbinic method of fences in these sections, and both have a focus on the Decalogue. While the Didache says that a minor sin *leads* to a major sin, the Master states that a minor sin *is equal to* a major sin.

Huub van de Sandt writes that "the similarities [between Didache 3.1–6 and the Sermon on the Mount] are extensive enough to establish an undeniable relationship between the two sections ... Both sections ... draw the same conclusions along the same line of reasoning. They share the method of applying the principle laid down in the preamble (Didache 3.1 and Matthew 5:17–19)."[50] David Flusser as well finds direct parallels between the Didache and Matthew 5 in the order and content for the Didache's first three verses:[51]

MATTHEW 5		DIDACHE 3	
5:17–20	Preamble: ... Do not set aside even the least of these commandments	3.1	My child, flee from all evil and everything like it.
5:21–22	Anger and murder	3.2	Anger leads to murder
5:27–28	One who looks at a woman lustfully has already committed adultery with her in his heart	3.3	Lust leads to sexual immorality

---

49 The Georgian version of the Didache opens with, "My son, I say to you," which seems to allude to the "I say to you" teachings of the Sermon on the Mount.
50 Van de Sandt, "Law and Ethics in Matthew's Antitheses and James's Letter," in Van de Sandt and Zangenberg, *Matthew, James, and Didache*, 329–330.
51 Van de Sandt and Flusser, *The Didache*, 171.

Indeed, in the *teknon* section we find an "affirmation of the Torah, ensuring the fulfillment of the major precepts by avoiding the minor infringements," which "also lies behind the 'greater righteousness' of the Antithesis of Matthew 5:17–18, rather than a rejection of the Torah in favor of the Gospel."[52]

While the *teknon* section also appears in the *Doctrina* (3.1–6), it is completely absent from the Epistle of Barnabas. The Epistle of Barnabas does not seem to incorporate any sayings of Yeshua into its Two Ways text, but the *Doctrina* does allude to sayings of Yeshua from time to time. This might indicate that the *teknon* section is based on no-longer-extant non-canonical sayings of the Master.[53] Didache 3.1–2 is also found in the *Oxyrhynchus Papyrus* fragments of the Didache. The *Oxyrhynchus Papyrus* contains only five verses of the Didache, and all of these verses seem likely to be non-canonical sayings of the Master.[54] Furthermore, some scholars suggest that the *teknon* section existed independently before it was incorporated into the Didache:

> The symmetrical strophic pattern of this unit has led many scholars to conclude that this passage existed as a separate block before it was incorporated into the Jewish Two Ways.[55]

It seems highly probable that the *teknon* material from chapter 3 of the Didache was based on some early version of the Sermon on the Mount that was later developed into the version that appears in the canonical Gospel of Matthew. This material could have been transmitted via a written or an oral source. It is even possible that both Matthew and the Didache draw upon a similar source that has not been preserved.

---

52   Jonathan A. Draper, "The Holy Vine of David Made Known to the Gentiles through God's Servant Jesus: 'Christian Judaism' in the Didache," in *Jewish Christianity Reconsidered: Rethinking Ancient Groups and Texts* (ed., Matt Jackson-McCabe; Minneapolis, MN: Fortress, 2007), 267. Additionally, there is also a strong link between the words of Yeshua's brother James (1:13–15, 19–21) and that of the *"teknon* section." See Van de Sandt, "Law and Ethics in Matthew's Antitheses and James's Letter," in *Matthew, James, and Didache* (ed. Van de Sandt and Zangenberg), 332.
53   The *teknon* section in the *Doctrina* opens with "son" which is equivalent to "my child" (Jefford, 24) but does not introduce each subsequent verse with this phrase as the Didache does. The *Doctrina* is also missing Didache 3.3. It could be that the *Doctrina* represents an initial stage in which sayings of the Master were beginning to be incorporated into the Two Ways and the Didache represents a stage in which those additions were more developed.
54   Didache 1.3b–4a, 2.7b–3.2a.
55   Van de Sandt and Flusser, *The Didache*, 133.

Commentary

🕭 *My child, flee from all evil and everything like it.*

(DIDACHE 3.1)

Chapter 3 opens up with a general admonition that serves as an introduction to the *teknon* section (3.1–6).[56] In a very rabbinic manner the Didache progresses from the general to the specific: Didache 3.1 states a general principle followed by the specific prohibitions of 3.2–6. "All evil" represents capitol offenses and prohibitions from the Ten Commandments: Murder, adultery, idolatry, theft, and blasphemy. The category of "everything like it" represents the seemingly minor sins listed which lead to the major ones. The *Doctrina* makes this about avoiding wicked individuals: "Son, flee from an evil man and from everyone like him" (3.1).[57]

Based upon the use of the word "evil" here, Charles Taylor suggests the possibility of an underlying Hebrew original.[58] It is quite possible that a Hebrew proverb of similar expression that was circulated at the time is here quoted or paraphrased by the Didache. For example, the Apostle Paul writes to the Thessalonians, "Abstain from every form of evil" (1 Thessalonians 5:22).

Participation in something "like evil" will lead to evil. For example, in *Derech Eretz Zuta*: "Be afraid of a light sin, for this may bring you to a grave sin," and, "If you neglect one commandment, you will finally be negligent of other commandments. The same is if you have overlooked the words of the Torah willingly: finally you will be overlooked, willingly or unwillingly."[59] Rebbe Nachman of Breslov taught:

---

56 The Apostolic Constitutions (7.5) seems to connect "evil" here to the lack of social justice when it quotes the book of Isaiah (54:14 Septuagint): "Abstain from injustice, and trembling shall not come near you."

57 One of the *Oxyrhynchus Papyrus* fragments of the Didache (Folio 2v) renders this, "My child, flee from every evil thing and its like." Interestingly, the exact text "from every evil thing" appears in the apocryphal book *Joseph and Asenath*, a work that may have been written by early believers. Cf. 26:2: "And Joseph said to her [Asenath], 'Take heart and do not be afraid, but go; for the Lord is with you and He will keep you from every evil thing (ἀπὸ παντὸς πράγματος πονηροῦ) as the apple of an eye.'"

58 Charles Taylor, "The Teaching of the Twelve Apostles with Illustrations from the Talmud," in *Didache: The Unknown Teaching of the Apostles* (ed. Brent S. Walters; San Jose, CA: The Anti-Nicene Archive, 1991), 162.

59 *Derech Eretz Zuta* 2:7 [58a]; 3:2–3 [58a]. *Avot DeRabbi Natan* combines both approaches: "Here it is said: 'You [plural] shall not approach' (Leviticus 18:6) and later it is said: 'You [singular] shall not approach' (18:19); hence, approach nothing that might lead to transgression, keep far from what is hideous and from what seems hideous. Therefore the Sages have said: 'Keep far from a minor sin lest it lead you to grievous sin; be quick to carry out a minor commandment for it will lead you to a major commandment'" (2 [A]). See Rabbi Nathan of Nemirov, *Rebbe Nachman's Wisdom*, 206–211.

[3.1]
My child, flee from all evil and everything like it.

"When a person does one sin, it then causes him to commit related offenses. The later sins are then responsible for still more related wrongs … The first sin along with the related ones following it, forms one package." Based on the line from the *Selichot* prayers, "remove the first one first," he stated that in order to be free from this package of sins the original root sin must be purged first.

The Master also stressed the observance of minor precepts: "Whoever relaxes one of the least of these commandments and teaches others to do the same will be called least in the kingdom of heaven, but whoever does them and teaches them will be called great in the kingdom of heaven" (Matthew 5:19).

◈ *Do not be an angry person, for anger leads to murder.*
(DIDACHE 3.2)

The Didache now lists five major sins and the sins that lead up to them.[60] Murder, adultery, and idolatry top the list as Judaism considers them to be the gravest of sins. The Master also paired murder and adultery together in the Sermon on the Mount.[61] Regarding murder he states, "You have heard that it was said to those of old, 'You shall not murder; and whoever murders will be liable to judgment.' But I say to you that everyone who is angry with his brother will be liable to judgment" (Matthew 5:21–22). Rabbinic texts of the period also make the same comparison: "He who hates his neighbor without cause is also considered a murderer."[62]

The Didache considers murder to be the prohibited "evil." Anger, envy, adversarial nature, and hot-temper fall into the category of "everything like it." The things that are like the evil lead to the evil.

In numerous biblical examples anger led to murder. The Apostolic Constitutions cites the stories of Cain, Saul, and Joab:

---

60   The *Doctrina* says, "Do not be an angry person, for anger leads to murder, nor be eager for malice, or proud, for all these things breed anger" (3.2–3).
61   Matthew 5:21–30.
62   *Kallah Rabbati* 8:7 54b. Cf. "Remove from you the spirit of envy, for this makes savage the soul and destroys the body; it causes anger and war in the mind, and stirs up unto deeds of blood" (Testament of Simeon 4:8); "If he transgresses, 'you shall love your neighbor as yourself' [Leviticus 19:18], he will eventually transgress, 'you shall not take vengeance or bear a grudge' [Leviticus 19:18], 'you shall not hate your brother' [Leviticus 19:17], and 'that your brother may live beside you' [Leviticus 25:36], until he ends up shedding blood" (*Sifrei*, Deuteronomy 186).

Do not be an angry person, nor spiteful, nor envious, nor furious, nor daring, lest you undergo the fate of Cain, and of Saul, and of Joab: for the first of these slew his brother Abel, because Abel was found to be preferred before him with God, and because Abel's sacrifice was preferred [Genesis 4]; the second persecuted holy David, who had slain Goliath the Philistine, being envious of the praises of the women who danced [1 Samuel 17–18]; the third slew two generals of armies—Abner of Israel, and Amasa of Judah [2 Samuel 3, 20]. (Apostolic Constitutions 7.5)[63]

[3.2]
Do not be an angry person, for anger leads to murder.

Also, in Jacob's rebuke of Simeon and Levi, he cursed their "anger" that had brought about the vicious slaughter in Shechem.[64]

The Scriptures are replete with warnings and admonitions against anger. Proverbs warns that "a man of quick temper acts foolishly," but exhorts, "Whoever is slow to anger has great understanding."[65] Paul exhorts the Ephesians to remove "bitterness and wrath and anger" and instead to "be kind to one another, tenderhearted, forgiving one another."[66] He also warns the Galatians that "fits of anger" are "works of the flesh," and that those who engage in them "will not inherit the kingdom of God."[67] As believers, we are to practice patience and forbearance and not easily be brought to anger and frustration. James, the brother of the Master, gives the sage-like advice, "Let every person be quick to hear, slow to speak, slow to anger" (James 1:19).

Jewish ethical teaching has strict warnings about the trait of anger (*ka'as*, כעס): "Anger is an evil trait. Just as scurvy is a disease of the body, so anger is a disease of the soul ... For anger deprives a man from reasoning ... Therefore, it is impossible for the angry man to escape great sins."[68] In the Talmud the sages equate unrighteous anger with idolatry.[69] The Mishnah urges, "Do not anger easily."[70]

The Apostle Paul warns us to handle anger in the correct manner: "Be angry and do not sin; do not let the sun go down on your anger" (Ephesians 4:26).

---

63 Cf. Wisdom of Solomon 10:3.
64 Genesis 49:7. According to the Testament of Dan, "the spirit of anger" also led to the near murder of Joseph (1:8).
65 Proverbs 14:17, 29; Cf. Ecclesiastes 7:9; Sirach 10:6, 28:7.
66 Ephesians 4:31–32. Cf. 1 Timothy 2:8; Colossians 3:8; Titus 1:7.
67 Galatians 5:18–21.
68 Rabbi Gavriel Zaloshinsky, *The Ways of the Tzaddikim* (trans. Rabbi Shraga Silverstein; 2 vols.; New York, NY: Feldheim, 1996), 1:237.
69 b.*Sanhedrin* 105b.
70 m.*Avot* 2:15.

◈ *Nor be envious.* (DIDACHE 3.2)

The theme of murder continues as the Didache lays out three sub-categories of anger. This is a gradual but steady progression that takes one from envy to murder.

"Envious" is the Greek word *zelotes* ("zealous," ζηλωτής). Envy, like anger, can be righteous or unrighteous. When it is used for good, the word is usually translated "zealous," for example, "zealous for the law" or "zealous for good works."[71] When it is used in the negative sense, it is often translated "jealous," as in "filled with jealousy."[72] The Apostle Paul warned against the dangers of envy in his epistles and stated that, as with anger, those who displayed jealousy would "not inherit the kingdom of God."[73] In Jewish ethical teaching it is taught that the trait of envy (*kin'ah*, קנאה) leads to "transgressing the Ten Commandments," which includes murder, because a man will do anything to obtain that for which he lusts.[74]

We disciples of the Master must guard ourselves against all forms of envy. Jealousy begins in the heart. The Talmud notes that the story of Saul's jealousy of David began within: "He had a sinking feeling and he envied him."[75] The murderous actions that Saul committed against David began with evil thoughts of jealousy. The Apostle Peter's disciple Clement states that envy caused Cain to kill Abel, Jacob to flee from Esau, Joseph almost to be killed by his brothers, Moses to flee from Pharaoh, Aaron and Miriam to slander Moses, Dathan and Abiram to be killed, Peter to suffer trials, and Paul nearly to be killed several times.[76]

◈ *Nor adversarial, nor hot-tempered, for from all of these things murder results.* (DIDACHE 3.2)

The admonitions not to be "adversarial" or "hot-tempered" do not appear in any other parallel literature with the same Greek words found in the Didache, nor their Hebrew equivalents.[77] Nevertheless, these two themes are similar to what has been discussed thus far in this chapter. The sages draw a prohibition against adversarial behavior from the story of Korah's rebellion: "He who is unyielding

---

71 Acts 21:20; Titus 2:14.
72 Acts 5:17, 13:45.
73 Galatians 5:20–21. Cf. Romans 13:3; 1 Corinthians 3:3; 2 Corinthians 12:20.
74 Rabbi Zaloshinsky, *The Ways of the Tzaddikim*, 265.
75 b.*Sanhedrin* 93b.
76 1 Clement 3.2–5.6. Cf. Testament of Simeon 2:6–3:6.
77 Niederwimmer, *The Didache*, 97.

in a dispute violates a negative command, as it is written: 'And let him not be as Korah, and as his company.'"[78] Hot-headedness is warned against in the comparison of two prominent sages: "A man should always be gentle like Hillel, and not hot-tempered like Shammai."[79]

[3.2]
Nor adversarial, nor hot-tempered, for from all of these things murder results.

The verse ends with a warning that out of all the behaviors against which it warns, murder is birthed. Envious, adversarial, and hot-tempered behavior are all offshoots of anger, which when exercised and not kept in check have the very real danger of leading us to acts of bloodshed.

◈ *My child, do not be a lustful person,*
for lust leads to sexual immorality. (DIDACHE 3.3)

The second major sin the Didache addresses is sexual immorality which was initially introduced in 2.2.[80] The Didache considers sexual immorality and adultery to be the prohibited "evil." Lust, inappropriate speech, and gazing on others with desire fall into the category of "everything like it." The things that are like the evil lead to the evil.

Lust can be defined as desire for something that is forbidden. Sexual desire in the mind leads to physical acts of sexual immorality. Lust and illicit sex are listed again side by side in Didache 5.1. The Apostolic Constitutions renders this, "Do not be foul-mouthed, nor one who casts eyes at women, nor be a drunkard; for from these things sexual immorality and adultery results."[81]

We once again find a parallel teaching in the words of the Master: "You have heard that it was said, 'You shall not commit adultery.' But I say to you that everyone who looks at a woman with lustful intent has already committed adultery with her in his heart" (Matthew 5:27–28). Rabbinic literature echoes Yeshua's words: "Unchaste imagination is more injurious than the sin itself" and, "One who lusts after a woman is as if he had sexual intercourse with her."[82]

The Greek word *epithumetes* ("lust," ἐπιθυμητής) appears in the Septuagint in the incident of Kibroth-hattaavah, in which the people craved meat. It literally

---

78   b.*Sanhedrin* 110a, citing Numbers 16:40.
79   b.*Shabbat* 30b.
80   Didache 3.3 is not found in the *Doctrina*. This verse could have been added by the Didache in reference to the Jerusalem Council's ruling against sexual immorality in Acts 15:20.
81   Apostolic Constitutions 7.6.
82   b.*Yoma* 29a; *Kallah* 7 (50b).

[3.3] *My child, do not be a lustful person, for lust leads to sexual immorality.*

says, "They buried the people who had the craving."⁸³ Paul uses this same word when he harkens back to the attitude of Israel in the wilderness: "These things took place as examples for us, that we might not desire evil [*epithumetes*] as they did" (1 Corinthians 10:6). In both cases the Israelites were lusting and craving for things that God had not given them, despite his tremendous provision for them.

The Testament of Issachar also connects fornication with lust of the mind: "Except my wife I have not known any woman. I never committed fornication by the uplifting of my eyes … The spirits of deceit have no power against him, for he looks not on the beauty of women, unless he should pollute his mind with corruption."⁸⁴ Paul, as well, exhorts the Ephesians against desires and immoral behavior: "Sexual immorality and all impurity or covetousness must not even be named among you" (Ephesians 5:3). As Paul later states, "the passion of lust" belongs to those "who do not know God."⁸⁵

The opposite of lust and a safeguard against it is the trait of modesty (*tzni'ut*, צניעות). The heart of this trait is distancing oneself "from all that is ugly and unseemly, from lust and from anything that causes people to be suspicious of you."⁸⁶ Modesty should be carried out in dress, speech, and action.⁸⁷ Sexual purity takes work, and it begins with the attitude of the heart. We must be vigilant against lust, lest it lead us down the path of physical transgression.

⁌ *Nor be foul-mouthed.* (DIDACHE 3.3)

A "foul-mouthed" (*aischrologos*, αἰσχρολόγος) person is someone who has filthy speech and enjoys uncouth humor.⁸⁸ The Apostle Paul tells the Colossians to put away "obscene talk from your mouth" (Colossians 3:8), and in Ephesians 5:4 he implores, "Let there be no filthiness nor foolish talk nor crude joking, which are out of place, but instead let there be thanksgiving." In rabbinic literature this kind of talk is known as obscene speech (*nivul peh*, ניבול פה), and the prohibition against it is taken seriously. The Talmud teaches that for the one who speaks

---

83   Numbers 11:34.
84   Testament of Issachar 4:4, 7:2–3. Cf. "No longer stubbornly follow a sinful heart and lustful eyes, committing all manner of evil" (Community Rule [1QS] I, 6).
85   1 Thessalonians 4:5.
86   Rabbi Levin, *Cheshbon HaNefesh*, 183.
87   E.g., 1 Timothy 2:9.
88   Niederwimmer, *The Didache*, 97. The same Greek word appears again in 5.1.

obscenely, "Gehenna is made deep for him."[89] Based upon Isaiah 9:16, it is said that "as a punishment for obscenity, troubles multiply, cruel decrees are proclaimed afresh, the youth of Israel's enemies die, and the fatherless and widows cry out and are not answered."[90] As disciples of the Master, we are to guard our tongues from such talk, as speaking and jesting about sexual immorality leads to thinking about the same, which leads to acting upon those thoughts. The Master tells us that "what comes out of a person is what defiles him."[91] Instead we should practice the principles of clean speech (*lashon naki*, לשון נקי). Our conversations should be filled with the words of Torah and our Master, as it is written in the *Shma*: "You ... shall talk of them when you sit in your house, and when you walk by the way, and when you lie down, and when you rise."[92]

[3.3] Nor be foul-mouthed.

⚜ Nor one who looks up at women, for from all of these things adultery results. (DIDACHE 3.3)

In this second admonition of sexual immorality, the Didache literally reads "one who looks up" (*upselophthalomos*, ὑψηλόφθαλμος), but we have supplied "at women," as the context involves sexual sin. This command doesn't describe one who is prideful but rather someone who is a lofty-eyed, lustful gazer.[93] The Apostolic Consitutions (7.6) has "Nor one who casts eyes [at women]."

We find similar language in the Tanach: "His master's wife cast her eyes on Joseph and said, 'Lie with me'" (Genesis 39:7). In fact, this is the reason that the LORD gave the commandment of tzitzit (ציצית) to the children of Israel: "It shall be a tzitzit for you to look at and remember the commandments of the LORD, to do them, not to follow after your own heart and your own eyes, which you are inclined to whore after" (Numbers 15:39).[94] In the New Testament the Apostle Peter speaks of false prophets and teachers who "have eyes full of adultery, insatiable for sin."[95] Rabbinic literature echoes the sentiment that thoughts, which are fed by

---

89 b.*Shabbat* 33a.
90 b.*Shabbat* 33a. "The youth of Israel's enemies" is a euphemism for the youth of Israel.
91 Mark 7:20.
92 Deuteronomy 6:7.
93 Niederwimmer, *The Didache*, 97.
94 Cf. Ezekiel 6:9; Testament of Issachar 7; Testament of Benjamin 6:3, 8:2; Sirach 23:4–5, 26:9; Psalms of Solomon 4:4.
95 2 Peter 2:14.

[3.3]
Nor one who looks up at women, for from all of these things adultery results.

what we gaze upon, lead to action: "He who gazes at a woman eventually comes to sin, and he who looks even at a woman's heel will beget degenerate children."[96]

To cope with these temptations, Judaism has developed halachah surrounding the principle of guarding the eyes (*shemirat enayim*, שמירת עינים). Purity of the eyes requires intense focus and discipline. The Talmud mentions the "bruised Pharisee," who accidentally runs into things because he is looking down in order to avoid looking upon women.[97] While this is hyperbolic and in some sense extreme, it is directly opposite the behavior of "one who looks up," against which the Didache warns.

We must not forget that our Master tells us that "everyone who looks at a woman with lustful intent has already committed adultery with her in his heart" (Matthew 5:28). He speaks so seriously of the matter that it would be better, he says, to lose an eye, a hand, or a foot that causes us to sin in this way than to face punishment for the sin in Gehenna.[98] Disciples of the Master need to guard their eyes with vigilance, looking away from anything that would cause sexual sin. If we are not careful, our sinful thoughts, speech, and desires can lead to sinful action such as masturbation or even adultery itself.[99]

The Apostolic Constitutions adds, "Nor be a drunkard," to the list of character traits that lead to adultery. Excessive quantities of alcohol lower one's inhibitions and have the ability to draw one into sexual sin. The Apostle Paul urges, "And do not get drunk with wine, for that is debauchery, but be filled with the Spirit" (Ephesians 5:18). The Torah gives us several examples of drunkenness leading to sexual immorality including the story of Lot and his daughters and some rabbinic interpretations of Ham's sin with Noah.[100] The sages also note the side-by-side conjunction in the Torah between the instructions regarding a *sotah* ("suspected

---

96 b.*Nedarim* 20a.
97 b.*Sotah* 22a.
98 Matthew 5:29–30; Mark 9:43–48. Cf. "The school of Rabbi Yishmael taught, 'You shall not commit adultery' implies 'You shall not practice masturbation either with hand or with foot ...' In the case of men, it ought to be cut off ... Come and hear what was taught. Rabbi Tarfon said, 'If his hand fondled his private member, let his hand be cut off below his belly ... It is preferable that his [hand be cut off] than that he should go down into the pit of destruction'" (b.*Niddah* 13b).
99 Certainly both our Master Yeshua and the Didache would have considered masturbation to be a transgression of the Torah. This is forbidden in rabbinic law (b.*Niddah* 13b) and is extended to Gentiles as well (Rabbi Moshe Weiner, *The Divine Code* [ed. Dr. Michael Schulman; 2d ed.; Pittsburgh, PA: Ask Noah International, 2011], 531–539). Masturbation falls under the prohibition of *zera levatala* ("[spilling] seed in vain," זרע לבטלה) and the sin of Onan (Genesis 38:8–10; b.*Niddah* 13a), which some authorities even extend to certain activities and birth control methods during intercourse between a married man and woman.
100 Genesis 19:31–36; b.*Sanhedrin* 29a.

adulteress," סוטה) and that of the Nazirite.[101] The injunction for the Nazirite to abstain from wine was a subtle reminder to avoid the sensual passions that lead to the woman's sexual immorality.[102]

My child, do not be a diviner because this leads to idolatry. (DIDACHE 3.4)

The third major sin addressed is idolatry, which is explicitly mentioned in the Didache only here and in 5.1. The Didache considers idolatry to be the prohibited "evil." Magic, spellcraft, and occult rituals fall into the category of "everything like it." The things that are like the evil lead to the evil.[103]

The Greco-Roman world was steeped in idolatry, both in public and private life, so exposure to idol worship was, to a certain extent, almost unavoidable. Because of the new Gentile initiate's previous pagan life, it was important to remind him early on of the dangers that could put him on a slippery slope back to idol worship. The instructions regarding the prohibition of idolatry play a vital role in preparing the candidate for immersion into the community.

Idolatry in Rabbinic Hebrew is known as *avodah zarah* ("foreign worship," עבודה זרה). While new Gentile believers were commanded at the Jerusalem Council only to "abstain from the things polluted by idols,"[104] the apostles surely meant this to include all forms of idolatry. It is in this spirit that Paul gave the injunction to "flee from idolatry."[105] The New Testament writers frequently admonished the

---

101 Numbers 5:11–31, 6:1–21.
102 b.*Sotah* 2a.
103 Cf. Pseudo-Clementine Recognitions 4.31.
104 Acts 15:20.
105 1 Corinthians 10:14.

[3.4]
My child, do not be a diviner because this leads to idolatry.

new Gentile believers to refrain from idol worship and reminded them that idolatry was part of their pre-Messiah life—something to be left behind.[106]

Over forty-five of the 613 commandments in the Torah deal exclusively with forbidding idolatry and what to do with those who practice it. In turn, the apostles would have viewed all these commandments as binding on the Gentile disciples coming into the community, although certain leniencies would have come into play, as was noted in the introduction to chapter 2.[107]

"Diviner" (*oionoskopos*, οἰωνοσκόπος) comes from the root *oionos*, meaning "bird omen," and is a typical method of divination using birds. The Apostolic Constitutions makes this explicit: "Do not be a soothsayer nor a diviner by great or little birds" (7.6). In the Roman Era people took the appearance and flight of birds as omens from the gods. "This method required some training and insight but was by no means restricted to professionals."[108] We find an example of this practice in Homer's *Iliad*: "Pallas Athena sent them a heron by the wayside upon their right hands; they could not see it for the darkness, but they heard its cry. Odysseus was glad at the omen and prayed to Athena."[109] Odysseus took this as a sign that he would be protected on his journey.

The Torah prohibits such practices, as a similar form of *oionoskopos* appears in the Septuagint: "You shall not interpret omens" (Leviticus 19:26), and, "There shall not be found among you anyone who … interprets omens" (Deuteronomy 18:10).[110] Both of these passages are alluded to in the Apostolic Constitutions:

---

106   1 Corinthians 12:2; 1 Thessalonians 1:9–10. Paul explicitly prohibits participation in pagan festivals in his epistle to the Galatians: "Formerly, when you did not know God, you were enslaved to those that by nature are not gods. But now that you have come to know God, or rather to be known by God, how can you turn back again to the weak and worthless elementary principles of the world, whose slaves you want to be once more? You observe days and months and seasons and years!" (Galatians 4:8–10). Why would they want to return to former pagan ways? Mark Nanos points out that because these Gentiles were not proselytes or candidates for ritual conversion to Judaism, they would not have been "protected from their pagan civic responsibilities by the authority of Jewish communal identity" (Mark D. Nanos, *The Irony of Galatians: Paul's Letter in First-Century Context* [Minneapolis, MN: Fortress, 2002], 268). Therefore, it would be a constant struggle with the authorities for them to maintain their abstention from *avodah zarah*.
107   According to several rabbis, the prohibition of idolatry in Noachide law contains many of the magic and sorcery practices mentioned in the Didache, such as divination, superstition, witchcraft, using incantations, consulting mediums and oracles, and necromancy. Indeed, transgressing any of these, if not immediately transgressing the prohibition of idolatry, will certainly lead to idolatry quite quickly. E.g., see Rabbi Menachem Azariah of Fano's *Asarah Maamarot* and Rabbi Shmuel ben Hofni, Gaon's list of thirty commandments incumbent on Noachides from the Cairo Genizah.
108   Milavec, *The Didache: Faith, Hope, and Life of the Earliest Christian Communities, 50–70 C.E.*, 151.
109   Homer, *Iliad* 10.274.
110   In the *Tosefta* Rabbi Yose adds this to the Noachide Laws (t.*Avodah Zarah* 8:6).

Do not be a diviner for this leads to idolatry; for says Samuel, "Divination is sin;" [1 Samuel 15:23 Septuagint] and, "There shall be no divination in Jacob, nor soothsaying in Israel" [Numbers 23:23 Septuagint]. Do not cast spells nor be one who performs purification rites for your child. Do not be a soothsayer nor a diviner by great or little birds. Nor shall you learn wicked arts; for all these things has the law forbidden [Deuteronomy 18:10–11; Leviticus 19:26, 31 Septuagint]. (Apostolic Constitutions 7.6)

[3.4]
My child, do not be a diviner because this leads to idolatry.

Followers of Messiah are not to participate in superstitious practices and events. All these, no matter how seemingly harmless, are minor forms of idolatry. Rabbi Moshe Weiner writes:

> Just as Gentiles are forbidden to practice idol worship itself, so too, they are forbidden to go in the customary ways of those who serve idols. These are the ways and schemes in which idol worshippers conduct themselves, that are connected to and strengthen their beliefs. The following are customary roles among those who worship idols: a magician, a diviner, a soothsayer, a witch, a charmer, a medium, a wizard or necromancer. All these, even when they do not actually include idol worship in their practices, are branches of idolatrous services, and they cause and bring a person to serve idols.[111]

Participating in the ways of idolaters will bring one to worship idols.

❧ *Nor be one who casts spells, nor one who studies astrology, nor one who performs purification rites.*
Do not even desire to see these things,
for from all of these things idolatry results. (DIDACHE 3.4)

Three more minor prohibitions are mentioned here, all of which lead to the major transgression of *avodah zarah*. The Didache instills in new Gentile disciples the truth that "nothing happens apart from God" (3.10). All these pagan practices are not only against Torah but are futile. Such superstitious rites have no real bearing on the future—but at the same time they do have the power to bring one into

---

111   Rabbi Moshe Weiner, *The Divine Code* [ed. Dr. Michael Schulman; 2d ed.; Pittsburgh, PA: Ask Noah International, 2011), 241.

[3.4]
Nor be one who casts spells, nor one who studies astrology, nor one who performs purification rites. Do not even desire to see these things, for from all of these things idolatry results.

idolatry.[112] The Apostolic Constitutions states, "Do not learn wicked arts; for all these things has the law forbidden" (7.6).

"One who casts spells," or an enchanter (*epaoidos*, ἐπαοιδός), was someone who "typically made use of incantations and spells, generally invoking the power of some god or angel for either beneficial or harmful ends."[113] The allure of this practice was alive and well in the Greco-Roman world, and even the Jewish historian Josephus offhandedly ascribed this ability to King Solomon.[114] The Torah outright prohibits spell casting and charming in Deuteronomy 18:10–11.

In classic Greek literature *mathematikos* (μαθηματικός) refers to "astrology." Astrology was prevalent in Greco-Roman society at the time of the Didache's composition, and it would have been a weighty temptation for new Gentile believers to fall back into this practice. While it appears that certain rabbinic circles accepted on some level the influence of the stars upon a person, most rejected astrology entirely and felt that it had no bearing upon the fate of Israel.[115] The rabbis cite Jeremiah 10:2 as a proof text: "Learn not the way of the nations, nor be dismayed at the signs of the heavens because the nations are dismayed at them"; in other words, the nations "are dismayed" by astrology, but Israel was not to be.[116] It is our Father in heaven who determines our destiny, not the stars.

The sin of "one who performs purification rites" might be midrashically linked to Deuteronomy 18:10: "There shall not be found among you anyone who burns his son or his daughter as an offering."[117] The Apostolic Constitutions (7.6) bolsters this connection adding, "Nor one who performs purification rites for your child." At any rate, this prohibition seems to involve various sacrifices and ceremonial purifications performed for the purpose of protection from disease and expiation.[118]

---

112 In the book of 1 Enoch, these kinds of occult activities were assigned to fallen angels that caused many to perish: "Amazarak taught all the sorcerers, and dividers of roots; Armers taught the solution of sorcery; Barkayal taught astrologers; Akibeel taught signs; Tamiel taught the constellations; and Asaradel taught the motion of the moon. And men, being destroyed, cried out; and their voice reached to heaven" (1 Enoch 8:3–9).

113 Milavec, *The Didache: Faith, Hope, and Life of the Earliest Christian Communities, 50–70 C.E.*, 151.

114 Josephus, *Antiquities of the Jews* 8:45–49/ii.5.

115 b.*Shabbat* 156a.

116 Cf. Deuteronomy 4:19; Isaiah 47:13; Luke 21:25. The sages find the prohibition against astrology in Leviticus 19:26: "You shall not … tell fortunes [*te'onenu*, תעוננו]," while *te'onenu* is related to the root *onah* ("season," עונה), i.e., interpreting the future by the season, determined by the constellations and planets. See Rashi to Leviticus 19:26. There is some debate in Judaism as to whether astrology was permitted for Gentiles. The Rambam rules that it was forbidden, while the *Shulchan Aruch* rules that it was permitted. See Rabbi Weiner, *The Divine Code*, 246–247.

117 In the *Tosefta* Rabbi Yose adds Deuteronomy 18:10 to the Noachide Laws.

118 See Schaff, *The Oldest Church Manual*, 172; Niederwimmer, *The Didache*, 98.

At the close of this verse, the Didache adds, "Do not even desire to see these things"; this phrase is stronger than any of the other *teknon* section closings.[119] The Apostolic Constitutions (7.6) renders this: "Be not one that wishes for evil, for you will be led into intolerable sins." A disciple of the Master should not only avoid performing any of these occult activities, but he should not even desire to see or be near them when they are carried out by anyone else. We must constantly flee from idolatry and anything like it, lest we be drawn into its snare.

[3.4] Nor be one who casts spells, nor one who studies astrology, nor one who performs purification rites. Do not even desire to see these things, for from all of these things idolatry results.

⸙ My child, do not be a liar because lying leads to theft.
(DIDACHE 3.5)

Fourth, the Didache addresses theft.[120] The Didache considers theft to be the prohibited "evil." Deceit, greed, and glory-seeking fall into the category of "everything like it." The things that are like the evil lead to the evil.

Lying and stealing have already been addressed by the Didache in 2.2–5, but here it is taught that there is a connection between the two: namely, false speech can lead to theft.

It seems strange to connect the two in this order, as normally it is stealing that leads to lying when one tries to cover things up. Compare, for example, Leviticus 6:2–4 and in the Decalogue, where lying appears to begin by theft. Yet, we find further support for the Didache's order in the book of Proverbs: "Do not add to his words, lest he rebuke you and you be found a liar … Remove far from me falsehood and lying … lest I be poor and steal and profane the name of my God" (Proverbs 30:6–9).

"Liar" (*pseusma*, ψεῦσμα) literally means "false." Kurt Niederwimmer proposes the possibility that "false" "here refers not so much to lying in the narrow sense as to dishonesty in the broader sense: deception, betrayal, treachery."[121] If this is true, then it is dishonesty in general (not merely lying) that leads to theft. Believers are to remove all falsehood from their midst, be it lying or any other form of dishonesty. The danger is that seemingly small-level deception will lead to much more grievous sins.

---

119 The Georgian version has "hear" instead of "see." The *Doctrina* has both: "do not desire to see or hear these things" (3.4).
120 The *Doctrina*'s version of this verse is nearly identical (3.5).
121 Niederwimmer, *The Didache*, 98.

[3.4]
My child, do not be a liar because lying leads to theft.

Clement of Alexandria appears to quote this verse from the Didache and refers to it as Scripture: "It is such a one that is by Scripture called a thief. It is therefore said: 'Son, be not a liar; for falsehood leads to theft.'"[122] This may indicate that Clement of Alexandria viewed the Didache as Scripture, or it may indicate that both Clement and the Didache quoted a now-lost saying of the Master from a source that Clement considered authoritative.

> *Nor be one who loves money, nor be glory-seeking, for from all of these things theft results.* (DIDACHE 3.5)

The love of money and the seeking of vainglory fit into the same category with theft because they are part of the broader definition of general dishonesty. The Didache warns that obsession with wealth and fame will cause many to attempt to gain both through unrighteous means. The Apostle Paul also connects these two traits when he states that in the last days many will be "lovers of self" and "lovers of money," and Philo speaks of those who are "lovers of money or covetous of glory."[123]

The Gospel of Luke speaks of some Pharisees as "lovers of money," which caused them to scoff at the Master's teaching on mammon: "No servant can serve two masters, for either he will hate the one and love the other, or he will be devoted to the one and despise the other" (Luke 16:13).[124] Likewise, the Apostolic Constitutions (7.6) has, "Nor be one who loves money, lest you 'serve mammon instead of God'" [Matthew 6:24; Luke 16:13], which bolsters the Didache's injunction. The love of possessions and money stands in direct contrast to serving our Father in heaven. We as disciples must make a choice between the two, because it is impossible to focus on both. Much like the choice between the Way of Life and the Way of Death, we must choose whether we will focus our attention on things earthly or things heavenly, and in the end only the heavenly things will endure.[125] Instead,

---

122 Clement of Alexandria, *Stromata* 1.20.
123 2 Timothy 3:2; Philo, *On the Posterity of Cain* 166. Cf. Testament of Levi 17:11.
124 Cf. Matthew 6:24.
125 "Yet, the Holy One blessed be He placed man in circumstances where many factors can distance him from the Blessed One, these being bodily desires; for if one is drawn toward them he progressively distances himself from the ultimate good" (Rabbi Moshe Chaim Luzzatto, *Path of the Just: Mesillas Yesharim* [trans. Yosef Leibler; Nanuet, NY: Feldheim, 2004], 9).

with what God has given us, we should practice the trait of frugality (*kimutz*, קִמוּץ), being careful how we serve as custodians of that which has been entrusted to us.¹²⁶

"Glory-seeking" (*kenodoxos*, κενόδοξος) describes someone who is not only boastful and self-centered but who is so bent on personal ambition and honor that he is willing to obtain it at all costs. The Apostolic Constitutions (7.6) expands this to, "Be not glory-seeking, nor haughty, nor high-minded." The Apostle Paul uses the same Greek word when he commands, "Let us not become conceited, provoking one another, envying one another" (Galatians 5:26). Philo also mentions the man who changes his life for the better and "no longer worries himself by entangling himself in the vain imaginations of the slaves of vain opinion."¹²⁷

Lust for prestige in the eyes of man can inspire a person to commit all sorts of evils, including stealing property and damaging other people's reputation in order to puff oneself up. As followers of Messiah, we must remember our Master Yeshua's words: "Whoever exalts himself will be humbled, and whoever humbles himself will be exalted" (Matthew 23:12).¹²⁸ Not only will "glory-seeking" lead us to sin, but in the end it will lead us to humiliation.

> [3.5] Nor be one who loves money, nor be glory-seeking, for from all of these things theft results.

◆ *My child, do not be a complainer because this leads to blasphemy.* (DIDACHE 3.6)

The fifth and final major sin addressed is blasphemy.¹²⁹ The Didache considers blasphemy to be the prohibited "evil." Complaining, egocentrism, and malevolence fall into the category of "everything like it." The things that are like the evil lead to the evil.

The Didache has moved from one speech infraction (lying) to another. Here a minor speech violation of complaining can lead to the most severe speech infraction of blasphemy.

"Blasphemy" (*blasphemia*, βλασφημία) refers to speaking impiously against God or profaning the sacred. This includes cursing the LORD and treating lightly

---

126 We find in 4 Maccabees that even if one is a "lover of money," when he takes on the ways of Torah, "he is forced to act contrary to his natural ways and to lend without interest to the needy and to cancel the debt when the seventh year arrives" (2:8). Indeed, the Torah's many regulations on tithing and money help to curb our appetite for material wealth. The sages remark, "Tithes form a fence to wealth [i.e., greed]" (m.*Avot* 3:13).
127 Philo, *On Dreams* 2.105.
128 Also Luke 14:11.
129 The *Doctrina*'s version of this verse is nearly identical (3.6).

[3.6]
My child, do not be a complainer because this leads to blasphemy.

divine and holy things.[130] Yet it can also refer to slander in general and not just that against God: "Let all ... slander [*blasphemia*] be put away from you."[131] Such utter disrespect for God as well as for others is to be guarded against and avoided at all costs by followers of the Master.

The Torah states that "whoever curses his God shall bear his sin. Whoever blasphemes the name of the LORD shall surely be put to death. All the congregation shall stone him. The sojourner as well as the native, when he blasphemes the Name, shall be put to death" (Leviticus 24:15–16). In the Mishnah, it is stated that, according to the written Torah, one is guilty of blasphemy only if he has actually pronounced God's name, that is, the Tetragrammaton,[132] but this was later extended to include circumlocutions, even if said in a non-Hebrew language. According to the *Mechilta*, the blasphemer could be forgiven only once he was executed: "For the LORD will not hold him guiltless who takes his name in vain."[133] Today the penalty for blasphemy, lacking a Sanhedrin, is excommunication.[134]

In the Septuagint the Greek word for "to complain" (*diagonguzo*, διαγογγύζω) corresponds to the Hebrew verbal root *l-v-n* (לון), which is a term that appears most infamously in the stories about the children of Israel complaining and murmuring in the wilderness.[135] In the Apostolic Constitutions version of this saying from the Didache, we read:

> Do not be a complainer, remembering the punishment which those underwent who murmured against Moses. Be not egocentric, nor malevolent, nor hard-hearted, nor passionate, nor mean-spirited, for from all these things blasphemy results. (Apostolic Constitutions 7.7)

---

130 The Georgian version of the verse reads "to blaspheming God."
131 Ephesians 4:31. Cf. Colossians 3:8; 1 Timothy 6:4; Jude 9; Revelation 2:9.
132 m.*Sanhedrin* 5:5.
133 *Mechilta*, Bachodesh 7, Exodus 20:7. In what appears to be a midrash on Exodus 20:7, the Master similarly teaches, "Whoever speaks a word against the Son of Man will be forgiven, but whoever speaks against the Holy Spirit will not be forgiven, either in this age or in the age to come" (Matthew 12:32). See Aaron Eby and Toby Janicki, *Hallowed Be Your Name: Sanctifying God's Sacred Name* (Marshfield, MO: First Fruits of Zion, 2008), 35–38. Also note that it is for the crime of blasphemy that Yeshua himself is falsely accused and then executed (Matthew 26:65. Cf. Mark 14:64; John 10:33).
134 The Talmud states that Gentiles are enjoined to this prohibition and that if they transgress it, they are to be decapitated. See b.*Sanhedrin* 56a. Rabbi Aaron Lichtenstein feels that for non-Jews "blasphemy" also includes the *mitzvot* to believe in God, fear God, pray to him, sanctify his name, not desecrate his name, study the Torah, and honor scholars and teachers. (*The Seven Laws of Noah* [3rd edition; New York, NY: Rabbi Jacob Joseph School Press, 1995], 86–87).
135 Exodus 15–17; Numbers 14–17.

The author of the Didache has in mind the stories of Israel complaining against Moses in the wilderness, and in this manner he may be addressing complaining about God-appointed leaders who are set up in believing communities. The Apostolic Constitutions (7.7) furthers this connection by adding "Nor hard-hearted" which Hebrews, drawing on Psalm 95:8, says was one of leading factors for Israel's sins in the wilderness: "Do not harden your hearts as in the rebellion, on the day of testing in the wilderness" (3:8).

[3.6]
My child, do not be a complainer because this leads to blasphemy.

Murmuring spreads discontentment: "A dishonest man spreads strife, and a whisperer separates close friends" (Proverbs 16:28). Therefore, the Apostle Paul urges disciples of the Master to "do all things without grumbling or disputing."[136] When we complain, be it about our jobs, our circumstances, or our leaders, we are in essence saying that God is not a good provider. We are criticizing him and what he has seen fit to give us as our lot in life. In turn, this is tantamount to blasphemy, whereby we slander the very essence of God as if he were something common, God forbid.

⁘ *Nor be egocentric, nor malevolent, for from all of these things blasphemy results.* (DIDACHE 3.6)

The Didache continues to warn against the downward hill that leads to blasphemy.

Someone who is "egocentric" (*authades*, αὐθάδης) is arrogant, conceited, and focused completely on oneself.[137] Therefore, being "egocentric" leads to blasphemy "insofar as attachment to one's own interests blocked one's ability to see events as promoting God's enterprise."[138]

Paul uses the same Greek word when he says that one of the characteristics of a congregational overseer is that "he must not be arrogant."[139] In 2 Peter 2:10 this word is connected to blasphemy: "Bold and willful [*authades*], they do not tremble as they blaspheme the glorious ones." Peter's disciple Clement also writes of disputes that had arisen because of "a few headstrong and self-willed persons."[140] Disputes among followers of Messiah actually cause blasphemy, because people

---

136 Philippians 2:14. Cf. Jude 16.
137 This negative character trait appears again in the vice list of 5.1.
138 Milavec, *The Didache: Faith, Hope, and Life of the Earliest Christian Communities, 50–70 C.E.*, 155. Cf. Proverbs 21:24.
139 Titus 1:7.
140 1 Clement 1.1.

[3.6]
Nor be egocentric, nor malevolent, for from all of these things blasphemy results.

on the outside see it as a reflection of the character of the LORD, and it profanes God's name to have the congregation torn apart.

A person who is "malevolent" (*ponerofron*, πονηρόφρων) is one who is "intent on evil" and gives "voice to a wicked intent."[141] This leads to "blasphemy" because the one who is bent on evil has the inability to see the good in things and blames everyone, including our Father in heaven, for his misfortunes and troubles. The Didache urges us instead to be drawn toward that which is holy and good and to look for the positive in everything that happens.

⁕ *Rather, be humble because the humble will inherit the earth.* (DIDACHE 3.7)

The Didache now transitions from the *teknon* section into injunctions for a lifestyle on humility.[142] This verse serves as a general introduction to this second section of chapter 3.[143]

"Rather" is a common expression in Rabbinic Aramaic (*adderabba*, אדרבא) that serves to contrast two points of view. Here in the Didache "rather" (*de*, δέ) is used in a similar manner. However, its use in this verse not only represents a change of topic, but it signals a shift from what we are to "put off" to what we are to "put on." The bad behavior to avoid has been mentioned (3.1–6); now we will be told how we should behave.

In Judaism Moses is considered the ultimate example of humility: "The man Moses was very meek, more than all people who were on the face of the earth" (Numbers 12:3). He endured the hardships of the wilderness and the complaints of the children of Israel on a regular basis while never murmuring about his own lot or putting his needs first. The Apostolic Constitutions mentions King David along with Moses as an example of humility.[144] King David's humility is presumably based upon his words, "O LORD, my heart is not lifted up; my eyes are not

---

141 Niederwimmer, *The Didache*, 99.
142 The Epistle of Barnabas has, "Be humble" (19.4), while the *Doctrina* has, "But be gentle (*manseutus*), for the gentle will possess the Holy Land" (3.7).
143 Cf. Jubilees 32:19; 1 Enoch 5:7. Also we find in rabbinic literature, "Great is the peace of the humble, as it is written [in Psalm 37:11], 'But the humble will inherit the land and delight themselves in abundant peace'" (*Sifrei*, Numbers 42).
144 The Apostolic Constitutions 7.7, quoting Psalm 37:11, adds its own interpretation within its quotation of the Didache: "Rather, be humble, as were Moses and David, 'because the humble will inherit the earth.'" This is typical rabbinic exegesis where a gloss is sandwiched within the verse itself.

raised too high; I do not occupy myself with things too great and too marvelous for me" (Psalm 131:1).[145]

The New Testament is replete with instructions about living a life of humility and meekness: "Put on then, as God's chosen ones, holy and beloved, compassionate hearts, kindness, humility, meekness, and patience" (Colossians 3:12); "Be kind to one another, tenderhearted, forgiving one another, as God in [Messiah] forgave you" (Ephesians 4:32); and, "We urge you, brothers, admonish the idle, encourage the fainthearted, help the weak, be patient with them all. See that no one repays anyone evil for evil, but always seek to do good to one another and to everyone" (1 Thessalonians 5:14–15). In imitation of Messiah himself, we are called to a life of humble submission to God and to one another.

In Jewish ethical teaching the character trait of humility is considered to be "the root of the Divine service," and from it flows all other godly character traits.[146] According to Judaism, one of the biggest aspects of humility is learning from others and constantly refining oneself: "Always seek to learn wisdom from every man, to recognize your failings and correct them. In doing so you will learn to stop thinking about your virtues and you will take your mind off your friend's faults."[147]

While the Didache quotes Psalm 37:11, "The humble will inherit the earth," the version in the *Doctrina* reads, "will possess the Holy Land."[148] This is a reference to dwelling in the land of Israel along with the Jewish people when Messiah returns. Samuel Lachs feels that the phrase "will inherit the earth" is synonymous with "theirs is the kingdom of heaven," which refers to the Messianic Era.[149] A close parallel in the Mishnah cites Isaiah: "All Israel have a share in the world to come, as it is written: 'And your people are all of them righteous; they shall inherit the earth forever' (Isaiah 60:21)."[150] The hope of which the Didache speaks is not for

[3.7]
Rather, be humble because the humble will inherit the earth.

---

145 Cited earlier in the Apostolic Constitutions in 7.6.
146 Rabbi Zaloshinsky, *The Ways of the Tzaddikim*, 1:57.
147 Rabbi Levin, *Cheshbon HaNefesh*, 145.
148 *Doctrina* 3.7. Although the Didache's quote is from Psalm 37:11, "The humble will inherit the land" (NASB), the choice of wording in Greek is closer to Matthew's quotation: "Blessed are the humble, for they shall inherit the earth" (5:5 WEB). The Greek *praus* (πραΰς) can mean "gentle," "humble," "meek," or even "unassuming," and the Hebrew *anav* (ענו), upon which the saying in both Matthew and the Didache are ultimately based, is best translated as "humble." Additionally, the Greek *ge* ("earth," γῆ) corresponds to the Hebrew *eretz* (ארץ), which when used with the definite article becomes *ha'aretz* (הארץ) and is used as an idiom for the land of Israel.
149 Samuel T. Lachs, *A Rabbinic Commentary on the New Testament: The Gospels of Matthew, Mark and Luke* (New York, NY: KTAV Publishing House, 1987), 74.
150 m.*Sanhedrin* 10:1.

this age but for the age to come; in the Messianic Era the humble will then receive their reward.

> ◈ *Be patient, merciful, gentle, quiet, and good-natured, always trembling at the words that you have heard.*
> (DIDACHE 3.8)

Now in verse 8 the Didache lists five character traits that describe a life of humility.[151] A similar list appears in the Dead Sea Scrolls' Two Ways material:

> These are their ways in the world for the enlightenment of the heart of man ... a spirit of humility, patience, abundant charity, unending goodness, understanding, and intelligence. (Community Rule [1QS] IV, 2–3)

To achieve humility, we must first attain the character trait of being "patient," which is a "fruit of the spirit."[152] The Apostle Paul tells us that Messiah exercised "perfect patience."[153] The Apostolic Constitutions renders this injunction, "Be patient; for such a one is very prudent, since 'he that is hasty of spirit is a very fool' [Proverbs 14:29]."[154] In Judaism patience (*savlanut*, סבלנות) is not just about keeping calm and not becoming aggravated when things go wrong; rather, it is about trusting completely that God controls our fate and that everything that happens is in his command. *Cheshbon HaNefesh* advises, "When something bad happens to you and you did not have the power to avoid it, do not aggravate the situation even more through wasted grief."[155] Patience brings us to humility because we are humbled by the fact that we are not in control.

The second character trait toward humility is "mercy." Mercy (*rachamim*, רחמים) is one of the thirteen attributes of the LORD.[156] The Didache enjoins us to be merciful like our Creator, not exacting the full weight of justice. The Apostolic

---

[151] The Epistle of Barnabas simply says, "Be quiet. Be one who trembles at the words that you have heard." (19.4), while the *Doctrina* says, "Be patient and upright in your business, trembling at the words you have heard" (3.8). Niederwimmer sees a connection in this to the ancient *anavim* ("poor ones"), whose piety consisted of "long-suffering, mercy, guiltlessness, quiet, goodness" (Niederwimmer, *The Didache*, 100–101).

[152] Galatians 5:22.

[153] 1 Timothy 1:16; *Exodus Rabbah* 19:4.

[154] Apostolic Constitutions 7.8.

[155] Rabbi Levin, *Cheshbon HaNefesh*, 117.

[156] Exodus 34:6–7.

Constitutions quotes the Master's words, "Be merciful, for 'blessed are the merciful, for they shall receive mercy' [Matthew 5:7]."[157] Mercy humbles us, because when we extend kindness, compassion, and forgiveness to others, we realize how much mercy God extends to us and how unworthy we are to receive it.

[3.8]
Be patient, merciful, gentle, quiet, and good-natured, always trembling at the words that you have heard.

Third, we attain humility through the character trait of "innocence." Messiah himself is referred to as innocent in the book of Hebrews: "It was indeed fitting that we should have such a high priest, holy, innocent, unstained, separated from sinners, and exalted above the heavens" (Hebrews 7:26). However, the word itself means more than just free from sin. The Greek word for "innocent" corresponds to the Hebrew term *tam* (תם). Noah is the first person in the Torah to be called such: "Noah was a righteous man, *blameless* in his generation."[158] In the Tanach this term often refers to one who is upright and honest: "The *integrity* of the upright guides them."[159] In turn, to be "innocent" is to act with integrity.[160] The Greek term also refers to someone who is gentle and harmless. If we are truly humble, we will act with full integrity, no matter what the circumstances or who is watching, knowing that God sees all and we will seek good and not harm for all God's creatures.

"Quiet" is listed as the fourth character trait of humility. In Jewish thought "silence" (*shtikah*, שתיקה) is one of the foremost virtues of a righteous individual. The great sage Shimon ben Gamliel used to say, "All my days I grew up among the sages, and I have found nothing better for a person than silence. Study is not the most important thing, but deed; whoever indulges in too many words brings about sin."[161] The wise man realizes that actions speak louder than words. Proverbs exhorts us that even those who are not wise can seem intelligent if they remain silent, which led the sages to say: "Silence is a fence to wisdom."[162] The eighteenth-century Jewish ethical work *Cheshbon HaNefesh* instructs, "Before you open your mouth, be silent and reflect: 'What benefit will my speech bring me and others?'"[163] Being quiet helps us to exercise humility by listening to others, which places their

---

157   Apostolic Constitutions 7.8. Cf. b.*Shabbat* 151b: "Who is merciful to others, mercy is shown to him by Heaven, while he who is not merciful to others, mercy is not shown to him by Heaven."
158   Genesis 6:9, emphasis added.
159   Proverbs 11:3, emphasis added. Cf. Job 2:3, 9. In Genesis 25:27 Jacob is called an *ish tam* ("innocent man" איש תם), which Rashi interprets as a man who speaks honestly and never acts with deception.
160   This is also very close to the character trait of truth (*emet*, אמת) in Jewish ethical teaching. See Rabbi Zaloshinsky, *The Ways of the Tzaddikim*, 2:395–407.
161   m.*Avot* 1:17.
162   Proverbs 17:28; m.*Avot* 3:17.
163   Rabbi Levin, *Cheshbon HaNefesh*, 165.

> [3.8]
> *Be patient, merciful, innocent, quiet, and good-natured, always trembling at the words that you have heard.*

needs before ours, and it helps us to realize that not everything we want to say is so important that it needs to be spoken.

The fifth character trait toward humility is being "good-natured." Similarly, the Master is called "a good man," and he likewise teaches, "The good person out of his good treasure brings forth good, and the evil person out of his evil treasure brings forth evil."[164] In the New Testament this refers to one who is faithful to the LORD and his commandments, but it is also related to the concept of *chesed* ("loving-kindness," חסד).[165] The fullness of *chesed* is seen in acts of complete humility, in which one reaches out to help others while at the same time expecting nothing in return.

Finally, this verse urges its audience to "always tremble at the words that you have heard."[166] The Apostolic Constitutions renders this, "Be innocent, quiet, good-natured, trembling at the word of God," alluding to the proof text of Isaiah 66:2: "This is the one to whom I will look: he who is humble and contrite in spirit and trembles at my word." The Didache probably alludes to the same passage.[167] Such language is reminiscent of the fear that came upon the Israelites as the Torah was given at Mount Sinai and the trembling that came upon the prophets as they encountered the words of God.[168] The sages said that just as there was dread, fear, trembling, and quaking at the giving of the Torah, so it should be when we study Torah.[169] Just as Yeshua took the Word of God seriously and said that "not an iota, not a dot will pass," so should we study the Torah and the words of our Master with reverence and fear.[170]

---

164 Matthew 12:35. Cf. John 7:12. Barnabas is also called a "good man" in Acts 11:24.
165 Tabitha is described as "full of good works and acts of charity" (Acts 9:36).
166 We also find a parallel in Paul's apocryphal beatitude list: "Blessed are they that tremble at the word of God, for they shall be comforted" (Acts of Paul and Thecla 6).
167 This passage from Isaiah is also quoted in 1 Clement after injunctions about humility, mercifulness, forbearance, and long-suffering (13.1–4). This similarity in content and the quoting of Isaiah 66:2 in both the Didache and 1 Clement caused Milavec to speculate that "it is possible that Isaiah 66:2 might have formed the rudimentary oral and mental template" from which the traits of humility and quietness resulted in "always trembling at the words that you have heard" (Milavec, *The Didache: Faith, Hope, and Life of the Earliest Christian Communities, 50–70 C.E.,* 158).
168 Exodus 19:16; Ezra 9:4; Isaiah 66:2; Habakkuk 3:16.
169 b.*Brachot* 22a. Based on Deuteronomy 4:9–10, one of the 613 commandments is to remember the giving of the Torah every day and to re-experience the awe and fear that Israel felt as they stood at base of Mount Sinai.
170 Matthew 5:18.

◈ *Do not aggrandize yourself nor give overconfidence to yourself.* (DIDACHE 3.9)

Continuing in the instructions on humility, the Didache now delivers a two-part saying with verse 9 that not only warns against arrogance but gives teaching on proper company. We find a close parallel saying in Romans: "Live in harmony with one another. Do not be haughty, but associate with the lowly. Never be wise in your own sight" (Romans 12:16). The Epistle of Barnabas adds, "But rather be humble-minded in everything" (19.3).[171]

In this first part of verse 9, "Do not aggrandize yourself" is an injunction to stay humble and avoid a conceited attitude. "Nor give overconfidence to yourself" (literally, "give your soul over to arrogance") means not to get carried away by feelings of boldness and self-importance. "Overconfidence" (*thrasos*, θράσος) is related to the Hebrew word *chutzpah* (חצפה), which refers to audacity that results in actions that go beyond socially acceptable behavior. The trait of chutzpah is the complete opposite of the trait of humility. The sages advise, "Do not seek greatness for yourself, and do not covet honor," and, "The brazen-faced to Geihinnom; the shame-faced to Gan Eden."[172]

The Apostolic Constitutions cites two proof texts to bolster the prohibition against arrogance:

> Do not be glory-seeking, nor haughty, nor high-minded. For from all these things arrogance results. Remember him who said: "O LORD, my heart is not lifted up; my eyes are not raised too high; I do not occupy myself with things too great and too marvelous for me, but I was humble" [Psalm 131:1–2]. (Apostolic Constitutions 7.6)

> Do not give overconfidence to yourself; for "a confident man shall fall into mischief" [Proverbs 13:17 Septuagint]. (Apostolic Constitutions 7.8)

Additionally, the Apostolic Constitutions refers to the Master's story of the Pharisee and the tax collector: "Do not exalt thyself, as did the Pharisee; for 'everyone who exalts himself will be humbled, but the one who humbles himself will be exalted' [Luke 18:14]; and 'For what is exalted among men is an abomination in the sight

---

171 This is in place of the Didache's line "nor give overconfidence to yourself." The *Doctrina* reads, "Do not aggrandize yourself or honor yourself among men, or admit arrogance to your soul" (3.9).

172 m.*Avot* 6:5; 5:20. However, not all boldness is bad. For example, "Be bold as a leopard, swift as an eagle, run like an antelope, and strong as a lion to do the will of your Father in heaven" (m.*Avot* 5:20). Chutzpah is good when it is to do the will of God but dangerous if it spills into other areas of life.

of God' [Luke 16:15]."[173] When we exalt ourselves, it leads to our own humiliation. Instead, we should humble ourselves before our Father in heaven, and, as James, the brother of the Master says, "he will exalt you."[174]

> *Do not connect yourself with the lofty,
> but rather associate with the righteous and lowly.*
> (DIDACHE 3.9)

In the second part of verse 9, the Didache literally warns us against joining our souls with the lofty. New Gentile believers were tempted to continue in the Roman mode of flattering and catering to the rich and powerful in hopes of material gain.[175]

The Torah warns that in court cases we should not "defer to the great" (Leviticus 19:15), and certainly this is applicable in everyday living as well. The sages point to the example of Korah's rebellion and how all who were involved with him in his wicked dispute lived in close proximity to him in the Israelite camp. Thus they warn us, "Woe to the wicked and woe to his neighbor."[176] We are to be exceedingly careful about with whom we associate and to be on guard not to pander to the wicked simply because of their prestige.

Instead we are advised to "associate with the righteous and lowly." The Apostolic Constitutions cites a proof text from Proverbs 13:20:

> Do not go along with the foolish, but with the wise and righteous; for "Whoever walks with the wise becomes wise, but the companion of fools will suffer harm." (Apostolic Constitutions 7.8)

The Master enjoins us to fellowship with the righteous: "The one who receives a righteous person because he is a righteous person will receive a righteous person's reward" (Matthew 10:41). Rabbinic Judaism stressed, "Let your house be a meetinghouse for the sages and sit amid the dust of their feet and drink in their

---

173 Apostolic Constitutions 7.8.
174 James 4:10.
175 Niederwimmer, *The Didache*, 101.
176 Numbers 16; *Numbers Rabbah* 3:12.

words with thirst."[177] According to the Didache, it was better to suffer with the righteous than to enjoy opulence with the proud.[178]

After all, in the kingdom it is the lowly who will eventually be exalted, as our Master says, "The last will be first, and the first last" (Matthew 20:16).[179] Similarly, the sages teach, "Where is the pious man, where is the humble man, one of the disciples of our father Abraham," and, "Three must not be provoked: an insignificant Gentile, a little snake, and a humble pupil. What is the reason? Because their kingdom stands behind their ears."[180]

[3.9] *Do not connect yourself with the lofty, but rather associate with the righteous and lowly.*

⫸ *Accept the things that happen to you as being for the good, knowing that nothing happens apart from God.* (DIDACHE 3.10)

Everything that happens, both good and bad, is from our Father in heaven. The Mishnah teaches that one must pronounce a blessing over bad things that happen just as one would for good.[181] This is a fitting closing statement for the section on humility, for as one lives out a humble life, troubles are sure to ensue. As disciples of our Master Yeshua, we are to walk in obedience to the Way of Life and trust that all that happens is the will of God. Nothing takes place in the universe that the LORD does not know about or allow to happen, and we are to trust that he is omnipotent. Appropriately, the Epistle of Barnabas adds before this verse, "Do not take credit for yourself," emphasizing that we are not really in control.[182]

---

177 m.*Avot* 1:4.
178 In rabbinic thought the suffering of the righteous (*tzaddikim*, צדיקים) is thought to bring merit to the nation of Israel (e.g., b.*Moed Katan* 28a; *Leviticus Rabbah* 20:12). The apostles speak similarly: "If when you do what is right and suffer for it you patiently endure it, this finds favor with God" (1 Peter 2:20 NASB); "I rejoice in my sufferings for your sake, and in my flesh I am filling up what is lacking in Messiah's afflictions for the sake of his body, that is, the church" (Colossians 1:24). It is therefore possible that when the Didache speaks of associating "with the righteous and lowly" it had in mind sharing in the afflictions of the righteous in order to gain merit and favor in God's sight. "Lowly" is the Greek word *tapeinos* (ταπεινός), which refers to those who have been brought low, are low in spirit, are humble. While this most certainly describes those who are humble, it may also allude to the poor and to those who suffer. The Didache's "righteous and lowly" could very well be a hendiadys meaning "the poor/suffering righteous." For a study on the use of hendiadys, see Ronald James Williams, *Williams' Hebrew Syntax* (ed. John C. Beckman; 3d ed.; Toronto, Canada: University of Toronto Press, 2007), 29–30.
179 Matthew 19:30; Mark 10:31; Luke 13:30.
180 b.*Brachot* 6b; b.*Pesachim* 113a.
181 m.*Brachot* 9:5.
182 Barnabas 19.3.

[3.10]
Accept the things that happen to you as being for the good, knowing that nothing happens apart from God.

The Apostolic Constitutions cites Job and Lazarus as examples for us: "Receive the afflictions that happen to you with an even mind, and the chances of life without over-much sorrow, knowing that a reward shall be given to you by God, as was given to Job and to Lazarus."[183] The Master illustrates, "Are not two sparrows sold for a penny? And not one of them will fall to the ground apart from your Father" (Matthew 10:29).[184] Paul writes, "We know that for those who love God all things work together for good, for those who are called according to his purpose" (Romans 8:28).

Parallels can be found in other Jewish literature. Nahum of Gamzu, despite his many sufferings, was famous for always trusting God and saying, "This also is for the good."[185] The sages taught that in the *Shma* the words "You shall love the LORD your God ... with all your might" could mean to love the LORD despite "whatever measure he metes out to you."[186] Judaism teaches that everything that happens is to be received with complete trust (*bitachon,* בטחון) that God is in control.[187]

This corresponds to the character trait of equanimity (*menuchat hanefesh,* מנוחת הנפש). *Cheshbon HaNefesh* teaches, "Rise above events that are inconsequential—both bad and good—for they are not worth disturbing your equanimity."[188] Jewish ethical teaching stresses that it is important that one does not lose his equilibrium over events that are beyond his control. It is important to always remain calm and in control, remembering that our Father in heaven is the one who ultimately directs our steps.

The Didache's saying has practical application for everyday life, and the new Gentile believers were sure to endure hardships as they began their journey in the

---

183 Apostolic Constitutions 7.8. The Apostle Peter is recorded as saying, "He who has apprehended that the world is regulated by the good providence of God ... is not vexed by things howsoever occurring, considering that things take their course advantageously under the providence of the Ruler. Whence, knowing that he is just, and living with a good conscience, he knows how by right reason to shake off from his soul any annoyance that befalls him, because, when complete, it must come to some unknown good" (Pseudo-Clementine Homilies 2.36.2. Cf. Pseudo-Clementine Recognitions 1.21.4).
184 Cf. Luke 12:7.
185 b.*Ta'anit* 21a.
186 b.*Brachot* 54a on Deuteronomy 6:5. "This is a homiletic explanation of the alliterative Hebrew words מדה, and מאד" (Philip Blackman, *Mishnayoth* [7 vols.; Gateshead, England: Judaica, 1983] 1:73).
187 Rashi drawing on the *Sifrei* (173) comments on "You shall be blameless before the LORD your God" (Deuteronomy 18:13): Conduct yourself with him with wholeheartedness and depend on him, and do not inquire of the future; accept whatever happens to you with wholeheartedness and then, you will be with him and to his portion." Interestingly, Rashi connects the concept of accepting one's lot in life with not inquiring into the future. Likewise, the Didache has this at the end of the chapter that also speaks against divination in 3.4.
188 Rabbi Levin, *Cheshbon HaNefesh,* 109.

path of discipleship. Whether suffering persecution, social pressure, life's hardships, heartaches, sickness, scarcity, disappointment, loss, bereavement, or even their own failings, the new Gentile disciples needed to know that everything came from heaven. The disciple must treat each trial as a learning experience, not blaming the LORD but rejoicing that God treats him as a son and disciplines him for his own good: "For the moment all discipline seems painful rather than pleasant, but later it yields the peaceful fruit of righteousness to those who have been trained by it" (Hebrews 12:11).[189]

[3.10]
Accept the things that happen to you as being for the good, knowing that nothing happens apart from God.

---

189 Both Origen (second century) and Dornotheus Abbas (sixth century) quote a form of this saying that is very close to Didcahe 3.10 ("Knowing that nothing happens apart from God") and credit it as coming from Scripture (*First Principles* 3:2:7; *Epistalue* 3). As with the quotation from Clement of Alexandria of 3.5, this could mean that at the time of Origen, and even in the sixth century, there were those who considered the Didache as Scripture, or perhaps they were both, along with the Didache, citing a now-lost non-canonical saying of the Master that they both considered authoritative.

Chapter Four

DIDACHE 4

4.1 My child, remember night and day the teacher who speaks the word of God to you,[1] and esteem him as the Lord, for where lordship is spoken of, there the Lord is.

4.2 And every day seek the presence of the righteous so that you may lean upon their words.

4.3 Do not crave conflict, but bring those who are quarrelling to peaceful reconciliation. Judge righteously;[2] do not show partiality[3] when rebuking transgressions.

4.4 Do not be indecisive as to whether or not your judgment is correct.

4.5 Do not be one who stretches out his hands to receive but then pulls them back in regard to giving.

4.6 If you have the means, give a ransom for your sins.

4.7 Do not hesitate to give, and do not complain when giving,[4] for you will find out who is the good payer of wages.

4.8 Do not turn away someone who is in need; rather, share all things in common with your brother.[5] Do not claim ownership, for if you are common partners in what is immortal, how much more so in what is mortal!

4.9 Do not withhold your hand from your son or daughter, but teach them the fear of God from their youth.

---

1 Hebrews 13:7.
2 Leviticus 19:15; Deuteronomy 1:16.
3 Leviticus 19:15; Deuteronomy 16:19.
4 2 Corinthians 9:7.
5 Acts 2:44, 4:32.

4.10 Do not harshly give orders to your servant or maid who put their hope in the same God, or else they might lose their fear of God, who is over both of you. For God does not intend to call anyone according to status; rather, he calls those whom the Spirit has prepared.

4.11 And as for you servants, submit yourselves to your masters in humility and fear, as they are an example of the authority of God.[6]

4.12 You shall hate every form of hypocrisy and everything that does not please the Lord.

4.13 Do not forsake the commandments of the Lord, but keep what you have received,[7] neither adding to nor subtracting from it.[8]

4.14 Confess your transgressions[9] in the assembly, and you will not draw near in prayer with a guilty conscience. This is the Way of Life.

---

6   Ephesians 6:5; Colossians 3:22.
7   1 Corinthians 11:2; 2 Thessalonians 2:15.
8   Deuteronomy 4:2, 12:32; Proverbs 30:6; Revelation 22:18–19.
9   James 5:16.

Overview

The Didache shows little concern over theology, doctrine, or Christology. It does not theologize regarding the nature of God, redemption from sin, or the role of Messiah. "These seem to be understood as implicit."[10] Instead, the Didache concerns itself almost exclusively with the disciples' obligations toward one another and toward other human beings. Chapter 4 is no exception to this rule.

The Didache's simplicity and lack of theological sophistication indicates its early date of authorship. The non-canonical Christian writings that littered the Christian world of the second and third centuries were full of fanciful theology, Gnostic musings, and harsh polemics. Unlike those later works, the Didache concerns itself with practical godly living, instructing the disciple as to how to walk in the Way of Life.

Structure of Chapter 4

The contents of chapter 4 seem at first glance to repeat what has already been covered in the earlier chapters of the Didache. It begins with "my son," reminiscent of the *teknon* section in chapter 3. Several themes from that chapter recur: respect for the Master's words, bonding with fellow believers, and trust in providence.[11]

The contents of chapter 4 can be divided into three distinct sections:[12]

4.1–8	Five congregational precepts
4.9–11	Three household rules
4.12–14	Epilogue (solemn final admonitions)

---

10 Tony Jones, *The Teaching of the Twelve: Believing & Practicing the Primitive Christianity of the Ancient Didache Community* (Brewster, MA: Paraclete, 2009), 86.
11 Didache 3.8 = 4.1, 3.9 = 4.2, and 3.10 = 4.4. Aaron Milavec, *The Didache: Faith, Hope, & Life of the Earliest Christian Communities, 50–70 C.E.* (New York, NY: Newman, 2003), 157.
12 Marcello del Verme, *Didache and Judaism: Jewish Roots of an Ancient Christian-Jewish Work* (New York, NY: T&T Clark, 2004), 116; William Varner, *The Way of the Didache: The First Christian Handbook* (New York, NY: University Press of America, 2007), 65–67.

The chapter begins with injunctions about living in community, and then it urges the disciple to exercise these commands by practicing righteous behavior at home. Godliness must be lived out both publicly and privately.

The chapter concludes with admonitions to hold on to the Master's teachings and not to add or subtract from them. Each new step of learning is to build on what one has gained previously. As disciples advance in their learning, they must not forget the fundamentals of the Way of Life.

Family, Community, and Fellowship

Despite its seeming similarity to earlier Didache chapters, a subtle transition takes place in chapter 4. The new Gentile initiate has, until this point, been instructed primarily on an individual level. The Didache now switches to instructions about life in community and family:

> Much of the teaching up to this point for the convert from paganism has been of an individual focus—the shedding of the convert's old life and putting on new attitudes and behavior patterns. But the convert is joining a family in this new life—a family with brothers and sisters and familial love—and also a family with potential quarrels and strife. So the life of the new believer in the body is stressed over the first few verses of chapter four.[13]

It's one thing for a believer to hold convictions and live a life of faith in isolation. It is quite another to live out one's convictions in interaction with a community of people. New believers need to be carefully taught how to fellowship properly with other believers in humility and self-sacrifice.

Assembling together for communal worship is an important part of Torah life. Leviticus states that the Shabbat is to be a "holy convocation" (*mikra kodesh*, מקרא קדש), which the Ramban interprets as an injunction to hold public gatherings on the Sabbaths for prayer and Torah study.[14] For thousands of years observant Jews have gathered together every Shabbat to worship the God of Israel and to hear the Scriptures read aloud.

---

13 Varner, *The Way of the Didache*, 65.
14 Leviticus 23:3; Ramban to Leviticus 23:2.

The Gospel of Luke tells us that the Master diligently attended synagogue every Shabbat "as was his custom."[15] The disciples as well fellowshiped on a regular basis:

> They devoted themselves to the apostles' teaching and the fellowship, to the breaking of bread and the prayers ... Day by day, attending the temple together and breaking bread in their homes, they received their food with glad and generous hearts, praising God and having favor with all the people. (Acts 2:42–47)

The community of disciples devoted themselves to "the fellowship" (*koinonia*, κοινωνία).[16] "The fellowship" refers to the community itself, not to mere congenial camaraderie. The Greek word implies common sharing or participation in a common cause. It speaks of the interdependency of people living and working together in a close-knit social unit. By devoting themselves to the fellowship, the early disciples devoted themselves to the day-to-day needs and concerns of the apostolic community in Jerusalem. The fellowship (*koinonia*) is the collective identity of local believers.

First-century Judaism contained other holy societies resembling the *koinonia* in Jerusalem. The Pharisees organized themselves into fellowships (*chavurot*, חבורות) whose members studied, ate, and prayed together. The sect of the Essenes lived collectively in holy fraternities resembling monastic orders. The disciples of the Jerusalem community seemed to arrange their priorities on the models of the Pharisaic fellowship (*chavurah*), the Essene brotherhood of the Qumran community, and other holy brotherhoods that shared meals and "divided the day into three parts—a third for Torah, a third for prayer, and a third for work."[17]

A form of the Greek word *koinonia* is used in Didache 4.8: "For if you are common partners [*koinonia*] in what is immortal, how much more so in what is mortal!" This indicates that the Didache was advocating a fellowship plan similar, if not identical, to that of the Jerusalem community. This pattern would include possible attendance at a local synagogue on Shabbat while fellowshiping with other believers on a near daily basis the rest of the week. At these gatherings believers would offer up prayers, break bread together, and learn the Scriptures.

---

15 Luke 4:16.
16 These next two paragraphs depend heavily upon D. Thomas Lancaster, *Torah Club: Chronicles of the Apostles* (6 vols.; Marshfield, MO: First Fruits of Zion, 2016), 1:66–67.
17 Ecclesiastes Rabbah 9:1. Hilary Le Cornu and Joseph Shulam, *A Commentary on the Jewish Roots of Acts* (2 vols.; Jerusalem, Israel: Academon/Netivyah, 2003), 1:146–147.

The book of Hebrews speaks of the importance of these gatherings and of community in general:

> Let us consider how to stir up one another to love and good works, not neglecting to meet together, as is the habit of some, but encouraging one another, and all the more as you see the Day drawing near. (Hebrews 10:24–25)

Even if the followers of Yeshua experienced doctrinal disagreements, interpersonal quarrels, or laziness, leaving fellowship was not an option. If community was an integral aspect of the believing community and one that helped these early believers survive those tumultuous years, how much more so do we need this today? The instructions in the Didache can aid us in keeping peace and community harmony. We are instructed to lay down our lives for our fellow congregants and to revere the Word of God.

The Church

The Greek word *ekklesia* (ἐκκλησία) appears in one form or another five times in the Didache, with its first appearance in 4.14.[18] The word also appears over one hundred times in the New Testament. We have chosen to translate this literally as "assembly," but most s prefer the common English "church." The word *ekklesia*, however, does not literally mean "church." Biblical Greek actually has no word equivalent to our English word "church."[19] The word *ekklesia* translates the Biblical Hebrew word *kahal* (קהל). *Kahal* means "assembly," "congregation," or "community." The word *ekklesia* is interchangeable with "synagogue," and it appears hundreds of times in the Septuagint to describe the congregation of the people of Israel.[20] For example, the Bible calls the children of Israel in the wilderness "the assembly." The Torah refers to the whole nation of the children of Israel as "the congregation of Israel." From a Jewish perspective the assembly of the Messiah will be the renewed nation of Israel, restored and gathered in from exile.

---

18   Didache 4.14, 9.4, 10.5, 11.11, 15.1.
19   This entire section depends heavily upon Lancaster, *Torah Club: Chronicles of the Apostles*, 1:108.
20   Jewish Greek used *ekklesia* almost interchangeably with *sunagoge* (συναγωγή), i.e., "synagogue." In the Septuagint the two terms translate, respectively, the Hebrew *kahal* (קהל) and *edah* (עדה), both of which translate into English as "assembly," "community," or "congregation," e.g., "the congregation of Israel." The Septuagint mostly translates *edah* as *sunagoge*, never as *ekklesia*, but it typically renders *kahal* as *ekklesia* and also quite often *sunagoge*.

The apostles did not think of themselves as a separatist movement. Rather, they envisioned Yeshua as the Messiah over all Israel—his assembly, or what we call the church. The Didache uses the word *ekklesia* to denote the assembly of the Messianic community within the larger Jewish nation, not something outside Israel.

Judges

Verses 3 and 4 of chapter 4 give instructions for judges in regard to handling conflicts that would arise within the community. In the synagogue each local Jewish community had a court (*beit din*, בית דין) comprised of a minimum of three judges. Court rulings had to have a majority for a decision to be passed. If the case was too difficult for a local court, the matter would be handled by higher courts and then ultimately by the seventy judges of the Sanhedrin in Jerusalem. The decisions that they made were considered as binding as the Torah itself: "According to the instructions that they give you, and according to the decision which they pronounce to you, you shall do. You shall not turn aside from the verdict that they declare to you, either to the right hand or to the left" (Deuteronomy 17:11).

The Master gave authority to his disciples to act as judges within the community:

> Truly, I say to you, whatever you bind on earth shall be bound in heaven, and whatever you loose on earth shall be loosed in heaven. Again I say to you, if two of you agree on earth about anything they ask, it will be done for them by my Father in heaven. For where two or three are gathered in my name, there am I among them. (Matthew 18:18–20)

Within the Didache communities these judges would have been overseers, about whom we will read in chapter 15. Here in chapter 4 they are briefly introduced as the new Gentile believer is being given an overview of community life.

The Household Code

Verses 9–11 deal with home-life instructions involving slaves and children. Scholars have labeled this list and others like it "household codes."[21] We find household codes dealing with similar issues in other works dedicated to educating Gentiles about Torah and Jewish values. For example:

---

21 Varner, *The Way of the Didache*, 66.

Do not be severe with your children, but be gentle. And if a child offends you, let the mother curtail the son, or the elders of the family or the leaders of the people ... Provide your servant with the portion owed to his stomach. Apportion to a slave what is appointed, so that he will be as you wish. Do not brand a servant, which insults him. Do not hurt a slave by slandering him to his master. Take the advice from a sensible house servant. (Pseudo-Phocylides 207–227)[22]

Household codes appear in the writings of the Apostles Paul and Peter.[23] Peter's disciple Clement also instructs,

> Let your children be partakers of the instruction of Messiah; let them learn of how great avail humility is with God—how much the spirit of pure affection can prevail with him—how excellent and great his fear is, and how it saves all those who walk in it with a pure mind. (1 Clement 21.8)[24]

Torah Judaism stresses the importance of piety within the family and home. While sections of the Bible such as the list of sexual sins in Leviticus 18 and 20 might seem redundant and excessive, the Torah emphasizes that a proper relationship between a husband and wife forms the backbone of a holy community. It is in the home that godly living and commandment-keeping begin.

The *Shma* instructs Israel to teach the Torah's words "diligently to your children" and to speak of its words "when you sit in your house."[25] Joshua declares, "As for me and my house, we will serve the LORD" (Joshua 24:15). It is on the foundation of godly families that healthy communities are formed.

Slavery

In the household code of chapter 4, the Didache gives instructions regarding how to treat slaves.[26] These injunctions are not unlike the numerous laws about slaves that we find in the Torah. To our modern ears this material feels not only archaic but disturbing. In North America—and in most of the world—the collective memory

---

22 See Pseudo-Phocylides 175–227; Philo, *The Decalogue* 165–167; Josephus, *Against Apion* 2:199–210/xxv.
23 Ephesians 5:22–6:9; Colossians 3:18–4:1; 1 Peter 2:18–3:7; 1 Timothy 2:8–15; Titus 2:1–10.
24 See 1 Clement 21.6–9. Cf. 1.3.
25 Deuteronomy 6:7.
26 This entire section depends heavily upon D. Thomas Lancaster, *Torah Club: Unrolling the Scroll* (6 vols.; Marshfield, MO: First Fruits of Zion, 2014), 1:287–289.

of slavery is ugly. People were kidnapped, maltreated, bought and sold, subjugated to all sorts of cruelties, and denied basic human dignities. By offering laws regarding slavery, did the Torah and the Didache condone slavery?

Two important matters of context must be considered in regard to laws about slavery in the Bible and in the Didache. First, we must remember that the Israelites themselves were slaves in Egypt and had experienced it in its ugliest form. It is only natural that God would address that institution and lay out rules to prevent the perpetuation of the maltreatment of slaves. Indeed, it is one of the first sets of instructions that he gave Israel after the exodus.[27] All the Bible's laws about slaves are meant for the protection and well-being of the people enslaved. God did not want the Israelites to treat their servants the way they themselves had been treated. The Torah commands the Jewish people five times, "You shall remember that you were a slave in the land of Egypt."[28] The Bible's laws on slavery are meant to break the pattern of the mistreatment of other human beings.

The second point of context is the realization that slavery in the ancient world was a real and normal part of the economy. In the days of the Torah, there was no standard of currency, and people did not ordinarily have jobs as we do. People lived primarily off the land. This meant that if a person was not a landowner or independently wealthy, owning his own flocks and herds, he probably had no secure means of supporting himself and his family. The concept of work for hire was risky, short term, and had no guarantees.

Later, in the first few centuries CE, the situation was not much different:

> The owning of slaves was not something reserved for the very rich; craftsmen of ordinary means frequently purchased one or more slaves to work with them in the family shop. Thus, the presence of slaves does not narrowly define the social status of the candidates.[29]

In pagan society no labor laws, minimum wage requirements, or retirement plans existed. For the landless lower class, servitude was an attractive option.

---

27 Exodus 21:1–11. "There is a beautiful hint in the text that is, perhaps, a key to understanding the Bible's intention regarding slavery. In Exodus 21's laws about slaves, the Hebrew word for "go out" (*yatza*, יצא) appears seven times. Seven is the number of divinity. In rescuing Israel from slavery, God indicated His will for human beings to be free. He desires for slaves to be able to go out from servitude. The theme of freeing one's servant is repeated in these passages" (Ibid., 1:288).

28 Deuteronomy 5:15, 15:15, 16:12, 24:18, 22.

29 Milavec, *The Didache: Faith, Hope, and Life of the Earliest Christian Communities, 50–70 C.E.*, 163.

It offered the acquisition of meaningful skills, lifelong employment, and food and shelter for a person and his dependents.

In most societies slaves had no rights. Judaism, as expressed in the Torah, the New Testament, and the Didache, sought to change that. Accordingly, slaves were to be treated as servants for hire rather than as property. The regulations on slavery were designed to prevent the type of enslavement experienced by many African Americans in North America prior to the Civil War.

Commentary

> My child, remember night and day the teacher who speaks the word of God to you and esteem him as the Lord, for where lordship is spoken of, there the Lord is. (DIDACHE 4.1)

As the new Gentile disciple was introduced to community living, he had to learn respect and honor for his teachers.

"Lord" (*kurios*, κύριος) in its present context is thought by most scholars to refer to our Master Yeshua.[30] However, the Apostolic Constitutions renders it, "Where the teaching concerning God is, there God is present."[31] The Torah teaches, "In every place where I cause my name to be remembered I will come to you and bless you" (Exodus 20:24), and in accordance, the Didache instructs that where the Master's teachings are present, there the Master's presence is as well. When the Master's words are spoken, his "lordship" abides, that is, "the Power," "the Name," or "the Presence of the Lord."[32] The opening words of chapter 4 illustrate "how close [the Didache] is to its Jewish background: to study God's law with a teacher is to come into the divine presence."[33]

According to the Didache, believers were to honor their teachers in the same way that the original disciples honored the Master. For example, Paul says that he

---

30   The Georgian version of the Didache has "Messiah" in place of "Lord."
31   Apostolic Constitutions 7.9. Wim J.C. Weren, "The 'Ideal Community' according to Matthew, James, and the Didache," in *Matthew, James, and Didache: Three Related Documents in Their Jewish and Christian Settings* (eds. Huub van de Sandt and Jürgen K. Zangenberg; Atlanta, GA: Society of Biblical Literature, 2008), 186 n.14. Milavec argues that every instance of "Lord" in the Didache refers to God. See Aaron Milavec, "The Distress Signals of Didache Research," in *The Didache: A Missing Piece of the Puzzle in Early Jewish Christianity* (eds. Jonathan A. Draper and Clayton N. Jefford; Atlanta, GA: Society of Biblical Literature, 2015), 70–72.
32   George Cantrell Allen, *The Didache: Or, the Teaching of the Twelve Apostles* (London, England: Astolat, 1903), 12. Cf. Ignatius, *To the Ephesians* 6.1. The Greek word *kuriotes* ("dominion, lordship" κυριότης) is used four times in the New Testament: Ephesians 1:21; Colossians 1:16; Jude 8; 2 Peter 2:10.
33   Thomas O'Loughlin, *The Didache: A Window on the Earliest Christians* (Grand Rapids, MI: Baker, 2010), 37. "But when two sit together and words of Torah pass between them, the Divine Presence rests between them, as it is written: 'Then those who revered the Lord spoke with one another. The Lord took note and listened, and a book of remembrance was written before him of those who revered the Lord and thought on his name' [Malachi 3:16]. Scripture speaks here of two. Whence do we learn that if even one sits and occupies himself in the Torah, the Holy One blessed be he, appoints him a reward? Because it is written 'to sit alone in silence when the Lord has imposed it' [Lamentations 3:28]" (m.*Avot* 3:3; Cf. 3:7).

> [4.1]
> My child, remember night and day the teacher who speaks the word of God to you and esteem him as the Lord, for where lordship is spoken of, there the Lord is.

was received by the Galatian believers "as an angel of God, as Messiah Yeshua."[34] The offices of those who spoke the "word of God" are later in the Didache divided into teachers, emissaries, prophets, overseers, and administrators.[35] The "word of God" would have been a divine message of Torah instruction most certainly focused on the words of Yeshua, and in that way his "lordship is spoken of." Just as the Torah itself should be meditated upon "night and day," so also the words of the teachers.[36]

This brings to mind several sayings of the Master. For example, "Whoever receives you receives me, and whoever receives me receives him who sent me" (Matthew 10:40), and, "Truly, truly, I say to you, whoever receives the one I send receives me, and whoever receives me receives the one who sent me" (John 13:20).[37] This teaching to honor one's leaders is also similar to our Master Yeshua's concept, "Where two or three are gathered in my name, there am I among them" (Matthew 18:20).[38] The writer of Hebrews echoes, "Remember your leaders, those who spoke to you the word of God. Consider the outcome of their way of life, and imitate their faith" (Hebrews 13:7).

This saying in Didache 4.1 to highly regard one's teachers may have originated as a proverb in the schools and study halls of the sages.[39] The Greek text lacks the definite article, so it literally reads "Esteem him as Lord." "Lord" finds the equivalent in the Aramaic term *mar* ("lord," מר), which is used in rabbinic literature as a title of respect for teachers.[40] We also find the title *kurios* being used in a similar way in the New Testament.[41] That being the case, the original saying might not have had any Christological implication. The mandate to esteem one's teacher "as lord" might have originally functioned as a rule of discipleship: Honor your teacher as your master.

---

34   Galatians 4:14.
35   Canon Spence, *The Teaching of the Twelve Apostles* (London, England: James Nisbet and Co., 1885), 19. E.g., Didache 11, 15.
36   Joshua 1:8. Putting "night" before "day" is the Jewish method of reckoning time (e.g., Genesis 1:5, etc.). Rambam used this Joshua passage as a proof text that one should study Torah in the morning and in the evening (*Mishneh Torah*, Talmud Torah 1:8).
37   Cf. Luke 9:48.
38   Cf. Gospel of Thomas 30. For the legal context of these sayings, see D. Thomas Lancaster, *Torah Club: Chronicles of the Messiah* (6 vols.; Marshfield, MO: First Fruits of Zion, 2010), 3:709.
39   Kurt Niederwimmer, *The Didache: Hermeneia—A Critical and Historical Commentary on the Bible* (Minneapolis, MN: Fortress, 1998), 104.
40   E.g., y.*Brachot* 1:1; y.*Sanhedrin* 2:1; b.*Brachot* 27b–28a; b.*Ta'anit* 23a–b. Also *adoni* ("my lord," אדני) in 1 Kings 18:13; 2 Kings 8:12.
41   John 12:21, 20:15; Acts 16:28–30.

In the Mishnah we find: "Let your reverence for your master be like the fear of heaven."[42] The Talmud interprets the Torah's commandment to "honor the face of an old man" (literally, "to honor an elder") as an obligation to honor one who has acquired wisdom—that is, a Torah scholar.[43] The rule of respecting teachers and Torah scholars, a rule that is incumbent upon Jews and Gentiles alike, prohibits disciples from publicly contradicting their teachers. It requires disciples to show their teachers the utmost deference, giving them first priority in all matters.[44] A Torah scholar was to be respected even more than one's own father, "since his father brought him only into the life of this world, whereas his teacher, who taught him wisdom [i.e., Torah], has brought him into the life of the World to Come."[45] In the same spirit, the Apostolic Constitutions adds, "Esteem him, not as the author of your birth, but as one that is made the occasion of your well-being" (7.9).

Several rabbinic axioms illustrate this principle: "Let the respect towards your teacher be as your reverence for God"; "Whoever quarrels with his teacher is as though he quarreled with the *Shechinah*"; and, "'You shall fear the Lord your God' is to include scholars."[46] It was taught that just as there was fear and trembling at Mount Sinai when the Torah was given, so there should be the same when studying Torah with a sage.[47]

The words "where lordship is spoken of, there the Lord is" find a parallel in Jewish teaching.[48] According to the Talmud, transmitting a teaching or an opinion from a previous scholar invokes the scholar's presence. A person must always honor the original teacher by citing his name: "When a teaching is said in their name in this world, their lips move gently in the grave."[49] The Chasidic movement developed the concept further, suggesting that a teacher is present in a mystical

[4.1]
My child, remember night and day the teacher who speaks the word of God to you and esteem him as the Lord, for where lordship is spoken of, there the Lord is.

---

42   m.*Avot* 4:12.
43   Leviticus 19:32; b.*Kiddushin* 32b.
44   *Mishneh Torah*, Talmud Torah 6; Rabbi Aaron Lichtenstein, *The Seven Laws of Noah* (3d ed.; New York, NY: The Rabbi Jacob Joseph School Press, 1995), 86–87.
45   m.*Bava Metzia* 2:11.
46   m.*Avot* 4:15; b.*Sanhedrin* 110a; b.*Pesachim* 22b.
47   b.*Brachot* 22a.
48   "And esteem him as the Lord, for where lordship is spoken of, there the Lord is" is not found in the Epistle of Barnabas. The *Doctrina* reads, "You shall esteem him as the Lord. For where the Lord is spoken of, there the Lord is." It is possible, since the Epistle of Barnabas does not seem to incorporate any sayings of the Master into its text but *Doctrina* does, that this saying, too, is linked to no-longer extant sayings of the Master. If we interpret "Lord" as referring to God, then Yeshua could have said this at any point during his life on earth; if we interpret "Lord" as referring to Yeshua, then it might have been something the Master said during the forty days he spent with his disciples after his resurrection. It is very similar to "Where two or three are gathered in my name, there am I among them" (Matthew 18:20).
49   b.*Sanhedrin* 90a.

[4.1]
My child, remember night and day the teacher who speaks the word of God to you and esteem him as the Lord, for where lordship is spoken of, there the Lord is.

sense when his words are spoken (even after his death). The Mittler Rebbe says that even if one did not know or serve a great rabbi in his lifetime, "but only studied the holy books that he left over as a blessing, and who bask in the radiance of his Torah teachings" have acquired connection with that rabbi in a personal way.[50]

In a similar way, the Gentile disciples to whom the Didache was originally addressed had never known the Master personally or even come into contact with him. Yet the disciple who heard the words of Yeshua read and taught experienced his presence. Therefore, the relationship between the disciple and the teacher was "shaped by the fundamental commandment of piety, which in turn is concretized in two ways: The pupil shall continually keep the teacher in mind, and shall honor him like the [Master] himself."[51]

The Epistle of Barnabas brings in the Hebrew idiom "apple of the eye" and changes the remembrance to the day of judgment: "You shall love as the apple of your eye all those teachers who speak the word of the Lord to you. Remember the Day of Judgment night and day."[52]

◈ *And every day seek the presence of the righteous so that you may lean upon their words.* (DIDACHE 4.2)

Once the Didache has established that disciples of the Master must respect their teachers, it stresses the need for them to remain in their teachers' constant presence, finding peace in their words. The Epistle of Barnabas has an expanded version:

> Every single day seek the presence of the righteous: either by laboring through your word and going out to encourage them as well as by

---

50 Rabbi Menachem Mendel Schneerson, *Proceeding Together: The Earliest Talks of the Lubavitcher Rebbe Rabbi Menachem M. Schneerson* (trans. Uri Kaploun; 4 vols.; Brooklyn, NY: Sichos in English, 1995), 1:15–16. Cf. "When a person succeeds in attuning his mind and opening his heart to the Torah and Mussar of the early Sages, he becomes one with them" (Rabbi Chaim Ephraim Zaitchik, *Sparks of Mussar: A Treasury of the Words and Deeds of the Mussar Greats* [Nanuet, NY: Feldheim, 2014], 3). Reb Noson of Breslov taught that "despite the fact that true *tzaddikim* leave this world, nevertheless their original Torah thoughts—the laws that they revealed—remain for us" (*Likutei Halachos* on *Parshat Shoftim*. from Dov Grant, "Learning Halachah: Likutei Halachos on Parshas Shoftim," n.p. [cited 6 September 2011]. Online: http://www.nanach.org/likutay-halachos/devarim/shoftim.html).

51 Niederwimmer, *The Didache*, 105.

52 Barnabas 19.9–10 quoting Proverbs 7:2: "Keep my commandments and live; keep my teaching as the apple of your eye." Therefore, the Epistle of Barnabas seems to be saying that a Torah teacher should be treated with the same respect as the written Torah, that is, as a living Torah. Cf. Deuteronomy 32:10; Lamentations 2:18; Psalm 17:8; Zechariah 2:8.

trying to save a life through your words; or work toward a ransom for your sins through your own means. (Barnabas 19.10)[53]

The Didache instructs its audience to "lean upon" the words of the righteous.[54] In this way the new believers would find rest and support in what the righteous teach. The sages offer similar instruction to frequent the company of the righteous:

> Yosi ben Yo'ezer used to say: "Let your house be a house of meeting for the sages and suffer thyself to be covered by the dust of their feet, and drink in their words with thirst." (m.*Avot* 1:4)

This verse finds a parallel backdrop in Judaism's concept of *devekut* ("attachment," דבקות). The Torah commands, "You shall fear the LORD your God … and hold fast [*davak*, דבק] to him" (Deuteronomy 10:20). The sages ask how one can "hold fast" to God, who "is a consuming fire" (Deuteronomy 4:24). The Talmud explains that one must hold fast to God by clinging to a righteous man. Maimonides codifies *devekut* in his *Book of the Commandments*:

> By this injunction we are commanded to mix and associate with wise men, to be always in their company, and to join with them in every possible manner of fellowship: in eating, drinking, and business affairs, to the end that we may succeed in becoming like them in respect of their actions and in acquiring true opinions from their words.[55]

[4.2]
And every day seek the presence of the righteous so that you may lean upon their words.

---

53 The line "so that you may lean upon their words" is absent from the Epistle of Barnabas but is found in the *Doctrina*. It is possible that, like the line "and esteem him as the Lord, for where lordship is spoken of, there the Lord is" (4.1), this, too, is linked to no-longer-extant sayings of the Master (see footnote 48). The Greek word *epanapauomai* (ἐπαναπαύομαι), which we have translated "lean upon," can also mean "rest," so the line could be translated "so that you may find rest in their words." This is similar to the Master's words: "Take my yoke upon you, and learn from me, for I am gentle and lowly in heart, and you will find rest [*anapausis*, ἀνάπαυσις] for your souls" (Matthew 11:29).

54 "Righteous" comes from the Greek word *hagioi* (ἅγιοι), which is commonly translated as "saints." It corresponds in the Septuagint to *kedoshim* ("set apart ones," קדושים) and is also related to the term *bechirim* ("chosen ones," בחירים). See Gedaliah Alon, "The Halacha in the Teaching of the Apostles," in *The Didache in Modern Research* (ed. Jonathan A. Draper; Leiden, The Netherlands: Brill, 1996), 166. Conceptually, however, the term seems to fit best with *tzaddikim* ("righteous ones," צדיקים). The *tzaddikim* are the "teachers" referred to in 4.1. Some scholars, based on the fact that "saints" in the New Testament often refers to all believers (e.g., Romans 1:7; 1 Corinthians 1:2), feel that here the Didache is merely stressing to the new initiate to remain in fellowship with the community. See Spence, *The Teaching of the Twelve Apostles*, 19. Yet others feel that this "can only refer to the teachers" of 4.1, and this perspective seems to place the verse in better context and show it more firmly rooted within Jewish thought. See Niederwimmer, *The Didache*, 106. Cf. Matthew 27:52.

55 Rambam, *Sefer HaMitzvot*.

[4.2]
And every day seek the presence of the righteous so that you may lean upon their words.

In this spirit Clement, the disciple of Peter, writes, "Cleave to the holy, for those that cleave to them shall be made holy."[56]

The Master taught his disciples to hold fast to him and thereby cling to God: "I am the way, and the truth, and the life. No one comes to the Father except through me. If you had known me, you would have known my Father also. From now on you do know him and have seen him" (John 14:6–7). Likewise, those who cling to his disciples cling to Yeshua, as he says, "Whoever receives the one I send receives me, and whoever receives me receives the one who sent me" (John 13:20).

⚜ *Do not crave conflict, but bring those who are quarrelling to peaceful reconciliation.* (DIDACHE 4.3)

The Didache continues with its instructions about community fellowship with warnings against causing division.[57] New Gentile disciples were to work hard to maintain peace in the congregation and avoid arguments. As a warning against schisms, the Apostolic Constitutions cites the division of Korah: "Do not make conflicts among the righteous, but be mindful of the followers of Korah" (7.10).[58]

Pirkei Avot also cites the example of Korah when teaching about the difference between godly arguments and arguments that originate from evil:

> Which is the [kind of] controversy that is in the name of heaven? Such as was the controversy between Hillel and Shammai; and which is the [kind of] controversy that is not in the name of heaven? Such as was the controversy of Korah and all his congregation. (m.*Avot* 5:17)

The Didache's sentiments echo the words of Yeshua: "Blessed are the peacemakers, for they shall be called sons of God" (Matthew 5:9); "Be at peace with one another" (Mark 9:50). Numerous parallels from the New Testament could be cited.[59]

The rabbis also stressed peacemaking and the way of peace as some of the most important virtues. The psalmist urges, "Turn away from evil and do good; seek peace and pursue it" (Psalm 34:14). The Mishnah teaches that "bringing peace

---

56   1 Clement 46.
57   There is a manuscript discrepancy regarding the word ποθήσεις ("you shall crave") in *Codex Hierosolymitanus* versus ποιήσεις ("you shall cause") in other manuscripts. Although the discrepancy occurs in just one letter (θ versus ι), the is still affected: "do not crave conflict" versus "do not cause conflict." The *Doctrina* has: "Do not create conflicts."
58   Numbers 16.
59   E.g., 1 Corinthians 1:10, 11:18–19; 1 Thessalonians 5:13; 2 Peter 3:14. Cf. 1 Clement 15.1, 22.5, 54.2.

between a man and his fellow" is one of the "fruits of which a man enjoys in this world, while the principle remains for him in the World to Come."[60]

"Hillel said, 'Be of the disciples of Aaron, loving peace and pursuing peace,'" and, "If someone cursed Aaron, he would respond, 'Peace be upon you!' Should a man argue with him, he remained silent."[61] The Apostolic Constitutions presents Moses also as a peacemaker: "Bring those who are quarrelling to peaceful reconciliation, as Moses did when he persuaded them to be friends" (7.10). This alludes to Moses' peacemaking efforts in Egypt: "When he went out the next day, behold, two Hebrews were struggling together. And he said to the man in the wrong, 'Why do you strike your companion?'" (Exodus 2:13).

[4.3] *Do not crave conflict, but bring those who are quarrelling to peaceful reconciliation.*

⫸ Judge righteously; do not show partiality when rebuking transgressions. (DIDACHE 4.3)

The Didache here turns its attention to standards of jurisprudence.[62] When arguments break out, the disputes are to be settled in a godly manner by the congregational leaders. The Didache juxtaposes two commandments from Leviticus 19:

> You shall not be partial to the poor or defer to the great, but in righteousness shall you judge your neighbor. (Leviticus 19:15)

> You shall not hate your brother in your heart, but you shall [surely rebuke] your neighbor, lest you incur sin because of him. (Leviticus 19:17)

The Apostolic Constitutions includes Deuteronomy 1:17: "For the judgment is God's."[63] This can be compared with Yeshua's saying, "Do not judge by appearances, but judge with right judgment" (John 7:24). Judgment should not be based

---

60   m.*Pe'ah* 1:1.
61   m.*Avot* 1:12; *Kallah Rabati* 3:4 52b. Cf. Psalm 133.
62   The *Doctrina* says, "Do not discourage anyone in his misfortune" (4.3). At least one source attributes "do not show partiality" to the Apostle Peter: "In the letter [to the Dontatists], Optatus states that the apostle Peter says in his epistle, 'Do not judge your brothers with partiality.' This quotation is not found in either of the two canonical Petrine epistles, nor is it attributed to Peter elsewhere in the New Testament … The Two Ways states 'Do not accuse with partiality anyone of a wrongdoing' (Barnabas 19:4) and 'Judge justly; do not accuse with partiality [anyone] of a wrongdoing' (Didache 4:3). This is undoubtedly the source of Optatus' quotation despite minor differences in wording" (Robert E. Aldridge, "Peter and the 'Two Ways,'" *Vigiliae Christianae* 53, no. 3 [August 1999]: 245–246).
63   Apostolic Constitutions 7.10. Cf. Exodus 23:1–3.

[4.3]
Judge righteously; do not show partiality when rebuking transgressions.

on superficial appearances or social status: "Open your mouth, judge righteously, defend the rights of the poor and needy" (Proverbs 31:9).

The Torah commands impartiality in judgment:

> I charged your judges at that time, "Hear the cases between your brothers, and judge righteously between a man and his brother or the alien who is with him. You shall not be partial in judgment. You shall hear the small and the great alike. You shall not be intimidated by anyone, for the judgment is God's. And the case that is too hard for you, you shall bring to me, and I will hear it." (Deuteronomy 1:16–17)[64]

God instructs judges to hear the words of both sides of a case and not to favor either side for any reason, sticking strictly to the facts of the situation. The *Mechilta* adds, "If a disreputable and a pious person stand before you in judgment do not say: 'Since he is a disreputable person, I shall view his cause unfavorably' but 'You shall not be partial to a poor man'—he who is poor in good works."[65] We are not to judge unfairly, even in regard to one's piety. James, the brother of the Master, teaches that those who show partiality are committing sin and are "convicted by the Torah as transgressors."[66]

These injunctions apply primarily to court cases within the community of faith, but they also apply to the disciple's personal life as well. The Master warns individuals against acting as judges: "Judge not, that you be not judged ... Why do you see the speck that is in your brother's eye, but do not notice the log that is in your own eye?" (Matthew 7:1–3). The *Doctrina* seems to quote Yeshua by rendering this verse, "Judge righteously, knowing that you will be judged."[67]

The sages state, "Judge everyone favorably."[68] Congregations and communities will be at peace only when disciples of the Master give each other the benefit

---

64   Cf. Leviticus 19:15. Based upon the Greek, there is a strong connection here between the Didache and these Torah *mitzvot*. Both Leviticus 19:15 and Deuteronomy 1:17 literally state, "You shall not be partial to face[s] [*pani(m)*, (פני(ם)]." The Greek behind the Didache's "do not show partiality" is literally "do not receive the face of [*ou lepse prosopon*, οὐ λήψῃ πρόσωπον]." The presence of this Hebrew idiom not only provides a linguistic link to these two Torah *mitzvot* but is also further evidence of a Hebrew background to the Didache. For the Hebrew usage of "face," see David Bivin and Roy Blizzard, Jr., *Understanding the Difficult Words of Jesus: New Insights from a Hebraic Perspective* (Shippensburg, PA: Destiny Image, 1994), 123–126.

65   *Mechilta*, Kaspa 3, Exodus 23:6.

66   James 2:9.

67   *Doctrina* 4.3. This is a rare instance in which the *Doctrina* uses a quote from the Master that is not present in the Didache.

68   m.*Avot* 1:6.

of the doubt and wait for all the facts before pronouncing someone guilty. When someone has clearly sinned and is in need of reproof, the steps of Matthew 18:15–17 should be carefully carried out, which begin with going to the offender in private. The Apostolic Constitutions warns us not to be partial if sin is present: "Do not show partiality when rebuking transgressions, but do as Elijah and Micaiah did to Ahab, and Ebed-melech the Ethiopian to Zedekiah, and Nathan to David, and John to Herod."[69] As disciples of the Master, we must not be afraid to rebuke sin; correction, however, should always be done in love and in the remembrance of Yeshua's words: "With the judgment you pronounce you will be judged, and with the measure you use it will be measured to you" (Matthew 7:1–2).

[4.3]
Judge righteously; do not show partiality when rebuking transgressions.

◈ *Do not be indecisive as to whether or not your judgment is correct.* (DIDACHE 4.4)

The Didache continues to instruct judges to administer justice fairly, warning now against indecisiveness. This saying in verse 4 should probably be understood as a commandment for judges to perform due diligence before rendering a decision. It corresponds to the rabbinic axiom, "Be deliberate in judgment."[70] A judge should not render a decision while he remains in a state of uncertainty. A judge must wait for evidence to be presented before making a ruling, and he must not render a judgment based on insufficient evidence.

The Apostolic Constitutions apparently misunderstood the Didache and interpreted this injunction in the context of prayer: "Do not be indecisive in your prayer, whether it shall be granted or not. For the Master said to Peter upon the sea: 'O you of little faith, why did you doubt?' [Matthew 14:31]."[71]

This saying of the Didache might also relate to Jewish teaching about the character quality of decisiveness (*haritzut*, הריצות). It is important when reaching decisions that one not take too much time deliberating, and once a decision is reached, one should be firm in his resolution. The eighteenth-century Jewish ethic work *Cheshbon HaNefesh* relates, "All of your acts should be preceded by deliberation;

---

69 Apostolic Constitutions 7.10. Cf. 1 Kings 18, 21, 22; 2 Samuel 12; Matthew 14.
70 m.*Avot* 1:1.
71 Apostolic Constitutions 7.11. Cf. Shepherd of Hermas, Mandate 9.4–6 (39.4–6). The Georgian version of the Didache connects this to the judgment of God: "But even about this you should not have any doubts as to whether God's judgment comes upon all men according to their deeds, or not."

[4.4] Do not be indecisive as to whether or not your judgment is correct.

when you reach a decision, act without hesitation."[72] Likewise, whether in the case of a court decision or everyday life, disciples of the Master should be firm in their decision-making process, not to the point of obstinacy but acting with confidence.

⚜ *Do not be one who stretches out his hands to receive, but then pulls them back in regards to giving.* (DIDACHE 4.5)

The Didache has already spoken about giving in 1.5, but now it begins to speak about charity within the community context. A new initiate needs to realize that although joining in fellowship with other believers provides him help and support in his time of need, he, too, needs to be generous when it comes to helping others. As the Master taught, "It is more blessed to give than to receive" (Acts 20:35).

The Wisdom of Sirach similarly warns, "Let not your hand be extended to receive, but withdrawn when it is time to repay."[73] The Torah commands that when we see a brother in need we are to help: "If among you, one of your brothers should become poor … you shall not harden your heart or shut your hand against your poor brother" (Deuteronomy 15:7).

In a community of believers, one is expected to be just as willing to help a brother in need as the community is willing to help him when he is in need: "For you always have the poor with you" (Mark 14:7).[74] There will always be those in need, and as disciples of the Master, we need to have our hands open to help.

⚜ *If you have the means, give a ransom for your sins.*
(DIDACHE 4.6)

Continuing on the theme of giving, the Didache instructs disciples to be generous with what they have earned in order to cover their sins. The Greek word for

---

72   Rabbi Menachem Mendel Levin, *Cheshbon HaNefesh: A Guide to Self-Improvement and Character Refinement* (trans. Rabbi Shraga Silverstein; New York, NY: Feldheim, 1995), 135.
73   Sirach 4:31. This passage from Sirach is similar to how the *Doctrina* renders 4.5: "Do not keep stretching out your hand to receive, and drawing them back when it comes to returning." It could be that "returning" here refers to returning the favor when charity is needed for others, or it could place the entire saying in the context of borrowing and returning an object. If it is in the context of borrowing and returning, it is in juxtaposition to "Love your enemies, and do good, and lend, expecting nothing in return, and your reward will be great, and you will be sons of the Most High, for he is kind to the ungrateful and the evil" (Luke 6:35).
74   Quoting Deuteronomy 15:11. Cf. Matthew 26:11; John 12:8.

188   The Way of Life

"ransom" (*lutrosis*, λύτρωσις) here has a similar connotation to the Hebrew word *kofer* (כפר), meaning "ransom" or "atonement." As repugnant as this may sound to Protestants, this concept is deeply embedded in the Scriptures. Proverbs teaches, "By steadfast love and faithfulness iniquity is atoned for" (Proverbs 16:6), and Daniel says to King Nebuchadnezzar, "Break off your sins by practicing righteousness, and your iniquities by showing mercy to the oppressed" (Daniel 4:27). The Apostolic Constitutions cites a midrashic paraphrased combination of verses from Proverbs as a proof text:

> If you have the means, give, that you may labor for the ransom for your sins: for "By alms and faithfulness iniquity is atoned for" (Apostolic Constitutions 7.12)[75]

Rabbinic literature develops this concept from two different arguments. First, we find the sages developing the idea of atonement through charity (*tzedakah*) based upon the sacrifices in the Temple and in particular the half-shekel offering, which was given "to make atonement for your lives."[76] Rabbi Eleazar states, "When the Temple stood, a man used to bring his shekel and so make atonement. Now that the Temple no longer stands, they give for charity."[77] Significantly, Rabbi Yochanan ben Zakkai states, "Just as the sin-offering makes atonement for Israel, so charity makes atonement for Gentiles."[78] If the Didache represents material from before the destruction of the Temple, these instructions may be seen as a means for Gentiles to offer sacrifices of charity in the Diaspora just as Jews offered sacrifices of animals in the Temple.

Second, this idea is developed out of a midrashic reading of Proverbs 10:2: "Righteousness delivers from death." "Righteousness" is the Hebrew word *tzedakah* (צדקה), which by the late Second Temple Period had taken on the narrower

---

75 The Apostolic Constitutions combines Proverbs 16:6 with the Septuagint version of Proverbs 15:27.
76 Exodus 30:12–16.
77 b.*Bava Batra* 9a. In a subtle shift over time, charity and sacrifice in the Temple were morphed. The sages reinterpret the *korban chagigah* (קרבן חגיגה), the sacrifice commanded to be brought on festivals in accordance with Exodus 23:15, 34:20, and Deuteronomy 16:16, as referring to *tzedakah* and not an actual sacrificial offering (*Mechilta deRabbi Shimon ben Yochai*, Kaspa 79, Exodus 23:15; *Sifrei*, Deuteronomy 143). Shmuel Safrai has suggested that the "moneybag" mentioned in John 13:29, which contained money for the poor, could have been for *tzedakah* in place of the *korban chagigah* (see Safrai, "Early Testimonies in the New Testament of Laws and Practices Relating to Pilgrimage and Passover," in *Jesus' Last Week: Jerusalem Studies in the Synoptic Gospels* [ed. R. Steven Notley, Marc Turnage, and Brian Becker; Boston, MA: Brill, 2006], 42–44).
78 b.*Bava Batra* 10b.

[4.6]
If you have the means, give a ransom for your sins.

meaning of "charity," as we see in rabbinic literature: "Charity delivers from death."[79] Already in the proto-rabbinic Wisdom of Sirach we find, "Water extinguishes a blazing fire: so almsgiving atones for sin."[80] Rabbi Eleazar quotes Proverbs 21:14, "A gift in secret averts anger," as a proof text that charity given in secret appeases God's anger over our sins.[81] The sages also connect charity and prayer, stating that if a man gives alms right before his prayers, "he is deemed worthy to receive the Divine Presence."[82]

In the New Testament we find examples of charity attracting our Father in heaven's attention. The angel of God told Cornelius, "Your prayers and your alms have ascended as a memorial before God" (Acts 10:4).[83] There is also a reference to this in the Master's words: "Give as alms those things that are within, and behold, everything is clean for you" (Luke 11:41).[84]

◈ *Do not hesitate to give and do not complain when giving.*
(DIDACHE 4.7)

Giving within the community was to be done immediately as the need arose and with a willing heart.[85] Giving was not only a commandment, but it was to be done with the proper attitude and promptness. Proverbs warns, "Do not say to your

---

79 E.g., b.*Shabbat* 156b; b.*Bava Batra* 10a; *Zohar* I, 199a; III, 111a, III, 113b.
80 Sirach 3:30. Cf. Tobit 4:10–11, 12:9.
81 b.*Bava Batra* 9b.
82 b.*Bava Batra* 10a. Orthodox Jews perform an interesting ritual on Erev Yom Kippur in which they swing a chicken or money around their heads three times while reciting a petition for atonement. The chicken or the money is then given to the poor. The ritual is called *Kapparot* ("Atonement," כפרות) and was practiced in some form as early as the Geonic Period. Although Judaism denies that this ritual is a type of sacrificial offering, it was developed in light of the absence of the Temple and the sacrifices that took place on Yom Kippur. The prayer recited ends by quoting Job 33:24: "I have found a ransom [*kofer*, כפר]."
83 It may be that Cornelius gave alms before he prayed just as Rabbi Eleazar did, who "used to give a coin to a poor man and straightway say a prayer, because, he said, it is written: 'in righteousness [*tzedakah*] shall behold your face'" (b.*Bava Batra* 10a, quoting Psalm 17:15). We also see the apostles speaking about both loving-kindness and suffering granting merit and cover for sins. Peter writes that "suffering unjustly" finds "favor" (*chen*, חן) before God (1 Peter 2:19–20 NASB). Additionally, the Apostle Peter states, "Above all, keep loving one another earnestly, since love covers a multitude of sins" (1 Peter 4:8). Cf. 2 Clement 16.4.
84 See Nathan Eubank, *Wages of Cross-bearing and Debt of Sin: The Economy of Heaven in Matthew's Gospel* (Berlin, Germany: Walter de Gruyte, 2013).
85 The Apostolic Constitutions (7.12) adds the clarifying clause "to the poor": "Do not hesitate to give to the poor." The Georgian version of the Didache says, "Do not hesitate in the giving of charity."

neighbor, 'Go, and come again, tomorrow I will give it'—when you have it with you" (Proverbs 3:28).

Giving freely and without complaining is foundational to Torah life. The Didache seems to draw upon the Scripture, "You shall give to him freely, and your heart shall not be grudging when you give to him, because for this the LORD your God will bless you in all your work and in all that you undertake" (Deuteronomy 15:10).[86] Maimonides in his *Mishneh Torah* lists reluctant giving as the least ideal and lowest form of charity.[87]

The New Testament also urges us as disciples to give with a joyful heart. Paul tells the Corinthians that once they have decided in their heart how much to give, their giving should be carried out neither "reluctantly or under compulsion, for God loves a cheerful giver" (2 Corinthians 9:7). Likewise the Apostle Peter states, "Show hospitality to one another without grumbling" (1 Peter 4:9). Peter's disciple Clement speaks highly of those who "never grudged any act of kindness, being 'ready unto every good work.'"[88]

⁌ *For you will find out who is the good payer of wages.*
(DIDACHE 4.7)

The Didache assures us that if we give, we will be rewarded by our Father in heaven. Our Master tells us, "Lay up ... treasures in heaven, where neither moth nor rust destroys and where thieves do not break in and steal" (Matthew 6:20). He will pay us back handsomely in the World to Come for what we have given in this world. Samuel Lachs, writes, "Wealth given away is wealth stored away; it actually ensures its existence."[89] This is especially true for gifts given in secret: "When you give to the needy, do not let your left hand know what your right hand is doing, so that your giving may be in secret. And your Father who sees in secret will reward you" (Matthew 6:3–4). The Apostolic Constitutions cites Proverbs 19:17: "Whoever is generous to the poor lends to the LORD, and he will repay him for his deed."[90]

---

86   Further evidence that the Didache may be drawing upon this passage is that Deuteronomy 15 goes on to address slavery, which is also discussed in Didache 4.10–11.
87   *Mishneh Torah*, Hilchot Matanot Aniyim 10:7–14.
88   1 Clement 2.7, quoting Titus 3:1. Cf. Pseudo-Phocylides 1:22; Sibylline Oracles 2.73.
89   Samuel Tobias Lachs, *A Rabbinic Commentary on the New Testament: The Gospels of Matthew, Mark, and Luke* (Jersey City, NJ: KTAV, 1987), 126.
90   Apostolic Constitutions 7.12.

[4.7]
For you will find out who is the good payer of wages.

Yeshua touches on this concept in the parable of the faithful servant, in which he instructs the disciples to be ready for his return.[91] They are to be prepared at all times, which means that they are to be constantly working for the kingdom. The Master has set his servants "over all his possessions," and they are to use these things wisely.[92] In the end they will need to give an account for how they used what they were given: "Everyone to whom much was given, of him much will be required, and from him to whom they entrusted much, they will demand the more" (Luke 12:48).

The sages of Israel liken God to an employer who will surely pay us the reward for our labors, and that reward will be paid to the righteous in the World to Come.[93] God will be faithful to give recompense to both his people Israel and the nations of the world:

> Rabbi Shabbetai said, "It is written: 'He is great in power and justice, he does not torment those abundant in righteousness' (Job 37:23). The Holy One, blessed be he, does not delay paying the reward to a Gentile who performs a religious duty." (m.*Pe'ah* 1:1)

This also brings to mind the Master's words, "Give, and it will be given to you. Good measure, pressed down, shaken together, running over, will be put into your lap. For with the measure you use it will be measured back to you" (Luke 6:38).[94] This is the rabbinic principle of measure for measure. We read in the Mishnah, "By the same measure with which a man measures out to others, they [i.e., heaven] measure it out to him."[95] When we give to others, our heavenly Father will give back to us with the same measure we use.

---

91   Luke 12:35–48. Cf. Matthew 24:42–51; Mark 13:34–47.
92   Luke 12:44.
93   m.*Avot* 2:14–16.
94   Cf. Matthew 7:2; Mark 4:24.
95   m.*Sotah* 1:7. Cf. Testament of Zebulun 8:1–5; *Exodus Rabbah* 25:9.

> *Do not turn away someone who is in need;
> rather, share all things in common with your brother.
> Do not claim ownership.* (DIDACHE 4.8)

The theme of giving charity without delay continues from Didache 4.7. We read in the Talmud that turning away a person who is in need is equivalent to idolatry.[96] The Apostolic Constitutions cites Proverbs 21:13: "Do not turn away someone who is in need, for says he: 'Whoever closes his ear to the cry of the poor will himself call out and not be answered.'"[97] "Do not turn away someone who is in need" is similar to the Master's words, "Do not refuse the one who would borrow from you," (Matthew 5:42) and may represent a non-canonical gospel saying.[98]

The Didache adds, "Share all things in common with your brother. Do not claim ownership."[99] The Apostolic Constitutions adds, "For the common participation of the necessaries of life is appointed to all men by God."[100] Marcello del Verme comments,

> Besides the call for charity ... the text appears to suggest a more radical form of giving, or even to refer to a precise institution: the practice of the community or sharing of goods among (some of) the members of the community.[101]

The precise meaning of this passage has baffled scholars, but it would seem that whatever is meant here is a parallel to the Jerusalem community of believers in the early chapters of Acts.[102]

Acts 4:32 states, "Now the full number of those who believed were of one heart and soul, and no one said that any of the things that belonged to him was his own, but they had everything in common." The early disciples in Jerusalem sold personal property and contributed the proceeds and their belongings to the collective body

---

96 b.*Ketuvot* 68a. Cf. b.*Bava Batra* 10a.
97 Apostolic Constitutions 7.12.
98 The line is absent from the Epistle of Barnabas but is found in the *Doctrina*, which may give further evidence that this is a no-longer extant saying of the Master. See footnote 48.
99 While the *Doctrina* also has "your brother" (4.8), the Epistle of Barnabas has "your fellow" (19.8). "Brother" implies another disciple of the Master Yeshua, whereas "fellow" (sometimes rendered "neighbor") is usually used to refer to everyone.
100 Cf. "Let all life be common, and all things in agreement" (Pseudo-Phocylides 30).
101 Del Verme, *Didache and Judaism*, 114.
102 Canon Spence writes, "The author of the 'Teaching' probably knew of and used the writings of S. Luke, both the Gospel and the Acts" (*The Teaching of the Twelve Apostles*, 22), but it could simply be that the writer of the Didache was familiar with the way the community operated in Acts as well.

[4.8]
Do not turn away someone who is in need; rather, share all things in common with your brother. Do not claim ownership.

of believers.[103] This was apostolic communal living, and it appears that the Didache is speaking about this as well. The Essenes also lived in a communal fashion, surrendering property and possessions to a common fund.[104]

The sages say, "What's mine is yours and what's yours is yours ... This is a righteous man."[105] This is the best expression of the Master's ideal for his disciples, of the type of economy that was practiced by the Jerusalem community, and of the model that we see espoused in the Didache. The early believers sold possessions and goods in order to help others as the need arose. This did not necessarily mean that everyone sold everything they owned as soon as they joined the community, but rather "from time to time those who owned land or houses sold them, brought the money from the sales and put it at the apostles' feet, and it was distributed to anyone who had need" (Acts 4:34–35 NIV).[106] Neither in the early Jerusalem community nor in the Didache did this consist of a onetime divesture of goods for everyone.

The community fund did not redistribute wealth; it provided for those in need from its surplus. Food was distributed to the poor and to the widows among the group.[107] The believers sought to fulfill the Torah's ideal, "There will be no poor among you; for the LORD will bless you in the land that the LORD your God is giving you for an inheritance to possess" (Deuteronomy 15:4).

Some disciples donated all their belongings and became dependent upon the community; others retained private ownership. The hospitality mentioned in Acts 2:46 and 4:34 indicates that in the Jerusalem community individuals continued to own their own homes, and we can assume that the same would hold true for those under the instruction of the Didache.[108]

---

103 This section depends heavily upon Lancaster, *Torah Club: Chronicles of the Apostles*, 1:100–101.
104 Josephus, *Jewish War* 2:122/viii.3; *Antiquities of the Jews* 18:20/i.5; Community Rule (1QS) VI, 19–23.
105 m.*Avot* 5:10.
106 "From time to time" correctly renders the imperfect tense verb. See Craig L. Blomberg, *Neither Poverty nor Riches: A Biblical Theology of Possessions* (Downers Grove, IL: Intervarsity Press, 1999), 165.
107 Acts 6:1. First Timothy 5:9–16 indicates that Pauline communities also distributed provision to widows who qualified for a widow's list. Young widows eligible for remarriage did not qualify for the list. The Pauline community's model assumes private ownership and responsibility: "If anyone does not provide for his relatives, and especially for members of his household, he has denied the faith and is worse than an unbeliever" (1 Timothy 5:8).
108 Twelve years later the disciples in Jerusalem gathered for prayer in the house of Mary, the mother of John Mark. Apparently, she had not surrendered her house to the common purse.

> *For if you are common partners in what is immortal, how much more so in what is mortal!* (DIDACHE 4.8)

The instructions on giving now appeal to the rabbinic argumentation of *kal vachomer* ("light and heavy," קל וחומר), which is used to say, "If A is true, then how much more so B." If by joining the community of faith a new disciple shares in things that are eternal, such as salvation and the promise of the coming kingdom of heaven, how much more so should the disciple share the things that are temporary, such as material wealth. New disciples should be happy to share their goods with the community as they are needed. According to the version in the *Doctrina*, giving charity is a holy act: "If we are partners in what is immortal, how much more ought we to consecrate from the mortal. For the Lord wants to give of his own gifts to everyone."[109]

The Didache's phrase "partners in the immortal" brings to mind Paul's words to the Gentile believers in Rome when he exhorts them to give charity to the Jewish believers in Jerusalem. He also uses the *kal vachomer* argument: "If the Gentiles have come to share in their spiritual blessings, they ought also to be of service to them in material blessings" (Romans 15:27). Since Gentile believers had now joined with the Jewish people and been grafted into the commonwealth of Israel, they now shared "in their spiritual blessings."[110] Therefore, it is only natural that as members of God's family, they would now give back by helping the Jewish believers in their time of need.

Combining Paul's words with the Didache's, new Gentile disciples had much to be grateful for, as they had now joined with Israel and the greater body of Messiah. As "fellow heirs" and "partakers of the promise in Messiah," they must now also share in taking care of the needs of the community.[111] It is equally important today that Gentile believers look for ways to support the Jewish people and the State of Israel.

---

109   *Doctrina* 4.8. The end of this saying is almost identical to: "For the Father wants to give of his own gifts to everyone" (Didache 1:5). Cf. James 1:5, 17. The Epistle of Barnabas has "incorruptible" and "corruptible" in place of the Didache's "mortal" and "immortal" (19.8).
110   Cf. Romans 11:17; Ephesians 2:12–23.
111   Ephesians 3:6.

> *Do not withhold your hand from your son or daughter, but teach them the fear of God from their youth.* (DIDACHE 4.9)

This verse begins the section of chapter 4 (4.9–11) that scholars refer to as a household code.[112] The instruction begins with the proper training and discipline of children, echoing the words of the psalm: "Come, O children, listen to me; I will teach you the fear of the LORD" (Psalm 34:11).

"Do not withhold your hand" refers not only to physical discipline; it is, additionally, an injunction that fathers and mothers should have an active presence in the lives of their children, instructing them in the ways of the Master. Other apostolic household codes offer similar sentiments. Paul states, "Fathers, do not provoke your children to anger, but bring them up in the discipline and instruction of the Lord" (Ephesians 6:4). The Apostle Peter's disciple Clement writes, "Let our children be partakers of the instruction which is in Messiah."[113] It is important that children, who represent the future of the community, be discipled along with the rest of the family. The Apostolic Constitutions adds Proverbs 19:18: "Correct your son, so shall he afford you good hope."[114]

The Torah enjoins Israel to teach their children the ways of the Lord: "You shall teach them diligently to your children, and shall talk of them when you sit in your house, and when you walk by the way, and when you lie down, and when you rise" (Deuteronomy 6:7). In Jewish ethical teaching education of children is of paramount importance. "Rav Yisrael Salanter asserts that the dead are judged in accordance with the deeds of their descendants, since they have had an active role in their children's education and spiritual development, be it positive or negative."[115]

Here in 4.9 and also in 4.10 we find the only mentions in the Didache of the "fear of God."[116] *Yir'at HaShem* ("fear of the Lord," יראת השם) is a direct commandment in the Torah and is found just a few verses down from the injunction to teach them

---

112 The *Doctrina* omits "or daughter" (4.9). Additionally the Apostolic Constitutions (7.12) adds the pronoun αὐτούς ("them"), which is not in the Greek text of the Didache but is implied in the . This discrepancy is probably explained by a later redactor who was likely much more proficient in Greek and smoothed over the author of the Didache's rough, broken Greek. This may give further evidence that the original author of the Didache was probably more proficient in Hebrew than Greek.
113 1 Clement 21.7. Cf. Shepherd of Hermas, Vision 1.3.1–2 (3.1–2).
114 Apostolic Constitutions 7.12.
115 Rabbi A.L. Scheinbaum, *Peninim on the Torah: An Anthology of Thought-Provoking Ideas, Practical Insights, and Review Questions & Answers on the Weekly Parsha Fifth Series* (Cleveland Heights, OH: Peninim, 1998), 75–76.
116 *Doctrina* 4.10 and the Georgian version of the Didache have "the fear of the Lord."

to your children: "It is the LORD your God you shall fear" (Deuteronomy 6:13).[117] The *Sefer HaChinnuch* states that this precept applies to "all of humanity."[118] Our Master urges his disciples: "But I will warn you whom to fear: fear him who, after he has killed, has authority to cast into hell. Yes, I tell you, fear him!" (Luke 12:5). Having the fear of the Lord means believing that God punishes sin and rewards righteousness. The fear of the Lord should result in keeping the commandments of God and avoiding sin. King Solomon sums up the duty of man this way: "Fear God and keep his commandments" (Ecclesiastes 12:13). The sages urged their disciples that their "fear of sin should precede their wisdom."[119]

The fear of the Lord was considered one of the backbone principles for good character: "All men must be informed that anyone who wishes to attain worthy character traits must intermix fear of HaShem with each trait, for the fear of HaShem is the common bond among all the traits."[120]

[4.9]
Do not withhold your hand from your son or daughter, but teach them the fear of God from their youth.

◈ *Do not harshly give orders to your servant or maid who put their hope in the same God, or else they might lose their fear of God who is over both of you.* (DIDACHE 4.10)

The household code now moves into instructions on the relationship between slaves and masters.[121] Slaves were not to be abused or mistreated in fits of rage. The Apostolic Constitutions renders this, "Do not harshly give orders to your servant or maid who put their hope in the same God, or else they groan against you, and wrath be upon you from God."[122] The disciple of the Master must set a righteous example of godly behavior even before his servants.

---

117 Deuteronomy 6:13.
118 *Sefer HaChinnuch* 432. See also Rabbi Aaron Lichtenstein who feels that this commandment is a subcategory of the Noachide commandment against blasphemy (*The Seven Laws of Noah*, 86).
119 m.*Avot* 3:9.
120 Rabbi Gavriel Zaloshinsky, *The Ways of the Tzaddikim* (trans. Rabbi Shraga Silverstein; 2 vols.; New York, NY: Feldheim, 1996), 1:17.
121 The *Doctrina* reads, "Do not give orders in your anger to your man or woman slave, who hope in the same Lord; let him fear both the Lord and you" (4.10).
122 Apostolic Constitutions 7.13. Although in our of both the Didache and the Apostolic Constitutions we have "harshly" for the Greek word *pichria* (πικρίᾳ), the Apostolic Constitutions adds *psuche* (soul, ψυχή), which then literally reads, "bitterness of soul." This preserves the Hebrew idiom *marat nafesh* (מרת נפש), which we find in various forms in 1 Samuel 1:10, Job 21:25, and Sirach 31:30. This may indicate that the Apostolic Constitutions is drawing on a version of the Didache that is older than *Codex Hierosolymitanus* 54 and that the Greek of the Didache was polished over time.

[4.10]
Do not harshly give orders to your servant or maid who put their hope in the same God, or else they might lose their fear of God who is over both of you.

When an owner was harsh with his slave, he committed the desecration of God's character (*chillul HaShem*), as the slave would begin to associate the behavior of his earthly master with that of his heavenly Master and in turn lose reverence for both. This brings to mind the words of our Master: "It is inevitable that stumbling blocks come, but woe to him through whom they come! It would be better for him if a millstone were hung around his neck and he were thrown into the sea, than that he would cause one of these little ones to stumble" (Luke 17:1–2 NASB).[123] It is significant here that both male and female slaves are mentioned. While both male and female servants were at risk of physical abuse, "Females were doubly at risk as objects of sexual exploitation by their owners."[124]

The Hebrew word for slave is *eved* (עבד), which can mean either "slave" or "servant." The Torah gives extensive instruction regarding the treatment of slaves. For example, they were to be set free after six years; the laws of adultery applied to female slaves in the same way as to free women; and a slave who escaped from his master was not to be returned.[125] Because the regulations in the Torah and rabbinic literature were so exhaustive and restrictive surrounding the ownership of slaves, the sages admitted, "Whoever buys a Hebrew slave is like buying a master for himself."[126] In fact, conditions were often so good for the slave that he would not want to leave, and the Torah makes provision for his permanent commitment to his master.[127]

In Jewish law a slave who was brought into a Jewish household was required to be circumcised (manservant) or immersed (maidservant) and observe Torah on the level of a Jewish woman: "Every precept which is obligatory on a woman is obligatory on a slave; every precept which is not obligatory on a woman is not obligatory on a slave."[128] A slave, male or female, would become a part of the Jewish nation and have certain legal rights. In turn, the Didache assumes this Jewish tradition of incorporating the slaves into the religion of the household. Slaves in Yeshua-following households are assumed to possess "the fear of God," (in other words,

---

123   "Little one" does not always refer to a young child. It is often used in rabbinic literature to refer to an unschooled and inexperienced student, e.g., m.*Avot* 4:20; b.*Sotah* 22a.
124   Jonathan A. Draper, "Children and Slaves in the Community of the Didache and the Two Ways Tradition," in *The Didache: A Missing Piece of the Puzzle in Early Christianity* (eds. Draper and Clayton N. Jefford; Atlanta, GA: SBL Press, 2015), 100.
125   Exodus 21:1–11; Leviticus 19:20–21; Deuteronomy 23:15–16. Cf. Exodus 21:20–21, 26–27, 32; Leviticus 25:39–40; Deuteronomy 15:15–17, 21:14, 24:7.
126   b.*Kiddushin* 22a.
127   Exodus 21:5–6; Deuteronomy 15:16–17.
128   b.*Chagigah* 4a.

they have become God-fearers) and to have joined in the community worship. As in Jewish law, this would then "preserve the ritual purity of the household."[129]

In the household codes of the New Testament, we find instructions regarding treatment of slaves. The Apostle Paul states, "Masters, treat your bondservants [slaves] justly and fairly, knowing that you also have a Master in heaven" (Colossians 4:1), and, "Masters, do the same to them, and stop your threatening, knowing that he who is both their Master and yours is in heaven" (Ephesians 6:9). Slaves were to be treated with respect and kindness as fellow human beings and as fellow disciples of the Master. They were not to be regarded as less, because both the master and the slave were equally subject to their Father in heaven.

[4.10] *Do not harshly give orders to your servant or maid who put their hope in the same God, or else they might lose their fear of God who is over both of you.*

> ⚜ *For God does not intend to call anyone according to status; rather, he calls those whom the Spirit has prepared.*
> (DIDACHE 4.10)

God does not make a distinction when calling people to discipleship.[130] Paul tells us that neither ethnicity, gender, nor social status affect a person's standing in Messiah: "There is neither Jew nor Greek, there is neither slave nor free, there is no male and female, for you are all one in Messiah Yeshua" (Galatians 3:28).[131] Everyone has equal access to salvation and right standing before God through the Master's atoning sacrifice. Paul writes that with God "there is no partiality."[132] Similarly, the sages say, "Before God, however, all are equal, women, slaves, poor and rich."[133] The Spirit upon the slave is a seal as to his or her equality with others before God.

The Didache's language in the phrase "he calls those whom the Spirit has prepared" speaks of a predestined call unto Messiah. The Apostle Paul also speaks similarly in Romans:

> Those whom he foreknew he also predestined to be conformed to the image of his Son, in order that he might be the firstborn among many brothers. And those whom he predestined he also called, and those

---

129 Draper, "Children and Slaves in the Community of the Didache and the Two Ways Tradition," 98.
130 The Georgian version of the Didache adds, "You should know that the Lord is not coming as a respecter of persons, but is rather coming for those who, by the Spirit of the Lord, have prepared a place for his Spirit."
131 Cf. Colossians 3:11.
132 Ephesians 6:9.
133 *Exodus Rabbah* 21:4.

[4.10]
For God does not intend to call anyone according to status; rather, he calls those whom the Spirit has prepared.

whom he called he also justified, and those whom he justified he also glorified. (Romans 8:29–30)

The Didache teaches that one can be called to Messiah only through the preparation of the Spirit, that is, the "work of the Spirit in the human heart."[134] Surprisingly, this is one of only two references to the Spirit in the Didache. The other appears in chapter 7 in the verbal formula used during immersion.

The mention of the Spirit here in connection with slaves also alludes to the Prophet Joel's words about the Spirit being poured out on all flesh in the Messianic Era: "Even on the male and female servants in those days I will pour out my Spirit" (Joel 2:29). This is supported in the *Doctrina*'s rendering of the Didache: "For the Lord came not to call men with partiality, but those in whom he found the Spirit."[135]

> *And as for you servants, submit yourselves to your masters in humility and fear as they are an example of the authority of God.* (DIDACHE 4.11)

After addressing the treatment of slaves by masters, the Didache now gives instructions for a slave's behavior toward his master. Slaves were to show respect and be submissive. The Apostolic Constitutions adds a proof text from Ephesians: "And as for you servants, submit yourselves to your masters in humility and fear as they are an example of the authority of God, 'as to the Lord and not to man' [Ephesians 6:7]."[136] The wording of both the Didache and Apostolic Constitutions is very similar to Ephesians 6:5: "Bondservants, obey your earthly masters with fear and trembling, with a sincere heart, as you would [Messiah]." Many slaves might resent their masters and resist being subject to them, but the Didache instructs slaves to submit to their masters anyway, as "they are an example of the authority of God."

---

134 Philip Schaff, *The Oldest Church Manual Called the Teaching of the Twelve Apostles* (Edinburgh, Scotland: T&T Clark, 1885), 178.
135 *Doctrina* 4.3.
136 Apostolic Constitutions 7.13.

Disrespect toward an earthly master could cause disrespect toward the heavenly Master. Instead, the master was to be treated as a godlike figure.[137]

In the apostolic household codes, we find a number of similar instructions as to how slaves should behave toward their masters. The Apostle Peter exhorts, "Servants, be subject to your masters with all respect, not only to the good and gentle but also to the unjust" (1 Peter 2:18). The Apostle Paul stresses that a slave's obedience to his master should be "not by way of eye-service, as people-pleasers, but with sincerity of heart, fearing the Lord," to which he adds, "as servants of [Messiah], doing the will of God from the heart."[138] Slaves are urged to "be well-pleasing, not argumentative, not pilfering" and must not be "disrespectful" to "believing masters," taking advantage of their common brotherhood in Messiah.[139]

Canon Spence sums up the instructions to masters and slaves:

> In the pagan world slavery was inextricably interwoven with all relations of society. All that the Christian teacher could do at first was, in the case of the master, to appeal to his consciousness of the universal brotherhood of man, and in the case of the slave, to remind him of his solemn duty to bear with brave patience whatsoever lot God hath ordained for him in this short period of trial called the earthly life. This quiet teaching has, we know, borne splendid fruit, and as a result of Christian teaching, the greatest curse of the old world, without any violent or destructive revolution, has well-nigh vanished from the face of the world.[140]

Much of the world has now banished slavery, but these principles regarding masters and slaves can be applied to employers and employees. Employers should treat their employees with respect and love, while employees, regardless of how they feel about their bosses, should work cheerfully for them with humble submission. These guidelines can help foster Messiah's love in the workplace and will further

[4.11]
And as for you servants, submit yourselves to your masters in humility and fear as they are an example of the authority of God.

---

137 There is a bit of ambiguity here in the Greek, and it could literally be rendered as "they are an example of God," which some have connected to the phrase "image of God" (*tzelem Elohim*, צלם אלהים), harkening back to Genesis 1.27: "God created man in his own image, in the image of God he created him; male and female he created them." For example, Thomas O'Loughlin translates this "as to an image of God" (O'Loughlin, *The Didache*, 164). If this is correct, the passage might be interpreted in light of this saying from m.*Avot* (3:18), which states: "Beloved is man since he was created in the image of God; an extra love is made known to him that he was created in God's image."
138 Colossians 3:22; Ephesians 6:5–8.
139 Titus 2:9–10; 1 Timothy 6:2.
140 Spence, *The Teaching of the Twelve Apostles*, 23.

spread the gospel of the kingdom, even without words. Just as the kingdom is to be characterized by humble submission, so must we as followers of King Messiah walk in humble submission now.

◈ You shall hate every form of hypocrisy and everything that does not please the Lord. (DIDACHE 4.12)

Having addressed community and home life, Didache 4 begins a closing summary section. Disciples of the Master are instructed to "hate every form of hypocrisy." As pointed out in the commentary to 2.6, the Greek word *hupokrites* ("hypocrite") refers to a "stage performer" or an "actor."[141] "Hypocrite" in the context of the Didache and the New Testament should be understood as someone who performs a religious obligation in an ostentatious way to attract attention, to be seen by others, and to be recognized as pious.

Disciples of the Master are urged not to perform their acts of righteousness for the sake of praise from men. They are to avoid "everything that does not please the Lord." The parallel in the Epistle of Barnabas adds, "You shall utterly hate that which is evil."[142] The *Doctrina* emphasizes action: "Everything that does not please God do not do."[143] This refers to the negative commandments of the Torah.[144] The Apostolic Constitutions renders this inversely: "Everything that pleases the Lord you shall do," which in turn refers to the positive commandments.[145] We find parallel examples in the Psalms: "Therefore I consider all your precepts to be right; I hate every false way" (Psalm 119:128), and, "I hate and abhor falsehood, but I love your law" (Psalm 119:163). In the Dead Sea Scrolls literature, we read, "Choose that which pleases him and reject that which he hates."[146]

---

141 It is also related to the Hebrew *chanaf* (חָנֵף), which has the broader connotation of "godless."
142 Barnabas 19.11.
143 *Doctrina* 4.12.
144 Cf. "At the same time as loving God, we must also remain in awe of his presence, i.e., be on guard against transgressing any of the negative commandments of the Torah. Under no circumstances are we to commit acts that we know to contradict his expressed wishes," (Rabbi Levi Yitzchak of Berditchev *Kedushat Levi* [trans. Eliyahu Munk; Brooklyn, NY: Lambda, 2009], 465.
145 Apostolic Constitutions 7.14.
146 Damascus Document[a] (4Q266) II, 15.

> *Do not forsake the commandments of the Lord, but keep what you have received, neither adding to nor subtracting from it.* (DIDACHE 4.13)

Disciples of the Master must not only loathe what is sinful but must love the Lord's commandments and not neglect them. The commandments of the Lord are the commandments of the Torah.[147]

The Didache urges one to "guard that which you have received," a turn of phrase that seems to imply oral transmission. This may indicate "those commandments of the Torah which you have received through apostolic teaching." The word "keep" corresponds to the Hebrew word *shamar* (שמר), which implies observance of a commandment.[148] Therefore, the phrase "keep what you have received" can be understood to mean "observe the commandments which have been entrusted to you." The Apostolic Constitutions adds, "Keep what you have received *from him*," which seems to emphasize that even the oral teachings should be viewed as from HaShem.[149]

The phrase "what you have received" finds congruency in the Apostle Paul's words, "I delivered to you as of first importance what I also received."[150] "Delivered" (*masorah*, מסרה) and "received" (*kabbalah*, קבלה) are technical terms used in rabbinic literature for the detailed process of the oral transmission.[151] This is evidence that even during the time of the Didache, some, if not the majority, of the Master's teachings were still being delivered orally. This is akin to the rabbinic practice of memorizing one's teacher's words. The Talmud praises the student who repeats his teacher's lesson over a hundred times.[152] In order for the disciple to guard and preserve the commandments of the Master, he must internalize them through memorization.

The Didache then instructs that nothing should be added to or taken away from the commandments. The Torah as well prohibits both adding to the commandments and subtracting from them. We find this admonishment repeated twice in

---

147 The *Doctrina* reads, "Therefore, my son, keep what you have heard and do not add to them what is contrary to them, nor subtracting from them" (4.13). It is notable that the *Doctrina* omits the word "commandments" that is found in the Epistle of Barnabas (9.2). The Didache might be adding "the commandments" to correct a false doctrine that had arisen.
148 The Greek word *phulasso* (φυλάσσω) used in the Didache corresponds to *shamar* in the Septuagint.
149 Apostolic Constitutions 7.14, emphasis added.
150 1 Corinthians 15:3.
151 E.g., m.*Avot* 1:1.
152 b.*Chagigah* 9b.

[4.13]
Do not forsake the commandments of the Lord, but keep what you have received, neither adding to nor subtracting from it.

the book of Deuteronomy: "You shall not add to the word that I command you, nor take from it, that you may keep the commandments of the LORD your God that I command you" (Deuteronomy 4:2), and, "Everything that I command you, you shall be careful to do. You shall not add to it or take from it" (Deuteronomy 12:32). Spence comments, "For a trained Jew, such as evidently the author of this treatise must have been, the Deuteronomy passage most likely was in his mind when he wrote this charge."[153] The Apostolic Constitutions cites Proverbs 30:6: "Do not add to his words, lest he rebuke you and you be found a liar."[154] In the minds of the earliest disciples, "the Torah must thus be seen as an organic whole and must be observed fully."[155]

⚜ *Confess your transgressions in the assembly, and you will not draw near in prayer with a guilty conscience.* (DIDACHE 4.14)

Naturally, one is bound to transgress the injunctions from time to time that 4.13 tells us to keep. When that happens, he is to confess his shortcomings in the community. Joshua Rudder points out that "the juxtaposition of these two tasks (confessing and praying) parallels James 5:16": "Confess your sins to one another and pray for one another, that you may be healed. The prayer of a righteous person has great power as it is working."[156] In Didache 14.1 we will see that confession is also required before a community meal.

Some have suggested that such confession was done publicly. However, the Apostolic Constitutions seems to indicate it was done privately: "Confess your transgressions unto the Lord your God; and do not add unto them, that it may be well with you from the Lord your God, who desires not the death of a sinner, but

---

153 Spence, *The Teaching of the Twelve Apostles*, 24.
154 Apostolic Constitutions 7.14. Cf. Proverbs 30:5; Revelation 22:18–19; 1 Enoch 104:10–13; Letter of Aristeas 310–311; Josephus, *Antiquities of the Jews* 1:17/0.3; *Against Apion* 1:42/viii. Also, "Whoever twists the sayings of the Lord to suit his own sinful desires and claims that there is neither resurrection nor judgment—well, that person is the firstborn of Satan" (Polycarp, *To the Philippians* 7.1).
155 Weren, "The 'Ideal Community' according to Matthew, James, and the Didache," 197.
156 Joshua Rudder, *The Two Ways: A Lost Early Christian Manual of Personal and Communal Ethics, Discipline and Morality* (Los Angeles, CA: Native Language, 2009), 37.

his repentance."[157] The Epistle of Barnabas omits "in the assembly," which is more evidence that the confession took place privately.[158]

In Judaism confession "is an essential part in the process of repentance."[159] In the Torah it is required that one confess his sin after realization of guilt: "He shall confess his sin that he has committed" (Numbers 5:7). The rabbis deemed that this confession is to be done privately. In most siddurim is a prayer entitled *Ashamnu*, recited on weekdays, that entails the confession of various sins. "In certain circumstances, however, where the sin involved public knowledge, a public confession is required."[160] Confession was also an integral part of offering a sin offering, a guilt offering, or a free-will burnt offering, when the one offering the sacrifice laid his hands upon the head of the sacrifice.[161]

The Greek word behind "draw near" (*proserchomai*, προσέρχομαι) is connected in the Septuagint to the Hebrew word *karav* (קרב). *Karav* means "to draw near" and is the root for the word *korban* ("sacrifice," קרבן). In Jewish thought sacrifice and prayer are intimately connected, and "draw near" can be used as an idiom for both.[162] This then connects this saying with the Master's words:

> If you are offering your gift at the altar and there remember that your brother has something against you, leave your gift there before the altar and go. First be reconciled to your brother, and then come and offer your gift. (Matthew 5:23–24)

Since the subject of both the Didache and our Master Yeshua's words here is that we are to deal with sin before drawing near to God, it is possible that the Didache's version is a kind of halachic midrash on the Master's words. The book of Hebrews stresses approaching the Lord with a clear conscience: "Let us draw near with a true heart in full assurance of faith, with our hearts sprinkled clean from an evil conscience and our bodies washed with pure water" (Hebrews 10:22).[163]

[4.14]
Confess your transgressions in the assembly, and you will not draw near in prayer with a guilty conscience.

---

157 Apostolic Constitutions 7.14. It is interesting that only here and in a scriptural quote in 7.15 are the only places that the Apostolic Constitutions uses the divine title "The Lord your God." This title is not found in the Didache.
158 Barnabas 19.12. The confession of sins is omitted entirely from the *Doctrina*.
159 Rabbi Adin Steinsaltz, *The Talmud Steinsaltz Edition: A Reference Guide* (New York, NY: Random, 1989), 185.
160 Ibid., 185.
161 Ibid.
162 For New Testament examples see Hebrews 4:16, 7:25, 10:1, 22, 11:6; 1 Peter 2:4.
163 Cf. Clement of Alexandria, *Stromata* 7.7.

[4.14]
Confess your transgressions in the assembly, and you will not draw near in prayer with a guilty conscience.

The phrase "in the assembly" (*en ekklesia*, ἐν ἐκκλησίᾳ) seems to refer to "a meeting in a local house-church ... probably for joint prayer."[164] It could also merely refer to "a place of prayer" such as that in Philippi where Lydia and the women gathered by the riverside on the Sabbath.[165]

◈ This is the Way of Life. (DIDACHE 4.14)

With this the section of the Didache detailing the Way of Life comes to a close. This sets up chapter 5, which explains the Way of Death. As in its parallel to chapter 1, the Epistle of Barnabas renders this with the more mystical language, "This is the Way of Light."[166] The Apostolic Constitutions adds some additional injunctions regarding parents, rulers, and prayer before concluding the Way of Life:

> You shall serve your father and mother as the causes of your being born, "that your days may be long in the land that the Lord your God is giving you" [Exodus 20:12]. Do not overlook your brethren or your kinsfolk, "Do not to hide yourself from your own flesh" [Isaiah 58:7]. You shall fear the king, knowing that his appointment is of the Lord. His rulers you shall honor as the ministers of God, for they are the revengers of all unrighteousness; to whom pay taxes, tribute, and every oblation with a willing mind. Do not proceed to your prayer in the day of your wickedness, before you have laid aside your bitterness. This is the Way of Life, in which may you be found, through Yeshua the Messiah our Master.[167]

---

164   Weren, "The 'Ideal Community' according to Matthew, James, and the Didache," 181. For the use of the word *ekklesia* as a meeting for prayer and teaching, see 1 Corinthians 14:19–35.
165   Acts 16:13.
166   Barnabas 19.12. The Georgian version of the Didache reads, "This is what until now has been said about the way of life."
167   Apostolic Constitutions 7.15–17. Despite this section not being found in the Didache it still appears to be very Jewish. For example, the injunction to "serve" one's father and mother is the rabbinic interpretation of honoring one's parents. See b.*Kiddushin* 31b.

Chapter Five

DIDACHE 5

5.1 But this is the Way of Death, which is first of all evil and full of curses: murder, adultery, lust, sexual immorality, theft, idolatry, magic, use of potions, robbery, false witness, hypocrisy, duplicity, deceit, arrogance, malice, egocentrism, greed, foul speech, jealousy, overconfidence, loftiness, and pretension.[1]

5.2 It is the way of those who persecute good; those who hate truth; those who love falsehood; those who are ignorant of the wages of righteousness; those who do not cling to what is good or to righteous judgment; those who keep watch not for good but for wickedness; those who are far from being considerate and persevering; those who love frivolous things; those who seek repayment; those who are merciless to the poor; those who do not trouble themselves for the oppressed; those who do not recognize the one who made them; those who murder children; those who corrupt what God has formed; those who turn away the needy; those who oppress the greatly distressed; those who are advocates of the wealthy; and those who are lawless judges of the poor—those who are utterly sinful. Children, may you be rescued from all of these![2]

---

[1] Matthew 15:19; Mark 7:21–22; Romans 1:29.
[2] Romans 1:29–31; 1 Corinthians 6:9–10; 1 Timothy 1:9–10; Revelation 21:8, 22:15.

Overview

In chapter 5 the Didache, as it continues the Two Ways section, turns from illustrating the Way of Life to expounding the Way of Death. Even though the Didache briefly mentions the Way of Death in the first verse of chapter 1, the book's contents thus far have dealt exclusively with the Way of Life. What is striking is not only how long it takes the Didache to address the Way of Death but the stark contrast between the amount of space it gives to the Way of Death and that given to the Way of Life. Tony Jones comments that "the Way of Life is explicated at great length, with both indicative descriptors and imperative commands"; in contrast, the Way of Death "is entirely indicative" and given one-fifth the treatment:

> Not necessarily an afterthought, the Way of Death is mainly a recapitulation of the litanies that were said not to be the Way of Life. Boiled down, the Way of Death is filled with behaviors that portray a lack of fear of God—those who put their trust in themselves rather than the Lord. "In a word," this section of the Didache concludes, "the way of death is full of those who are steeped in sin. Be delivered, children, from all of this!"[3]

Although the new Gentile believers did not need as elaborate a description of the Way of Death as of the Way of Life, it was important that the new believers knew exactly what behavior would not be tolerated within the Messianic communities. In essence, chapter 5 defines the lifestyle and character traits of those who are completely wicked and far from God. Such behavior should not be found among followers of the Master.

Evil Traits

Teachings on Jewish ethics prescribe a study of both good character traits and bad character traits in order to discern proper behavior. We find in the sixteenth-century Jewish ethical work *Orchot Tzaddikim*:

---

[3] Tony Jones, *The Teaching of the Twelve: Believing & Practicing the Primitive Christianity of the Ancient Didache Community* (Brewster, MA: Paraclete, 2009), 88.

> The righteous man must recognize good and evil and be an expert in the value of each trait. He must properly observe and reflect upon them and exert himself physically and intellectually to rid himself of folly and to embrace understanding and remove admixture of dross.[4]

Only through the study and contemplation of evil traits can we completely rid these qualities from our lives. If we don't know how to recognize wrongdoing, we will not be able to purge it.

Messianic luminary Paul Philip Levertoff comments on the order of the prayers in the *Amidah* where the prayer for knowledge is before the prayer for repentance:

> First it says, "You grant knowledge to mankind." After the petition for knowledge, we ask for repentance. Without knowledge of sins, one cannot differentiate between good and evil. Without knowledge, a person would not come to repentance.[5]

It is this knowledge of sin and then recognizing where it is in our own lives that brings us to complete repentance.

Additionally, if we do not continually eradicate evil traits from our lives, thereby allowing these qualities to gain the upper hand in our nature, we will eventually come to despise good character traits. *Orchot Tzaddikim* continues:

> Know and understand that one who by nature inclines to an evil trait or has become habituated to such a trait and does not take it upon himself to forsake it, but constantly strengthens himself in it—such a one will come to despise and abhor the corresponding positive traits.[6]

For this purpose the Didache exposes the Way of Death so that the new disciples would be wary of its traps and exercise healthy introspection, examining the evil traits that could ensnare them and removing them from their lives.

---

4 Rabbi Gavriel Zaloshinsky, *The Ways of the Tzaddikim* (trans. Rabbi Shraga Silverstein; 2 vols.; New York, NY: Feldheim, 1996), 1:15.
5 Paul Philip Levertoff, *Religious Ideas of the Chasidim* (trans. Kevin Hanke; Marshfield, MO: First Fruits of Zion, forthcoming).
6 Rabbi Zaloshinsky, *The Ways of the Tzaddikim*, 1:13.

STRUCTURE AND STYLE

The material of chapter 5, typically portioned into only two verses, is considerably shorter than that of the Didache's first four chapters. It can be neatly divided into three sections: a list of twenty-two vices, a list of eighteen types of evildoers, and a final summary statement.[7]

Section	Content
5.1	List of twenty-two vices
5.2	List of eighteen evildoers
5.2	Summary statement

The chapter, for the most part, lacks conjunctions and can thus be described in a grammatical sense as the "least attractive of the sections of the Didache."[8] Yet its terse style betrays a distinctly Hebrew flavor:

> The grammatical form of the chapter, rugged as it is and Hebraic, makes for the opinion that the *Teaching* emanates from a Jewish source. Notice the abrupt way in which the series of evil things is introduced, and the suddenness of the transition from these to evil men, of which an apt illustration may be found in the sixth chapter of the Jewish Fathers.[9]

The example Taylor is citing is from *Pirkei Avot*. It begins with good characteristics by which the Torah is acquired:

> The Torah [is acquired by] forty-eight things, and these they are in: study, attentive listening, ordered presentation of the lips, reasoning of the heart, intelligence of the heart, awe, fear, humility, joyousness,

---

[7] Scholars number the evildoer and vice lists differently. While our reflects twenty-two vices, some count "evil and full of curses" as a vice for a total of twenty-three. Others add "those who are utterly sinful" for a total of nineteen evildoers instead of eighteen, and some also split "those who do not cling to what is good or to righteous judgment" into two, making a total of twenty evildoers.

[8] William Varner, *The Way of the Didache: The First Christian Handbook* (New York, NY: University Press of America, 2007), 67.

[9] Charles Taylor, "The Teaching of the Twelve Apostles with Illustrations from the Talmud," in *Didache: The Unknown Teaching of the Twelve Apostles* (ed. Brent S. Walters; San Jose, CA: Anti-Nicene Archive, 1991), 169. All this is significantly smoothed out and softened in the later version of this section in the Apostolic Constitutions (7.18).

ministering unto the sages, painstaking examination together with one's colleagues, fine argumentation of disciples, sedateness, scripture, the oral learning, moderation in sleep, moderation in conversation, moderation in pleasure, moderation in hilarity, moderation in worldly affairs, long-suffering, a good heart, the conscientiousness of the sages, acceptance of chastisements. (m.*Avot* 6.5)

It then, in the next section continuing in the list of forty-eight things by which the Torah is acquired, switches to descriptions of good people:

The possessor of Torah is one who recognizes his place, who rejoices in his portion, who makes a fence to his words, who claims no credit for himself, is loved, loves the all-present, loves mankind, loves righteous ways, welcomes reproofs, loves uprightness, keeps himself far from honor, lets not his heart become swelled on account of his learning, delights not in giving legal decisions, shares in the bearing of a burden with his colleague, uses his weight with him on the scale of merit, places him upon truth, places him upon peace, composes himself at his study, asks and answers, listens, and adds, learns in order to teach, learns in order to practice, makes his teacher wiser, notes with precision that which he has heard, and says a thing in the name of him who said it. (m.*Avot* 6.6)

Some have argued that Didache chapter 5 is "dependent upon an early Jewish source which was known to the Didachist."[10] The structural parallels between the

---

10   Clayton N. Jefford, *The Sayings of Jesus in the Teaching of the Twelve Apostles* (New York, NY: Brill, 1989), 83.

Didache and *Pirkei Avot* are so strong that it could be that the contents of this chapter originally circulated as a counterpart to the list in *Pirkei Avot*.[11]

But whether or not this section was based upon older sources, the composers of the Didache were Jewish, and they thought in Hebrew. It is thus only natural that this chapter, as well as the entire book, be structured grammatically in the style of the Hebrew language.

Vice Lists

The first half of the chapter (5.1) finds its parallel in what scholars call "vice lists." These lists of sins are found in intertestamental Jewish literature as well as in the New Testament and rabbinic writings:

> There reigned in all men without exception blood, manslaughter, theft, and dissimulation, corruption, unfaithfulness, tumults, perjury, disquieting of good men, forgetfulness of good turns, defiling of souls, changing of kind, disorder in marriages, adultery, and shameless uncleanness. (Wisdom of Solomon 14:25–26)[12]

---

[11] The rabbis mused about the significance of the number forty-eight in connection with this passage from *Pirkei Avot*. For example the Midrash states: "The word, 'well' is found in the Torah forty-eight times, corresponding to the forty-eight qualities by which knowledge of the Torah is acquired" (*Midrash Song of Songs* 4:31). The homily being that each of the forty-eight aspects takes us deep into the depths of the Torah like a well. There is also the tradition that there were a total of forty-eight prophets in Israel (b.*Megillah* 14a) and that Abraham was forty-eight years old when he recognized HaShem as his Maker (*Pesikta Rabbati* 21:12). See Rabbi Yosef Stern, *Pirkei Avos with Ideas and Insights from Sfas Emes and Other Chassidic Masters* (Brooklyn, NY: Artscroll, 2008), 459–461. In Didache 5 we have forty evil traits and individuals. While it is pure speculation to make connections, the number forty in Scripture is often associated with sin, testing, and repentance. Israel journeyed in the wilderness for forty years as punishment for their sin (Numbers 32:13); Jonah warned Nineveh that they had forty days to repent (Jonah 3:4); Ezekiel laid on his right side for forty days to symbolize the sin of Judah (Ezekiel 4:6); and the Master was tempted in the wilderness for forty days (Matthew 4:2; Mark 1:13; Luke 4:2). There is also the requirement that a mikvah have forty *se'ah* of water in order to purify (m.*Mikva'ot* 1:4). J. Rendel Harris connects the twenty-two vices to the same number of vices found in Romans 1:29–32 and the *Vidui* (confession, ודוי) prayer of Yom Kippur. He writes: "There is ground for suspicion that the Vidui of the Day of Atonement, the catalogue of vices in the [Didache], and the catalogue of vices in the first chapter of Romans, are all derived from a lost alphabetical catalogue of sins" (*The Teaching of the Apostles* [London, England: C.J. Clay and Sons, 1887], 82–86). Building off the connection between the Vidui prayer and Didache 5.1, E. Bruce Brooks feels that similar lists of sins found in Mark 7:21–22, Galatians 5:13–6:10, and Barnabas 18:1–20:2 along with Didache 5.1 all go back to a proto-form of this Vidui prayer, which is best preserved in the Didache ("The Two Ways," *Alpha: Studies in Early Christianity* vol. 1 [2017]: 39–47).

[12] Cf. Testament of Asher 2:1–10; 3 Baruch 4:17, 8:5, 13:4.

They were filled with all manner of unrighteousness, evil, covetousness, malice. They are full of envy, murder, strife, deceit, maliciousness. They are gossips, slanderers, haters of God, insolent, haughty, boastful, inventors of evil, disobedient to parents, foolish, faithless, heartless, ruthless. (Romans 1:29–31)[13]

Teach us, our Rabbi: For how many things is a person afflicted by plagues? So did our Rabbis teach: A plague [of *tzora'as*] afflict a person for [one of the following] eleven things: Idolatry, blaspheming the Name, immorality, theft, spreading evil gossip, testifying falsely, a judge who corrupts justice, swearing in vain, extending into someone else's domain, thinking false thoughts, and causing an argument between brethren. (*Midrash Tanchuma*, Metzora 4)[14]

Most notable is the list in the Two Ways material of the Dead Sea Scrolls, which scholars feel is similar to the strain of tradition found in the Didache:

The ways of the spirit of falsehood are these: greed, and slackness in the search for righteousness, wickedness and lies, haughtiness and pride, falseness and deceit, cruelty and abundant evil, ill-temper and much folly and brazen insolence, abominable deeds (committed) in a spirit of lust, and ways of lewdness in the service of uncleanness, a blaspheming tongue, blindness of eye and dullness of ear, stiffness of neck and heaviness of heart, so that man walks in all the ways of darkness and guile. (Community Rule [1QS] IV, 9–11)

The vice list in the Didache offers a window into the godless behaviors of the Roman world in the first centuries CE. Descriptions of Roman society from contemporary historians and writers such as Seneca and Tacitus offer corroboration.[15] The Didache's list of debauchery and sin is not merely theoretical; it accurately depicts the social context from which the new Gentile disciples came.

---

13   Cf. 1 Timothy 1:9–10; Shepherd of Hermas, Mandate 8.3 (38.3).
14   from Rabbi Yaakov Y.H. Pupko ed., *The Metsudah Midrash Tanchuma* (trans. Rabbi Avrohom Davis; Lakewood, NJ: Israel Book Shop, 2006), 4:287–288. Cf. b.*Arachin* 16a.
15   Philip Schaff, *The Oldest Church Manual Called the Teaching of the Twelve Apostles* (Edinburgh, Scotland: T&T Clark, 1885), 179.

Words of the Master

Some scholars have proposed a loose connection between the first section of the vice list in 5.1 and the words of the Master. In Mark 7, Yeshua enumerates thirteen sins that come from within the heart of man: "evil thoughts, sexual immorality, theft, murder, adultery, coveting, wickedness, deceit, sensuality, envy, slander, pride, foolishness."[16] Quite a few of these appear in Didache 5. A parallel passage in Matthew 15 offers seven sins that nearly identically parallel the Didache's list. See the italicized parallels below:

Matthew 15:19	Didache 5.1
"evil thoughts, *murder, adultery, sexual immorality, theft, false witness*, slander"	"*murders, adulteries*, lusts, *sexual immorality, thefts*, idolatry, magic, use of potions, robbery, *false witness*"

Both the Didache and Matthew have arranged the similar items in a parallel order, following the same general structure as the second tablet of the Decalogue:

> You shall not murder. You shall not commit adultery. You shall not steal. You shall not bear false witness. (Exodus 20:13–16)[17]

Some suggest that Matthew and the Didache compiled their lists independently of one another and merely followed the second half of the Decalogue,[18] but it seems quite possible that the Didache used a no-longer-extant oral or written gospel source from which Matthew drew as well.[19]

Evildoers

In 5.2 the Didache switches from listing evil traits to listing evildoers. This type of abrupt transition is found often in rabbinic literature.[20] This second section of

---

16 Mark 7:21–22.
17 Cf. Deuteronomy 5:17–20.
18 Jefford, *The Sayings of Jesus in the Teaching of the Twelve Apostles*, 84.
19 R.H. Connolly sees the "run of plurals" at the beginning of the Didache's list (which ends halfway through 5.1) as a further parallel with the list in Matthew. See Connolly, "The Didache in Relation to the Epistle of Barnabas," *Journal of Theological Studies* XXXIII (1932): 240–241.
20 Cf. m.*Avot* 6:5–6; Taylor, "The Teaching of the Twelve Apostles with Illustrations from the Talmud," 169.

chapter 5 reveals the severity of all kinds of sin. The new Gentile believer needed to recognize what types of people would not be found in the kingdom of heaven: those who committed grievous sins such as murder and adultery but also those whose sin seemed less obvious, such as turning their hand from the poor and ignoring the downtrodden of society:

> The Didache seems to be fully aware of the phenomenon of those who saw morality in terms of the avoidance of specific sinful acts by the individual, while not ignoring the social nature of sin and the social demands that are made on those who seek God. Christians were not to ignore the demands of seeking justice in society and showing a constant concern for the poor, and still imagine that they were not on the Way of Death.[21]

It was just as easy in the first few centuries CE as it is today to feel righteous by avoiding certain heinous transgressions while at the same time neglecting "the weightier matters of the law: justice and mercy and faithfulness" (Matthew 23:23). The Didache teaches that disciples of Yeshua are to strive for perfection in all areas of life and not to turn away from those in need.

---

[21] Thomas O'Loughlin, *The Didache: A Window on the Earliest Christians* (Grand Rapids, MI: Baker, 2010), 38.

Commentary

⚜ But this is the Way of Death. (DIDACHE 5.1)

The Didache introduces the Way of Death in the first verse of chapter 1 ("There are two ways: one of life and one of death"), but it is not until here in chapter 5 that it elaborates upon the term. In turn, chapter 5 "contrasts neatly" with 1.2 ("The Way of Life is this: first, you shall love God who made you. Second, you shall love your fellow as yourself") and serves as a kind of bookend to the opening chapter and its description of the Way of Life.[22] The contents of this chapter stand in direct juxtaposition to everything that has been presented previously regarding the Way of Life. The *Doctrina* states, "the Way of Death is opposite to [the Way of Life]."[23] The Epistle of Barnabas renders this with the more metaphoric language, "the Way of Darkness."[24]

This contrasting pattern is recognized by scholars as inherently Jewish in style.[25] For example, we find in the Two Ways material of the Community Rule, "These are their ways in the world for the enlightenment of the heart of man, and that all the paths of true righteousness may be made straight before him ... But the ways of the spirit of falsehood are these."[26]

The new Gentile disciples needed to be warned about the dangers and enticements of reverting to the Way of Death. Proverbs tells us that if we do not guard ourselves, our own hearts can lead us down the path of evil: "There is a way that seems right to a man, but its end is the way [of] death" (Proverbs 16:25). Every day we have two choices: "Thus says the LORD: 'Behold, I set before you the way of life and the way of death'" (Jeremiah 21:8). We must cling daily to our Father in heaven and our Master Yeshua by always choosing life.

---

22 Joshua Rudder, *The Two Ways: A Lost Early Christian Manual of Personal and Communal Ethics, Discipline and Morality* (Los Angeles, CA: Native Language, 2009), 38.
23 *Doctrina* 5.1.
24 Barnabas 20.1.
25 Oskar Skarsaune, *In the Shadow of the Temple: Jewish Influences on Early Christianity* (Downers Grove, IL: InterVarsity Press, 2002), 361.
26 Community Rule (1QS) IV, 2, 9.

◈ *Which is first of all evil and full of curses.* (DIDACHE 5.1)

The Way of Death is presented first of all as entirely evil and wicked. The Apostolic Constitutions expands this: "The way of death is known by its wicked practices: for therein is the ignorance of God, and the introduction of many evils, and disorders, and disturbances."[27] The Epistle of Barnabas reads, "The Way of Darkness is perversely twisted and full of curses. For it is the way of eternal death with punishment in which are the things that destroy their souls."[28] Nothing good comes from walking in the Way of Death—it leads only to more sin.

The Way of Death is also described as "full of curses." The warning about "curses" invokes the divine punishments that fall upon those who violate the Torah.[29] Deuteronomy 27 and 28 detail the curses that HaShem would mete out on the Jewish people if they turned against his commandments:

> All these curses shall come upon you and pursue you and overtake you till you are destroyed, because you did not obey the voice of the LORD your God, to keep his commandments and his statutes that he commanded you. (Deuteronomy 28:45)

At the same time, just as the Way of Death is "full of curses," so the Way of Life is full of blessings:[30]

> If you faithfully obey the voice of the LORD your God, being careful to do all his commandments that I command you today, the LORD your God will set you high above all the nations of the earth. And all these blessings shall come upon you and overtake you, if you obey the voice of the LORD your God. (Deuteronomy 28:1–2)

This contrast of "blessing" and "curse" is a frequent theme in the book of Deuteronomy and dovetails nicely with the Didache's contrast between the Way of Life and the Way of Death. The choice between blessing and cursing is laid before Israel in much the same way as are the paths of life and death. Moses tells Israel, "See, I am setting before you today a blessing and a curse" (Deuteronomy 11:26), and, "I call heaven and earth to witness against you today, that I have set before

---

27 Apostolic Constitutions 7.18.
28 Barnabas 20.1.
29 Kurt Niederwimmer, *The Didache: Hermeneia—A Critical and Historical Commentary on the Bible* (Minneapolis, MN: Fortress, 1998), 114.
30 Ibid. Cf. Deuteronomy 28.

you life and death, blessing and curse. Therefore choose life, that you and your offspring may live" (Deuteronomy 30:19). Both the children of Israel and the audience of the Didache are urged to choose the life and blessing found in obedience to God over the death and cursing found in sin.

[5.1]
Which is first of all evil and full of curses.

◈ Murder, adultery, lust, sexual immorality, theft. (DIDACHE 5.1)

The Didache now begins its list of vices with the enumeration of commandments six, seven, and eight of the Decalogue; number nine, "false witness," will be listed a few vices later.[31] This is similar to the version of the second half of the Decalogue that we saw in Didache 2.2.

The Apostolic Constitutions (7.18) adds "swear falsely" (*epiorkeo*, ἐπιορκέω) after "sexual immorality" and the adjective "unlawful" to "lust." "Swear falsely" was already mentioned in Didache 2.3.

A similar list of sins is found in Matthew 15:19: "Out of the heart come evil thoughts, murder, adultery, sexual immorality, theft, false witness, slander."[32] The Master taught that all the sins of the Way of Death begin first in the evil thoughts of the heart.

◈ Idolatry, magic, use of potions. (DIDACHE 5.1)

The list here continues on the theme of the Decalogue with an allusion to the second commandment, "You shall have no other gods before me."[33] The sin of idolatry has already been mentioned in Didache 3.4. "Magic" and "potions," which are characteristics of idolatry, were mentioned in 2.2.

The pagan world of the first century was steeped in idolatry and idolatrous institutions. The new Gentile believers needed to be reminded repeatedly of the dangers of turning back to these accursed practices.

---

31 Exodus 20:13–16; Deuteronomy 5:17–20.
32 Cf. Mark 7:21–22.
33 Exodus 20:3–5; Deuteronomy 5:7–10.

⹋ Robbery. (DIDACHE 5.1)

The Greek word *arpagai* (ἁρπαγαί) is quite rare and not found in the Septuagint or the New Testament.[34] It is therefore difficult to ascertain its precise meaning here. While it is commonly translated in this verse as "robbery," others render it "rapines"[35] or "plunderings,"[36] and it can even have the connotation of "greediness."

Since "theft" has already been mentioned earlier in this verse in relation to the Decalogue, Kurt Niederwimmer suggests that "robbery" might correspond to 2.2: "Nor shall you covet the things of your fellow."[37] If this is so, this vice may be an allusion to the tenth commandment of the Decalogue, "You shall not covet."[38]

⹋ False witness. (DIDACHE 5.1)

The prohibition on false witness alludes to the ninth commandment of the Decalogue, "You shall not bear false witness against your neighbor."[39] It concludes the various vices that 5.1 draws from the Ten Commandments. "Do not bear false witness" is also found in 2.3.

⹋ Hypocrisy, duplicity. (DIDACHE 5.1)

Both these sins are also found in 2.4–6. "Hypocrisy" refers to putting on a show and performing a religious obligation in an ostentatious way to attract attention, to be seen by others, and recognized as pious. "Duplicity" (*diplokardia*, διπλοκαρδία) can mean "double-heartedness," "double-mindedness," or "deception." The duplicitous person only pretends to be pious. His righteousness is a façade behind which he conceals his true nature.

The hypocrite uses his piety, genuine though it may be, to garner the praise of men. The duplicitous man creates a show of false piety to deceive others into believing that he is righteous. When others are not watching, he is not pious. Both men walk on the Way of Death.

---

34   It is found in 1 Maccabees 13:34.
35   Alexander Roberts and James Donaldson, *Fathers of the Third and Fourth Centuries* (vol. 7 of *The Ante-Nicene Fathers*; ed. A Cleveland Cox et al.; New York, NY: Christian Literature Publishing, 1886), 379.
36   J.B. Lightfoot, *The Apostolic Fathers* (London, England: Macmillan, 1898), 231.
37   Niederwimmer, *The Didache*, 116.
38   Exodus 20:17; Deuteronomy 5: 21.
39   Exodus 20:16; Deuteronomy 5:20.

⫷ *Deceit.* (DIDACHE 5.1)

"Deceit" or "trickery" (*dolos*, δόλος) is quite common in vice lists.[40] This sin is not directly mentioned in chapter 2 but is similar in theme and content to what we read in 2.5: "Let not your word be false or empty, but let it be put in practice by action."

"Deceit" is the opposite of the character quality of truth (*emet*, אמת). It betrays the trust of others and seeks quick gain through falsehood. In the end it does not pay off:

> Deceit is a tool we use to achieve quickly things we want. However, its benefits do not last too long. Truth therefore, is the better tool. While it may work slower, what it produces is permanent. (*Otiyot deRebbe Akiva*)[41]

Disciples of Yeshua are to be known for honesty and forthrightness. Deceptiveness, however small, must be far from our lives. Instead we are to walk in the light of truth. The Apostle Peter's disciple Clement writes that "if we follow the way of truth," we will "cast away from us all unrighteousness and iniquity, along with all … deceit."[42]

⫷ *Arrogance, malice, egocentrism.* (DIDACHE 5.1)

"Arrogance" and "malice" can be found in 2.6, and "egocentric" is mentioned in 3.6. These three traits can be grouped together based upon the connection between "arrogance" and "egocentrism." The Epistle of Barnabas adds "willful transgression," referring to someone who brazenly and knowingly sins without fear of consequence.[43]

⫷ *Greed.* (DIDACHE 5.1)

Greed is found in 2.6.

---

40 Mark 7:22; Romans 1:29.
41 from Rabbi Avraham Tzvi Schwartz, "Deceit and Truth," n.p. [cited 02 October 2013]. Online: https://sharings.wordpress.com/2009/05/21/self-growth-keep-smiling-27th-iyar-5769/.
42 1 Clement 35.5.
43 Barnabas 20.1.

◈ *Foul speech.* (DIDACHE 5.1)

Foul speech is discussed in 3.3.

◈ *Jealousy.* (DIDACHE 5.1)

Jealousy is mentioned in 3.2.

◈ *Overconfidence, loftiness.* (DIDACHE 5.1)

Both overconfidence and loftiness are found in 3.9. The Epistle of Barnabas renders this as "overconfidence, loftiness of one's power."[44] The Apostolic Constitutions (7.18) has "haughtiness" (*hepselophrosune*, ὑψηλοφροσύνη) in place of "loftiness."

◈ *And pretension.* (DIDACHE 5.1)

This is the last of the vices of 5.1. "Pretension" (*alazoneia*, ἀλαζονεία), which refers to the sin of boastfulness, is the only evil in this list not mentioned previously in the Didache. It does, however, appear frequently in vice lists found in other works.[45]

Pretension stands in complete opposition to the character trait of humility (*anavah*) and is directly connected to the character trait of pride (*ga'avah*). James addresses this sin in his epistle: "You boast in your arrogance [*alazoneia*]. All such boasting is evil" (4:16). The Apostle John also links "pretension" with the desires of the world: "All that is in the world—the desires of the flesh and the desires of the eyes and pride [*alazoneia*] of life—is not from the Father but is from the world" (1 John 2:16).

As believers in Yeshua, we are to be humble in our self-accounting, much like the tax-collector in the Master's parable who prayed, "God, be merciful to me, a sinner!"[46] We should approach God with humility, in the spirit of the self-effacing confession of synagogue liturgy: "What are we? What is our life? What is our devotion? What are our righteous acts? … What can we say before You, O LORD, our

---

44 Ibid.
45 E.g., Romans 1:30; 1 Clement 35.5; Shepherd of Hermas, Mandates 6.2.5 (36.5), 8.5 (38.5). "Pretension" is frequently found throughout 1 Clement.
46 Luke 18:13.

God? Are not all the powerful men as if they are nothing before You?" Disciples of the Master must realize that it is only by the grace of his shed blood that we can approach the King of the universe.

[5.1]
And pretension.

This same humility should be true of our interactions with our fellow man. We should not behave boastfully or in pride, seeking praise from men for our deeds. Rather, our words, particularly about ourselves, should be filled with modesty and humility. The Master urges that even our deeds of righteousness should be done in secret.[47] In this manner our treasure and reward will be with our Father in heaven.

At the end of this first section, the Epistle of Barnabas adds "irreverence of God."[48] This appears not just to be an additional evil trait but a summary of all the wicked character flaws that have been listed. All these traits can be linked back to a lack of the fear of the Lord. Reward and punishment are fundamental concepts in Judaism and find their full expression in the concept of the fear of God. Without the fear of God, one has no motivation to follow his ways.

[The Way of Death is] the way of those who persecute good.
(DIDACHE 5.2)

The Didache now switches from listing evil traits to listing evildoers. It begins with "those who persecute good." These are people who mock and seek to destroy that which is righteous.[49]

The Master warned his followers that they would be persecuted for his name's sake: "Remember the word that I said to you: 'A servant is not greater than his master.' If they persecuted me, they will also persecute you. If they kept my word, they will also keep yours" (John 15:20). When persecution came, the disciples were to consider themselves blessed and were to pray for their persecutors.[50]

The Apostle Peter's disciple Clement gives an account of "those who persecute good": "The righteous were indeed persecuted, but only by the wicked. They were cast into prison, but only by the unholy; they were stoned, but only by transgressors; they were slain, but only by the accursed, and such as had conceived an unrighteous envy against them."[51]

---

47   Matthew 6:1–6.
48   Barnabas 20.1. The Apostolic Constitutions (20.1) simply has "irreverence" (*aphobia*, ἀφοβία).
49   The Georgian version of the Didache has, "All these things are done by those who persecute good."
50   Matthew 5:11, 44, 10:23, 23:34; Luke 21:12. Cf. Romans 12:14.
51   1 Clement 45.4.

◈ *Those who hate truth; those who love falsehood.* (DIDACHE 5.2)

The description of these two evildoers forms a type of Hebrew parallelism that uses antithetical word pairs in which the second line expresses the same idea as the first, for example, hate good/love evil.[52] This dovetails with the previous type of evildoer, "those who persecute good," since those who hate truth and love falsehood are hostile toward righteousness and drawn toward wickedness.

Similar themes are expressed throughout the Scriptures: "How long will you love vain words and seek after lies?" and, "Outside are the dogs and sorcerers and the sexually immoral and murderers and idolaters, and everyone who loves and practices falsehood."[53] Followers of the Master, conversely, are expected to be people who hate evil and love what is good. The Apostle Paul speaks of the wicked as those who "refused to love the truth and so be saved."[54]

The Prophet Zechariah urges:

> These are the things that you shall do: Speak the truth to one another; render in your gates judgments that are true and make for peace; do not devise evil in your hearts against one another, and love no false oath, for all these things I hate, declares the LORD ... Therefore love truth and peace.[55]

To love truth is to love God, for God is truth. We find in *Orchot Tzaddikim*, "There is no falsehood above, in the place of the Holy of Holies, but all is truth, as it is written [Jeremiah 10:10]: 'And HaShem God is truth.'"[56] In order for us to maintain a close relationship with our Father in heaven, we need to remain in truth, for falsehood and deception cannot stand in his presence.

---

52 This is called *parallelismus membrorum*. For a complete study on parallelism as it relates to Hebrew poetry, see Wilfred G.E. Watson, *Classical Hebrew Poetry: A Guide to Its Techniques* (Sheffield, England: JSOT, 1986), 114–159.
53 Psalm 4:2; Revelation 22:15. Cf. Isaiah 59:4.
54 2 Thessalonians 2:10.
55 Zechariah 8:16–19.
56 Rabbi Zaloshinsky, *The Ways of the Tzaddikim*, 2:396. In rabbinic literature "truth" (*emet*, אמת) is one of the names for God. See A. Marmorstein, *The Old Rabbinic Doctrine of God* (New York, NY: KTAV, 1968), 73.

◈ *Those who are ignorant of the wages of righteousness.*
(DIDACHE 5.2)

The wicked practice wickedness because they do not possess the fear of the Lord; in other words, they fail to understand that God rewards righteousness and that he punishes sin as well. The wages of righteousness are blessing and life, but "the wages of sin is death."[57] One heavenly reward for righteousness, that for giving charity, was discussed in 4.7. The Apostolic Constitutions (7.18) generalizes this to "ignorant of righteousness."

Our Master Yeshua teaches that there is reward for acts of righteousness: for being persecuted on his account, for loving one's enemies, for giving to the needy, for praying and fasting in secret, and for receiving one of his followers, whether they be great or small.[58] He tells his disciples, "Love your enemies, and do good, and lend, expecting nothing in return, and your reward will be great, and you will be sons of the Most High" (Luke 6:35). It is the Master himself who will come and bring reward in kind: "Behold, I am coming soon, bringing my recompense with me, to repay each one for what he has done" (Revelation 22:12).

The sages taught that God is faithful to reward righteous behavior, partially in this world, but primarily in the World to Come.[59] In this world the reward for keeping a commandment is the opportunity to keep another commandment and lay up more reward in heaven, but "the wages of sin is death."[60]

◈ *Those who do not cling to what is good or to righteous judgment.* (DIDACHE 5.2)

The Apostolic Constitutions (7.18) renders this, "They who do such things do not cling to what is good or to righteous judgment." This stands in contrast to 4.2, in which disciples are told to "every day seek the presence of the righteous." "Cling" (*kollao*, κολλάω) is reminiscent of the Jewish concept of *devekut* and is discussed in the commentary to 4.2. When the wicked let go of righteousness and goodness, they instead cling to that which is evil and wicked.[61]

---

57 Romans 6:23.
58 Matthew 5:11–12, 6:1–6, 16–18, 10:41–42; Mark 9:41; Luke 6:22–23, 35. Cf. Luke 23:41.
59 m.*Avot* 2:21.
60 m.*Avot* 4:2; Romans 6:23.
61 Niederwimmer states that this saying is "captive to the Jewish (-Christian) milieu in its phrasing" (*The Didache*, 117).

[5.2]
Those who do not cling to what is good or to righteous judgment.

"Good" here refers to righteous things in general, including upright character traits. It could, additionally, be a circumlocution for the name of God (*Tov*, טוב), a circumlocution that appears in rabbinic literature.[62] Therefore, one who does not cling to "Good" does not cling to "God." In Romans Paul admonishes his audience to "abhor what is evil; hold fast [cleave] to what is good."[63] Likewise, the Testament of Asher urges, "Cleave unto goodness only, for God has his habitation therein, and men desire it."[64]

The Torah commands that the judges "shall judge the people with righteous judgment."[65] In the context of the Didache, "righteous judgment" refers to godly justice both in courts and in everyday life, meaning not judging others' actions too quickly, before all the facts are known, and not being too harsh in our judgment. The Master states, "Do not judge by appearances, but judge with right judgment" (John 7:24). The Epistle of Barnabas interprets "righteous judgment" in light of the care of widows and orphans: "Those who do not cling to what is good or to righteous judgment; those who are not mindful of the widow and orphan."[66]

◆ *Those who keep watch, not for good but for wickedness.*
(DIDACHE 5.2)

The Didache speaks metaphorically of those whose hearts are constantly set on all things evil. These people seem to be looking out and waiting for evil to happen. Ecclesiastes speaks of the "heart" of the sinner as "fully set to do evil."[67] A disciple of Yeshua, conversely, "does not rejoice at wrongdoing, but rejoices with the truth."

The sages warn against "one who lays awake at night," that is, one who spends the evening thinking about wicked thoughts and committing sin.[68] Paul urges us

---

62 This idea is based on Psalm 145:9, "The LORD is good," and Psalm 25:8, "Good and upright is the LORD"; b.*Menachot* 53b; y.*Ta'anit* 2:1; *Genesis Rabbah* 57:2; Marmorstein, *The Old Rabbinic Doctrine of God*, 85–86. See Matthew 19:17; Mark 10:18; Luke 18:19. Additionally, "good" is a name for righteous individuals such as Moses, Joshua, and Israel as a whole (e.g., b.*Menachot* 53b) and is also a name for Messiah (Tzvi Sadan, *The Concealed Light: Names of Messiah in Jewish Sources* [Marshfield, MO: Vine of David, 2012], 98–99).
63 Romans 12:9.
64 Testament of Asher 3:1.
65 Deuteronomy 16:18.
66 Barnabas 20.2.
67 Ecclesiastes 8:11.
68 m.*Avot* 3:4. Kirsopp Lake translates the passage, "Spending wakeful nights not for good but for wickedness" (Lake, *The Apostolic Fathers* [New York, NY: Macmillan, 1912], 319).

instead to watch and remain "alert [awake] with all perseverance, making supplication for all the saints."[69]

⫸ *Those who are far from being considerate and persevering; those who love frivolous things.* (DIDACHE 5.2)

This is directly opposite the character traits enumerated in 3.7–8: humility, patience, and gentleness. The wicked here are insensitive, impatient, and focused on that which is fleeting. The parallel passage in the Epistle of Barnabas reads, "Those who are far, even far-removed, from being considerate and persevering; those who love frivolous things."[70]

The Didache's character trait of being "considerate" speaks of one who selflessly puts the needs of others before himself—a courteous person. In Jewish ethics this character trait is similar to that of deliberation (*metinut*, מתינות). Judaism teaches that one must not get caught up in the emotions of his heart or the desires of his flesh. Instead, we should deliberate before taking action and speaking, careful to be considerate of those around us. *Cheshbon HaNefesh* states, "Let your heart not be precipitate nor your mouth be hasty. Rather, pause several times while speaking or acting so as to deliberate and calm yourself."[71] The Way of Death, on the other hand, is filled with those who "follow after their own heart";[72] by this they are led astray as they put themselves before their fellow. This leads only to "frivolous things."

"Perseverance" is the ability to maintain a steady course toward a goal despite difficulties that one may encounter. This quality is related to the character trait of patience (*savlanut*), which is spoken of in 3.8. To persevere requires patience—not giving up in the face of difficult circumstances and trusting in the providence of God. Patience allows one to endure pain and burdens while maintaining a course toward righteousness. In *Chochmah U'Mussar* we read, "A well-known saying of the wise: 'pain and joy are interlaced with one another'—that is, after pain will come joy and the joy will be much greater than if one hadn't experienced the pain before the joy."[73] This is the Way of Life.

---

69 Ephesians 6:18.
70 Barnabas 20.1.
71 Rabbi Menachem Mendel Levin, *Cheshbon HaNefesh: A Guide to Self-Improvement and Character Refinement* (trans. Rabbi Shraga Silverstein; New York, NY: Feldheim, 1995), 183.
72 Numbers 15:39.
73 from "*Savlanut*—Patience 2," 21, n.p. [cited 3 October 2013]. Online: http://www.mussarleadership.org/pdfs/Savlanut%202.pdf.

[5.2]
Those who are far from being considerate and persevering; those who love frivolous things.

Those who follow the Way of Death give up their pursuit of worthwhile things because the challenges of seeking good prove too difficult for them. Instead they set their eyes on the quick gains of "frivolous things," which they love. The psalmist declares, "O men, how long shall my honor be turned into shame? How long will you love vain words and seek after lies?" (Psalm 4:2). In the end frivolity proves fleeting, but the righteous hold on to true treasures that are eternal in nature.

The second half of this part of verse 2, "those who love frivolous things," may be a midrashic-style combination of two passages from the Septuagint version of the Psalms and Proverbs: "Wherefore do you love vanity, and seek falsehood?" (Psalm 4:2) and, "They that pursue vanities are void of understanding" (Proverbs 12:11).

◈ *Those who seek repayment.* (DIDACHE 5.2)

Most scholars interpret this phrase as referring to individuals who seek to be rewarded for their good deeds. Earlier in verse 2 the Didache speaks of "those who are ignorant of the wages of righteousness." It may be that the Didache is midrashically citing the Septuagint again: "Your princes are rebellious ... seeking after rewards."[74] Similarly, the sages warn of the danger of those who serve God only for reward: "Be not like servants who minister unto their master for the sake of receiving a reward, but be like servants who serve their master not upon the condition of receiving a reward."[75] The Master likewise states, "When you have done all that you were commanded, say, "We are unworthy servants; we have only done what was our duty" (Luke 17:10).

Yet it might be better to interpret this phrase in light of 1.4, where the Didache commands disciples of Yeshua, "Restrain yourselves from natural and physical inclinations," and tells them to turn the other cheek:

> If someone strikes you on the right cheek, turn the other to him, and you will be complete. If someone forces you to go one mile, go with him two. If someone takes away your cloak, give him your tunic also. If someone takes away what is yours, do not demand it back, for you are not even able to get it back.

---

74 Isaiah 1:23.
75 m.*Avot* 1:3.

New Gentile believers are commanded not to retaliate or demand repayment for wrong done to them but instead to return evil with good. "Those who seek repayment" are the wicked who try to retaliate and who demand justice for every insult and wrong done to them. The Master tells us, "Do not resist the one who is evil" (Matthew 5:39). This is in line with the Torah's injunction: "You shall not take vengeance or bear a grudge" (Leviticus 19:18).

[5.2]
Those who seek repayment.

"Those who seek repayment" can relate as well to those who seek repayment for charity. We read in 1.5, "Give to whoever asks, and do not demand it back." The way of evil is to loan money or give charity to the needy and then demand repayment. As it says in Sirach, "Today he lends, tomorrow he will demand it back; hateful is such a one" (20:15).

The sages combined these interpretations and taught that the ultimate remedy for this current exile as we long for the arrival of the Messianic Kingdom is to go "beyond the letter of the law" (*lifnim m'shurat hadin*, לפנים משורת הדין) and serve God merely out of love:

> Concerning those who are insulted but do not insult others [in revenge], who hear themselves reproached without replying, who [perform good] work out of love of the Lord and rejoice in their sufferings, Scripture says: "But they that love Him be as the sun when he goes forth in his might [Judges 5:31]." (b.*Yoma* 23a)

The Talmud adds, "There are three whom the Holy One, blessed is he, loves: one who does not get angry; one who does not get drunk; and one who does not insist on his due measure."[76]

⁌ *Those who are merciless to the poor; those who do not trouble themselves for the oppressed.* (DIDACHE 5.2)

The Didache here uses Hebrew parallelism again to stress the wickedness of ignoring the needy and disenfranchised.[77] Those who are on the path of evil ignore the needs of the poor and oppressed. The obligation to give charity has already been addressed in 1.5 and 4.6–8. The true disciple of the Master will tend to those who

---

76 b.*Pesachim* 113b.
77 The Georgian version of the Didache states, "Those who are not compassionate toward the needy and sick."

[5.2] *Those who are merciless to the poor; those who do not trouble themselves for the oppressed.*

are in need. The *Doctrina* reads, "Those without mercy for the poor; those not grieving for one who is grieved."[78]

"Those who are merciless to the poor" are criticized throughout the book of Proverbs and contrasted against those who take care of the needy.[79] For example, "Whoever despises his neighbor is a sinner, but blessed is he who is generous to the poor" (Proverbs 14:21), and, "Whoever oppresses a poor man insults his Maker, but he who is generous to the needy honors him" (Proverbs 14:31).[80]

God is known as the one "who executes justice for the oppressed, who gives food to the hungry" (Psalm 146:7). Likewise Isaiah, in the passage that our Master Yeshua read in the synagogue in Nazareth, declares that God has anointed the Messiah "to bring good news to the poor … and the opening of the prison to those who are [oppressed]" (Isaiah 61:1). He also speaks of the true fast, which means "to let the oppressed go free, and … to share your bread with the hungry and bring the homeless poor into your house" (Isaiah 58:6–7). Unlike those who follow the Way of Death, we are to imitate our Father in heaven and his Son Yeshua by caring for the poor and meeting the needs of the oppressed.

To ignore the downtrodden is to ignore the Master, and to meet their needs is to meet the needs of the Master:

> I was hungry and you gave me food, I was thirsty and you gave me drink, I was a stranger and you welcomed me, I was naked and you clothed me, I was sick and you visited me, I was in prison and you came to me … Truly, I say to you, as you did it to one of the least of these my brothers, you did it to me. (Matthew 25:35–40)

The Epistle of Barnabas adds, "Those who are prone to slander" (20.2). This ties in the Way of Death with the speech prohibitions of Didache 2:3–5.

⁌ *Those who do not recognize the one who made them.*
(DIDACHE 5.2)

The Didache now describes those who wickedly follow the Way of Death as people who have forgotten God completely.[81] This harkens back to 1.2: "You shall love God

---

78   *Doctrina* 5.2.
79   Niederwimmer, *The Didache*, 117.
80   Cf. Proverbs 19:17, 22:9, 28:8.
81   Niederwimmer, *The Didache*, 117.

who made you." The wicked do not love God; more than that, they have completely removed him from their minds. One who forgets his Maker also forgets his brother, as we saw with the previous evildoer listed in this verse. But Proverbs reminds us that the rich and poor are of equal worth: "The rich and the poor meet together; the LORD is the maker of them all" (Proverbs 22:2).

[5.2] Those who do not recognize the one who made them.

A similar lament appears in the apocryphal book Wisdom of Solomon: "He knew not his Maker, and him that inspired into him an active soul, and breathed in him a living spirit."[82] The book of Hosea connects grievous sin with a lack of knowledge of God: "Their deeds do not permit them to return to their God. For the spirit of whoredom is within them, and they know not the LORD" (Hosea 5:4).

The Apostle Paul tells us that those who do not recognize the Creator are without pardon: "For his invisible attributes, namely, his eternal power and divine nature, have been clearly perceived, ever since the creation of the world, in the things that have been made. So they are without excuse" (Romans 1:20). As disciples of Yeshua, we should constantly acknowledge our Father in heaven.

While the context of the Didache's words here is most likely that of idolators, they equally apply to atheists, who are much more prevalent today. The sages combine both heresies in their exegesis of the *Shma*:

> It has been taught: "After your own heart" [Numbers 15:29]: this refers to atheism; and so it says, "The fool has said in his heart, 'There is no God'" [Psalms 14:1] ... "which you are inclined to whore after" [Numbers 15:29]: this refers to the hankering after idolatry; and so it says, "And they went astray after the Baalim" [Judges 8:33]. (b.*Brachot* 12b)

In Jewish tradition atheists are worse off than idolators. The late Lubavitcher Rebbe Menachem Mendel Schneerson writes:

> The atheist, too, has a god, and it is himself. The idolater at least understands there is something greater than him, something beyond the grasp of his physical senses, some external forces to which he is subject. But for the atheist, all the universe is defined by his own understanding, all ethics are subject to his approval, and even he himself is an artifact of his own mind. He is a self-made man, for he creates his own universe and squeezes himself inside it.[83]

---

82 Wisdom of Solomon 15:11.
83 Rabbi Tzvi Freedman, *Bringing Heaven Down to Earth: Book Two* (Lavergne, TN: CreateSpace, 2012), 334.

- *Those who murder children; those who corrupt what God has formed.* (DIDACHE 5.2)

This is a clear reference to infanticide and abortion. Unborn and newborn innocent children are perfect representations of the "poor" and "oppressed" mentioned above. Both of these are mentioned in 2.2: "You shall not murder children through infanticide; nor shall you murder them after having been born." A similar sentiment is expressed in the Wisdom of Solomon, describing "merciless murderers of children, and devourers of man's flesh, and the feasts of blood."[84]

"Those who corrupt what God has formed" connects back to the previous evildoers: "those who do not recognize the one who made them," and both of these statements connect back to "You shall love God who made you" (1.2). Because the wicked do not recognize that it is God who formed and created human beings, they have no reservations about destroying his workmanship. In turn, a lack of the acknowledgement of God in one's life leads to devaluing the sanctity of life.

- *Those who turn away the needy; those who oppress the greatly distressed.* (DIDACHE 5.2)

Here we see another Hebrew parallelism that expresses an evildoer similar to another described earlier in this verse: "Those who are merciless to the poor; those who do not trouble themselves for the oppressed."[85]

Turning away from the needy and oppressed is a behavior addressed often in the Hebrew Scriptures: "Whoever oppresses the poor to increase his own wealth, or gives to the rich, will only come to poverty" (Proverbs 22:16).[86] In fact, this was the sin of Sodom and Gomorrah as described by the Prophet Ezekiel: "She and her daughters had pride, excess of food, and prosperous ease, but did not aid the poor and needy" (Ezekiel 16:49). The Master teaches:

> I was hungry and you gave me food, I was thirsty and you gave me drink, I was a stranger and you welcomed me, I was naked and you

---

84   Wisdom of Solomon 12:5.
85   The *Doctrina* renders this, "Those who turn away from good works; who oppress the greatly distressed" (5.2). "Good works" could go back to the Hebrew *tzedakah* ("righteousness," צדקה), which is idiomatically used for "charity."
86   Cf. Ezekiel 18:12, 22:29; War Scroll (1QM) XI, 13–14.

clothed me, I was sick and you visited me, I was in prison and you came to me. (Matthew 25:35–36)

[5.2]
Those who turn away the needy; those who oppress the greatly distressed.

When a disciple of Yeshua passively turns away from the needy and oppressed, it is tantamount to turning away from Messiah. In the same way, if we actively "oppress the greatly distressed," it is as if we are oppressing Yeshua.

⁂ *Advocates of the wealthy; and lawless judges of the poor.*
(DIDACHE 5.2)

Here another parallel statement continues on the previous theme.[87] The language in this phrase is reminiscent of "the prophetic style of cursing."[88] In this example of an evildoer, the sin of ignoring the poor and oppressed is amplified by corruptly championing the cause of the rich against those who are in need. These evildoers are described as *anomia* ("lawless," ἀνομία)—lacking in Torah. They are lawless in that they have not followed the Torah's commandment to practice "righteous judgment."[89] The Master says to those who are lawless, "Depart from me ... I never knew you."[90]

Patrick Hartin points out the irony here:

> The phrase ["advocates of the wealthy"] is ironic since the word ["advocate"] refers to how someone acts on behalf of another. They should in fact be supporting the poor in the spirit of the Hebrew Scriptures as well as of Jesus. Instead, they support the rich.[91]

The Torah warns that justice should be served by judges in all situations: "You shall do no injustice in court. You shall not be partial to the poor or defer to the great, but in righteousness shall you judge your neighbor" (Leviticus 19:15).[92]

Being an advocate of the wealthy falls under the character trait of flattery (*chanifut*, חניפות). "Flattery" in Jewish teaching takes on various forms: Keeping

---

87 The *Doctrina* says, "Those who avoid advocating for the upright" (5.2).
88 Niederwimmer, *The Didache*, 118.
89 Deuteronomy 16:18.
90 Matthew 7:23.
91 Patrick J. Hartin, "Ethics in the Letter of James, the Gospel of Matthew, and the Didache: Their Place in Early Christian Literature," in *Matthew, James, and Didache: Three Related Documents in their Jewish and Christian Settings* (ed. Huub van de Sandt and Jürgen K. Zangenberg; Atlanta, GA: Society of Biblical Literature, 2008), 307.
92 Cf. Isaiah 11:4.

[5.2]
Advocates of the wealthy; and lawless judges of the poor.

company with slanderers is one; being in a position to stand up for righteousness but not doing so out of fear is another. One of the worst forms of flattery can be seen when we "recognize someone as wicked and deceitful, as spreading evil reports about the innocent, and stealing from others," yet instead of rebuking the person, we praise him, telling him that he has committed no wrongdoing.[93] "Advocates of the wealthy" practice this type of flattery in order to gain wealth and prestige, even at the expense of justice for others. Proverbs speaks against this type of flatterer: "He who justifies the wicked and he who condemns the righteous are both alike an abomination to the LORD" (Proverbs 17:15).

◈ *Those who are utterly sinful.* (DIDACHE 5.2)

Those who pursue the Way of Death are filled with an abundance of wickedness. There is no righteousness or life in them. The Greek word for "utterly sinful" (*panthamartetoi*, πανθαμάρτητοι) is rare and found elsewhere only in the Apostolic Constitutions and the Epistle of Barnabas.[94]

◈ *Children, may you be rescued from all of these!* (DIDACHE 5.2)

The final line of chapter 5 serves as both a summary statement and a prayer.[95] It is reminiscent of the Master's prayer: "Lead us not into temptation, but deliver us from evil" (Matthew 6:13). Just as the author of the Didache shudders at the thought of these sins and sinners, so should we, as we read his words, desire to be saved from such wickedness.[96]

---

93 Rabbi Zaloshinsky, *The Ways of the Tzaddikim*, 2:409.
94 Apostolic Constitutions 7.18; Barnabas 20. A similar word is found in 2 Clement 18.2.
95 The *Doctrina* says, "Children, rescue yourselves from all of these." The Georgian version of the Didache says, "Keep us away, O Son of God, from all those who are not walking in this way."
96 Marcello del Verme notes that "the presence of the term *tekna* (vocative plural, "oh sons") allows us to establish a parallel with the genre of the 'testaments'" (Del Verme, *Didache and Judaism: Jewish Roots of an Ancient Christian-Jewish Work* [New York, NY: T&T Clark, 2004], 2440). The Testament of the Twelve Patriarchs uses the phrase "my children" throughout, and this also gives us a connection with the *teknon* sayings of chapter 3.

Chapter Six

DIDACHE 6

6.1 See that no one leads you astray[1] from this way of teaching, because he does not teach you according to God.

6.2 If you can bear the whole yoke of the Lord, you will be complete;[2] but if you cannot, then do what you can.

6.3 Concerning food, bear what you can, but scrupulously guard yourself from what has been offered to idols,[3] because it is the worship of dead gods.

---

1 Matthew 24:4; Mark 13:5; Luke 21:8.
2 Matthew 5:48, 19:21.
3 Acts 15:20, 29, 21:25.

Overview

Chapter 6 is the shortest chapter of the Didache. It serves as a bridge and a segue from the Two Ways section to the ritual and community instructions that make up the rest of the work. This also marks the end of the parallels with the Epistle of Barnabas, and only 6.1 finds a parallel in the *Doctrina*.

A clear change in the Didache's grammar is seen beginning in this chapter. In chapters 1 through 5, the words "you shall" appear in the second-personal singular form, but in chapter 6 the Didache switches primarily to the second-personal plural.[4] This switch seems to indicate a shift in focus from individualized instruction to more community-oriented teaching, which we find in the remaining chapters.

As chapter 6 closes out the Two Ways section, it harkens back to the book's opening chapter. "Teaching" is mentioned in 6.1 for the first time since 1.3. Being "perfect" is mentioned in 1.4 and here in 6.2. Additionally, the term "yoke of the Lord" in chapter 6 may allude back to 1.2, in which love of God and love of neighbor are mentioned as the central tenets of the Way of Life. The Master summed up the entire Torah (which is "the yoke of the Lord") as comprising these two commandments.[5]

Acts 15

David Flusser and Huub van de Sandt feel that the content of chapter 6 represents "some form of a common, widespread, and authoritative instruction, circulating in early Christian communities" similar to the Apostolic Decree in Acts 15.[6] Taking this a step further, some correlation can be established between Didache 6 and Acts 15, as if the author of the Didache had the ruling of the Apostolic Decree in mind and intentionally attempted to elucidate it in chapter 6. Both texts deal with the subject of the Gentile believer's relationship to the Torah. Notice the following similarities in content:

---

4   With the exception of 6.2–3, 7.2–4, 13.3, 5–7.
5   Matthew 22:37–39; Mark 12:30–31; Luke 10:27.
6   Huub van de Sandt and David Flusser, *The Didache: Its Jewish Sources and Its Place in Early Judaism and Christianity* (Minneapolis, MN: Fortress, 2002), 242.

Acts 15	Didache 6
We have heard that some persons have gone out from us and troubled you with words, unsettling your minds, although we gave them no instructions. (15:24)	See that no one leads you astray from this way of teaching because he does not teach you according to God. (6.1)
Now, therefore, why are you putting God to the test by placing *a yoke* on the neck of the disciples that neither our fathers nor we have been able *to bear*? (15:10)	If you can *bear the whole yoke of the Lord*, you will be complete; but if you cannot, then do what you can. (6.2)
For it has seemed good to the Holy Spirit and to us to lay on you no greater burden than these requirements: that you abstain *from what has been [offered] to idols*. (15:28–29)	Concerning food, bear what you can, but scrupulously guard yourself *from what has been offered to idols* because it is the worship of dead gods. (6.3)

Didache 6.1 opens the chapter with a warning against those who lead disciples astray with false teachings. The main issue in Acts 15 likewise concerns those who had spread unauthorized instructions and caused confusion among the believers.

Verse 2 of chapter 6 deals with Gentile believers and their ability or inability to "bear the whole yoke of the Lord." In Acts 15 the apostles similarly felt that placing the full yoke of the Torah upon the Gentile believers as a requisite of discipleship was too much for them to "bear." An additional similarity between the Didache and the Apostolic Decree is that both bind Gentile believers to the prohibition of food sacrificed to idols:

> A number of scholars who have commented upon Didache 6 have noted the possible association of the chapter with the Apostolic Decree of Acts 15 … The style of the Didache as it reflects upon these three themes is by no means polemical or emphatic, but it is merely a brief comment upon what presumably is authoritative for the readers of the

text. It is not difficult to envision that the Apostolic Decree served as that community standard upon which Didache 6 was composed.[7]

Furthermore, the entire instruction of the Didache is the natural outworking of the ruling of the Jerusalem Council in Acts chapter 15.

Torah for Gentiles

Jewish believers, even after coming to faith in Messiah, were to continue in their full covenantal responsibility toward the Torah and its commandments. On the other hand, at the Jerusalem Council the apostles decided that they would "not trouble those of the Gentiles who turn to God" by requiring them to legally convert to Judaism and, in turn, bear the full yoke of Torah as Jews. Instead, the Gentile believers were given four prohibitions: they were to avoid idolatry, sexual immorality, things strangled, and blood:[8]

> Therefore my judgment is that we should not trouble those of the Gentiles who turn to God, but should write to them to abstain from the things polluted by idols, and from sexual immorality, and from what has been strangled, and from blood. (Acts 15:19–20)

However, these prohibitions were not to be considered the upper limit of Torah observance. Paul and the rest of the apostles laid out many other commandments and instructions for Gentiles throughout the New Testament.[9] Flusser writes,

> The Noachide precepts were only seen as the minimal condition for Gentiles to be recognized as God-fearers. They were so understood by the God-fearers themselves, who were attracted by the Jewish way of life and accepted many Jewish commandments without becoming full proselytes. This was the attitude of many Christian God-fearers

---

[7] Clayton N. Jefford, *The Sayings of Jesus in the Teaching of the Twelve Apostles* (New York, NY: Brill, 1989), 96–97. Cf. Charles Taylor, "The Teaching of the Twelve Apostles with Illustrations from the Talmud," in *Didache: The Unknown Teaching of the Apostles* (ed. Brent S. Walters; San Jose, CA: Anti-Nicene Archive, 1991), 170–171.

[8] Acts 15:20, 29, 21:25. Cf. "Keep yourselves from the religion of demons and from gods, and from dead things keep, and from blood and things strangled, and further, a bone shall not be broken. But concerning Apostles and Prophets according to the ordinance of the Gospel you shall do" (*The Statutes of the Apostles* 52).

[9] See Toby Janicki, *God-Fearers: Gentiles & the God of Israel* (Marshfield, MO: First Fruits of Zion, 2012), 49–72.

... many of which wished to observe as many Jewish precepts as they could. It is evident that, while the leadership of the Mother Church decided to lay no burden upon the Gentile believers beyond the Noachide precepts ... it did not object to their voluntarily observing more.[10]

The fourth-century Jewish-Christian Clementine literature of the prohibitions of Acts 15:

Be this therefore the first step to you of three; which step brings forth thirty commands, and the second sixty, and the third a hundred, as we shall expound more fully to you at another time. (Pseudo-Clementine Recognitions 4.36)

The four prohibitions of the Apostolic Decree (Acts 15) set a minimum standard for non-Jews within the Messianic community that went beyond the minimums proscribed by the Noachide commandments. The Didache pushes the standard even further. The Didache seems to encourage Gentile believers to move beyond the seven Noachide laws and four apostolic decrees and to embrace as much of the Torah's lifestyle as they are able. It encourages its audience to move toward embracing "the whole yoke of the Lord" but then graciously concedes that if they are not able, they should do what they can. Jonathan Draper writes that "since the Didache is directed to gentiles, the performance of Torah is not an obligation but a goal towards which one should strive."[11]

Dietary Restrictions

Three of the four prohibitions of the Jerusalem Council are dietary in nature, so it is not surprising that chapter 6 of the Didache addresses dietary laws. The first prohibition, eating food contaminated by idols, is the only one from Acts 15 also mentioned directly in the Didache. In 6.3, this prohibition is established as the bare minimum of dietary restrictions for Gentiles, to which it adds, "Concerning food, bear what you can."

The remaining two dietary prohibitions of the Apostolic Decree, avoiding strangled meat and blood, are not mentioned in the Didache. Both commandments

---

10 David Flusser, *Judaism and the Origins of Christianity* (Jerusalem, Israel: Magnes, 1988), 630.
11 Jonathan A. Draper, "Do the Didache and Matthew Reflect an 'Irrevocable Parting of the Ways' with Judaism?" in *Matthew and the Didache: Two Documents from the Same Jewish-Christian Milieu?* (ed. Huub van de Sandt; Minneapolis, MN: Fortress, 2005), 229.

deal with the same issue: the kosher slaughter of meat.¹² The first, abstinence from "what is strangled," refers to meat that has been improperly slaughtered. The second prohibition, to refrain from consuming blood, is connected to the prohibition on strangulation.¹³ Without proper method of slaughter, Jewish law considers the lifeblood to remain in the meat of the animal.

In the Torah the prohibition against consuming blood is universal. The commandment was initially given to Noah when God first permitted him to eat meat: "Every moving thing that lives shall be food for you. And as I gave you the green plants, I give you everything. But you shall not eat flesh with its life, that is, its blood" (Genesis 9:3–4).¹⁴ It is reiterated for Israel and also for the stranger who dwells in their midst: "No person among you shall eat blood, neither shall any stranger who sojourns among you eat blood" (Leviticus 17:12).¹⁵

Ample evidence points to the fact that Gentile believers observed the prohibitions on blood and things strangled beyond the Apostolic Era. In his apologetic work *Octavius*, Minucius Felix (160–250 CE) responds to those who accuse Christians of drinking human blood by saying, "We do not use the blood even of eatable animals in our food" (30.6).¹⁶ Oskar Skarsaune finds evidence in early church literature that Christians in Gaul (present-day France) at the end of the second century still purchased kosher-slaughtered meat even after the church had begun severing its ties from Judaism:

> Under torture, a girl named Biblias in a sudden burst of indignation said, "How can those eat children, who are forbidden to eat the blood

---

12   See Aaron Eby, *Biblically Kosher: A Messianic Jewish Perspective on Kashrut* (Marshfield, MO: First Fruits of Zion, 2012), 79–83.
13   m.*Chullin* 1:2.
14   Although rabbinic interpretation sees Genesis 9:4 as a prohibition against eating the flesh of a living animal (*ever min ha-chai*, אבר מן החי), both Ibn Ezra and the Ramban interpret this as referring to the prohibition of consuming blood. While Rebbe Nachman of Breslov would certainly have adhered to the talmudic interpretation of Genesis 9:4, it is interesting that in his *Likkutei Halachot* he interprets it on a *peshat* level: "Thus, from Noah's time onward mankind was permitted to eat meat—as long as the animal had undergone kosher slaughter, which brings about a rectification" (*Rebbe Nachman's Torah: Genesis* [ed. Y. Hall; New York, NY: Breslov Research Institute, 2011], 143).
15   At least one rabbinic source makes the observance of the precept of kosher-slaughtered meat the marker for the *ger toshav* ("resident proselyte," גר תושב): "What is a 'resident proselyte'? Whoever undertakes to abstain from idolatry, in the view of Rabbi Meir; Rabbi Judah said: Whoever undertakes not to eat meat that has not been ritually slaughtered" (*Gerim* 3:1 [61a]). Eating blood is also spoken against in the universal Jewish work Pseudo-Phocylides 31, "Do not eat blood; abstain from what is sacrificed to idols," although most scholars feel this verse is an interpolation. Philo refers to eating meat with blood still in it as "injurious and likely to cause disease" (*On the Special Laws* 4.119).
16   Cf. A.M. Harmon, trans., *Lucian* (8 vols.; Cambridge, MA: Harvard University Press, 1936), 5:18.

even of brute beasts?" This clearly indicates that the community of Lyons [France] still observed the apostolic decree of Acts 15 concerning kosher meat. As Frend aptly remarks, "The question arises, where did the Christians get their meat from? The only possible answer is, from a kosher market established for the Jews, and this in turn indicates fairly close personal relations between the Jews and Christians in the City."[17]

The third-century church father Origen gives instructions on the apostolic dietary prohibitions in his writings,[18] and we even find a passage from Jerome (fourth century) in which he is concerned about the proper slaughter of certain birds.[19]

Given the universal application of the prohibition against blood in the Scriptures and the history of its observance in the early church, it is curious that the Didache completely omits it.

Significantly, the prohibition is mentioned in the section of the Didache preserved in *The Ethiopic Church Order*:

> Keep yourselves from the religion of demons and from gods, and from dead things keep, and from blood and things strangled, and further, a bone shall not be broken.[20]

We also find it in the Apostolic Constitutions' version of Didache 6:

> Concerning food, the Lord says to you, "You shall eat the good things of the earth" [Isaiah 1:19], and, "All sorts of flesh shall you eat, as the green herb" [Genesis 9:3]; but, "You shall pour out the blood" [Deuteronomy 15:23]. (Apostolic Constitutions 7.20)

---

17 Oskar Skarsaune, *In the Shadow of the Temple: Jewish Influences on Early Christianity* (Downers Grove, IL: InterVarsity Press, 2002), 239.
18 *Contra Celsum* 8.30. Cf. 8.24.
19 Peter J. Tomson, *Paul and the Jewish Law: Halakha in the Letters of the Apostle to the Gentiles* (Minneapolis, MN: Fortress, 1990), 184. The pseudepigraphical Clementine literature (written by Jewish followers of Yeshua in the second century) says that non-Jews, in their service of God, were "to abstain from the table of devils, that is, from food offered to idols, from dead carcasses, from animals which have been suffocated or caught by wild beasts, and from blood" (Pseudo-Clementine Homilies 7.8. Cf. Pseudo-Clementine Recognitions 4.36).
20 G.W. Horner, *The Statutes of the Apostles or Canones Ecclesiastici* (London, England: Williams & Norgate, 1904), 193.3–6. "Because this section immediately precedes the two distinct extracts of Didache 11.3–13.7 and Didache 8.1–2a, it presumably was incorporated here in association with Didache 6.2–3. There is a strong possibility, then, that the translator of the Didache or tradition which preserved Didache 6.2–3 until its into Ethiopic, has connected this passage with the wording of the Decree in Acts 15" (Van de Sandt and Flusser, *The Didache*, 243).

These passages prove that despite the omission of this prohibition in the Didache, the communities that continued in the Didache's instructions adhered to the prohibitions against consuming blood and things strangled. It is highly unlikely that a fourth-century church document such as the Apostolic Constitutions would have created such a thoroughly Jewish prohibition in its reworking of the Didache, let alone cited a proof text from the Torah to support its observance. Evidence rather points to the fact that the original version of the Didache most likely included both the Apostolic Decree's prohibitions of blood and of things strangled. It may have been subsequently removed by a later Christian copyist who might have viewed the commandment to eat only kosher-slaughtered meat as too cumbersome in non-Jewish contexts or no longer applicable.

Commentary

> ※ *See that no one leads you astray from this way of teaching because he does not teach you according to God.* (DIDACHE 6.1)

The Didache begins chapter 6 with a warning against false teachers who lead people away from God and the Way of Life.[21] This is a continuation of the exhortation at the end of 5.2: "Children, may you be rescued from all of these!" All that has been taught so far is to be carefully guarded, and new Gentile disciples are to watch out for those who would lead them astray from the Way of Life.

This warning is reminiscent of Deuteronomy 11:

> Take care lest your heart be deceived, and you turn aside and serve other gods and worship them ... I am setting before you today a blessing and a curse: ... the curse, if you do not obey the commandments of the LORD your God, but turn aside from the way that I am commanding you today, to go after other gods that you have not known. (Deuteronomy 11:16, 26, 28)

Deuteronomy speaks of being deceived to the point that one worships "other gods." Similarly to this Deuteronomy passage, Didache 6 begins with a warning about being led astray and ends with strong warnings against food offered to idols (idolatry).

The Apostolic Constitutions cites a proof text from Deuteronomy 5:

> See that no one leads you astray from piety; for he says: "You may not turn aside from it to the right hand, or to the left, that you may have understanding in all that you do" [Deuteronomy 5:32]. For if you do not turn out of the right way, you will not be ungodly. (Apostolic Constitutions 7.19)[22]

---

21   In the Georgian version of the Didache, chapter 6 begins with "Walk now."
22   The Apostolic Constitutions seems to be quoting a no-longer extant targumic version of Deuteronomy 5:32 that adds "that you may have understanding in all that you do." It could also be that it is midrashically combining Deuteronomy 5:32 with 4:6: "Keep them and do them, for that will be your wisdom and your understanding in the sight of the peoples."

[6.1]
See that no one leads you astray from this way of teaching because he does not teach you according to God.

Draper sees in Didache 6.1 two distinct groups that could have threatened to lead members of the Didache communities "astray from this way of teaching." On one side he observes "Christians depicted as sheep turned to wolves, led astray by the anti-Christ, who wish to lead the community away from its traditional way of teaching which 'breaks down [Torah],'" and on the opposite side "other Jews, labeled as hypocrites."[23] The Odes of Solomon expresses a similar concern:

> And the corrupting of the Corruptor, I saw when the bride who was corrupting was adorned, and the bridegroom who corrupts and is corrupted. And I asked the Truth, Who are these? And He said to me: This is the Deceiver and the Error. And they imitate the Beloved and His Bride, and they cause the world to err and corrupt it. (Odes of Solomon 39:9–11)

The community must seek to preserve the Torah and traditions as handed down by the apostles and must not fall prey to those who said it had been done away with or who sought to impose their own interpretations and variant halachah. In the mind of the Apostle Peter, it would have been better never to have "known the way of righteousness" than to come to the truth and then be led astray.[24]

Several parallel sayings to 6.1 can be found in the New Testament: "Little children, let no one deceive you" (1 John 3:7), and, "Forsaking the right way, they have gone astray" (2 Peter 2:15).[25] Didache 6.1 is very close to Yeshua's saying, "See that no one leads you astray"; as such, it may be that the Didache is drawing from a no-longer-extant teaching of the Master.[26]

Some feel that the end of the *Doctrina* might represent a version of the original ending of the Two Ways section. Indeed, the "language and way of thinking are Jewish or Jewish-Christian."[27] Whether or not this is true, the *Doctrina*'s ending is interesting to note, as the first section parallels Didache 6.1:

> See that no one leads you astray from this teaching; otherwise, you will be taught outside the true instruction. If you do these things daily with

---

23 Draper, "Do the Didache and Matthew Reflect an 'Irrevocable Parting of the Ways' with Judaism?" 219.
24 2 Peter 2:21.
25 E.g., Romans 1:17–18; 1 Corinthians 6:9; 2 Peter 2:21; James 1:16. Cf. Testament of Gad 3:1.
26 Matthew 24:4. Cf. Mark 13:5; Luke 21:8; Jefford, *The Sayings of Jesus in the Teaching of the Twelve Apostles*, 93.
27 Kurt Niederwimmer, *The Didache: Hermeneia—A Historical and Critical Commentary on the Bible* [Minneapolis, MN: Fortress, 1998], 120–121.

reflection,[28] you will be near the Living God, but if you do not do them, you will be far from the truth. Lay up all these things in your mind, and you will not be disappointed in your hope, but through these sacred contests you will attain the crown. (*Doctrina* 6.1–6)[29]

[6.1]
See that no one leads you astray from this way of teaching because he does not teach you according to God.

⁌ *If you can bear the whole yoke of the Lord.* (DIDACHE 6.2)

As the Way of Life section comes to a close, the Didache now speaks more broadly about the full "yoke of the Lord." The Didache did not view its instruction as an end unto itself. This verse alludes to a broader spectrum of teaching that needed to be studied and observed—that of the Hebrew Scriptures and the teachings of Yeshua that had been transmitted through the apostles.

"Lord" here is the Greek word *kurios* (κύριος). In the Didache, as in the New Testament, it refers sometimes to God the Father and other times to the Master, oftentimes making it difficult to decipher the usage, even from the context. Those who interpret "Lord" as God the Father here in 6.2 also point out that "yoke of the Lord" would refer specifically to the Torah.[30] Supporting this is the fact that of the five times the word "yoke" (*zugos*, ζυγός) is used in the New Testament, four of those refer to the Torah.[31] Furthermore, in rabbinic literature the term "yoke" (*ol*, עוֹל) is synonymous with the Torah. For example, "Whoever takes upon himself the yoke of Torah, they remove from him the yoke of government and the yoke of worldly concerns."[32] Another rabbinic phrase synonymous with "yoke of Torah" is "yoke of heaven," in which "heaven" (*shamayim*, שמים) is a circumlocution for the

---

28   Cf. Joshua 1:8: "You shall meditate on it day and night." "The possibility cannot be excluded that *Doctrina* 6:4a originates from Joshua 1:8" (Van de Sandt and Flusser, *The Didache*, 139).
29   Niederwimmer writes that the last section of the *Doctrina*—"through our Master Yeshua the Messiah, who reigns and rules with God the Father and the Holy Spirit forever and ever. Amen"—was added later when this Two Ways source was adapted by the *Doctrina*. See the reconstruction in Joshua Rudder, *The Two Ways: A Lost Early Christian Manual of Personal and Communal Ethics, Discipline and Morality* (Los Angeles, CA: Native Language, 2009), 40–41.
30   Cf. Barnabas 21.1–2, 8. Wim J.C. Weren, "The 'Ideal Community' according to Matthew, James, and the Didache," in *Matthew, James, and Didache. Three Related Documents in their Jewish and Christian Settings* (ed. Huub van de Sandt and Jürgen K. Zangenberg; Atlanta, GA: Society of Biblical Literature, 2008), 186.
31   References to "yoke" in Matthew 11:29–30 (twice), Acts 15:10, and Galatians 5:1 refer to Torah; "yoke" in 1 Timothy 6:1 does not. See Jonathan A. Draper, "Torah and Troublesome Apostles in the Didache Community," *Novum Testamentum* 33, no. 4 (October 1991): 363–364.
32   m.*Avot* 3:5. Cf. 2 Baruch 41:3; Sirach 51:23–28.

[6.2]
If you can bear the whole yoke of the Lord.

Tetragrammaton.³³ Verse 2 then could be seen as a direct parallel to the Didache's "yoke of the Lord," giving further evidence that this phrase refers to the Torah. We also find the rabbinic expression "yoke of him who spoke and the world came into being" in reference to a potential convert to Judaism.³⁴

However, those who interpret "Lord" as referring to Yeshua point to the Master's words: "Take my yoke upon you, and learn from me, for I am gentle and lowly in heart, and you will find rest for your souls. For my yoke is easy, and my burden is light" (Matthew 11:29–30).³⁵ In this light, the "yoke of the Lord" is the "yoke of Yeshua," that is, discipleship.³⁶

Both interpretations of "Lord" have merit, and they are not mutually exclusive. The Master's yoke was not separate from the Torah but rather represented his halachah and interpretations of the Torah. Clayton Jefford writes that the Didache "did not seek to replace the 'yoke of Torah' with the 'yoke of Jesus,' but instead … the Didachist was anxious to weld the two yokes into a single system."³⁷ The "yoke of the Lord," then, is the Torah as it was interpreted by the Master and henceforth his apostles.

⁌ *You will be complete; but if you cannot, then do what you can.* (DIDACHE 6.2)

Gentile disciples are instructed that the "whole yoke of the Lord" is the goal to which they should attain, but the Didache acknowledges that not every Gentile believer will be in a position to accomplish this.³⁸ If Gentile believers are unable to observe the Torah in full, they should do what they are able. Flusser aptly points

---

33 E.g., b.*Sotah* 47b; b.*Sanhedrin* 111b. See Aaron Eby and Toby Janicki, *Hallowed Be Your Name: Sanctifying God's Sacred Name* (Marshfield, MO: First Fruits of Zion, 2008), 29.
34 *Gerim* 1:2 (60a). (Note this line does not appear in all manuscripts.)
35 Cf. Gospel of Thomas 90; "yoke of love" Odes of Solomon 42:6–8; 1 Clement 16.17; Justin, *Dialogue with Trypho* 53.1.
36 "The fact that this document takes so much of its exegetical doctrine on church life from teachings that other first-century Christians attributed to Jesus corroborates the claim that the Didache aims to transmit exegetical doctrine that goes back to the origin of the Christian movement. Draper has argued for interpreting 'the Lord' mentioned in Didache 6.2 as a reference to Jesus' interpretation of the Torah. If he is right, then the whole of Didache 1–6 is thus attributed to Jesus' teaching" (Joseph G. Mueller, "The Ancient Church Order Literature: Genre or Tradition?" *Journal of Early Christian Studies* 15, no. 3 [Fall 2007]: 363).
37 Jefford, *The Sayings of Jesus in the Teaching of the Twelve Apostles*, 102.
38 The Georgian version of the Didache adds, "If only your faith is genuine and sincere, and knows what is good."

out that "an observant Jew does not have the choice mentioned here."[39] The Epistle of Barnabas' Two Ways section has two passages that are similar in content:[40]

[6.2]
You will be complete; but if you cannot, then do what you can.

> Be pure as much as you can for your life's sake. (Barnabas 19.8)

> It is good therefore that he who has learned the ordinances of the Lord as many as have been written should walk in them. For he who does these things shall be glorified in the kingdom of God, but he who chooses the others shall perish with his works. For this reason there will be resurrections, for this reason there is a recompense. (Barnabas 21.1)

It is possible that some of the language of this verse in the Didache finds its roots in instructions given to the God-fearers in the synagogue.[41] These were Gentiles who had attached themselves to Judaism on various levels without converting. Their Torah observance, which usually went beyond the moral commandments, was completely voluntary and therefore paralleled the status of Gentiles granted by the Jerusalem Council in Acts 15.[42]

The Didache teaches that those who can handle the "whole yoke of the Lord" will be "complete" (*teleios*, τέλειος). "Complete" was used in 1.4 to describe those who turn the other cheek, and it is used in 16.2 to describe those who remain faithful until the Master returns. Disciples of Yeshua are to constantly strive toward this state of completion. The Greek word *teleios* corresponds to the Hebrew *tamim* ("unblemished"), which in the Torah is the required state for animals that are offered as sacrifices upon the altar.[43]

Additionally, Noah was called *tamim*, "blameless," in Genesis 6:9, and Jacob is designated *tam* ("blameless") in Genesis 25:27. God tells Abraham: "I am God

---

39 Van de Sandt and Flusser, *The Didache*, 238.
40 Because there are not direct parallels either in the Epistle of Barnabas or the *Doctrina* to Didache 6.2–3, many scholars feel that this section was added on to the original Two Ways document as 1.3–5 was. Nevertheless, as was stated in the introduction, this section feels very apostolic and seems to be connected to the rulings of Acts 15.
41 Skarsaune, *In the Shadow of the Temple*, 361. Cf. Van de Sandt and Flusser, *The Didache*, 240.
42 See Janicki, *God-Fearers*, 39–47. Alfred Stuiber feels that this reflects a progression that eventually leads to "complete conversion" (Stuiber, "'Das ganze Joch des Herrn' (Didache 6, 2–3)," in *Studia Patristica* 4.2 (TU 79; Berlin, Germany: Akademie-Verlag, 1961), 328, as quoted in Niederwimmer, *The Didache*, 122), while Solomon Schechter and Kaufmann Kohler feel that this represents the "two classes of proselytes Judaism recognized: the full proselyte, who accepted all the laws of the Torah, including circumcision, Sabbath, and the dietary laws; and the semi-proselyte, who accepted only the Noachian laws as binding. For the latter verse 3 contains the warning not to eat meat which has been offered to idols, which is forbidden also to the Noachide" (Schechter and Kohler, "Didache," *Jewish Encyclopedia* 4:585–588).
43 E.g., Exodus 12:5; Leviticus 1:3, 10.

[6.2]
You will be complete; but if you cannot, then do what you can.

Almighty; walk before me, and be blameless [*tamim*], that I may make my covenant between me and you, and may multiply you greatly" (Genesis 17:1–2). Nahum Sarna notes, "As applied to human beings, *tamim* acquired a moral dimension connoting 'unblemished' by moral default—hence a person of unimpeachable integrity."[44] King David asks, "Who shall dwell on your holy hill? He who walks blamelessly and does what is right and speaks truth in his heart" (Psalm 15:1–2).[45] The Master ends the first discourse in the Sermon on the Mount with the injunction, "You therefore must be perfect, as your heavenly Father is perfect" (Matthew 5:48).[46]

The Didache points the Gentile believer in the direction of fuller observance of the Torah in light of the teachings of the Master and the apostles, but at the same time it leaves room for those to whom this would be unbearable and too difficult in their current situation. In a similar way the Master says, "Not everyone can receive this saying, but only those to whom it is given" (Matthew 19:11), and the Apostle Paul adds, "I wish that all were as I myself am. But each has his own gift from God, one of one kind and one of another" (1 Corinthians 7:7).

⫸ *Concerning food, bear what you can.* (DIDACHE 6.3)

The Didache now moves from the broad generality of Torah observance as a whole to specific commandments surrounding a kosher diet. The word "concerning" (*peri*, περὶ) is used here, elsewhere in the Didache, and in the letters of Paul for

---

44 Nahum M. Sarna, *The JPS Torah Commentary: Genesis*, (New York, NY: Jewish Publication Society, 1989), 50.
45 Cf. Psalm 101:6.
46 Cf. Matthew 19:21; James 3:2. Because Matthew is the only gospel to use the term "yoke," and "perfection" is a major theme in Yeshua's teachings therein, some scholars feel that 6.2 is drawing from the Matthean tradition (Jefford, *The Sayings of Jesus in the Teaching of the Twelve Apostles*, 94). Cf. Matthew 19:21. Jonathan Draper finds a connection between *teleios* and Jewish debates about the application of Torah. For example, in the Dead Sea Scrolls, "'perfection' means keeping the Torah according to the community halachot (E.g., Community Rule [1QS] 1:8ff, 2:2, 3:9ff, 8:1ff). "In turn, the 'perfect' or complete Christian in the Didache, then, is the one who keeps the whole Torah according to Christian *halakah*" (Draper, "Torah and Troublesome Apostles in the Didache Community," *Novum Testamentum* 33, no. 4 [October 1991]: 365–366).

the purpose of introducing a new topic.[47] It corresponds to similar expressions in rabbinic literature that introduce new sections of halachah.[48]

Kurt Niederwimmer states, "['Concerning food'] refers obviously to the commandments and prohibitions regarding food in the Old Testament and Jewish tradition ... [which further solidifies the idea that] there is no fundamental abrogation of the foods laws here."[49] This would include the full gamut of dietary laws as given in the Torah, which addresses clean and unclean meats, kosher slaughter, separation of meat and dairy, and avoidance of food sacrificed to idols.[50] Even though Acts 15 required only that Gentile disciples of the Master eat kosher-slaughtered meat and avoid food sacrificed to idols, the Didache encouraged them to take on more than the bare minimum; the Apostolic Decree was given as a starting point and not as a maximum.

This seems to be the spirit of the apostles' decision at the Jerusalem Council. In light of their ruling that Gentile believers were required to eat kosher-slaughtered meat, it is hard to believe that the apostles would have imagined setting up ritual slaughter (*shechitah*, שחיטה) for swine and other animals that are not kosher. If a person eats only kosher-slaughtered meat, then by default he will be limited to kosher species of livestock. This might suggest that it was already obvious to the apostolic community that Gentiles should eat only kosher animals; at the very least, the council seemed to push them in this direction.

Additionally, the Jerusalem Council writes, "From ancient generations Moses has had in every city those who proclaim him, for he is read every Sabbath in the synagogues" (Acts 15:21). As the Gentiles attended synagogue, they would learn more about the ways of Torah and the kosher diet given to the Jewish people. Many of the new Gentile believers, such as Cornelius, were already God-fearers

[6.3]
Concerning food, bear what you can.

---

47   Didache 7.1, 9.1, 11.3; 1 Corinthians 7:1, 25, 8:1, 12:1, 16:1, 12; 1 Thessalonians 4:9, 5:1.
48   על זה נאמר, עליו. Jonathan A. Draper, "Weber, Theissen and 'Wandering Charismatics' in the Didache," *Journal of Early Christian Studies* 6, no. 4 (Winter 1998): 563, n. 109. Additionally, the word "concerning" corresponds to the Hebrew *al* (על), which is in blessing formulas for commandments: "Blessed are you, HaShem our God, King of the universe, who commands us concerning ..." Also, "A Hebrew parallel to this formation has come to light in the halakic letter from Qumran (*we-'al* ..., 4QMMT, *passim*)" (Peter J. Tomson, *'If This Be from Heaven ...' Jesus and the New Testament Authors in Their Relationship to Judaism* [Sheffield, England: Sheffield Academic Press, 2001], 387).
49   Niederwimmer, *The Didache*, 123.
50   E.g., Exodus 23:19, 34:26; Leviticus 7:10–17, 26–27, 11:1–47; Deuteronomy 12:21, 14:1–29. Robert Kraft feels that "concerning food" is not referring to the Torah but "represents a larger, older source which listed the various relevant food laws which Christianity had adopted from the Jewish 'Noachic Laws' for sympathetic Gentiles" (Kraft, *Barnabas and the Didache* [vol. 3 of *The Apostolic Fathers: A New and Commentary*; ed. Robert M. Grant; New York, NY: Thomas Nelson, 1965], 163).

[6.3]
Concerning food, bear what you can.

embedded within the Jewish community and would have kept a kosher diet on some level before the Apostolic Decree was delivered.[51]

The rabbis themselves had in mind that many Gentiles would take on aspects of the Jewish dietary laws:

> In the future, the blessed Holy One will send a herald to announce, "Let anyone who has never eaten the flesh of a pig in his life come and receive his reward." Many people from the nations of the world who have never eaten the flesh of a pig in their lives will come and receive their reward. (*Ecclesiastes Rabbah* 1:28)

Nevertheless, the Didache could only encourage Gentiles in the direction of accepting dietary laws that went beyond the minimums of the Apostolic Decree. A plethora of issues would have made the higher standards of Jewish law difficult, if not impossible, for many Gentile believers to observe. For example, many believers lived in the same home and ate at the same table with non-believing family members. Many were slaves. Many lived far outside Jewish communities, where the standards of Jewish law could not be observed. Non-Jewish disciples of the Master were to make their best effort at the Torah's dietary laws, and they were not to be condemned for a failure to meet the whole burden of obligation.

The Apostolic Constitutions renders this with the prohibition on blood and a general admonition to partake of the provisional blessings that our Father in heaven has given us in thanksgiving:

> Concerning food, the Lord says to you, "You shall eat the good things of the earth" [Isaiah 1:19], and, "All sorts of flesh shall you eat, as the green herb" [Genesis 9:3]; but, "You shall pour out the blood" [Deuteronomy 15:23]. For "not those things that go into the mouth, but those that come out of it, defile a man" [Matthew 15:11]; I mean blasphemies, evil-speaking, and if there be any other thing of the like nature. But "you shall eat the fat of the land" with righteousness [Genesis 45:18]. For "if there be anything pleasant, it is his; and if there be anything good, it is his. Wheat for the young men, and wine to cheer the maids" [Zechariah 9:17 Septuagint]. For 'who shall eat or who shall drink without Him?" [Ecclesiastes 2:25 Septuagint]. Wise Ezra does also admonish thee and

---

51 Chris A. Miller, "Did Peter's Vision in Acts 10 Pertain to Men or the Menu?" *Bibliotheca Sacra* 159, no. 635 (2002): 302–317.

say: "Go your way, and eat the fat, and drink the sweet, and be not sorrowful" [Nehemiah 8:10]. (Apostolic Constitutions 7.20)

⁌ But scrupulously guard yourself from what has been offered to idols because it is the worship of dead gods. (DIDACHE 6.3)

Even if one is not able to keep all the laws of kosher, he must absolutely avoid idolatrous food. The Apostolic Constitutions renders this command, "But guard yourself from what has been offered to idols, for they offer them in honor of demons, that is, to the dishonor of the one God, that you may not become partners with demons," which colors this prohibition with Paul's language in 1 Corinthians 10:20–21.[52] This alone among the dietary restrictions was never to be transgressed among Gentile believers, because it concerned more than food—it was directly linked to worshiping idols. As disciples of the Master, we are to avoid idolatry at all costs.

Some have suggested that once initiated into the community, believers were limited to purchasing "food and drink ... from within the (Jewish) Christian community to ensure strict compliance, since most meat would have been slaughtered in temples before being sold and wine would have been offered in libation before being retailed."[53] It is also probable that the early believers who adhered closely to dietary restrictions of food sacrificed to idols and kosher meat would have had access to Jewish merchants and markets as well.[54] When such options were not available, the Gentile believers adopted dietary standards similar to those of Daniel and his friends in Babylon.[55]

Although there is no explicit commandment in the Torah to refrain from food sacrificed to idols, the rabbis derive the prohibition from several passages: "You shall not bring an abominable thing into your house," and, "Take care, lest you ... whore after their gods and sacrifice to their gods and ... you eat of his sacrifice."[56] The prohibition included not only food but anything that had been tainted with idolatry. It became forbidden to derive any benefit from such an item. The Lord chastises Israel, saying, "Where are their gods, the rock in which they took refuge,

---

52 Apostolic Constitutions 7.21.
53 Jonathan A. Draper, "Ritual Process and Ritual Symbol in Didache 7–10," *Vigiliae Christianae* 54, no. 2 (2000): 124.
54 See W.H.C. Frend, *Martyrdom & Persecution in the Early Church: A Study of a Conflict from the Maccabees to Donatus* (Garden City, NY: Anchor, 1967), 17.
55 Daniel 1:8–14.
56 Deuteronomy 7:26; Exodus 34:12, 15. Cf. Leviticus 17:8–9.

[6.3]
But scrupulously guard yourself from what has been offered to idols because it is the worship of dead gods.

who ate the fat of their sacrifices and drank the wine of their drink offering?" (Deuteronomy 32:37–38). From this passage the rabbis derived the prohibition against drinking wine offered to idols, and in rabbinic literature the concern over idolatrous food deals almost exclusively with wine.

The prohibition of food sacrificed to idols was one of the four bestowed upon Gentiles by the Jerusalem Council.[57] It was so important that it merits an almost three-chapter discussion in Paul's first epistle to the Corinthians.[58] Paul states emphatically, "You cannot drink the cup of the Lord and the cup of demons. You cannot partake of the table of the Lord and the table of demons" (1 Corinthians 10:21).[59] The prohibition is brought up twice in the book of Revelation, where it is linked with "sexual immorality."[60] It is also spoken against in other early church literature outside the Didache such as in Justin Martyr's *Dialogue with Trypho the Jew*.[61] No less influential leaders in the early church than Clement of Alexandria, Irenaeus, Tertullian, and the fifth-century church father Augustine also spoke strongly against the eating of food sacrificed to idols.[62]

Jewish law treats this prohibition with utmost stringency, and it is significant that the wicked Greek king Antiochus IV Epiphanes and his armies tested the loyalty of the Jewish people by forcing them to "eat pork and food sacrificed to idols."[63] This command is extended to Gentiles in Noachide law, and we find it again in the universal Sibylline Oracles: "Eat not blood, and abstain from things offered to idols."[64]

We are to avoid eating food offered to idols, because to consume it is to participate in the worship of dead gods. The Prophet Jeremiah laments those who worship false gods, which are in fact not alive but dead, and the psalmist speaks of

---

[57] Acts 15:20, 29, 21:25.

[58] 1 Corinthians 8–10. For a study on why Paul's words here should not be viewed as dismissing the need to avoid food, see Toby Janicki and D. Thomas Lancaster, "Paul and Idol Food," *Messiah Journal* 114 (Fall 2013): 15–32.

[59] Cf. Baruch 4:7; Jubilees 1:11, 22:16 – 17; 1 Enoch 19:1; Pseudo-Clementine Homilies 7.3; Pseudo-Clementine Recognitions 2.71–72.

[60] Revelation 2:14, 20.

[61] Justin, *Dialogue with Trypho the Jew* 35.

[62] E.g., Ignatius, *To the Magnesians* 8–10; Tertullian, *Apology* 9.13–14. See Tomson, *Paul and the Jewish Law*, 180–181.

[63] 4 Maccabees 5:1–2.

[64] Rabbi Moshe Weiner, *The Divine Code* (ed. Dr. Michael Schulman; 2d ed.; Pittsburgh, PA: Ask Noah International, 2011), 224–235; Sibylline Oracles 2.115. This law is also found in the equally universal Pseudo-Phocylides (31): "Do not eat blood; abstain from what is sacrificed to idols," although most scholars feel that this verse is an interpolation. See P.W. van der Horst, ed., *The Sentences of Pseudo-Phocylides* (Leiden, The Netherlands: Brill, 1978), 135–136.

idolaters who eat "sacrifices offered to the dead."⁶⁵ The Didache's phrase "worship of dead gods" is related to the rabbinic expression "sacrifices of the dead" (*zivchei meitim*, זבחי מתים), which is also used as an argument against idolatrous food.⁶⁶ The sages used the phrase metaphorically to speak of idolatry in general: "Rabbi Simeon said: 'If three have eaten at one table and have not spoken thereat words of Torah, [it is] as if they had eaten sacrifices of the dead.'"⁶⁷

[6.3]
But scrupulously guard yourself from what has been offered to idols because it is the worship of dead gods.

---

65   Jeremiah 10:3–5; Psalm 106:28. Cf. Deuteronomy 4:28.
66   E.g., m.*Avodah Zarah* 2:3. Van de Sandt and Flusser, *The Didache*, 260.
67   m.*Avot* 3:3. Cf. *Seder Eliyahu Rabbah* 9; *Avot DeRabbi Natan* 34 (B). Similar language such as "sacrifices to gods that are dead" is also found in pseudepigraphic and early church literature. See 2 Clement 3.1; Diognetus 2.4–5; Sibylline Oracles 8.522–524; Wisdom of Solomon 13–15; Philo, *On the Decalogue* 52–82.

Chapter Seven

DIDACHE 7

7.1 Concerning immersion, immerse in this way: Having first said all these things, immerse in the name of the Father and the Son and the Holy Spirit[1] in living water.

7.2 But if you do not have living water, immerse in other water; and if you cannot immerse in cold water, then immerse in warm water.

7.3 But if you do not have either in sufficient quantity to immerse, pour water on the head three times in the name of the Father and the Son and the Holy Spirit.[2]

7.4 Prior to the immersion, the one performing the immersion and the one being immersed should fast beforehand, and also any others if they can. Require the one being immersed to fast one or two days prior to the immersion.

---

1 Matthew 28:19.
2 Ibid.

Overview

At this point in the Didache, Gentile believers have completed the training in the Two Ways (chapters 1–6), and now they are ready to be initiated into the Messianic community through immersion. Chapter 7 presents legal instructions for carrying out the immersion procedure. Its contents represent the earliest legal instructions for immersion outside the New Testament, and it is probable that they are older than much of the New Testament itself.

Additionally, chapter 7 begins what many refer to as the liturgical, or ritual, section of the Didache, which comprises chapters 7–10. This chapter continues the trend begun in chapter 6 of using mainly the second-person plural form of "you" in its teachings,[3] perhaps indicating that the Didache has moved into more community-minded instructions as opposed to the more individualized material of chapters 1–5.

Immersion Instructions

Most striking about the immersion injunctions is their simplicity. The Didache deals only with the type of water to be used and the rules for fasting beforehand:

> The Didache's teaching about the water to be used for baptism is attention grabbing, primarily because it's so different than the way Paul wrote about baptism. We're familiar with Paul's highly theological, and even esoteric, comments on baptism. In contrast, the Didache's advice is purely pragmatic, even mundane.[4]

The instructions are completely devoid of theological or mystical teachings about being born again or the death of Messiah. They read more like a section out of the Mishnah than from one of Paul's epistles.

While this certainly lends evidence to the antiquity of the material, at least two other reasons exist for this archaic simplicity. First, as we pointed out early on, the Didache's teaching is focused on practical application rather than on theology. The hope of its authors is that "right practice would lead to right experience,

---

3 The notable exception is 7.2–4.
4 Tony Jones, *The Teaching of the Twelve: Believing & Practicing the Primitive Christianity of the Ancient Didache Community* (Brewster, MA: Paraclete, 2009), 99.

and right experience would lead to right theology."[5] While the Didache does not discredit the spiritual meaning of immersion, its thrust is on making sure that the procedure is done properly.[6]

Second, as Jonathan Draper points out, these types of instructions are exactly what we would expect to see "in a Jewish community admitting Gentiles into its fellowship. The concern is fundamentally with ritual purity."[7] In the early Messianic Jewish community, it was essential that Gentiles be admitted into fellowship in a state of purity and that issues of ritual ablution be dealt with. This is the focus of chapter 7, specifically as it pertains to regulations surrounding "living water," which was the cornerstone of Jewish immersion and ritual purity.

Gentile Impurity

Jewish law declares that the Torah's twenty-plus commandments surrounding ritual purity are never applicable to Gentiles, whether a Temple is standing or not. Because many of the purity injunctions begin with "Speak to the people of Israel … ," the sages reasoned, "The people of Israel are the subjects of these matters and not Gentiles."[8] Although this is the prevailing rabbinic opinion today, it appears that the apostles did not fully agree, since they extended purity concerns to the Gentile believers.[9] According to the book of Acts, when Gentiles began coming to faith in Messiah, the initial pressing concern was whether or not they could be considered ritually clean. This is the reason for Peter's vision of the sheet and his trip to Cornelius' house in Acts 10.

The Master commanded his Jewish followers to go and make disciples from all the nations, and the initial sign of people's repentance was to be immersion.[10]

---

5 Aaron Milavec, *The Didache: Faith, Hope, & Life of the Earliest Christian Communities, 50–70 C.E.* (New York, NY: Newman, 2003), 282.
6 Jonathan A. Draper, "The Holy Vine of David Made Known to the Gentiles through God's Servant Jesus: 'Christian Judaism' in the Didache," in *Jewish Christianity Reconsidered: Rethinking Ancient Groups and Texts* (Matt Jackson-McCabe, ed.; Minneapolis, MN: Fortress, 2007), 269.
7 Ibid.
8 E.g., Leviticus 15:2, 12:2. *Sifra* on Leviticus 12:2. See Christine Elizabeth Hayes, *Gentile Impurities and Jewish Identities: Intermarriage and Conversion from the Bible to the Talmud* (New York, NY: Oxford University Press, 2002), 109–122.
9 Some rabbinic texts seem to disagree as well. E.g., in m.*Machshirin* 2:3, Gentiles are referred to as "unclean persons" and in m.*Oholot* 18:7, "the dwelling places of Gentiles are unclean." However, these statements seem to relate more to the impurity of idolatry than to the ritual purity regulations of the Torah.
10 Matthew 28:19.

In first-century Judaism immersion was directly connected with ritual purity. While immersion has a symbolic meaning as well, it is always associated with the removal of ceremonial uncleanness. The fact that Gentiles were required to immerse in order to become disciples of Yeshua shows that they were in some sense moving from a state of being "unclean" (*tamei*, טמא) to a state of being "clean" (*tahor*, טהור).[11] Before coming to Messiah, the non-Jews were tainted with idolatry and immorality. Therefore, the Torah's laws of ritual purity must, in some sense, apply to non-Jewish disciples of the Master. A tradition even exists that Peter himself would not eat with Gentiles unless they repented and were immersed.[12] It is noteworthy as well that rabbinic law does prescribe immersion for Gentiles as a component of conversion to Judaism.

Upon close examination, the minimum injunctions that make up the Apostolic Decree are largely, if not entirely, about ritual purity. The dietary restrictions against idolatrous food and improperly slaughtered meat certainly have a tone of ritual purity about them.[13] Not only was participation in *avodah zarah* (idolatry) grounds for severe punishment, but so was eating blood, according to the Lord's command: "If any one of the house of Israel or of the strangers who sojourn among them eats any blood, I will set my face against that person who eats blood and will cut him off from among his people" (Leviticus 17:10). Both transgressions affected the purity of Israel. Additionally, some scholars argue that the prohibition against "sexual immorality" was also linked to ritual purity, such as the injunctions of the period of separation associated with the menstrual cycle (*niddah*, נדה) and purification after marital relations.[14]

Even moving beyond the Apostolic Period, we find evidence for concern over ritual purity in the church. Early Christian baptismal pools found in "Israel, Turkey, Greece, and Rome were built on the same principle as *mikva'ot*."[15] The *Canons of Hippolytus* give instructions similar to those in the Didache about "living water"

---

11 Cf. "I took courage and became strong and captured the world, and the captivity became mine for the glory of the Most High, and of God my Father. And the Gentiles who had been dispersed were gathered together, but I was not defiled by my love for them, because they had praised me in high places. And the traces of light were set upon their heart, and they walked according to my life and were saved, and they became my people for ever and ever. Hallelujah" (Odes of Solomon 10:4–6).
12 Pseudo-Clementine Homilies 13.4; Pseudo-Clementine Recognitions 2.71–72.
13 Acts 15:20, 29.
14 See Marcel Simon, "The Apostolic Decree and Its Setting in the Ancient Church," *Bulletin of the John Rylands Library* 52, no. 2 (1969–1970): 437–460.
15 Gordon Moyes, "*A Fresh Look at New Testament Baptism*," n.p. [cited 30 November 2011]. Online: http://www.gordonmoyes.com/wp-content/uploads//FreshLookatBaptism.pdf.

and add that one must remove anything that hinders complete contact with the water, including clothing and jewelry—instructions in complete accordance with rabbinic law.[16] In the Jewish Christian Clementine literature, we find the injunction to Gentiles "not to live any longer impurely; to wash after intercourse; that the women on their part should keep the law of purification" (Pseudo-Clementine Homilies 7.8).[17] All this evidence points to early Gentile believers observing some level of purity law, and the Didache's instructions focusing on ritual purity for immersion echo this sentiment.

Jewish Roots of Baptism

The origins of immersion practices in the early believing community were firmly rooted in the Judaism of the Second Temple Period. The instructions in the Didache are no exception. The closest Jewish parallel to the immersion of new Gentile believers into Messiah is the Jewish practice of proselyte immersion. While Jewish law required a convert to Judaism to be circumcised and, when the Temple was still standing, to offer a sacrifice, undergoing immersion was the key turning point in the proselyte process.[18] Therefore, proselyte immersion becomes the natural backdrop for the immersion of Gentiles who were entering into the Messianic community.

Jewish proselyte immersion was to be done in "living water" (*mayim chayim*, מים חיים), which meant natural, flowing water.[19] But it could also be done in a *mikvah* (מקוה), a specially designed ritual bath that collected rainwater. The Didache falls in line with these prescriptions by requiring immersion to be done in "living water," although it makes concessions for its Gentile audience by listing a series of other options. "Immerse in other water" (7.2) very likely refers to the waters of a *mikvah*. In its concern over the kind of water used in immersion, chapter 7 strikes a legal tone.

Even the regulations surrounding the period of training and fasting just prior to immersion find their counterpart in Judaism. While the specifics of each of the

---

16   *Canons of Hippolytus* 21; b.*Bava Kama* 82a–b.

17   This is in accordance with Leviticus 15:18, etc. This practice is still carried out today in Judaism through a ritual washing of hands after intercourse, though some have the custom of immersing in a *mikvah* or showering. See Rabbi Simcha Bunim Cohen, *Laws of Daily Living* (1 vol.; Brooklyn, NY: ArtScroll, 2007), 1:45.

18   Cf. b.*Yevamot* 46a; b.*Brachot* 47b; Maimonides, *Mishneh Torah*, Issurei Biah 8:5.

19   *Sibylline Oracles* 4.162–170.

parallels will be discussed at greater length in the commentary, the chart below compares Jewish proselyte immersion and that of apostolic practice:[20]

Jewish Proselyte Immersion	Didache
Introduction to some of the heavier and some of the lighter commandments (b.*Yevamot* 47a)	Pre-baptismal instruction in ethical and moral teachings (7.1)
Baptism in "flowing water" (Sibylline Oracles 4.162–170) or in a mikvah	Baptism preferably in "living [running] water" but allowable in a basin (7.1)
Proselyte Aseneth praying and fasting (Joseph and Aseneth 10–13)	Prayer and fasting immediately before baptism (7.4)

The requirements for a new believer to receive previous instruction, to be immersed in living water, and even to fast before immersion all find parallel in Jewish sources of the period. Even the concessions that we will see detailed in 7.2–3 (using "other water" or "warm water") have a ring similar to rabbinic discussions about what constitutes minimum standards for purification.[21]

In Hippolytus' *Apostolic Tradition* (third century), we find even more parallels with Jewish law:[22]

---

[20] Created from Oskar Skarsaune, *In the Shadow of the Temple: Jewish Influences on Early Christianity* (Downers Grove, IL: InterVarsity Press, 2002), 359–360.

[21] Cf. m.*Mikva'ot* 1:8, 3:4; m.*Yoma* 3:5; y.*Brachot* 3:4; b.*Brachot* 22a. Some have even speculated, based upon the order in which the Didache presents its material, that the "Thanksgiving" meal of Didache 8–9 was eaten by the new Gentile initiate immediately after immersion. According to David Flusser, this also finds its counterpart in the popular custom of proselytes to Judaism completing their conversion process just in time to eat of the Passover sacrifice. "It is an unknown fact that the custom of baptism of neophytes at the night of Easter is the sequel of the Jewish custom of baptism of proselytes in the evening of Passover … This custom is well attested in Jewish sources, and it's clear why the proselyte liked to be baptized at the evening of Passover, having been circumcised some days before: they were permitted to eat the Passover lamb, which is, according to the Law of Moses, forbidden to the uncircumcised" (David Flusser, "Some Notes on Easter and the Passover Haggadah," *Immanuel* 7 [Spring 1977]: 52–60). Cf. m.*Pesachim* 8:8.

[22] Created from Skarsaune, *In the Shadow of the Temple*, 359–360.

Jewish Proselyte Immersion	Apostolic Tradition
Candidates asked about motives for conversion (b.*Yevamot* 46b)	Candidates asked about motives for conversion (15.2)
Two or three witnesses required at baptism (b.*Yevamot* 46b)	Candidates required to have witnesses to guarantee their sincerity (15.2)
Aseneth renounces the devil and idols (Joseph and Aseneth 10:8–13, 12:9–12)	Candidates renounce devil, equaling rejection of idolatry (21.9)
Water to touch every part of body; women untie their hair; nobody may let an object come between the water and their body (b.*Bava Kama* 82a–b)	Water to touch every part of body; women loosen their hair and take off all jewelry; nobody may bring an alien object with them (21.5)
After-baptism participation in first Passover meal, bringing of sacrifice (m.*Pesachim* 8:8; m.*Keritot* 2:1)	After-baptism participation in bread and wine as first offering (20.10, 21.27)[23]

It is likely that the practices and regulations mentioned in the *Apostolic Tradition* were employed in the early apostolic communities.[24] The instructions are too Jewish to have been absorbed into the church at a late date. At the time of the writing of the Didache, however, they may have circulated only orally.

In the Didache "the connection with Jewish purification ritual is still strong and the modes of the ritual have not lost their prominence yet."[25] The immersion instructions in chapter 7 are thoroughly Jewish and almost certainly go back in some form to the apostles.

---

[23] Cf. Justin, *First Apology* 65. "Hippolytus's whole initiation rite is recognizably derived from the initiation of Jewish proselytes. His baptismal rite is derived directly from the baptismal rite for Jewish proselytes … Lastly, the Jewish proselyte was strictly obliged forthwith to provide his first sacrifice. So Hippolytus requires that every Christian neophyte shall bring with him to baptism his own personal προσφορά (oblation of bread and wine) to be forthwith at the Baptismal Mass" (Gregory Dix and Henry Chadwick, eds., *The Treatise on the Apostolic Tradition of St. Hippolytus of Rome, Bishop and Martyr* [New York, NY: Routledge, 1991], xi).

[24] Cf. "And then according to the initiation of Moses, he that is to deliver the books should bring him to a river or a fountain, which is living water, where the regeneration of the righteous takes place, and should make him, not swear—for that is not lawful—but to stand by the water and adjure, as we ourselves, when we were re-generated, were made to do for the sake of not sinning." (The Epistle of Peter to James 4.1).

[25] Huub van de Sandt, "'Do Not Give What Is Holy to the Dogs' (Did 9:5d and Matt 7:6a): The Eucharistic Food of the Didache in Its Jewish Purity Setting," *Vigiliae Christianae* 56, no. 3 (August 2002): 241.

Spiritual Conversion

In addition to all its ritual and legal considerations, the immersion into Yeshua symbolizes a change of status: not a legal conversion to become Jewish but a spiritual conversion and regeneration. The immersion into Yeshua represents repentance, the forgiveness of sins in Yeshua's name, and a symbolic identification with Yeshua as a new member in his school of disciples. The Didache does not bring up the concept of spiritual transformation in connection with immersion, but neither does it in any way contradict the New Testament's teachings on the subject. The Didache seems to assume that new disciples already understand the symbolism.

The Jerusalem Council in Acts 15 did not require new Gentile believers to be circumcised and become legally Jewish, but the apostles did follow the Master's injunction to "make disciples of all nations, baptizing them," which, as we pointed out, was an important ceremonial feature in Jewish proselyte conversion.[26]

In rabbinic law Gentiles did not receive immersion except upon conversion to Judaism. An interesting discussion in the Talmud details what constitutes a full proselyte:

> Our Rabbis taught: "If a proselyte was circumcised but had not performed the prescribed ritual ablution, R. Eliezer said, 'Behold he is a proper proselyte; for so we find that our forefathers were circumcised and had not performed ritual ablution.' If he performed the prescribed ablution but had not been circumcised, R. Joshua said, 'Behold he is a proper proselyte; for so we find that the mothers had performed ritual immersion but had not been circumcised.'" (b.*Yevamot* 46a)

At the end of the discussion, the sages ruled that one must undergo both circumcision and immersion to be considered a legal convert. Nevertheless, this passage records the alternate opinion that one had only to be immersed. (This stands to reason, since circumcision applies to only half the human species.) Some rabbinic texts even make reference to a type of convert who only immerses:

> [In Tractate *Gerim*] a distinction is made between those who bathe only, those who have bathed and been circumcised, and those who have been circumcised but not bathed (1:6). This seems to me to reflect the differing situation of the *ger toshav* and the *ger tsedek*. The bath is required to put the Gentile in a minimum state of purity to share in

---

26 Matthew 28:19.

the life of the Jewish community, together with other minimum observances of the Noachic laws and abstention from what has been offered to idols (and meat which has not been ritually slaughtered; *Gerim* 3:1 [61a]). This enables table fellowship: "his bread, his oil and his wine are clean."[27]

In light of all this, we may deduce that a Gentile immersed into Messiah attained a legal status different from that of other Gentile believers (for example, Noachides or first-century God-fearers).[28] While immersion into Yeshua's name certainly did not imply formal, legal conversion in the halachic sense, the immersion did indicate that some type of conversion had taken place. The Gentile immersed in Messiah was purified and had undergone a change of legal status regarding his relationship to Israel. Hence, in the Didache only those "immersed in the name of the Lord" could partake in communal meals (9.5).

Paul uses the ceremonial language of conversion to describe the spiritual transformation that the Gentile believer undergoes when he comes to Messiah. He describes the new believer's spiritual transformation with language borrowed from the physical ceremonies of conversion (that is, circumcision and immersion). This conversion is not accomplished by human hands but by faith in God: "In him also you were circumcised with a circumcision made without hands ... the circumcision of Messiah."[29] Commenting on Paul's words in Ephesians 2:19 that Gentiles in Messiah are "no longer strangers and aliens," Rabbi Yechiel Tzvi Lichtenstein states, "They were complete proselytes through faith in the righteous Messiah."[30]

In Judaism a formal convert is called a son of Abraham (*ben Avraham*, בן אברהם) or a daughter of Abraham (*bat Avraham*, בת אברהם).[31] This is precisely the language

---

27 Jonathan A. Draper, "A Continuing Enigma: the 'Yoke of the Lord' in Didache 6:2–3 and Early Jewish-Christian Relations," in *The Image of the Judaeo-Christians in Ancient Jewish and Christian Literature* (ed. Peter J. Tomson and Doris Lambers-Petry; Tübingen, Germany: Mohr Siebeck, 2003), 119. Cf. "When a Jew purchased a non-Jew (man or woman) as a slave, the slave had to be immersed in a *mikvah* in order to acquire the new status of *eved c'na'ani*. Once an *eved c'na'ani* had undergone immersion in a *mikvah* he was obligated to observe all the Torah's commandments that had no specific time for their performance" (Rabbi Adin Steinsaltz, *The Talmud Steinsaltz Edition: A Reference Guide* [New York, NY: Random, 1989], 195–196). Cf. b.*Yevamot* 45b, 47b.
28 See D. Thomas Lancaster, *Grafted In: Israel, Gentiles, and the Mystery of the Gospel* (Marshfield, MO: First Fruits of Zion, 2009).
29 Colossians 2:11–12.
30 Rabbi Yechiel Tzvi Lichtenstein, *Commentary on the New Testament* (trans. Aaron Eby and Robert Morris; Marshfield, MO: Vine of David, unpublished) on Acts 15:7; trans. of *Bi'ur Lesifrei Brit HaChadashah* (8 vols.; Leipzig, Germany: Professor G. Dahlman, 1891–1904).
31 Cf. y.*Bikkurim* 1:4; b.*Chagigah* 3a; *Mechilta*, Nezikin 18, Exodus 22:21; *Peskita Rabbati* 43:4.

that Paul used to describe new Gentile believers. He told them that they were now "sons of Abraham" (Galatians 3:7), and when addressing the mixed congregation in Corinth, he even referred to the Israelites who came out of Egypt as "our fathers" (1 Corinthians 10:1).[32] This indicates that the Patriarchs and the exodus from Egypt had now become a part of the Gentile believer's spiritual heritage. Draper writes that the new Gentile initiates in the Didache "identify themselves socially with the God of Israel and the people of the covenant, Israel and its history, regardless of the fact that they are not racially Jews."[33]

Paul continues on this theme of spiritual conversion in Romans:

> No one is a Jew who is merely one outwardly, nor is circumcision outward and physical. But a Jew is one inwardly, and circumcision is a matter of the heart, by the Spirit, not by the letter. His praise is not from man but from God. (Romans 2:28–29)

In Messiah all believers undergo a spiritual conversion that, figuratively speaking, can be compared to the type of legal conversion Gentile converts undergo when they become Jewish. This "spiritual conversion" in no way makes Gentile believers Jewish in the flesh, either physically or legally. Nor does it diminish the legal and practical distinctions between a Jewish person and a Gentile believer. Rather, the apostles borrow the symbolic language of the conversion ritual to speak about the new believer's inner spiritual transformation in Messiah.

According to the apostles and the Didache, Gentiles who come to faith in Messiah and undergo immersion in his name fulfill "the requirement of moral, not halakhic conversion."[34] Through their expression of faith in Yeshua, believing Gentiles find themselves grafted into the people of God and members of the commonwealth of Israel. While all the legal distinctions between Jewish and

---

[32] Cf. 1 Clement 4. Also note Caroline Johnson Hodge, who sees Romans 9:7 ("Not all are children of Abraham because they are his offspring, but 'Through Isaac shall your offspring be named'") as indicating that Gentiles are spiritually descended through Isaac (Hodge, *If Sons, Then Heirs: A Study of Kinship and Ethnicity in the Letters of Paul* (New York, NY: Oxford University Press, 2007), 94.

[33] Jonathan A. Draper, "Mission, Ethics, and Identity in the Didache," in *Sensitivity towards Outsiders: Exploring Dynamic Relationship between Mission and Ethics in the New Testament and Early Christianity* (Tübingen, Germany: Mohr Siebeck, 2014), 478.

[34] Paula Fredriksen, "Judaism, the Circumcision of Gentiles, and Apocalyptic Hope: Another Look at Galatians 1 and 2," *Journal of Theological Studies* 42 (1991): 561. It is a common Jewish teaching that Jewish people are born with a unique divine soul but that converts receive this divine soul upon conversion. In a similar manner, "Augustine ... speculate[d] that the rite [of baptism] conferred a 'spiritual character' permanently marking the soul" (Milavec, *The Didache: Faith, Hope, & Life of the Earliest Christian Communities, 50–70 C.E.*, 277). Cf. Romans 6:6–7; 2 Corinthians 5:17; 1 Peter 1:23.

Gentile believers remain, the new Gentile believers become coheirs of the kingdom spiritually. Both Jewish and Gentile believers are full-fledged members of the Messianic community.

Pre-Baptism Training

According to the Didache, immersion into Messiah is not to be done in haste but requires extensive preparation. The candidate must undergo a period of training in the Way of Life and undertake a fast of "one or two days prior" to immersion (7.4). The words "having said all these things" at the start of chapter 7 implies that the candidate has gone through an intensive study program before now preparing for immersion.

This training would have included at least the material that comprises chapters 1–6 of the Didache (maybe even the entire document) and other oral or written material that contained "the elementary doctrine of Messiah," that is, the "instruction about immersions" alluded to in the book of Hebrews.[35] Before his spiritual conversion, the Gentile entering the community needed to learn the expectations, terms, and conditions of the new faith. He needed to learn the Way of Life—the ways of the Master and how to walk them out in everyday life. Immersion was then the seal on this period of studying and training, after which the Gentile believer would become a full participant in meals and all community events.

Some have pointed out that this seems inconsistent with the stories of immersion told in the book of Acts. For example, when Philip encountered the Ethiopian eunuch, after he briefly explained a passage of Isaiah 53 and told him the good news about Yeshua, the eunuch was immersed:

> As they were going along the road they came to some water, and the eunuch said, "See, here is water! What prevents me from being baptized?"
> And he commanded the chariot to stop, and they both went down into the water, Philip and the eunuch, and he baptized him. (Acts 8:36–38)

We see, too, the case of the Philippian jailer. When Paul and Silas were bound in chains in the prison, and the prison doors and their shackles miraculously opened

---

[35] Hebrews 6:1–3, author's . For a full discussion of the "elementary principles," see D. Thomas Lancaster, *Elementary Principles: Six Foundational Principles of Ancient Jewish Christianity* (Marshfield, MO: First Fruits of Zion, 2013).

in the middle of the night, the jailer was so taken aback by the miracle and also by Paul and Silas' reluctance to escape that he was brought to the point of repentance:

> Then he brought them out and said, "Sirs, what must I do to be saved?" And they said, "Believe in the Lord Yeshua, and you will be saved, you and your household." And they spoke the word of the Lord to him and to all who were in his house. And he took them the same hour of the night and washed their wounds; and he was baptized at once, he and all his family. (Acts 16:30–33)

In both of these stories, each apostle offered simple instruction about what Messiah had done to bring salvation to all mankind, and then the candidates were immersed.

Some speculate that the Didache and the New Testament represent two opposing views regarding immersion, but that does not necessarily have to be the case. Like the Jewish people in Acts 2 who immediately received immersion into Messiah, some of these individuals who were immersed as soon as they believed were already practicing Judaism in some form. God-fearing Gentiles would not need extensive training before immersion. The Ethiopian eunuch was either born Jewish or was a proselyte; Acts makes no mention of a Gentile background.[36] The jailer, who was a Gentile, may have been a God-fearer and knowledgeable in the Torah. Cornelius, who was also immersed immediately upon hearing the good news along with his family, was most definitely a God-fearer, since he is described as "a devout man who feared God with all his household, gave alms generously to the people, and prayed continually to God."[37]

Moreover, these stories may be exceptions to the general rule. All the examples in the book of Acts of immediate immersion upon a person hearing the good news

---

[36] "The Ethiopian eunuch is sometimes considered the first Gentile convert. That seems unlikely. Luke makes no issue about his non-Jewish status as he does regarding Cornelius in Acts 10. Ethiopia was home to a continuous Jewish presence from the days of Solomon up until the modern era. *Beta Israel* Jews, also known as Ethiopian Jews, claim Jewish ancestry reaching back to the Solomonic Era. One may safely assume that an Ethiopian who went to the trouble of making a pilgrimage to Jerusalem to worship the LORD in His Temple was Jewish. Luke says, 'He had come to Jerusalem to worship' (Acts 8:27). The eunuch had traveled a great distance to reach Jerusalem, more than a month's travel time. He had probably come to attend one of the pilgrimage festivals. While in Jerusalem, he purchased several Greek versions of the scrolls of the prophets—reading material for the trip home" (D. Thomas Lancaster, *Torah Club: Chronicles of the Apostles* [6 vols.; Marshfield, MO: First Fruits of Zion, 2016], 1:194). Cf. D.A. Hubbard, "Ethiopian Eunuch," in *The New Bible Dictionary* (J.D. Douglas, ed.; Westmont, IL: InterVarsity Press, 1962), 398, in which it is suggested that the eunuch was a proselyte.

[37] Acts 10:2.

are special cases under special circumstances that should not constitute the normal standard for entrance into a community of faith. A candidate should not undergo immersion before fully knowing the terms of discipleship.

This precedent was established with the immersions conducted by John the Baptist. When John saw unrepentant people coming to be immersed, he turned them away, telling them first to "bear fruit in keeping with repentance."[38] In other words, one must show signs of repentance before coming to be immersed. The immersion was to be an outward seal of an inner transformation that had already taken place. Josephus wrote of John:

> [He] commanded the Jews to exercise virtue, both as to righteousness toward one another, and piety toward God, and so to come to baptism; for that the washing [with water] would be acceptable to him, if they made use of it, not in order to the putting away [or the remission] of some sins [only], but for the purification of the body: supposing still that the soul was thoroughly purified beforehand by righteousness. (*Antiquities of the Jews* 18.5.2 §117)

Some may fear that this prolongs becoming "saved," but that is to miss the point of the entire process. As C.S. Lewis comments, "Don't bother at all about that question of a person being 'made a Christian' by baptism."[39] Faith in Messiah is a journey, one that begins the moment we realize that Yeshua is the Son of God, the Redeemer of Israel, and even before that. Immersion into his name is one step

---

38 Matthew 3:8; Luke 3:8. Cf. "Wherefore as man, having something more than the irrational animals, namely, rationality, purify your hearts from evil by heavenly reasoning, and wash your bodies in the bath. For purification according to the truth is not that the purity of the body precedes purification after the heart, but that purity follows goodness. For our Teacher also, dealing with certain of the Pharisees and Scribes among us, who are separated, and as Scribes know the matters of the law more than others, still he reproved them as hypocrites, because they cleansed only the things that appear to men, but omitted purity of heart and the things seen by God alone" (Pseudo-Clementine Homilies 11.28).

39 Wayne Martindale and Jerry Root, eds., *The Quotable Lewis: An Encyclopedic Collection of Quotes from the Complete Published Works of C.S. Lewis* (Carol Stream, IL: Tyndale, 1990), 64. It is worth noting that there was a strain of tradition amongst the early Jewish believers that immersion was a necessary prerequisite for the forgiveness of sins and entrance into the kingdom of heaven (Pseudo-Clementine Recognitions 1.55.3–4 [Syriac], 1.69.5 [Syriac]; Pseudo-Clementine Homilies 11.27; Shepherd of Hermas, Vision 3.2.3, 9, 11 [10.3, 9, 11.5]).

that brings us closer to being conformed into God's image, but it should not be considered the mechanism of salvation.[40]

Practical Application

The halachah of Didache 7 can serve as a model for the immersion of new Gentile believers into Messiah today. The injunctions for a training period beforehand, the specification of water types, and preliminary fasting can serve as a blueprint for meaningful practice that is rooted in the teachings of the apostles.

For one thing, since immersion in "living water" is not always practical throughout the year in most climates, Messianic congregations should consider building ritual immersion pools (*mikva'ot*) within the guidelines of Jewish law. As the Didache contains the earliest ritual instructions outside the New Testament on immersion, its injunctions should be taken seriously and adopted for observance today.

Additionally, if we move slightly beyond the original intent of the authors of the Didache, these instructions can also serve as a guideline for non-Jews wishing to implement some of the Torah's regulations on ritual purity in their lives. The Didache's guidelines can help us recover apostolic practice in regard to immersion ceremonies in general, not just immersion for the sake of initiation into the Yeshua movement.

Without a Temple in our day, most of the laws pertaining to being clean (*tahor*) and unclean (*tamei*) have no direct application today, even for Jewish people. To a certain extent everyone is in a state of impurity (*tamei*) because the ritual mechanism for purification (which requires the ashes of a red heifer) is no longer available. Furthermore, the specifics of a Gentile believer's obligation to purity laws are difficult to ascertain and certainly beyond the scope of this commentary.[41]

---

40   This, of course, raises the issue of infant baptism, which is prominent in some Christian denominations. The rigorous pre-immersion training coupled with fasting makes it almost certain that the Didache does not have in mind this practice. The practice itself is not first mentioned until the late second/early third century by Tertullian, who in fact argues against such a practice. It is not until the mid-third century that we find writings actually speaking for the practice of infant baptism (e.g., Origen, *Commentary on Romans* 5.9; Hippolytus, *Apostolic Tradition* 21.4). For a full discussion on this issue, see Milavec, *The Didache: Faith, Hope, & Life of the Earliest Christian Communities, 50–70 C.E.*, 259–261.

41   While the Gentile's obligation to purity laws becomes a moot point in light of the destruction of the Temple, it is certainly something that will need to be considered for the Messianic Kingdom. After all, the book of Revelation tells us that "nothing unclean will ever enter" the New Jerusalem (Revelation 21:27).

Nevertheless, some purity-related injunctions have direct application to Messianic Jews and Messianic Gentiles today. For example, the commandment of *niddah*, the injunction for a man to separate from his wife during her menstruation period, retains some aspects of ritual purity concern.[42] While the laws of family purity are certainly binding upon Jewish believers, they are also applicable to Gentile believers under the prohibition of sexual immorality that appears both in the decision of the Jerusalem Council and in the Didache.[43] According to Jewish law, when the period of *niddah* is over, a woman must undergo a ritual immersion before renewing relations with her husband.[44] This is to be done in living water or in a kosher mikvah.

Most Messianic believers today do not have access to a mikvah, and in many cases immersing openly in "living water" is not an option either due to climate or geographical location.[45] In such situations the instructions of the Didache can be of assistance. If one does not have living water, other water may suffice; if one has not cold water, one may use warm; and finally, if one has none of the above, having

---

42 Leviticus 15:19–24.
43 Acts 15:20, 29, 21:25; Didache 2.2.
44 According to the Torah, the period of separation for a woman in *niddah* is seven days from the time that she begins her menstruation (Leviticus 15:19). However, if her bleeding is not due to menstruation but to an abnormal flow (*zavah gedolah*, זבה גדולה), the seven-day count begins once she has stopped her bleeding, meaning that the couple is separated for the entire time she bleeds plus seven "clean days" (Leviticus 15:25–28). In rabbinic tradition the two injunctions are combined so that even during menstruation a woman waits to count the seven days until she has stopped bleeding, and since typically this count cannot begin until after five days, this results in a twelve-day separation period. Additionally, although the Torah's restrictions for a husband not to come into any physical contact with his wife while she is in *niddah* are related to the Temple laws of *tahor* and *tamei*, in Orthodox Judaism today couples still refrain from even non-affectionate touch and sleeping in the same bed as a safeguard against transgressing the prohibition of sexual relations during *niddah*. See Meira Svirsky, *A Woman's Mitzvah: A Fully Sourced Guide to the Laws of Family Purity* (Jerusalem, Israel: Old City, 2007). For a historical study on the lengthening of the period of *niddah*, see David C. Kraemer, "A Developmental Perspective on the Laws of Niddah," in *Exploring Judaism: The Collected Essays of David Kraemer* (ed. David C. Kraemer; Atlanta, GA: Scholars, 1999), 235–243.
45 Most kosher Jewish *mikva'ot* facilities dissuade both Messianic Jews and non-Jews from immersing in their pools. It should also be pointed out that Jewish law does not require "living water" for immersion after *niddah*, but "living water" certainly qualifies for immersion after *niddah*, as it is considered more perfunctory than a mikvah.

water poured over the head, which might constitute a shower, would suffice.⁴⁶ A creative reworking of chapter 7 allows Messianic believers to apply the practice of family purity to the best of their ability. While these alternatives are not completely acceptable for Jewish women under the strict interpretations of Jewish law, they do provide viable Apostolic-era alternatives in a majority of cases, and they should certainly suffice for Gentile believers observing the commandment of family purity.

---

46 In halachah the example of the *ba'al keri* might suffice as well. A *ba'al keri* (בעל קרי) is a male who has had a nocturnal emission or sexual relations, and according to the Torah he must immerse in order to become clean (Leviticus 15:16–18; Deuteronomy 23:10–11). While a *ba'al keri's* uncleanness specifically applies to entering the Temple, the sages extended it to prayer and Torah study. As a result, the issue arose of the impractical nature of a man immersing every time he becomes a *ba'al keri*. In concession the sages of the Talmud declared, "A *ba'al keri* on whom nine *kavim* of water have been thrown is clean" (b.*Brachot* 22a). Some Orthodox Jews still observe the obligation to cleanse oneself when in a state of *ba'al keri* by going to a mikvah, while others do so in light of the Talmud's ruling by taking a shower and letting the water run for two minutes or so. While this is not an acceptable alternative in Jewish halachah for a woman's immersion after *niddah*, it can serve as practical application for Messianic Gentiles in the absence of any suitable option. For sources and a halachic discussion on this, see "Halacha Highlight: Immersing in a Mikveh before Studying Torah," *Daf Yomi Digest* 22 (August 23, 2012): 2. Cited 8 October 2013. Online: http://www.dafdigest.org/berachos/Berachos%20022.pdf.

Commentary

⚜ Concerning immersion, immerse in this way. (DIDACHE 7.1)

The Didache begins its instructions on immersion with this simple introductory statement. Some scholars believe that these instructions are derived from an earlier Jewish source or from oral tradition in circulation during the Apostolic Era.[47]

The phrase "concerning" (*peri*), as we have noted previously, is used in the Didache to introduce a new topic.[48] This phrase corresponds to similar expressions in rabbinic literature that introduce new topics of halachah.[49] Additionally, an equivalent Hebrew word for "concerning" (*al*, על) is included in the blessing formula before performing commandments. For example, the Talmud renders the blessing before immersion, "Blessed be he who has sanctified us with his commandments and commanded us concerning immersion."[50]

The Apostolic Constitutions cites the Master's commandment in the Great Commission:

> Concerning immersion ... you shall so immerse as the Lord commanded us, saying: "Go therefore and make disciples of all nations, immersing them in the name of the Father, and the Son, and the Holy Spirit, teaching them to observe all that I have commanded you" [Matthew 28:19–20]: of the Father who sent, of Messiah who came, of the Comforter who testified. (Apostolic Constitutions 7.22)

The Apostolic Constitutions then adds: "But you shall beforehand anoint the person with the holy oil, and afterward immerse him with the water, and in the conclusion shall seal him with the ointment; that the anointing with oil may be the participation of the Holy Spirit, and the water the symbol of the death of Messiah, and the ointment the seal of the covenants. But if there be neither oil nor ointment,

---

47 Kurt Niederwimmer, *The Didache: Hermeneia—A Critical and Historical Commentary on the Bible* (Minneapolis, MN: Fortress, 1998), 126.
48 Didache 6.3, 9.1, 11.3; 1 Corinthians 7:1, 25, 8:1, 12:1, 16:1, 12; 1 Thessalonians 4:9, 5:1.
49 על זה נאמר, עליו. Jonathan A. Draper, "Weber, Theissen and 'Wandering Charismatics' in the Didache," *Journal of Early Christian Studies* 6, no. 4 (Winter 1998): 563, n. 109. Also, "A Hebrew parallel to this formation has come to light in the halakic letter from Qumran (*we-'al* ... , 4QMMT, *passim*)" (Peter J. Tomson, *'If This Be from Heaven ...' Jesus and the New Testament Authors in Their Relationship to Judaism* [Sheffield, England: Sheffield Academic Press, 2001], 387).
50 b.*Brachot* 51a.

water is sufficient both for the anointing, and for the seal, and for the confession of him that is dead, or indeed is dying together with Messiah."

⸙ Having first said all these things. (DIDACHE 7.1)

Prior to its teaching on immersion, the Didache emphasizes the need for instruction and for learning in the Way of Life. The new Gentile believer entering the community needed first to learn the Way of Life as taught in chapters 1–6 and in the Scriptures, making them part of his life and understanding. Immersion then confirmed this period of studying and training.

The Apostolic Constitutions gives a detailed list of pre-immersion instructions so that the new believer "might hate every way of iniquity, and walk in the way of truth, that he might be thought worthy of the laver of regeneration":

> Let him, therefore, who is to be taught the truth in regard to piety be instructed before his immersion in the knowledge of the unbegotten God, in the understanding of his only begotten Son, in the assured acknowledgment of the Holy Spirit. Let him learn the order of the several parts of the creation, the series of providence, the different dispensations of your laws. Let him be instructed why the world was made, and why man was appointed to be a citizen therein; let him also know his own nature, of what sort it is; let him be taught how God punished the wicked with water and fire, and did glorify the righteous ones in every generation—I mean Seth, and Enos, and Enoch, and Noah, and Abraham and his posterity, and Melchizedek, and Job, and Moses, and Joshua, and Caleb, and Phineas the priest, and those that were holy in every generation; and how God still took care of and did not reject mankind, but called them from their error and vanity to the acknowledgment of the truth at various seasons, reducing them from bondage and impiety unto liberty and piety, from injustice to righteousness, from death eternal to everlasting life. Let him that offers himself to immersion learn these and the like things during the time that he is a catechumen; and let him who lays his hands upon him adore God, the Lord of the whole world, and thank him for his creation, for his sending Messiah his only begotten Son, that he might save man by blotting out his transgressions, and that he might remit ungodliness and sins, and

might purify him "from every defilement of body and spirit" [2 Corinthians 7:1], and sanctify man according to the good pleasure of his kindness, that he might inspire him with the knowledge of his will, and enlighten the eyes of his heart to consider of his wonderful works, and make known to him the judgments of righteousness, that so he might hate every way of iniquity, and walk in the way of truth, that he might be thought worthy of the laver of regeneration, to the adoption of sons, which is in Messiah, that being "united with him in a death like Messiah's" [Romans 6:5], in hopes of a glorious communication, he may be mortified to sin, and may live to God, as to his mind, and word, and deed, and may be numbered together in the book of the living. And after this thanksgiving, let him instruct him in the doctrines concerning our Lord's incarnation, and in those concerning his passion, and resurrection from the dead, and assumption. (Apostolic Constitutions 7.39)

[7.1]
Having first said all these things.

The wording of the Greek in the Didache here almost implies that this instruction was recited immediately prior to immersion. The Greek word *proeipontes* (προειπόντες) comes from the root word *proeipon* (προεῖπον), which means "to say before," and in this context some have rendered it "repeat," that is, "after you have repeated these things."[51] This implies that the initiate needed to prove himself ready for immersion by reciting the teachings of the Didache. In rabbinic literature *mishnah* ("repeat," משנה) is a common idiom meaning "to study." In turn, this could simply imply that the initiate was to thoroughly study the Way of Life before immersion.

In the Talmud a potential proselyte is asked, "What reason have you for desiring to become a proselyte?" and then he is instructed "with some of the minor, and with some of the major commandments."[52] In the minor talmudic tractate *Gerim*, we read, "If, however, he undertakes [to be a proselyte], they take him down to the place of immersion, cover him in water up to his middle, and tell him some details of the precepts … As they say to a man, so they say to a woman."[53]

---

51 Walter Bauer, *A Greek-English Lexicon of the New Testament and Other Early Christian Literature* (eds. William Arndt, Frederick W. Danker, and F. Wilbur Gingrich; Chicago, IL: University of Chicago, 1958), 705.
52 b.*Yevamot* 47a–b.
53 *Gerim* 1:3–4 (60a). from Dr. Abraham Cohen, *The Minor Tractates of the Talmud* (2 vols.; London, England: Soncino, 1965), 2:603.

[7.1]
Having first said all these things.

In rabbinic tradition these pre-immersion instructions included the commandments of not collecting forgotten sheaves after harvesting one's field, leaving the corners of the field for the poor, and offering the poor man's tithe. The sages feared a non-Jew might be attracted to Judaism solely to benefit from these provisions for the needy. In turn, they also taught the potential proselyte the punishments for the transgression of the commandments and the penalty for breaking the Sabbath to ensure that he was sincere in his desire to convert. Oskar Skarsaune writes:

> In the pre-baptismal instruction, the proselyte is reminded that as a full fledge Israelite he is first and foremost obliged to do to others what he himself might crave for himself. In other words, the teaching about gleanings, etc. was probably to be seen as a concretization of Leviticus 19:18, "Love your neighbor as yourself."[54]

In this then we have a connection to the Didache, which begins with and focuses on the injunction to love one's fellow as oneself.

⁌ *Immerse in the name of the Father and the Son and the Holy Spirit.* (DIDACHE 7.1)

The Didache instructs that new Gentile believers in Messiah be immersed "in the name of the Father and the Son and the Holy Spirit," which is rendered almost identically to the Greek of the Master's commandment in Matthew 28:19.[55] The Didache could be quoting oral or written gospel material or sourcing some well-known liturgy.[56] This citation directly connects the immersion of the new Gentile believer to our Master Yeshua's injunction, "Go therefore and make disciples of all nations … teaching them to observe all that I have commanded you" (Matthew 28:19–20) and the Apostolic Constitutions (7.22) quotes this verse in its reworking of the Didache.

---

54 Skarsaune, *In the Shadow of the Temple*, 362.
55 Justin Martyr preserves, "On the name of God, the Father and Master [*despotes*, δεσπότης] of all, and of our Savior Yeshua the Messiah, and of the Holy Spirit." Some believe this is quite old based upon the distinctly Jewish language. Cf. "God who feeds and provides for all" (*Birkat HaMazon*); "God of the spirits of all flesh" (Numbers 27:16).
56 "It is uncertain as to whether the second redactor of the Didache simply has drawn upon the same tradition as that from which the Matthean redactor also has borrowed, or whether s/he in fact relies upon this particular form of the text as it appears in the Matthean Gospel" (Clayton N. Jefford, *The Sayings of Jesus in the Teaching of the Twelve Apostles* [New York, NY: Brill, 1989], 136).

The phrase "in the name of" (*leshem*, לשם) "is a Jewish technical term which means 'for the purpose of,' 'for the sake of,' 'with reference to.'"[57] For example, the mishnaic expression "in the name of heaven" means "for the sake of God."[58] Additionally, when a non-Jewish servant is acquired by a Jew, the slave must initially immerse "in the name of slavery"; when he is set free, he immerses "in the name of freedom."[59] Compare this also with Paul's rhetorical question, "Were you baptized in the name of Paul?"[60] One who immerses "in the name of the Father and the Son and the Holy Spirit" immerses for the sake of God and in mind of his mission of redemption through Yeshua the Messiah by the work of the Spirit. "By means of baptism a human being thus enters into that relationship which one has 'in mind' when performing the ritual ... ['Into the name of'] expresses the intention of cultic action."[61]

The expression "in the name of the Father and the Son and the Holy Spirit" is one of the only Christological references in the Didache. Some scholars have thus speculated that this passage was interpolated by church writers under the influence of later Trinitarian doctrines. As we have pointed out, the expression is directly related to Matthew 28:19, which contains exactly the same wording. While no manuscript textual variants of this passage in Matthew exist, some scholars have pointed to the writings of Eusebius (260–340), who often quotes a shorter version of

[7.1]
Immerse in the name of the Father and the Son and the Holy Spirit.

---

57 Huub van de Sandt and David Flusser, *The Didache: Its Jewish Sources and Its Place in Early Judaism and Christianity* (Minneapolis, MN: Fortress, 2002), 285. For a good survey of the usage of the phrase "in the name of" in Jewish literature, see Lars Hartman, "Baptism 'Into the Name of Jesus' and Early Christology," *Studia Theologica* 28 (1974): 21–48.
58 Cf. m.*Avot* 4:11, 5:17.
59 b.*Yevamot* 45b, 47b. Cf. b.*Avodah Zarah* 27a.
60 1 Corinthians 1:13. Cf. "And [Paul] said, 'Into what then were you baptized?' They said, 'Into John's baptism'" (Acts 19:3).
61 Van de Sandt and Flusser, *The Didache*, 285.

[7.1]
Immerse in the name of the Father and the Son and the Holy Spirit.

this passage: "Go and make disciples of all nations in my name."[62] We find evidence of a shorter version in a handful of other non-canonical gospel citations as well.[63]

However, every textual witness to a version of Matthew 28:19 contains the tripartite formula. We find similar three-part expressions in other New Testament passages as well: "The grace of the [Master Yeshua the Messiah] and the love of God and the fellowship of the Holy Spirit be with you all" (2 Corinthians 13:14), and, "According to the foreknowledge of God the Father, in the sanctification of the Spirit, for obedience to [Yeshua the Messiah]" (1 Peter 1:2).[64] There is no reason then to believe that the texts of Matthew 28:19 and Didache 7.2 are a later interpolation. It could very well be that the version Eusebius quotes and the other textual witnesses of this phrase existed side by side with the canonical version, or they could have been truncated or paraphrased traditions of the canonical texts.[65]

---

62 In all sixteen of Eusebius' references to this passage before the council of Nicaea (325), he quotes this shorter version. It is not until after Nicaea that he quotes the canonical longer version. This has caused some to speculate that this change was influenced by the Trinitarian doctrines of the council. See Fred C. Conybeare, "The Eusebian Form of the Text of Matthew 28:19," *Zeitschrift für Neutestamentlich Wissenschaft* (1901): 275–288.

63 For example, Hebrew University scholar Shlomo Pines uncovered the work of an Arabic writer from the eleventh century who quotes a Hebrew version of the gospel that he claims goes back to early Jewish believers: "[Yeshua] and his companions behaved constantly in this manner, until he left this world. He said to his companions: 'Act as you have seen me act, instruct people in accordance with instructions I have given you, and be for them what I have been for you.' His companions behaved constantly in this manner and in accordance with this" (Shlomo Pines, *The Jewish Christians of the Early Centuries of Christianity According to a New Source* [Jerusalem, Israel: Central, 1966], 25). Additionally, in the fourth-century *Prophecy of the Tiburtine Sibyl*, we read, "Go, and the teaching that you have received from me, teach to all the peoples, subjecting all the nations by means of seventy-two languages"; and in the Coptic *Discourse on Mary Theotokos* by Cyril Archbishop of Jerusalem (mid-sixth century or earlier), we find, "The Messiah said, 'You shall go into all the world, and teach all the nations in my name in every place.'"

64 Also 1 Corinthians 12:4–6; 2 Thessalonians 2:13–14.

65 Flusser and Van de Sandt see a parallel between "Go and make disciples of all nations in my name" and the common rabbinic practice of reciting a teaching in the name of the teacher who taught it first: "The possessor of Torah is one who ... notes with precision that which he has heard, and says a thing in the name of him who said it. For you have learned: Everyone that says a thing in the name of him who said it, brings deliverance into the world, as it is said: 'and Esther told the king thereof in Mordecai's name'" (m.*Avot* 6:6). "The rabbinic expression בשם ('in the name of') is commonly used in the context of handing down a teaching ... The resurrected Jesus is said to have commanded his disciples to instruct all nations *in his name*, which means that the disciples should teach the doctrine of their master (all that he has commanded) after his death" (*The Didache*, 289).

Furthermore, the threefold formula presented in the Didache and Matthew do not represent the "full-blown developed doctrine of the Trinity as it was later defined."[66]

David Flusser and Huub Van de Sandt argue that the tripartite immersion formula may have been influenced by the rabbinic custom to immerse three times.[67] The Apostolic Constitutions instructs that the new initiate be immersed three times based upon the three-part formula.[68] This then is supported by 7.3: "Pour water on the head three times in the name of the Father and the Son and the Holy Spirit."

Another matter concerning the Didache's immersion formula "in the name of the Father and the Son and the Holy Spirit" is the complete absence of its use from the immersions performed in the book of Acts and in the rest of the New Testament. There we find "in the name of Yeshua the Messiah" and "in the name of the Master Yeshua."[69] Some scholars are quick to use this as evidence that Matthew's version is indeed a later addition, but there is no reason to suppose that these different versions could not have been in use simultaneously. The apostles and early believers were "not bound by precise 'formulas' and felt no embarrassment at a multiplicity of them, precisely because Jesus' instruction, which may not have been in these precise words, was not regarded as a binding formula."[70]

One possible reason for the various immersion formulas is that they were used for different circumstances. Willy Rordorf suggests that the formula "in the name of Yeshua" was used for Jewish immersion into Messiah, whereas "in the name of the Father and the Son and the Holy Spirit" was used when immersing Gentiles. Gentiles "had to confess, first of all, the one God, Father of Jesus Christ, in order to

[7.1] *Immerse in the name of the Father and the Son and the Holy Spirit.*

---

66   Van de Sandt and Flusser, *The Didache*, 287. "It is my argument, then, that neither formula in the Didache can be taken, without qualification, as evidence for a deliberate, distinctive christological content in the baptism rite" (Nathan Mitchell, "Baptism in the Didache," in *The Didache in Context: Essays on Its Text, History & Transmission* [ed. Clayton N. Jefford; Leiden, The Netherlands: Brill, 1995], 227–255). Whatever the triune theology of some early Jewish believers, it was fairly widespread, e.g., Odes of Solomon 23:5–6, 21–22; Martyrdom and Ascension of Isaiah 1:7, 8:16–18, 9:27–42; Pseudo-Clementine Recognitions 1.69.5.
67   Van de Sandt and Flusser, *The Didache*, 290. See Daniel Sperber, *Why Jews Do What They Do: The History of Jewish Customs Throughout the Cycle of the Jewish Year* (Hoboken, NJ: KTAV, 1999), 173–174.
68   Apostolic Constitutions 8.47. Cf. Tertullian, *Against Praxeas* 26.
69   Acts 2:38, 8:16, 10:48, 19:5; Romans 6:3. Cf. Galatians 3:27; Shepherd of Hermas, Vision 3.7.3 (15.3).
70   D.A. Carson, "Matthew," in *The Expositor's Bible Commentary: Matthew, Mark, Luke* (ed. Frank E. Gaebelein; 12 vols.; Grand Rapids, MI: Zondervan, 1990), 8:598. "It would be misleading here to imagine that one has here a 'baptismal formula' ... Had such a formula been used, one would have expected some such entire formula to be spelled out as in the case of the eucharistic prayers" (Milavec, *The Didache: Faith, Hope, & Life of the Earliest Christian Communities, 50–70 C.E.*, 266).

[7.1]
Immerse in the name of the Father and the Son and the Holy Spirit

be baptized."[71] Non-Jews needed to be brought into monotheism, whereas Jewish people already adhered to this belief and needed only to be brought into Messiah.[72] This also sheds light on why in 9.5 we find the shorter formula "in the name of the Lord," since Gentile disciples by that point in the Didache had accepted the Lord as their Father and as the one true God.

◈ *In living water.* (DIDACHE 7.2)

The Didache prefers that immersion be done in "living water" (*udor zon*, ὕδωρ ζῶν), a phrase equivalent to the Hebrew expression *mayim chayim* (מים חיים). *Mayim chayim* refers to non-stagnant water that has not been manipulated by plumbing, meaning sources such as rivers, springs, and lakes. For water to be classified in Jewish law as "living water," it must consist of "water that issues out of the ground with a natural force that makes it 'alive.' It must be good tasting, i.e., not salty or warm."[73] Additionally, it was required that the water be flowing.

In the Gospels we read that John was immersing "at Aenon near Salim, because water was plentiful there," which is most likely a reference to the fulfillment of the requirement of "living water."[74] In the book of Acts, immersion often took place near a natural body of water, fulfilling the requirement of "living water."[75] Justin

---

71   Willy Rordorf, "Baptism According to the Didache," in *The Didache in Modern Research* (ed. Jonathan A. Draper; Leiden, The Netherlands: Brill, 1996), 217–218. Rordorf also states, "One notes the same change of viewpoint in Justin: in *Dial* 39:2 when he addressed himself to Jews, he speaks of baptism in the name of Jesus alone; in *1 Apol* 61:3, 10, 13, when he addresses himself to Gentiles, he uses the Trinitarian formula" (218, n. 28).

72   "I would add the possibility that 'baptized in the name of the Lord' (9:5), might be heard as 'in the name of the Lord God' by gentiles and 'in the name of the Lord Jesus' by Jews. Either way, the hearer would approve the formulation and embrace it as his/her own" (Milavec, *The Didache: Faith, Hope, & Life of the Earliest Christian Communities, 50–70 C.E.*, 272).

73   Rabbi Nosson Sherman and Rabbi Meir Lebowitz, eds., *Yad Avraham Mishnah Series: Seder Tohoros* (10 vols.; Brooklyn, NY: Mesorah, 2001), 4b:39.

74   John 3:23; William Sanford La Sor, "Discovering What Jewish Miqva'ot Can Tell Us about Christian Baptism," *Biblical Archaeology Review* 13, no. 1 (January–February 1987): 52–59.

75   Acts 8:36, 16:13.

Martyr's writings as well as the Jewish Christian Clementine literature and other sources continue to show precedence for immersing in living water.[76]

[7.2] *In living water.*

In Jewish law living water usually refers to a "spring" (*ma'ayan*, מעין) and is the most superior form of purification waters.[77] "Living water" is mentioned in the Torah in regard to the purification procedures of a person or house cured from a disfiguring disease (*tzara'at*, צרעת), the immersion of one who has been cured of a discharge affliction (*zav*, זב), and the requirement to mix it with the ashes of the red heifer to purify someone who has come in contact with a dead body (*tamei met*, טמא מת).[78] Therefore, Jewish law requires that immersion be done only in "living water" for these three impurities.

However, there is evidence that some Jewish authorities extended the requirement of living water to conversion immersions.[79] This is not surprising, since "the rabbis argued that 'the uncleanness of idols' was analogous to leprosy or corpse defilement."[80] The Didache mirrors this tradition by showing its preference for living water. The Scriptures reveal a deeply spiritual meaning in the expression "living water."

It is found in Song of Songs 4:15: "a garden fountain, a well of living water." This phrase was interpreted as an allegory for the blessings that flow forth from the *Shechinah*.[81] Zechariah foretold, "On that day living waters shall flow out from

---

76   "They are brought by us where there is water" (Justin, *1 Apology* 61:2–3). In Clementine literature we see this statement most notably here: "For thus the prophet has sworn to us, saying, 'Truly I say to you, unless you be regenerated by living water into the name of the Father, Son, and Holy Spirit, you shall not enter the kingdom of heaven'" (Pseudo-Clementine Homilies 11.26). This statement appears to be an altered form of John 3:5, perhaps even influenced by Pseudo-Clementine Recognitions 1.69.5. Cf. Pseudo-Clementine Homilies 9.19, 11.35–36; Pseudo-Clementine Recognitions 4.32. Also note the injunction of Hippolytus, *Apostolic Tradition* (21:2): "When they come to the water, the water shall be pure and flowing, that is, the water of a spring or a flowing body of water."
77   m.*Mikva'ot* 1:8. Living water is also attested to in Community Rule (1QS) IX and the universal Jewish Sibylline Oracles 4.165. There seem to be texts that imply some Gentiles would have preferred "living water" in religious ceremony from their own pagan background. Cf: "(I would like to ask) to take some running water in pitchers, so we may pour a (proper) libation to the gods. The trickles of stagnant water are not clear, and are being all churned up by our numerous host" (Euripides, *Hypsipyle* frg. 752h.29–32).
78   Leviticus 14:5–9, 50–53, 15:13; Numbers 19:17. See Rabbi Steinsaltz, *The Talmud Steinsaltz Edition: A Reference Guide*, 215.
79   Sibylline Oracles 4.162–170.
80   Milavec, *The Didache: Faith, Hope, & Life of the Earliest Christian Communities, 50–70 C.E.*, 262, citing y.*Pesachim* 9:1; b.*Avodah Zarah* 32b; b.*Chullin* 13b.
81   *Zohar* I, 135b. Cf. I, 132a, III, 201b. "This verse also refers to the Torah, both Written and Oral parts, which is a source of sustenance; 'a garden storing, a well of living water *which streams* from Lebanon'—i.e., which emanates from God who dwells in the Temple referred to as Lebanon (*Ibn Aknin*)" (Rabbi Meir Zlotowitz, *Shir HaShirim: Song of Songs/A New with a Commentary Anthologized from Talmudic, Midrashic and Rabbinic Sources* [Brooklyn, NY: Mesorah, 2000], 142).

[7.2]
In living water.

Jerusalem" (Zechariah 14:8). "Living water" is then an "expression of eschatological cleansing, renewal, and fertility."[82] The Master uses this term to express the foretaste of the kingdom of heaven that is available to all those who abide in him: "If you knew the gift of God, and who it is that is saying to you, 'Give me a drink,' you would have asked him, and he would have given you living water" (John 4:10); "Whoever believes in me, as the Scripture has said, 'Out of his heart will flow rivers of living water'" (John 7:38). When believers immerse in living water, we symbolically come into contact with the blessings of the Messianic Era.

◈ *But if you do not have living water, immerse in other water.* (DIDACHE 7.2)

Didache 7.2 begins with the phrase "But if" (*ean de*, ἐὰν δὲ), which seems to betray an underlying Semitism.[83] Although the ideal is to immerse in "living water," concessions are made: If living water is not available, then "other water" will suffice; if one does not have cold, then warm is acceptable. If all else fails, water is to be poured over the head three times. The fourth-century *Canons of Hippolytus* makes similar provision: "The stream shall flow through the baptismal tank or pour into it from above when there is no scarcity of water; but if there is a scarcity, whether constant or sudden, then use whatever water you can find."[84]

Despite the Didache's acquiescence regarding immersion in living water, its injunctions still fall within the fold of Jewish immersion instructions. The entire discussion of water preferences sounds as if it originates in rabbinic discourse. In the Mishnah we find a teaching on the "six degrees of gathering of water" used in purification: the water of pits, rainwater that has not been collected, a mikvah of

---

82 Jonathan A Draper, "Ritual Process and Ritual Symbol in Didache 7–10," *Vigiliae Christianae* 54, no. 2 (2000): 144.

83 "The short instruction concerning apostles in [Didache] 11:3–6 bears the same casuistic structure and tone as the instructions in Didache 6, 7, 9–10: first the statement of the general principle in the imperative, then particular specifications and qualifications of the general principle, followed by a statement of the limit of what is permissible. The casuistic style is marked by expressions reflecting underlying semitisms: πᾶς, ἐὰν δὲ, as well as a negative formulation. (G. Schille ["Das Recht der Propheten und Apostel—gemeinderechtliche Beobachtungen zu Didache Kapitel 11–13," *Theologische Versuche* I, eds. P. Wätzel and G. Schille (Berlin: Evangelische Verlaganstalt, 1966), 89–90] sees these reflecting the Semitic כל and כי אם.) "It has a restrained and undeveloped tone very different from the instructions about the prophets, which bear the stamp of a burning issue" (Draper, "Weber, Theissen and 'Wandering Charismatics' in the Didache," 565).

84 *Canons of Hippolytus* 21.

forty *se'ah*, a spring (*ma'ayan*) to which water has been added, water that is living but not drinkable (*mayim mukkin*, מים מוכין), and living water (*mayim chayim*).[85] Each water listed is inferior to the next.

The following chart compares the rabbinic list to the Didache's list:

M.MIKVA'OT 1:1–8	DIDACHE 7.1–3
Living water	Living water
Spring water that is bitter	Other water
A spring to which water is added	Cold water
Mikvah of forty *se'ah*	Warm water
Rainwater not collected	Drawn water poured over the head three times
Water of pits	

[7.2] *But if you do not have living water, immerse in other water.*

Skarsaune writes:

> The prescriptions about different kinds of immersion water are very close to the ruling of the Mishnah, at least in the evaluating principles applied. From the outside, no big difference would be observed between Jewish and Christian immersion of converts. If the community to which the Didache is addressed had no suitable river in the neighborhood and decided to build a baptismal pool, they would very likely build it according to the same standards as the Jewish ritual baths.[86]

Once again this displays the Didache's concern with ritual purity.[87] It was not until the time of Tertullian (160–225) that the spirit of the Didache's concessions were misinterpreted to mean, "It makes no difference whether a man be washed in a sea or a pool, a stream or a fount, a lake or a trough."[88]

It is difficult to know for sure to what "other water" (*allo udor*, ἄλλο ὕδωρ) the Didache refers. Kurt Niederwimmer feels that it "probably means water taken or

---

85   m.*Mikva'ot* 1:1–8.
86   Skarsaune, *In the Shadow of the Temple*, 366.
87   Van de Sandt and Flusser, *The Didache*, 283.
88   Tertullian, *On Baptism* 4.3.

[7.2]
But if you do not have living water, immerse in other water.

diverted from a spring or river but still possessing its original 'cool' temperature."[89] However, it seems most probable that the Didache is referring to a mikvah.

A mikvah "in the strict sense of the word refers only to a pool of rainwater (not of spring water)."[90] The Torah states, "A spring or a cistern holding water shall be clean."[91] Rabbinic halachah interprets a "spring" (*ma'ayan*) as classifying as living water (*mayim chayim*), which must be used in the three cases mentioned above. In all other cases, immersion in a "cistern" (i.e., mikvah) is acceptable, which is interpreted as a pool of rainwater attached to the ground. For a pool of rainwater to be classified as a mikvah and valid for immersion, it must contain a minimum of forty *se'ah* (approximately 77.6 gallons) of water, and the water must not be flowing.[92] Once this minimum quantity of rainwater is present, drawn water (*sh'uvin*, שאובין) can be added.[93]

In the days of the Second Temple Era, *mikva'ot* could be manmade following detailed halachah, and, if needed, non-rainwater could be added to the forty *se'ah* of rainwater through a special process. It is the same today. In the book of Acts, the three thousand who were immersed on Shavu'ot would have been immersed in the numerous manmade *mikva'ot* on the southern end of the Temple Mount. Most of these *mikva'ot* were of the rainwater variety.[94] Early Christian baptismal pools found in "Israel, Turkey, Greece, and Rome were built on the same principle as *mikva'ot*."[95]

◉ *And if you cannot immerse in cold water, then immerse in warm water.* (DIDACHE 7.2)

The Didache now concedes that if cold water cannot be used, warm should be used instead. Cold water seems to be the ideal state for living water in Jewish literature. Josephus records that the Jewish ascetic Banus, who lived a life similar to John the

---

89 Niederwimmer, *The Didache*, 127–128.
90 Rabbi Sherman and Rabbi Lebowitz, *Yad Avraham Mishnah Series: Seder*, 4b:36. Cf. "The waters that were gathered together [*mikvah*] he called Seas" (Genesis 1:10).
91 Leviticus 11:36.
92 "The Torah specifies *a pit of gathered waters*. 'Gathered' means still water" (Rabbi Sherman and Rabbi Lebowitz, *Yad Avraham Mishnah Series: Seder*, 4b:10).
93 Water poured from a vessel takes on the Jewish legal category of drawn water (*sh'uvin*).
94 Acts 2:41. In Jerusalem alone archeologists have uncovered over 150 *mikva'ot*. See Ronny Reich, "Design and Maintenance of First-century Ritual Immersion Baths," *Jerusalem Perspective* 56 (July/September 1999): 14–19.
95 Moyes, "*A Fresh Look at New Testament Baptism.*"

Baptist, immersed "himself in cold water frequently, both by night and by day, in order to preserve his chastity."⁹⁶ Also the the Elcesaites, who were Jewish disciples of Yeshua, instructed those afflicted with disease to immerse "in cold water forty times during seven days."⁹⁷ In some modern Jewish movements, immersion in cold water and covering oneself in snow is thought to inspire true repentance.⁹⁸

[7.2]
And if you cannot immerse in cold water, then immerse in warm water.

Scholars debate the reason for the allowance of warm water in the Didache. Some feel that "warm water" refers to water that has been intentionally heated for a variety of reasons. For example, Rordorf and André Tuilier suggest that this might be done because of cold weather.⁹⁹ Others feel that the water could be heated "in the event of sickness or weakness" of the one who was about to be immersed.¹⁰⁰ For example, if the high priest performing services in the Temple (who needed to immerse several times during his service on Yom Kippur) was "old or extremely sensitive they would prepare for him hot water ... to temper its chill."¹⁰¹

More likely the Didache refers to water heated naturally by the sun. Niederwimmer writes, "This does not mean water that has been 'warmed' (perhaps out of concern for the sick), but probably standing water in cisterns or the like, that is, water that no longer has its fresh temperature."¹⁰²

In the Mishnah's list of preferred types of water, "bitter water" from a spring (*mayim mukkin*) ranks second.¹⁰³ This refers to water that is "salty or warm and hence not good tasting."¹⁰⁴ "Bitter water" is a step down from "living water," because in Jewish law living water (*mayim chayim*) in the Torah is interpreted as "sweet [i.e., palatable] water."¹⁰⁵ In turn, when the Didache references "warm" water, it might be referring to spring water that is warm or bitter, which is not as ideal as clean, cold, living water.

---

96   Josephus, *The Life* 11/ii.
97   Hippolytus of Rome, *The Refutation of All Heresies* 9.16.
98   While Rebbe Nachman of Breslov was still in his youth he would roll around undressed in the snow in order to achieve self mastery. See Rabbi Nathan of Nemirov, *Rebbe Nachman's Wisdom* (trans. Rabbi Aryeh Kaplan; Monsey, NY: Breslov Research Institute, 1973), 26.
99   Willy Rordorf and André Tuilier, *La Doctrine des Douze Apôtres (Didachè)* (Paris, France: Cerf, 1978), 171, as translated in Michelle Murray, *Playing A Jewish Game: Gentile Christian Judaizing in the First and Second Centuries CE* (Waterloo, Ontario: Wilfred Laurier University Press, 2004), 65.
100 Canon Spence, *The Teaching of the Twelve Apostles* (London, England: James Nisbet and Co., 1885), 32.
101 m.*Yoma* 3:5.
102 Niederwimmer, *The Didache*, 127–128. See also Van de Sandt, "Do Not Give What Is Holy to the Dogs," 241; Arthur Vööbus, *Liturgical Traditions in the Didache* (Wetteren, Belgium: Cultura, 1968), 24.
103 m.*Mikva'ot* 1:8.
104 Rabbi Sherman and Rabbi Lebowitz, *Yad Avraham Mishnah Series: Seder*, 4b:39.
105 Ibid.

[7.2]
And if you cannot immerse in cold water, then immerse in warm water.

It is not improbable that the Didache has all the above in mind. Chapter 7 therefore sanctions in special circumstances, when living water cannot be found or used (because of the state of the one immersing or the season), that warm (or bitter) water may be substituted.

> *But if you do not have either in sufficient quantity to immerse, pour water on the head three times in the name of the Father and the Son and the Holy Spirit.*
> (DIDACHE 7.3)

Didache 7.3, like 7.2, opens with the Semitic phrase "But if" (*ean de*).[106] In its final concessions regarding immersion, the Didache allows, if nothing else is available, water to be poured three times over the head of the one being immersed. The issue here concerned the unavailability of a sufficient amount of water, which fact is reinforced by the Georgian version of the Didache: "If, however, you do not have enough of either, then pour out some water three times over the head."[107] Water poured from a vessel takes on the Jewish legal category of drawn water (*sh'uvin*).

In Jewish thought the "head" is the "seat of intelligence" and is used as an idiom in the Hebrew Scriptures to represent the entire man.[108] William Varner writes, "The aspiration of the head was the nearest substitute for total immersion, since the head is the chief part of man."[109] However, this does not mean that the rest of the body was not drenched, only that the water was to be applied, beginning at the head.

The water was to be poured on the head three times, likely in imitation of the oral tradition to immerse three times—a regular practice in Judaism and mentioned in the Apostolic Constitutions.[110] The formula "in the name of the Father and the Son and the Holy Spirit," is almost identical to the tripartite formula in 7.2 and in Matthew 28:19, with the exception of the missing definite articles in Greek.

---

106   See Draper, "Weber, Theissen and 'Wandering Charismatics' in the Didache," 565.
107   Rordorf, "Baptism According to the Didache," 219.
108   Philip Schaff, *The Oldest Church Manual Called the Teaching of the Twelve Apostles* (Edinburgh, Scotland: T&T Clark, 1885), 186; Judges 5:30.
109   William Varner, *The Way of the Didache: The First Christian Handbook* (New York, NY: University Press of America, 2007), 73–74.
110   Apostolic Constitutions 8.47. Cf. Tertullian, *Against Praxeas* 26.

Pouring water over the head in lieu of full immersion is not foreign to Jewish law. For example, the sages ruled that under constraint a male who has had a seminal emission (*ba'al keri*, בעל קרי) was permitted to be purified by having nine *kavim* of water poured on his head from a vessel.¹¹¹ Additionally, according to the Torah, when an Israelite came into contact with a human corpse, he could be purified only through the sprinkling of a mixture of living water and ashes from a completely red heifer.¹¹² Skarsaune feels that this ritual "is one of the closest analogies to Gentile defilement, that of corpses, [which] required sprinkling with purifying water. This could be the background for the emergency alternative of baptism by effusion in the Didache."¹¹³

[7.3]
But if you do not have either in sufficient quantity to immerse, pour water on the head three times in the name of the Father and the Son and the Holy Spirit.

Another parallel to Jewish law is found in the water having to be poured from a vessel and not from a faucet or the like. Jonathan Draper points out that by requiring a vessel, "there is no contact with the source of the water and the person being baptized [so that] it cannot become a 'father of impurity' and ritual purity is maintained (cf. m.*Tohorot* 4:11)."¹¹⁴ Therefore, even in allowing the pouring of water in special circumstances, the Didache maintains its concerns about ritual purity.

In actual practice the amount of water poured needed to be enough to drench the entire body so that all areas of the body were covered equally, as if the person had immersed:

> The very notion of "pouring" must have been perceived as approximating "flowing water" … The presumption would be in the direction of assuming that as much water was poured as possible—taking due account of the availability of water and the strength of the one baptizing.¹¹⁵

Full drenching was ensured by carrying out the process three times. The concession of pouring allowed the one being immersed to be fully covered with water, even when a sufficient pool was not available. Archeological evidence suggests that this

---

111 Leviticus 15:16–18; Deuteronomy 23:10–11; m.*Mikva'ot* 3:4; y.*Brachot* 3:4; b.*Brachot* 22a. However, the one pouring must be ritually clean himself. See Van de Sandt and Flusser, *The Didache*, 283; Gedaliah Alon, "The Halacha in the Teaching of the Twelve Apostles," in *The Didache in Modern Research* (ed. Jonathan A. Draper; Leiden, The Netherlands: Brill, 1996), 190–191.
112 Numbers 19.
113 Skarsaune, *In the Shadow of the Temple*, 366.
114 Draper, "Ritual Process and Ritual Symbol in Didache 7–10," 133.
115 Milavec, *The Didache: Faith, Hope, & Life of the Earliest Christian Communities, 50–70 C.E.*, 264. "It can hardly be expected that so little water would have been used as to interpret this instruction as allowing for mere sprinkling with water or pouring only a token quantity—practices that appear to have emerged no earlier than the mid-third century."

procedure took place as the one having water poured upon his or her head stood either in running water such as a shallow stream or in a basin to collect the water.[116]

> ◈ *Prior to the immersion, the one performing the immersion and the one being immersed should fast beforehand, and also any others if they can. Require the one being immersed to fast one or two days prior to the immersion.* (DIDACHE 7.4)

In this concluding instruction on immersion, the Didache enjoins both the one being immersed and the one overseeing the immersion to fast.[117] Others in the community could join in the fasting to support the new initiate if they wished to, but for them it was optional. In the Bible a fast is an abstention from both food and water, as we read in the book of Esther: "Hold a fast on my behalf, and do not eat or drink" (Esther 4:16).

Although the injunction to fast before immersion is not found in the New Testament, it is highly improbable that it was invented by the writers of the Didache. Aaron Milavec points out that "the presentation is so low key, so matter of fact, that it must be surmised that the Didache is merely giving voice to a tradition already practiced."[118] The Apostolic Constitutions strengthens the Didache's injunction with the example of our Master:

> But before immersion, let him that is to be immersed fast; for even the Lord, when he was first immersed by John, and abode in the wilderness, did afterward fast forty days and forty nights [Matthew 3:16–4:2]. But he was immersed, and then fasted, not having himself any need of cleansing, or of fasting, or of purgation, who was by nature pure and holy; but that he might testify the truth to John, and afford an example to us. Wherefore our Lord was not immersed into his own passion, or death, or resurrection—for none of those things had then

---

116 For images of early Christian art depicting immersion by pouring, see Frederick van der Meer and Christine Mohrmann, *Atlas of the Early Christian World* (London, England: Nelson, 1966), plates 45, 396–397. In these images the one being immersed stands in ankle deep water while having water poured over his head.

117 The Jewish believers' Clementine literature is also adamant that the one being immersed fast a day before immersion. See Pseudo-Clementine Homilies 3.73, 13.11, 12, 13.9, 10, 11.35; Pseudo-Clementine Recognitions 3.67, 7.34, 35, 37.

118 Milavec, *The Didache: Faith, Hope, & Life of the Earliest Christian Communities, 50–70 C.E.*, 253.

happened—but for another purpose. Wherefore he by his own authority fasted after his immersion, as being the Lord of John. But he who is to be initiated into his death ought first to fast, and then to be immersed. For it is not reasonable that he who has been buried with Messiah, and is risen again with him, should appear dejected at his very resurrection. For man is not lord of our Savior's constitution, since one is the Master and the other the servant. (Apostolic Constitutions 7.22)[119]

Judaism even has a precedent for fasting before proselyte immersion. The first-century Jewish work Joseph and Aseneth is an apocryphal account of Joseph's marriage to Aseneth, the daughter of an Egyptian priest. In the account Aseneth converts to Judaism before her marriage to Joseph. Prior to her immersion she fasts for seven days and offers up prayers of repentance: "I have sinned, O Lord, I have sinned. I have transgressed your law and acted impiously, and I have spoken things evil before you. My mouth, O Lord, has been defiled by things offered to idols, and by the table of the gods of the Egyptians."[120] Like Aseneth, the new Gentile disciple certainly needed to take a deep look into his past life and confess all those areas in which he had sinned before coming to faith in Messiah.[121] Fasting served as a time for one to search out his heart and make a clean break with the past.

In Judaism fasting also served as a tool for "preparing and fine-tuning" oneself to meet with the Almighty.[122] As Daniel prepared to receive a vision from God, he "ate no delicacies, no meat or wine entered [his] mouth, nor did [he] anoint [himself] at all, for the full three weeks" (Daniel 10:3). In the book of Acts, it was during a period of fasting that the Holy Spirit spoke to the believers in Antioch and said, "Set apart for me Barnabas and Saul for the work to which I have called them" (Acts 13:2).[123] Likewise, the new Gentile believer readied his soul through fasting to experience the transforming power of God.

Finally, fasting before immersion had the effect of ritually purifying the believer and preparing him for fellowship with the community. According to the Epistle of

[7.4]
Prior to the immersion, the one performing the immersion and the one being immersed should fast beforehand, and also any others if they can. Require the one being immersed to fast one or two days prior to the immersion.

---

119 Additionally, John, for his part, preached the message that one must repent (*teshuvah*, תשובה) before being immersed, which to Jewish ears most likely included some fasting. We also find that Paul "for three days ... neither ate nor drank," after which "he rose and was baptized" (Acts 9:9, 18).
120 Joseph and Aseneth 10:20, 12:5.
121 Justin Martyr teaches that the one being immersed is "instructed to pray and to entreat God with fasting, for the remission of their sins that are past" (*First Apology* 61.2). Cf. Tertullian, *On Baptism* 20.
122 Thomas O'Loughlin, *The Didache: A Window on the Earliest Christians* (Grand Rapids, MI: Baker, 2010), 62.
123 Cf. Acts 14:23.

[7.4]
Prior to the immersion, the one performing the immersion and the one being immersed should fast beforehand, and also any others if they can. Require the one being immersed to fast one or two days prior to the immersion.

Barnabas, before coming to God an individual was "a temple truly built by hands; for it was full of idolatry and was a house of demons."[124] As with Aseneth, the new believer's past behavior included partaking of food and drink offered to idols. The fasting ensured "that food eaten in the state of idolatry [was] purged."[125] After immersion the new Gentile initiates totally refrained from idolatrous food and things tainted with idolatry and henceforth were included in the communal meals.

It is important to point out that contrary to current church practice, the one performing the immersion did not dunk or touch the one being immersed.[126] According to Jewish law, it is imperative that the water touch all parts of the naked human body during the immersion—that no garments or accessories be worn and that nothing touch the body. These items are considered a *chatzitzah* ("barrier," חציצה), and if they touch the body, the immersion is considered invalid.[127] In keeping with Jewish law, the *Apostolic Tradition* rules, "They shall take off all their clothes ... the women, after they have unbound their hair, and removed their jewelry. No one shall take any foreign object with themselves down into the water ... They shall stand in the water naked."[128] "The one performing the immersion" served rather as a witness to the immersion to ensure that it was done properly and that the one being immersed was submerged completely beneath the water. This was the practice of John the Baptist and the apostles.[129]

---

124 Barnabas 16.7. The connection of baptism with the casting out of demons (and in later cases, renouncing allegiance to the devil) is strong early on. Jewish believers maintained this connection into the third and fourth centuries as evidenced by Pseudo-Clementine Homilies (8.22–23).
125 Draper, "The Holy Vine of David Made Known to the Gentiles through God's Servant Jesus," 270.
126 Additionally, the Didache gives no instructions on who can perform the immersion but the Apostolic Constitutions adds, "Concerning immersion, O overseer, or elder, we have already given direction, and we now say, that you shall immerse ..." (7.22).
127 m.*Mikva'ot* 8:5.
128 Hippolytus, *Apostolic Tradition* 21.3–11.
129 Commenting on the phrase "baptized by him" (Luke 3:7), Samuel Lachs writes, "MS D reads 'to be baptized before him' ... If this is the correct reading it might well stem from the Heb. *lifanav*, meaning by the 'authority of' or 'by the direction of' John" (Lachs, *A Rabbinic Commentary on the New Testament: The Gospels of Matthew, Mark, and Luke* [Hoboken, NJ: KTAV, 1987], 42). Cf., "They both went down into the water, Philip and the eunuch, and he baptized him. And when they came up out of the water ..." (Acts 8:38–39).

Chapter Eight

DIDACHE 8

8.1 Your fast days should not coincide with those of the hypocrites,[1] for they fast on the second day of the week and on the fifth day.[2] But you are to fast on the fourth day and on the preparation day.[3]

8.2 Nor should you pray like the hypocrites[4] but just as the Lord commanded in his good news.

This is what you should pray:[5]

> Our Father, who is in heaven,
> Let your name be sanctified.
> Let your kingdom come;
> Let your will be done—as in heaven, so on earth.
> Our bread of tomorrow, immediately give us today,
> And pardon us our debt,
> As we also pardon those indebted to us.
> And do not bring us into testing,
> But rescue us from what is evil.
> For yours is the power and the glory, forever and ever.[6]

8.3 This is what you should pray three times a day.[7]

---

1. Matthew 6:16.
2. Luke 18:12.
3. Matthew 27:62; Mark 15:42; Luke 23:54; John 19:14, 31, 42.
4. Matthew 6:5.
5. Matthew 6:9.
6. Matthew 6:9–13; Luke 11:2–4.
7. Daniel 6:10, 13.

Overview

Chapter 8 continues with the legal material of the Didache. It contains two short sections, one on fasting (8.1) and one on prayer (8.2–3). We see a link between this chapter and the previous one with the instructions in 7.4 regarding a fast before immersion and the current chapter's further legal injunctions on fasting.

The instructions here are short and simple. As with the instructions regarding immersion in the previous chapter, the Didache offers no explanations or spiritual meanings behind the legal injunctions. This indicates that the Didache is not introducing new practices but rather citing already-established customs within the Messianic communities. The Didache delivers its instructions regarding prayer and fasting "as the Lord commanded in his good news"; in other words, it simply delivers the established practice as commanded by Yeshua.

Fasting and prayer are central tenets of Jewish practice and intimately connected with one another. Rabbinic literature contains extensive legal discussions on both of these topics, and the Mishnah includes separate tractates about them.[8] Some of the instructions pertaining to prayer and fasting in the Didache at first glance appear to contradict Jewish law. However, nothing in chapter 8 puts the Didache outside the broad umbrella of Judaism.

The Commandment of Fasting

Fast days and fasting, the focus of Didache 8.1, occur commonly in Judaism. These took on heightened significance and frequency in the decades before and after the destruction of the Second Temple. The Hebrew Scriptures use several different words for fasting. *Tzom* (צוֹם) is the most popular one, but we also find the descriptive *innui nefesh* (עינוי נפש), meaning "affliction of the soul," which is an idiom for fasting.[9] Additionally, we find the later biblical Aramaic and rabbinic term *ta'anit* (תענית).[10] The variety of terms indicates the importance of fasting in Jewish culture.

In the Scriptures fasting usually meant refraining from both food and water, as we read in the book of Esther: "Hold a fast on my behalf, and do not eat or

---

8   Tractates *Brachot* ("Blessings") and *Ta'anit* ("Fasts").
9   Leviticus 16:29, 23:27; Psalm 35:13; Isaiah 58:3, 10.
10 Ezra 9:5.

drink."[11] The sages record that fasting could also entail refraining from bathing, anointing oneself, wearing leather shoes, and marital relations.[12] It was customary as well to give charity on a fast day.[13] Fasting usually lasted from dawn until nightfall, with the exception of Yom Kippur and *Tisha B'Av*, which both began at sunset the night before.

In the Bible fasting was at times a sign of mourning, such as when Ahab heard from the Prophet Elijah of the imminent disaster approaching him and his wife Jezebel.[14] David took on a fast for his sick child: "David therefore sought God on behalf of the child. And David fasted and went in and lay all night on the ground" (2 Samuel 12:16). Fasting was also taken on as preparation to receive revelation from God, as can be seen in the examples of Moses and Daniel.[15]

The primary goal of fasting is to deny ourselves material gratification in order to spiritually connect with our heavenly Father. In the Talmud, Rav Sheshet equates "afflicting one's soul" with offering up one's soul on the Temple altar: "May it be your will to account my fat and blood which have been diminished as if I had offered them before you on the altar."[16] The Didache assumes that fasting will be a regular practice of believers, both Jew and Gentile.

Annual Fasts

The biblical calendar makes annual national fast days incumbent upon all Jewish people. The most prominent is Yom Kippur, which, as we see in the book of Acts, Jewish people often simply called "the Fast."[17] Zechariah mentions "the fast of the fourth month and the fast of the fifth and the fast of the seventh and the fast

---

11   Esther 4:16.
12   m.*Yoma* 8:1. Cf. Targum Pseudo-Jonathan to Leviticus 23:27: "On the tenth day of this seventh month is the Day of Atonement; a holy convocation shall it be to you, and you shall humble your souls, [abstaining] from food, and from drink, and from the use of the bath, and from anointing, and the use of the bed, and from sandals." Jacob Milgrom adds, "Indeed that the psalmist must specify *'inniti ba-tsom nafshi*, 'I afflicted myself with a fast' (Psalm 35:13), means that there are other forms of self affliction, some of which were mandatory for the day. Finally, Daniel's attempt *le hit 'annot* [to afflict himself] consisted of three weeks of mourning during which he says, 'I ate no tasty food, nor did any meat or wine enter my mouth. I did not anoint myself' (Daniel 10:3, 12). Thus his 'self denial' consisted of a partial fast; otherwise it resembled the rabbinic definition" (Milgrom, *The JPS Torah Commentary: Numbers* [New York, NY: Jewish Publication Society, 1990], 246–247).
13   "The merit of a fast day lies in the charity dispensed" (b.*Brachot* 6b). Cf. b.*Sanhedrin* 35a.
14   1 Kings 21:27. CF. 1 Samuel 31:13.
15   Exodus 34:28; Deuteronomy 9:9; Daniel 9:3.
16   b.*Brachot* 17a.
17   Leviticus 23:27–32; Acts 27:9.

of the tenth" (Zechariah 8:19), four additional fasts that commemorate events surrounding the destruction of the Temple. A fast was also established before Purim to remember Esther's fast.[18]

Fast Name	Calendar Date[19]	Biblical Reference
Tzom Tammuz	Seventeenth of Tammuz	Zechariah 8:19
Tisha B'Av	Ninth of Av	Zechariah 8:19
Tzom Gedalyah	Fourth of Tishrei	Zechariah 8:19
Yom Kippur	Tenth of Tishrei	Leviticus 23:27–32
Asarah B'Tevet	Tenth of Tevet	Zechariah 8:19
Ta'anit Esther	Thirteenth of Adar	Esther 4:16

Jewish law requires all Jewish males over thirteen years old and all females over twelve to fast on these days, but the rabbis instituted some leniencies for certain situations.[20] In a *mishnah* for Yom Kippur we read,

> If a woman with child smells food and becomes faint, she must be given to eat until she feels satisfied. A sick person is fed at the word of experts

---

18 Esther 4:16. Another fast day is *Ta'anit Bechorot* (the Fast of the Firstborn) on the eve of Passover, on which firstborn males fast for being spared in the tenth plague. Today it is customary for those who are obligated to fast to find a halachic loophole, an example of which allows them to attend a *simchah* (a joyous celebration) in order to avoid the fast. It is interesting that early church tradition had a custom to fast on the day before Passover in remembrance of the Master's suffering and death on the cross: "There is one only Sabbath to be observed by you in the whole year, which is that of our Lord's burial, on which men ought to keep a fast, but not a festival. For inasmuch as the Creator was then under the earth, the sorrow for Him is more forcible than the joy for the creation; for the Creator is more honorable by nature and dignity than his own creatures" (Apostolic Constitutions 7.23). "Many other fasts, in memory of certain troubles that befell Israel, were added in the course of time, a full list of which is given at the end of *Megillat Ta'anit*. These were not regarded as obligatory, and they found little acceptance among the people" (Julius H. Greenstone, Emil G. Hirsch, and Hartwig Hirschfeld eds., "Fasting and Fast-Days," *Jewish Encyclopedia* [1906]. Cited 15 November 2014. Online: http://www.jewishencyclopedia.com/articles/6033-fasting).
19 All fasts, if they fell on Shabbat, were moved, with the exception of Yom Kippur. All fasts are also moved from Friday (Erev Shabbat) except *Asarah B'Tevet*, because Ezekiel says "this very day" (Ezekiel 24:2) in reference to the event that happened on the day the fast commemorates.
20 "One should not afflict children at all on Yom Kippur. But one trains them a year or two before in order that they become used to religious observances" (m.*Yoma* 8:4).

and if no experts are there, one feeds him at his own wish until he says: enough. (m.*Yoma* 8:5)

The sages offered special exemptions for pregnant women, the infirm, and others in difficult physical circumstances. We do not have space here to discuss all the legal details surrounding this subject, but their end result is that one is generally exempt from the requirement to fast if fasting might cause detriment to one's health.[21]

Monday and Thursday

Fasts, from earliest Jewish history, could be taken on personally and privately.[22] This could be done for a variety of reasons such as "in memory of certain events in his own life, or in expiation of his sins, or in time of trouble to arouse God's mercy."[23] Traditionally, one formally declares a private fast at the time of the afternoon prayers on the day before undertaking the fast.[24] Yet the sages of Israel cautioned against fasting that would lead to lack of productivity at work, hinder Torah study, or put one in physical danger.[25] As the Talmud relates, "One who fasts even though it weakens him is termed a sinner" (b.*Ta'anit* 11a).

It was also common for the leadership of Israel to call community fasts:

> More frequent, however, were the occasional fasts instituted for the whole community, especially when the nation believed itself to be under divine displeasure (Judges 20:26; 1 Samuel 7:6, where it is conjoined with the pouring out of water before the Lord; Jeremiah 36:9; Nehemiah 9:1), or when a great calamity befell the land (Joel 1:14, 2:12), as when pestilence raged or when drought set in; and sometimes also when an important act was about to be carried out by the officials of the land (1 Kings 21:12; comp. 1 Samuel 14:24).[26]

---

21 b.*Yoma* 85b.
22 We see evidence of private fasts already in the Torah: "Any vow and any binding oath to afflict herself [literally 'afflict her soul'], her husband may establish, or her husband may make void" (Numbers 30:13). Also Judith 8:6; 1 Maccabees 3:47; 2 Maccabees 13:12.
23 "Fasting and Fast-Days," *Jewish Encyclopedia*.
24 Rabbi Adin Steinsaltz, *The Talmud Steinsaltz Edition: A Reference Guide* (New York, NY: Random, 1989), 273.
25 E.g., b.*Ta'anit* 11a.
26 "Fasting and Fast-Days," *Jewish Encyclopedia*.

In the late Second Temple Period, these public fasts were limited primarily to Monday and Thursday, which were both market days and times when public court hearings were held. In extreme cases, particularly in the case of drought in Israel, the leadership would call upon the community to take on a series of three fast days: Monday, the subsequent Thursday, and the following Monday:

> If the seventeenth of Marcheshvan [Cheshvan] came and no rain fell the Jews begin to fast three fasts [Monday, Thursday, and Monday]. (m. Ta'anit 1:4)

This series of fasts was considered optional. If it failed to bring rain, however, the leadership could declare a second, mandatory, series.[27] If this failed, they could proclaim another with stricter regulations. Finally, if that failed, a fourth fast series would be called with even more stringencies.[28]

Some pious individuals took to fasting on Monday and Thursday every week regardless of whether or not public fasts had been declared. The evidence for this appears in the Gospels, in which a Pharisee in one of the Master's parables boasts, "I fast twice a week."[29] These are the fast days to which the Didache refers when it says, "Your fast days should not coincide with those of the hypocrites, for they fast on the second day of the week and on the fifth day" (8.1). In modern times Jewish liturgy carries on a liturgical memory of this practice with the recital of a longer version of *Tachanun* ("supplications," תחנון) prayers on Monday and Thursday.

In later generations, especially among the Ashkenazi Jews, there developed the custom of the fast of *Behab*. Behab (בה״ב) is an acronym for the fast days Monday (ב [*bet*], second day of the week), Thursday (ה [*heh*], fifth day of the week), and Monday (ב). This fast sequence took place in the months of Cheshvan, after Sukkot, and Iyyar, after Passover. It was said to be a time of penitence for possible excessive celebration during the two festivals preceding it.[30] Most in Judaism no longer fast on these days.

---

27 m. Ta'anit 1:5.
28 m. Ta'anit 1:6.
29 Luke 18:12.
30 Some cite the basis of fasting after a festival from Job: "When the days of the feast had run their course, Job would send and consecrate them, and he would rise early in the morning and offer burnt offerings according to the number of them all. For Job said, 'It may be that my children have sinned, and cursed God in their hearts'" (Job 1:5).

The Commandment of Prayer

Like fasting, prayer plays a major role within Judaism. The Didache introduces its prayer instructions in 8.2 by teaching the believers to pray "as the Lord commanded." Likewise, the sages of Israel considered prayer one of the 613 commandments based on the Torah's phrase "You shall serve the LORD."[31] The Torah also commands, "Serve the LORD your God with all your heart."[32] The Talmud asks, "What is the service of the heart?" to which the people answer, "Prayer."[33]

In Judaism prayers are to be offered up in times of need, for thanksgiving, or just to communicate with and draw close to God. Prayer can be in the form of liturgical texts or can be spontaneous, from the heart. Prayer meets the deepest needs of the human soul as we long to connect with God and have relationship with him. In Jewish thought prayer bonds us with our Father in heaven.

Liturgical Set-Time Prayer

Liturgical prayer plays a prominent role in biblical and Jewish culture. The book of Psalms, for example, contains one of the largest collections of liturgical prayers and songs from antiquity. As evidenced by the many snippets of liturgy and hymns throughout the New Testament and early Messianic Jewish literature, the early believing community employed liturgical prayers.

In the Second Temple Period and at the time of the writing of the Didache, the two most prominent liturgical prayers were the *Shma* ("Hear," שמע) and the *Shmoneh Esreh* ("Eighteen," שמנה עשרה). The *Shma* consists of three scriptural passages from Deuteronomy and Numbers and is recited twice daily, in the morning and in the evening, in accordance with the verse, "You ... shall talk of them ... when you lie down, and when you rise."[34] The *Shmoneh Esreh* is the central prayer

---

31 Exodus 23:25; Deuteronomy 6:13, 11:13, 13:4. See *Sefer HaChinnuch* 433.
32 Deuteronomy 10:12, 11:13.
33 b.*Ta'anit* 2a. According to some halachic authorities, the commandment of prayer is considered obligatory upon both Jews and Gentiles. See Rabbi Aaron Lichtenstein, *The Seven Laws of Noah* (3d ed.; New York, NY: Rabbi Jacob Joseph School Press, 1995), 86. See also page 118 on which it is related that Rabbi Samuel ben Holfni, Gaon, includes the commandment to pray in his list of the thirty obligations incumbent upon Noachides. He derives this from Genesis 20:7, "He will pray for you." Cf. Sibylline Oracles 3.285, 7.88. The Apostle Paul exhorts Gentile believers to "pray without ceasing" (1 Thessalonians 5:17), to "be constant in prayer" (Romans 12:12), and to "continue steadfastly in prayer" (Colossians 4:2). All these passages imply that the apostles considered the Torah's commandment to pray as incumbent upon Gentile believers.
34 Deuteronomy 6:4–9, 11:13–21; Numbers 15:37–41.

of Judaism and contains eighteen benedictions on weekdays and seven on Shabbat. It is traditionally said to have been created around 560 BCE by the men of the Great Assembly, which included Ezra and the last of the prophets.[35] It may indeed be this old, for we find the structure and outline of the *Shmoneh Esreh* in the books of 2 Maccabees and of Sirach, both of which date to around the second century BCE.[36] The Master and the earliest disciples would have been intimately familiar with early forms of these liturgical prayers from the synagogue and the Temple.[37]

Closely connected to the recitation of liturgical prayers is the traditional thrice-daily times of prayer. The Didache alludes to this when it says, "This is what you should pray three times a day" (8.3). These times of prayer are derived from the Torah's injunction in Numbers 28:2 to offer up the daily sacrifices in the Temple at the "appointed time" (*mo'ed*, מועד), a phrase that designates a specific meeting time with the Lord and that is also used in connection with the feasts. Because the commandment is prefaced by the words "Command the people of Israel," the Torah indicates that this appointment is not only for the priests offering the sacrifices but for the entire nation. Hence, the twice-daily times of sacrifice, morning and afternoon (to which was eventually added a third time in connection with the recitation of the evening *Shma*) became times of prayer (specifically for praying the *Shmoneh Esreh*). In Jewish law the Torah's obligation on the people to pray is specifically fulfilled by praying at the daily times of sacrifice.

Time of Prayer	Hebrew Name	Main Prayers Recited	Temple Activity
Morning	*Shacharit* (שחרית)	Shma, Shmoneh Esreh	Morning lamb offered
Afternoon	*Minchah* (מנחה)	Shmoneh Esreh	Afternoon lamb offered
Evening	*Ma'ariv* (מעריב)	Shma, Shmoneh Esreh	Leftover offerings burned

---

35   b.*Megillah* 17b.
36   2 Maccabees 1:24–29; Sirach 36:1–11.
37   For the use of the *Shma* in the New Testament, see Birger Gerhardsson, *The Shema in the New Testament: Deuteronomy 6:4–5 in Significant Passages* (Uppsala, Sweden: Almqvist and Wiksell, 1996). For references to the *Shmoneh Esreh* in the New Testament, see Toby Janicki, "The Apostolic Constitutions: A Christian Sabbath Amidah," *Messiah Journal* 114 (Fall 2013): 76–88.

We see this rhythm of prayer carried out throughout the New Testament. As Zechariah offered up incense in the Temple, "the people were waiting" outside for his return as they prayed at the time of sacrifice.[38] The Holy Spirit fell upon the disciples on Shavu'ot as they were gathered in the Temple at the "third hour of the day," which was the time of the *Shacharit* prayers.[39] Peter and John headed to the Temple "at the hour of prayer."[40] Even the Gentile Cornelius received his angelic visitation as he was praying at "about the ninth hour of the day," which was the time of the *Minchah* service.[41] It is no wonder then that this practice is found in the Didache as well.

THE CONNECTION BETWEEN FASTING AND PRAYER

It is of note that the Didache addresses the practices of fasting and prayer in the same chapter. In Jewish thought fasting and prayer are closely connected one to the other. The Bible often links fasting with prayer. For example,

> As soon as I heard these words I sat down and wept and mourned for days, and I continued fasting and praying before the God of heaven. (Nehemiah 1:4)

> Then I proclaimed a fast there ... that we might humble ourselves before our God ... So we fasted and implored our God for this, and he listened to our entreaty. (Ezra 8:21–23)[42]

Thomas O'Loughlin aptly comments,

> Prayer without fasting seemed to lack seriousness: words seem such fluffy things! But when you feel something in your stomach, then you are in earnest with your words. Then you are taking prayer seriously and asking God to take your needs seriously.[43]

---

38 Luke 1:21.
39 Acts 2:15.
40 Acts 3:1.
41 Acts 10:3.
42 Cf. Jeremiah 14:11–12.
43 Thomas O'Loughlin, *The Didache: A Window on the Earliest Christians* (Grand Rapids, MI: Baker, 2010), 70.

Practical Application

Fasting

The Didache instructs believers "to fast on the fourth day and on the preparation day"—Wednesday and Friday—rather than on the traditional second and fifth days of the week as practiced in Judaism (8.1). It is difficult to know whether the Didache imagines its audience fasting on these days every week or rather merely points out that if one does decide to take on a personal fast or the community calls for a public fast, it should ideally be on those two days. We can approach both interpretations and offer a few suggestions based upon the way modern Judaism handles fasting and liturgy on Monday and Thursday.

These fasts on Wednesday and Friday, in accordance with Jewish practice, lasted from dawn until nightfall. They were complete fasts, calling for abstinence from both food and water. However, in traditional Judaism today the current generation is viewed as much weaker than those of the past, and most do not observe the fast of *Behab* at all, let alone fast every Monday and Thursday. Fasting is most certainly not done if it affects one's daily performance at work and in Torah study. It is customary for some to observe the fast of *Behab* by refraining from eating as much as they do on regular days, and some choose to avoid meat.[44]

Because the Didache was a Jewish document written by Jewish believers, halachic developments can be brought into its instructions on fasting. Applying Judaism's standards to the Didache's injunctions on fasting on Wednesday and Friday offers us a few options. Certainly, as we saw in chapter 7, the Didache employs leniency with fasting: the believers are to "fast ... if they can." If we interpret chapter 8 as referring to an ongoing, twice-weekly fast, one could observe the fast days by fully fasting from dawn until nightfall or perhaps by refraining from certain foods such as meat. In traditional churches today in which this twice-weekly fast is still observed, the practice is to refrain from "meat, fish, dairy products, eggs, oil, wine, and sex" but not to undertake a total fast.[45]

For those interpreting these days not as ongoing fasts days but rather as the ideal days on which to call fasts, a similar approach could be taken. For example, one could observe fasts around the time of *Behab* (during the months of Iyyar and Cheshvan after Pesach and Sukkot, respectively) but focus them on Wednesday,

---

44 Halachic customs in this paragraph taken from Rabbi Ari Enkin, "The Fast of Behab," n.p. [cited 19 November 2013]. Online: http://hirhurim.blogspot.com/2008/05/fast-of-behab.html.
45 O'Loughlin, *The Didache*, 84.

Friday, and Wednesday. These fasts could then be observed with the varying degrees of stringency mentioned above. Additionally, these two days could serve as ideal times for community-wide fasts called for by the leadership in times of trouble or hardship.

Regardless of the interpretation we accept, it is clear that the Didache is communicating to its audience that the days most effective for followers of the Master to fast are Wednesday and Friday. Likewise, disciples of Yeshua who pray the traditional Jewish liturgy out of the Siddur and want to incorporate this practice of the early Messianic community could move the longer recitation of *Tachanun* from Monday and Thursday to Wednesday and Friday.

Prayer

The injunction to pray the *Our Father* three times a day serves as a minimum requirement for Gentile believers at the times of prayer. This is in line with the debates in the Mishnah about what is actually required at the set times, in which Rabbi Eliezer argues for short prayers and Rabbi Joshua allows for an "abbreviated" version of the *Shmoneh Esreh*.[46] If such debates occurred about what was required of Jewish people, who had grown up with these prayers, how much more so for Gentiles who were trying to initiate themselves into the rhythm of Jewish prayer life. As the Didache says in 6.2, "Do what you can."

As for the actual times of prayer, the Didache merely states, "This is what you should pray three times a day" (8.3). This indicates that the Didache did not attempt to start a new tradition but simply adopted the practices of Judaism. Believers wishing to follow the injunctions of the Didache and pray at the three set times of prayer should determine those times in accordance with Jewish law.

---

46 m.*Brachot* 4:3.

Commentary

> *Your fast days should not coincide with those of the hypocrites.* (DIDACHE 8.1)

The Didache begins chapter 8 by admonishing believers not to fast along with the "hypocrites." In saying "your fast days should not," it implies that the members of the believing community, without need for an explanation, would fast on a regular basis.

The Greek term *hupokrites* (ὑποκριτής) refers to a "stage performer" or an "actor."[47] Although most commentators define "hypocrite" as someone who behaves in a disingenuous manner, creates a façade of piety, or says one thing and does another, it is better defined in the context of the Didache and the New Testament as someone who puts on a show and performs a commandment in an ostentatious way to attract attention, to be seen by others, and recognized as pious. The hypocrite performs the good deed for the sake of his appearance in the eyes of men, not in order to bring glory to his Father in heaven but to glorify himself. In his effort to seek reward in the present, he loses it in the kingdom.

Scholars have struggled to identify the "hypocrites" of the Didache. Some have connected them with the Pharisees, others implicate the whole of the Jewish people, and still others identify the hypocrites with an opposing Messianic Jewish sect that was prone more toward Pharisaic tradition than the Didache community. The best solution connects the instructions on fasting and the term "hypocrite" back to the Master's halachah on fasting in the Sermon on the Mount:

> When you fast, do not look gloomy like the hypocrites, for they disfigure their faces that their fasting may be seen by others. Truly, I say to you, they have received their reward. But when you fast, anoint your head and wash your face, that your fasting may not be seen by others but by your Father who is in secret. And your Father who sees in secret will reward you. (Matthew 6:16–18)

Yeshua condemned turning fast days into an ostentatious show of one's piety, seeking reward from men and not God. This practice is condemned in rabbinic

---

47   It is also related to the Hebrew *chanaf* (חנף), which has the broader connotation of "godless."

[8.1]
Your fast days should not coincide with those of the hypocrites.

literature as well: "In no case should one boast of his fasts to others, and even though he is asked he should try to evade the question."[48] Fasting on Monday and Thursday was the practice of the very pious, as is evidenced in the prayer of the Pharisee, "I fast twice a week."[49] The Master's warnings seem to indicate that many of the supposedly pious ascetics did their righteous deeds for men's accolades.[50] The "hypocrites," therefore, were those who used fasting as a way to show off their piety.

How were disciples of Yeshua to ensure that they did not fast in a hypocritical manner? In the Gospels they were told to wash and prepare themselves for the day as they normally did so that no one would suspect that they were fasting. Fasting twice weekly itself was not considered problematic but only one's efforts to be lauded for it. Marcello del Verme points out, "The optional and bi-weekly fast of the Pharisees (lacking a specific mandate in the Torah!) ... is not condemned by Jesus, but is welcomed as an expression of interior devotion along with prayers."[51]

◉ *For they fast on the second day of the week and on the fifth day.* (DIDACHE 8.1)

In Jewish communities of the late Second Temple and Post Destruction Periods, Monday and Thursday were both market days and times when public court hearings were held.[52] Public reading of the Torah was also customary on these days.[53]

---

48 *Shulchan Aruch,* Orach Chayyim 565:6.
49 Luke 18:12. Cf. Kurt Niederwimmer, *The Didache: Hermeneia—A Critical and Historical Commentary on the Bible* (Minneapolis, MN: Fortress, 1998), 132.
50 This does not refer to community fast days such as Yom Kippur and *Tisha B'Av,* on which everyone would be fasting and thus to do so would not make one appear more pious.
51 Marcello del Verme, *Didache and Judaism: Jewish Roots of an Ancient Christian-Jewish Work* (New York, NY: T&T Clark, 2004), 171.
52 b.*Bava Kama* 82a. The sages speculate as to why Monday and Thursday were particularly favorable days on which to fast and read from the Torah. In the Talmud it is believed that because the earthly court meets on this day, so did the heavenly court likewise assemble (b.*Shabbat* 129b). In turn, mystical Judaism later taught that these were the days when man is judged by heaven; therefore they are appropriate for fasting and prayer (Rabbi Nosson Scherman, *The Complete ArtScroll Siddur: Nusach Ashkenaz* [Brooklyn, NY: Mesorah, 2007], 124). Other sources have it that the Temple was destroyed on Thursday or that Monday and Thursday were special "because Moses broke the first set of tablets on a Thursday, and the Israelites were forgiven for the sin of the golden calf on a Monday" (Rabbi Lawrence A. Hoffman, ed., *My People's Prayer Book: Traditional Prayers, Modern Commentaries* [10 vols.; Woodstock, VT: Jewish Lights, 2002], 6:54–55).
53 m.*Ta'anit* 1:6, 2:9; m.*Megillah* 3:6, 4:1.

These, in turn, became ideal days to hold both public and private fasts.⁵⁴ For example, public fasts were appointed in times of drought in successions of three days: Monday, Thursday, and Monday.⁵⁵ Some pious individuals voluntarily chose to fast on these days every week as well.⁵⁶

Although, as we have pointed out, the Didache contains no instructions for observing Shabbat or other festivals of Israel, its time-keeping instructions are rooted completely in the Jewish calendar.⁵⁷ The practice of numbering the days of the week is inherently Jewish and points back to creation: "the first day," "the second day," etc.⁵⁸ Judaism has no names for the individual six days of the week. The word for "week" here is *sabbaton* (σαββάτων), which renders the phrase "second day of the week," literally "second day of Shabbat."⁵⁹

[8.1]
For they fast on the second day of the week and on the fifth day.

---

54 Scholars differ in opinion as to whether the Didache refers to public or private fasts or both. E.g., "The text of the Didache alludes to the fasting customs of pious enlightened Jews that established individual, private days of fasting in addition to those that were obligatory for all ... The rules for Jewish-Christian liturgical praxis copied by the Didachist probably refer also to freely chosen private fasting, not to obligatory fasting by the entire community" (Niederwimmer, *The Didache*, 132); and, "The instruction in Didache 8.1 does not seem to presuppose a situation in which Jews and Christians fasted two days every week but rather implies a discussion as to which two days are preferable once an individual or a community has indeed decided to fast" (Huub van de Sandt and David Flusser, *The Didache: Its Jewish Sources and Its Place in Early Judaism and Christianity* [Minneapolis, MN: Fortress, 2002], 293).
55 m. *Ta'anit* 1:4–6.
56 Luke 18:12; "They fasted twice a week, on the second and fifth days" (Epiphanius, *Panarion*, 1.16.1.5).
57 For the influence of the Jewish calendar in early Christian literature, see Gerhard Friedrich, "σάββατον, σαββατισμός, παρασκευή," *TDNT* 7:32.
58 Genesis 1:5, 8, etc.
59 In Hebrew this translates nicely to *sheni bashabbat* (שני בשבת). Cf. "The nations of the world count the first day in the week, the second, the third, the fourth, the fifth, and [the sixth], which Israel terms the eve of the Sabbath, but the Sabbath itself the nations do not count as a day of rest" (*Pesikta Rabbati* 23).

[8.1]
For they fast on the second day of the week and on the fifth day.

Jewish Name[60]	Roman Name	English Name
First day	Day of the sun	Sunday
Second day	Day of the moon	Monday
Third day	Day of Mars	Tuesday
Fourth day	Day of Mercury	Wednesday
Fifth day	Day of Jupiter	Thursday
Preparation Day	Day of Venus	Friday
Shabbat	Day of Saturn	Saturday

This points to a seven-day week that measures its days by the passing of Shabbat. "Neither the Romans nor the Greeks had a Sabbath day of rest or a seven-day week; accordingly, neither Latin nor Greek has a term for these things."[61] Therefore, built within the fabric of the Didache's instructions is the time-keeping mechanism of Israel, so "every gentile joining the Didache community had to become acquainted with the Jewish calendar."[62]

◈ *But you are to fast on the fourth day and on the preparation day.* (DIDACHE 8.1)

The Didache instructs that followers of Messiah are to fast on Wednesday and Friday instead of on Monday and Thursday.[63] These days are offered as sectarian alternatives to normative Jewish practice. It is possible that at certain times and places the fast days of Monday and Thursday were dominated by individuals looking to make a show of their righteousness.

Fasting on the alternate days of Wednesday and Friday further safeguarded against making fasting an ostentatious show of piety, because no one in the broader

---

60 Based on O'Loughlin, *The Didache*, 73.
61 Aaron Milavec, *The Didache: Faith, Hope, & Life of the Earliest Christian Communities, 50–70 C.E.* (New York, NY: Newman, 2003), 290.
62 Ibid., 291.
63 It could be that these fasts were related to the Didache's teaching on fasting "for those who persecute you" (1.3).

Jewish community would suspect anyone of fasting then. This reference in Didache 8.1 is the oldest reference to the Christian tradition of fasting on Wednesdays and Fridays. Some branches of Christianity still fast on Wednesday and Friday today.[64] The Apostolic Constitutions renders this, "Do you either fast the entire five days, or on the fourth day of the week, and on the day of the Preparation."[65]

[8.1]
But you are to fast on the fourth day and on the preparation day.

The Didache does not appear to be introducing a new practice. Instead it seems to report one already established among believers. At some early stage the leadership of the believing community may have made a deliberate decision to switch the weekly fast days to those mentioned here.

Our Master Yeshua expected his disciples to practice fasting, and as we pointed out above, he gave them instructions for doing so. In response to the question, "Why do John's disciples and the disciples of the Pharisees fast, but your disciples do not fast?" Yeshua answered, "Can the wedding guests fast while the bridegroom is with them? As long as they have the bridegroom with them, they cannot fast. The days will come when the bridegroom is taken away from them, and then they will fast in that day" (Mark 2:18–20). As long as the disciples had Yeshua with them, they were tasting the joy of the Messianic Era, and it would not be appropriate for them to frequently fast. However, once he left them, they indeed would fast once again while they were waiting for his second coming.

Aaron Milavec writes that "given the Jewish roots of the Didache, it can safely be assumed that members of the Didache observed their fasts in the same way as the Jews of their day."[66] During these fasts one refrained from both food and drink in accordance with biblical and rabbinic teaching. The fasts probably took place from dawn until nightfall. Most likely, if 8.1 is a reference to the private twice-weekly fast, this fast was encouraged but viewed as optional.[67] The Didache

---

64 "Fasting on Wednesdays and Fridays from meat, fish, dairy products, eggs, oil, wine, and sex is still the official teaching governing Christians in the Orthodox world. And even though not many people follow this rule in everyday life, quite a lot do! It also became the standard practice for Latin Christians. We have a curious piece of evidence that confirms this from the Latin Church's most westerly region in the Middle Ages: Ireland. Most European languages (including Welsh which, like Irish, is a Celtic language) have the days of the week based on the Latin names linked to the seven planets. But the seven-day week arrived in Ireland with Christianity and three of the days are named after the practice of fasting. Wednesday is called *Céadaoin* which means 'first fast day,' Friday is called *Aoine* which means 'the fast day,' while Thursday is called *Déadaoine* which comes from 'between the fasts'" (O'Loughlin, *The Didache*, 84).
65 Apostolic Constitutions 7.23.
66 Milavec, *The Didache: Faith, Hope, & Life of the Earliest Christian Communities, 50–70 C.E.*, 296.
67 For the opinion that these fasts were not optional, see Del Verme, *Didache and Judaism*, 173.

[8.1]
But you are to fast on the fourth day and on the preparation day.

certainly displays leniency when it comes to fasting for those new initiates who are soon to be immersed, who are to "fast … if they can" (7.4).

But why Wednesday and Friday? "To compare the [Didache] with the Talmud, we may say that the clause in question is like a Mishnah, and that its explanatory Gemara is to be found in the *Apostolic Constitutions*."[68] The Apostolic Constitutions states:

> Because on the fourth day the condemnation went out against the Lord, Judas then promising to betray him for money; and you must fast on the preparation day, because on that day the Lord suffered the death of the cross under Pontius Pilate. (Apostolic Constitutions 7.23)[69]

"The preparation day" (*paraskeue*, παρασκευή) is Friday, which in Judaism is referred to as *Erev Shabbat* (ערב שבת).[70] The version in *The Ethiopic Church Order* literally has "the evening," in other words, "the evening" before the Sabbath, which seems to correspond with *Erev Shabbat* (literally "The Eve of the Sabbath").[71] As with the reference to each day of the week as "the first [or second, or third] of Shabbat," this reference to Friday as "the preparation day" is another indication that the new Gentile believers were well aware of the Sabbath day and marked it out weekly. Some have suggested that fasting on "the preparation day" may have been a criticism of Sabbath observance. After all, as the sages state, "On Friday [the lay representatives at the Temple] did not fast out of respect for the Sabbath; and certainly not on the Sabbath."[72] For example, although while a widow Judith fasted just about every day of the week, she respectfully refrained on "the eves of the Sabbaths, and the Sabbaths."[73] Yet we find in later Jewish literature that it was "the custom of pious men … to fast the entire *Erev Shabbat*" in order that the

---

68 Charles Taylor, "The Teaching of the Twelve Apostles with Illustrations from the Talmud," in *Didache: The Unknown Teaching of the Twelve Apostles* (ed. Brent S. Walters; San Jose, CA: Anti-Nicene Archive, 1991), 175.

69 As was noted above, in Jewish tradition the sequence of fast days of Monday, Thursday, and Monday are given the acronym *Behab* (בה״ב) based on the Hebrew letters associated with the number of each day: Monday (ב [*bet*], second day of the week), Thursday (ה [*heh*], fifth day of the week), and Monday (ב). Applying this same naming schematic to the Didache's sequence of fast days of Wednesday (ד [*dalet*] fourth day of the week), Friday (ו [*vav*] sixth day of the week), Wednesday (ד) results in David (דוד).

70 This phrase appears in the Gospels in Matthew 27:62; Mark 15:42; Luke 23:54; John 19:14, 31, 42. Also Josephus, *Antiquities of the Jews* 16:163/vi.2 and Judith 8:6.

71 See G.W. Horner, *The Statutes of the Apostles or Canones Ecclesiastici* (London, England: Williams & Norgate, 1904), 194.26.

72 b. *Taʿanit* 27b.

73 Judith 8:6.

first thing that they would taste after their fast were the delicacies of Shabbat.⁷⁴ Accordingly, fasting on Friday in no way indicates a desecration of Shabbat. The Apostolic Constitutions actually uses the instructions on fasting on the fourth day and on preparation day as a catalyst to mandate resting on Shabbat: "Keep the Sabbath, and the Lord's Day festival; because the former is the memorial of the creation, and the latter of the resurrection" (7.23).

[8.1]
But you are to fast on the fourth day and on the preparation day.

◖ *Nor should you pray like the hypocrites but just as the Lord commanded in his good news.* (DIDACHE 8.2)

The Didache, with verse 2, moves into instructions on prayer. As with fasting, the audience of the Didache is urged not to act in accordance with the hypocrites but instead to follow the instructions of the Master.

We have discussed in other places that "Lord" is the Greek word *kurios* (κύριος). Both the New Testament and the Didache sometimes use the word *kurios* to mean "master" and sometimes as a circumlocution for the name of God. In the context of Didache 8.2, when coupled together with "good news," the word clearly refers to the Master, that is, to Yeshua as teacher.⁷⁵

The term "good news" comes from the Greek word *euanggelion* (εὐαγγέλιον), which is often translated "gospel."⁷⁶ It translates the Hebrew term *besorah* (בשורה), which appears in the Prophets to refer to the good news of Israel's future redemption—when her enemies will be vanquished, the exiles will return to the land,

---

74   *Shulchan Aruch*, Orach Chayyim 249:3–4. While Rebbe Nachman of Breslov was still in his youth he would often fast from Sabbath to Sabbath (Rabbi Nathan of Nemirov, *Rebbe Nachman's Wisdom* [trans. Rabbi Aryeh Kaplan; Monsey, NY: Breslov Research Institute, 1973], 10).

75   That "good news" refers to Yeshua himself is the almost unanimous opinion of scholars; however, contrary to this, Milavec argues that in every instance of "Lord" in the Didache, it refers to God. See Aaron Milavec, "The Distress Signals of Didache Research," in *The Didache: A Missing Piece of the Puzzle in Early Jewish Christianity* (eds. Jonathan A. Draper and Clayton N. Jefford; Atlanta, GA: Society of Biblical Literature, 2015), 70–72. "This accords well with the understanding of the Christian Scriptures that Jesus proclaimed 'the good news of God' (Mark 1:14; Romans 1:1; 2 Corinthians 11:7; 1 Thessalonians 2:2, 9; 1 Peter 4:17)—never the 'good news of Jesus.' Thus, in the four places within the Didache wherein 'good news' (εὐαγγέλιον) is found (Didache 8.2, 11.3, 15.3, and 15.4), it must be supposed that this refers to an oral source and that it comprises the 'good news of our Lord God' (Didache 15.4) transmitted by his servant, Jesus ... Furthermore, the Didache doesn't stop with saying, 'as the Lord ordered,' but continues with 'in his good news.' The good news, of course, is God's good news of his plans to establish his kingdom on earth as it is already established in heaven" (11, 13).

76   Εὐαγγέλιον appears first in Homer's *Odyssey* 14.152.

[8.2]
Nor should you pray like the hypocrites but just as the Lord commanded in his good news.

and the Lord will establish his kingdom on earth.[77] This is the broader meaning of Yeshua's message of "the gospel of the kingdom."[78] Additionally, while believers often do not think of the gospel message as including practical instructions for living, the Qumran community viewed preparing the way of the Lord and his good news as the path of "the study of Torah."[79] In the Didache, then, "good news" does not refer to a specific written gospel but rather to the living oral tradition of the teachings of the Master. His teachings included not only the message of the coming kingdom but practical instructions on how to prepare for and live in that kingdom.[80] This included instructions on prayer.

Most scholars feel that when the Didache states, "Nor should you pray like the hypocrites," and then instructs believers to pray the *Our Father*, it means to replace the traditional recitation of the *Shmoneh Esreh* with the *Our Father*. That is to say that when believers "pray three times a day," they should not pray the traditional prayers of the synagogue, according to most scholars, but instead should simply pray the *Our Father*. However, this misses the point of the Didache's instructions.

Evidence indicates that the early believers prayed the *Shmoneh Esreh*. The Master and the disciples attended synagogue services and participated in the Temple worship, where the *Shmoneh Esreh* was prayed regularly.[81] In the book of Acts, we read that the apostles were dedicated to "the prayer," which was another name for *Shmoneh Esreh*, that is, *HaTefillah* (התפילה).[82] Furthermore, we find a Christianized form of the Sabbath version of the prayer in the Apostolic Constitutions right after the section that contains a reworked version of the Didache.[83]

---

77 E.g., Isaiah 40:9, 52:7, 60:6, 61:1.
78 Matthew 4:23, 9:35, 24:14; Mark 1:15.
79 Community Rule (1QS) VIII, 14–15.
80 Jürgen K. Zangenberg, "Reconstructing the Social and Religious Milieu of the Didache: Methods, Sources, and Possible Results," in *Matthew, James, and Didache: Three Related Documents in Their Jewish and Christian Settings* (ed. Huub van de Sandt and Jürgen K. Zangenberg; Atlanta, GA: Society of Biblical Literature, 2008), 66, and Jens Schröter, "Jesus Tradition in Matthew, James, and the Didache: Searching for Characteristic Emphases," in ibid., 239. Milavec points out that "historically speaking, the term εὐαγγέλιον referred to an oral production and, only in the latter third of the second century, were books recording the 'good news' first designated by this name" ("The Distress Signals of Didache Research—Quest for a Viable Future," 11, n. 40).
81 E.g., Luke 4:16, 24:53.
82 Literally "the prayers" in Acts 2:42 and "the prayer" in Acts 6:4.
83 For a discussion of the *Shmoneh Esreh* in the Apostolic Constitutions and the use of the *Shmoneh Esreh* in the early believing community, see Janicki, "The Apostolic Constitutions: A Christian Sabbath Amidah," 76–88. Also see Yehudah Liebes, "Who Makes the Horn of Jesus to Flourish" (*Immanuel* 21 [1987]: 55–66), in which he argues that disciples of the Master attending synagogue influenced the wording of the *Malchut Beit David* blessing in the *Shmoneh Esreh*.

Additionally, the Didache is addressing new Gentile believers. Rather than supplanting Jewish liturgical traditions, the Didache offers God-fearing Gentile believers the option of praying the *Our Father* three times a day as a way to meet their minimum obligation to the liturgical traditions. This does not replace longer liturgical forms of synagogue liturgy for Jewish believers; it simply provides the individual Gentile believer with a reasonable minimum threshold.

[8.2] Nor should you pray like the hypocrites but just as the Lord commanded in his good news.

Once again, "hypocrite" in the Didache should be defined not as a disingenuous pretender who says one thing and does another but in the sense of an actor or performer—one who uses good deeds to bring glory to himself and not God. As was the case with instructions on fasting, the Didache's instructions about prayer and the identification of "hypocrites" should be linked back to the Master's halachah on prayer in the Sermon on the Mount. Our Master Yeshua teaches:

> When you pray, you must not be like the hypocrites. For they love to stand and pray in the synagogues and at the street corners, that they may be seen by others ... But when you pray, go into your room and shut the door and pray to your Father who is in secret ... When you pray, do not heap up empty phrases as the Gentiles do, for they think that they will be heard for their many words. (Matthew 6:5–7)[84]

The Master's rulings on prayer are much the same as they are for fasting. We are not to make an ostentatious show of our prayer life. Furthermore, the hypocrites that Yeshua criticized as those who "heap up empty words" were Gentiles, not Jews. It is hypocrisy and showmanship that the Didache urges us to avoid, not traditional Jewish prayer, worship, or liturgy. In turn, the Didache's instructions "Nor should you pray like the hypocrites but just as the Lord commanded in his good news" should be viewed as a stand-alone teaching that is not directly clarified by "This is what you should pray." The Master's teaching on prayer in Matthew 6 follows this same order and train of thought.

⁕ *This is what you should pray.* (DIDACHE 8.2)

The Didache now introduces a short prayer to be prayed by the members of the community. This opening line matches exactly with the Greek of Matthew 6:9.[85]

---

84   Cf. Luke 20:46–47.
85   Cf. Luke 11:2.

[8.2] *This is what you should pray.*

By beginning with the line, "This is what you should pray," the Didache is including the *Our Father* in the legal instructions of the Master on prayer.

The Greek of the *Our Father* in the Didache matches almost word-for-word with the Greek of Matthew 6:9–13.[86] Below is a comparison chart between Matthew, the Didache, and Luke. The slight differences between Matthew and the Didache are in italics.[87]

Matthew 6:9–13	Didache 8.2	Luke 11:2–4
Our Father, who is in the *heavens*, let your name be sanctified; let your kingdom come; let your will be done—as in heaven, so on earth. Our bread of tomorrow, immediately give us today, and pardon us our *debts*, as we also *pardoned* those indebted to us,	Our Father, who is in the *heaven*, let your name be sanctified; let your kingdom come; let your will be done—as in heaven, so on earth. Our bread of tomorrow, immediately give us today, and pardon us our *debt*, as we also *pardon* those indebted to us,	Father, let your name be sanctified; let your kingdom come. Our bread of tomorrow, continually give us every day, and pardon us our sins, for we ourselves pardon everyone who is indebted to us,
and do not bring us into testing, but rescue us from what is evil.	and do not bring us into testing, but rescue us from what is evil.	and do not bring us into testing.
(For yours is *the kingdom and* the power and the glory, forever and ever.)	For yours is the power and the glory, forever and ever.	

The virtually identical versions in Matthew and the Didache have led some scholars to speculate that the author of the Didache had a copy of Matthew as a

---

86   The Didache has "in the heaven" (τῷ οὐρανῷ) instead of "in the heavens" (τοῖς οὐρανοῖς), "our debt" (τὴν ὀφειλὴν) instead of "our debts" (τὰ ὀφειλήματα), "we forgive" (ἀφίεμεν) instead of "we forgave" (ἀφήκαμεν), and "the glory and the power" (ἡ δύναμις καὶ ἡ δόξα) instead of "the kingdom and the power and the glory" (ἡ βασιλεία καὶ ἡ δύναμις καὶ ἡ δόξα).

87   The is the author's (with help from Aaron Eby) and has been brought into the style of the Didache for comparison's sake.

reference.[88] Most agree that it is more probable that the Didache and Matthew are working from a similar oral or written source or even more likely working from memory from the regularly practiced liturgy of the Messianic community.

[8.2]
This is what you should pray.

In Luke's introduction to the *Our Father*, the disciples ask the Master, "Teach us to pray, as John taught his disciples," indicating that what the Master then taught them is not something outside Jewish tradition but rather firmly rooted within it.[89] David Flusser and Huub Van de Sandt correctly observe that "the halachic instructions in 8.3, in any event, clearly associate the *Our Father* with the regular Jewish *tefillah* because, like the *tefillah*, it had to be said three times a day."[90] So if we do not accept the theory that the *Our Father* is a replacement for the *Shmoneh Esreh*, how are the two prayers connected?

The *Our Father* may originally have been recited as a short meditation at the conclusion of the *Shmoneh Esreh*. In the Markan introduction to the *Our Father*, Yeshua says, "Whenever you stand praying," "standing" being both the English of the Hebrew *amidah* (עמידה), another name for the *Shmoneh Esreh*, and the posture in which the prayer is recited. Philip Segal has concluded that the *Our Father* was the Master's version of a private prayer to be recited after the *Shmoneh Esreh*:

> The Lord's Prayer was probably intended to be a private prayer the worshipper was to recite after the *'amidah* [*Shmoneh Esreh*] such as those offered as examples of closing private prayers by ancient rabbis (b.*Brachot* 16b–17a). Thus in Luke 11:2 "Say this when you pray," signifies "when you recite the *tefilah*" (that is, the *'amidah*), use this as a closing private prayer.[91]

Therefore, the *Our Father* does not replace the *Shmoneh Esreh* but is a closing prayer to be recited after it by disciples of the Master.[92]

---

88 E.g., Clayton Jefford feels that this shows that the author of the Didache had some knowledge of Matthean gospel here. See Jefford, *The Sayings of Jesus in the Teaching of the Twelve Apostles* (New York, NY: Brill, 1989), 138, n. 142.
89 Luke 11:1.
90 Van de Sandt and Flusser, *The Didache*, 294.
91 Philip Segal, "Early Christian and Rabbinic Liturgical Affinities," *New Testament Studies* 30 (1984): 73.
92 Note also that it was after the Master was "finished" praying (i.e., after the recital of the *Shmoneh Esreh*) that the disciples asked him, "Lord, teach us to pray, as John taught his disciples" (i.e., "Teach us your version of how to end the *Shmoneh Esreh*, as John taught his disciples his version") (Luke 11:1). See D. Thomas Lancaster, *Torah Club: Chronicles of the Messiah* (6 vols.; Marshfield, MO: First Fruits of Zion, 2014), 2:510; Aaron Eby, *First Steps in Messianic Jewish Prayer* (Marshfield, MO: First Fruits of Zion, 2014), 105–106.

[8.2]
This is what you should pray.

The *Our Father* itself is dually focused both on the present world and on the future Messianic Era. It is prayed in the first-person common plural form. Milavec writes that "as in the case of rabbinic prayers, which can be used when one person is alone—the prayer in such circumstances unites itself with all those who share the same prayer and look forward to the same kingdom."[93] O'Loughlin likewise concludes, "By using the plural, this prayer meant that the individual was not to see herself/himself praying alone, but always, at least virtually, as part of the whole."[94] The *Our Father*, wherever recited, whether alone or in a group, connects disciples of the Master to the broader Jewish community with prayers for today and hopes for the coming kingdom.

⸙ Our Father, who is in heaven. (DIDACHE 8.2)

The opening of the *Our Father* addresses God as "Father." "Father in heaven" was a common way of addressing God in Jewish prayer and also a popular circumlocution for the Tetragrammaton. For example, "The chasidim of old used to wait an hour before praying in order that they might focus their thoughts upon their Father in heaven" (b.*Brachot* 30b); and, "A blind man, or one who cannot tell which direction to pray, should direct his heart towards his Father in Heaven" (b.*Brachot* 30a).[95]

Yeshua often referred to God as "Father" or "Father in heaven." The concept of God as a father is common in the Scriptures, first appearing in Exodus 4:22: "Thus says the LORD, 'Israel is my firstborn son.'" The Master emphasized the paternal aspect of God frequently throughout his ministry, even comparing God's care for his people to that of a loving earthly Father: "If you then, who are evil, know how to give good gifts to your children, how much more will your Father who is in heaven give good things to those who ask him!" (Matthew 7:11).

"Our Father" is used in the mealtime prayers of chapter 9 and 10 as well. It is striking that the Didache maintains this title for God for Gentile recitation. Normally, "Our Father" was reserved for the Jewish people in light of passages such as "Israel, my firstborn" (Exodus 4:22) and "You are the sons of the LORD your God" (Deuteronomy 14:1). In turn, the Didache is making a strong statement echoing

---

[93] Milavec, *The Didache: Faith, Hope, & Life of the Earliest Christian Communities, 50–70 C.E.*, 333.
[94] O'Loughlin, *The Didache*, 81.
[95] Cf. m.*Yoma* 8:6; m.*Sotah* 9:15; b.*Sotah* 10a, 12a, 38b; b.*Shabbat* 116a; b.*Pesachim* 112a; b.*Rosh HaShanah* 29a; b.*Sanhedrin* 101–102. See also Aaron Eby and Toby Janicki, *Hallowed Be Your Name: Sanctifying God's Sacred Name* (Marshfield, MO: First Fruits of Zion, 2008), 28–29.

the New Testament that Gentiles in Messiah have been "predestined ... for adoption as sons through [Yeshua the Messiah], according to the purpose of his will" (Ephesians 1:5).[96] The Apostolic Constitutions makes this connection implicit:

[8.2] Our Father, who is in heaven.

> This is what you should pray three times a day, preparing yourselves beforehand, that you may be worthy of the adoption of the Father; lest, ... you call him Father unworthily. (Apostolic Constitutions 7.24)

⬥ Let your name be sanctified. (DIDACHE 8.2)

The prayer begins with a petition, the first of six. This first one is a petition of praise to sanctify the name of God.[97] Similar wording is found in the traditional *Kaddish* prayer, "Let his name be magnified and sanctified," and in the third benediction of the *Shmoneh Esreh*, "You are holy and holy is your name." The petition for God's name to be sanctified alludes to passages in Ezekiel that describe the redemption of Israel as a sanctification of God's name, whereas the exile of Israel profanes God's name among the nations.[98]

"Name" (*shem*, שם) in Hebrew refers to the essence and character of a person. The name of God refers to his reputation and person. To sanctify God's name is to make his true essence and character known in the earth. On a practical level, we "sanctify" God's name when we conduct ourselves in a manner that reflects well on his reputation. Likewise, we profane God's name when we conduct ourselves in a manner inconsistent with his character. When we operate in disobedience to his Torah, we profane his name and blemish his character. This is the concept of sanctification of the Name (*kiddush HaShem*, קידוש השם), which is the inverse of profaning the Name (*chillul HaShem*, חלול השם).[99] Sanctifying the Name (*kiddush HaShem*) can also be accomplished through the actions of the Lord as he fulfills his words and promises. When we pray for God's name to be sanctified, we are praying that his true character will be known throughout the earth.

"Let your name be sanctified" also points to the Messianic Era, when God's name will be sanctified once and for all. The Prophet Isaiah prophesies of that day, "They will sanctify my name; they will sanctify the Holy One of Jacob and will stand

---

96 Cf. 2 Corinthians 6:18; Galatians 3:26.
97 For the commentary on the *Our Father*, I have drawn heavily from D. Thomas Lancaster, *Torah Club: Chronicles of the Messiah*, 2:509–517.
98 Ezekiel 20, 36.
99 Leviticus 22:32–33 commands us to sanctify God's name and prohibits us from profaning it.

[8.2]
Let your name be sanctified.

in awe of the God of Israel" (Isaiah 29:23). To pray "Let your name be sanctified" is to pray for the arrival of the Messianic Kingdom, which we as disciples of Messiah should be eagerly awaiting.

The Apostolic Constitutions adds two scriptural citations at the end of the *Our Father*:

> This is what you should pray three times a day, preparing yourselves beforehand, that you may be worthy of the adoption of the Father; lest, when you call him Father unworthily, you be reproached by him, as Israel ... his first-born son was told: "If then I am a father, where is my honor? And if I am a master, where is my fear?" [Malachi 1:6]. For the glory of fathers is the holiness of their children, and the honor of masters is the fear of their servants, as the contrary is dishonor and confusion. For says he: "Through you my name is blasphemed among the Gentiles" [Isaiah 52:5 Septuagint]. (Apostolic Constitutions 7.24)

The Apostolic Constitutions stresses that God is to be honored by all those who call themselves his children. Although the immediate context of Isaiah 52 is that of Israel causing God's name to be blasphemed among the nations, it appears that the Apostolic Constitutions reads the text midrashically to refer to Gentiles profaning God's name. These additional citations, therefore, combined with the prayer "Let your name be sanctified," constituted a call for these new Gentile believers to leave behind their former ways that profaned God's name and to become sanctifiers of his name through their actions.

⁍ *Let your kingdom come.* (DIDACHE 8.2)

The *Our Father* continues with a second petition, this one asking that God's kingdom come down to earth both now and in the coming kingdom of heaven. This also echoes the traditional *Kaddish* prayer: "May he cause his Kingdom to reign." When we pray, "Let your kingdom come," we are asking God to bring about the prophetic day of the Lord, the final redemption, and the Messianic Era.

As we pointed out above, this is the good news as proclaimed by Yeshua: "Repent, for the kingdom of heaven is at hand."[100] He came to announce the arrival of the messianic redemption. The nation did not receive the summons to repent

---

100   Matthew 3:2, 4:17; Mark 1:15.

and to prepare for the kingdom. After Yeshua's resurrection his disciples asked him, "Lord, will you at this time restore the kingdom to Israel?" He responded, "It is not for you to know times or seasons that the Father has fixed by his own authority."[101] The Master did not deny that the kingdom of heaven was a real, literal kingdom, but he told the disciples that they would have to wait for its arrival. Nevertheless, the coming kingdom was his central message, and as his disciples today, we eagerly await and pray for that day. "Let your kingdom come" is a "summary of the message and the hope of the Didache community."[102]

[8.2]
Let your kingdom come.

Additionally, we have the opportunity to taste of the Messianic Era now as disciples of Messiah. The Master teaches, "Behold, the kingdom of God is in the midst of you" (Luke 17:21). Although we long for the kingdom of heaven to arrive in all its fullness, we can experience a firstfruits of it now as we submit our lives daily to the King and live according to his Torah.

⌖ Let your will be done—as in heaven, so on earth.
(DIDACHE 8.2)

The third petition asks God to fulfill his will on earth so that all creation will be subject to him just as the angels are subject to him in the heavenly realms. It is a prayer that God will infuse the world with his presence. Similarly, Rabbi Eliezer prays, "Do your will in heaven above, and grant relief to them that fear you below and do that which is good in your eyes."[103]

This is directly connected to the petition "Your kingdom come" but is also linked to "Let your name be sanctified." Rabbi Yechiel Tzvi Lichtenstein writes,

> It is to say, "May your name be sanctified, may your kingdom come, and may your will be done—as it is in heaven—for your name *is* sanctified, and the kingdom of God *is* there, and his will *is* done by 'his ministers, who do his will' (Psalm 103:21). So may your name be sanctified on the earth, may your kingdom come, and may your will be done."[104]

---

101 Acts 1:6–7.
102 Milavec, *The Didache: Faith, Hope, & Life of the Earliest Christian Communities, 50–70 C.E.*, 318.
103 b.*Brachot* 29b.
104 Yechiel Tzvi Lichtenstein, *Commentary on the New Testament* (trans. Aaron Eby and Robert Morris; Marshfield, MO: Vine of David, unpublished) on Matthew 6:10; trans. of *Bi'ur Lesifrei Brit HaChadashah* (8 vols.; Leipzig, Germany: Professor G. Dahlman, 1891–1904).

[8.2]
Let your will be done—as in heaven, so on earth.

Yet this is not just a prayer; it must also be carried out in the disciples' daily lives. In accordance with praying for God's will to be done on earth, we must be *doing* God's will on earth, that is, living out his commandments. In Chasidic thought, when each commandment of the Torah is performed, it brings down an aspect of godliness into the world.[105] In the *Sfas Emes*, Rabbi Yehudah Lieb Alter teaches that "when we do a mitzvah ... we prepare a place on earth for the glory of His Kingship to rest."[106] By doing God's will as his followers, we sanctify his name, cause his will to be done on earth, and help prepare an abode for his kingdom.

⬥ Our bread of tomorrow, immediately give us today.
(DIDACHE 8.2)

After prayers for God to bring his kingdom down to earth comes a petition to bring some of the abundant provision of that kingdom into the present. Ezekiel prophesies that in the Messianic Era the Lord "will provide for them renowned plantations so that they shall no more be consumed with hunger in the land, and no longer suffer the reproach of the nations" (Ezekiel 34:29).

The Greek word for "bread" (*arton*, ἄρτον) corresponds to the Hebrew *lechem* (לחם), which can stand for food in general. The prayer addresses the very practical day-to-day needs and worries of disciples of the Master; as the sages say, "Where there is no bread, there is no Torah."[107] This prayer teaches us to rely daily on God for provision. Just as an earthly father provides for his children, how much more so does our Father in heaven? As the Master says,

> Which one of you, if his son asks him for bread, will give him a stone? Or if he asks for a fish, will give him a serpent? If you then, who are evil, know how to give good gifts to your children, how much more will your Father who is in heaven give good things to those who ask him! (Matthew 7:9–11)

Although the Greek word *epiousios* (ἐπιούσιος) is usually translated "daily," it also has the connotation of "coming day." The "bread of tomorrow" is supported with

---

105 Rabbi Yitzchok Dovid Wagshul, "Torah Or: Exodus" (New York, NY: Purity Press, unpublished book), 3.
106 Rabbi Yosef Edelstein, "Insights into Exodus: Parshat Tetzaveh," n.p. [cited 21 November 2013]. Online: http://www.ou.org/torah/savannah/5760/tetzaveh60.htm.
107 m.*Avot* 3:17.

a version of the *Our Father* that appeared in the now-lost Gospel of the Hebrews: "Give us today bread for tomorrow."[108] In turn, the prayer for the "bread of tomorrow" asks our Father in heaven "to grant sustenance today from the abundance of the Messianic Era—a realized eschatology that complements the beatitudes and the kingdom message: 'Blessed are you who are hungry now, for you shall be satisfied' (Luke 6:21)."[109]

[8.2]
Our bread of tomorrow, immediately give us today.

⚜ And pardon us our debts, as we also pardon those indebted to us. (DIDACHE 8.2)

This fifth petition is one for forgiveness, a frequent theme in Jewish prayer. Sins are compared to debts that a man owes, and the Hebrew/Aramaic word *chovah* (חובה) can mean both "sin" and "debt."[110] As with financial debt, sin can become insurmountable, but if we repent and confess our sins to the Father, we can find forgiveness in the blood of his Son: "If we confess our sins, he is faithful and just to forgive us our sins and to cleanse us from all unrighteousness" (1 John 1:9).

In the Sermon on the Mount, the *Our Father* ends, "If you forgive others their trespasses, your heavenly Father will also forgive you, but if you do not forgive others their trespasses, neither will your Father forgive your trespasses" (Matthew 6:14–15). We learn in the Master's parable of the unforgiving servant that if we do not have mercy on others' sins, God will not have mercy on us.[111] This is the principle of "measure for measure" that was mentioned in the commentary on Didache 4.7. Similarly, Rabba teaches, "He who forgoes his right [to exact punishment] is forgiven all his iniquities, as it says, 'Forgiving iniquity and passing by

---

108 Jerome (*On Matthew* 6.11) says, "In the Gospel which is called according to the Hebrews, I found [*machar*, מחר] ... which means 'for tomorrow.'" Whether or not this represents the original Hebrew of the *Our Father* remains uncertain. The Gospel of the Hebrews passage appears to be a midrashic expansion on the *Our Father* rather than a literal rendering. In *Treatise on the Psalms* 135, Jerome reports the passage as follows: "In the Hebrew Gospel according to Matthew it is said in this way: 'Give us today our bread for the following day; that is the bread which will be given in your kingdom, give us today.'" A.F.J. Klijn, *Jewish-Christian Gospel Tradition* (Supplements to *Vigiliae Christianae* 17; Leiden, The Netherlands: Brill, 1993), 86–87.
109 Lancaster, *Torah Club: Chronicles of the Messiah*, 2:513; see also Eby, *First Steps in Messianic Jewish Prayer*, 113–116.
110 Eby, *First Steps in Messianic Jewish Prayer*, 116–119.
111 Matthew 18:23–35.

[8.2]
And pardon us our debts, as we also pardon those indebted to us.

transgression' (Micah 7:18). Who is forgiven iniquity? One who passes by transgression [against himself]."[112]

Forgiveness was a major part of the message and mission of our Master Yeshua. He taught us that we must forgive a brother who has transgressed against us with the same sin "seventy-seven times."[113] The Master was always extending forgiveness to those who needed it, from the adulterous woman who was almost stoned to death to the crippled man who was lowered through Peter's roof. Yeshua came to offer forgiveness to the world, and as his disciples, we must emulate him by always being quick to forgive those who offend us. Joshua Tilton writes, "According to Jesus there is a correlation between the way we forgive and our own experience of forgiveness: God's forgiveness is activated in our lives when we forgive the debt of others."[114] In turn, if we are unforgiving toward others, we cannot experience the forgiveness of our Father in heaven.

Putting this into the kingdom perspective, these prayers for forgiveness not only address the current needs of the petitioner, but as with all the other petitions in the *Our Father*, they will find their ultimate fulfillment in the Messianic Era. In his first coming Messiah purchased forgiveness through his atoning death. Individuals who cast allegiance with him receive forgiveness in his name on the merit of his suffering. When he returns, he will bring national forgiveness to Israel, which will result in the restoration of the Jewish people to their land. Messiah will establish his kingdom, and the Lord promises: "On the day that I cleanse you from all your iniquities" (Ezekiel 36:33); "I will forgive their iniquity, and I will remember their sin no more" (Jeremiah 31:34); "I will remove the iniquity of this land in a single day" (Zechariah 3:9).[115] This idea was put into a liturgical hymn by early Jewish believers: "And I bore their bitterness because of humility; that I might redeem my nation and instruct it. And that I might not nullify the promises to the patriarchs, to whom I was promised for the salvation of their offspring. Hallelujah."[116]

---

112 b.*Rosh HaShanah* 17a. Cf. b.*Yoma* 23a, 87b; b.*Megillah* 28a.
113 Matthew 18:22.
114 Joshua N. Tilton, *Jesus' Gospel: Searching for the Core of Jesus' Message* (Joshua N. Tilton, 2013), 83, available here: http://www.jerusalemperspective.com/products-page/ebooks/jesus-gospel/.
115 Cf. Isaiah 1:18; Ezekiel 36:25.
116 Odes of Solomon 31:12–13.

◈ *And do not bring us into testing, but rescue us from what is evil.* (DIDACHE 8.2)

The first part of this sixth and final petition might give the impression that we are to ask God to spare us from temptation to sin. This is often translated "lead us not into temptation." The Greek (*peirasmon*, πειρασμόν) and corresponding Hebrew (*nissayon*, נסיון) for "testing" found here in 8.2 can both mean "enticement to sin," but they also refer to "trial" or "testing."

James, the brother of the Master, writes, "Let no one say when he is tempted, 'I am being tempted by God,' for God cannot be tempted with evil, and he himself tempts no one. But each person is tempted when he is lured and enticed by his own desire" (James 1:13–14). God does not tempt us; rather, we are tempted by our own evil inclination (*yetzer hara*). Therefore, to pray that God not lead us into being tempted by sin would be erroneous. D. Thomas Lancaster adds, "He may lead us into difficulties that test our character and try our faith and allegiance. The petition beseeches God to lead us not into difficulties, evil occurrences, tragedy, misfortune, disease, and so forth."[117] The Master tells us that we must keep "watch and pray" so that we will "not enter into temptation. The spirit indeed is willing, but the flesh is weak."[118]

The second part of this petition, "rescue us from what is evil," is parallel to the first. The Master urges us to pray that we be led not into testing but that if we are, we be rescued from it. It is a petition "for deliverance from any evil circumstance, a prayer for deliverance from persecution, or a prayer for deliverance from the evil one—the Satan."[119] A close parallel is found in the Siddur:

> Do not lead us into the power of sin, nor into the power of trespass or iniquity, nor into the power of temptation, nor into the power of disgrace, and do not let the evil inclination control us. Distance us from an evil person or an evil friend. Cause us to cling to the good inclination and to good deeds, and compel our inclination to submit itself to you.[120]

These prayers for protection and deliverance, while all important themes for this age, find their ultimate fulfillment in the Messianic Kingdom, at whose advent

---

117 Lancaster, *Torah Club: Chronicles of the Messiah*, 2:516.
118 Mark 14:38.
119 Lancaster, *Torah Club: Chronicles of the Messiah*, 2:516.
120 In the *Morning Blessings* section of the *Shacharit* prayers based on a prayer by Rabbi Yehuda HaNasi in b.*Brachot* 60b.

God will forever deliver his people Israel, along with the Gentiles who have been grafted in, from their enemies and will bring them the salvation and deliverance for which they have been longing and praying.

⁌ *For yours is the power and the glory, forever and ever.*
(DIDACHE 8.2)

Having finished its petitions, the *Our Father* closes here with a short doxology that appears in a similar form in the mealtime prayers of Didache 9 and 10. It is slightly shorter than the ending that appears in some manuscripts of Matthew 6. It is also missing the "kingdom" phrase from the version in Matthew.[121] William Varner notes that "it is very similar to a common ending to prayers in the Jewish liturgy which exists even today."[122] It is much like the prayer of David in 1 Chronicles, which is included in the traditional Jewish daily morning prayers:

> Yours, O LORD, is the greatness and the power and the glory and the victory and the majesty, for all that is in the heavens and in the earth is yours. Yours is the kingdom, O LORD, and you are exalted as head above all. (1 Chronicles 29:11)

Similar doxologies appear throughout the New Testament.[123]

In Matthew this doxology "is absent in the best and oldest manuscripts, and the earliest patristic commentaries on the *Our Father* (Tertullian, Origen, and Cyprian) do not know it."[124] In light of this, most scholars feel that the doxology "represents a later addition to the *Our Father*, a liturgical adaptation to render the prayer more suitable for corporate prayer services."[125] Further evidence for this is the fact that the Didache and Matthew have variant versions pointing to other-than-canonical origins.

---

121   The "kingdom" phrase is also missing in the version of the *Our Father* in Gregory of Nyssa, *On the Lord's Prayer*, Homily 5.
122   William Varner, "The Didache's Use of the Old and New Testaments," *The Master's Seminary Journal* 16, no. 1 (Spring 2005): 134– 135.
123   E.g., Romans 11:36, 16:27; Galatians 1:5; Ephesians 3:21; Philippians 4:20; 1 Timothy 1:17, 6:16; 2 Timothy 4:18; Hebrews 13:21; 1 Peter 4:11, 5:11; 2 Peter 3:18; Jude 25; Revelation 1:6, 5:13–14, 7:12.
124   Van de Sandt and Flusser, *The Didache*, 294. A similar concluding blessing is recited in the Temple service as well (m.*Brachot* 9:5).
125   Lancaster, *Torah Club: Chronicles of the Messiah*, 2:516. See also Van de Sandt and Flusser, *The Didache*, 295.

The doxology functions as an "amen." It is a final concluding line that reminds the petitioner that ultimately all glory and honor belong to the Lord. At the end of our prayers, all we can do is place those things for which we have asked in our Father's care. Ultimately, it is up to him how he chooses to answer our petitions.

⁌ *This is what you should pray three times a day.* (DIDACHE 8.3)

The Didache closes chapter 8 with instructions to pray the *Our Father* three times a day. The Apostolic Constitutions adds, "You should pray three times a day, preparing yourselves beforehand, that you may be worthy of the adoption of the Father."[126] The Scriptures provide examples of praying thrice daily: "Evening and morning and at noon I utter my complaint and moan, and he hears my voice" (Psalm 55:17); "Daniel ... got down on his knees three times a day and prayed and gave thanks before his God" (Daniel 6:10). We find similar practices in apocryphal literature and at Qumran.[127] Most prominently we find praying three times a day in Jewish law laid down by the sages of Israel.[128]

As stated in the overview of this chapter, the first two times of daily prayer are based upon the two daily appointed times (*mo'adim*, מועדים), when the daily sacrifices were to be offered up in the Temple. The third time of prayer is based upon the recitation of the evening *Shma*. The three times of prayer were called *Shacharit*, *Minchah*, and *Ma'ariv* (sometimes *Aravit* or *Arvit* [ערבית]). In the oldest reckoning of the halachic times for these prayers, we find, "The morning prayer [can be said] until midday ... The afternoon prayer [can be said] till evening [sundown]. ... The evening prayer has no fixed limit."[129] The sages added more specifications about the ideal hours for the times of prayer to occur.

Milavec writes, "Here again, one can presume that the rhythms of prayer were taken over from Judaism, and one can accordingly learn something of the practice of the Didache by examining first-century Judaism."[130] Because the Didache mentions no specific times of prayer, "it is logical to assume that the writer of the book was

---

[126] Apostolic Constitutions 7.24. Cf. m.*Brachot* 5:1, in which it is stated that the ancient Chasidim would meditate for an hour in preparation for prayer.
[127] 2 Enoch 51:5; Community Rule (1QS) ix, 26–x, 2.
[128] E.g., m.*Brachot* 4:1.
[129] m.*Brachot* 4.1. The section here is paraphrased to reflect what was believed to be present in the first century, according to David Instone-Brewer, *Traditions of the Rabbis from the Era of the New Testament* (2 vol.; Grand Rapids, MI: Eerdmans Publishing Company, 2004), 1:53.
[130] Milavec, *The Didache: Faith, Hope, & Life of the Earliest Christian Communities, 50–70 C.E.*, 308.

referring to the dawn prayer (as *Halacha* has ruled) and to *Minha* and to *Aravit*."[131]

[8.3]
This is what you should pray three times a day.

Disciples of the Master wishing to follow the prayer instructions of the Didache should follow the legal times as they are interpreted today by traditional Judaism.

It can also be assumed that, as in Judaism, the Didache endorsed praying toward the Temple, which is accomplished most frequently today by praying to the east.[132] In the Apostolic Constitutions we find:

> Let him pray towards the east. For this also is written in the second book of the Chronicles, that after the temple of the Lord was finished by King Solomon, in the very feast of dedication the priests and the Levites and the singers stood up towards the east, praising and thanking God with cymbals and psalteries, and saying, "Praise the Lord, for he is good; for his mercy endures forever" [2 Chronicles 5:13 Septuagint]. (Apostolic Constitutions 7.44)

It may be that by the time the Apostolic Constitutions was committed to writing the original reason for praying toward the east was forgotten and that congregations prayed eastward regardless of their orientation to Jerusalem. In turn, praying toward the east continues to be the practice in many liturgical church traditions today without any reference to the Temple. Nevertheless, the custom of praying toward the east in the Apostolic Constitutions and in many churches today comes from the biblical and Jewish custom to pray toward the Temple whether it was standing or not.

O'Loughlin summarizes the importance of the thrice-daily prayers:

> With their communal prayer, recited as a group (physical or virtual) every day—at the beginning, middle and end—wherever they were,

---

131   Gedaliah Alon, "The Halacha in the Teaching of the Twelve Apostles," in *The Didache in Modern Research* (ed. Jonathan A. Draper; Leiden, The Netherlands: Brill, 1996), 180–81. Alon adds that from the Didache, "ostensibly, from this we have irrefutable evidence for the *Halacha* which fixed prayer three times a day, *Shacharit*, *Minha* and *Aravit*, and corroboration for the opinion of Rabban Gamaliel against Rabbi Joshua who says that the *Aravit* prayer is optional."

132   E.g., m.*Brachot* 4:5–6.

they were praying that the kingdom would grow, and were that new kingdom in their action.¹³³

Praying three times a day, whether together with the community or alone as an individual, establishes a rhythm of prayer in the daily life of a believer. It keeps us in constant contact with our Father in heaven, allows us to saturate our day with praise, prayer, and petition unto his name, and keeps his coming kingdom at the forefront of our minds.

[8.3]
This is what you should pray three times a day.

---

133   O'Loughlin, *The Didache*, 82. He prefaces this with, "The prophets looked forward to a time when Israel would offer a pure sacrifice in all places (>Malachi 1:11, quoted in Didache 14.3), and there would be a time when God would be offered mercy and steadfast love and not sacrifice (>Hosea 6:6; and Matthew 9:13 and 12:7). At the core of this vision was that of a holy, pure people offering prayer without ceasing: all people would behave as if they were priests. This is, indeed, the standard by which the Pharisees sought to live. Jesus takes over this notion and his community of disciples are seen as a priestly people, who can call on God—as the Levitical priests did—and even call him 'Father.'"

Chapter Nine

DIDACHE 9

9.1 Now concerning the giving of thanks, give thanks in this way:

9.2 First, concerning the cup:

> We thank you, our Father, for the holy vine of your servant David that you made known to us through your servant Yeshua. Yours is the glory forever.[1]

9.3 Next, concerning the piece of bread:

> We thank you, our Father, for the life and the knowledge that you made known to us through your servant Yeshua. Yours is the glory forever.[2]

9.4 Just as this piece of bread was scattered over the mountains and gathered together, so may your assembly be gathered from the ends of the earth[3] into your kingdom. For yours is the glory and the power through Yeshua the Messiah forever.[4]

9.5 But do not let anyone eat or drink by means of your giving of thanks except those immersed in the name of the Lord, for the Lord even said concerning this, "Do not give what is holy to the dogs."[5]

---

1 Matthew 6:13.
2 Ibid.
3 Deuteronomy 30:4; Isaiah 11:11–12; Zechariah 2:10(6); Nehemiah 1:9; Matthew 24:31.
4 Matthew 6:13.
5 Matthew 7:6.

Overview

The Didache continues the liturgical section that began in chapter 7 and extends through chapter 10. Chapter 9 contains prayers to be recited before a meal, and chapter 10, in a similar manner, contains prayers to be recited after a meal. The ends of both chapters 9 and 10 contain brief halachic instructions on who can be present at these meals and who is to lead the prayers.

These instructions regarding meals are intentionally placed after instructions about immersion into Messiah (chapter 7). Only after a new Gentile believer had completed the process of water immersion could he participate in the community's ceremonial meals. Eating with fellow believers was a major step in the initiation process. Jonathan Draper writes, "While washing established a state of separate ritual community or holiness, it is above all eating and drinking together which expresses it." In other words, the liturgy of these ceremonial meals both "symbolizes and effects" the incorporation of Gentiles into the commonwealth of Israel.[6] It is in dining together with the community that real fellowship begins.

Throughout history and throughout the world, meals bring family and friends together. A meal involves more than just eating:

> Nothing bonds us as human beings like sharing a meal: We are the only animals who cook our food—and this indicates that eating is always something more significant to us than just inputting nourishment. Around the table we become families, friends, and communities. Meals mark what is significant in life: a life without festive meals marking the events of our lives would point to a very dull life indeed. Meals make us human.[7]

In the Didache ceremonial meals are about sharing in fellowship and community, but they are also a sacrificial celebration of the past, present, and future. They are a taste of the kingdom of heaven and the mark of true discipleship. The prayers

---

[6] Jonathan A. Draper, "Ritual Process and Ritual Symbol in Didache 7–10," *Vigiliae Christianae* 54, no. 2 (2000): 134; and "The Holy Vine of David Made Known to the Gentiles through God's Servant Jesus: 'Christian Judaism' in the Didache," in *Jewish Christianity Reconsidered: Rethinking Ancient Groups and Texts* (ed. Matt Jackson-McCabe; Minneapolis, MN: Fortress, 2007), 269–273.

[7] Thomas O'Loughlin, *The Didache: A Window on the Earliest Christians* (Grand Rapids, MI: Baker, 2010), 103.

of chapters 9 and 10 ensure that every time believers eat together, their focus is not just nourishment and pleasure but an encounter with the divine.

Antiquity

The simplicity and brevity of these prayers cause many scholars to speculate that these chapters contain some of the earliest liturgical prayers of the Messianic community, possibly created within the first few years after the Master's ascension.[8] Kurt Niederwimmer states that these prayers "offer an archaic liturgical formula without peer in the early period of Christian liturgy."[9] They reflect the austerity of the believing community in the book of Acts: "Day by day, attending the temple together and breaking bread in their homes, they received their food with glad and generous hearts" (Acts 2:46).

Because of the antiquity of these prayers in the Messianic community, it should go without saying that their composition is entirely Jewish. They seem to be molded in part after the traditional fixed Jewish blessings recited over wine and bread with an additional prayer similar to the tenth benediction of the *Amidah* about the ingathering of the exiles.[10] In the Didache the blessings over the wine and the bread (9.2–4) have received a "poetic expansion" treatment similar to the Jewish liturgical poems that eventually became known as *piyyutim* (פיוטים).[11] They are "aggadic in character"[12]—homiletic and expanded. It is interesting to note that

---

8   Enrico Mazza, "Didache 9–10: Elements of a Eucharistic Interpretation," in *The Didache in Modern Research* (ed. Jonathan A. Draper; Leiden, The Netherlands: Brill, 1996), 283.
9   Kurt Niederwimmer, *The Didache: Hermeneia—A Critical and Historical Commentary on the Bible* (Minneapolis, MN: Fortress, 1998), 139.
10 Huub van de Sandt and David Flusser, *The Didache: Its Jewish Sources and Its Place in Early Judaism and Christianity* (Minneapolis, MN: Fortress, 2002), 310–325; Oskar Skarsaune, *In the Shadow of the Temple: Jewish Influences on Early Christianity* (Downers Grove, IL: InterVarsity Press, 2002), 406–407.
11 Draper, "The Holy Vine of David Made Known to the Gentiles through God's Servant Jesus," 272.
12 Joseph G. Mueller, "The Ancient Church Order Literature: Genre or Tradition?" *Journal of Early Christian Studies* 15, no. 3 (Fall 2007): 356.

similar Hebrew prayers that date to the late third century CE or earlier were found in parchment in the Dura-Europos synagogue.[13]

The prayers in Didache 9 and 10 move beyond simply thanking God for the physical sustenance of food; they expand to include the spiritual blessings that the food represents. A similar spiritualization of food is found throughout the Scriptures. For example, "Your words were found, and I ate them, and your words became to me a joy and the delight of my heart, for I am called by your name, O LORD, God of hosts" (Jeremiah 15:16), and, "Come, everyone who thirsts, come to the waters; and he who has no money, come, buy and eat! Come, buy wine and milk without money and without price ... Incline your ear, and come to me; hear, that your soul may live" (Isaiah 55:1–3).[14] The apocryphal Sirach says of the Torah, "They that eat me shall not be hungry, and they that drink me shall not thirst."[15] Likewise, the Master praises those who "hunger and thirst for righteousness, for they shall be satisfied."[16]

This spiritualization does not subvert giving thanks for physical food but rather augments it. Oskar Skarsaune observes,

> The Jewish prayers thank God for the physical drink and nourishment enjoyed by the body through wine and bread; the Didache prayers thank God for the spiritual gifts conveyed through the cup and the bread. These spiritual gifts, however, are described in such a way as to keep the reference to wine and bread intact.[17]

The prayers in the Didache enable us to thank our Father in heaven simultaneously for both the physical and the spiritual nourishment.

---

13 J.L. Teicher, "Ancient Eucharistic Prayers in Hebrew (Dura-Europos Parchment D. Pg. 25)," *Jewish Quarterly Review* 54, no. 2 (October 1963): 99–109. Teicher attempts to identify these as Christian in origin, but this seems unlikely. In a similar fashion the eighteenth-century work *Kedushat Levi* also allegorizes the traditional blessing over the bread: "The benediction which ends with the words "who brings forth bread from the earth," is accordingly understood as raising of something that was merely earthly, bread, to a progressively higher status through the thoughts that will course through our hearts and minds while we eat the bread, i.e., the meal. The deeper meaning of the benediction is that although it is apparently pronounced over the most basic material component of the physical earth, bread, the staff of life, it contains within it, though being sublimated, the potential to enable one of the exiled sparks from heaven to begin its journey homeward, to its roots in the celestial spheres" Rabbi Levi Yitzchak of Berditchev *Kedushat Levi* (trans. Eliyahu Munk; Brooklyn, NY: Lambda, 2009), 206.
14 Cf. Psalm 16:5; Amos 8:11.
15 Sirach 24:21. Cf. John 6:35.
16 Matthew 5:6.
17 Skarsaune, *In the Shadow of the Temple*, 409.

This gives further evidence that when these prayers were composed and used within the Messianic community, a strong connection to Judaism and its environment remained. The liturgy was not composed by someone outside Jewish tradition; rather, the composer was deeply steeped in and living amid the Jewish community. This fact must be taken strongly into consideration as we attempt to decipher the meaning and purpose of these prayers.

The archaic nature of the prayers and their strong ties to Jewish practice make this section of the Didache one the most heavily studied and debated. Do chapters 9 and 10 represent the oldest form of the Eucharist, or are the prayers contained in them simply meant to be used for an ordinary meal? We will attempt to answer these questions from a Messianic Jewish perspective. To begin we need to examine the Jewish tradition of reciting fixed blessings (*brachot*) at mealtimes.

THE COMMANDMENT TO GIVE THANKS

The custom of reciting blessings over food is not unique to Israel and existed in many ancient societies and religions. Although it is difficult to determine exactly when the blessings developed fixed forms in Israel, the custom of blessing before and after the meal goes back to a very early time.[18] Already in the Letter of Aristeas (200 BCE) we find mention of a set custom and procedure for blessing.[19]

The commandment to bless God after eating is found in Deuteronomy 8:10; this will be discussed in the overview of chapter 10. Although the injunction to thank God before partaking of anything is not explicitly commanded in the Torah, the sages found an allusion to it in Psalm 24:1:

> Rabbi Yehudah said in the name of Shmuel: "To enjoy anything of this world without a benediction is like making personal use of things consecrated to heaven, since it says: 'The earth is the LORD's and the fullness thereof.'" (b.*Brachot* 35a)[20]

---

18   Joseph Heinemann, *Prayer in the Talmud: Forms and Patterns* (Studia Judaica 9; New York, NY: De Gruyter, 1977), 115.

19   Letter of Aristeas 158, 183–186. Cf. Josephus, *Jewish War* 2:131/viii.5; Philo, *On the Special Laws* 4.99; *On the Contemplative Life* 66; Community Rule (1QS) VI, 4–5, X, 14–15.

20   Cf. t.*Brachot* 4:1. The sages also drew a conclusion that they were to bless before the meal, through the argument of *kal vachomer* ("inference from a minor to a major," קל וחומר), based upon the command to bless after the meal: "If he says a blessing when he is full, how much more so ought he to do so when he is hungry?" (b.*Brachot* 35a).

In the mind of the sages, to benefit from something without first giving thanks to God for it is to show ingratitude; worse, it is like stealing from God by profaning something holy, since everything belongs to him. The Apostle Paul used Psalm 24:1 in a similar way to discuss food and the prohibition of eating meat sacrificed to idols.[21]

Throughout the Gospels we frequently see Yeshua observing this standard by offering thanks before eating. We may assume that this was his regular practice. He followed it at the feeding of the four thousand, at the feeding of the five thousand, at the Last Seder, and even after his resurrection:[22]

> When he was at table with them, he took the bread and blessed and broke it and gave it to them. And their eyes were opened, and they recognized him. And he vanished from their sight. (Luke 24:30–31)

The Master's standard practice was to take bread, give thanks, and then break the bread for distribution. Although our English s of the Gospels often give the impression that Yeshua was blessing the bread, this is a mis of the Greek. For example, in Luke 24:30 the New American Standard Bible says that the Master "blessed it," referring to the bread. However, the word "it" is not in the original Greek, but has been added by the translators.[23] Thus, Yeshua simply "blessed." The blessing was always directed to the Lord and not to the item; the Scriptures do not portray anyone asking God to bless food. Rather, offering a blessing is a way of offering thanks before enjoying something that he has given to us.

Samuel Lachs points out, "Jesus follows the rabbinic procedure at table."[24] At his Last Seder he was careful not only to make a blessing for bread but also for the wine.[25] Jewish law stipulated that the wine for the recitation of Kiddush (the blessing over wine that declares the sanctity of the holy day or Sabbath) was

---

21 1 Corinthians 10:25–26.
22 Matthew 14:19, 15:36, 26:26; Mark 6:41, 8:7, 14:22; Luke 9:16, 22:19; John 6:11.
23 Luke 9:16 reads, "He blessed them" (NASB). While "them" (αὐτοὺς) is in the Greek text, an important manuscript variant in Codex Bezae reads "over them" (ἐπ' αὐτοὺς). See Reuben J. Swanson, ed., *New Testament Greek Manuscripts: Luke* (Sheffield, England: Sheffield Academic Press, 1995), 163. This represents a Hebrew idiom that shows that blessing concerning an item is directed to God and not to the item itself. It is possible that this Hebrew idiom preserved in Codex Bezae is the original, and that it confused Greek translators. Brad Young writes, "In reality, to recite a blessing 'over' them seems awkward in Greek and does preserve the original Hebrew idiom." See Young, *Jesus the Jewish Theologian* (Peabody, MA: Hendrickson, 1995), 125, n. 8.
24 Samuel Tobias Lachs, *A Rabbinic Commentary on the New Testament: The Gospels of Matthew, Mark and Luke* (Hoboken, NJ: KTAV, 1987), 241.
25 Luke 22:17.

to be blessed before the bread in honor of the day. The wine and the bread each required a separate blessing, and at a Passover Kiddush the wine blessing came first.[26] If the Master followed Jewish tradition by giving thanks before partaking of something (including maintaining the specified order of bread and wine), we have no legitimate reason to doubt that he followed the rest of the halachah in regard to blessings. In turn, we see these same sensitivities in the Didache.

Communion or an Ordinary Meal?

Most scholars agree that the mealtime blessings of the Didache developed out of the Jewish blessings (*brachot*) tradition (which proscribed various blessings on food), but the type of meal to which the Didache refers is debated.[27] Were these prayers intended specifically for a communion, or Eucharist, service? Or were they merely the prescribed blessings to be recited before any meal? Scholarship is divided into many opinions on this issue, with the majority falling into three camps:

1. Those who suggest that the Didache describes a Eucharist celebration
2. Those who suggest that the Didache describes an ordinary (or *agape*) meal
3. Those who suggest that the Didache describes some combination of the two[28]

Many scholars suggest that chapters 9 and 10 of the Didache definitely represent a Eucharist but not in a sacramental sense. During the nascent stage in the development of Christianity in which the Didache was written, the weekly Eucharist ritual was simply a continuation of the traditional Jewish communal meal. It may have had associations with Passover and our Master's injunctions at

---

26 Although in both Matthew (26:26–29) and Mark (14:22–25) it appears that Yeshua blessed the bread before the wine, this must be read in light of Luke (22:15–20) who has wine/bread/wine. Luke's second cup of wine is "the cup after they had eaten," which is used to represent Messiah's blood. First Corinthians 11:25 also has "he took the cup, after supper." Matthew and Luke omit mention of the first cup before the meal because they are focused on the bread representing his body and the cup representing his blood. Therefore, Matthew and Mark do not contradict the rabbinic order of cup then bread on Passover.

27 For the next several sections I have drawn heavily from Aaron Eby and Toby Janicki, *Breaking Bread: In Everything Give Thanks* (Marshfield, MO: First Fruits of Zion, 2013), 25–32.

28 Those who suggest that the liturgy of the Didache represents both the Eucharist and an ordinary meal are generally divided between two theories: The first is that 9.1–10.5 represents an ordinary meal, and that the Eucharist begins in 10.6. The second is that the Eucharist does not begin until chapter 14. For a full survey of opinions in scholarship, see Niederwimmer, *The Didache*, 141–142.

the Last Supper, however, if it did, those associations are absent from the Didache version of the ritual.

Turning to the text itself, at first glance we see a few notable elements that might incline us toward a Eucharist interpretation:

- The Greek word from which we get "Eucharist" is used (*eucharistia*, εὐχαριστία).
- Bread and wine are present, which on some level represent Messiah.
- It is found in a liturgical section of the document following instructions regarding immersion, fasting, and daily prayer.

However, the word translated "Eucharist" simply means "giving of thanks." It corresponds to the Hebrew word *todah* (תודה).[29] Even in modern Greek the way to say "thank you" is *eucharisto* (εὐχαριστῶ, pronounced today *efharisto*). Nothing requires us to translate the word into the technical term "Eucharist"; thus 9.1 could easily read, "Now concerning the giving of thanks." In fact, the same word and its related forms are employed frequently in the Gospels to describe blessings for ordinary meals.[30] In Greek-speaking Judaism and among the earliest believers, the term simply referred to blessing God before and after meals.

The combination of blessings for bread and wine does not necessarily indicate a Eucharist ritual either. First, bread and wine have been common components of every meal since ancient times in Mediterranean and Near Eastern cultures. Second, consider that observant Jewish people eat three meals containing bread and wine every Sabbath. Each of these meals also begins with appropriate blessings. Perhaps the reason that the Didache text does not mention other foods is that, according to Jewish law, when a blessing is made over the bread, no other blessings are required for the rest of the meal (except for those over wine or grape juice). Third, the Didache blessings of wine first and then of bread do not follow the order of a traditional Eucharist service, which usually blesses bread first and then wine.[31] This order was so important in the traditional Eucharist that in the

---

29 *Eucharistias* could also correspond to the Hebrew term *brachah* ("blessing," ברכה). See Skarsaune, *In the Shadow of the Temple*, 407.
30 See Matthew 15:36; Mark 8:6; Luke 22:17; John 6:11, 23; Acts 27:35. Cf. 1 Corinthians 14:16–17.
31 The earliest attestation of this order is from Justin Martyr's *First Apology* 65–67 (Justin lived from about 110–165 CE). Some have suggested that the Didache is following here an alternate rabbinic practice of wine and then bread such as that found in m.*Brachot* 8:8. Cf. Matthew 26:26–29; Mark 14:22–25; Luke 22:15–20; 1 Corinthians 11:23–28.

Apostolic Constitutions (fourth century CE) reworking of the Didache prayers, the order was switched to bless bread, and then wine in order to line up with the Eucharist.[32]

The Didache's inclusion of these prayers in connection with other rituals (chapters 7–8) should not be surprising either. Simply because these chapters on prayers follow shortly after a discussion about immersion does not necessarily indicate that we are dealing with the Lord's Supper. In fact, the placement of chapters 9–10 within the Didache is an appropriate context for meal blessings, considering that food is a recurring theme in nearby chapters. Chapter 6 instructs the reader to avoid meat offered to idols, and chapter 8 gives instructions regarding fasting. While the blessings of chapters 9 and 10 do not constitute a "sacrament" in the Catholic or Orthodox sense, the Jewish mealtime blessings, as with fasting and baptism, comprise a ritual having important religious significance.

We find at least one more serious difficulty with interpreting these prayers for a Eucharist. Although the blessings here are extensive, they do not contain any of the themes that we would expect to be present in a Eucharist ceremony. Namely, the text does not mention the suffering, death, or resurrection of Yeshua; sin, sacrifice, atonement, or forgiveness; the final Passover meal; or Yeshua's blood, Yeshua's body, the new covenant, or the phrase "in remembrance of me."[33] A number of scholars have noted this jarring omission:

> That is to say, there is no question of a memorial of the death of Jesus, of his body and the blood of the covenant, or of a remembrance of the Last Supper on the night of his betrayal.[34]

> In the same way, the instructions on the Eucharist contain no reference to the words of institution, the Last Supper, or Jesus' sacrificial death on the cross.[35]

---

32 Apostolic Constitutions 7.25.
33 We do find these themes in the rendering of these prayers in the Apostolic Constitutions (7.35).
34 See Hans Lietzmann, *Mass and Lord's Supper: A Study in the History of the Liturgy* (Leiden, The Netherlands: Brill, 1979), 188–194.
35 Draper, "The Holy Vine of David Made Known to the Gentiles through God's Servant Jesus," 269–273.

The text does not say that the meals in which the εὐχαριστίαι ["giving of thanks"] featured has a specifically sacramental content, nor do the prayers imply any reference to Jesus' Last Supper.[36]

Except for the association that we might make with bread and wine, the prayers in chapters 9 and 10 do not mention anything that would connect them with the ceremony that our Master Yeshua performed at the Last Supper.

Breaking Bread

Interpreting the Didache blessings as part of a Eucharist celebration of the Last Supper also raises the problem of anachronism. At the time that the Didache was written, believers still celebrated their formal remembrance of the Last Supper within its original Passover context.[37] The ritual Eucharist of Holy Communion had not yet fully developed within Christianity. But if the Didache text represents Jewish mealtime blessings rather than a Eucharist ritual, how was it employed?

The early believers regularly ate together at communal meals:

> They devoted themselves ... to the breaking of bread and the prayers ... Breaking bread in their homes, they received their food with glad and generous hearts. (Acts 2:42, 46)

"Breaking bread" (*paras lechem*, פרס לחם) is a common term in rabbinic literature for the beginning of a meal, when the blessing was recited.[38] Each time that they gathered, blessed God, and broke bread together, the earliest disciples would have remembered meals that they had enjoyed together with Yeshua. In addition to the many daily meals that they had shared with the Master, they would have remembered how he had miraculously fed the multitudes and changed water into wine. They would have remembered the Sabbath and festival meals that he had shared with them over the years.

---

36 Jürgen K. Zangenberg, "Reconstructing the Social and Religious Milieu of the Didache: Methods, Sources, and Possible Results," in *Matthew, James, and Didache: Three Related Documents in Their Jewish and Christian Settings* (ed. Huub van de Sandt and Jürgen K. Zangenberg; Atlanta, GA: Society of Biblical Literature, 2008), 59.

37 One example of believers who celebrated the Last Supper at Passover is the Quartodecimans. See Oskar Skarsaune and Reidar Hvalvik, *Jewish Believers in Jesus: The Early Centuries* (Peabody, MA: Hendrickson, 2007), 516–528.

38 E.g., b.*Brachot* 46a and b.*Shabbat* 117b.

Jewish tradition mandates three festive meals every Sabbath. It is easy to imagine the earliest believers gathering on the Sabbaths and festivals to break bread, enjoy one another's fellowship, and encourage one another with the words of Yeshua. Table fellowship was extremely important in the apostolic communities, so much so that many disputes arose among the early believers over issues related to meals.[39]

Agape Meals

The tradition of communal meals among the believers continued through the Apostolic Era. Jude 12 refers to these community meals as "love feasts" (*agapais*, ἀγάπαις). Gedaliah Alon suggests that the background of the apostolic *agape* feasts is the rabbinic custom of sages and their disciples often dining together. He feels that the word *agape* itself is connected to the Hebrew *ahavah* ("love," אהבה) and to the joyous feasts (*simchat merei'ut*, שמחת מריעות) written about in the Talmud.[40] These gatherings took place in synagogues and in the house of study on holy days and weekdays alike, where meals took on a sacred tone of joyous celebration and Torah.[41]

The apostles continued a tradition similar to that which they had observed with their Master. Hans Lietzmann paints the picture:

> As it had been in the happy days of their journey in Galilee, so it came to be again: a Jewish [*chavurah*] they gathered together around the Master for the common meal. The old "table-fellowship" (κοινωνία) which had begun in the time of the historic Jesus was continued with the risen Lord ... Thus, had it been formally, when the Lord had presided at the table in the flesh. Now he was with his disciples "in the

---

39 Acts 15:20; Romans 14; 1 Corinthians 11:23–34; Colossians 2:16–23; 1 Timothy 4:3–5.
40 "As can be seen, the name itself, ἀγάπη (אהבה), proves its Jewish origins ... the *agape* is but the Hebrew word *meriyot*, which is found in the *Baraita* in the Talmud (b.*Moed Katan* 22b), and its contents refer to a supper with companions, which was initially, undoubted, referred to as *seudat-reyim* (fellowship-meal), but with time the name was shortened, as usual, and only the term *meriyot* remained" (Gedaliah Alon, "The Halacha in the Teaching of the Twelve Apostles," in *The Didache in Modern Research* [ed. Jonathan A. Draper; Leiden, The Netherlands: Brill, 1996], 185).
41 This practice finds expression in the modern day Chasidic movement with customs such as the *Farbrengen* ("joyous gathering," פארברענגען) and a rebbe's *tisch* ("table," טיש). These communal festive meals take place on Shabbats and other special occasions. At these joyous meals, filled with singing and dancing, the rebbe would divulge some of the most treasured and intimate of all his Torah teachings. When the rebbe passes, in some cases a new leader does not take over and instead, the teachings of the deceased rebbe are taught by his disciples in an effort to make him symbolically present at the meal with his disciples.

spirit," for where two or three were gathered together in his name there he was in the midst of them (Matthew 18:20). And soon, the community fervently believed, he would come again in the clouds of heaven, like Daniel's Son of man, and set up the Messianic Kingdom on earth. This belief made them joyful; the meal was celebrated "with gladness"; and in answer to the "Maranatha," the "Come, Lord Jesus," of their leader, the company of the table hailed the longed-for Lord with glad hosannas.[42]

The members of the Messianic community under the leadership of the apostles continued to eat their meals with the presence of our Master Yeshua in their hearts. As the Master himself had said, "Behold, I am with you always, to the end of the age" (Matthew 28:20).

A Messianic Banquet

The believers would have found it completely natural to remember Messiah every time they broke bread and drank wine in the context of a community meal. The Didache blessings seem to reflect that consciousness, yet they steer away from invoking the explicit Last Supper language of "This is my body" and "This is my blood." Why? Perhaps the believers reserved that language for the celebration of Passover. Instead of using the bread as a symbol for Messiah's body and the wine as a symbol for his blood, the Didache blessings use the wine as a symbol for the Davidic monarchy and the bread as a symbol for the believers scattered across the earth. Both look forward to Messiah's second coming, when the scattered assembly will be "gathered from the ends of the earth," and the Davidic monarchy ("the holy vine of your servant David") will be reestablished.

The language of the Didache's pre-meal prayers make every meal that the disciples of the Master share together a taste of the Messianic banquet that will take place at the inauguration of the kingdom of heaven upon the Master's return.[43] Norman Perrin writes, "We must see the table-fellowship of that ministry as a table-fellowship 'of the Kingdom' and as anticipating a table-fellowship 'in the Kingdom.'"[44] Furthermore, this is even evidenced in placing the mealtime blessings right after the *Our Father*: In chapter 8 disciples are taught to pray a prayer

---

42   Lietzmann, *Mass and Lord's Supper*, 204.
43   For more details on the Messianic banquet, see Aaron Eby, trans., *Meal of Messiah: The Wedding Supper of the Lamb* (Marshfield, MO: Vine of David, 2013), viii–ix.
44   Norman Perrin, *Rediscovering the Teaching of Jesus* (New York, NY: Harper & Row, 1976), 107.

in expectation of the coming kingdom, in chapter 9 and 10 they get a taste of that kingdom in a meal that foreshadows the Messianic banquet.

The prophets foretell this great and awesome day when the Lord will gather Israel and "bring them into their own land" and "feed them on the mountains of Israel" (Ezekiel 34:13). In that day he will "make for all peoples a feast of rich food, a feast of well-aged wine, of rich food full of marrow, of aged wine well refined" (Isaiah 25:6).[45] While this banquet is centered on the Jewish people, it will include many from the nations. The Master spoke of the universal aspect of this feast: "I tell you, many will come from east and west and recline at the table with Abraham, Isaac, and Jacob in the kingdom of heaven" (Matthew 8:11). In the meal of the Didache, this prophetic future becomes a present reality when Jew, Gentile, man, woman, slave, and free all sit down to eat together as disciples of the Master:[46]

> What set this community apart was that the sharing of food cut right across the social stratifications of the ancient world and indeed its dining practice. The poor and the rich ate together, the slaves shared a table with their masters, women ate with men, the outcasts with the righteously pure, the gentile sat next to the Jew, and all prayed to the Father and thanked him for sending his Son.[47]

This is a picture of God's kingdom. The book of Revelation states, "Blessed are those who are invited to the marriage supper of the Lamb."[48] It is at this feast that we will be united in the Master's company, and that he will "drink again" of the fruit of the vine.[49]

It appears that the Didache blessings were the standard liturgical text for the Messianic community's communal meals. When the believers gathered on Sabbaths and festivals they prayed these blessings over bread and wine in remembrance of Yeshua, the bread of life and the true vine, who gave them spiritual food and drink.

---

45 Cf. Isaiah 65:13.
46 Cf. Isaiah 55:1–5.
47 O'Loughlin, *The Didache*, 91.
48 Revelation 19:9. Cf. Revelation 3:20, 19:7.
49 Matthew 26:29. Cf. Luke 22:15–18, 29–30; Mark 14:25. Also note the parable of the bridesmaids in Matthew 22:1–14.

Practical Application

One of the overarching themes that we can derive from chapter 9 is the importance of giving thanks before we eat. The community of the Didache, in step with the Judaism of its day, viewed offering blessings before partaking of food as a mitzvah.

Judaism has created six different pre-meal blessings for various foods.[50] Some modern rabbinic authorities recommend that even Gentiles follow much of the laws surrounding blessings.[51] Paul, writing to non-Jewish believers, taught them to "partake with thankfulness," implying that they said blessings before they ate.[52] Most likely he was referring to the traditional blessings or some form of them.

Based upon the stress that the Didache places on blessing God at mealtimes, Gentile disciples should certainly follow the custom of Yeshua by blessing God before a meal as an important part of discipleship and Torah practice.

But what about the pre-meal blessings of Didache 9? When exactly should these specific prayers be used? It seems that Sabbath and festival meals are appropriate occasions on which to recite the Didache's blessings, as these meals begin with bread and wine. The Didache text naturally augments Judaism's traditional bread and wine blessings. For example, the precedence of wine over bread in the pre-meal blessings corresponds to the order of a Kiddush service and not to that of an ordinary meal. The Didache text adds a heightened level of sanctity to the Sabbath meals by introducing a remembrance of Messiah and an eschatological view toward the kingdom.

---

50   m.*Brachot* 6:1.
51   Rabbi Yoel Schwartz, *Service from the Heart: Renewing the Ancient Path of Biblical Prayer and Service* (ed. Rabbi Michael Katz et al.; Rose, OK: Oklahoma B'nai Noah Society, 2007); Rabbi Moshe Weiner and Rabbi J. Immanuel Schochet, *Prayers, Blessings, Principles of Faith, and Divine Service for Noahides* (ed. Dr. Michael Schulman; Pittsburgh, PA: Ask Noah International, 2010).
52   1 Corinthians 10:30.

Commentary

⹋ Now concerning the giving of thanks, give thanks in this way. (DIDACHE 9.1)

Chapter 9 opens with instructions for giving thanks. The second word here is identical to that in the beginning of 7.1, "Concerning immersion …" As we have noted before, this construction is formulaic for introducing halachic instruction.[53] The equivalent Hebrew word for "concerning" (*peri*, περὶ) in this context is *al* (עַל), and it is significant that this term is included in the Jewish blessing formula before performing commandments. The Apostolic Constitutions adds to this statement, "Be always thankful, as faithful and honest servants" (7.25), reminiscent of Paul's words to "give thanks in all circumstances."[54]

The root word here for "the giving of thanks" and "give thanks" is *eucharistia* (εὐχαριστία), which quite literally means "to give thanks." Although in later literature the term takes on the technical meaning, usually transliterated as *Eucharist* and referring to Communion, here in this early stage of the Messianic community, it simply referred to offering thanks to God. It reflects the language of Jewish blessings: *levarech* ("to bless," לְבָרֵךְ) and *lehodot* ("to give thanks," לְהוֹדוֹת).[55] As such, the Didache is giving instruction about blessings at fellowship meals and not Communion.

⹋ First, concerning the cup. (DIDACHE 9.2)

The liturgy begins with the first of two blessings: that given for the cup. The opening language is reminiscent of rabbinic literature. The Greek word *peri* ("concerning," περὶ) corresponds in the Septuagint to *al* (עַל), similar to the way the Mishnah

---

53 Niederwimmer writes that "['give thanks in this way'] is to be understood: the following is the manner in which you are to pray the benedictions" (*The Didache*, 144). Flusser and Van de Sandt suggest that these blessings might have been given in place of the traditional Jewish blessings: "In the same way the Lord's Prayer in Didache 8 is supposed to take the place of the Jewish *tefilla*, so the full text of the eucharistic prayers may have been inserted in the Didache as a replacement for the Jewish table prayer" (*The Didache*, 325).
54 1 Thessalonians 5:18.
55 Peter J. Tomson, *Paul and the Jewish Law: Halakha in the Letters of the Apostle to the Gentiles* (Minneapolis, MN: Fortress, 1990), 140.

[9.2]
First, concerning the cup.

introduces a legal topic: "Over (על) wine one says ..."⁵⁶ Additionally, "cup" (*poteriou*, ποτηρίου) corresponds to the Hebrew word *kos* (כוס), which is used in rabbinic discussions about blessings over wine.⁵⁷

The order of wine before bread here follows the prescribed order for Shabbat and festival Kiddush meals, whereas on regular weekdays the order is bread before wine. This may indicate that these blessings were intended to be recited on Sabbaths and festivals.

Typically either the head of the house or an honored guest led the blessing.⁵⁸ The blessings would have been recited in a melodic chant. As he pronounced the blessing, the master of ceremony would have held the cup in his right hand, raising it above the table. The Didache specifies "the cup" in the singular, implying a common cup. After the leader tasted a sip of the wine, he would pass the cup around so that all present could partake. This is similar to the practice of the Master at his Last Seder: "He took a cup, and when he had given thanks he gave it to them, saying, 'Drink of it, all of you.'"⁵⁹ The rabbis believed that the cup over which the blessing (*brachah*) was recited imparted a blessing to those who drank of it.⁶⁰

⌘ We thank you, our Father. (DIDACHE 9.2)

The Didache's blessing over the cup is thought by many to be a poetic expansion on the traditional Jewish blessing over wine. David Flusser and Huub Van de Sandt point out:

> First, the concept of the vine, directly bound up with the contents of the cup, is also found in the Jewish benediction over the cup. Second, the formula "for the holy vine" (ὑπὲρ τῆς ἁγίας ἀμπέλου) takes up the Jewish expression "fruit of the vine" (*pri hagafen*, פרי הגפן), which indicates the dependence on the traditional blessing.⁶¹

---

56 m.*Brachot* 6:1. Karl-Gustav Sandelin suggests that the original Hebrew source of the Didache's introductory formula could have been לפנים על הכוס (*lefanim al hakos*) (*Wisdom as Nourisher* [Turku, Finland: Åbo Akademi, 1986], 190).
57 m.*Brachot* 8:2.
58 b.*Pesachim* 46a.
59 Matthew 26:27. Cf. Mark 14:23; Luke 22:17.
60 b.*Brachot* 51b.
61 Van de Sandt and Flusser, *The Didache*, 310. Vööbus feels that the phrase ἁγίας ἀμπέλου (*agias aupelou*, holy vine) is reminiscent of the Jewish Kiddush (*Liturgical Traditions*, 163).

This blessing over the cup is divided into three parts: thanksgiving to God, which we are examining now; a description of the item of blessing; and a concluding doxology. Likewise, the traditional Jewish blessing over wine can be divided in a similar tri-part fashion:

[9.2]
We thank you, our Father.

Didache 9.2	Rabbinic Blessing over Wine[62]
We thank you, our Father,	Blessed are you, O LORD, our God, King of the universe,
for the holy vine of your servant David that you made known to us through your servant Yeshua.	who creates the fruit of the vine.
Yours is the glory forever.	Amen.

While the traditional rabbinic blessing begins with "Blessed are you," the Didache blessing begins with "We thank you." Although the "Blessed are you" form was the most popular one used in the Temple and in the synagogue, we find evidence of "We [or 'I'] thank you" from Jewish literature and prayers, including the Dead Sea Scrolls.[63] Note also Psalm 118:21: "I thank you that you have answered me." This phrase is found on the lips of our Master several times in the Gospels, which most certainly influenced the Didache's choice of wording.[64] "The fact that the formula is chosen in the Didache is thus no sign of distance from Judaism; it is rather an indication of the antiquity of these prayers."[65]

Another difference between the blessing over the cup in the Didache and that of traditional Judaism is the Didache's use of "our Father" rather than the Tetragrammaton found in the traditional blessing.[66] "Our Father" (*Avinu*, אבינו) as a title for God is found sprinkled throughout rabbinic literature, usually coupled

---

62 m.*Brachot* 6:1.
63 E.g., Sirach 51:1; m.*Brachot* 4:2; the *Hoda'ah* benediction of the *Genizah Amidah*; Thanksgiving Hymns (1QH[a]). For a full discussion, see J.M. Robinson, *The Sayings Gospel Q: Collected Essays* (ed. C. Heil and J. Verheyden; Bibliotheca Ephemeridum Theologicarum Lovaniensium; Leuven, Belgium: Peeters, 2005), 75–118.
64 Matthew 11:25; Luke 10:21; John 11:41. "I thank you" also begins the Pharisee's prayer in Luke 18:11.
65 Skarsaune, *In the Shadow of the Temple*, 407.
66 One of the key characteristics of rabbinic prayer of the period is that it is not addressed to an intermediary such as an angel or holy figure. This matches the "character of prayers of the Didache" (Aaron Milavec, *The Didache: Faith, Hope, & Life of the Earliest Christian Communities, 50–70 C.E.* [New York, NY: Newman, 2003], 403). Indeed, throughout the New Testament all prayers are directed to the Father.

[9.2] We thank you, our Father.

with the phrase "in heaven."[67] This title for God finds its roots in Exodus 4:22, in which the Lord states, "Israel is my firstborn son." This title for the Lord, in various permutations, was Yeshua's favorite in his teachings about the paternal nature of God and in many of his prayers. This again most certainly influenced the Didache's choice of "our Father."

As was pointed out in the commentary on the *Our Father* in chapter 8, "our Father" as a title for God was usually reserved for the Jewish people because of their unique relationship with HaShem. By instructing Gentiles to use this epithet in their prayers the Didache was echoing the New Testament's sentiments that Gentiles in Messiah have been adopted as sons and daughters of the King.[68]

> *For the holy vine of your servant David that you made known to us through your servant Yeshua.*
> (DIDACHE 9.2)

The Didache takes the image of the cup of wine and transforms it into a symbol of the prophetic expectations of the Messiah and the Messianic Kingdom. Flusser and Van de Sandt suggest that the composer of this prayer worked with an already existing liturgical version used in Jewish communities and simply added the phrase "that you made known to us through your servant Yeshua."[69] The blessing is rich in the imagery of the Hebrew Scriptures and of Judaism.

"Holy vine" is reminiscent of the traditional phrase "fruit of the vine." In Jewish symbolism the vine represents the nation of Israel: "You brought a vine out of Egypt; you drove out the nations and planted it. You cleared the ground for it; it took deep root and filled the land" (Psalm 80:8–9).[70] In some instances, however,

---

67 E.g., m.*Avot* 5:20; m.*Kilayim* 9:8; b.*Brachot* 30a; b.*Shabbat* 116a.
68 Cf. 2 Corinthians 6:18; Galatians 3:26; Ephesians 1:5.
69 "The fact that identical designations were ascribed to Jesus and David, though one would have expected a clear inferiority of David, makes it hard to believe that the text of Didache 9.2a was conceptualized in Christian circles" (Van de Sandt and Flusser, *The Didache*, 324).
70 Also Hosea 10:1; Jeremiah 2:21; Ezekiel 15:1–8, 17:6, 19:10–14. Stephan Filan feels that the connection between Israel and the vine could have been based originally on Numbers 13:23: "They came to the Valley of Eshcol and cut down from there a branch with a single cluster of grapes, and they carried it on a pole between two of them." See Filan, "Identity in the Didache Community," in *The Didache: A Missing Piece of the Puzzle in Early Jewish Christianity* (eds. Jonathan A. Draper and Clayton N. Jefford; Atlanta, GA: Society of Biblical Literature, 2015), 27.

it symbolizes the Davidic King.⁷¹ The Didache combines these two themes. In it the vine becomes a "metaphor for the salvation and blessing of the messianic kingdom."⁷² Isaiah tells us that "aged wine" will be served at the messianic banquet. The sages say that the "aged wine" has been preserved since the days of creation.⁷³ In this way the vine represents Israel and its Messianic expectations.

[9.2]
For the holy vine of your servant David that you made known to us through your servant Yeshua.

The Master also speaks of the vine in the Gospel of John: "I am the true vine, and my Father is the vinedresser … Abide in me, and I in you … I am the vine; you are the branches. Whoever abides in me and I in him, he it is that bears much fruit, for apart from me you can do nothing" (John 15:1–5). Our Master Yeshua is the fulfillment of the Messianic expectation symbolized by the vine. He identified himself as the vine of Israel. He is King Messiah in accordance with the vine/kingship prophecy about Judah in Genesis 49:11. Combining this image with "your servant David," Draper states that "the vine of David is a reference to the covenant people of Israel of which David is the king, as well as to David's own royal house that is restored by Jesus."⁷⁴ The Master is the "son of David," "the root of Jesse," "the root and the descendant of David," and "a horn of salvation for us in the house of

---

71 2 Baruch 36–37; Targum to Psalm 80:15. In b.*Chullin* 92 the vine is referred to as the world, Torah, Israel, and Jerusalem.
72 Skarsaune, *In the Shadow of the Temple*, 409.
73 Isaiah 25:6. See Raphael Patai, *The Messiah Texts: Jewish Legends of Three Thousand Years* (Detroit, MI: Wayne State University, 1988), 244–245. See also D. Thomas Lancaster, "Life of the Party: The Miracle of Changing Water to Wine," *Messiah Journal* 100 (Spring 2009): 21–25. HaRav Eliyahu Tzvi Soloveitchik (*Kol Kore* to Matthew 26:29) feels that Yeshua alludes to this wine at his Last Seder: "*I will drink it with you*—and so it says in the Talmud (b.*Brachot* 34b): 'Rabbi Chiya said: "Rabbi Yochanan said: 'All the prophets did not prophesy about anything except the days of Messiah. However, in the world to come, "No eye has seen, O God, but you" (Isaiah 64:4).' This means: you have not been seen nor revealed to any prophet. 'What does it mean that no eye has seen you? Rabbi Yehoshua son of Levi said: "This is the wine that has been preserved in its grapes from the six days of creation."' This means: this is an example of the goodness that is reserved for the righteous from the six days of creation, and this is what he [Yeshua] meant when he said, 'which I will drink with you in the kingdom of my father.'"
74 Draper, "The Holy Vine of David Made Known to the Gentiles through God's Servant Jesus," 272. Also, "The kingdom of David is presented as the fulfillment of the divine promise in the gift of the land, which in the Old Testament is the most important theme. David is the 'blessed' of God and 'wherever he went, God gave him victory' (2 Samuel 8:14). Above all, we note that the victories of David are crowned with the taking of Jerusalem, which will be called the City of David, and so David and the House of Israel form a single people around their God. All this has, through Christ, a new sense and a deeper meaning, which nevertheless does not separate itself nor oppose itself to the salvation history of Israel" (Enrico Mazza, "Didache 9–10: Elements of a Eucharistic Interpretation," in *The Didache in Modern Research* [ed. Jonathan A. Draper; Leiden, The Netherlands: Brill, 1996], 280).

[9.2]
For the holy vine of your servant David that you made known to us through your servant Yeshua.

his servant David."⁷⁵ He is the fulfillment of the Messianic prophecies of "the holy vine of your servant David."⁷⁶

The Didache refers to both David and the Messiah as "your servant." The expression "David your servant" (*David avdecha*, דוד עבדך) appears in the Hebrew Scriptures, the New Testament, and in Jewish liturgy.⁷⁷ "The servant" is an important prophetic title for Messiah in the book of Isaiah, and Yeshua is subsequently referred to often as "my servant."⁷⁸ Yeshua is the servant who takes over the scepter of kingship in the royal line of the servant David.

"Servant" becomes a central and important early Christological image for the Messianic community.⁷⁹ Yeshua is called Messiah in the Didache only once, in 9.4, and some scholars feel that even this is a textual variant.⁸⁰ In the minds of the apostles, Yeshua was the Messiah-elect—he was indeed the Anointed One but had not yet completely fulfilled his role. He had come this first time in the role of the suffering servant in the book of Isaiah. Peter, speaking to his fellow Jewish brothers, refers to the Messiah as yet to come, saying that God would "send the Messiah appointed for you, Yeshua."⁸¹ New Testament scholar John Robinson paraphrases Peter:

> Jesus is still only the Christ-elect; the messianic age has yet to be inaugurated … We know who the Messiah will be; there is no need to look for another … Jesus has already been sent, as the forerunner of the Christ he is to be, in the promised role of the Servant and the Prophet, with the offer of the covenanted blessing and a preaching of repentance. Accept that therefore … you may be able to receive him in due time as the Christ, the bringer of God's new age.⁸²

---

75 Matthew 1:1, 12:23; Isaiah 11:10; Revelation 22:16; Luke 1:69.
76 In Clement of Alexandria's *Quis Dives Salvetur* 29 we find what appears to be a quote of a more developed version of this blessing: "He it is that poured wine on our wounded souls the blood of David's vine."
77 Psalm 132:10; Luke 1:69; Acts 4:25; *Malchut Beit David* and *Y'rushalayim v'David* benedictions of the *Genizah Amidah*; the festival prayer *Ya'aleh Veyavo*; and the *Baruch She'amar*.
78 E.g., Isaiah 42:1; Matthew 12:18; Acts 3:13, 26, 4:27, 30; 4 Ezra 7:28–29, 13:32, 37; 1 Clement 59.2–4; Barnabas 6.1, 9.2.
79 Mazza, "Didache 9–10: Elements of a Eucharistic Interpretation," 284; Niederwimmer, *The Didache*, 147–148; Skarsaune, *In the Shadow of the Temple*, 409.
80 The Apostolic Constitutions (7.25) omits διὰ Ἰησοῦ Χριστοῦ altogether. In turn, some scholars, such as Kirsopp Lake, have chosen to omit Χριστοῦ from the text (Lake, *The Apostolic Fathers* [New York, NY: Macmillan, 1912], 323).
81 Acts 3:20.
82 John A.T. Robinson, *Jesus and His Coming* (2d ed.; Philadelphia, PA: Westminster, 1979), 144.

In turn, the Didache lays great stress upon Yeshua's role as God's servant as we await the day when he will return as King Messiah.

"The holy vine of your servant David" (Israel and its messianic expectation of salvation and redemption) has been "made known" to Gentiles as well through Yeshua. This is reminiscent of the words of the psalm, "The LORD has made known his salvation [*yeshuah*, ישועה]; he has revealed his righteousness in the sight of the nations" (Psalm 98:2). Draper summarizes,

[9.2]
For the holy vine of your servant David that you made known to us through your servant Yeshua.

> This cannot be construed as supersessionism, since it is not that the Gentiles have replaced the people of Israel as the heirs of the covenant, but that Israel is "made known to them" by their baptism. In other words, they become members of Israel by adoption through Jesus as the heir of David … They fulfill the prophecy that Gentiles will associate themselves with Israel in the eschatological age.[83]

Draper argues that Gentiles actually find identity in God's ongoing covenantal faithfulness with the Jewish people:

> The continuity with God's covenant with Israel lends stability and its firm ethical basis in the stereotypes of the Decalogue (as opposed to the enumerated ethical failures of their previous Gentile identity), and provides legitimation for the new social identity and the differentiation from the old identity ('we-they').[84]

In the fellowship meals of the early believers, the grafting in of Gentiles to the commonwealth of Israel was sealed: "Drinking the cup of the holy vine, therefore,

---

[83] Jonathan A. Draper, "Do the Didache and Matthew Reflect an 'Irrevocable Parting of the Ways' with Judaism?" in *Matthew and the Didache: Two Documents from the Same Jewish-Christian Milieu?* (ed. Huub van de Sandt; Minneapolis, MN: Fortress, 2005), 238–239; Draper, "The Holy Vine of David Made Known to the Gentiles through God's Servant Jesus," 273. Draper also states, "The vine of David is a reference to the covenant people of Israel of which David is the king, as well as to David's own royal house that is restored by Jesus … In other words, the Gentile Christians who are the addressees of the text are associated with Israel in some way, which stops short of full incorporation, since they do not become the vine but come to know it. This, in my opinion, relates to the admission of Gentiles to community meals without requiring full conversion to Judaism and circumcision; that is, they do not have to 'be perfect' and 'take upon themselves the full yoke of the Lord' (6:2)" (Ibid., 272).

[84] Jonathan A. Draper, "Mission, Ethics, and Identity in the Didache," in *Sensitivity towards Outsiders: Exploring the Dynamic Relationship between Mission and Ethics in the New Testament and Early Christianity* (Tübingen, Germany: Mohr Siebeck, 2014), 478.

[9.2]
For the holy vine of your servant David that you made known to us through your servant Yeshua.

enabled Gentiles to join in fellowship with Israel and to partake of their messianic expectations."[85]

The Apostolic Constitutions' version of the Didache's blessing over the bread was expanded and modified to be brought into the context of the Eucharist:

> We also thank you, our Father, for the precious blood of Yeshua the Messiah, which was shed for us and for his precious body, of which we celebrate this representation, as he himself appointed us, to proclaim his death.[86] For through him glory is to be given to you forever. Amen. (Apostolic Constitutions 7.25)

⚜ Yours is the glory forever. (DIDACHE 9.2)

The blessing for the cup (as well as that for the bread) ends with a doxology. Both are similar in content to other doxologies within Jewish liturgy, such as that found in 1 Chronicles 29:11, "Yours, O LORD, is the greatness and the power and the glory," and the *Yishtabach* prayer, which closes the *Pesukei Dezimra* section: "It is fitting for You, O LORD our God and God of our fathers, to receive ... blessings and thanks from this moment and to eternity." The phrase "Yours is the glory forever" also appears in the *Prayer of Manasseh*.[87] It is similar as well to the end of the Lord's Prayer.[88]

A doxology functions as an extended "amen." Doxologies appear frequently in the New Testament and in early Patristic literature. A proper doxology follows a rigid formula:

1. An address to God,
2. An ascription of glory,
3. A statement of terms,
4. A concluding "amen."

For example, Romans 11:36 preserves the formula in its simplest form: "To him be the glory forever. Amen." Variations on the theme include embellishments in the

---

85 Milavec, *The Didache: Faith, Hope, & Life of the Earliest Christian Communities, 50–70 C.E.*, 364.
86 Cf. 1 Corinthians 11:26.
87 Prayer of Manasseh 1:15.
88 Matthew 6:13.

address, the ascription, or the term, but all doxologies follow this format. When the concluding "amen" is omitted, as it is in the Didache, it may be assumed as a matter of course.

[9.2] *Yours is the glory forever.*

It has been suggested that the doxology here in 9.2 was recited by those who had gathered for the meal in response to the first part of the prayer, which had been recited by the leader.[89] Most likely the traditional "amen" (אמן) was originally part of the response.[90] In the Temple, the doxology "Blessed is the name of the glory of his kingdom for ever and ever" was said in response to prayers instead of "amen,"[91] but this is an anomaly, and the phrase may have been punctuated by an "amen." Scholars assume that the doxology formula that appears so frequently in the New Testament derives from Temple liturgy. Skarsaune asks the question, "Could it be that the repeated doxology—'yours is the glory [and the power] forever'—in the Didache prayers is reminiscent of those early days when the first believers would 'meet together in the temple courts' (Acts 2:46)?"[92]

◉ Next, concerning the piece of bread. (DIDACHE 9.3)

The second blessing of chapter 9 is for the bread, and it begins with instruction and language similar to that of the cup. Once again, as in 9.1, we find the word "concerning" (*peri*), an introduction to legal instruction in rabbinic literature. In Jewish law the blessing over bread covered the whole meal, and no other blessings were necessary to recite except that over wine or grape juice. The Didache follows this protocol.

Some controversy exists over the interpretation of the word *klasma* (κλάσμα), which we have translated "piece of." Some feel that it should be translated as "broken piece," but in Jewish practice, at least on Sabbath and festivals, the bread is not broken before the blessing is said. Note the practice of the Master: "He took

---

89 Niederwimmer, *The Didache*, 148.
90 Ibid., n.28.
91 m.*Brachot* 9:5; b.*Brachot* 63a.
92 Skarsaune, *In the Shadow of the Temple*, 407–408. In Jewish thought a blessing is not complete if it does not mention God's kingship (b.*Brachot* 40b). The rabbinic pre-meal blessings accomplish this through the phrase "Lord our God, King of the universe." It could be that the Didache's doxology, "Yours is the glory forever," is meant to express that same sentiment of the kingdom of heaven. However, it is equally as probable that the opinion expressed in the Talmud is a later development in Jewish liturgy that shaped the currently recognized blessing formula, and it would be anachronistic to push it back onto the Didache.

[9.3]
Next, concerning the piece of bread.

the bread and blessed and broke it and gave it to them."[93] Flusser suggests that the Greek term *klasma* is related to the Mishnaic Hebrew word *pat* ("a piece, or loaf, of bread," פת), which is used in Jewish legal discussions about blessings.[94] This could then be rendered in Hebrew "concerning the piece [of bread]" (*v'al hapat*, ועל הפת).[95] In turn, as with the cup of wine, the opening instructions are reminiscent of rabbinic legal language.

> We thank you, our Father,
> for the life and the knowledge that you
> made known to us through your servant Yeshua.
> Yours is the glory forever. (DIDACHE 9.3)

The Didache's blessing over the bread, like the blessing over the cup, is modeled after the traditional Jewish blessing over bread and has been expanded. It, too, can be broken up into a tripartite structure:

---

[93] Luke 24:30. Some have suggested that the bread being broken before blessing is in line with an alternate halachah: "We learn that the blessing preceded the breaking of the bread, as is the ruling which the *Halacha* ordained in the *Gemara* (*b.Brachot* 39b). However, from the words of Rabbi Ḥiyya bar Ashi (39a) we learn that there were those who instructed that the blessing should be said over the bread which had been broken" (Alon, "The Halacha in the Teaching of the Twelve Apostles," 186).

[94] "The term κλάσμα might simply be a of the Hebrew equivalent פת as this is mostly rendered in the Septuagint by κλάσμα. This background seems to be corroborated in m.*Brachot* 6:1, where specific blessings are listed: 'What benediction do they say over the fruit? Over the fruit of the trees one says: ... except for the bread, for over the bread (חוץ מן הפת, שעל הפת) one says "who brings forth bread (לחם) from the earth"' and another example in 6:5: 'If one said the benediction over the bread (ברך על הפת) he need not say it over the savoury; but if he said it over the savoury he is not exempt from saying it over the bread (לא פטר את הפת)'" (Van de Sandt and Flusser, *The Didache*, 298).

[95] Sandelin, *Wisdom as Nourisher*, 199. We find the expression "piece of bread" (*pat lechem*, פת לחם) in Genesis 18:15: "[Abraham says:] ... while I bring a morsel of bread, that you may refresh yourselves." In Jewish tradition Abraham is a model of hospitality but he also taught his guests Torah. Rabbi Levi Yitzchak of Berditchev writes "The word פת refers to the written Torah, whereas the word לחם refers to the oral Torah" (*Kedushat Levi*, 91). This fits into the further allegorical imagery of the bread in the Didache's blessings.

Didache 9.3	Rabbinic Blessing over Bread[96]	[9.3]
We thank you, our Father,	Blessed are you, O LORD, our God, King of the universe,	We thank you, our Father, for the life and the knowledge that you made known to us through your servant Yeshua. Yours is the glory forever.
for the life and the knowledge that you made known to us through your servant Yeshua.	who brings bread out of the earth.	
Yours is the glory forever.	Amen.	

See the commentary on 9.2 regarding the opening address "We thank you, our Father," the title "your servant," and the concluding doxology.

The bread represents revelation of "the life and the knowledge," which is "made known to us through your servant Yeshua."[97] This harkens back to the Garden of Eden (*Gan Eden*), in which grew the "tree of life" and the "tree of the knowledge of good and evil."[98] It is through the Messiah that believers are brought back to the Edenic state of bliss to which all creation longs to return.[99] This theme of the earth returning to a state like that of the Garden of Eden at the end of the age is expressed in the book of Revelation and in apocryphal literature. For example, "To the one who conquers I will grant to eat of the tree of life, which is in the paradise of God."[100] In this vein Yeshua tells the thief on the cross, "Today you will be with me in Paradise ['garden of pleasure,' פרדס]" (Luke 23:43).

For the audience of the Didache, bread represented "life" in a very real way. "In the first century, bread was a staple at every meal. Not to have bread was to

---

[96] m.*Brachot* 6:1.

[97] It has been suggested that "the life and the knowledge" (*zoes kai gnoseos*, ζωῆς καὶ γνώσεως) is a hendiadys, the delivery of an idea in which "one meaning is expressed by means of two words." For a study on the use of the hendiadys, see Ronald James Williams, *Williams' Hebrew Syntax* (3d ed.; ed. John C. Beckman; Toronto, Canada: University of Toronto, 2007), 29–30.

[98] Genesis 2:9. Joan Hazelden Walker notes some interesting connections between eating/food and knowledge, as we find in the Didache, in both Genesis and Luke: "[Eve] took of its fruit and ate, and she also gave some to her husband who was with her, and he ate. Then the eyes of both were opened, and they knew that they were naked" (Genesis 3:6–7); "[Yeshua] took the bread and blessed and broke it and gave it to them. And their eyes were opened, and they recognized him" (Luke 24:30–31). See Walker, "A Pre-Marcan Dating for the Didache: Further Thoughts of a Liturgist," *Studia Biblica* 3 (1978): 407.

[99] Johannes Betz, "The Eucharist in the Didache," in *The Didache in Modern Research* (ed. Jonathan A. Draper; Leiden, The Netherlands: Brill, 1996), 260–263.

[100] Revelation 2:7. Cf. Revelation 22:2, 14, 19; 2 Enoch 65:9–10; 2 Baruch 4:6; Apocalypse of Moses 13:2; 4 Ezra 8:52; Testament of Levi 18:10.

[9.3]
We thank you, our Father, for the life and the knowledge that you made known to us through your servant Yeshua. Yours is the glory forever.

go hungry or, in extreme cases, to starve. Bread, therefore, preserved life."[101] In a spiritual sense then, without Messiah, "the bread of life," one cannot fully live.[102] Certainly the Didache here means to draw our thoughts back to its opening verse: "There are two ways: one of life and one of death" (1.1). In Yeshua is true life in the fullest sense of the Hebrew word *chayim* (חיים).

The "knowledge" of which the Didache speaks "does not mean intellectual apprehension of objects, but the revealed knowledge of God, the insights into the hidden meaning of life and the universe that is bestowed by revelation, the uncovering of what would otherwise be radically alien and hidden from the human being."[103] Paul Philip Levertoff speaks of two kinds of knowledge (*da'at*, דעת) that exist in Chasidic thought: the knowledge that "anyone may acquire by studying creation and acquainting themselves with the character imprinted thereon," and the knowledge "of the inner being of God ... [that] leads to love of Him ... It is a consummation which will not be reached until the Messianic Age, but it is surely promised then."[104] It is this latter type of knowledge of which the Didache speaks. For its fullness we must wait for the Messianic Age, but at present we can have a taste of it in Messiah.[105]

In Jewish thought both "the life and the knowledge" are associated with the Torah.[106] Proverbs 8:35 states, "Whoever finds [Torah] finds life," and likewise the sages of Israel stated, "The words of Torah which I have given to you are life unto you."[107] In the fourth benediction of *Genizah Amidah* we find, "Favor us with your knowledge, our Father; and with your Torah's understanding and wisdom."[108]

---

101   Milavec, *The Didache: Faith, Hope, & Life of the Earliest Christian Communities, 50–70 C.E.*, 372.
102   John 6:35, 48.
103   Niederwimmer, *The Didache*, 149.
104   Paul Philip Levertoff, *Love and the Messianic Age* (Marshfield, MO: Vine of David, 2009), 32.
105   Compare the development of this idea within Chabad: "The manna that our ancestors ate in the Sinai Desert contained all possible flavors. Spiritually, the manna is associated with the revelation of spiritual pleasure that will occur in the future era. For the Torah is compared to bread, and its innermost dimension—the deepest reason behind all of its commandments—is the bread of pleasure, the bread that will emerge from the heavens only in the future era. In order for the ultimate spiritual pleasures of the future to be drawn into our tangible reality during the era of redemption, we must prepare the tangible world now with physical commandments and spiritual refinement" (Rebbe Menachem Mendel Schneerson).
106   Skarsaune, *In the Shadow of the Temple*, 409.
107   *Mechilta*, Vayassa 1, Exodus 15:26. Cf. Acts 7:38; *Tanchuma*, Shemot 25; Leviticus 18:5; *Deuteronomy Rabbah* 7:3. Yeshua alludes to the giving of the Torah when he says, "For the bread of God is he who comes down from heaven and gives life to the world" (John 6:33). Cf. "The earth trembled when He gave life to the world [i.e., the giving of the Torah]" (*Exodus Rabbah* 29:9).
108   Rabbi Lawrence A. Hoffman, *The Amidah* (vol. 2 of *My People's Prayer Book: Traditional Prayers, Modern Commentaries*; Woodstock, VT: Jewish Lights, 1998), 39. Cf. Sirach 17:11, 45:5.

Indeed, "in the face of Yeshua the Messiah" is "the knowledge of the glory of God," and as the living Torah, the Master teaches "the words of eternal life."[109] Messiah has "made known" to the Gentiles "the life and the knowledge" by having them "brought near" to "the commonwealth of Israel" and to the "covenants of promise [i.e., the Torah]."[110]

As with the blessing over the bread, the Apostolic Constitutions' version of the Didache's blessing over the wine has been expanded and modified to be brought into the context of the Eucharist:

> We thank you, our Father, for the life that you made known to us through your servant Yeshua,[111] by whom you made all things,[112] and took care of the whole world; whom you sent to become man for our salvation; whom you permitted to suffer and to die; whom you raised up, and were pleased to glorify and set down on your right hand; by whom you have promised us the resurrection of the dead. (Apostolic Constitutions 7.25)

[9.3] *We thank you, our Father, for the life and the knowledge that you made known to us through your servant Yeshua. Yours is the glory forever.*

⁕ Just as this piece of bread was scattered over the mountains and gathered together. (DIDACHE 9.4)

In the second half of the blessing over the bread, we find a prayer that calls upon God to gather together his congregation from the places where they have been scattered throughout the world. This theme is found again in chapter 10 in the third petition of the *Grace after Meals* prayer. The Apostolic Constitutions renders this prayer:

---

109 2 Corinthians 4:6; John 6:68. Cf. John 6:63; 1 Clement 59.2.
110 Ephesians 2:12–3.
111 The first section of the prayer matches the Greek of the Didache except for the omission of "and the knowledge."
112 This phrase is reminiscent of the traditional *Shehakol* blessing, "by whose word all things came to be" (m.*Brachot* 6:2).

[9.4]
Just as this piece of bread was scattered over the mountains and gathered together.

O Lord Almighty, everlasting God,[113] may your assembly be gathered from the ends of the earth into your kingdom, as this grain was once scattered, and is now become one piece of bread.[114] (Apostolic Constitutions 7.25)

The Didache's prayer here is like a parable about the kingdom, and, because it is so similar to certain of the Master's teachings, some have suggested that it might go back to a now-lost non-canonical gospel teaching or parable.[115] The Galilean hills where Yeshua walked lend themselves well to the imagery of seed being "scattered over the mountains."[116]

This prayer invokes the themes of exile (*galut*, גלות) and redemption (*g'ullah*, גאולה), symbolizing them in an agricultural metaphor. Just as seeds of grain are scattered as they are planted and then their fruit gathered into one group when it is harvested, so God's people Israel, who were exiled into the Diaspora, will be gathered back to their land in the Messianic Kingdom. Psalm 126, recited before *Grace after Meals* on Shabbat and festivals, contains the theme of scattering and gathering seed as it speaks of the ingathering of the exiles and redemption:

> Those who sow in tears shall reap with shouts of joy! He who goes out weeping, bearing the seed for sowing, shall come home with shouts of joy, bringing his sheaves with him (Psalm 126:5–6)

Second Chronicles uses comparable imagery to describe the dispersion of Israel: "I saw all Israel scattered on the mountains, as sheep that have no shepherd" (2 Chronicles 18:16); this is the imagery pictured as well in the "gathering up" of

---

113 The Apostolic Constitutions expanded the Didache's pre-meal prayers to adapt them to the sacramental Eucharist, but this particular line seems to have been created by a Hebrew thinker. The Hebrew for "O Lord, Almighty, Everlasting God" would almost certainly be *HaShem Tzeva'ot, El Olam* ("Lord of Legions, God of the World," יי צבאות אל עולם), which are both biblical phrases. The Greek words for "almighty" (*pantokrator*, παντοκρατορ) and "everlasting" (*aionios*, αἰώνιος) do not have the connotations that the Hebrew does of "legions" and "world," which seems to fit the rest of the line: "May your assembly be gathered from the ends of the earth into your kingdom." The line also bears some minor similarity to the blessing before the *Shma*, "He who illuminates the earth." This prayer refers to God as "Eternal God" (*Elohei Olam*, עאלהי עולם), refers to his "legions" (*tzeva'av*, צבאיו), and calls him by the name *Shaddai* (שדי), which is another possible Hebrew interpretation of *pantokrator* ("almighty").

114 Cf. 1 Corinthians 10:17.

115 Canon Spence, *The Teaching of the Twelve Apostles* (London, England: James Nisbet and Co., 1885), 43. Cf. Matthew 13:1–44 and other kingdom parables in which Yeshua compares the kingdom to seed that has been sown.

116 Charles Taylor, "The Teaching of the Twelve Apostles with Illustrations from the Talmud," in *Didache: The Unknown Teaching of the Twelve Apostles* (ed. Brent S. Walters; San Jose, CA: Anti-Nicene Archive, 1991), 194.

the fragments of bread at the feedings of the four and five thousand.[117] Also note the Master's words: "Behold, the hour is coming, indeed it has come, when you will be scattered" (John 16:32), and, "Whoever does not gather with me scatters" (Matthew 12:30).

The exile is a punishment for Israel's sin, but it also serves a redemptive process for all mankind:

> Eleazar also said: "The Holy One, blessed be he, did not exile Israel among the nations save in order that proselytes might join them, for it is said: 'And I will sow her unto Me in the land' (Hosea 2:23); surely a man sows a *se'ah* in order to harvest many *kor*!" (b.*Pesachim* 87b)

[9.4]
Just as this piece of bread was scattered over the mountains and gathered together.

One *kor* is equal to thirty *se'ah*, and therefore this saying is a metaphor for the knowledge of God being multiplied in the world through the exile of Israel. We indeed see this taking place through the dispersion of believers throughout the world. Nevertheless, both the sages and the Didache community longed for the period of exile to end. William Varner writes, "A local community, gathered around what is but a small fragment, recognizes that it is part of a larger loaf, or body, to change the metaphor, that will be gathered into the future kingdom"—that is, at the end of the exile.[118]

While the idea of being in exile might seem foreign to followers of Messiah, the concept is deeply embedded in the New Testament. James, the brother of the Master, addresses his epistle "to the twelve tribes in the Dispersion" and the Apostle Peter likewise in his first epistle "to those who are elect exiles of the Dispersion."[119] Peter urges his non-Jewish readers, "Conduct yourselves with fear throughout the time of your exile" (1 Peter 1:17). So long as the Temple remains destroyed and there is no Davidic king enthroned in Israel, even Gentile believers are in exile. The corrupt high priest Caiaphas prophesied that the Master must die not only for the nation of Israel, "but also to gather into one the children of God who are scattered abroad."[120]

---

117 See Matthew 14:20; Mark 6:43, 8:19–20; John 6:12–13. All use a form of the word κλάσμα ("fragment"), that is found in Didache 9.3.
118 William Varner, *The Way of the Didache: The First Christian Handbook* (New York, NY: University Press of America, 2007), 79. Some have suggested a connection of this idea to 1 Corinthians 10:17: "Because there is one bread, we who are many are one body, for we all partake of the one bread."
119 James 1:1; 1 Peter 1:1.
120 John 11:52.

> *So may your assembly be gathered from the ends of the earth into your kingdom. For yours is the glory and the power through Yeshua the Messiah forever.* (DIDACHE 9.4)

The Greek word for "gather" (*sunago*, συνάγω) is related in the Septuagint to the Hebrew word *kibbutz* (קבץ), which points to the important Jewish concept of the ingathering of the exiles (*kibbutz galuyot*, קיבוץ גלויות). The tenth benediction of the *Amidah* runs parallel in thought to this passage of the Didache: "Sound a great shofar for our freedom, and lift up a banner for the gathering of our exiles. Blessed are you, O Lord, who gathers the dispersed among his people Israel."[121] The Apostolic Constitutions renders this similarly, "O Lord Almighty, everlasting God, may your assembly be gathered from the ends of the earth into your kingdom" (7.35).[122]

The Didache's prayer is deeply rooted in the biblical prophecies that speak about the ingathering of the Jewish people back to their land, which is to take place in the Messianic Era: "If your outcasts are in the uttermost parts of heaven, from there the LORD your God will gather you, and from there he will take you" (Deuteronomy 30:4); "Behold, I will gather them from all the countries ... I will bring them back to this place, and I will make them dwell in safety" (Jeremiah 32:37).[123]

According to the Prophets, this is one of the main roles of the Messiah. The Rambam writes, "The Messianic King will arise in the future and restore the Davidic Kingdom to its former state and original sovereignty ... and gather the dispersed of Israel."[124] Yeshua himself, in the last week before his death, spoke of the time he would fulfill this task: "He will send out his angels with a loud trumpet call, and they will gather his elect from the four winds, from one end of heaven to the other."[125] The Master was ready to accomplish this and would have done so if Israel had accepted his message and repented. Yeshua stated, "How often would I have gathered your children together as a hen gathers her brood under her wings, and you were not willing!" (Matthew 23:37). When we pray this prayer of the Didache,

---

[121] This version of the passage is from the *Genizah Amidah* as found in Hoffman, *The Amidah*, 40. The theme of the ingathering is also found in the *Ahavah Rabbah* prayer of Shacharit services and in the *Mussaf* liturgy of Rosh HaShanah and Yom Kippur.

[122] See footnote 113.

[123] Also Psalm 147:2; 2 Chronicles 18:16; Isaiah 11:11–12; Zechariah 2:6; Nehemiah 1:9; Ezekiel 11:17; b.*Brachot* 49a. For a full list of references from the Hebrew Scriptures and Apocryphal literature, see Niederwimmer, *The Didache*, 151, n.55. Also Van de Sandt and Flusser, *The Didache*, 311, n.118.

[124] *Mishneh Torah*, Hilchot Melachim 11:1.

[125] Matthew 24:31; Mark 13:27. Cf. John 11:52; Revelation 14:14–16.

we are not only calling for the gathering of the exiles but also for the return of the Messiah, the inauguration of the Messianic Kingdom, and the end of the exile.

In the Didache the gathering of "the assembly" is one and the same as the gathering of Israel.[126] As was pointed out in the overview of chapter 4, the Greek word for "assembly" (*ekklesia*) is used in the Septuagint for *kahal*, which means "assembly," "congregation," or "community." It appears one hundred times in the Septuagint in reference to Israel, which is the sense in which it should be taken here—that is, the assembly of both those who are Jewish by birth and those who have been grafted into the commonwealth of Israel through Messiah.

In prophecies like that found in Ezekiel 47–48, which speaks of the Jewish people's return to the land of Israel, provision is made for Gentiles to have an inheritance in the land:

> You shall allot it as an inheritance for yourselves and for the sojourners who reside among you and have had children among you. They shall be to you as native-born children of Israel. With you they shall be allotted an inheritance among the tribes of Israel. In whatever tribe the sojourner resides, there you shall assign him his inheritance, declares the Lord GOD. (Ezekiel 47:22–23)

The Odes of Solomon, written by early Jewish believers, anticipated that Gentiles would be gathered along with the Jewish people: "And the Gentiles who had been dispersed were gathered together" (10:5).[127] The gathering of the Jewish exiles back to Israel is intimately connected with the redemption of all the nations of the earth: "Bring back the preserved of Israel; I will make you as a light for the nations, that my salvation may reach to the end of the earth" (Isaiah 49:6).[128]

While a specific reference to the land of Israel is absent from this blessing in the Didache, its reference to the ingathering and the phrase "into your kingdom" clearly anticipate the arrival of the Messianic Era, in which Messiah will rule and

[9.4]
So may your assembly be gathered from the ends of the earth into your kingdom. For yours is the glory and the power through Yeshua the Messiah forever.

---

126 Van de Sandt and Flusser, *The Didache*, 327. Although later church writings would view the ingathering as strictly for the church, that is not the case here in the Didache. See Niederwimmer, *The Didache*, 149.
127 Cf. Odes of Solomon 11:15–24.
128 Rabbi Yoel Schwartz has created a version of the *Kibbutz Galuyot* prayer for non-Jews: "Sound the great shofar for the freedom of Your People Israel. Raise the banner to gather the exiles of Israel, and may we merit this prophecy, 'Let us go with you, for we have heard that G-d is with you' (Zechariah 8:23) at its appointed time. Be mindful of us, O Lord, when You favor Your People; take note of us when You deliver them, that we may enjoy the prosperity of Your chosen ones, share the joy of Your Nation, glory in Your very own People (Psalm 106:4). Blessed are You, O Lord, Who gathers the dispersed of His People Israel" (*Service from the Heart*, 74–75).

[9.4] *So may your assembly be gathered from the ends of the earth into your kingdom. For yours is the glory and the power through Yeshua the Messiah forever.*

reign from Jerusalem. In Jewish thought these concepts are inseparable from the land of Israel. The Didache might have had in mind the disciples' question, "Lord, will you at this time restore the kingdom to Israel?" to which the Master replied it was not for them to know, but that instead they should spread his message "to the end of the earth."[129] In turn, the gathering "from the ends of the earth into your kingdom" is about the inclusion of Gentiles in the kingdom of heaven.

> *But do not let anyone eat or drink by means of your giving of thanks except those immersed in the name of the Lord, for the Lord even said concerning this, "Do not give what is holy to the dogs."* (DIDACHE 9.5)

Having laid out blessings for the cup and the bread, chapter 9 ends with a prohibition on allowing the uninitiated to participate in the ceremonial fellowship meals of the community. This is similar to the apocryphal traditions about the Apostle Peter, of whom it was said that he would not eat with Gentiles unless they had renounced idolatry and been immersed.[130] The Apostolic Constitutions expounds on the Didache:

> Do not let anyone eat of these things that is not initiated; except those immersed into the death of the Lord. But if any one that is not initiated conceal himself, and partake of the same, he eats eternal judgment;[131] because, being not of the faith of Messiah, he has partaken of such things as it is not lawful for him to partake of, to his own punishment. But if anyone is a partaker through ignorance, instruct him quickly, and initiate him, that he may not go out and despise you. (Apostolic Constitutions 7.25)[132]

---

129 Acts 1:6–8.
130 Pseudo-Clementine Homilies 13.4; Pseudo-Clementine Recognitions 2.70–71.
131 Cf. 1 Corinthians 11:29.
132 Because the Apostolic Constitutions is eager to add proof texts from Scripture to bolster the Didache's words, it is curious that we do not find the citation of Matthew 7:6. In turn, Clayton Jefford feels this indicates that this quote from the Master "has been secondarily added into the text at this point by a later hand and was never actually known to the author of the Apostolic Constitutions and *Canons* as part of the Didache source" (Jefford, "Authority and Perspective in the Didache" in *The Didache: A Missing Piece of the Puzzle in Early Jewish Christianity* [eds. Jonathan A. Draper and Clayton N. Jefford; Atlanta, GA: Society of Biblical Literature, 2015], 42).

The Didache's quotation is word for word what we find in Matthew 7:6, "Do not give dogs what is holy"; thus "the Lord" here in 9.5 refers to Yeshua.[133] While a few scholars suggest that the Didache is quoting Matthew, it is more probable that both Matthew and the Didache drew from a similar oral tradition.[134] In the original context of the Master's saying, the prohibition deals with teaching Torah to Gentiles, but here it is repurposed to forbid non-believers from participation in a holy meal.[135]

The saying "Do not give what is holy to the dogs" goes back to a halachic rule about the sacred foods and sacrifices of the Temple. Both the Master and the Didache use the rule in a metaphorical sense. "Holy" (*hagios*, ἅγιος) is linked to the Hebrew word *kadosh* (קדוש), which is "applied in biblical tradition to those places, objects, and things that were separated from the profane because they belong to God."[136] It can also be used in reference to sacrificial meat.[137] In turn, we find a parallel saying to "not give what is holy to dogs"[138] in rabbinic literature: "One may not redeem dedicated sacrifices [holy things] in order to give food to dogs."[139] "Dogs" were considered "despicable, insolent, and unclean animals, scouring for refuse and eating things that disgusted human beings." It was unacceptable to offer them things that were *kadosh*.[140]

The Torah states, "A lay person shall not eat of a holy thing; no foreign guest of the priest or hired worker shall eat of a holy thing" (Leviticus 22:10). In the Didache the communal meals take on a sacrificial character. To paraphrase Draper, the background has to do with a question of Jewish law regarding the sanctity of

[9.5]
But do not let anyone eat or drink by means of your giving of thanks except those immersed in the name of the Lord, for the Lord even said concerning this, "Do not give what is holy to the dogs."

---

133 The only difference between Didache 9.5 and Matthew 7:6 is a minor spelling variation in the Greek word for "dogs." Matthew uses *kusin* (κυσίν), and the Didache uses *kusi* (κυσί). Cf. Gospel of Thomas 93. Milavec argues that every instance of "Lord" in the Didache refers to God. See Aaron Milavec, "The Distress Signals of Didache Research," in *The Didache: A Missing Piece of the Puzzle in Early Jewish Christianity* (eds. Jonathan A. Draper and Clayton N. Jefford; Atlanta, GA: Society of Biblical Literature, 2015), 70–72.
134 Niederwimmer, *The Didache*, 153; Clayton N. Jefford, *The Sayings of Jesus in the Teachings of the Twelve Apostles* (New York, NY: Brill, 1989), 140. Cf. "The word of God must not depart from you among those in impurity" (Barnabas 19.4).
135 Toby Janicki, *God-Fearers: Gentiles & the God of Israel* (Marshfield, MO: First Fruits of Zion, 2012), 17–18.
136 Huub van de Sandt, "'Do Not Give What Is Holy to the Dogs' (Did 9:5d and Matt 7:6a): The Eucharistic Food of the Didache in Its Jewish Purity Setting," *Vigiliae Christianae* 56, no. 3 (August 2002): 231–232.
137 Niederwimmer, *The Didache*, 154.
138 Translation from Aaron Eby.
139 E.g., m.*Trumot* 6:5; b.*Bechorot* 15a; b.*Trumot* 17a. This principle is debated but generally accepted.
140 Van de Sandt, "Do Not Give What Is Holy to the Dogs," 231. Cf. Exodus 22:31; Joseph and Aseneth 10:14; *Liber Antiquitatum Biblicarum* (Pseudo-Philo) 39:11.

[9.5]
But do not let anyone eat or drink by means of your giving of thanks except those immersed in the name of the Lord, for the Lord even said concerning this, "Do not give what is holy to the dogs."

the sacrificial portions from the Temple. That is to say, the holiness of the sacrificial portions offered in the Temple is being extended to the sacred, shared meal in the community. The Septuagint of Leviticus 22:10 prohibits a foreigner from eating that which is offered in the Temple with very similar words. The Pharisees had similar reservations about sharing meals with non-observant Jews living in Israel, i.e., "sinners and tax collectors."[141]

We see concerns regarding the purity of wine and oil in connection with the resident alien (*ger toshav*) in tractate *Gerim*.[142] Not unlike the Didache, Qumran literature required an initiation period before one could eat meals with the community.[143]

Van de Sandt writes:

> The dog represents the gentiles in their impure state. The admittance of gentiles to the holy food would amount to the release of sacrificed things ... to stray street roamers consuming the unclean. The rabbinic view of gentile uncleanness—referring to people who were affected by a corpse impurity, or some other defilement because of their idolatry—must have persisted in the (early stages of) the Didache community.[144]

In summary, if the Master "forbade giving what is holy to the dogs, he thus forbade (*also* at any rate) the giving of the sacred food to the unbaptized."[145]

According to the apostles, this prohibition should extend even to believers who continue in sin. For example, Paul forbids eating or associating with one who "is guilty of sexual immorality or greed, or is an idolater, reviler, drunkard, or swindler."[146] The Didache itself, in chapter 14, requires the confession of sins and resolution of arguments before one partakes of a fellowship meal. In regard to those not in Messiah, we follow the example of our Master who "came not to call the righteous, but sinners" (Matthew 9:13); but with those who claim to be of Messiah yet continue in sin without repentance, we must be careful not to fellowship.

---

141 Draper, "The Holy Vine of David Made Known to the Gentiles through God's Servant Jesus," 271.
142 *Gerim* 1:9 (60b), 3:2 (61a).
143 Community Rule (1QS) VI, 16–21. Cf. Pseudo-Clementine Homilies 13.4; Pseudo-Clementine Recognitions 2.71–72.
144 Van de Sandt, "Do Not Give What Is Holy to the Dogs," 238–239.
145 Niederwimmer, *The Didache*, 153.
146 1 Corinthians 5:11. Cf. 2 Peter 2:22; Philippians 3:2; Revelation 22:15.

Chapter Ten

DIDACHE 10

10.1 After you have been satisfied, give thanks in this way:

10.2 We thank you, our holy Father, for your holy name that you have caused to dwell in our hearts; and for the knowledge, faithfulness, and eternal life that you have made known to us through your servant Yeshua. Yours is the glory forever.[1]

10.3 You, O Lord of Legions, created all things[2] for the sake of your name; you gave nourishment and drink for human beings to enjoy in order that they would give thanks to you. You also bestowed upon us spiritual nourishment and drink and eternal life through your servant.

10.4 And for all things we thank you because you are powerful. Yours is the glory forever.[3]

10.5 Remember, O Lord, your congregation,[4] to rescue her from all evil and to make her complete in your love. Gather her, the sanctified, from the four winds[5] to your kingdom that you have prepared for her.[6] For yours is the power and the glory forever.[7]

10.6 May grace come, and may this world pass away. *Hoshana* to the God of David![8] Everyone who is holy, let him come. Everyone who is not, let him repent. *Maran etha!*[9] Amen.

10.7 Permit the prophets to lead the giving of thanks as much as they desire.

---

1. Matthew 6:13.
2. Revelation 4:11.
3. Matthew 6:13.
4. Psalm 74:2.
5. Deuteronomy 30:4; Isaiah 11:11–12; Zechariah 2:10(6); Nehemiah 1:9; Matthew 24:31.
6. Matthew 25:34.
7. Matthew 6:13.
8. Matthew 21:9, 15.
9. 1 Corinthians 16:22.

Overview

Chapter 10 continues the mealtime liturgy. Having presented blessings to be recited before meals in chapter 9, the Didache now offers blessings to be recited after one eats. The prayers in Didache 10 are similar to the traditional *Grace after Meals* prayer that Judaism proscribes for recitation after a meal containing bread.[10]

The post-meal liturgy here in chapter 10 has similar language to that of the pre-meal blessings in chapter 9. Both liturgies demonstrate a cohesive thematic pattern of four liturgical units. Both 9.4 and 10.5 call for the ingathering of the congregation. The injunction "Do not let anyone eat or drink ... except those immersed in the name of the Lord" (9.5) has a parallel in the closing invitation of chapter 10: "Everyone who is holy, let him come. Everyone who is not, let him repent" (10.6). Together "the prayers before and after the meal form a coherent and complementary whole."[11]

Additionally, like the prayers of chapter 9, these in chapter 10 do not represent a Eucharist meal in the traditional sacramental sense but instead contain blessings that thank God for the physical and spiritual nourishment enjoyed at fellowship meals among believers. The Didache's prayers were created so that Gentile believers could fulfill the commandment of saying grace after meals.

The Commandment of Grace after Meals

Although the injunction to bless God before eating food is derived from rabbinic tradition, the commandment to bless after the meal is based upon a scriptural injunction. It is derived from Deuteronomy 8:10, where God tells the Jewish people,

> You shall eat and be full, and you shall bless the LORD your God for the good land he has given you.[12]

When one is finished eating and is satiated, he is required to bless the Creator. Reciting a thanksgiving prayer after a meal is the customary way to fulfill this

---

10   Huub van de Sandt and David Flusser, *The Didache: Its Jewish Sources and Its Place in Early Judaism and Christianity* (Minneapolis, MN: Fortress, 2002), 297.
11   Jonathan A. Draper, "Ritual Process and Ritual Symbol in Didache 7–10," *Vigiliae Christianae* 54, no. 2 (2000): 139.
12   y.*Brachot* 7:1; b.*Brachot* 21a.

obligation. This traditional prayer is called the *Birkat HaMazon* (ברכת המזון), which literally means "the blessing for food." We will simply refer to it henceforth as *Grace after Meals*.

The traditional liturgical prayer of the *Grace after Meals* today consists of four sections, but in the days of the apostles and the Didache, it had only three.[13] Rabbinic tradition ascribes the authorship of these first three blessings to Moses, Joshua, and David (with the help of Solomon), respectively.[14] Remarkably, both the apocryphal book of Jubilees and the Talmud imagine Abraham reciting a form of this prayer after he had eaten.[15] It may be fanciful to ascribe such antiquity to the blessings after meals, but modern scholar Abraham Millgram remarks that the first three blessings of *Grace after Meals* "are among the most ancient prayers in Jewish Liturgy."[16] Although the first complete written form of *Grace after Meals* was not found until around 1000 CE, literary evidence points to a much older origin.[17]

The Gospels never explicitly mention the Master praying *Grace after Meals*, but there is absolutely no reason to suppose that he did not. After he fed both the four thousand and the five thousand, the Synoptic Gospel narratives state, "They all ate and were satisfied."[18] This is a direct reference to Deuteronomy 8:10: "You

---

13   m.*Brachot* 6:8; b.*Brachot* 48b. See David Instone-Brewer, *Traditions of the Rabbis from the Era of the New Testament* (2 vols.; Grand Rapids, MI: Eerdmans, 2004), 1:75–77.
14   b.*Brachot* 48b.
15   Jubilees 22:5–10; b.*Sotah* 10a–b.
16   Abraham Millgram, *Jewish Worship* (Philadelphia, PA: Jewish Publication Society, 1971), 293.
17   The oldest complete rabbinic texts are found in the Rabbi Amram Gaon Siddur and the Cairo Genizah. For early examples of *Grace after Meals* texts that are similar to the rabbinic version, see Jubilees 22:6–10; Sirach 36:12–14, 17–19; 4QDeutn; 4QDeutj; Barchi Nafshia (4Q434).
18   Matthew 14:20, 15:37; Mark 6:42, 8:8; Luke 9:17.

shall eat and be full, and you shall bless the LORD your God." This citation in the Gospels is an indication that the Master and his disciples recited *Grace after Meals*.[19]

The importance of this commandment to bless after the meal is underscored by the passage that follows it:

> Take care lest you forget the LORD your God by not keeping his commandments and his rules and his statutes, which I command you today, lest, when you have eaten and are full … then your heart be lifted up, and you forget the LORD your God, who brought you out of the land of Egypt, out of the house of slavery … Beware lest you say in your heart, "My power and the might of my hand have gotten me this wealth." (Deuteronomy 8:11–17)

When we fail to give the Father thanks in times of plenty, we begin to think that provision comes from our own strength. We forget that we depend upon his daily provision. It is easy to remember God when we experience times of need, but when things are going well, it is crucial for us to stay focused on him so that we do not get haughty. Ingratitude turns us away from him, and we wander into sin.

The Grace after Meals and the Didache

Like the traditional *Grace after Meals*, the prayer of Didache 10 fulfills the commandment to bless the Lord after one eats. It contains similar wording and form to the traditional *Grace after Meals*. Both prayers contain three succinct liturgical blessings (while Didache 10 adds a closing prayer calling for the Messianic Age in

---

[19] Instone-Brewer, *Traditions of the Rabbis from the Era of the New Testament*, 1:81. The way the people sat down before the feeding of the five thousand offers another clue that they may have recited the *Grace after Meals*. The Gospels record that the Master instructed them to sit in groups of fifties and hundreds (Mark 6:39–40; Luke 9:14–15). The Mishnah dictates specific formulas for the invitation (*zimmun*, זימון) to the *Grace after Meals* (m.*Brachot* 7:3). The number of adult males present determines which formula is to be used. Instone-Brewer sees a connection here: "The different blessings for different sizes of gatherings may explain the reason why the Gospels are particularly interested in the number of people who sat down to eat the miraculous loaves and fishes with Jesus. Mark 6:40 says that they were sat down in groups of fifty and one hundred and Luke 9:14 says that this was the specific instruction of Jesus, so it was presumably done to facilitate counting. Part of the reason for giving the numbers was, no doubt, that 4,000 and 5,000 were impressive, but it would have been more impressive to give total numbers, and not just the number of men. Matthew specifically says on both occasions that the women and children were not counted (14:21, 15:38), which suggests that they were counting the number of eligible people for the saying of Grace, in order to decide the form of blessing" (1:81). The organization of the people into specific group sizes based on males present points strongly to the recital of the *Grace after Meals*.

10.6). This chart compares the three distinct post-meal blessings of Didache 10 and the oldest complete form of the *Grace after Meals* as found in the Cairo Genizah.[20]

Didache 10	Cairo Genizah Grace after Meals
[10.2]	**Birkat HaZan** (He Who Nourishes, ברכת הזן)
We thank you, our holy Father, for your holy name that you have caused to dwell in our hearts and for the knowledge, faithfulness, and eternal life that you have made known to us through your servant Yeshua. Yours is the glory forever.	Blessed are you, O LORD our God, King of the universe, who nourishes the whole world in his kindness, grace, and mercy. He gives food to all flesh, because his favor toward us and his great kindness are everlasting. For the sake of his great name, no good thing has ever been lacking to us nor ever will be, because he nourishes and feeds all. Blessed are you, O LORD, who nourishes all.
[10.3–4]	**Birkat HaAretz** (Blessing of the Land, ברכת הארץ)
You, O Lord of Legions, created all things for the sake of your name; you gave nourishment and drink for human beings to enjoy in order that they would give thanks to you. You also bestowed upon us spiritual nourishment and drink and eternal life through your servant. And for all things we thank you because you are powerful. Yours is the glory forever.	We thank you, O LORD, our God, because you have given us as an inheritance a desirable, good, and spacious land, the covenant and the Torah, life and peace. For all these we thank you and bless your great and holy name, eternally and always. Blessed are you, O LORD, for the land and for the food.
[10.5]	**Birkat Yerushalayim** (Blessing of Jerusalem, ברכת ירושלים)
Remember, O Lord, your congregation, to rescue her from all evil and to make her complete in your love. Gather her, the sanctified, from the four winds to your kingdom that you have prepared for her. For yours is the power and the glory forever.	Have mercy, O LORD, our God, on Israel your people, on Jerusalem your city, on the house of David, your anointed one, and on the great and holy house upon which your name has been invoked. Hasten to restore the kingdom of the house of David to its place in our time. Rebuild Jerusalem quickly; restore us to its midst and give us joy in it. Blessed are you, O LORD, who in your mercy rebuilds Jerusalem. Amen.

---

20 from Enrico Mazza, *The Celebration of the Eucharist: The Origin of the Rite and the Development of Its Interpretation* (Collegeville, MN: Liturgical, 1999), 308.

We find some striking parallels between these two prayers: thanksgiving to God for his nourishment of all creation, mention of God's holy name, and prayers for the coming kingdom. However, the rabbinic requirement to mention the land of Israel, the covenant that God made with the Jewish people, and the Torah in the *Grace after Meals* does not influence the Didache's version.[21] One reason for the omission of these elements may be that the version in the Didache reflects a much earlier form of *Grace after Meals* that predates those rabbinic forms. Like other elements of Jewish liturgy, the *Grace after Meals* with which we are familiar probably received its current form in the generations following the destruction of the Temple. Alternatively, the absence of those specific elements, which are decidedly Jewish themes, might indicate that this prayer was constructed specifically for Gentile believers. Non-Jewish disciples of the Master do not have the same relationship with the land, the covenant, and the Torah that the Jewish people do.

A few other differences exist between the prayers as well. For example, as in the pre-meal blessings, Didache 10.2 uses the opening formula "We thank you," whereas the rabbinic version has "Blessed are you, O LORD." As we noted in the commentary to chapter 9, evidence indicates that both forms were used in the Judaism of the first few centuries CE.

Some scholars have also noted that the order of the first two blessings in Didache 10 are reversed from those in the *Grace after Meals*. David Flusser and Huub van de Sandt speculate that Diaspora Judaism might have used an alternate version of the *Grace after Meals* that also flipped the order of the first two blessings and in turn influenced the Didache.[22] Additionally, it must be remembered that the wording of Jewish liturgy was not as fixed in the first century as it is today.

---

21 b.*Brachot* 49a.
22 Van de Sandt and Flusser, *The Didache*, 322–323.

An interesting textual variant on Didache 10 reflects some of the variety of first-century Judaism's table liturgy.[23]

The last notable difference between the two prayers is that while the *Grace after Meals* primarily focuses on thanking God for the physical nourishment and gifts that he provides, the Didache also adds thanksgiving for the mystical and spiritual blessings that God has given through Messiah. This also finds its roots in Judaism. Food and drink are associated with knowledge and understanding in Proverbs and Sirach.[24] Additionally, a similar poetically expansive prayer was found in Hebrew from the Dura-Europos synagogue that dates to the third century CE.[25] Jonathan Draper finds these poetic expansions of the Didache similar to liturgical poetry

---

23   In the Coptic version of Didache 10, an additional thanksgiving prayer appears regarding oil: "We offer you thanks, Father, for the aroma (ointment) that you have made known to us through your Son Yeshua. For yours is the glory forever." Incidentally, in Hebrew the biblical word for aroma is *reyach* (ריח), which is a form of *ruach* ("spirit," רוח). This could point to a play on words in the blessing. We also find this prayer in the Apostolic Constitutions 7.27: "Concerning the ointment give thanks in this manner: we thank you, O God, the Creator of the whole world, both for the good smell of the ointment, and for the immortality which you have made known to us through your servant Yeshua. For yours is the glory and the power forever. Amen." The language seems to relate to 2 Corinthians 2:15: "We are the aroma of Messiah to God among those who are being saved and among those who are perishing." For a study on the debates and issues surrounding this prayer, see Stephen Gero, "The So-Called Ointment Prayer in the Coptic Version of the Didache: A Re-evaluation," *Harvard Theological Review* 70, no. 1–2 (April 1977): 67–84, and Joseph Ysebaert, "The So-Called Coptic Ointment Prayer of Didache 10.8 Once More," *Vigiliae Christianae* 56, no. 1 (February 2002): 1–10. While scholars debate as to whether or not this prayer was a later addition to the Didache, it does have some Jewish parallels. Gedaliah Alon writes, "We have already had the privilege of deriving confirmation from the differences of opinion among the sages, as we learnt in *Tosefta* (t.*Brachot* 6:5): 'The School of Shammai says that with a glass of wine on his right and pleasant oil on his left he blesses the wine and afterwards the oil and the School of Hillel says you bless the oil ...' (the reference is to oil and wine after the food). And this blessing has not been elucidated, although we found several formulas in the Talmud ('Creator of pleasant oil,' 'Creator of oil of land,' b.*Brachot* 43a; 'who infused good aroma into pleasant oil, who infused good aroma into the trees of spices, and others,' y.*Brachot* 6:6). From this we can apparently establish that the blessing of Rabbi Zera ('who infused good aroma into pleasant oil') is the essence of the prayer" ("The Halacha in the Teaching of the Twelve Apostles," in *The Didache in Modern Research* [ed. Draper; Leiden, The Netherlands: Brill, 1996], 189). Today, there is a similar custom among Mizrachi Jews to begin Shabbat by walking clockwise around the Shabbat table with a fragrant oil, branch, or spices before Kiddush and in Sephardic custom fragrant spices or oil are smelled after a meal kind of like a dessert. The blessing transmitted by the Coptic Didache would then most likely be for aromatic oil used to fill the room with a pleasant fragrance for Shabbat before Kiddush, after a meal before *Grace after Meals*, at Havdalah, and/or some sort of ceremony after immersion.

24   Proverbs 9:5–6; Sirach 15:1–3.

25   J.L. Teicher, "Ancient Eucharistic Prayers in Hebrew (Dura-Europos Parchment D. Pg. 25)," *Jewish Quarterly Review* 54, no. 2 (October 1963): 99–109. Teicher attempts to identify these prayers as Christian in origin, but this conclusion seems unlikely.

that later became known in Jewish circles as *piyyutim*.²⁶ We also find thanksgiving for both the physical and the spiritual in the writings of Philo.²⁷

Despite some differences in wording and sequence, the Didache version and *Grace after Meals* share enough similarities to indicate a common origin in Jewish liturgical tradition.²⁸

Practical Application

The Didache views the requirement to give thanks after eating as fully incumbent upon Gentile believers. Likewise, some modern rabbinic authorities today recommend that Gentiles bless God after they eat, most suggesting that non-Jews recite only the first blessing of the *Grace after Meals*. The first blessing has universal application; the subsequent blessings are more specific to the Jewish people.²⁹

The prayers of Didache 10 represent an authentic *Grace after Meals* prayer used by the earliest Gentile followers of Messiah. This provides an exciting link back to the time of the apostles, but it is not so easy to determine how these prayers were originally implemented or how they should be implemented today. For example, were these blessings employed universally among believers to the exclusion of other traditional Jewish forms of *Grace after Meals*? Were they used only by Gentile believers, and if so, what form of thanksgiving liturgy did the community use when both Jewish and Gentile believers were present at the meal?

Another important factor to consider is that Messianic Jewish communities today do not live in a religious and cultural vacuum. In Messianic Judaism we not

---

26 Jonathan A. Draper, "The Holy Vine of David Made Known to the Gentiles through God's Servant Jesus: 'Christian Judaism' in the Didache," in *Jewish Christianity Reconsidered: Rethinking Ancient Groups and Texts* (ed. Matt Jackson-McCabe; Minneapolis, MN: Fortress, 2007), 272. Cf. "There are reasons to think of a Hellenistic Jewish tradition underlying this deviation from the *Birkat HaMazon*" (Van de Sandt and Flusser, *The Didache*, 323).

27 Philo, *On the Special Laws* 1.209.

28 Flusser and Van de Sandt suggest that the Didache's prayer has been modified from "one coherent Jewish liturgical source" (*The Didache*, 313).

29 Rabbi Michael Katz et al., eds., *Service from the Heart: Renewing the Ancient Path of Biblical Prayer and Service* (Rose, OK: Oklahoma B'nai Noah Society, 2007), 131. Cf. Rabbi Moshe Weiner and Rabbi J. Immanuel Schochet, *Prayers, Blessings, Principles of Faith, and Divine Service for Noahides* (Pittsburgh, PA: Ask Noah International, 2010), 29. It should be pointed out that there are two other post-meal blessings in Judaism for meals and snacks that do not include bread. For a discussion on the history and legal rulings surrounding these blessings, see Aaron Eby and Toby Janicki, *Breaking Bread: In Everything Give Thanks* (Marshfield, MO: First Fruits of Zion, 2013). For the text of these prayers in Hebrew and English, see *We Thank You: Blessings of Thanks before and after Meals* (trans. Aaron Eby; Marshfield, MO: Vine of David, 2008).

only desire to maintain consistency with the early believers but also with current Jewish practice.

Several options exist for those attempting to implement the Didache's prayers at mealtime. Some may wish to recite the post-meal prayers of the Didache as they stand. Others, who may perhaps be those among a mixed group of Messianic Jews and Gentiles, might want to integrate the Didache version throughout the traditional *Grace after Meals*, reciting the two together.[30] Some Gentile believers may wish to recite the first blessing of the traditional *Grace after Meals*, as many modern Jewish authorities recommend, while others might prefer to do so in combination with the Didache's prayers.

---

30 For a version that integrates the two prayers, see *We Thank You*, 6–25.

Commentary

ⵊⵊ *After you have been satisfied, give thanks in this way.*
(DIDACHE 10.1)

The prayers of chapter 10 are introduced with the instruction that they are to be recited when the participants are "satisfied" after a full meal. As we noted earlier, this evokes the injunction of Deuteronomy 8:10, "You shall eat and be full, and you shall bless the LORD your God," from which the sages derived the commandment to recite *Grace after Meals*.[31] This is again alluded to in Didache 10.3: "You gave nourishment and drink for human beings to enjoy in order that they would give thanks to you." Like the Apostle Paul, who stated that food is to be received "with thanksgiving" and "prayer," the Didache views the prayer after the meal as the fulfillment of a commandment.[32]

In rabbinic practice, it was often customary to recite the *Grace after Meals* over a cup of wine called the "cup of blessing" (*kos shel brachah*, כוס של ברכה).[33] Paul alludes to the technical name of this cup in his first epistle to the Corinthians, and it was over this cup, "after [the disciples] had eaten," that the Master stated, "This is my blood."[34] Although we can only speculate, this may have been the practice of the Didache community as well.

---

[31] y.*Brachot* 7:1; b.*Brachot* 48b. The Greek word for "satisfied" (*empimplemi*, ἐμπίμπλημι) in the Didache is the same word used in the Septuagint version of Deuteronomy 8:10. Van de Sandt and Flusser argue that *empimplemi* (Septuagint = *sheva*, שבע) "appears to be a technical formula in the Bible aiming at the prosperous situation in the Promised Land," which shows a further connection to Deuteronomy 8:10, "good land" (*The Didache*, 312). The Apostolic Constitutions removes "satisfied" and renders this, "After the participation, give thanks in this way" (7.26).

[32] 1 Timothy 4:3–4. "The use of the term ἐμπλησθῆναι [*euplesthenai*] at the end of the meal may indicate that now the duty of reciting the prayer, enjoined in Deuteronomy 8:10, is performed" (Van de Sandt and Flusser, *The Didache*, 312).

[33] See m.*Brachot* 7:5; b.*Pesachim* 107a; b.*Sotah* 38b.

[34] Luke 22:20; Matthew 26:27–28; Mark 14:23–24. Cf. 1 Corinthians 10:16, 11:25.

> *We thank you, our holy Father, for your holy name that you have caused to dwell in our hearts.* (DIDACHE 10.2)

This first of three blessings of the Didache's *Grace after Meals* focuses on thanking God for the spiritual blessings that Gentile disciples have received through Messiah Yeshua. This blessing is more similar in form and content to the second blessings of the traditional *Grace after Meals*, which begins similarly: "We thank you, O Lord our God, because you have given us ..."[35] The Apostolic Constitutions expands this slightly: "We thank you, O God and Father of Yeshua our Savior, for your holy name that you have caused to dwell among us" (7.26).[36]

The use of "We thank you" over "Blessed are you" has already been discussed in the commentary on chapter 9.[37] However, the Didache here uses the title "holy Father" rather than "Father" alone. The title parallels "holy name" in the phrase that follows it.[38] "Holy Father" as a title for God appears in the Odes of Solomon and in the Acts of Peter.[39] The Master uses this designation in his prayer in John 17:11, which also includes language about being kept in God's name: "Holy Father, keep them in your name, which you have given me."

"Name" (*shem*, שם) in this context refers to the Dwelling Presence or Holy Spirit of God, known in rabbinic writings as the *Shechinah* (שכינה).[40] The Scriptures speak of Jerusalem and in particular the Temple as the place where God chose to cause his name to dwell.[41] The Talmud mentions that the watchmen in the Temple greeted one another on the Sabbath by saying, "May he who caused his name to dwell in this house cause love, brotherhood, peace, and friendship to dwell among you."[42] In the Didache's prayers God's name equates to his Dwelling Presence.

---

35 Cf. Jubilees 22:7.
36 The expression "God and Father of Yeshua our Savior" is similar to Paul's "God and Father of our Lord Yeshua the Messiah" (2 Corinthians 1:3) and his "God, the Father of our Lord Yeshua the Messiah" (Colossians 1:3).
37 The Georgian version of the Didache has "I thank you" instead of "We thank you."
38 For the use of "holy name" in the Hebrew Scriptures, see Leviticus 20:3, 22:32; Psalm 111:9; Luke 1:49. Cf. 1 Clement 64.1.
39 Odes of Solomon 31:5; Acts of Peter 27.
40 Solomon Schechter and Kaufmann Kohler, "Didache," *Jewish Encyclopedia* 4:585–588. In the Septuagint *kataskenoo* (κατασκηνόω) is equal to *shachan* ("dwell," שכן), which is the root of the word *Shechinah*.
41 Deuteronomy 12:11, 14:23, 16:2, 6, 26:2; Jeremiah 7:12; Ezekiel 43:7. Cf. Sirach 24:8; Psalms of Solomon 7:6.
42 b.*Brachot* 12a.

According to the Didache, God's Dwelling Presence will also rest on believers in Messiah. This is important, because in Jewish thought the Holy Spirit could not rest on Gentiles unless they formally converted to Judaism.[43] The apostles spoke of all believers as "the temple of the Holy Spirit," where God's presence dwelled within them.[44] The book of Revelation states, "Behold, the dwelling place of God is with man."[45] This concept does not replace the presence of God in the Temple (when it stands) but instead was understood by some rabbis as the complementary interpretation of Exodus 25:8, "Let them make me a sanctuary, that I may dwell in their midst," in which the Hebrew for "in their midst" (*betocham*, בתוכם) can be interpreted as "in them."[46] The version of this blessing in the Apostolic Constitutions seems to allude to this Exodus passage by changing "dwell in our hearts" to "dwell among us."[47]

[10.2] We thank you, our holy Father, for your holy name that you have caused to dwell in our hearts.

The indwelling of the *Shechinah* finds its ultimate manifestation in Messiah: "The Word became flesh and dwelt among us, and we have seen his glory, glory as of the only Son from the Father, full of grace and truth" (John 1:14). While we have a measure of the Lord's Spirit within us, "in him all the fullness of God was pleased to dwell" (Colossians 1:19). Just as "the knowledge, faithfulness, and eternal life" is made known through Yeshua, so is the Lord's "holy name": "I made known to them your name, and I will continue to make it known, that the love with which you have loved me may be in them, and I in them" (John 17:26).[48]

The Dwelling Presence of God rests specifically in the "heart" (*lev*, לב), which in Judaism is the figurative source of one's will and decision-making capabilities. That means that "this indwelling of the 'holy Father' is not to be reduced to a pious fiction or to sentimental feelings. 'Holiness,' for the framers of the Didache, was firmly attached to knowing the way of life revealed by the Father and putting it into practice."[49] For these newly immersed Gentile initiates, the indwelling of God's name symbolized "the conferring of a new identity and a new kin ... Speaking the

---

43   See Toby Janicki, "Gentiles and the Holy Spirit," in *Gifts of the Spirit* (Marshfield, MO: First Fruits of Zion, 2013), 135–159.
44   1 Corinthians 6:19. Cf. Romans 8:9; 1 Corinthians 3:16, 6:16; James 4:5.
45   Revelation 21:3.
46   See Rabbi Shloma Majeski, *A Tzaddik and His Students: The Rebbe-Chassid Relationship* (Brooklyn, NY: Sichos in English, 2008), 30.
47   Apostolic Constitutions 7.26.
48   Cf. John 17:6, 11–12. Knowledge and Messiah making himself and God known to believers is a big theme in the Odes of Solomon, e.g., Odes of Solomon 4:7, 7:16–26, 18:9–10, 33:13.
49   Aaron Milavec, *The Didache: Faith, Hope, & Life of the Earliest Christian Communities, 50–70 C.E.* (New York, NY: Newman, 2003), 386.

Name has the power to effect the transformation of the Gentile believer into a member of the renewed kingdom."[50] To receive the holy name was to be received into the commonwealth of Israel.

> And for the knowledge, faithfulness,
> and eternal life that you have made known to us
> through your servant Yeshua. Yours is the glory forever.
> (DIDACHE 10.2)

The language here, again, is similar to the pre-meal blessings for the wine and bread in chapter 9.[51] Both blessings have the expression "through your servant Yeshua" along with a comparable doxology, and 9.3 has the almost identical "for the life and the knowledge that you made known to us." The difference between the two blessings is that here we have the addition of "faithfulness" and the descriptive "eternal life." As in the prayers of chapter 9, God is thanked for the blessings he has bestowed upon believers through Yeshua the Messiah. The Apostolic Constitutions renders this, "And for the knowledge, faithfulness, love, and eternal life that you have given us through your servant Yeshua" (7.26).

"Faithfulness" in Hebrew is the word *emunah* (אמונה) and refers not just to belief but to trust, loyalty, and steadfastness that is carried out in action. As James, the brother of the Master, said, "Faith by itself, if it does not have works, is dead" (James 2:17). We show our faith through our works. After all, we were "justified by the faithfulness of Messiah," and it is our duty as disciples to follow in the example of his obedience.[52] In that way we received "faithfulness" through God's "servant Yeshua."

We also find "faithfulness" mentioned again in Didache 16 in the context of the end of days. There "faithfulness" also means having trust and hope for the coming Messianic Era and living in that reality now, persevering in this present age. In the twelfth of his thirteen principles of faith, Maimonides states, "I believe with perfect faith in the coming of the Messiah, and though he may tarry, still I await him every day." Like the Didache, Judaism teaches that faith in the coming of the

---

50   Draper, "Ritual Process and Ritual Symbol in Didache 7–10," 146.
51   The Georgian version of the Didache has "I thank you for the knowledge" and omits "to us."
52   Lloyd Gaston, *Paul and the Torah* (Vancouver, BC: University of British Columbia, 1987); D. Thomas Lancaster, *The Holy Epistle to the Galatians* (Marshfield, MO: First Fruits of Zion, 2011), 93.

Messiah is expressed in living a life of faithfulness to the commandments, which thereby demonstrates trust in and anticipation of his arrival.

In addition to "knowledge" and "faithfulness," we also receive "eternal life" through Messiah Yeshua. The Master foretold this in the Gospels and the Apostle John writes explicitly: "God so loved the world, that he gave his only Son, that whoever believes in him should not perish but have eternal life" (John 3:16).[53] Peter declared to Yeshua, "You have the words of eternal life" (John 6:68). "Eternal life" (*chayei olam*, חיי עולם) refers primarily to the resurrection of the dead; that is, to receive eternal life is to be brought back to life in the great eschatological resurrection of the dead.

The Apostle Paul states that believers will receive "eternal life through Messiah Yeshua" and that through Messiah "has come also the resurrection of the dead."[54] Maimonides' thirteenth principle of faith states, "I believe with perfect faith that there will be a resurrection of the dead at the time when it shall please the Creator." The resurrection of Messiah was the firstfruits of that final resurrection of the dead.[55] In Messiah we receive salvation from the Way of Death in this world (*olam hazeh*, עולם הזה) as a pledge of the physical salvation that we will receive from physical death in the World to Come (*olam haba*, עולם הבא).

> ⁌ *You, O Lord of Legions, created all things*
> *for the sake of your name; you gave nourishment and drink*
> *for human beings to enjoy in order that*
> *they would give thanks to you.* (DIDACHE 10.3)

Here begins the second blessing of the Didache's *Grace after Meals*. This section matches more closely the first blessing of the traditional *Grace after Meals*. Both prayers focus on thanking God for his nourishment of all mankind and include the line "for the sake of your [great] name." The major difference between them is that the Didache adds a section at the end that thanks the Lord for his spiritual nourishment.

[10.2]
And for the knowledge, faithfulness, and eternal life that you have made known to us through your servant Yeshua. Yours is the glory forever.

---

53   Cf. Matthew 19:29, 25:46; Mark 10:30; Luke 18:30; John 3:15, 36, 4:14, 36, 5:24, 39, 6:27, 40, 47, 54, 10:28, 12:25, 50, 17:2–3.
54   Romans 5:21; 1 Corinthians 15:21.
55   1 Corinthians 15:20.

[10.3]
You, O Lord of Legions, created all things for the sake of your name; you gave nourishment and drink for human beings to enjoy in order that they would give thanks to you.

This section is greatly expanded in the Apostolic Constitutions:

> You, O Lord of Legions, the God of the universe, created the world, and the things that are in it, through him; and have planted Torah in our souls, and beforehand prepared things for the convenience of human beings. O God of our holy and blameless fathers, Abraham, and Isaac, and Jacob, your faithful servants; you, O God, who are powerful, faithful, and true, and without deceit in your promises; who sent upon earth Yeshua your Messiah to live with men, as a man, when he was God the Word, and man, to take away error by the roots. (Apostolic Constitutions 7.26)[56]

The title "Lord of Legions" appears in the Didache only here, but it appears frequently in the Scriptures, especially in the Prophets.[57] It expresses the imagery of God as the commander of a great army and asserts that he is Israel's protector and defender. The Didache uses it to emphasize that God is all-powerful and the provider for his people.

Unlike in the first blessing, "name" here is used in the more typical Jewish sense to refer to God's reputation and character (see commentary on 8.2).[58] The Didache is communicating that the greatness of God's character is seen in the way that he provides for creation on a daily basis. A similar expression is found in the traditional *Grace after Meals*: "For the sake of his great Name, no good thing has ever been lacking to us nor ever will be, because he nourishes and feeds all."[59] Additionally, his name is exalted when those for whom he provides give "thanks" to him for his care: "Worthy are you, our Lord and God, to receive glory and honor and power, for you created all things, and by your will they existed and were created" (Revelation 4:11).

---

56 Even though the prayer was expanded by a later editor and heavily Christianized, the Apostolic Constitutions adds a few distinctly Jewish phrases. The phrase "and have planted Torah in our souls" is similar to the blessing after the reading of the Torah: "who gave to us the Torah of truth, and planted eternal life in our midst." The phrase "O God of our holy and blameless fathers, Abraham, and Isaac, and Jacob, your faithful servants" is similar to the *Avot* benediction of the *Amidah*: "Our God and God of our forefathers, God of Abraham, God of Isaac, God of Jacob."

57 E.g., Psalm 24:10; Isaiah 1:9. Cf. 2 Corinthians 6:18.

58 Some feel that "name" here refers to Messiah. Yeshua is spoken of by the apostles as the revealer of God's name and in some cases he himself is the name of God. Cf. John 17:6; Philippians 2:9–11; 1 Clement 59.2; Shepherd of Hermas, Similitude 9.14.5 (91.5).

59 of Cairo Genizah *Grace after Meals* from Mazza, *The Celebration of the Eucharist*, 308. Cf. the line from the post-meal prayer *Borei Nefashot*: "We thank you for all the things that you made that keep your creatures alive."

Contrary to many ascetic beliefs, God desires that we "enjoy" the nourishment that he gives to us.[60] The Apostle Paul enjoins us not to be haughty in our material gains, for it is God "who richly provides us with everything to enjoy."[61] The Jerusalem Talmud even contains the opinion that "in the future a man is going to have to give an account for everything [permissible pleasure] that his eye saw and he did not eat" (y.*Kiddushin* 4:12). In Jewish tradition Shabbat meal gatherings are called *oneg* ("delight," עונג), and in them delicious food and drink are served to increase the level of celebration and enjoyment. Ultimately this manner of eating is not about gluttony or hedonism but instead is meant to result in our giving thanks and praise to our Father in heaven for all that he has created and given us to enjoy.

[10.3] You, O Lord of Legions, created all things for the sake of your name; you gave nourishment and drink for human beings to enjoy in order that they would give thanks to you.

> *You also bestowed upon us spiritual nourishment and drink and eternal life through your servant.*
> (DIDACHE 10.3)

In addition to thanking God for the physical food and drink, this second post-meal prayer also thanks God for his spiritual nourishment.[62]

Although this type of spiritualization is not present in the traditional *Grace after Meals*, it is not foreign to Jewish thought. As was noted in this chapter's overview, Torah teachings and divine knowledge are often compared with food and drink.[63] The Prophet Isaiah states, "Why do you spend your money for that which is not bread, and your labor for that which does not satisfy? Listen diligently to me, and eat what is good, and delight yourselves in rich food. Incline your ear, and come to me; hear, that your soul may live" (Isaiah 55:2–3). Likewise, the Master quotes the famous passage from Deuteronomy about manna: "Man does not live by bread alone, but man lives by every word that comes from the mouth of the LORD."[64]

---

60   The Coptic version of the Didache has a fragmented remnant of this line reading "you gave them to the sons of men to enjoy." Thus it preserves the Semitic idiom "sons of men," while the Greek simply has "human beings" (*anthropois*, ἀνθρώποις).

61   1 Timothy 6:17.

62   The Georgian version of the Didache reads, "But for those of us who have been immersed by you, you have offered us this spiritual food and drink, and have given us eternal life through your Son Yeshua the Messiah." The Coptic version of the Didache also has "your Son Yeshua" instead of "your servant Yeshua," but that could just be because the Greek word *pais* (παῖς) can be defined as "son" as well as "servant."

63   Proverbs 9:5–6; Sirach 15:1–3.

64   Deuteronomy 8:3; Matthew 4:4; Luke 4:4.

[10.3]
You also bestowed upon us spiritual nourishment and drink and eternal life through your servant.

There seems to be a strong connection between the Didache's words and the narrative of the manna in the Torah. The Midrash connects the manna in the wilderness to the nourishment of Torah: "The Holy One, blessed be he, said, 'I will lead them about in the desert for forty years that they may eat manna and drink the water of the well and [thereby] the Torah will be united with their body.'"[65] The Apostle Paul's words about manna in 1 Corinthians 10:3–4 are strikingly similar to the Didache's expression "spiritual nourishment and drink": "All ate the same spiritual food, and all drank the same spiritual drink. For they drank from the spiritual Rock that followed them, and the Rock was Messiah."

In the Gospel of John, Yeshua states that he is the "bread of life" and the true manna: "I am the living bread that came down from heaven. If anyone eats of this bread, he will live forever. And the bread that I will give for the life of the world is my flesh" (John 6:51). Just as the Didache thanks God for the "spiritual nourishment" and "eternal life," the Master states that anyone who "feeds on [his] flesh and drinks [his] blood has eternal life."[66] We need to thank our Father in heaven not only for the food and drink with which he sustains us daily but also for the spiritual sustenance and life he provides us through Yeshua, the living Torah.

⁕ *And for all things we thank you because you are powerful. Yours is the glory forever.* (DIDACHE 10.4)

Although most published versions of the Didache break the text to make these words the beginning of a new verse, they actually function as the closing section and doxology for the blessings of 10.3.[67] They describe God as powerful, which

---

65   *Mechilta*, Beshallach 1, Exodus 13:17. Cf. Philo, *Allegorical Interpretation* 3.169–177. Cf. the words of Rabbeinu Bachya: "The manna that fell from heaven for the Jews in the desert was not a regular food. It was a highly refined substance, a material crystallization of a supernal, lofty divine light. It was provided to the Jews who received the Torah in order to refine their minds and elevate their perception so they could properly internalize the Torah. The same is true of the foods that our Sages associate with the final redemption, such as the Leviathan fish, the *bar yochani* bird, the "animal that pastures on the thousand mountains," and so on. These are similarly material distillations of extremely sublime divine light and consequently, they are highly refined forms of materiality that will serve to sharpen our minds in the era of redemption to a far greater extent than even the manna in the desert, for at that time, wisdom will flow freely and Godly knowledge will fill the earth."

66   John 6:54.

67   The Coptic version of the Didache adds "Amen" to the end of the doxology.

parallels the opening of 10.3 in which God is addressed as the "Lord of Legions."[68] God demonstrates his strength not through war and destruction but by lovingly caring for his children. The language is reminiscent of the phrase from the *Grace after Meals*: "For all these we thank you and bless your great and holy name, eternally and always."[69]

In several of the Didache's doxologies, "power" is attributed to the Lord, and in chapter 16 it is said that "the earth will be delivered into his power."[70] In rabbinic literature and in the Targums, one of the names for God is "the Power" (*HaGevurah*, הגבורה).[71] Yeshua uses the title in his trial before the high priest Caiaphas: "I tell you, from now on you will see the Son of Man seated at the right hand of Power."[72] God is also described as "powerful" in the second benediction (*Gevurah*) of the *Amidah*. This benediction is largely centered on the resurrection of the dead, which fits into the Didache's reference to "eternal life." These doxologies are absent from the version of the post-meal prayers in the Apostolic Constitutions.

[10.4]
And for all things we thank you because you are powerful. Yours is the glory forever.

◈ *Remember, O Lord, your congregation,*
to rescue her from all evil and to make her complete
in your love. (DIDACHE 10.5)

The third section of the Didache *Grace after Meals*, beginning here in verse 5, is identical in theme to the ingathering prayer recited over bread in 9.4. The Apostolic Constitutions expands this slightly: "Even now, through him [i.e., Messiah], remember your holy congregation, which you have purchased with the precious blood of your Messiah, and rescue her from all evil, and make her complete in your love and your truth" (7.26). A prayer for the ingathering is also found in the post-meal prayer section of Sirach.[73] While the traditional *Grace after Meals* prayer does not mention the ingathering of the exiles, this third blessing here in 10.5 parallels

---

68 The Georgian version of the Didache adds, "You are powerful and good." The goodness of God is a prominent theme in the *Grace after Meals*: "The Good King, who does good to all, and day after day, he did good, he does good, and he will do good for us" (Fourth Blessing: The Good and Beneficent One).
69 of Cairo Genizah *Grace after Meals* from Mazza, *The Celebration of the Eucharist*, 308. The version in the Apostolic Constitutions prayer for the righteous is even more similar: "For all which things do we give you thanks" (7.38).
70 Didache 8.2, 9.4, 10.4, 5, 16.4.
71 b.*Sotah* 37a; *Avot deRabbi Natan* 37 (A); Targum Isaiah 33:21, 48:13. The Greek words *dunatos* (δυνατός) and *dunamis* (δύναμις) are related to the Hebrew *gevurah* ("power," גבורה) in the Septuagint.
72 Matthew 26:64. Cf. Mark 14:62.
73 Sirach 36:11.

[10.5]
Remember, O Lord, your congregation, to rescue her from all evil and to make her complete in your love.

the third blessing of the traditional *Grace after Meals*, the blessing for Jerusalem, in that they both speak about the restoration of the kingdom. It seems likely therefore that "the Didache prayer traces its origin" back to this traditional blessing.[74]

Similarly, the *Ya'aleh Veyavo* prayer inserted into the *Amidah* on festivals and New Moons calls upon God to remember and take notice of his people by bringing about the Messianic Age. "Remember" (*zachar*, זכר) in Biblical Hebrew idiom can mean "to act upon an obligation." When we pray for God to remember his congregation, we are asking him to fulfill his promise to bring about the redemption and restore the kingdom of David.

Ekklesia is translated here as "congregation" instead of "assembly" as in 4.14, 9.4, and 11.11, because it appears that the Didache is actually quoting Psalm 74:2, "Remember your congregation," which uses *edah* ("congregation," עדה) instead of *kahal* ("assembly," קהל).

Like the *Our Father*'s "rescue us from what is evil," this third blessing of the Didache's *Grace after Meals* petitions God to rescue his people from all evil and to bring relief from troubles. This is a prelude to the ingathering of the exiles and the Messianic Age and is a major theme throughout the Scriptures.[75] *Ruomai* ("rescue," ῥύομαι) is related to the Hebrew word *go'el* ("redeem," גואל). The Didache then is petitioning God to bring the final redemption in the same manner that we find in the *Ge'ulah* benediction of the *Amidah*: "See our affliction and fight our fight; redeem us for the sake of your name. Blessed are you, O LORD, who redeems Israel."[76] Our prayer is also that we might experience a foretaste of this deliverance now. As the Master prayed, "I do not ask that you take them out of the world, but that you keep them from the evil one" (John 17:15).

Once the congregation is rescued, they will be "complete in" God's "love." "Complete" (*teleios*) appears three other times in the Didache and has the sense of "unblemished" or "perfect."[77] This is reminiscent of the Master's prayer: "I in them and you in me, that they may become perfectly one, so that the world may know that you sent me and loved them even as you loved me" (John 17:23). The Apostle John writes, "Whoever keeps his word, in him truly the love of God is perfected. By this we may know that we are in him" (1 John 2:5); "No one has ever seen God;

---

74 Van de Sandt and Flusser, *The Didache*, 316.
75 For a full set of passages from the Bible that deal with redemption and deliverance, see Karl-Gustav Sandelin, *Wisdom as Nourisher* (Turku, Finland: Åbo Akademi, 1986), 218.
76 Rabbi Lawrence A. Hoffman, *The Amidah* (vol. 2 of *My People's Prayer Book: Traditional Prayers, Modern Commentaries*; Woodstock, VT: Jewish Lights, 1998), 39.
77 Didache 1.4, 6.2, 16.2.

if we love one another, God abides in us and his love is perfected in us" (1 John 4:12).[78] In the final redemption we will be complete and fulfilled in God's love, in perfect unity with one another.

> *Gather her, the sanctified, from the four winds to your kingdom that you have prepared for her. For yours is the power and the glory forever.* (DIDACHE 10.5)

The third post-meal blessing of Didache 10 continues by asking God to gather the sanctified into his kingdom.[79] In step with 9.5, it calls for the ingathering of the exiles back to the land of Israel, where the Messianic Kingdom will be established. The prayer ends with a doxology. The Apostolic Constitutions truncates this: "And gather us all together to your kingdom that you have prepared" (7.26). Rabbi Nachman mentions the ingathering of the exiles in a discussion about the *Grace after Meals* and the ingathering is the theme of Psalm 126, which is recited before *Grace after Meals* on Shabbat and festivals.[80]

In this prayer "sanctified" is related to the Hebrew term *mekudeshet* (מקודשת), which is used in the context of marriage to mean "betrothed." In a Jewish wedding, when a ring is placed on the bride's hand, the groom says, "Behold, you are sanctified to me by means of this ring." Therefore, the Didache alludes to the bride of Messiah.[81] The Master tells us that he consecrates himself and sanctifies (betroths) us in truth.[82] Paul states, "I betrothed you to one husband, to present you as a pure virgin to [Messiah]" (2 Corinthians 11:2).

The expression "four winds" is found in the book of Zechariah, also in the context of the ingathering: "Up! Up! Flee from the land of the north, declares the LORD. For I have spread you abroad as the four winds of the heavens, declares the LORD" (Zechariah 2:6). Yeshua uses this expression in a prophecy about the final ingathering: "He will send out his angels with a loud trumpet call, and they

---

78   Cf. 1 John 4:13–18.
79   The Coptic version of the Didache adds "Amen" to the end of the doxology.
80   b.*Brachot* 49a.
81   Revelation 18:23, 19:7, 21:2, 9, 22:17. Joel Willitts argues that the bride of Messiah throughout Revelation refers to Israel, not specifically the *ekklesia* as elsewhere in the New Testament. See Willitts, "The Bride of Messiah and the Israel-ness of the New Heavens and New Earth," in *Introduction to Messianic Judaism* (ed. David Rudolph and Willitts; Grand Rapids, MI: Zondervan, 2013), 245–254.
82   John 17:19; Hebrews 10:10.

[10.5] *Gather her, the sanctified, from the four winds to your kingdom that you have prepared for her. For yours is the power and the glory forever.*

will gather his elect from the four winds, from one end of heaven to the other" (Matthew 24:31).[83]

When the great ingathering of the exiles takes place, the redeemed will be brought to the Holy Land of Israel to dwell in the kingdom that our Father in heaven has already prepared. The Master says that we will be greeted by the King, who will say, "Come, you who are blessed by my Father, inherit the kingdom prepared for you from the foundation of the world" (Matthew 25:34).

We must not confuse the Didache's fervent petitions for the imminent inauguration of the Messianic Age as endorsing the idea of an escapism eschatology. The Didache firmly lays out the Way of Life with a call to all followers of Messiah to walk in the Torah daily. As we await and long for the arrival of the Messianic Era, through our lives and actions, we experience and bring about a foretaste of the kingdom of heaven in this present age. When we perform commandments, we are "hastening the coming of the day of God."[84] We all have much work to do in preparing the way for the arrival of the King and his kingdom.

> *May grace come, and may this world pass away. Hoshana to the God of David!* (DIDACHE 10.6)

The Didache's *Grace after Meals* ends with a closing prayer that, like the blessing in 10.5, calls for the swift arrival of the redemption and the Messianic Age. The Apostolic Constitutions states, "*Maran etha! Hoshana* to the Son of David! Blessed is he who comes in the name of the Lord" (7.6).[85] It seems quite possible that last section was influenced by the Psalms of Solomon:

> May the salvation of the Lord be upon Israel his servant for ever; May the sinners perish together at the presence of the Lord; May the Lord's pious ones inherit the promises of the Lord. (Psalms of Solomon 12:6)

---

83 Cf. Mark 13:27.
84 2 Peter 3:12.
85 Matthew 21:9; Mark 11:10; John 12:13. Cf. 1 Corinthians 16:22. The Apostolic Constitutions then adds, "God the Lord, who was manifested to us in the flesh." Notice how the Apostolic Constitutions has "Son of David" in place of the Didache's "God of David." "Son of David" is the form we find in the Gospels and in use among the early Jewish believers. The Coptic version of the Didache has "Hoshana to the house of David." This is a reference to the Davidic dynasty from which King Messiah has emerged in Yeshua. E.g., Psalm 122:5; Zechariah 12:7–8; Luke 1:69.

Some scholars feel that this could be the response of the meal's participants to the leader after he has recited the first three blessings or that it constitutes a series of back-and-forth responses between the leader and the participants.[86]

[10.6]
May grace come, and may this world pass away. Hoshana to the God of David!

To be shown "grace" (*chen*, חן) is to be shown God's favor. "May grace come" is a petition that Israel find favor in the eyes of God, which then will bring the arrival of the Messianic Era.[87] At Yeshua's birth the angels proclaimed, "Glory to God in the highest, and on earth peace among those with whom he is pleased!" (Luke 2:14). "May grace come" expresses the same desire as the petition in the Lord's Prayer, "May your kingdom come."

"May this world pass away" parallels "may grace come." No deprecation of the physical world is implied here, nor a Gnostic hope to escape the physical world. Instead, the prayer petitions God to bring the reign of Messiah down to earth. It is not a prayer to escape the world; it is a call to transform it. What will pass away is the old order, the *olam hazeh*, this present age, and what will arrive is the new order, the *olam haba*, the age to come. The Apostle Paul writes, "The present form of this world is passing away" (1 Corinthians 7:31). In the meantime the Apostle Peter urges us, "Preparing your minds for action, and being sober-minded, set your hope fully on the grace that will be brought to you at the revelation of [Yeshua the Messiah]" (1 Peter 1:13). With this prayer we cry out for the redemption while we "groan inwardly as we wait eagerly for adoption as sons, the redemption of our bodies" (Romans 8:23).

"*Hoshana*" (הושע נא) is an Aramaic word shortened from Hebrew that is transliterated into the Greek of the Didache. It appears in Psalm 118:25, "Save us [*hoshia na*, הושיעה נא], we pray, O LORD! O LORD, we pray, give us success!" and it is found frequently in the *Hoshanot* liturgy for Sukkot.[88] Originally it was used as a cry for help, but eventually it became an expression of praise and even a salutation.

---

86 Draper feels that this fourth prayer is an addition to the regular Didache *Grace after Meals* in the same vein as "the much later Jewish practice of inserting poetic *piyyutim* at the end of the *berakoth*." See "Ritual Process and Ritual Symbol in Didache 7–10," 141.

87 The Coptic version of the Didache reads, "May the Lord come and let this world pass away. Amen." (G.W. Horner, "A New Papyrus Fragment of the 'Didache' in Coptic," *Journal of Theological Studies* 25 [1924]: 230).

88 "The liturgy of the Feast of Tabernacles becomes a key to the combination, 'Hosanna … Maranatha. Amen.' For the 'Hosanna' verse, which was the cry of the people as they encompassed the altar on the successive days of the feast, is followed immediately in Psalm 118 by, 'Blessed be he who comes in the name of the Lord'; so that the 'Maranatha' in its Hebrew form is linked on the one side to the 'Amen' in the hymn, and on the other to the 'Hosanna' in the psalm" (Charles Taylor, "The Teaching of the Twelve Apostles with Illustrations from the Talmud," in *Didache: The Unknown Teaching of the Twelve Apostles* [ed. Brent S. Walters; San Jose, CA: Anti-Nicene Archive, 1991], 183).

[10.6]
May grace come, and may this world pass away. Hoshana to the God of David!

"*Hoshana* to the God of David" finds its parallel in the Gospels in "*Hoshana* to the Son of David." As Yeshua entered Jerusalem, the crowds greeted him with, "Hosanna to the Son of David! Blessed is he who comes in the name of the Lord! Hosanna in the highest!" (Matthew 21:9).[89] "*Hoshana* to the Son of David" functioned as a petition and greeting among the early Jewish believers.[90]

The original version of the Didache's prayer may well have read "Hosanna to the Son of David," as is preserved in the Apostolic Constitutions, but later may have undergone an emendation to read "God of David." If this is so, the phrase functioned as a petition for the arrival of King Messiah and even as a greeting to be offered him on his arrival. This sentiment completes the thought that began in the preceding expression, "May grace come, and may this world pass away," and it is echoed at the conclusion of the prayer with the petition "Maranatha."

According to the Jerusalem Talmud, it was a requirement to mention the "God of David who rebuilds Jerusalem" in the fourteenth benediction of the *Amidah*, which corresponds to "O Lord, who builds Jerusalem" in the third blessing of the traditional *Grace after Meals*.[91] The expression "God of David" represents the Messiah and the Messianic Kingdom—the fulfillment of the Davidic line.[92] Draper calls this "Davidic Christology."[93] In turn, the expression "*Hoshana* to the God of David" is essentially voicing the sentiment, "May we greet King Messiah."

◈ *Everyone who is holy, let him come. Everyone who is not, let him repent. Maran etha! Amen.* (DIDACHE 10.6)

This final line of the prayer gives a welcome and a warning. It is an invitation to enter the kingdom of heaven and join in the Messianic banquet, which the community meals of the Didache foreshadowed. It reminds us of the Master's words, "Come, you who are blessed by my Father, inherit the kingdom prepared for you from the foundation of the world ... Depart from me, you cursed, into the eternal fire prepared for the devil and his angels" (Matthew 25:34, 41).

---

89   Cf. Matthew 21:15.
90   Eusebius, *Ecclesiastical History* 2.23.14. See D. Thomas Lancaster, *Torah Club: Chronicles of the Messiah* (6 vols.; Marshfield, MO: First Fruits of Zion, 2014), 4:1235–1237.
91   y.*Brachot* 4:6. In b.*Brachot* 48b it is said that it is a requirement to mention "the kingdom of the house of David" in the third blessing of the *Grace after Meals*.
92   The Coptic version of the Didache has "house of David," which some feel probably better reflects the original version. See footnote 85.
93   Draper, "The Holy Vine of David Made Known to the Gentiles through God's Servant Jesus," 272.

"Everyone who is holy" refers to those who are followers of Messiah and have also been properly immersed in accordance with the instructions of chapter 7. The term harkens back to 9.5: "But do not let anyone eat or drink by means of your giving of thanks except those immersed in the name of the Lord." This further solidifies that Gentiles in Messiah have been sanctified and made holy through the Spirit and immersion. Those who are "holy" are welcome to enter into the joys and blessings of the kingdom of heaven.

> [10.6]
> *Everyone who is holy, let him come. Everyone who is not, let him repent. Maran etha! Amen.*

For the unholy this is not a declaration of damnation but a call to repentance. In Hebrew "repentance" (*teshuvah*, תשובה) means not only "to feel remorse for one's sins" but to completely change one's behavior so that it is in line with the Torah. This was the message of John the Baptist, who prepared the way for the arrival of Messiah and for the message of the gospel of Yeshua: "Repent, for the kingdom of heaven is at hand" (Matthew 4:17). In other words, the kingdom is about to arrive, and we need to prepare ourselves to enter into it.

"*Maranatha*" (מרן אתא) is a transliterated Aramaic phrase that appears in the Greek (μαρὰν ἀθά) of the Didache.[94] It means "O, Master, come!" and is parallel to the expression "*Hoshana* to the God of David." The Apostle Paul uses it in a similar context: "If anyone has no love for the Lord, let him be accursed. Our Lord, come!" (1 Corinthians 16:22). It closes the Didache's *Grace after Meals* with a fervent desire to see the Master return quickly to inaugurate the Messianic Kingdom.

The Didache prayer closes with the traditional Jewish response to blessings, "*amen*" (אמן), which is also a transliterated word that appears in the Greek. As a liturgical rule of thumb, all doxologies conclude with "amen." The "amen" does not appear in the earlier examples of chapters 9 and 10, but one may assume the implied "amen" in each instance simply on the basis of universal custom. The Didache includes this final amen to indicate its conclusion of the series of blessings that constitute its *Grace after Meals*.

Jewish law requires its adherents to respond with "amen" to a variety of blessings and prayers, even if they are merely overheard. The Apostle Paul alludes to this legal ruling in 1 Corinthians 14:16. The Talmud teaches that it stands for the acronym *El melech ne'eman* ("God faithful King," אל מלך נאמן).[95] Here in the Didache it functions as the congregational response in affirmation of the entire prayer.

---

94   The Coptic version omits *Maranatha* and has, "The Lord has come! Amen." Similarly, the Georgian version has, "The Lord has come, and his kingdom lasts forever."
95   b.*Shabbat* 119b; b.*Sanhedrin* 111a.

> *Permit the prophets to lead the giving of thanks as much as they desire.* (DIDACHE 10.7)

The Apostolic Constitutions (7.27) renders this as: "Whoever comes to you, and gives thanks in this manner, receive him as a disciple of Messiah. But if he teaches another kind of teaching, different from that which Messiah by us has delivered to you, such a one you must not permit to give thanks; for such a one rather affronts God than glorifies him."

Many scholars interpret this passage of the Didache to mean that the prophets of the community were permitted to add to the Didache's *Grace after Meals* with extemporaneous thanksgiving and praise. However, there might be a better way to view this passage in light of the Didache's Jewish background.

In the commentary to chapter 13, we will argue that when the Didache assigns privileges and dues granted to prophets, the category also includes emissaries and teachers. This should be understood in this case as well. The Apostolic Constitutions supports this theory by rendering 10.7 as, "Permit also to your elders to give thanks" (Apostolic Constitutions 7.26). By the time of the writing of the Apostolic Constitutions, there were no prophets, and in turn, this can be seen as a general injunction to allow the honored ones in the community to offer the *Grace after Meals*.

As will be explained in the commentary to chapter 11, prophets, emissaries, and teachers played major roles in the early believing communities and were shown a high level of honor. In many ways they stood in relation to the Gentile believers as the Levitical priests (*kohanim*, כהנים) did to the Jewish people. For example, prophets and teachers in the Didache were given the "first part" in much the same way that priests received priestly gifts from the Jewish nation. In 13.3 we read, "The prophets ... are your high priests."

Like the prophets, emissaries, and teachers of the Didache, the Levitical priests continue to hold a special place of honor in the Jewish community even today. When the Torah is read in the synagogue, descendants of the priesthood are always given the opportunity to read first, and on special days they still recite the Aaronic benediction (Numbers 6:24–26) over the congregation.[96] Additionally, at a meal at which *Grace after Meals* is recited, a priest (*kohen*, כהן) is honored by being

---

96 *Shulchan Aruch*, Hilchot Kriat Sefer Torah 135.14.3.

permitted to lead the prayer. However, if a Torah scholar is present, he might be given the honor in the place of the priest.⁹⁷

In the same way, it seems that when a prophet, emissary, or teacher (like the priest or Torah scholar) was present at a meal of the early believers, he would have been offered the privilege of leading the post-meal prayer. In this way the community honored prophets, emissaries, and teachers at their meals.

[10.7]
Permit the prophets to lead the giving of thanks as much as they desire.

---

97 *Shulchan Aruch*, Hilchot Birkat HaMazon 201.4.2.

Chapter Eleven

DIDACHE 11

11.1 Now receive whoever comes to teach you in all that has just been said.

11.2 But if this teacher, having turned aside, were to teach a different kind of teaching to undermine this teaching, do not obey him.[1] However, if his teaching serves to promote righteousness and knowledge of the Lord, receive him as the Lord.

11.3 Concerning the emissaries and prophets, according to the ordinance of the good news, this is what you should do:

11.4 Let every emissary who comes to you be received as the Lord.[2]

11.5 He shall stay only one day, but if it is absolutely necessary, he may stay another day. However, if he stays three days, he is a false prophet.

11.6 And when the emissary leaves, let him take nothing except bread to sustain him until he finds a new place to stay. But if he asks for money, he is a false prophet.

11.7 Do not put to the test nor pass judgment on any prophet who speaks in the Spirit, for every sin will be forgiven, but this sin will not be forgiven.[3]

11.8 Yet not everyone who speaks in the Spirit is a prophet; rather, only if he has the conduct of the Lord. Therefore, the false prophet and the true prophet should be recognized by this conduct.[4]

11.9 Any prophet who orders in the Spirit that a dining table be set may not eat from it; otherwise, he is a false prophet.

11.10 If any prophet who teaches the truth does not do what he instructs, he is a false prophet.

---

1 Deuteronomy 13:1–3.
2 Matthew 10:40–41; Luke 10:16; John 13:20.
3 Matthew 12:31–32; Mark 3:28–29.
4 Deuteronomy 13:1–3; Matthew 7:15–20.

11.11 Any prophet who, after having been proven to be true, acts in accordance with the earthly mystery of the assembly but does not instruct you to do what he himself does, shall not be liable to judgment before you, because his judgment remains with God, for all the ancient prophets did so as well.

11.12 But whoever might say in the Spirit, "Give me money," or something else, do not obey him. However, if he should say to give on behalf of others who are poor and in need, let no one judge him.

Overview

Chapter 11 of the Didache begins a new section of material concerned with congregational order and legal rulings. This section continues through chapter 15. The last line of chapter 10, with its instructions for honoring prophets (and teachers) by allowing them to lead the *Grace after Meals*, creates a smooth transition to chapter 11, which speaks about teachers, emissaries, and prophets. Chapter 11 also deals with the issue of hospitality toward different types of travelers, as does chapter 12.

The community instruction that makes up this section of the Didache seems simple and unsophisticated; it provides structure and order for congregational life, with rules applying to those who live within a particular community as well as to those visiting.

Receiving as the Lord

Chapter 11 offers rules pertaining to three different offices within the apostolic community: teachers, emissaries (that is, apostles), and prophets. The content is generally organized as follows:

11.1–2	Teachers
11.3–6	Emissaries
11.7–12	Prophets

These categories often overlap, however; we do not always find clear distinctions between the three groups. Some of the instructions apply to those filling these offices within the local community, while a good portion of the material deals with visitors and travelers who claim to occupy these offices.

Chapter 11 does not communicate sayings of Yeshua but rather attempts to clarify his instructions on hospitality and respect toward those appointed by God. Yeshua enjoined his followers to receive emissaries, prophets, and teachers with open arms:

> Whoever receives you receives me, and whoever receives me receives him who sent me. The one who receives a prophet because he is a

prophet will receive a prophet's reward, and the one who receives a righteous person because he is a righteous person will receive a righteous person's reward. (Matthew 10:40–41)

Truly, truly, I say to you, whoever receives the one I send receives me, and whoever receives me receives the one who sent me. (John 13:20)

These sayings of the Master laid down a principle that required disciples to receive agents of Yeshua who came in his name, offer them hospitality and sustenance, and heed their instruction. While hospitality and respect for teachers, prophets, and emissaries were important parts of discipleship, they could not be practiced without discretion and regulation. Hospitality exercised without discernment could quickly be abused. If every teacher, emissary, and prophet were accepted outright and without qualification, they could pose potential problems for the health of the community. Laws, criteria, and instructions had to be put in place to ensure that Christ-mongers, impostors, and frauds were weeded out.

The Didache uses language echoing the Master's injunction: "Now receive whoever comes to teach you in all that has just been said" (11.1); "Receive him as the Lord" (11.2); and, "Let every emissary who comes to you be received as the Lord" (11.4). The text then comments upon these statements, clarifying them and giving further instructions on them to ensure that the community's generosity and respect toward leaders and teachers would not be trampled upon. In these chapters (11–15) we clearly see how the Didache treats Yeshua's words like the Mishnah and creates a Gemara-like commentary upon them.

Traveling Emissaries and Prophets

Visiting prophets, emissaries, and teachers were an important part of the early Messianic community. Although the local community had an autonomous identity, its members also realized that they were part of a greater community of disciples:

> This larger unity was not just notional but made itself felt in many ways. Churches welcomed visitors from other churches; apostles moved around; and evangelists went from church to church preaching "the

gospel" (the recordings on papyrus of these preachers would become our four Gospels).[5]

Visiting teachers had a celebrated role in the Messianic community.[6] They brought news from other groups of believers. They introduced sayings of Yeshua and the apostles with which the local congregation might not have been familiar. They introduced new epistles and documents that were in circulation in the broader apostolic community. They brought a fresh voice of inspiration and teaching from someone outside the immediate area. All these things contributed to the local community's growth and health.

The Didache teaches that it was the responsibility of the community to honor traveling teachers and offer them hospitality. The Talmud interprets the verse "honor the face of an old man" [*zaken* (זָקֵן), literally "elder"] as referring to one who has acquired wisdom, that is, a Torah scholar.[7] "Honor" encompassed more than just respect but required providing for the needs and sustenance of these teachers. The traveling prophets and emissaries of the Didache were equivalent to Torah scholars and deserved the same level of respect and care.

False Teachers and Prophets

However, hospitality could be abused. Religion in general "seems to attract charlatans, then as now: people who want to make a living out of the generosity of God and his people."[8] There was a danger that the instructions regarding generous charity in Didache 1 and 4 could be taken advantage of. False teachers and prophets traveled around preying upon the hospitality of early believers, making a living from false pretenses. The role of the itinerant emissary and prophet "was easily copied by charlatans and hucksters, and the fakes who could be difficult to sniff out, especially for a new initiate who might be especially susceptible to the wiles of

---

5   Thomas O'Loughlin, *The Didache: A Window on the Earliest Christians* (Grand Rapids, MI: Baker, 2010), 108.
6   Note the idealized portrayal of hospitality in the Pseudo-Clementine writings, where Peter visits a town with his entourage and the town is saddened that there are more hosts than there are guests (Pseudo-Clementine Homilies 8.1–2; Pseudo-Clementine Recognitions 4.1–2).
7   Leviticus 19:32; b.*Kiddushin* 32b.
8   O'Loughlin, *The Didache*, 115.

a con man."[9] Even within one's own community, self-appointed false teachers and prophets could rise up, seeking financial support and leading the believers astray.

In the New Testament Simon Magus offered Peter and John money in the hopes that he, too, could perform miracles.[10] The apostles speak against such "peddlers of God's word" and "false prophets" who "will secretly bring in destructive heresies."[11] Later church writings refer to this kind of self-aggrandizing prophecy as the sin of Simony.

Pseudo-Clementine literature also warns against charlatans who attempt to earn a living through false teaching.[12] New believers needed to be careful about listening to self-proclaimed teachers who were either delusional or intentionally deceitful. They were to be on guard against those seeking to take advantage of them.

It appears that believers in Messiah early on had a reputation for being duped by swindlers and con-men. The second-century Greek writer Lucian of Samosata tells of a false teacher named Peregrinus Proteus who lived an opulent lifestyle among believers for some time:

> [Proteus] now an adroit, unscrupulous fellow, who has seen the world, has only to get among these simple souls, and his fortune is pretty soon made; he plays with them ... The Christians were meat and drink to him; under their protection he lacked nothing, and this luxurious state of things went on for some time. (Lucian, *The Passing of Peregrinus* 13, 16)

The fact that the Didache dedicates a whole chapter to these issues indicates that false teachers and prophets posed a real problem among the early disciples. The Didache establishes guidelines to ensure that counterfeits did not take advantage of the community, and that at same time, the community honored the true teachers, emissaries, and prophets:

> So the Didache teaches discernment—generosity chastened with wisdom—when it comes to the prophets and teachers ... The Didache does not abolish the role of the itinerant preacher. To the contrary, the amount of space used in setting forth the guidelines for dealing with

---

9   Tony Jones, *The Teaching of the Twelve: Believing & Practicing the Primitive Christianity of the Ancient Didache Community* (Brewster, MA: Paraclete, 2009), 107–108.
10 Acts 8:18–24.
11 2 Corinthians 2:17; Matthew 7:15, 24:11, 24; Mark 13:22; Luke 6:26; 1 John 4:1; 2 Peter 2:1.
12 Pseudo-Clementine, Letter on Virginity 1.10, 2.1.

them betrays just how important these wanderers were to the early church.[13]

THREE OFFICES OF THE COMMUNITY

The three types of offices mentioned in chapter 11—teachers, emissaries, and prophets—are the same three mentioned by the Apostle Paul: "God has appointed in the church first apostles, second prophets, third teachers" (1 Corinthians 12:28). Despite some overlap in the text between these categories, we will introduce each group separately.

TEACHERS

Didache 11.1–2 discusses those who hold the title of teacher: "Now receive whoever comes to teach you in all that has just been said." "Teachers" are mentioned in the book of Acts, and the Apostle Paul said that, along with that of emissary and prophet, the office of teacher was one of the appointed positions of God.[14] The Greek word *didaskalos* (διδάσκαλος) is equivalent to the Semitic title *rabbi* (רבי).[15] "The term *didaskalos* thus has a distinctively rabbinic character and is linked with the sage of early Judaism whose work lies within the sphere of the community."[16] Some have even suggested that there was "an early Jewish-Christian Pharisaic teaching office."[17]

"Teachers" were primarily responsible for instructing the community in the words of Scripture and concerning religious legal rulings. They were deserving of the community's "honor" (15.1–2), and they were to be remembered "day and night" because they spoke "the word of God" (4.1). Teachers, along with prophets and emissaries, were to be honored by being given the privilege of leading *Grace after Meals* (10.7) and being given the "first part" of the people's harvest, livestock,

---

13 Jones, *The Teaching of the Twelve*, 107–108.
14 E.g., Acts 13:1–2; 1 Corinthians 12:28.
15 See John 1:38: "They said to him, 'Rabbi [ῥαββί] (which means Teacher [διδάσκαλος]), where are you staying?'" In turn, everywhere in the Gospels where the Master is called "Teacher" (διδάσκαλος), the Hebrew word "Rabbi" lies underneath. E.g., Mark 10:17; Luke 18:18. Of the fifty-eight times the word διδάσκαλος appears in the New Testament, forty-eight are in the Gospels.
16 Huub van de Sandt and David Flusser, *The Didache: Its Jewish Sources and Its Place in Early Judaism and Christianity* (Minneapolis, MN: Fortress, 2002), 356.
17 Kurt Niederwimmer, *The Didache: Hermeneia—A Critical and Historical Commentary on the Bible* (Minneapolis, MN: Fortress, 1998), 190.

and possessions (13.1–7).[18] The Didache assigns teachers, emissaries, and prophets the same honor, privilege, and due that the Torah grants to the Aaronic priests (13.3). In turn, these "teachers" were found primarily living and functioning within the local communities as permanent residents.

Unproven itinerant teachers, on the other hand, like unproven traveling "emissaries" and "prophets," were to be limited to a stay of two days and were not permitted to ask for money. They were to be given only enough food for their journey when they left. The general warnings of 11.1–2 apply equally to all three offices.

Emissaries

The next group discussed (11.3–6) is the "emissary," commonly translated as "apostle": "Let every emissary who comes to you be received as the Lord" (11.4). The Greek term *apostolos* (ἀπόστολος) is related to the Hebrew term *shaliach* (שליח), meaning "sent one." *Shaliach* refers to a legal agent or representative that a man has dispatched on a mission to represent him and his interests. In Judaism *shlichim* (plural form, "sent ones," i.e., "apostles") did not occupy religious office but acted as agents of a sender.[19] The Talmud states, "A man's *shaliach* has the same legal authority as the man himself."[20] This concept is echoed, as we saw previously, in the words of our Master Yeshua: "Whoever receives you receives me, and whoever receives me receives him who sent me" (Matthew 10:40). A similar term is still used today in Chasidic Judaism, in which agents of a rebbe (rabbi) are called *shluchim*.

Emissaries were sent out with a specific mission to accomplish, such as relaying a legal decision or aiding in a community problem. Huub Van de Sandt and David Flusser provide some rabbinic background:

> The *shaliach* was sent around to the communities of the Diaspora as an envoy of the central authorities in Jerusalem. Authorized by the Sanhedrin or the *nasi* (נשיא), i.e., the patriarch, these distinguished emissaries preserved the connection between the motherland and the congregation outside of Israel. Their commission was multifaceted. They preached in public, exercised surveillance, solved halakic problems and conveyed circular letters. An additional important task

---

18   Cf. Didache 15.2.
19   D. Thomas Lancaster, *Torah Club: Chronicles of the Messiah* (6 vols.; Marshfield, MO: First Fruits of Zion, 2014), 2:358.
20   m.*Brachot* 5:5. E.g., b.*Nedarim* 72b.

was the collection of tributes for the patriarch, who used the funds to maintain courts, the academics, and needy students ... [Even after the destruction of the Temple] the *shlichim*, the emissaries, would gather these monies from the scattered Jewish communities and transport them to Jerusalem.[21]

Jonathan Draper adds,

> The instructions would serve those on a specific embassy, with letters of recommendation from the community which sent them. The important feature of the Jewish *shlichim* is that they were appointed for a specific task, and only for the duration of that task did they have their plenary function. They were not missionaries (in our modern sense of religious evangelism) nor necessarily even teachers, although rabbis seem usually to have been chosen for religious delegations. Hospitality toward such prestigious sages (*talmid hachamim*) was enjoined as especially meritorious (b.*Brachot* 10b; b.*Sanhedrin* 92a). They were not regular officers of the community, yet they must have been a common feature of life in the Jewish Diaspora, keeping communities in touch with one another and with the center of Jewish religious life in Palestine.[22]

The activities of the Apostle Paul reflect that of an emissary. He was sent out by James and the Jerusalem Council to go to communities and spread the good news of the coming kingdom and also to deliver the decision of the Jerusalem Council in Acts 15.[23] He was sent out to teach, answer questions, and bring correction to legal issues. Additionally, Paul collected monies for the Jerusalem community.[24] He was never a permanent member of the communities he visited.

However, in the New Testament and in the Didache, the term "emissary" is used specifically to refer to the apostles who had been directly commissioned by the Master to testify to his resurrection. In the New Testament, to qualify as an apostle, one needed to be an eyewitness of the risen Messiah and commissioned by him as an agent to testify to his resurrection.[25]

---

21 Van de Sandt and Flusser, *The Didache*, 353.
22 Jonathan A. Draper, "Weber, Theissen and 'Wandering Charismatics' in the Didache," *Journal of Early Christian Studies* 6, no. 4 (Winter 1998): 567.
23 Acts 15:22.
24 Romans 15:25–28; 1 Corinthians 16:1–4; 2 Corinthians 8–9; Galatians 2:10.
25 Acts 10:40–41.

This included the original twelve disciples minus Judas Iscariot, who was replaced by Matthias in Acts 1; the seventy-two, who were also appointed and sent out by the Master (Luke 10:1); the Apostle Paul, who was directly commissioned by Yeshua in Acts 9; and the "more than five hundred brothers" to whom the Master appeared after his resurrection (1 Corinthians 15:6). Also included were women apostles such as Mary Magdalene and the other Mary (mother of James the Less), to whom Yeshua first appeared after his resurrection.[26]

There is quite a bit of overlap between the offices of emissary and prophet. While not all the apostles operated in the gift of prophecy, each of them at the very least operated in the authority of a prophet, that is, they spoke on behalf of the Lord. Both emissaries and prophets were limited to a two-day visit within a community, and many of the same tests that were applied to a prophet would also have been applied to the emissary. In turn, if the emissary was proven to be true and desired to become a permanent resident in the community, he, like the prophet and teacher, was "entitled to his sustenance" (13.1–2) and would be given the "first part" gifts of chapter 13.

At the time the Didache was written, some of the apostles were still alive and operating within the Messianic community, but false emissaries were probably more common than were visits from authentic apostles. When the Didache was reworked in the Apostolic Constitutions, the office of the emissary was completely removed from the discussion, because by that time (fourth century) the generation of the apostles had long since died.

Prophets

The third category the Didache addresses in chapter 11 is the "prophet": "Do not put to the test nor pass judgment on any prophet who speaks in the Spirit" (11.7). In Hebrew a prophet is called a *navi* (נביא). This title does not necessarily connote one who predicts the future. Rather, the term refers to someone commissioned by God to speak on his behalf through the ecstatic inspiration of the Holy Spirit. In the Hebrew Scriptures we find both male and female prophets, and in the New Testament the office of prophet was held by both men and women in fulfillment

---

26 Matthew 28:1, 9–10; Mark 16:9; Romans 16:6.

of the Prophet Joel's words about the Messianic Era: "Your sons and daughters shall prophesy" (Joel 2:28).[27]

The sages taught that the office of the biblical prophet ceased when the last of the prophets of the Hebrew Scriptures passed away: "After the later prophets Haggai, Zechariah, and Malachi had died, the Holy Spirit departed from Israel, but they still availed themselves of the voice of God [*bat kol*, בת קול]" (b.*Yoma* 9b).[28] Prophecy would not return until the arrival of the Messianic Kingdom:

> Veritable prophecy was dead and no one could claim the title "prophet" until God was to fully realize the kingdom. Although some rabbis were held to be worthy of the title "prophet," the iniquity of the present age made it impossible for even the holiest of men, such as Hillel the Elder and Rabbi Akiva, to be called so.[29]

However, with the arrival of Messiah Yeshua, the Messianic Age was at hand. The events in Acts 2 confirmed that believers in Messiah could receive a pledge of the great outpouring of the Holy Spirit that was to characterize the Messianic Kingdom.[30] The book of Acts identifies Judas, Silas, and Agabus as "prophets."[31] Paul speaks of the office of prophet in his letters and uses the doublet "holy apostles and prophets," indicating that these two positions were often combined.[32]

In the Didache speaking "in the Spirit" means that the prophet was established and spoke words that "inspired" and were "inspiring."[33] The prophet functioned much like the teacher, sharing the Word of God and speaking forth truth, but additionally he performed miracles and operated more heavily under the ecstatic inspiration of the Spirit.[34] Although the offices of emissary and prophet are closely connected, not every prophet was an emissary, that is, not every prophet was an eyewitness of the risen Messiah directly commissioned by the Master to testify of

---

27 For women prophets, see Exodus 15:20; Judges 4:4; 2 Kings 22:14; 2 Chronicles 34:22; Nehemiah 6:14; Isaiah 8:3; Luke 2:36; Acts 21:8–9.
28 Cf. "Until then, the prophets prophesied by means of the Holy Spirit. From then on, give ear and listen to the words of the sages" (*Seder Olam Rabbah* 30). Also 1 Maccabees 4:46, 9:27, 14:41.
29 Van de Sandt and Flusser, *The Didache*, 357.
30 For more on this, see *Gifts of the Spirit* (Marshfield, MO: First Fruits of Zion, 2013).
31 Acts 15:32, 21:10.
32 Ephesians 3:5. Cf. 1 Corinthians 12:12, 14:29–32; Ephesians 4:11.
33 Aaron Milavec, *The Didache: Faith, Hope, & Life of the Earliest Christian Communities, 50–70 C.E.* (New York, NY: Newman, 2003), 458.
34 The Martydom and Ascension of Isaiah describes a prophetic school similar to what the Didache seems to have in mind here.

his resurrection. The Didache seems to distinguish between two types of prophets: the one who is proven and the one who is unproven.

The proven and established prophet was "not put to the test" (11.7). Like teachers and emissaries, he was to be shown honor and respect and was entitled to the provisions of chapter 13.[35] These true prophets would have been tried and tested thoroughly in accordance with the Didache, and many were permanent residents in the community.

It was a different story for the unproven prophets. Self-proclaimed and unproven prophets might rise up within the local communities. They were not to be accepted outright as one "who speaks in the Spirit" (1.7). They had to prove the veracity of the divine inspiration they claimed to wield. More often unproven prophets visited the congregation from the outside as itinerant seers and teachers. In the first few centuries CE, many Messianic prophets traveled from town to town, sharing and teaching the way of the Master through the influence of the Holy Spirit, much in the same way the traveling *maggid* (מגיד) of the Chasidic movement went around teaching, telling inspirational stories, and performing wonders. Both Jewish and Hellenistic sources attest "that the mobility of preachers was not unusual or exceptional in the first and second century CE."[36] This was the lifestyle of Yeshua and his disciples as well; they traveled from village to village in the land of Israel as itinerant teachers and miracle workers.[37]

The prophets of which the Didache warns were those who had not been verified. The prophetic office of these alleged prophets needed to be validated. Certain regulations had to be put in place to ensure that the self-proclaimed charlatans were not merely trying to profit from the gospel. For instance, they were not to ask for charity or provision for themselves. If a prophet was proven "true," however, he would then receive the privileges and dues outlined in chapter 13 (food, money, and clothing). If he was not already a permanent resident in the community and he desired to settle down, he, like the emissary, would be "entitled to his sustenance" (13.1) as an office holder within the community.

Interestingly enough, outside of the New Testament, the Didache, and Shepherd of Hermas the office of the prophet is not mentioned in congregational instructional

---

35 Cf. Didache 15.2.
36 Van de Sandt and Flusser, *The Didache*, 340.
37 See David Bivin, "The Traveling Teacher," *Jerusalem Perspective* 10 (July 1988): 1, 4. Cf. "Yeshua said: Become passers-by" (Gospel of Thomas 42).

type works.[38] The Apostolic Constitutions completely omits content similar to Didache 11.7–12 and only offhandedly mentions prophets: "Every true prophet or teacher that comes to you is entitled to his sustenance, as being a worker in the word of righteousness" (7.28). It appears that only a short while after the New Testament Era, as was the case with the emissary, the office of the prophet within the believing community all but disappeared.

Practical Application

Modern-day congregations and communities exist in a much different environment than did the communities depicted in the Didache, but many of the principles from chapter 11 apply to our current situation. Let's briefly examine the three offices—teacher, emissary, and prophet—in today's context:

- **Teachers.** Teachers should be honored, respected, and received with grace and recompense. Their needs should be provided for as they labor within the community. Their teachings, however, must remain consistent with the Torah and with the teachings of our Master. If they do not, a teacher should not be heeded or obeyed.

- **Emissaries.** The office of emissary no longer exists today because this role specifically refers to the apostles who were eyewitnesses of the resurrected Messiah and directly commissioned by the Master to testify of his resurrection. Anyone today claiming to operate in the office of an apostle has misunderstood the New Testament definition of an emissary.

- **Prophets.** As with the emissary, the office of prophet seems to have disappeared early on in the Messianic community. That is not to say that the spiritual gift of prophecy does not function today, but those who truly speak in the Spirit are few and far between. Modern-day prophets within the Messianic community should be tested and examined in line with the Didache's instructions. If they are proven true, they should be honored and respected; if they are found false, they should be dismissed.

---

38 E.g., Shepherd of Hermas, Mandate 11 (44). See William Varner, *The Way of the Didache: The First Christian Handbook* (New York, NY: University Press of America, 2007), 85–86. Note that the *Martyrdom of Polycarp* does mention the "apostolic and prophetic teacher" (16.2).

In general, the Didache calls on believers to exercise discernment and a healthy dose of skepticism. We need to be diligent students of the Word, knowing what lines up with the Torah and what does not. However, everything must be done with a spirit of grace and humility. We must render respect where it is due and, if necessary, rebuke where it is due. Every rebuke should be done with love and in proper order.

Commentary

> ❖ **Now receive whoever comes to teach you in all that has just been said.** (DIDACHE 11.1)

The Didache opens chapter 11 with an exhortation to honor and receive teachers of the truth. This continues on the theme of 4.1: "Remember night and day the teacher who speaks the word of God to you."

This opening statement of chapter 11 is reminiscent of our Master Yeshua's words, as we noted in the overview:

> Whoever receives you receives me, and whoever receives me receives him who sent me. The one who receives a prophet because he is a prophet will receive a prophet's reward, and the one who receives a righteous person because he is a righteous person will receive a righteous person's reward. (Matthew 10:40–41)[39]

> Truly, truly, I say to you, whoever receives the one I send receives me, and whoever receives me receives the one who sent me. (John 13:20)

By referencing language similar to that of Yeshua in several places in chapter 11, the Didache is attempting to expound on Yeshua's words and offer guidelines to ensure that false teachers, emissaries, and prophets were exposed. While verses 1–2 address the office of teacher, the principles apply equally to emissaries and prophets as well.

Teachers are one of the central pillars of Torah life. They speak "the word of God" and deserve to be received "as the Lord" (4.1). In Judaism the study of the Scriptures is considered the highest form of worship: "The more Torah the more life, the more schooling the more wisdom ... he has acquired words of the Torah, he has attained life in the world to come" (m.*Avot* 2:7).[40] The teachers brought this life to the believing community, and in turn they were worthy of honor.

To "receive" a teacher implied both accepting his teaching and providing for his needs.[41] Didache 13 requires the community to provide for the teacher's "suste-

---

[39] Cf. Mark 6:11; Luke 10:8; 2 Corinthians 7:15; Colossians 4:10.
[40] Cf. "And the study of Torah is equivalent to them all" (m.*Pe'ah* 1:1).
[41] Cf. Matthew 10:14.

[11.1]
Now receive whoever comes to teach you in all that has just been said.

nance," and along with the prophets and emissaries, teachers were to be given the "first part" of one's harvest, livestock, and possessions. This rule may be derived from the Master's rule: "The laborer deserves his food" (Matthew 10:10).[42] The principle also reflects broader Judaism, which teaches that we are to honor Torah scholars and take care of their needs: "Let your house be a meeting place for the sages, cleave to the dust of their feet, and drink thirstily their words" (m.*Avot* 1:4).

"All that has just been said" refers to all that has been taught in the Didache up to this point. This includes the ethical instructions and the teachings on immersion, prayer, fasting, and mealtime blessings. Not that the teacher needed to limit his teachings to those topics covered in chapters 1–10, but rather those teachings were to form the standard by which every teaching must be measured.

> *But if this teacher, having turned aside, were to teach a different kind of teaching to undermine this teaching, do not obey him.* (DIDACHE 11.2)

Didache 11.2 begins with the phrase "But if" (*ean de*, ἐὰν δὲ), which seems to betray an underlying Semitism. This phrase and its parallel, *pas ho* ("everyone who," πᾶς ὁ), is used throughout chapter 11:

> The short instruction concerning apostles in 11:3–6 bears the same casuistic structure and tone as the instructions in Didache 6, 7, 9–10: first the statement of the general principle in the imperative, then particular specifications and qualifications of the general principle, followed by a statement of the limit of what is permissible. The casuistic style is marked by expressions reflecting underlying semitisms: [*pas, ean de*], as well as a negative formulation.[43]

So in a very rabbinic manner the Didache has moved from a general rule about accepting teachers (11:1) to an specific exception to that rule if they are false teachers (11:2). Although teachers were to be honored and respected, the community was not to turn a blind eye to suspicious doctrine. Not every teacher conveys the truth, and

---

42 Cf. 1 Corinthians 9:4, 7–14; 1 Timothy 5:18.
43 Draper, "Weber, Theissen and 'Wandering Charismatics' in the Didache," 565. Gottfried Schille ["Das Recht der Propheten und Apostel—Gemeinderechtliche Beobachtungen zu Didache Kapitel 11–13," in *Theologische Versuche* 1 (ed. P. Wätzel and Gottfried Schille; Berlin, Germany: Evangelische Verlagsanstalt, 1966), 89–90] sees these reflecting the Semitic כל and כי אם.

some even seek deliberately to lead the flock astray. In the spirit of Deuteronomy 13, the believers were to test and measure a teacher's words against the Torah. These instructions are a continuation of what is taught in the Two Ways section:

> Do not forsake the commandments of the Lord, but keep what you have received, neither adding to nor subtracting from it. (4.13)

> See that no one leads you astray from this way of teaching, because he does not teach you according to God. (6.1)

[11.2]
But if this teacher, having turned aside, were to teach a different kind of teaching to undermine this teaching, do not obey him.

The language of "turned aside" is reminiscent of "You shall not turn aside to the right hand or to the left. You shall walk in all the way that the LORD your God has commanded you" (Deuteronomy 5:32–33). It continues in the imagery of the "Way of Life" as the straight and narrow path to righteousness.[44] The false teacher leads people away from the commandments of God and onto the "Way of Death."

The Didache addresses those who taught that the Torah had been abolished. "Undermine" is the Greek word *kataluo* (καταλύω), which is used as "a technical reference to undermining Torah."[45] It is similar to the Mishnaic Hebrew term *batel* (בטל), which often has the connotation of "abolishing commandments": "Whoever fulfills the Torah in poverty, will fulfill it later on in wealth; and whoever abolishes [*batel*] the Torah in wealth, will abolish it later in poverty" (m.*Avot* 4:9); "If, however, they ruled that a part [of a commandment] was to be annulled [*batel*] and a part retained, they are liable" (m.*Horayot* 1:3).[46] To "undermine this teaching" of the Didache is to abolish the Torah and the commandments. The Didache harkens back to the Master's words: "Do not think that I have come to abolish the Law or the Prophets; I have not come to abolish them but to fulfill them" (Matthew 5:17).

If the community encountered such a teacher, they should not "obey him." The Greek here literally says that one should not "listen to him," a Hebraism for obedience. The Hebrew word *shma* (שמע) can mean both "to listen" and "to obey."[47] If a teacher taught false doctrine, one should neither listen to nor obey him. This echoes the injunction about a false prophet in Deuteronomy 13:3: "You shall not listen to [literally 'obey'] the words of that prophet." The Apostolic Constitutions

---

44 The Georgian version of the Didache further connects "turning aside" with a departure from the teachings of the Didache itself by rendering this "turning aside from all of this."
45 Jonathan A. Draper, "Torah and Troublesome Apostles in the Didache Community," *Novum Testamentum* 33, no. 4 (October 1991): 357. Cf. 2 Maccabees 2:22; Josephus, *Antiquities of the Jews* 16:35/ii.4; Philo, *On the Special Laws* 3.182.
46 Cf. y.*Ta'anit* 2:12.
47 *Akouo* (ἀκούω) is directly related to *shma* in the Septuagint.

[11.2] *But if this teacher, having turned aside, were to teach a different kind of teaching to undermine this teaching, do not obey him.* adds, "And even when a false teacher comes, you shall provide for his needs, but do not receive his error. Nor indeed may you pray together with him, lest you be defiled as he is."[48] On the other hand, if the teacher was proven true, it was required that he be listened to and obeyed. The Master told his emissaries that in places where people would "not listen to [them]," they should "shake off the dust" from their feet and leave.[49]

> *However, if his teaching serves to promote righteousness and knowledge of the Lord, receive him as the Lord.*
> (DIDACHE 11.2)

If the teaching of the visiting teacher supported and upheld the Torah, he should be received as the Lord.[50] Like the first part of 11.2 this section also offers another specific rule to the general principle of 11.1 to receive teachers.[51] "Lord" (*kurios*, κύριος) in its present context refers to Yeshua.[52] The language echoes Didache 4.1, "Esteem him as the Lord," as well as the saying of Yeshua, "Truly, truly, I say to you, whoever receives the one I send receives me, and whoever receives me receives the one who sent me" (John 13:20).[53] The true teacher should be received as a messenger of the Master. The Apostolic Constitutions states:

> Let anyone who comes to you first be scrutinized, and then be received: for you will know if he is true, because you will be able to discern between right and wrong, and to distinguish false teachers from true teachers. (Apostolic Constitutions 7.28)

---

48 Apostolic Constitutions 7.28.
49 Mark 6:11.
50 The Georgian version of the Didache reads, "But if it serves for a better understanding of his righteousness, and better knowledge of the Lord, receive him as the Lord."
51 The Greek behind "however" is *de* ("but," δὲ).
52 Wim J.C. Weren, "The 'Ideal Community' according to Matthew, James, and the Didache," in *Matthew, James, and Didache: Three Related Documents in Their Jewish and Christian Settings* (ed. Huub van de Sandt and Jürgen K. Zangenberg; Atlanta, GA: Society of Biblical Literature, 2008), 186, n. 14. Contrary to this, Milavec argues that every instance of "Lord" in the Didache refers to God. See Aaron Milavec, "The Distress Signals of Didache Research," in *The Didache: A Missing Piece of the Puzzle in Early Jewish Christianity* (eds. Jonathan A. Draper and Clayton N. Jefford; Atlanta, GA: Society of Biblical Literature, 2015), 70–72.
53 Cf. Matthew 10:40–41.

Just as "undermine" is related to the concept of abolishing the Torah, "to promote" (*prostithemi*, προστίθημι) is related to upholding or fulfilling the Torah. Hence, this once again draws us back to the Master's words: "Do not think that I have come to abolish the Law or the Prophets; I have not come to abolish them but to fulfill them" (Matthew 5:17). "Righteousness" recalls Yeshua's continued teaching: "I tell you, unless your righteousness exceeds that of the scribes and Pharisees, you will never enter the kingdom of heaven" (Matthew 5:20). The true teacher upholds the Torah and the commandments.

[11.2]
However, if his teaching serves to promote righteousness and knowledge of the Lord, receive him as the Lord.

The "righteousness and knowledge of the Lord" refers to the Torah, as interpreted in light of the teachings of the Master.[54] Considering Matthew 5:20, "righteousness" should be interpreted here in an ethical sense to mean following the Torah and keeping the commandments.[55] This indicates "that teachers should be received only if their teaching reaffirms the Jewish Torah and promotes the 'Christian halachah.'"[56]

"Knowledge" was mentioned in 9.3 and 10.2 as being the divine knowledge of God as revealed through Yeshua.[57] The teacher's instruction must line up with Torah and with the teachings of the Master, upholding the commandments and divine wisdom.

The Didache has stern warning for "teachers" who would lead disciples astray. The Apostle John echoes these sentiments: "If anyone comes to you and does not bring this teaching, do not receive him into your house or give him any greeting, for whoever greets him takes part in his wicked works" (2 John 1:10–11).

> ⁌ *Concerning the emissaries and prophets, according to the ordinance of the good news, this is what you should do.* (DIDACHE 11.3)

Didache 11.3 begins a section on "emissaries and prophets." The wording here is identical to the beginning of 7.1 and 9.1, "Concerning immersion" and "Concerning

---

54 Much as we see in Matthew 5:21–47.
55 Draper, "Torah and Troublesome Apostles in the Didache Community," 358.
56 Van de Sandt and Flusser, *The Didache*, 333.
57 Even though in the Septuagint *gnosis* (γνῶσις) corresponds to *yada* ("know," ידע), in Hebrew the mystical Jewish term *da'at* seems to better express the sense of knowledge that is expressed in the Didache.

[11.3]
Concerning the emissaries and prophets, according to the ordinance of the good news, this is what you should do.

the giving of thanks," and is a formula to introduce a new section of halachic instruction.[58]

Although 11.3–6 focuses primarily on emissaries and 11.7–12 on prophets, some of the instructions in both sections can be applied to both offices. The distinction between the two is not always clear-cut. Aaron Milavec notes that there is no definite article in front of "prophets" and suggests therefore that the Greek could be rendered "apostle-prophets," which would mean that when the Didache speaks about emissaries and prophets, it is referring to one and the same office.[59] This is further supported in 11.5, in which a visiting emissary who stays in a community three days is deemed a "false prophet." Even the instructions of Yeshua conflate the two offices and apply the same standards to both.[60] While overlap and even confusion do at times appear between the roles of emissary and prophet, for simplicity's sake we will treat them as two separate offices.

"Ordinance" (*dogma*, δόγμα) is at times used in the New Testament to refer to Jewish or apostolic halachah.[61] It corresponds in the Septuagint to *dat* (דת), a term that in rabbinic literature usually refers to Jewish custom and Torah law (*dat Mosheh*). (*Dat* is the root of the Modern Hebrew word *dati* (דתי), which means "religious.") The phrase "according to the ordinance of the good news" means "according to the halachah of the Master," that is, according to Yeshua's instructions about receiving one sent in his name:[62]

> Whoever receives you receives me ... The one who receives a prophet because he is a prophet ... the one who receives a righteous person because he is a righteous person .... and whoever gives one of these

---

58 The equivalent Hebrew word for "concerning" (*peri*, περὶ) in this context could be *al* (על), e.g., על זה נאמר, עליו. See Draper, "Weber, Theissen and 'Wandering Charismatics' in the Didache," 563, n. 109. Additionally, this corresponds to the Hebrew *al* (על), which we find in blessing formulas for commandments: "Blessed are you, HaShem our God, King of the universe, who commands us concerning ..." Also, "A Hebrew parallel to this formation has come to light in the halakic letter from Qumran (we-'al ..., 4QMMT, *passim*)" (Peter J. Tomson, *'If This Be from Heaven ...' Jesus and the New Testament Authors in Their Relationship to Judaism* [Sheffield, England: Sheffield Academic Press, 2001], 387).
59 Milavec, *The Didache: Faith, Hope, & Life of the Earliest Christian Communities, 50–70 C.E.*, 438–441.
60 Additionally, the Master seems to equate the twelve emissaries with prophets: "Whoever receives you receives me, and whoever receives me receives him who sent me. The one who receives a prophet because he is a prophet will receive a prophet's reward, and the one who receives a righteous person because he is a righteous person will receive a righteous person's reward" (Matthew 10:40–41).
61 Ephesians 2:15. Cf. Acts 16:4; Colossians 2:20.
62 In the Didache "good news" does not refer to a specific written gospel but rather to the full oral living teachings of the Master, which included the message of the coming kingdom and practical instructions for how to prepare for and live in that kingdom. See comments on "good news" in Didache 8.2.

little ones even a cup of cold water because he is a disciple. (Matthew 10:40–42)

When the Didache states "according to the ordinance of the good news, this is what you should do," it is informing us that it will now expound upon this saying of the Master.

[11.3] *Concerning the emissaries and prophets, according to the ordinance of the good news, this is what you should do.*

⑅ *Let every emissary who comes to you be received as the Lord.* (DIDACHE 11.4)

The Didache now specifically addresses rulings for receiving emissaries. *Apostolos* ("emissary") is related to the Hebrew term *shaliach* (שליח), meaning "sent one." Like the teacher who promotes the "righteousness and knowledge of the Lord," the emissary is to be "received as the Lord." "Lord," again, in this context refers to the Master and is reminiscent of his words: "Truly, truly, I say to you, whoever receives the one I send receives me, and whoever receives me receives the one who sent me" (John 13:20).[63] The itinerant emissaries depended on the hospitality of the believing community, especially in the Diaspora, where access to kosher food and drink and other things untainted by idols might be difficult.

Legitimate "emissaries" carried letters with them to authenticate their mission and credentials. The emissary "would normally be unknown personally to the community, so that the letters would be crucial to prevent the exploitation of the community's resources by frauds."[64] Examples of this practice are found in the New Testament: "When I arrive, I will send those whom you accredit by letter to carry your gift to Jerusalem" (1 Corinthians 16:3); "We ought to support people like these, that we may be fellow workers for the truth. I have written something to the church" (3 John 1:8–9).[65]

In the New Testament and in the Didache, "emissary" specifically refers to the apostles who were directly commissioned by the Master to testify to his resurrection:

---

63   Cf. Matthew 10:40–41.
64   Jonathan A. Draper, "The Holy Vine of David Made Known to the Gentiles through God's Servant Jesus: 'Christian Judaism' in the Didache," in *Jewish Christianity Reconsidered: Rethinking Ancient Groups and Texts* (ed. Matt Jackson-McCabe; Minneapolis, MN: Fortress, 2007), 278.
65   Cf. Acts 9:1–2, 15:22–35; 2 Corinthians 3:1–3.

[11.4]
Let every emissary who comes to you be received as the Lord.

God raised him on the third day and made him to appear, not to all the people but to us who had been chosen by God as witnesses, who ate and drank with him after he rose from the dead. (Acts 10:40–41)

As explained above, to qualify as an apostle, one needed to be an eyewitness of the risen Messiah and commissioned by him as an agent to testify to his resurrection. The list of emissaries included not only the Twelve but "more than five hundred brothers" to whom the Master appeared after his resurrection (1 Corinthians 15:6) and a number of other specified individuals.[66] In turn, because the Apostolic Constitutions was not composed until the fourth century, long after these qualifications expired, the office of emissary is omitted.

◈ *He shall stay only one day, but if it is absolutely necessary, he may stay another day. However, if he stays three days, he is a false prophet.* (DIDACHE 11.5)

Although the believers were to provide for the traveling "emissary," limits were to be placed on how long he could stay in one community if he was yet unproven.[67] Our Master gave his disciples similar instructions for when they traveled: "Remain in the same house, eating and drinking what they provide, for the laborer deserves his wages. Do not go from house to house" (Luke 10:7).[68] This means that according to the Master, the wage that an emissary was entitled to receive was food and lodging, which is what the Didache proscribes. The community was to be hospitable, but at the same time, these emissaries were "subjected to examination" so as "to prevent charlatans from taking advantage of its hospitality."[69]

Logically, this injunction applied to the traveling prophet as well. If an apostle commissioned directly from the Master was allowed to stay only two days, how much more so the traveling prophet? Also, while not all emissaries were prophets,

---

66 Matthew 28:1, 9–10; Mark 16:9; Luke 10:1; Acts 1:12–26, 9:10–15; Romans 16:6.
67 The verse can be divided into three sections beginning with a general principle followed by two clarifying principles that are each introduced with the Semitism *ean de* ("but if," ἐὰν δὲ):

General Principle	He shall stay one day.
Clarifying Principle	But if absolutely necessary, he may stay another day.
Clarifying Principle	However, if he stays three days, he is a false prophet.

68 Cf. 1 Corinthians 9:14; 1 Timothy 5:17–18.
69 Van de Sandt and Flusser, *The Didache*, 334. Cf. 2 John 8–11; Sirach 11:29, 34.

they all operated in the authority of a prophet. We find a further connection between emissaries and prophets in that the emissary who stayed too long was called a "false prophet." Additionally, it seems that these regulations also applied to the traveling teacher.

[11.5]
He shall stay only one day, but if it is absolutely necessary, he may stay another day. However, if he stays three days, he is a false prophet.

The unproven emissary or prophet was permitted one day of hospitality and two at the most if absolutely necessary.⁷⁰ While the stay of an extra day might be required if the emissary's mission within the community needed more than one day, some have suggested that it provided for the possibility of his arriving on the eve of the Sabbath.⁷¹ Travel is forbidden on the Sabbath, and thus two nights' lodging and provision would have been essential. Flusser and Van de Sandt believe that this latter conclusion might be derived from rabbinic legal rulings on aiding poor travelers:

> One must not give the wandering poor man less than a loaf worth a *pondion* at a time when four *se'ahs* [of wheat cost] one *sela'*. If he spends the night [at a place], one must give him the cost of what he needs for a night. If he stays over the Sabbath he is given food for three meals. (m.*Pe'ah* 8:7)⁷²

If an unproven emissary's or prophet's stay went beyond two days, he was labeled a "false prophet." This rule indicates that by the time of the writing of the Didache, the believing communities had already suffered from false apostles and prophets who had overstayed their welcome and abused communal hospitality. Curiously, in Didache 12.2 we see that an ordinary traveler is allowed a stay of three days, not just two. It is possible that the stricter rule for supposed emissaries and prophets represents a later redaction and that at an earlier stage an across-the-board limit of two or three days was in place for all visitors.

The injunction, as we have discussed, limited the stay for an unknown and unproven emissary or prophet. If, however, the emissary or prophet was established and known to be legitimate, we can assume that he was permitted to stay much longer. For example, the Apostle Paul stayed much longer than two days in the communities he visited. He was in Corinth for an eighteen-month stint and in Ephesus

---

70   The version in *The Ethiopic Church Order* has, "Every apostle who comes to you shall not remain except one day or the next; and if need, the third also; and if he stays longer he is a false prophet" (G.W. Horner, *The Statutes of the Apostles or Canones Ecclesiastici* [London, England: Williams & Norgate, 1904], 193.8–11).
71   Draper, "The Holy Vine of David Made Known to the Gentiles through God's Servant Jesus," 278.
72   Van de Sandt and Flusser, *The Didache*, 355, n. 81.

[11.5]
He shall stay only one day, but if it is absolutely necessary, he may stay another day. However, if he stays three days, he is a false prophet.

for two years.⁷³ Paul had a reputation as an established and well-known apostle in the Messianic community. Additionally, when Paul stayed with communities, he worked to earn his keep, although he states that this practice of his was an exception to the rule of the congregation providing for an emissary.⁷⁴ If an emissary was validated and wished to settle within a community, he, like the prophet and teacher, had entitlement to the community support and provisions of chapter 13.

An emissary or a prophet who was suspect was called a "false prophet." "False prophet" (*navi sheker*, נביא שקר) was a familiar expression in Jewish vernacular and could be applied to a variety of charlatans and religious swindlers. The terms "false prophet" and "false apostle" appear frequently in both the New Testament and other early church works outside the Didache.⁷⁵

In the Torah the punishment for a false prophet was death:

> If a prophet or a dreamer of dreams arises among you and gives you a sign or a wonder, and the sign or wonder that he tells you comes to pass, and if he says, 'Let us go after other gods,' which you have not known … you shall not listen to the words of that prophet … But that prophet or that dreamer of dreams shall be put to death … So you shall purge the evil from your midst. (Deuteronomy 13:1–5)

The Didache's rule does not call for the false prophet's execution. (In fact, a false prophet was not technically considered as such according to the Torah's definition until he uttered a prophecy that contradicted the Torah or that failed to come to pass.) The Mishnah states that the penalty of death for the "false prophet" was not applicable outside Israel.⁷⁶ Instead, it can be assumed that, as with the false teacher of 11.2, one simply need "not obey him." This rule echoes Deuteronomy 13:3: "You shall not listen to [literally 'obey'] the words of that prophet." Additionally, the hospitality would have ceased, and the false emissary would have been asked to leave the community.

---

73   Acts 18:11, 19:10.
74   E.g., 1 Corinthians 9:4–15.
75   False prophet: Matthew 7:15, 24:11, 24; Mark 13:22; Luke 6:26; 2 Peter 2:1; 1 John 4:1; Pseudo-Clementine Homilies 16.21; Acts of Thomas 79; Shepherd of Hermas, Mandate 11 (43). False apostle: 2 Corinthians 11:13; Revelation 2:2, 20; Pseudo-Clementine Homilies 16.21; Acts of Thomas 79.
76   m.*Makkot* 11:5.

> *And when the emissary leaves, let him take nothing except bread to sustain him until he finds a new place to stay. But if he asks for money, he is a false prophet.* (DIDACHE 11.6)

Conditions are now established for the provision of an emissary or prophet when he leaves a community. He is to be provided with food for his journey and nothing else. "Bread" (*lechem*) is used in Hebrew to refer to food in general and in this context means enough food for his journey. If the emissary asked for payment, he was, as in 11.5, to be deemed a "false prophet."[77]

Similarly, rabbinic literature warns that one who says, "I will flatter this man that he may give me to eat; I will flatter this man that he may give me to drink; I will flatter this man that he may clothe me," exhibits "the conduct of a false prophet."[78] The sages warn against teaching Torah with the expectation of monetary gain:

> Do your teaching of Torah gratuitously and accept no remuneration for it; because the Omnipresent gave it gratuitously and one may not take a fee for the teaching of words of Torah, you will consequently destroy the moral constitution of the entire world. Say not, "I have no money," since all money is his, as it is stated, "The silver is mine, and the gold is mine, declares the LORD of hosts" [Haggai 2:8]. (*Derech Eretz Zuta* 4:3 [58b])

The Didache's instructions are in line with the Master's when he instructed his apostles: "Acquire no gold or silver or copper for your belts, no bag for your journey, or two tunics or sandals or a staff, for the laborer deserves his food" (Matthew 10:9–10);[79] and, "You received without paying; give without pay" (Matthew 10:8). In other words, the emissary or prophet was not to teach or testify for money; he was only to be provided with food on his journey.

Kurt Niederwimmer writes that "the special character of the apostolic itinerancy emerges once again here; it is a life based on willing abandonment of everything beyond what is really and absolutely necessary."[80] An emissary was to live out the petition of the Lord's Prayer: "Give us the bread we need today" (8.2).

---

77   But if he asks for money, he is a false prophet" is introduced by the Semitic *ei de* ("but if," εἰ δὲ). The line can be seen as a stand alone clarifying statement to address the prophet who goes against the injunction of the first part of the verse.
78   *Kallah Rabbati* 4:16 (53b).
79   Cf. Mark 6:8; Luke 9:3.
80   Niederwimmer, *The Didache*, 176.

He was to trust daily in the provision of his Father in heaven and to literally live out a foreshadowing of the abundant supernatural provision of the Messianic Era. As our Master Yeshua taught, "Blessed are you who are hungry now, for you shall be satisfied" (Luke 6:21).

> *Do not put to the test nor pass judgment on any prophet who speaks in the Spirit, for every sin will be forgiven, but this sin will not be forgiven.* (DIDACHE 11.7)

A new section now begins in which prophets are discussed, and it continues through the end of chapter 11. It begins by addressing instructions regarding an established prophet: a "prophet who speaks in the Spirit" refers to a proven-true prophet.[81]

The Didache teaches that a true prophet is not to be tested, a rule that is in line with rabbinic exegesis of the Torah. The sages interpreted "You shall not put the LORD your God to the test" (Deuteronomy 6:16) as a prohibition against demanding a sign from a known prophet. They reasoned that demanding a sign from a true prophet is, in essence, demanding a sign from God, and the Torah forbids us from so testing the LORD. Instead, a true prophet is to be obeyed as if God himself:

> I will raise up for them a prophet like you from among their brothers. And I will put my words in his mouth, and he shall speak to them all that I command him. And whoever will not listen to my words that he shall speak in my name, I myself will require it of him. (Deuteronomy 18:18–19)

Judaism interprets this commandment as the obligation to heed a known and established prophet. To disobey an established prophet or to question his authority was a grievous sin. In the same manner, the Apostle Paul writes, "Do not quench the Spirit. Do not despise prophecies" (1 Thessalonians 5:19–20). "The prophet

---

81   A slightly different version appears in *The Ethiopic Church Order*: "And every prophet who speaks in the spirit shall be proved, and he shall be examined that there may be no sin in him" (Horner, *The Statutes of the Apostles or Canones Ecclesiastici*, 193.12–14). The Georgian version of the Didache has "in the Holy Spirit" for "in the Spirit."

may not be tested or judged, since God's word is in his mouth and it would be blasphemy to contradict God's word."[82]

The warning against passing judgment on a verified prophet's words finds close parallel in the Master's words: "Therefore I tell you, every sin and blasphemy will be forgiven people, but the blasphemy against the Spirit will not be forgiven" (Matthew 12:31).[83] Both deal with blaspheming against God's Spirit by questioning the legitimacy of the manifestation. At points the Greek text here in Didache 11.7 is identical with the saying in Matthew. Some scholars suggest that both sayings "derive from common tradition."[84]

Because speaking "in the Spirit" is not defined here, we can assume that this concept was well known to the Didache community. Similar language is found in several places in the New Testament in 1 Corinthians and Revelation.[85] While some suggest that speaking "in the Spirit" refers to one being "in ecstasy, or in a highly exalted state of mind when it is the organ of the Holy Spirit,"[86] such may not be the case here. Milavec writes:

> Presumably, one is not dealing with glossolalia or with obscure poetic predictions of the future: forms of speech that would demand an interpreter. Nor should it be supposed that "speaking in the Spirit" necessarily implied some paranormal ecstatic state wherein voluntary control was surrendered to "the Holy Spirit" who spoke through the prophet. Rather, "speaking in the Spirit" (*en pneumati*) must carry with it the notion of speech that is "inspired" and "inspiring."[87]

[11.7]
Do not put to the test nor pass judgment on any prophet who speaks in the Spirit, for every sin will be forgiven, but this sin will not be forgiven.

---

82 Jonathan A. Draper, "Apostles, Teachers, and Evangelists: Stability and Movement of Functionaries in Matthew, James, and the Didache," in *Matthew, James, and Didache: Three Related Documents in Their Jewish and Christian Settings* (ed. Huub van de Sandt and Jurgen K. Zangenberg; Atlanta, GA: Society of Biblical Literature, 2008), 158.
83 Cf. Mark 3:28–30; Luke 12:10.
84 Draper, "Apostles, Teachers, and Evangelists," 159. "The Didache's wording agrees exactly with Matthew's redaction of Mark in Mt 12:31/Mk 3:28. (Matthew πᾶσα ἁμαρτία … ἀφεθήσεται; Mark πάντα ἀφεθήσεται … τὰ ἁμαρτήματα). The second half of the saying in the Didache has been modelled very precisely on the first half. Ἁμαρτία in the second half has no precise parallel in any synoptic version, though οὐκ ἀφεθήσεται agrees with Matthew again (Matthew 12:31b, 32b also Luke 12:10b)" (Christopher M. Tuckett, "Synoptic Tradition in the Didache," in *The Didache in Modern Research* [ed. Jonathan A. Draper; Leiden, The Netherlands: Brill, 1996], 105).
85 1 Corinthians 12:3, 14:2; Revelation 1:10, 4:2.
86 Philip Schaff, *The Oldest Church Manual Called the Teaching of the Twelve Apostles* (Edinburgh, Scotland: T&T Clark, 1885), 200.
87 Milavec, *The Didache: Faith, Hope, & Life of the Earliest Christian Communities, 50–70 C.E.*, 458.

> *Yet not everyone who speaks in the Spirit is a prophet; rather, only if he has the conduct of the Lord. Therefore, the false prophet and the true prophet should be recognized by this conduct.* (DIDACHE 11.8)

The Didache now addresses what to do with an unknown prophet, be he a traveler passing through or one who has risen up within the community. While a true prophet was never to be tested, an unproven prophet was to be tested by his conduct. The version in *The Ethiopic Church Order* has, "Everyone who speaks in the spirit is a prophet; if he lives the life of God, he is a true prophet. His life up until now reveals whether he is a false prophet or true prophet."[88] Prophets were not accepted outright but were to be judged in order to protect the community against frauds and swindlers: "Beloved, do not believe every spirit, but test the spirits to see whether they are from God, for many false prophets have gone out into the world" (1 John 4:1). In turn, "It is only the words of genuine prophets that cannot be criticized without sinning against the Holy Spirit."[89]

The New Testament frequently warns that false prophets will arise and that disciples should be on guard lest they fall under their spell. Yeshua warns, "Beware of false prophets, who come to you in sheep's clothing but inwardly are ravenous wolves" (Matthew 7:15). The Torah says that even if a prophet's words came to pass, he was deemed a false prophet if he led people away from observing the commandments.[90] In Deuteronomy 13, in which we find these warnings about prophets, the Lord reemphasizes, "You shall walk after the LORD your God and fear him and keep his commandments and obey his voice, and you shall serve him and hold fast to him" (Deuteronomy 13:4). The true prophet should lead the community to keep the commandments that he in turn should be keeping. If he did not, he was a false prophet. Deuteronomy tells us that God specifically placed false prophets within Israel to test their loyalty to Torah.[91]

---

88 Horner, *The Statutes of the Apostles or Canones Ecclesiastici*, 193.14–17. The Georgian version of the Didache has "in the Holy Spirit" for "in the Spirit" and "the false and the true prophet" for "every false prophet or true prophet."
89 Varner, *The Way of the Didache*, 85.
90 Deuteronomy 13:1–3.
91 Deuteronomy 13:3.

A prophet must have "the conduct of the Lord." "Lord" here refers to Yeshua.[92] He must walk in the righteousness of the Torah—the Way of Life as interpreted by the Master and the apostles. The Didache is drawing from the words of Yeshua:

> You will recognize [false prophets] by their fruits. Are grapes gathered from thornbushes, or figs from thistles? So, every healthy tree bears good fruit, but the diseased tree bears bad fruit. A healthy tree cannot bear bad fruit, nor can a diseased tree bear good fruit. Every tree that does not bear good fruit is cut down and thrown into the fire. Thus you will recognize them by their fruits. Not everyone who says to me, "Lord, Lord," will enter the kingdom of heaven, but the one who does the will of my Father who is in heaven. (Matthew 7:16–21)

[11.8] Yet not everyone who speaks in the Spirit is a prophet; rather, only if he has the conduct of the Lord. Therefore, the false prophet and the true prophet should be recognized by this conduct.

Not every disciple is endowed with gifts of the Spirit such as prophecy, but everyone should demonstrate the fruits of the Spirit: "Love, joy, peace, patience, kindness, goodness, faithfulness, gentleness, self-control" (Galatians 5:22–23). If every Spirit-filled believer was expected to display such characteristics, how much more so the divinely appointed prophet. We find similar injunctions toward prophets in the Shepherd of Hermas:

> Try the man who has the Divine Spirit by his life ... He who has the Divine Spirit proceeding from above is meek, and peaceable, and humble, and refrains from all iniquity and the vain desire of this world, and contents himself with fewer wants than those of other men. (Mandate 11.7–8 [43.7–8])[93]

These instructions probably applied on some level to an unproven emissary as well. Like the prophet, the unproven emissary was to be judged on the merit of his behavior—whether or not he measured up to "the conduct of the Lord."

---

92 See Weren, "The Ideal Community according to Matthew, James, and the Didache," 186, n. 14. As mentioned above, contrary to Weren's conclusion, Milavec argues that every instance of "Lord" in the Didache refers to God. See Milavec, "The Distress Signals of Didache Research," 70–72.
93 Cf. Shepherd of Hermas, Mandate 11.12 (43.12).

> ⸎ *Any prophet who orders in the Spirit that a dining table be set may not eat from it; otherwise, he is a false prophet.*
> (DIDACHE 11.9)

Didache 11, continuing its section on prophets, now has several verses (11.9–12) dealing with specific prophetic transgressions. The examples cited must have been issues common in the believing community and therefore needed to be addressed. Didache 11.9 begins by giving instructions about a prophet who asks for the setting of a table. This has been a difficult passage for scholars to understand, and different ones have proposed varying interpretations.

"Table" here refers to a full meal.[94] While some have suggested that this might refer to the liturgical communal meal of chapters 9 and 10, it seems probable that what is meant here is a normal meal. Understanding it as a normal meal is more consistent with the restriction that we see in 11.12 ("Whoever might say in the Spirit, 'Give me money,' or something else, do not obey him.").[95] Others have suggested that this might be a meal ordered for the poor and needy.[96] The prophet could order that a meal be prepared for the poor, but if he partook in such a meal, he betrayed ulterior motives, proving himself to be a false prophet who did not really speak in the Spirit.[97]

The basic premise of this rule was that a true prophet should not invoke divine authority for his own benefit. The principle applies beyond the preparation of meals. We find similar instructions regarding prophets in the Shepherd of Hermas:

> First, the man who seems to have the Spirit exalts himself, and wishes to have the first seat, and is bold, and impudent, and talkative, and lives in the midst of many luxuries and many other delusions, and takes rewards for his prophecy; and if he does not receive rewards, he does not prophesy. Can, then, the Divine Spirit take rewards and prophesy? It is not possible that the prophet of God should do this, but prophets of this character are possessed by an earthly spirit. (Mandate 11.12 [43.12])

---

94 Cf. Acts 6:2.
95 Varner, *The Way of the Didache*, 85.
96 Niederwimmer, *The Didache*, 179.
97 "Otherwise, he is a false prophet" is introduced by the Semitic *ei de* ("but if," εἰ δὲ). The line can be seen as a stand-alone clarifying statement to address the prophet who goes against the injunction of the first part of the verse.

A prophet was to come as Messiah did, "not to be served but to serve."[98] This rule indicates that even if a prophet's words sounded consistent with the Torah and even if his predictions seemed to come to pass, he was not to be received if he misused his spiritual authority for his own benefit.

> *If any prophet who teaches the truth does not do what he instructs, he is a false prophet.* (DIDACHE 11.10)

Here we find another overlap between teachers and prophets. All true teachers, whether they be prophets, emissaries, or anything else, are required to practice what they preach. This is the very criticism that the Master offered some of the Pharisees of his day: "The scribes and the Pharisees sit on Moses' seat, so do and observe whatever they tell you, but not the works they do. For they preach, but do not practice" (Matthew 23:2–3). If a prophet does not back up his words with his actions by observing his own proclamations, he is a false prophet.

In Jewish thought a teacher instructs others primarily through his actions: "This rule enforces the traditional rabbinic notion that a rabbi is a 'living Torah' and trains his disciples as much by what he does as by what he says."[99] Paul states, "Be imitators of me, as I am of Messiah" (1 Corinthians 11:1). A prophet could lead people astray with his actions as much as with his words. Our Master Yeshua speaks of the great sin of causing others to stumble through our actions: "Whoever causes one of these little ones who believe in me to sin, it would be better for him to have a great millstone fastened around his neck and to be drowned in the depth of the sea" (Matthew 18:6).[100]

---

98 Mark 10:45.
99 Milavec, *The Didache: Faith, Hope, & Life of the Earliest Christian Communities, 50–70 C.E.*, 464.
100 Note that "little one" (*katan*, קטן) does not refer to a child but to an unschooled, inexperienced disciple. See m.*Avot* 4:20; b.*Sotah* 22a.

> *Any prophet who, after having been proven to be true, acts in accordance with the earthly mystery of the assembly but does not instruct you to do what he himself does, shall not be liable to judgment before you, because his judgment remains with God, for all the ancient prophets did so as well.* (DIDACHE 11.11)

This is perhaps one of the most enigmatic verses of the entire Didache. The passage describes a proven prophet who "acts in accordance with earthly mysteries of the assembly," a cryptic reference to some type of ascetic practice or spiritual devotion. The context is now lost to us. The version in *The Ethiopic Church Order* completely removes the enigmatic phrase:

> Every prophet proved in truth, who acts in the assembly of men and acts unlawfully, shall not be judged by you for his judgment is from God; because thus did the ancient prophets.[101]

Scholars have struggled to decipher exactly to what "earthly mystery of the assembly" refers. The language is similar to that found in Kabalistic literature in which "every 'upper mystery' corresponds to a mystery in the 'lower' world, which is the 'cosmos.'"[102] We find this concept used in the book of Hebrews, in which the earthly Tabernacle is a copy of the one in the heavens.[103] This theme also appears throughout rabbinic literature.[104] Therefore, it could be that the Didache is refer-

---

[101] Horner, *The Statutes of the Apostles or Canones Ecclesiastici*, 193.22–25. The Coptic version supports this tradition: "having taught and testified to an orderly tradition in the church" (F. Stanley Jones and Paul A. Mirecki, "Considerations on the Coptic Papyrus of the Didache," in *The Didache in Context: Essays on Its Text, History & Transmission* [ed. Clayton N. Jefford; Leiden, The Netherlands: Brill, 1995], 55). Jones and Mirecki write: "The lexical alteration between μαρτύριον (testimony) and μυστήριον (mystery) could have been initiated as a copyist error in a previous Greek manuscript, but it is impossible to determine which came first. Perhaps the easier reading of "having taught and testified to an orderly tradition in the church" (as supported by the Coptic text) is to be preferred over the enigmatic and classically problematic Greek phrase "[acts in accordance with the earthly mystery of the assembly]" (68). The Georgian version of the Didache on the other hand preserves something closer to what we find in the Greek: "Earthly mystery of the assembly of Messiah."

[102] Charles Taylor, "The Teaching of the Twelve Apostles with Illustrations from the Talmud," in *Didache: The Unknown Teaching of the Twelve Apostles* (ed. Brent S. Walters; San Jose, CA: Anti-Nicene Archive, 1991), 185.

[103] Hebrews 9.

[104] E.g., b.*Ta'anit* 5a; b.*Chagigah* 12b; b.*Menachot* 110a; *Pesikta d'Rav Kahana* 1:7; *Tanchuma*, B'chukotai 65; *Exodus Rabbah* 35:6; *Numbers Rabbah* 12:12. Cf. Testament of Levi 5:1; Testament of Levi 3:4–6; 4 Ezra 8:52–54, 10:32–57; 3 Baruch 11:1, 11:8–12:5; 2 Baruch 4:1–6; 4 Baruch 5:35.

ring to a prophet who has had a specific mystical/esoteric teaching revealed to him but he is unwilling to share it with others. We see this type of behavior with the later chasidic rebbes and teachers.

However, the phrases "earthly mystery of the assembly" and "for all the ancient prophets did so as well" are connected. In them the Didache seems to be speaking about some of the strange ascetic-type practices and sign acts that the prophets of the Hebrew Scriptures performed at the command of the Lord. For example, Isaiah walked around naked and barefoot for three years. Ezekiel was instructed to cook his food over human excrement and to lie on his side for 390 days. Jeremiah was told to hide his loincloth under a rock.[105] These mysterious actions were earthly representations of heavenly truths. The prophets were never instructed to induce other people to imitate their actions.

Likewise, in the Didache "if the prophet did strange things, like the prophets of the Old Testament, it was for God to judge him, provided that he did not try to incite his hearers to behave likewise."[106] The strange behavior of the prophet was to be judged by God and not by man. "The prophets of today are treated like the prophets of old; the false prophets of today are treated like the false prophets of old."[107]

> [11.11] Any prophet who, after having been proven to be true, acts in accordance with the earthly mystery of the assembly but does not instruct you to do what he himself does, shall not be liable to judgment before you, because his judgment remains with God, for all the ancient prophets did so as well.

※ *But whoever might say in the Spirit, "Give me money," or something else, do not obey him. However, if he should say to give on behalf of others who are poor and in need, let no one judge him.* (DIDACHE 11.12)

Chapter 11 closes with a final behavioral statute for the prophet. A prophet who was supposedly speaking in the Spirit but asked for something for himself was

---

105 Isaiah 20:3; Ezekiel 4:12; Jeremiah 13:4. Cf. Ezekiel 4:4–5, 5:1–2; Jeremiah 27:2; Matthew 3:4.
106 Varner, *The Way of the Didache*, 85. Some think this points to actions that were otherwise forbidden but were permitted at certain times by certain people, e.g., "Or have you not read in the Law how on the Sabbath the priests in the temple profane the Sabbath and are guiltless?" (Matthew 12:5). "Dr. Taylor further illustrates the point by quoting Barnabas (Epistle chap, xii.) and Justin Martyr (Dial, c, Trypho), both of whom refer to the serpent of brass made by Moses for the healing of the people, and as a type of Christ, although he had himself delivered to Israel the commandment, 'Ye shall have neither molten nor graven image,' and 'Cursed be the man that maketh a molten or graven image.' Both Barnabas and Justin seem to refer to an oral Didache existing previous to any written treatise" (Canon Spence, *The Teaching of the Twelve Apostles* [London, England: James Nisbet and Co., 1885], 55).
107 Jonathan Reed, "The Hebrew Epic and the *Didache*," in *The Didache in Context: Essays on Its Text, History & Transmission* (ed. Clayton N. Jefford; New York, NY: Brill, 1995), 223.

[11.12]
But whoever might say in the Spirit "Give me money" or something else, do not obey him. However, if he should say to give on behalf of others who are poor and in need, let no one judge him.

deemed a false prophet. While the established prophet in a community received the benefits that the instructions in chapter 13 entitled him, a true prophet never used his prophetic office for personal benefit. [108]

The book of Micah chastises prophets who "practice divination for money; yet they lean on the LORD and say, 'Is not the LORD in the midst of us? No disaster shall come upon us'" (Micah 3:11). The Master stated to his disciples as they went out, "Heal the sick, raise the dead, cleanse lepers, cast out demons. You received without paying; give without pay" (Matthew 10:8). The office of the prophet was not to be cheapened and used for material gain, nor was the Holy Spirit.

As we saw in 11.2, the Greek of the phrase "do not obey him" literally reads "do not listen to him," a Hebraism that means both "to listen" and "to obey."[109] This echoes the injunction about a false prophet in Deuteronomy 13:3: "You shall not listen to [literally 'obey'] the words of that prophet."

While the prophet could not ask for money or other earthly rewards, he was permitted to take up a collection for those in need. But even in this the Didache provides protection for the community. Milavec writes: "On the one hand, the prophet's message was not to be challenged; on the other hand, the community was not to be mobilized. The result was left up to the freewill offering for those who wished to participate."[110] The community could not judge the prophet for asking for charity for the poor, but neither were they forced to give.[111]

---

108 "However, if he should say to give on behalf of others who are poor and in need, let no one judge him" is introduced by the Semitic *ean de*, ("but if," ἐὰν δὲ). The line can be seen as a stand-alone clarifying statement to address the prophet does not ask money for himself.
109 *Akouo* (ἀκούω) is directly related to *shma* (שמע) in the Septuagint.
110 Milavec, *The Didache: Faith, Hope, & Life of the Earliest Christian Communities, 50–70 C.E.*, 470.
111 The Georgian version of the Didache adds at the end, "For this is from the Lord God, and what has been done by him, he has ordained."

Chapter Twelve

DIDACHE 12

12.1 Let anyone who comes in the name of the Lord[1] be received, but then after you have scrutinized him, you will know if he is true, because you will be able to discern between right and wrong.

12.2 If the one who comes is a traveler, help him as much as you can, but he may not stay with you more than two, or if necessary three, days.

12.3 But if he wants to live among you and is a craftsman, let him work and eat.

12.4 If he does not have a skill, according to your discernment take into consideration how he will avoid living idly among you[2] as a follower of the Messiah.

12.5 But if he is not willing to do so, he is a Messiah peddler. Guard yourselves from people like this!

---

1 Psalm 118:26; Matthew 21:9, 23:39; Mark 11:9; Luke 13:35, 19:38; John 12:13.
2 2 Thessalonians 3:6–12.

Overview

Chapter 12 continues with instructions on hospitality for travelers. Unlike chapter 11, however, the travelers discussed in this chapter are not teachers, emissaries, or prophets but rather ordinary disciples. The Didache gives instructions for providing for these strangers' needs, including procedures for integrating them into community life if they so desired.

The order of the contents of chapters 11 and 12 appear to follow the order of the Master's words about receiving guests in Matthew 10. Chapter 11 speaks of receiving teachers, emissaries, and prophets, which corresponds to Yeshua's instructions on receiving prophets and righteous ones (Matthew 10:41). Chapter 12 speaks of receiving ordinary disciples, which corresponds to Yeshua's instructions on giving a cup of cold water to little ones because they are disciples (Matthew 10:42).

STRUCTURE

The chapter follows a pattern of moving from a general opening instruction to addressing four distinct cases:

12.1	General instructions for receiving a traveler
12.2	The traveler who is passing through
12.3	The traveler who desires to stay and has a trade
12.4	The traveler who desires to stay but does not have a trade
12.5	The traveler who desires to stay but not work

As in the previous chapter, Didache 12 expounds upon the Master's injunctions regarding receiving disciples:

> Whoever receives you receives me, and whoever receives me receives him who sent me. The one who receives a prophet because he is a prophet will receive a prophet's reward, and the one who receives a righteous person because he is a righteous person will receive a righteous person's reward. And whoever gives one of these little ones even

a cup of cold water because he is a disciple, truly, I say to you, he will by no means lose his reward. (Matthew 10:40–42)

Truly, truly, I say to you, whoever receives the one I send receives me, and whoever receives me receives the one who sent me. (John 13:20)

While Yeshua commands his disciples to be hospitable and charitable toward fellow disciples, this was to be done with discernment. In the current chapter the Didache establishes principles to ensure that the Master's injunction was not abused by charlatans and freeloaders.

Receiving Guests

As with all instruction in the Didache, the basis for its hospitality teachings are found within Jewish tradition. In Judaism the practice of hospitality is more than proper social etiquette but is elevated to the level of a divine mandate. In Hebrew it is called *hachnasat orechim* (הכנסת אורחים), which literally means "bringing in guests." The Talmud states, "Hospitality to wayfarers is greater than welcoming the presence of the *Shechinah*."[3] Abraham is considered the father of hospitality because of the kindness he showed to the three mysterious guests in Genesis 18.

The Master mentions three aspects of hospitality in Matthew 25:35: feeding the hungry, giving drink to the thirsty, and inviting in strangers. Likewise, the Apostle Paul exhorts us to "contribute to the needs of the saints and seek to show hospitality."[4] Hospitality is one of the key characteristics that Paul required for one to be an overseer as well as for a widow to be eligible to receive support.[5]

While the commandment to be hospitable certainly applies to friends and relatives, the true heart of hospitality is found in extending kindness to strangers. Several times throughout the Torah, God reminded the Israelites of their former slavery. He did this so that the Jewish people, after entering into their own land, would in turn treat strangers with care and compassion:

---

3   b.*Shabbat* 127a.
4   Romans 12:13.
5   1 Timothy 3:2, 5:10; Titus 1:8. Cf. Clement's letter to the Corinthians, in which he praises them for their hospitality (1 Clement 1.2).

> You shall treat the stranger who sojourns with you as the native among you, and you shall love him as yourself, for you were strangers in the land of Egypt: I am the LORD your God. (Leviticus 19:34)[6]

One way to love the stranger as oneself was to provide him with hospitality. Why does the commandment end with "I am the LORD your God"? Rashi comments, "I am your God and his God."[7] The stranger who had nowhere to go and no one to protect him was just as much one of God's children as the Israelites were. The people of Israel were to take him in as one of their own. The writer of the book of Hebrews repeats the command to entertain strangers:

> Do not neglect to show hospitality to strangers, for thereby some have entertained angels unawares. (Hebrews 13:2)

The Scriptures have harsh criticism for those who do not show hospitality. The rabbis taught that the worst sin of Sodom and Gomorrah was not their abhorrent sexual practice but rather their lack of hospitality:

> Behold, this was the guilt of your sister Sodom: she and her daughters had pride, excess of food, and prosperous ease, but did not aid the poor and needy. (Ezekiel 16:49)

Ramban taught that the repulsive behavior of the people of Sodom toward the visiting strangers was not a result of their sexual desires, but rather of their desire to keep out travelers so that they would not have to share their wealth.[8]

Therefore, the hospitality injunctions we find in the Didache are grounded in the Torah and Jewish tradition. Although the Didache imposes some restrictions and cautions, every stranger who came in the name of the Master, whether he was a teacher, prophet, or disciple, was to be welcomed and received with joy.

The Idle Messiah Peddlers

As was the case in chapter 11 regarding teachers, emissaries, and prophets, the open-handed hospitality of the community and their generous charity to strangers

---

6   Cf. Deuteronomy 24:17.
7   Rashi notes that the suffix meaning "your" is plural (*chem*, כם); therefore it refers to God being both the Israelite's and the stranger's God. See Rabbi Yisrael Isser Zvi Herczeg, *The Torah: With Rashi's Commentary Translated, Annotated and Elucidated, The Sapirstein Edition* (5 vols.; Brooklyn, NY: Mesorah, 2002), 3:248.
8   Rabbi A.J. Rosenberg, *Genesis: A New English* (3 vols.; New York, NY: Judaica, 1993), 1:225c–225d.

invited abuse. The Didache warns: "If he is not willing to do so [i.e., work], he is a Messiah peddler. Guard yourselves from people like this!" (12.5). There was and always will be those who abuse the kindness of others in an attempt to support their idle lifestyle. Thomas O'Loughlin laments,

> Everyone who has been involved in running a charity knows this dilemma in one way or another. Welcome and support is something that Christians should give; but at the same time no one should be allowed to abuse the generosity and sponge rather than work. Such people are not brothers who should be welcomed in Christ as coming in the Lord's name but people who are using the name of Christian for their own ends.[9]

This was especially true for the budding communities of new believers, who could easily be swayed and abused due to their innocence and childlike trust. Furthermore, Didache 1 and 4 are filled with admonishments for the believers to be generous and to give freely to those in need; to balance this, chapter 12 now stresses the importance of the disciples being on guard against falsehood even in their giving. It contains clear-cut guidelines so that hospitality would not be trampled upon and abused.

This was especially important in a community that depended on a collectivist model: "The community was based on all pulling together and sharing the task of welcome: so no individual was to live within a community and take advantage of it."[10] To have lazy members mooch off the hard work of others could ruin the delicate balance of the community and quickly deplete its resources. Everyone needed to pull his or her own weight.

Practical Application

The Didache's instructions on hospitality are pertinent for believers today. Open and generous hospitality should be the norm for Messianic communities. Whether it be hosting people for dinner or for lodging in our homes, we should receive anyone "who comes in the name of the Lord." It is important as well, however, that we use discernment in dealing with friends and strangers alike.

---

9 Thomas O'Loughlin, *The Didache: A Window on the Earliest Christians* (Grand Rapids, MI: Baker, 2010), 122.
10 Ibid.

It is also true today, as mentioned above regarding the early believers, that everyone in a community needs to do their share. While most people will not admit outright that they do not want to work to provide for themselves and their families, many do use excuses and sometimes even "spiritual" pretenses as to why they are unable to find and hold a job. In such cases the community should be on guard not to overburden its members by continually providing for the needs of a few individuals who are fully capable of doing so themselves. The instructions of the Didache provide a solid foundation on this matter to help us use discernment and common sense in our acts of charity and hospitality.

Commentary

◈ *Let anyone who comes in the name of the Lord be received, but then after you have scrutinized him, you will know if he is true, because you will be able to discern between right and wrong.* (DIDACHE 12.1)

Chapter 12 begins with the Greek phrase *pas ho* ("anyone who," πᾶς ὁ), a Semitism often used to introduce a general principle that is then followed by specifics and qualifications of that broad statement.[11] The general principle here is that every believer who visits the community is to be received with open arms and shown hospitality.[12] The traveler need not be a teacher, prophet, or emissary. In some ways the rules about extending hospitality toward the average visitor are more magnanimous than those regarding the visiting teacher. This spirit is very much in line with that of our Master Yeshua, who chastised those of his day who sought the honor of the elite and were kind only to those who had something to offer them.[13] James, the brother of the Master, writes, "My brothers, show no partiality as you hold the faith in our Lord [Yeshua the Messiah], the Lord of glory" (James 2:1).

"Lord" (*kurios*) here refers to Yeshua.[14] The phrase "who comes in the name of the Lord" (*haba b'shem Adonai*, הבא בשם ה') designates one who is a disciple of Yeshua; such a "guest is under the special protection of the Lord."[15] This phrase is first found in Psalm 118:26: "Blessed is he who comes in the name of the LORD!

---

11 Jonathan A. Draper, "Weber, Theissen and 'Wandering Charismatics' in the Didache," *Journal of Early Christian Studies* 6 no. 4 (Winter 1998): 565. Also, Gottfried Schille ("Das Recht der Propheten und Apostel—gemeinderechtliche Beobachtungen zu Didache Kapitel 11–13," *Theologische Versuche* I [eds. Paul Wätzel and Gottfried Schille; Berlin, Germany: Evangelische Verlagsanstalt, 1966], 89–90) sees these reflecting the Semitic כל and כי אם.
12 The Georgian version of the Didache adds, "The one who is coming among you should be accepted according to his worth."
13 E.g., Matthew 5:47, 23:6–7.
14 Wim J.C. Weren, "The 'Ideal Community' according to Matthew, James, and the Didache," in *Matthew, James, and Didache: Three Related Documents in Their Jewish and Christian Settings* (eds. Huub van de Sandt and Jürgen K. Zangenberg; Atlanta, GA: Society of Biblical Literature, 2008), 186, n. 14. Contrary to Weren's perspective, Aaron Milavec argues that every instance of "Lord" in the Didache refers to God. See Milavec, "The Distress Signals of Didache Research," in *The Didache: A Missing Piece of the Puzzle in Early Jewish Christianity* (eds. Jonathan A. Draper and Clayton N. Jefford; Atlanta, GA: Society of Biblical Literature, 2015), 70–72.
15 Kurt Niederwimmer, *The Didache: Hermeneia—A Critical and Historical Commentary on the Bible* (Minneapolis, MN: Fortress, 1998), 183.

[12.1]
Let anyone who comes in the name of the Lord be received, but then after you have scrutinized him, you will know if he is true, because you will be able to discern between right and wrong.

We bless you from the house of the LORD."[16] It is quoted by the pilgrims in Jerusalem who welcomed the Master as he entered the city before Passover and again by our Master Yeshua himself as he started toward Jerusalem: "I tell you, you will not see me again, until you say, 'Blessed is he who comes in the name of the Lord'" (Matthew 23:39).[17] This is also found at the end of the Apostolic Constitutions (7.6) version of the Didache's *Grace after Meals*.

But taking in travelers, as we have noted, was not to be done naïvely. Once a visitor had been shown hospitality, he was then to be "scrutinized." No doubt instructions to do this were given in light of past experiences in which freeloaders had taken advantage of the hospitality of the believing communities. It is of note that this testing was not the job of community officials but was to be done by those showing the hospitality. It was they who would have the closest contact with the stranger and be in the best position to pass judgment. Despite the Didache's emphasis on charity and hospitality, the believing communities were not to be pushovers who were easily abused. The Apostolic Constitutions actually places the emphasis on scrutiny over hospitality:

> Let anyone who comes to you first be scrutinized, and then be received: you will know if he is true, because you will be able to discern between right and wrong, and to distinguish false teachers from true teachers. (Apostolic Constitutions 7.28)[18]

The Apostle John urges his audience, "Beloved, do not believe every spirit, but test the spirits to see whether they are from God, for many false prophets have gone out into the world" (1 John 4:1).[19] The discernment process, as with the assessment of the teacher, prophet, or emissary, involved examining the actions of the stranger: "Thus you will recognize them by their fruits" (Matthew 7:20).

The phrase "discern between right and wrong" is literally translated "discern between right and left," a Semitic idiom for right and wrong. The version in *The Ethiopic Church Order* preserves the idiom even more closely with "the right hand and the left."[20] In wicked Nineveh, the Hebrew Scriptures relate, the people did

---

16 Cf. 1 Samuel 17:45.
17 Matthew 21:9, 23:39; Mark 11:9; Luke 13:35, 19:38; John 12:13.
18 The Georgian version of the Didache adds, "And you will know whether what he has in his heart is from the Lord."
19 Cf. 1 Clement 42.4.
20 G.W. Horner, *The Statutes of the Apostles or Canones Ecclesiastici* (London, England: Williams & Norgate, 1904), 194.1–2.

"not know their right hand from their left," and the Master similarly states, "He will place the sheep on his right, but the goats on the left."[21] The Didache indicates that the Spirit of God will grant discernment in hospitality: "The Lord will give you understanding in everything" (2 Timothy 2:7).

> ◆ *If the one who comes is a traveler, help him as much as you can, but he may not stay with you more than two, or if necessary three, days.* (DIDACHE 12.2)

In a rabbinic manner the Didache moves on from the general to specifics, going on from its general opening injunction to deal with four distinct cases.[22] The first is that of the traveler who is passing through. The regulations regarding such a visitor are similar to what we find in the Mishnah regarding the poor wanderer:

> One must not give the wandering poor man less than a loaf worth a *pondion* at a time when four *se'ahs* of wheat cost one *sela'*. If he spends the night at a place, one must give him the cost of what he needs for a night. If he stays over the Sabbath he is given food for three meals. (m.*Pe'ah* 8:7)

Unlike the itinerant teacher, emissary, or prophet, who was permitted to stay a maximum of two days, the regular traveler could stay three days if necessary. It is possible that, at an earlier stage in community development, an across-the-board rule allowing for two or three days of hospitality applied to all travelers but that abuses by itinerant wanderers claiming to be teachers, prophets, and emissaries motivated the communities to place special limits on anyone making claim to those offices. Additionally, the Didache here instructs, "Help him as much as you can," implying that more than simply food and shelter could be provided—perhaps new clothing and other provisions as needed.[23] The community was to provide a place where the traveler could rest and be refreshed physically and spiritually before resuming his travels.

---

21 Jonah 4:11; Matthew 25:33. Cf. Deuteronomy 17:20, 28:14; 2 Corinthians 6:7.
22 In Semitic style verse 2 begins with *ei* ("if," εἰ) and verses 3 through 4 begin with *ei de* ("but if," εἰ δὲ).
23 The Coptic version of the Didache has, "But if one comes to you on the the road, help him" (F. Stanley Jones and Paul A. Mirecki, "Considerations on the Coptic Papyrus of the Didache," in *The Didache in Context: Essays on Its Text, History & Transmission* [ed. Clayton N. Jefford; Leiden, The Netherlands: Brill, 1995], 57).

[12.2]
If the one who comes is a traveler, help him as much as you can, but he may not stay with you more than two, or if necessary three, days.

As was pointed out in the overview of this chapter, such hospitality is grounded in the Jewish practice of *hachnasat orechim* ("bringing in guests"). The book of Hebrews tells us that sometimes we do not realize the identity of our guests: "Do not neglect to show hospitality to strangers, for thereby some have entertained angels unawares" (Hebrews 13:2). The Master teaches:

> I was hungry and you gave me food, I was thirsty and you gave me drink, I was a stranger and you welcomed me, I was naked and you clothed me, I was sick and you visited me, I was in prison and you came to me … Truly, I say to you, as you did it to one of the least of these my brothers, you did it to me. (Matthew 25:35–40)

Yeshua assures us that we "will be repaid at the resurrection of the just" for our hospitality and kindness toward the poor and strangers.[24]

⟐ *But if he wants to live among you and is a craftsman, let him work and eat.* (DIDACHE 12.3)

The second case concerns the traveler who wishes to become a permanent resident within the community and has a trade. He was more than welcome to stay but with the stipulation that he must use his trade to earn a living. The community, no doubt, would help him find employment and get him established, but the gracious hospitality of 12.2 would end after three days. He would then be responsible for his own livelihood. "Let him work and eat" finds its antithesis in the Apostle Paul's command: "If anyone is not willing to work, let him not eat" (2 Thessalonians 3:10).[25]

From the very beginning man was created to work: "The LORD God took the man and put him in the garden of Eden to work it and keep it" (Genesis 2:15). God established the week as six days of work and one day for a Sabbath rest (Leviticus 23:3). Paul instructs about those who are idle, "Such persons we command and encourage in the Lord, [Yeshua the Messiah], to do their work quietly and to earn their own living" (2 Thessalonians 3:12).

Not working puts a burden on the community to provide unnecessarily for an able-bodied person. Additionally, it leads to trouble, as the old saying tells us: "The

---

24 Luke 14:14.
25 The Georgian version of the Didache adds after "Let him work and eat," "with everyone among you in unity and peace."

devil finds work for idle hands." A life of laziness can only lead to evil and poverty. The book of Proverbs instructs, "A little sleep, a little slumber, a little folding of the hands to rest, and poverty will come upon you like a robber, and want like an armed man" (Proverbs 6:10–11). Paul laments regarding the idle among the Thessalonians: "We hear that some among you walk in idleness, not busy at work, but busybodies" (2 Thessalonians 3:11). Similarly we find in the *Didascalia*, "Be always working, for idleness is a blot for which there is no cure."[26] The sages state: "Torah study together with a worldly occupation keeps one from sin."[27]

[12.3]
But if he wants to live among you and is a craftsman, let him work and eat.

The Apostle Paul himself established an example as he ministered long term in communities while at the same time supporting himself as a tentmaker.[28] This was despite the fact that Paul was an emissary and that he himself argued that those who shared the gospel should be provided for. Despite that rule, he chose to live above and beyond reproach.[29] Paul stated:

> I coveted no one's silver or gold or apparel. You yourselves know that these hands ministered to my necessities and to those who were with me. In all things I have shown you that by working hard in this way we must help the weak and remember the words of the Lord [Yeshua], how he himself said, "It is more blessed to give than to receive." (Acts 20:33–35)

Paul and the Didache teach us that we are commanded to work and to provide for ourselves and our families.

> *If he does not have a skill, according to your discernment take into consideration how he will avoid living idly among you as a follower of the Messiah.* (DIDACHE 12.4)

In this third situation the traveler desired to live within the community, but at the same time he did not have a specific trade. In this circumstance the community was to assist him in finding work—a proceeding that would take more effort than helping the traveler who came with a particular trade or craft. Nevertheless, because of this traveler's willingness to work, he should be assisted.

---

26 *Didascalia* 13.2.63. Cf. Pseudo-Clementine, Letter on Virginity 1.11.
27 m.*Avot* 2:2.
28 Acts 18:3.
29 1 Corinthians 9:1–18; 1 Thessalonians 2:9; 2 Thessalonians 3:8–9; 1 Timothy 5:17–18.

[12.4]
If he does not have a skill, according to your discernment take into consideration how he will avoid living idly among you as a follower of the Messiah.

The community was to make sure that the able-bodied worker found work and was not idle. The Apostle Paul exhorted the Thessalonian believers to be hard workers and to keep far from idleness:

> You yourselves know how you ought to imitate us, because we were not idle when we were with you, nor did we eat anyone's bread without paying for it, but with toil and labor we worked night and day, that we might not be a burden to any of you. (2 Thessalonians 3:7–8)

The *Didascalia* exhorts parents to teach their children a trade in order that they may avoid idleness:

> Teach your children crafts that are agreeable and befitting to religion, lest through idleness they give themselves to wantonness. For if they are not corrected by their parents, they will do those things that are evil, like the heathen. (*Didascalia* 22.4.11)

The Didache seeks to guard the name and character of the term "follower of Messiah." The Greek word *christianos* (Χριστιανός), commonly translated "Christian," is one of the earliest names for followers of Messiah.[30] The disciples of the Master first picked up the name in Syrian Antioch, but it spread widely among Greek-speaking Jews.[31] The name "Christian" became the Greek appellation for the sect of Judaism that revered Yeshua as the Messiah (*Christos*, Χριστός).

It was not a derogatory term. The word "Christian" implied allegiance to the Messiah and functioned as the Greek equivalent to the English word "Messianic." Originally the name did not indicate the Christian religion. Gentile Christianity had not yet developed outside the Jewish community or in antithesis to Judaism: "No distinction had been made between Judaism and 'Christianity.'"[32] Rather, the name referred to association with Messiah: "If anyone suffers as a Christian, let him

---

30 Acts 11:26, 26:28; 1 Peter 4:16. "Follower of Messiah/Christian" is omitted from the version of the Didache in *The Ethiopic Church Order*: "But if he works not he shall not be supported, and if he has no trade and works not, according to your wisdom devise for him that he shall not remain with you idle" (Horner, *The Statutes of the Apostles or Canones Ecclesiastici*, 194.6–9). This might reflect a more ancient version of the oral tradition of the Didache before the term was wide spread.

31 D. Thomas Lancaster, *Torah Club: Chronicles of the Apostles* (6 vols.; Marshfield, MO: First Fruits of Zion, 2016), 3:814–815.

32 Hilary Le Cornu and Joseph Shulam, *A Commentary on the Jewish Roots of Acts 1–15* (Jerusalem, Israel: Academon/Netivyah, 2003), 623. Magnus Zetterholm writes, "That a Messianic Jewish community would be given a name by other Jews that manifested this is quite natural and does not imply any break with Judaism—rather the opposite" (*The Formation of Christianity in Antioch: A Social-Scientific Approach to the Separation Between Judaism and Christianity* [London, England: Routledge, 2005], 95).

not be ashamed, but let him glorify God in that name" (1 Peter 4:16). Writing near the end of the first century, Josephus testified to the growing popularity of the new name for the sect when he referred to the believers as the "tribe of the Christians."³³

> *But if he is not willing to do so, he is a Messiah peddler. Guard yourselves from people like this!* (DIDACHE 12.5)

The fourth and final situation involves the traveler who wanted to stay long term but did not desire to work. Such travelers were not welcomed. The Didache urges the community to be on guard against such individuals lest they deplete the resources and morale of the community by spreading idleness. Likewise the Apostle Paul urges:

> We command you, brothers, in the name of our [Master Yeshua the Messiah], that you keep away from any brother who is walking in idleness and not in accord with the tradition that you received from us. (2 Thessalonians 3:6)

Such a lazy person was called a "Messiah peddler" (*christemporos*, χριστέμπορός). *The Ethiopic Church Order* has "seller of the name of Messiah."³⁴ While we do find this term in later church literature, its mention here in the Didache is its first occurrence, and it is possible that the author of the Didache invented it.³⁵ It is a word play on "follower of Messiah" (*christianos*), combining *christianos* with *emporos* ("peddler," ἔμπορος). Kurt Niederwimmer defines *emporos* thus:

> In the broad sense, someone who travels, and then specifically (and this is the basis of the didachistic construction of the word) a merchant, more properly a wholesale merchant who undertakes business journeys to distant places, in contrast to κάπηλος [*kapelos*], the small local merchant. A χριστέμπορός [*christemporos*] is apparently someone who "deals in" Christ, that is, who misuses Christian faith and the name of Christ for personal enrichment.³⁶

---

33 Josephus, *Antiquities of the Jews* 18:63–64/iii.3.
34 Horner, *The Statutes of the Apostles or Canones Ecclesiastici*, 194.9–10.
35 For a list of sources that include this term, see Niederwimmer, *The Didache*, 187.
36 Niederwimmer, *The Didache*, 187.

[12.5] *But if he is not willing to do so, he is a Messiah peddler. Guard yourselves from people like this!*

The creative word has in view traveling freeloaders who, like merchants peddling their wares, travel from village to village, selling themselves to local communities as worthy disciples deserving of hospitality and community support.

Followers of Messiah are not to take discipleship lightly. Paul warns against believers who imagine "that godliness is a means of gain."[37] According to the Didache, idle and lazy members of our communities who rely on the benevolence of believers are not true followers of the Master. They blaspheme the name of God by using faith as a crutch for indolence.

---

37   1 Timothy 6:5. Cf. 2 Clement 20.4.

Chapter Thirteen

DIDACHE 13

13.1 Every true prophet who wants to live among you is entitled to his sustenance.[1]

13.2 Likewise, a true teacher is also entitled, just as the worker is entitled to his sustenance.[2]

13.3 Therefore, you shall take every first part of the produce of the wine press and threshing floor,[3] and of both cattle and sheep,[4] and give it to the prophets, because they are your high priests.

13.4 But if you do not have a prophet, give it to the poor.

13.5 When you make a batch of bread dough, take the first part and give it according to the commandment.[5]

13.6 Likewise, when you open a vessel of wine or oil, take the first part and give it to the prophets.

13.7 Also of money and clothing and any other possession, take the first part as it seems fitting to you, and give it according to the commandment.

---

1 Matthew 10:10; 1 Timothy 5:18; 1 Corinthians 9:13–14.
2 Matthew 10:10; 1 Timothy 5:18; 1 Corinthians 9:13–14.
3 Deuteronomy 18:4, 26:2.
4 Exodus 22:30; Numbers 18:15; Deuteronomy 18:1–4.
5 Numbers 15:18–21.

Overview

*D*idache 13 continues the legal section that began in chapter 7 and introduces a new section about supporting prophets and teachers. The chapter offers practical halachic advice on fulfilling the Master's mandate that "the laborer deserves his food" (Matthew 10:10). Establishing this system of gifts for prophets and teachers ensured that the community would provide for the needs of its leaders, and it gave the Gentile believers of the Diaspora a way to participate in the Torah's commandments regarding priestly gifts.

STRUCTURE

The first two verses of the section introduce general principles on providing for prophets and teachers. The remaining five verses give specific regulations regarding gifts given to prophets and teachers. If a prophet or teacher was not present within a community, the "first part" was given to the poor.

GENERAL PRINCIPLE	
13.1–2	Prophets and teachers should be provided for
SPECIFICS OF GENERAL PRINCIPLE	
13.3	First part of winepress, threshing floor, and cattle and sheep given to prophets and teachers
13.4	If no prophet or teacher, given to poor
13.5	First of dough given to prophets and teachers
13.6	Portion of newly opened wine or oil given to prophets and teachers
13.7	First of money, clothing, or other possessions given to prophets and teachers

The Laborer Deserves His Food

When Yeshua sent out his disciples, he told them not to take extra money with them on their missions because "the laborer deserves his food" (Matthew 10:10). They were to seek hospitality in the villages they visited.

Later in the same passage, Yeshua says that those who provide for the needs of his disciples receive the reward of prophets and righteous men:

> The one who receives a prophet because he is a prophet will receive a prophet's reward, and the one who receives a righteous person because he is a righteous person will receive a righteous person's reward. (Matthew 10:41)

This saying of Yeshua forged an association between his disciples (teachers and apostles) and the office of prophets, at least in regard to compensation and communal support. Didache 13 reflects that same relationship. All the rules of community support for true prophets apply equally to community teachers: "Likewise, a true teacher is also entitled" (13.2).

The apostles interpreted the Master's teaching about a laborer deserving his wages to mean that community elders who serve well and labor in preaching and teaching should receive the double honor of compensation for their efforts. Paul cites the teaching of Yeshua to establish this principle:

> Let the elders who rule well be considered worthy of double honor, especially those who labor in preaching and teaching. For the Scripture says, "You shall not muzzle an ox when it treads out the grain," and, "The laborer deserves his wages." (1 Timothy 5:17–18)

Paul's mention of "elders who rule well" and "labor in preaching and teaching" refers to those who functioned in the place of the Master's disciples as leaders over their respective communities. The apostles taught that these local leaders should receive compensation to cover their living expenses while they labored for the community.

In a similar passage that makes an obvious allusion to Yeshua's teaching, the Apostle Paul invokes the Master's injunction about paying a laborer in order to justify his own right to community support from the congregations in which he taught:

> The plowman should plow in hope and the thresher thresh in hope of sharing in the crop. If we have sown spiritual things among you, is it too much if we reap material things from you? If others share this rightful claim on you, do not we even more? (1 Corinthians 9:10–12)

Further on in the same discussion, Paul compares teachers of the gospel to priests at work in the Temple. Just as the priests received compensation for their service in the Temple in the form of sustenance derived from the sacred service, so too, the proclaimers of the gospel should receive their living from their proclamation of the gospel:

> Do you not know that those who are employed in the temple service get their food from the temple, and those who serve at the altar share in the sacrificial offerings? In the same way, the Lord commanded that those who proclaim the gospel should get their living by the gospel. (1 Corinthians 9:13–14)

With these words Paul unambiguously interprets Yeshua's original saying about the workman deserving his food to mean that the teacher of the gospel should obtain his living through his teaching. That is to say, he should be compensated. Didache 13 takes this analogy a step further by stating that teachers and prophets were entitled to community support because they were the community's "high priests" (14.7).

Tithing

Based on the words "They shall not profane the holy things of the people of Israel, which they contribute to the LORD" (Leviticus 22:15), Jewish law teaches that it is a violation of the Torah for an individual to consume un-tithed produce (*tevel*, תבל).[6] Rabbinic literature is filled with detailed legal rulings surrounding tithing and what to do with doubtfully tithed food.[7] These details regarding tithing were

---

[6] Rabbi Yisrael Meir HaKohen, *The Concise Book of Mitzvoth: The Commandments Which Can Be Observed Today* (New York, NY: Feldheim, 1990), 291–293.

[7] David Instone-Brewer, *Traditions of the Rabbis from the Era of the New Testament* (2 vols.; Grand Rapids, MI: Eerdmans, 2004), 1:169–194.

so important that, much as in the Didache, they were among the first commandments taught to new converts to Judaism.[8]

The principle of tithing first appeared when Abraham met the mysterious Melchizedek:

> Melchizedek king of Salem brought out bread and wine. (He was priest of God Most High.) And he blessed him ... and Abram gave him a tenth of everything. (Genesis 14:18–20)

The Hebrew word for tithe is *ma'aser* (מעשר), which literally means a "tenth part." Later on in Genesis, we see Jacob promise God that if he will keep him safe and provide for him, Jacob will "give a full tenth" back to God (Genesis 28:22). Although no specific legal instructions are given, the concept of giving back to God from that with which he blesses us is established.

It was not until the Torah was given at Sinai that specific regulations on tithing were delivered. The tithing system of the Bible is complex, but we can find a few overarching principles that apply to most of the commandments on tithing:

- The Torah imposes tithes only on agricultural produce, and most of the laws of tithing apply only in the land of Israel.

- According to the majority interpretation of Numbers 18:12, the biblical tithe applies only to grain, grapes, and olives: "All the best of the oil and all the best of the wine and of the grain" (Numbers 18:12).[9]

- The majority of the Torah's laws on tithing were not considered incumbent upon Gentiles.[10]

---

8   *Gerim* 1:3 (60a). See Jonathan A. Draper, "A Continuing Enigma: the 'Yoke of the Lord' in Didache 6:2–3 and Early Jewish-Christian Relations," in *The Image of the Judaeo-Christians in Ancient Jewish and Christian Literature* (ed. Peter J. Tomson and Doris Lambers-Petry; Tübingen, Germany: Mohr Siebeck, 2003), 118.

9   Cf. Deuteronomy 18:4. See Rabbi Nosson Scherman and Rabbi Meir Zlotowitz, ed., *Yad Avraham Mishnah Series: Seder Zeraim* (8 vols.; Brooklyn, NY: Mesorah, 2003), 4b:5.

10 Compare Jubilees in which Noah is commanded, "For three years the fruit of everything that is eaten will not be gathered: and in the fourth year its fruit will be accounted holy [and they will offer the first-fruits], acceptable before the Most High God, who created heaven and earth and all things. Let them offer in abundance the first of the wine and oil [as] first-fruits on the altar of the Lord, who receives it, and what is left let the servants of the house of the Lord eat before the altar which receives [it]. And in the fifth year make the release so that you release it in righteousness and uprightness, and you shall be righteous, and all that you plant shall prosper" (7:36–37).

Although most Christians think of tithing as merely the obligation to give 10 percent of their income to the church, the Torah's system involved a lot more.

The First Part

Readers of the Didache might naturally assume that the legislation in chapter 13 imposes a system of tithing, but on closer examination the reader will realize that the chapter does not refer to the gifts that are set aside for prophets and teachers as tithes. The usual Greek word for "tithes" is *apodekatou* ("a tenth," ἀποδεκατόω), but the Didache uses the term "first part" *aparche* (απαρχή). The Septuagint uses this word *aparche* for both *trumah* ("offering," תרומה) and *reishit* ("first or best part," ראשית). In other Jewish literature it can refer to the various tithes or simply to firstfruits (*bikkurim*, בכורים).[11] In turn, there are three main possible meanings for "first part" (*aparche*):

1. *Trumah* (offering): an initial first-part offering that is given to a priest

2. *Bikkurim* (firstfruits): a first part of crops (after the *trumah* is removed) that is offered in Jerusalem

3. *Ma'aser* (tithe): an offering of 10 percent given to the Levites

Despite this semantic flexibility, the word *aparche* seems to have a specific meaning in the Didache. The context indicates that the Didache uses *aparche* as an equivalent for the Hebrew *trumah*, the sacred first-part portions that were offered to the Levitical priests, rather than to the 10-percent tithe, or *ma'aser*. Before the Israelite removed any tithes from his new crops, he removed a "first part" portion for the priests. This portion was called the *trumah gedolah* (תרומה גדולה), or just *trumah*.

When the Torah refers to *trumah*, it specifically mentions it in reference to grain, wine, and oil, the same three types of produce specified by the Didache:[12]

---

11   Cf. Josephus, *Antiquities of the Jews* 16:172/vi.7; Philo, *On Dreams* 2.75, *On the Embassy to Gaius* 156–157. *Aparche* "can refer, depending on circumstances, to ראשית, תרומה ראשון or מעשר עני" (Marcello del Verme, *Didache and Judaism: Jewish Roots of an Ancient Christian-Jewish Work* [New York, NY: T&T Clark, 2004], 220). See also Gedaliah Alon, "The Halacha in the Teaching of the Twelve Apostles," in *The Didache in Modern Research* (ed. Draper; Leiden, The Netherlands: Brill, 1996), 191; William Varner, *The Way of the Didache: The First Christian Handbook* (New York, NY: University Press of America, 2007), 220; Huub van de Sandt and David Flusser, *The Didache: Its Jewish Sources and Its Place in Early Judaism and Christianity* (Minneapolis, MN: Fortress, 2002), 361.

12   See Rabbi Scherman and Rabbi Zlotowitz, ed., *Yad Avraham Mishnah Series: Seder Zeraim*, 4b:5.

> All the best of the oil and all the best of the wine and of the grain, the firstfruits of what they give to the LORD, I give to you. (Numbers 18:12)
>
> The firstfruits of your grain, of your wine and of your oil, and the first fleece of your sheep, you shall give him. (Deuteronomy 18:4)

According to Numbers 18:12, *trumah* is the best portion of the firstfruits but is a separate offering from the firstfruits. The Didache's laws of setting aside a first part for the priests draw heavily from the legislation in Numbers 18:11–20.

The sages derived a rule of thumb from Ezekiel 45:13 for measuring *trumah*. They understood the Hebrew to imply that a person must set aside at least one sixtieth of his entire produce (a legally insignificant amount of the whole) as *trumah*. This was the minimum amount, but a generous person could give more. In reality, the Torah does not specify an actual amount necessary to fulfill the law of giving *trumah* to the priests. This fits with the Didache's injunction to give "as seems fitting." In fact, the amount of *trumah* a person chose to give provided a sort of barometer to indicate his generosity:

> This is the amount of *trumah*: the man with a good eye [that is, the generous man] gives a fortieth; Beit Shammai says, one thirtieth. The average man one fiftieth and the man with a bad eye [that is, the stingy man] gives one sixtieth. (m.*Trumot* 4:3)

Didache 13 obviously is not discussing the Torah's laws of giving one's firstfruits (*bikkurim*). Firstfruits can be ruled out because, in Jewish law, firstfruits were to be taken from the seven species of Israel (wheat, barley, grapes, figs, pomegranates, olives, and dates).[13] Also, the law did not apply outside the land. Furthermore, in the Torah, the firstfruits had to be brought to Jerusalem, whereas tithes (which included *trumah*) could be distributed anywhere.[14]

Aparche cannot refer to a *ma'aser* (tithe) because unlike in 13.7 ("as seems fitting to you"), *ma'aser* is a specified amount of 10 percent.[15] Additionally, tithes in the Torah were primarily given to the Levites, consumed by the owner, or given to the poor. Although a small portion of the first tithe to the Levite was given to the priest, *trumah* is wholly dedicated to the priest. In the Didache, prophets who

---

13 m.*Bikkurim* 1:3.
14 Deuteronomy 26:2.
15 "Rabban Gamaliel used to say: '... Make not a habit of tithing by guesswork'" (m.*Avot* 1:16).

receive the "first part" are said to be the believers' "high priests" (13.3). In turn, something akin to *trumah* best fits the context.

Halachah for Gentiles

According to the Didache, the Gentile believers do not give the sacred gifts to priests and Levites but rather to prophets and teachers. The Didache reasons that the "first part" should be given to the prophets because, as the writer indicates to the believers, "They are your high priests" (13.3).

Some scholars interpret this as a replacement of the Levitical system, but the New Testament does not teach substitution or replacement of Old Testament laws and institutions, as Christian interpretation usually assumes. On the contrary, the New Testament assumes that the Torah's laws of priestly gifts are being upheld. The New Testament contains several metaphorical references to tithing that assume that the system is in place.[16] In fact, the Master did not even take issue with the Pharisees' extension of the laws of tithing to include "mint and dill and cumin" so long as they did not subvert "weightier matters of the law." Rather, our Master Yeshua taught, "These you ought to have done, without neglecting the others" (Matthew 23:23). If the Master had not been strict about the laws of priestly offerings himself, he would not have been invited to dine with the Pharisees. Even in other apostolic tradition 1 Clement, we find that the apostolic community preserved a positive view of the Temple and the ongoing hierarchical nature of the Levitical system:

> To the High Priest were assigned special services, and to the priests a special place hath been appointed; and on the Levites special duties are imposed. But he that is a layman is bound by the ordinances of laymen. (1 Clement 40.5)

So why did the Didache direct its readers to give their gifts to prophets and teachers rather than to Levitical priests? It must be remembered that the Didache was written to Gentile believers in Messiah who lived in the Diaspora. The laws of *trumah* in the Torah apply only within the land of Israel and only to Jews. Additionally, many of the communities in which the Gentile believers lived did not have qualified Levitical priests to whom *trumah* could be paid. Therefore, the Didache's instructions are intended as special legislation for Gentile believers, teaching them how they may participate in the principles of the Torah's priestly

---

16 See Toby Janicki, *What about Tithing?* (Marshfield, MO: First Fruits of Zion, 2014), 33–46.

gift commandments. The tithing legislation of Judaism is here "artfully adopted for Gentiles."[17] In this way the Didache reinterprets the *trumah* commandments of the Torah and makes them applicable to these new non-Jewish initiates.

This points not to a break with the people of Israel and normative Judaism but rather displays continuity with the Jewish people as the Didache seeks to apply the principles of the Torah to the nations. Marcello del Verme writes that Didache 13 "is a clear sign that the 'parting of the ways' between Judaism and Christianity is still far away."[18] Even the twice-repeated phrase "according to the commandment" points toward a loyalty to Judaism and the Torah and not to a separation:

> The natural and straightforward way in which the Didachist refers to the assistance to be given to the prophets as being "according to the commandment" says something about the way in which the Didachist (and his audience) understood their relationship to the Torah ("according to the commandment") and to Judaism (the priest being replaced by the prophets).[19]

In the spirit of Matthew 16:19, "I will give you the keys of the kingdom of heaven, and whatever you bind on earth shall be bound in heaven, and whatever you loose on earth shall be loosed in heaven," the Didache reinterprets and adapts the *trumah* commandments of Judaism to make them applicable to Gentiles living outside the land of Israel. If the Didache represents, in some shape or form, the teachings of the apostles, then what is preserved here are legal rulings that were "bound" upon new non-Jewish disciples. The teachings were based on and in continuity with Jewish law, not created in opposition to it.

---

17 Aaron Milavec, *The Didache: Faith, Hope, & Life of the Earliest Christian Communities, 50–70 C.E.* (New York, NY: Newman, 2003), 518. Some believe that the entire section is a reworking of Jewish oral *halachah*: "Both the symmetrical structures of our passage and the recurrence of the same stereotyped wording, facilitating memorization, may indicate that this unit has been transmitted orally. It would be a reasonable hypothesis that a Jewish oral tradition was the section's original form since the specification of the firstfruits and the wording itself have the characteristic marks of a Jewish halachic tradition. This basic tradition may have circulated in Jewish communities as a teaching about the firstfruits and tithes before it was reworked and incorporated in the *Didache*" (Van de Sandt and Flusser, *The Didache: Its Jewish Sources and Its Place in Early Judaism and Christianity* [Minneapolis, MN: Fortress, 2002], 361). Cf. "The norms, laid down in Didache 13.3–7, preserve traditional material of great antiquity. Whether they are understood as being contributed by the Didachist himself, or whether they are considered as interpolations made in the course of the transmission of the text, in both cases the Jewish background to the passage is beyond dispute" (Del Verme, *Didache and Judaism*, 199).

18 Del Verme, *Didache and Judaism*, 116, 220.

19 Ibid., 199.

From Prophets to Priests

The prophets spoken of in chapter 13 are the verified prophets who have been tested, according to chapter 11: "You shall take every first part ... and give it to the prophets because they are your high priests" (Didache 13.3). For purposes of chapter 13's rules about *trumah*, the Didache includes teachers in the same legal category as the prophets. It does so by introducing the legislation as applicable to both prophets and teachers:

> Every true prophet who wants to live among you is entitled to his sustenance. Likewise, a true teacher is also entitled. (13.1–2)

That is to say that the legislation in chapter 13 applies equally to both teachers and prophets, even when the text specifically mentions only the entitlements of a prophet. The community's teachers are also in view.

The Didache places prophets and teachers in the Gentile communities in the position of honor and entitlement that Judaism reserved for the Aaronic priesthood. Like the priests, the prophets and teachers received the first honor of leading the *Grace after Meals*, and like the priests, they were to receive support in the form of tithes from the community. Perhaps the Didache chose prophets and teachers as the recipients of *trumah* from Gentile believers because most of the Diaspora communities of Gentile believers had no Levites or Levitical priests within their congregations.

Additionally, we find a biblical precedent for giving prophets tithes and firstfruits: "A man came from Baal-shalishah, bringing the man of God bread of the firstfruits, twenty loaves of barley and fresh ears of grain in his sack" (2 Kings 4:42). "The man of God," Elisha the prophet, was given firstfruits. Huub van de Sandt and David Flusser point out that even after the destruction of the Temple,

the rabbis encouraged the people to continue to offer priestly gifts. They speculate that tithes were specifically given to Levites who were also rabbis (i.e., teachers).[20]

Practical Application

How do the laws of priestly gifts apply today? Ideally, Messianic Jews should follow the Torah's laws as they are interpreted today in modern Jewish law. Messianic Gentiles would do well to adhere to the injunctions of Didache 13. However, practically applying the Didache's injunctions can prove to be difficult.

Being so far removed from the time and economy for which the Didache was written makes it difficult to decipher what the text is directing its reader to do. The early church seems to have maintained a 10-percent system similar to tithing legislation. "Origen had already commanded that the priestly gifts mentioned in the Torah, are among those commandments which were not to be abolished, that even Christians are obligated to observe (in their fashion)."[21] Furthermore, the Didache's instructions on giving the "first part" are embellished and expanded on in the Apostolic Constitutions, the *Didascalia*, and *The Apostolic Tradition of Hippolytus of Rome*.[22] Nevertheless, the practice of contributions to prophets disappeared (along with the office of prophets) by the fourth century, and there remains no universally attested practice of giving a portion of anything but money to the church in Christian practice today. This leaves us with no current church tradition to draw upon for practical application.

---

20   E.g., b.*Pesachim* 72b–73a. See Van de Sandt and Flusser, *The Didache*, 361–362. Jewish tradition also records that many of the priests, in particular high priests, possessed prophetic powers. In the apocryphal Testament of the Twelve Patriarchs, Levi receives a vision of seven men in white garments who tell him, "Arise, put on the robe of the priesthood, and the crown of righteousness, and the breastplate of understanding, and the garment of truth, and the plate of faith, and the turban of the head, and the ephod of prophecy" (Testament of Levi 8:1–3, cf. Testament of Levi 8:1–38, 11–15). Josephus records that the second-century BCE high priest John Hyrcanus is said to have had several prophetic dreams and even says of him, "He was esteemed by God worthy of three of the greatest privileges: the government of his nation, the dignity of the high priesthood, and prophecy" (Josephus, *Antiquities of the Jews* 11:322, 327/viii.4, 13:299–300/x.7). In the New Testament, Caiaphas the high priest unknowingly prophesied about the death of the Master (John 11:49–51). Rabbinic literature also records that both the high priests Yochanan and Simeon the Righteous received a prophetic word from the "house of the Holy of Holies" (t.*Sotah* 13:5–6).

21   Alon, "The Halacha in the Teaching of the Twelve Apostles," 192.

22   Apostolic Constitutions 7.28–29; *Didascalia* 2.25.1–25, 2.27.1–4, 2.35.1–4; *The Apostolic Tradition of Hippolytus of Rome* 31–32. See Milavec, *The Didache: Faith, Hope, & Life of the Earliest Christian Communities, 50–70 C.E.*, 520–523.

Even so, some broad principles can be derived from Didache 13. Most importantly, the Didache sees the giving of a percentage of one's income to support teachers and ministry as a commandment incumbent upon every disciple. Both Jewish and Christian tradition have set the percentage at 10 percent in imitation of the biblical laws of the tithe, yet the Didache leaves it at, "Take the first part as it seems fitting to you."[23] Jewish and Christian tradition agree that giving a percentage of one's income should be the norm for God-fearing people—certainly for believers in Messiah today. The teachings of the Didache further emphasize this discipline, particularly in conjunction with supporting teachers and leadership.

The general principles of Didache 13 can be translated into our modern economy. The Didache assumes an agricultural economy in which people were accustomed to trading in crops, livestock, and produce. The donation of the "first part" of agriculture functioned as a type of tithe (so to speak) on the person's income. If the Didache were to be written for today's readers, the apostles would tell us to give a percentage of our income to support our teachers, Bible-teaching ministries, local assemblies, and the poor among us.

---

[23] Although early churchmen such as Clement of Alexandria, Irenaeus, and Chrysostom stressed the tithing principles, tithing was not fully mandated by the church until about the sixth century, when it became canon law at the Third Council of the Synod of Mâcon in 585.

Commentary

⫸ Every true prophet who wants to live among you is entitled to his sustenance. (DIDACHE 13.1)

The Didache begins its instructions on tithing with two general prescriptions for providing for true prophets and teachers. *The Ethiopic Church Order* adds the injunction, "Then support him."[24] The Apostolic Constitutions combines verses 1 and 2 together: "Every true prophet or teacher that comes to you is entitled to his sustenance, as being a worker in the word of righteousness" (7.28).[25] The prophets and teachers that the Didache has in view are those who functioned as leaders and clergy over a local community.

The itinerant prophet was given the option to settle down within the community if he so desired. But the description "true" indicates that he first had to be tested and proven worthy of the title "prophet" before being allowed to stay permanently. Chapter 11 states that a prophet was recognized as true or false by his "conduct." Only the "true prophet" had the "conduct of the Lord." He deserved to have his needs provided for so that he could serve the community full-time as a teacher.

The Greek for the phrase "entitled to his sustenance" is similar to the Master's words "for the laborer deserves his food." Didache 13.1–2 may be based on no-longer extant sayings attributed to Yeshua.[26] "Sustenance" (*trophe*, τροφή) indicates food or nourishment and is used in the Septuagint for *lechem* ("bread," לחם) and *ochel* ("food," אכל), but here in the Didache it might be better expressed by the Hebrew word *parnasah* (פרנסה), which is used in rabbinic literature more generally to refer to livelihood and income. The prophet would need more than food to survive. Verse 7 states that he was to receive "also of money and clothing and any other possession."

The Didache uses the title "prophet" categorically here to include prophets, apostles, and teachers. Didache 13.2 indicates that "true" teachers fall into the same category as worthy of community support. This is consistent with the teachings

---

24 G.W. Horner, *The Statutes of the Apostles or Canones Ecclesiastici* (London, England: Williams & Norgate, 1904), 194.12.
25 Cf. Matthew 10:41.
26 Matthew 10:10. Cf. Luke 10:7; Pseudo-Phocylides 1:19; Sibylline Oracles 2.74. See Kurt Niederwimmer, *The Didache: Hermeneia—A Critical and Historical Commentary on the Bible* (Minneapolis, MN: Fortress, 1998), 188–189.

[13.1]
Every true prophet who wants to live among you is entitled to his sustenance.

of the New Testament. As noted above, the Apostle Paul taught that those who ministered within the community were to be supported, just as the priesthood received their share from the sacrificial offerings brought to the altar: "In the same way, the Lord commanded that those who proclaim the gospel should get their living by the gospel" (1 Corinthians 9:14).

Likewise, we noted that in 1 Timothy Paul uses the Torah's commandment "You shall not muzzle an ox when it is treading out the grain" (Deuteronomy 25:4) midrashically to prove that those "who labor in preaching and teaching" deserve community support.[27] Similar injunctions are found in Pseudo-Clementine literature.[28] As followers of the Master, we are to provide for and take care of those who nourish us spiritually.

◉ *Likewise, a true teacher is also entitled, just as the worker is entitled to his sustenance.* (DIDACHE 13.2)

Like prophets, resident teachers were to be provided for. "Likewise" might represent the Mishnaic phrase *vechen* ("and likewise," וכן), which is used to infer "that the second halachah resembles the one preceding it."[29] Just as the prophet needed to be provided for so that he could operate in his office full-time, the teacher also needed to be given his sustenance so that he could study and teach. In *Pesikta DeRav Kahana*, we find an injunction to tithe money to Torah teachers: "The words 'tithe all' (Deuteronomy 14:22), according to R. Abba bar Kahana, are a hint to merchants and seafarers that they are to set aside a tithe of earnings for men who labor in the Torah."[30]

Once again, the descriptive "true" is applied, indicating that a teacher must be proven worthy to receive his sustenance from the community. His teaching must "promote righteousness and knowledge of the Lord" and not "undermine" the Master's teachings or turn students aside from what is being taught in the Didache (11.2). Once the community had tested and proved him as a teacher of the truth, its members were to support him for his service.

---

27   1 Timothy 5:17–18.
28   Pseudo-Clementine Homilies 3.71.
29   Rabbi Adin Steinsaltz, *The Talmud Steinsaltz Edition: A Reference Guide* (New York, NY: Random, 1989), 92.
30   *Pesikta DeRav Kahana* 10:10.

🔊 *Therefore, you shall take every first part ... and give it to the prophets, because they are your high priests.* (DIDACHE 13.3)

The Didache now moves from the general statements of 13.1–2 into specific instructions regarding how the prophet and teacher were to be provided for.

"First part" is the Greek word *aparche* (ἀπαρχή), which can have a variety of connotations, but in chapter 13 of the Didache it refers to the portion set aside from produce to be given to the priests, or the *trumah*. (See the discussion in the overview of this chapter.)

Unlike the *trumah* commandments of the Torah by which the priests received a portion of the firstfruits from the children of Israel, in the Didache the "prophets" (and teachers) received the gifts.[31] As was discussed in the overview, this does not imply a replacement of the priesthood and the Temple or even a separation from Judaism. Rather, since the Torah's commandments on priestly gifts were inapplicable to Gentiles and because many believing communities in the Diaspora would not have a priest dwelling among them to whom one might offer a gift, the Didache created a quasi-*trumah* system based on injunctions that Gentiles could follow. It should be reiterated that "the term 'high priests' applies metaphorically to the prophets only insofar as they received the people's gifts and first parts. No one imagined, for example, that the community's prophets or teachers were the sons of Aaron or that they were ordained."[32] The Apostolic Constitutions replaces "prophets" with "priests," probably referring to ecclesiastical leadership from a later era.[33] In the Didache era, Christianity had not yet developed a "priesthood." The Didache says that the "prophets" stand in for the "high priests."[34]

---

[31] In 13.3, the Georgian version of the Didache has "your theologians" in place of "the prophets."
[32] Milavec, *The Didache: Faith, Hope, & Life of the Earliest Christian Communities, 50–70 C.E.*, 478.
[33] Apostolic Constitutions 7.29.
[34] "High priests" might have been referenced because of the strong tradition in Judaism of linking the high priest to prophecy (Testament of Levi 8:1–3, 11–15; Josephus, *Antiquities of the Jews* 11:322, 327/viii.4, 13:299–300/x.7; John 11:49–51; t.*Sotah* 13:5–6). Milavec speculates that the choice was deliberate as a clarification for the Didache's Gentile audience: "Accommodating his gentile readers, Philo uses the term 'second rank' to designate Levites, who are not priests, and, following upon this designation, refers to those receiving the first fruits as 'priests of superior rank' ([*On the Special Laws*] 1.157) ... One might wonder whether the term *archiereis* (*archē* + *hieres* 'first' + 'priest') was used by the framers of the Didache to designate 'priests of the superior rank.' If so, the use of *archiereis* ('first priests') could be seen as providing a more accurate impression to gentiles than would the term 'priests,' and ... a helpful clarification for gentiles" (Milavec, *The Didache: Faith, Hope, & Life of the Earliest Christian Communities, 50–70 C.E.*, 513).

[13.3]
Therefore, you shall take every first part ... and give it to the prophets, because they are your high priests.

The command "you shall take" comes from the sphere of halachic language surrounding *trumah*, firstfruits, and tithing. Regarding the firstfruits brought to Jerusalem, the Torah states, "*You shall take* some of the first of all the fruit of the ground" (Deuteronomy 26:2, emphasis added). In rabbinic dialogue about firstfruits, the technical term *mevi'in* ("bring," מביאין) is used, for example: "There are some who bring [*mevi'in*] the firstfruits."[35] Additionally, the Mishnah in tractate *Trumot* uses the technical term "separate" (*taram*, תרם) in regard to the *trumah gedolah*. The Greek word for "take" *lambano* (λαμβάνω) can also have the sense of "bring" as well as the connotation "to choose, select."[36] The choice of the wording "you shall take" may also reflect Jewish legal interpretation of "Speak to the people of Israel, that they take for me a contribution" (Exodus 25:2). Because the Torah uses "take" instead of "give" the sages ruled this meant that "the Jewish people were commanded to assign solicitors who can receive the donations according to each person's generosity."[37] It may be that the Didache is enforcing the same practice for the "first part."

> *You shall take every first part of the produce of the wine press and threshing floor, and of both cattle and sheep.*
> (DIDACHE 13.3)

The Didache specifies that a "first part" of produce, grain, and animals is to be given to the prophets and teachers. The language here sounds biblical. The expression "first part of the produce of the wine press and threshing floor" appears in reverse order in Numbers: "When you have offered from it the best of it, then the rest shall be counted to the Levites as produce of the threshing floor, and as produce of the winepress" (Numbers 18:30), and similar language occurs in conjunction with *trumah*: "All the best of the oil and all the best of the wine and of the grain, the firstfruits of what they give to the LORD, I give to you" (Numbers 18:12). This chapter of the Didache draws heavily from the legislation about priestly gifts.

---

35 m.*Bikkurim* 1:1.
36 E.g., Matthew 16:7–8. See Joseph H. Thayer, *Thayer's Greek-English Lexicon of the New Testament* (Peabody, MA: Hendrickson, 2000), 370–371.
37 Mark Greenspan, "T'rumah and Tz'dakah: How We Define Synagogue Dues," *The Rabbinical Assembly* (Parashat T'rumah): 2. Cited 16 September 2015. Online: http://www.rabbinicalassembly.org/sites/default/files/public/resources-ideas/source-sheets/tol-parashot/t-rumah.pdf

Similarly, the Torah's "of your herd and of your flock" parallels the Didache's "of both cattle and sheep."[38]

The Apostolic Constitutions adds a blessing for obedience similar to Deuteronomic blessings. Compare:

> Every part of the produce of the winepress, the threshing-floor,[39] of both the oxen and the sheep, you shall give to the priests, that your storehouses and garners and the produce of your land may be blessed, and you may be strengthened with grain and wine and oil, and the herds of your cattle and flocks of your sheep may be increased. (Apostolic Constitutions 7.29)

> If you will indeed obey my commandments ... [the LORD your God] will give the rain for your land in its season, the early rain and the later rain, that you may gather in your grain and your wine and your oil. And he will give grass in your fields for your livestock, and you shall eat and be full. (Deuteronomy 11:13–15)

As explained above, the Didache's "first part" of the produce and grain refers to *trumah*. In accordance with Jewish law, "the produce of the wine press" refers to both grapes and wine. Rabbinic law designates a specific time when produce was required to be tithed. Grapes that were consumed as fruit reached the tithing stage when they were "in the early stages of ripening." Grapes used for wine became liable for tithing during the wine-making process after the liquid had "been skimmed."[40] "The produce ... of the threshing floor" is a general term for grain that included wheat, barley, oats, spelt, and rye.[41] In rabbinic law, grains reached their tithing stage "after they [were] one-third ripe."[42]

The "first part" of "both cattle and sheep" refers to something similar to the Torah's law of offering up the firstborn (*bechor*, בכור) of animals. We find this injunction in Numbers 18:

> Everything that opens the womb of all flesh, whether man or beast, which they offer to the LORD, shall be yours. Nevertheless, the firstborn of man you shall redeem, and the firstborn of unclean animals

[13.3]
You shall take every first part of the produce of the wine press and threshing floor, and of both cattle and sheep.

---

38 Deuteronomy 12:6, 17.
39 Cf. Numbers 18:27, 30.
40 m.*Ma'aserot* 1:2, 7.
41 Rabbi Scherman and Rabbi Zlotowitz, ed., *Yad Avraham Mishnah Series: Seder Zeraim*, 4b:5.
42 m.*Ma'aserot* 1:3.

[13.3] *You shall take every first part of the produce of the wine press and threshing floor, and of both cattle and sheep.*

you shall redeem. And their redemption price (at a month old you shall redeem them) you shall fix at five shekels in silver, according to the shekel of the sanctuary, which is twenty gerahs. But the firstborn of a cow, or the firstborn of a sheep, or the firstborn of a goat, you shall not redeem; they are holy. You shall sprinkle their blood on the altar and shall burn their fat as a food offering, with a pleasing aroma to the LORD. (Numbers 18:15–17)

The domesticated firstborn animal was offered up on the altar in Jerusalem, and the priest was required to eat its flesh there.[43] Animals offered as gifts to prophets and teachers did not have the sacred status of Levitical sacrifices. They were intended as food or livestock for the recipients to use as they saw fit. Considering that even Noah offered only ritually clean animals upon the altar, it seems safe to assume the Gentiles of the Didache would not offer unclean animals to the prophets or teachers.

The general principle is that the Lord should be honored with a portion from the blessings that he has bestowed upon his people and that the prophets and teachers are to be the recipients of those gifts.

⁕ But if you do not have a prophet, give it to the poor.
(DIDACHE 13.4)

The Didache now brings forth a specific clarifying statement to the general injunction to offer the "first part" to the priest.[44] If there was not a true prophet or qualified teacher present within a community, the "first part" was given over to the poor.[45] This principle seems to be based, in part, on the Torah's commandment to give the second tithe to the poor (*ma'aser ani*, מעשר עני) in the third and sixth years of the Sabbatical cycle:

> At the end of every three years you shall bring out all the tithe of your produce in the same year and lay it up within your towns. And the

---

43 Numbers 18:15–18. If the animal developed a blemish, it was then not offered up on the altar, but it was given to the priest nonetheless. Today, without a Temple, the firstborn of an animal is usually left to graze by itself until it develops a blemish, and it is then given to a priest. See Rabbi HaKohen, *The Concise Book of Mitzvoth*, 71.
44 This statement begins with the Semitic *ean de* ("but if," ἐὰν δὲ).
45 In 13.4, the Georgian version of the Didache has "theologian" in place of "prophet."

Levite, because he has no portion or inheritance with you, and the sojourner, the fatherless, and the widow, who are within your towns, shall come and eat and be filled, that the LORD your God may bless you in all the work of your hands that you do. (Deuteronomy 14:28–29)

[13.4] *But if you do not have a prophet, give it to the poor.*

This is a general principle that not only applies to the produce and livestock mentioned in 13.3, but to all the "first part" instructions of chapter 13.

The Apostolic Constitutions turns this into a general prescription to give a tithe to the needy: "You shall give the tenth of your increase to the orphan, and to the widow, and to the poor, and to the stranger" (Apostolic Constitutions 7.29). This is in accordance with the Torah commandments that specifically forbid oppressing these groups: "You shall not mistreat any widow or fatherless child" (Exodus 22:22); "You shall not oppress a sojourner" (Exodus 23:9); "You shall not oppress a hired worker who is poor and needy" (Deuteronomy 24:14).[46]

When you make a batch of bread dough, take the first part and give it according to the commandment. (DIDACHE 13.5)

Some scholars mistake this practice of offering up a first part of the bread as a double tithe based upon the fact that a "first part ... of the threshing floor" is already offered (13.4). On the contrary, this commandment to take the "first part ... [of] a batch of bread dough" finds its context in the Torah's commandment of *challah* ("portion," חלה), which was a form of *trumah*.[47] In the writing of Philo, we find a precedent for referring to this commandment as "first part" *aparche*.[48] The Apostolic Constitutions renders this: "All the first part of your hot bread ... you shall give to the priests" (Apostolic Constitutions 7.29).

Originally, when the Temple stood in Jerusalem, a portion of each batch of dough was given to the priests. This allowed even the non-farmer to offer up a sort of firstfruits. This commandment was considered so important that its performance is said by the Prophet Ezekiel in 44:30 to cause a blessing to rest on the house of the one who obeyed it. The portion of the dough for the priest was called *challah*,

---

46   Cf. Jeremiah 7:6.
47   Numbers 15:17–21.
48   Philo, *On the Special Laws* 1.132.

[13.5]
When you make a batch of bread dough, take the first part and give it according to the commandment.

and the commandment was called "the separation of *challah*." "Since the *challah* is a form of *trumah*, the law does not apply to God-fearing Gentiles."[49]

Additionally, because the *challah* portion had the status of priestly *trumah*, the priests could not eat it unless they were in a state of ritual purity. After the destruction of the Temple, when the priesthood was no longer Levitically fit to receive *challah*, the custom of destroying the *challah* portion developed. Instead of giving it to the priesthood, the baker burned the *challah* portion in the oven or in the fire. This is still practiced today by observant Jews.[50]

While the expression "as the Lord commanded in his good news" (8.2; cf. 11.3, 15.3–4) is an unambiguous reference to the teachings of the Master, the phrase "according to the commandment" seems to invoke the authority of the Torah.[51] It might not have a specific commandment in mind. In Jewish vernacular, "the commandment" is shorthand for the whole Torah (cf. 1 Timothy 6:14). By invoking the authority of "the commandment," the Didache alludes to the principle of giving a portion of one's increase expressed in the Torah's numerous laws of tithing, charity, and sacred gifts. Alternatively, it might be an explicit reference to the injunction to separate the *challah*.

If the Didache is referencing the latter, this indicates that it seeks to reapply the commandment of *challah* for Gentiles who are not otherwise obligated to this Torah injunction. The *challah* portion of Gentile believers would not have the same sanctity as if it were from Jewish dough, so it could be given to a prophet or teacher and did not need to be given to a priest or be burned. This allowed Gentile believers to participate in the commandment of *challah* in a distinctive manner that honored Jewish tradition.[52]

---

49 D. Thomas Lancaster, *Torah Club: Depths of the Torah* (6 vols.; Marshfield, MO: First Fruits of Zion, 2017), 2:729–730.

50 The separation of *challah* today is only performed if more than 2 lbs. 8 oz. of flour is used. For details on the procedure and technical guidelines see Rabbi Dovid Weinberger, *The Artscroll Women's Siddur: Sefard* (Brooklyn, NY: Artscroll, 2005), 196–197.

51 The Greek clause "according to the commandment" most likely reflects "the Hebrew or Aramaic wording כמצוה or כמצוותא because the word מצוה or מצוותא ('commandment/precept') was well established in similar contexts in the language of the Sages" (Van de Sandt and Flusser, *The Didache*, 362).

52 The phrase "according to the commandment" appears here in the context of the giving of the first part of the dough as well as the commandment to tithe on all one's possessions in 13.7. In Jewish law, both of these injunctions were applicable both within the land of Israel and in the Diaspora. The Didache's phrase "according to the commandment" may imply that these are the only two commandments in chapter 13 that legally apply for the Jewish people outside the land of Israel.

> *Likewise, when you open a vessel of wine or oil, take the first part and give it to the prophets.* (DIDACHE 13.6)

Just as with a batch of dough, the first of a wine bottle and of a jar of oil was to be given to the prophets and teachers.[53] Unlike the Didache's previous injunctions, we have no direct parallels to this commandment in Jewish law. The Apostolic Constitutions states: "All the first part ... of your barrels of wine, or oil, or honey, or nuts, or grapes, or the first part of other things, you shall give to the priests" (Apostolic Constitutions 7.29). Again, in the Apostolic Constitutions the "priests" in view are not Levitical priests but ecclesiastical authorities.

The tithing of wine and grapes was discussed in 13.3.

"Oil" here undoubtedly refers to olive oil. Jewish law designates olives as one of the three items (along with grain and grapes) from which a person is biblically obligated to remove *trumah* and tithes.[54] Depending upon how the olives are used, they reach the tithing stage at two different times. Olives that are used for food are tithed "after they grow one-third ripe," and olives used for oil are to be tithed "after [the oil] has dripped through the trough."[55] The mention of olive oil here may imply that olives are included in the injunction to tithe grain in 13.3. The two are combined in a Mishnaic discussion on tithing.[56]

Jewish legal literature does not contain instructions about tithing either oil or wine after it has been bottled. It could be that the Didache is speaking of a case in which the wine or the oil falls under the category of doubtfully tithed food (*demai*, דמאי). *Demai* refers to situations in which, for various reasons, the buyer might be unsure of whether the tithes have been removed.[57] Tractate *Demai* discusses the various procedures for tithing such food and when it can be done. It was generally assumed that if produce had been bought from a Jewish merchant, at the very least *trumah gedolah* had been removed. It is possible then that the Didache refers to wine and oil purchased from the non-Jewish market, in which case it would have been certain that the "first part" had not been removed. Under this scenario, it was to be removed at the opening of the "vessel."

---

53 *The Ethiopic Church Order* adds honey to this command and replaces "prophets" with "the poor": "Likewise an earthenware vessel of wine or of oil, and of honey, having opened it, having taken the first-fruits of it, give it to the poor" (Horner, *The Statutes of the Apostles*, 194.18–20).
54 Rabbi Scherman and Rabbi Zlotowitz, ed., *Yad Avraham Mishnah Series: Seder Zeraim*, 4b:5.
55 m.*Ma'aserot* 1:3, 7.
56 m.*Ma'aserot* 1:3.
57 Instone-Brewer, *Traditions of the Rabbis from the Era of the New Testament*, 1:169.

[13.6]
Likewise, when you open a vessel of wine or oil, take the first part and give it to the prophets.

Another possibility is that this refers to an otherwise undocumented Jewish legal practice in which the "first part" of wine and oil was separated for the priest in a similar manner to the separation of *challah* from a loaf of bread dough. As was discussed in the commentary to 13.2, "likewise" might represent the talmudic phrase *vechen* ("and likewise," וכן), which is used to infer "that the second halachah resembles the one preceding it."[58] In turn, 13.6 should be viewed in a similar vein to 13.5.

By commanding the Gentiles to take the "first part" of "a vessel of wine or oil," the Didache's legislation allowed the non-farmer to participate in the commandment of *trumah*. He, too, desired to give thanks to God for his bountiful provision and to take care of the prophets and teachers.

> *Also of money and clothing and any other possession, take the first part as it seems fitting to you, and give it according to the commandment.* (DIDACHE 13.7)

Lastly, the Didache extends the commandment of the "first part" to "money and clothing and any other possession." This could be a general injunction to give to prophets and teachers from all of one's income and/or possessions.[59] This appears to be alluding once again to Numbers 18: "Every devoted thing in Israel shall be yours" (Numbers 18:14).

As with the commandment to give the "first part" of the dough in 13.5, the surrendering of the first part of one's non-agricultural possessions was also to be done "according to the commandment."[60] The "commandment" refers to the Torah.[61] The Didache could be making a general reference to the Torah's injunctions on tithing, charity, and sacred gifts. Alternatively, "according to the commandment" could refer more specifically to the rabbinic interpretation of the Torah's laws about giving a percentage of one's income, namely that everyone is obligated to give a

---

58   Rabbi Steinsaltz, *The Talmud Steinsaltz Edition: A Reference Guide*, 92.
59   Niederwimmer, *The Didache*, 193.
60   "And perhaps we can discern in the wording *kemitzvah*, which only applies to the *Halachot* pertaining to gifts for [their] priests and for the poor, a hint of the word *Mitzvah*, *metzavta* which is used by the Amoraim and the Tanaim in Israel, and denotes *ketzedaka*, the giving of money" (Alon, "The Halacha in the Teaching of the Twelve Apostles," 192).
61   Note the version in *The Ethiopic Church Order* renders "according to the commandment" here as "according to the commandment of the Lord." See Horner, *The Statutes of the Apostles*, 194.22–23.

tithe of his income to charity.[62] Supporting this view, the Apostolic Constitutions seems to interpret "give it according to the commandment" as an injunction to give a monetary tithe to the poor:

> All the first parts of your hot bread, of your barrels of wine, or oil, or honey, or nuts, or grapes, or the first part of other things, you shall give to the priests; but those of money, and of clothing, and any other possessions, to the orphan and to the widow. (Apostolic Constitutions 7.29)

[13.7]
Also of money and clothing and any other possession, take the first part as it seems fitting to you, and give it according to the commandment.

Although most of the Torah's injunctions on tithing involve agricultural products, by the Second Temple Period the sages of Israel began extending tithing to one's income (*ma'aser kesafim*, מעשר כספים). Both Abraham and Jacob offered a tithe to the Lord on all their possessions.[63] We find evidence of this practice in Yeshua's parable about the Pharisee and the tax collector in which the Pharisee declares, "I give tithes of all that I get" (Luke 18:12). The midrash *Sifrei* finds support for tithing beyond agriculture through a creative exegesis of Deuteronomy 14:22:

> "You shall definitely tithe all your agricultural produce which comes forth in the field every year." From this we could deduce that only agricultural produce must be tithed. How can we deduce that it applies to loan interest, trading, and all other profits? From the word "all"; for the verse could have stated "your agricultural produce." What is the significance of "all"? To include loan interest, trading, and all other profits.[64]

It is difficult to discern with any certainty what taking the "first part" of "clothing" implies. It could be used in the general sense of referring to giving an offering on all one's income, no matter in what form, be it money or goods or it could specifically refer to the materials from which clothing is made: wool, linen, and

---

62 "In 13:7, however, a wider separation of tithes, like money, clothes, and chattel is recorded. Also in this respect, however, the Didache reflects established Jewish halakha. In a later period, the custom of tithing was extended to apply to other types of income as well, to goods and money in general, although this custom never was really widespread. Judging by Jewish sources indicating this practice, it is likely that this tendency to tithe all profits had already emerged in the Second Temple period. In a time when trade, in addition to pasturage, became an important component of the nation's economy, this measure probably served as a means to treat the farmer and traders equally in the matter of tithes. The conclusion appears to be that the regulation in the Didache reflects contemporary Jewish halachah" (Van de Sandt and Flusser, *The Didache*, 362).
63 Genesis 14:20, 28:22. Cf. Jubilees 32:2.
64 *Sifrei* on Deuteronomy 14:22 as quoted in *Tosafot Ta'anit* 9a as translated in Cyril Domb, ed., *Maaser Kesafim: Giving a Tenth to Charity* (New York, NY: Feldheim, 1982), 20. Cf. *Community Rule* (1QS) XIV, 11–15; y.*Pe'ah* 1:1; b.*Ketubot* 51a; *Pesikta Rabbati* 25; *Pesikta DeRav Kahana* 10.

[13.7]
Also of money and clothing and any other possession, take the first part as it seems fitting to you, and give it according to the commandment.

flax. In turn, it might even allude to the commandment in Deuteronomy 18:4 to give "the first fleece of your sheep" to the priest.[65]

The Didache adds the qualifying instruction to "take the first part ... as it seems fitting to you"—that is to say, there is no fixed amount. This should be taken as a clarifying statement to the term "first part" that can then be applied generally to the rest of the "first part" injunctions of chapter 13. This is reminiscent of the Mishnaic axiom: "These are matters that do not have a specific limit: the corner of a field, the first fruits, the pilgrimage, acts of generosity, and Torah study" (m.*Pe'ah* 1:1).

In the Didache's system of tithing, everyone was to give a "first part," regardless of whether they were farmers, bakers, or day laborers. In this way, the Didache expands and modifies the Torah's system of priestly gifts to adapt it to Gentile believers living in the Diaspora, allowing them to participate in this important set of commandments. Thomas O'Loughlin comments:

> Among the Jews this offering was a way both of honoring God for his goodness and of supporting the praise of God through supporting the priesthood. Now, in the Didache, it is carrying on these two functions: it praises God and supports the work of the prophets who seem to have inherited the rights of the "high priest."[66]

---

65 The sages ruled that this offering of fleece should be one sixtieth in quantity, and it is still observed today in the land of Israel, where the wool tithe is still given to the priests (Rabbi Yisrael Meir HaKohen, *The Concise Book of Mitzvoth*, 69–71).

66 Thomas O'Loughlin, *The Didache: A Window on the Earliest Christians* (Grand Rapids, MI: Baker, 2010), 124.

Chapter Fourteen

DIDACHE 14

14.1 On the day of the Lord, being gathered together, break bread and give thanks after having confessed your transgressions,[1] so that your sacrifice may be pure.

14.2 But do not let anyone who has a quarrel with his fellow come together with you until they have reconciled,[2] so that your sacrifice may not be impure.

14.3 For this is what was spoken by the Lord: "'In every place and time, offer me a pure sacrifice … because I am a great king,' says the Lord, 'and my name is awesome among the Gentiles.'"[3]

---

1 1 Corinthians 11:28–29.
2 Matthew 5:23–24.
3 Malachi 1:11, 14.

Overview

Chapter 14 is one of the shortest sections in the entire Didache, comprising only three verses. It continues in the broader section of legal rulings (chapters 11–15). The contents of this chapter are concerned with resolving community sins and quarrels and maintaining the purity and unity of the congregation.

STRUCTURE

Specific instructions are given in this chapter on how to maintain the holiness of community gatherings and meals. The chapter can be divided into three sections—a general principle, specifics of the general principle, and a proof text—but the theme is consistent throughout: "God requires that the community offer him a pure sacrifice."[4]

GENERAL PRINCIPLE	
14.1	Confessing transgressions before coming together as a community
SPECIFICS OF GENERAL PRINCIPLE	
14.2	Reconciling with fellow before coming together as a community
PROOF TEXT	
14.3	Citation from Malachi enforcing the idea that community meals are like sacrifices

The holy nature of ceremonial meals and prayer was alluded to in both 9.5, "Do not let anyone eat or drink by means of your giving of thanks except those immersed," and 10.6, "Everyone who is holy, let him come. Everyone who is not, let him repent." In chapter 14, the Didache appears to elaborate further on the instructions given

---

[4] Jonathan A. Draper, "Pure Sacrifice in Didache 14 as Jewish Christian Exegesis," *Neotestamentica* 42, no. 2 (2008): 230.

in 4.14: "Confess your transgressions in the assembly, and you will not draw near in prayer with a guilty conscience. This is the Way of Life."[5]

While the basic principle of making amends before gathering as a community is mentioned before the instructions on immersion, details of what this looks like are now given, as the new initiate would now be engaging frequently in prayer, ceremonial meals, and fellowship with the community after his immersion. Purity of the community must be maintained through constant confession and introspection.

Some scholars have wondered why these instructions were not given immediately after chapters 9 and 10, which give important instructions for the new disciple's first fellowship meal with the community. But because the believer had been newly immersed and had confessed his sin beforehand, he did not need to confess his transgressions again and should have had no grievances with community members. Instead, the focus at that stage was on learning the blessings. Chapter 14 represents a point at which the new disciple was fully integrated into the community and fellowshiping with the community on a regular basis. The stress here lies on community holiness and harmony among its members.

Offering Your Gift

In chapter 14, the Didache once again draws from and exegetes the teachings of the Master. Yeshua teaches in the Sermon on the Mount:

> If you are offering your gift at the altar and there remember that your brother has something against you, leave your gift there before the altar and go. First be reconciled to your brother, and then come and offer your gift. (Matthew 5:23–24)

The Didache applies this teaching spiritually to fellowship meals within the community.

When believers meet together for worship or any sacred function, it should be in a holy atmosphere devoid of sin and conflict. When things are not right between brothers and sisters, animosity taints their gatherings, and the spiritual sacrifice is defiled, so to speak. Instead, grievances between parties should be resolved before assembling for public prayer or a ceremonial meal. This is the responsibility not

---

5 Aaron Milavec, *The Didache: Faith, Hope, & Life of the Earliest Christian Communities, 50–70 C.E.* (New York, NY: Newman, 2003), 531.

just of the leadership but of "every member of the community: Everyone is to be on guard that reconciliation happens before worship."[6]

Temple Replaced?

The Didache likens the ceremonial community meals to ceremonial meals that took place around the sacrifices that were offered in the Temple. When Jewish worshipers came together for a ceremonial meal to eat a peace offering, a thanksgiving offering, a vow offering, or a Passover offering, they needed to ensure that all the participants were in a state of ritual purity. To participate in such a meal while in a state of Levitical impurity was a serious sin that incurred excision from the community:

> All who are clean may eat flesh, but the person who eats of the flesh of the sacrifice of the LORD's peace offerings while an uncleanness is on him, that person shall be cut off from his people. And if anyone touches an unclean thing, whether human uncleanness or an unclean beast or any unclean detestable creature, and then eats some flesh from the sacrifice of the LORD's peace offerings, that person shall be cut off from his people. (Leviticus 7:19–21)

The Didache derives a spiritual principle from the Torah's legislation regarding Levitical purity at sacrificial meals. Much as the Jewish worshiper needed to be Levitically pure before participating in a sacrificial meal, so the disciple of Yeshua should have a clean conscience before God and with his fellow before participating in a ceremonial community meal.

Similar to the way that the priesthood needed to ensure the purity of a sacrifice before offering it on the altar in Jerusalem, the community must be certain that the spiritual sacrifice of their meal was without blemish. The language connecting community meals and sacrifice is already found in previous chapters of the Didache:

> Guard yourself from what has been offered to idols because it is the worship of dead gods. (6.3)

---

[6] Tony Jones, *The Teaching of the Twelve: Believing & Practicing the Primitive Christianity of the Ancient Didache Community* (Brewster, MA: Paraclete, 2009), 109.

> Do not let anyone eat or drink by means of your giving of thanks except those immersed in the name of the Lord, for the Lord even said concerning this, "Do not give what is holy to the dogs." (9.5)

Some scholars view the sacrificial language of chapter 14 as a rejection of the Temple and the priesthood in Jerusalem. However, the Didache represents a time when believers were still firmly rooted within Judaism and Torah. A major theme throughout the Didache is the longing for the prophesied arrival of the Messianic Era. These prophecies included defeating Israel's enemies, gathering the Jewish people back to their land, establishing the kingdom in Jerusalem, and last but not least, rebuilding the Temple. These were all to be accomplished by Messiah Yeshua upon his return.

The Master referred to the Temple as his "Father's house" (Luke 2:49). He cleared out the money changers who were defiling its courts,[7] and he referenced the Messianic prophecy "My house shall be called a house of prayer for all the nations" (Mark 11:17 quoting Isaiah 56:7), which pointed to the future time when Gentiles of all nationalities will flock to the Temple to worship the God of Israel.

The apostles, who could be referred to as a Temple sect, often referred to the service of God as a spiritual sacrifice:

> I appeal to you therefore, brothers, by the mercies of God, to present your bodies as a living sacrifice, holy and acceptable to God, which is your spiritual worship. (Romans 12:1)

> God [gave me grace] to be a minister of [Messiah Yeshua] to the Gentiles in the priestly service of the gospel of God, so that the offering of the Gentiles may be acceptable, sanctified by the Holy Spirit. (Romans 15:15–16)

> Through him then let us continually offer up a sacrifice of praise to God, that is, the fruit of lips that acknowledge his name. (Hebrews 13:15)

The book of Hebrews also speaks of hospitality and brotherly love as that which we "offer to God" as "acceptable worship, with reverence and awe" (Hebrews 12:28). In all these examples, spiritually applying the sacrifices does not replace the physical Temple and priesthood.[8]

---

7   Matthew 21:12–17; Mark 11:15–19; Luke 19:45–48; John 2:13–16.
8   Cf. Testament of Levi 3:5.

We find this same type of allegorization in other Jewish literature as well. The Jewish philosopher Philo of Alexandria spiritualizes the sacrificial service:

> Even if they bring nothing else, still when they bring themselves, the most perfect completeness of virtue and excellence, they are offering the most excellent of all sacrifices, honoring God, their Benefactor and Savior, with hymns and thanksgivings; the former uttered by the organs of the voice, and the latter without the agency of the tongue or mouth, the worshippers making their exclamations and invocations with their soul alone. (*Special Laws* 1.272)[9]

Table as Altar

The Jewish concept of the miniature sanctuary (*mikdash me'at*, מקדש מעט) sheds further light on the sacrificial imagery around communal meals. The sages developed the concept of the miniature sanctuary from Ezekiel 11, where Ezekiel cries out for the Jewish people in exile: "Ah, Lord GOD! Will you make a full end of the remnant of Israel?" (Ezekiel 11:13), to which God promises:

> Though I removed them far off among the nations, and though I scattered them among the countries, yet I have been a sanctuary [*mikdash me'at*] to them for a while in the countries where they have gone. (Ezekiel 11:16)

God is reassuring the Jewish people that while they are in exile, they will have little sanctuaries among them to remind them that in the coming Messianic Era, the Temple will be rebuilt and they will be gathered back. Jewish tradition interprets these little sanctuaries as the synagogue, the house of study, and the home.[10] The idea is a logical outworking of the Pharisaic understanding that all Israelites are priests, and they therefore tried to emulate Temple practices in their own homes.

When the home is compared to a sanctuary, the table upon which one eats becomes like the Temple altar (*mizbeach*, מזבח), and the food we eat upon it becomes like sacrifices. The sages said, "As long as the Temple stood, the altar atoned for Israel, but now a man's table atones for him."[11] And at this table spiritual sacrfices were offered up:

---

9   Cf. *On the Special Laws* 1.248.
10   b.*Megillah* 29b.
11   b.*Brachot* 55a. Cf. b.*Chagigah* 27a.

Rabbi Shimon says: "Three who ate at a single table and did not say upon it words of Torah, it is as though they ate from the offerings of the dead, as it is said: 'For all of the tables are full of vomit and feces without the Omnipresent' [Isaiah 28:8]. However, three who ate at one table and said upon it words of Torah, it is as though they ate from the table of the Omnipresent, blessed be He, as it is said: 'And he said to me, this is the table that is before the Lord' [Ezekiel 41:22]." (m.*Avot* 3:3)

This is especially true on Shabbat, when the loaves of *challah* are symbolic of the bread of the Presence, the wine represents the drink offerings, the Sabbath candles are like the golden Menorah, and the special clothes that are worn recall the priestly garments. The bread is even salted in remembrance of the fact that every sacrifice made on the altar must be salted. The priestly blessing recited in the Temple is read over the children, and the table songs are similar to the Levitical choir. This imagery informs the Didache's ceremonial meals, connecting the community's breaking bread with the Temple sacrifice.

Similarities can be found in the modern-day Chasidic movement with customs such as the *Farbrengen* ("gathering," פארברענגען) and a rebbe's *tish* ("table," טיש). These communal and ceremonial meals take place on Shabbat and other special occasions. The meals assume an elaborate and sacred tone, often mimicking the service of the priests in the Temple:

> Once, Rabbi Monele Karliner entered the *tish* [table] of Rabbi Shmuel of Karlin and the Ratner Maggid was cutting the meat for him. His face was burning like a torch, and he took a piece of meat and put it in his mouth and said: I eat this with the same intent as the High Priest in the Holy Temple would eat the sin offering; then he took another piece and said, this one, as a burnt offering.[12]

The Chasidic masters point out that in the Torah's mention of "consuming fire" (Deuteronomy 4:24), the Hebrew phrase literally translates as "eating fire" (*aish ochelah*, אש אכלה), and in turn connect the act of eating with the fire that consumes sacrifices on the altar.

While some of these concepts in Judaism may have developed at a later time than the Didache, there is no reason to doubt that similar ideas existed in the

---

12 Allan Nadler, "Holy Kugel: The Sanctification of Ashkenazic Ethnic Foods in Hasidism," in *Food and Judaism* (vol. 15 of *Studies in Jewish Civilization*; ed. Leonard J. Greenspoon, Ronald A. Simkins, and Gerald Shapiro; Omaha, NE: Creighton University Press, 2005), 193–214.

first century, especially with the Temple services in recent memory. The communal ceremonial meals of the Didache and these later ideas both draw from the same well of Jewish thought. The writers of the Didache saw community meals as sacrificial and holy, likened to the service in the Temple. In this way, much like with the "first part" gifts of chapter 13, they found a way to reinterpret the laws of the offerings in the Temple in such a way as to allow Gentile disciples of Yeshua to offer a type of sacrifice wherever they were located throughout the world. As they prayed for the ingathering, the symbolic sacrificial meal reminded them of the sacrifices offered in the Temple, the metaphorical sacrifice of Yeshua, and the future sacrifices of the Messianic Era, when the Temple will become a house of prayer for all nations:

> These I will bring to my holy mountain, and make them joyful in my house of prayer; their burnt offerings and their sacrifices will be accepted on my altar; for my house shall be called a house of prayer for all peoples. (Isaiah 56:7)

Practical Application

The contents of chapter 14 provide sober instructions for table fellowship among believers. Before we come together at ceremonial meals such as Sabbath meals, holiday meals, Seder meals, and commemorations of the Master's Last Supper, we should ensure that we have confessed and repented from our sins and that we have reconciled with our brothers and sisters. Sometimes this might involve making restitution or seeking counsel and intervention from an elder. Our holy meals carry a sacred tone and should not be treated as merely an opportunity to fill our bellies. They are the equivalent of our Temple service unto our Father in heaven.

Disciples of Yeshua would profit by learning some of the Jewish traditions surrounding the concept of a miniature sanctuary, especially in regard to honoring the Sabbath through ceremonial meals.[13] By implementing these customs into our homes and fellowship meals, we bring visible reminders to the table that help us remember that our ceremonial meals have a sacred tone.

---

13   Jewish tradition sees festive meals on the Sabbath as a fulfillment of "If you ... call the Sabbath a delight (*oneg*, עֹנֶג)" (Isaiah 58:13). Joyous meals enhance the delight (*oneg*) of Shabbat and hence meals and gatherings on the Sabbath are often called *oneg* Shabbat.

Commentary

⁌ On the day of the Lord, being gathered together. (DIDACHE 14.1)

Chapter 14 opens up with one of the most controversial phrases in the entire Didache. Without any introduction or explanation, the Didache states that the community will be gathered together on "the day of the Lord." This is not presented in command form but rather assumes that the audience knows exactly what this term means and is well aware of the practice. The Apostolic Constitutions renders this in command form: "Gather together, without fail" (7.30).

Although the opening words of chapter 14 are usually translated into English as "the day of the Lord" or "the Lord's day," the Greek is more ambiguous. *Kuriaken de kuriou* (κυριακὴν δὲ κυρίου) is a redundant phrase that can literally be translated as "Lord's of the Lord," which is something to the effect of "Lord's day of the Lord" or "the Lord's own day." Some scholars have suggested that this is a Semitism based upon the Torah's phrase "Sabbath of the Lord," where the Didache replaces "Sabbath" with "Lord's" in order to mimic the Hebrew designation.[14]

Many commentators are quick to see this as an early reference to Christian veneration of the first day of the week. This is how it is rendered in the Apostolic Constitutions: "On the day of the resurrection of the Lord, that is, the Lord's day" (7.30). Yet the evidence may not be that clear cut. The appearance of "the day of the Lord" in the Didache is the first witness of the title. The phrase "the Lord's day" (*te kuriake hemera*, τῇ κυριακῇ ἡμέρᾳ) does appear one time in the New Testament in the book of Revelation, but no designation is given as to which day it refers to. "It is not until the second century CE that unequivocal references to weekly Sunday worship can be found" and the phrase "the Lord's Day" is directly connected to

---

[14] Cf. the Septuagint of Exodus 20:10 "τῇ σάββατα κυρίῳ" and Leviticus 23:38 "τῶν σαββάτων κυρίου." See Charles Taylor, "The Teaching of the Twelve Apostles with Illustrations from the Talmud," in *Didache: The Unknown Teaching of the Twelve Apostles* (ed. Brent S. Walters; San Jose, CA: Anti-Nicene Archive, 1991), 176. Some have suggested that "Sabbath day of the Lord" was the original in the Didache before it was altered by a scribe.

[14.1]
On the day of the Lord, being gathered together.

the first day of the week.[15] Furthermore, in the New Testament, Sunday is always referred to as "the first day of the week."[16]

Aaron Milavec feels that the Greek could be translated as "every divinely instituted day of the Lord" or "divinely instituted day."[17] He adds, "Given that the Jewish calendar dominates the Didache, the 'divinely instituted day' could refer either to the Sabbath or the first day of the week."[18] It's possible then that "the Lord's day" "might have been an uncommon, apostolic way of referring to the Sabbath day, as Yeshua said, 'For the Son of Man is Lord of the Sabbath' (Matthew 12:8). This explanation is attractive for Sabbatarians, and it might find corroboration in the *Acts of John at Rome*: 'on the seventh day, the Lord's day.'"[19]

A few other suggestions have been proposed as well. Some who hold that the expression "the Lord's day" refers to Sunday view the double repetition in the Didache "the Lord's day of the Lord" as an emphasis that this is not just any Sunday but specifically Resurrection Sunday (Easter Sunday).[20] Neville Tidwell feels that the phrase is a reference to Yom Kippur. The language of "Lord's of the Lord" is similar to the Torah's description of Yom Kippur as the Sabbath of Sabbaths (*Shabbat Shabbaton*, שבת שבתון), both phrases emphasizing the day of which they are speaking as "the most solemn of days."[21] Yom Kippur is about atoning for sins against God and making things right with one's fellow, which parallels the instructions of Didache 14.[22] This opinion, however, is difficult to reconcile with the biblical prohibition to eat or drink on that day.

Samuele Bacchiocchi, citing Jean Baptiste Thibaut, states that "'Lord's—*kuriaken*' is used as an adjective and not as a substantive and that the issue is not the time

---

15 Draper, "Pure Sacrifice in Didache 14 as Jewish Christian Exegesis," 223–252. E.g., Ignatius, *To the Magnesians* 9; Barnabas 15.9; Gospel of Peter 1.9, 12; Apostolic Constitutions 7.30, 36. Justin Martyr mentions holding a "common assembly" (*First Apology* 67) on Sunday, and Tertullian was the first to mention resting on Sunday, "on which day it is our duty to free ourselves from all worldly care and trouble, even postponing business, lest we should give place to the devil" (George Cantrell Allen, *The Didache or the Teaching of the Twelve Apostles* [London, England: Astolat, 1903], 23).

16 Matthew 28:1; Mark 16:2, 9; Luke 24:1; John 20:1, 19; Acts 20:7; 1 Corinthians 16:2.

17 Milavec, *The Didache: Faith, Hope, & Life of the Earliest Christian Communities, 50–70 C.E.*, 533–534.

18 Ibid., 573.

19 D. Thomas Lancaster, *Torah Club: Chronicles of the Apostles* (Marshfield, MO: First Fruits of Zion 2012), 1215.

20 Kurt Niederwimmer, *The Didache: Hermeneia—A Critical and Historical Commentary on the Bible* (Minneapolis, MN: Fortress, 1998), 195, n. 8.

21 Neville Tidwell, "Didache XIV:1 (*Kata Kuriaken de Kuriou*) revisited," *Vigiliae Christianae* 53, no. 2 (1999): 197–207.

22 Daniel Stökl Ben Ezra, *The Impact of Yom Kippur on Early Christianity: The Day of Atonement from Second Temple Judaism to the Fifth Century* (Tübingen, Germany: Mohr Siebeck, 2003), 217.

but the manner of the celebration."[23] Furthermore, based on its close proximity to the end of chapter 13, "according to the commandment," he insists that the opening word *kata* (κατὰ) should be translated as "according to" as it is in 1.5; 2.1; 4.13; 6.1, 11; and 13.6, resulting in "according to the sovereign doctrine of the Lord."[24]

[14.1]
On the day of the Lord, being gathered together.

The most probable answer is that "the day of the Lord" refers to a ceremonial community meal that took place on Saturday night after the Sabbath concluded. Varner writes:

> It follows that the meal was taken in the evening, since that would be when a meal is taken and [since] work obligations would have prevented something as important as this in the daytime ... I am not convinced that Sunday evening was the practice of the Didache believers, since in Jewish custom, evening marks the beginning of the next day.[25]

We see the custom of gathering on Saturday evening in Acts 20:7. "On the first day" and "after the Sabbath" is the time of the Master's resurrection, that is, Saturday night. The early believers seem to have gathered after the Sabbath to commemorate the resurrection and to share a special meal. While the believers may have attended their local synagogues on Shabbat, they could then have gathered together in the evening without the encumbrances of the Sabbath's prohibitions.

The custom of holding a meal on Saturday night after the Sabbath, called *Melaveh Malkah* (מלווה מלכה), is still kept today in many Jewish circles.[26] As Christianity separated from Judaism and lost its Jewish associations, Sunday became

---

23   Samuele Bacchiocchi, *From Sabbath to Sunday: A Historical Investigation of the Rise of Sunday Observance in Early Christianity* (Rome, Italy: Pontifical Gregorian University, 1977), 125–126.
24   Stökl Ben Ezra, *The Impact of Yom Kippur on Early Christianity*, 217.
25   William Varner, *The Way of the Didache: The First Christian Handbook* (New York, NY: University Press of America, 2007), 78.
26   "After explaining that [those not scheduled to make the pilgrimage to the Temple] avoided fasting on Friday and Saturday because of the Sabbath, the Talmud questions why [some] did not fast on the first day of the week. One explanation was 'on account of the *Notzrim* (b.*Ta'anit* 27b).' *Notzrim* means 'Nazarenes,' and refers to the followers of Yeshua. This suggests that the followers of Yeshua would have considered the first day of the week to be a time of rejoicing and an inappropriate time for fasting" (Aaron Eby, *The Sabbath Table* [Marshfield, MO: Vine of David, 2014], 151–152). The earliest reference to *Melaveh Malkah* is in the Talmud: "R. Hanina said: One should always set his table on the termination of the Sabbath, even if he merely requires as much as an olive. Hot water after the termination of the Sabbath is soothing; fresh [warm] bread after the termination of the Sabbath is soothing" (b.*Shabbat* 119b).

[14.1]
On the day of the Lord, being gathered together.

associated with the Lord's Day, but originally the disciples would have gathered on Saturday night.[27]

In addition to meeting at the conclusion of the Sabbath in memory of the resurrection of the Master, it is possible that the community expected his return at this time. Jewish tradition states that Messiah will not come on the Sabbath because there is much work to do upon his arrival.[28] Therefore, the first possible time for his appearance would be at *Melaveh Malkah*. Appropriately, this meal is also known as *Seudata d'David Malka Meshicha* (The Meal of David, King Messiah, סעודתא דדוד מלכא משיחא). Furthermore, upon the return of Messiah, there will be a great banquet.

⊪ *Break bread and give thanks.* (DIDACHE 14.1)

Believers should gather together and share a meal; but before they do that, they must ensure the purity of their hearts and actions. "Gathered together" (14.1) is from the root word *sunago* (συνάγω), which corresponds to the Hebrew verbal root *k-b-tz* ("to assemble, to gather," קבץ). From *sunago* the Greek language derives the term "synagogue." Here the verb implies not only assembling in one location but gathering in a spirit of unity, as in the psalm: "Behold, how good and pleasant it is when brothers dwell in unity!" (Psalm 133:1). In order for that unity to be complete, grievances must be made right before God and with one's fellow.

The Apostolic Constitutions expands this by giving a reason for the thanksgiving:

---

27 There is evidence of Jewish believers celebrating both Shabbat and Sunday: "The Sabbath and the rest of the discipline of the Jews they observed just like them, but at the same time, like us, they celebrated the Lord's days as a memorial of the resurrection of the Saviour" (Eusebius *Ecclesiastical History* 3.27.5). For a while this seemed to be a common practice even in Gentile churches: "Nor is there less variation in regard to religious assemblies. For although almost all churches throughout the world celebrate the sacred mysteries on the sabbath of every week, yet the Christians of Alexandria and at Rome, on account of some ancient tradition, have ceased to do this" (Socrates Scholasticus, *Ecclesiastical History* 5.22). Note especially how the historian Socrates Scholasticus (fifth century) mentions that the "mysteries" (Eucharist of sorts) took place on the evening after Shabbat: "The Egyptians in the neighborhood of Alexandria, and the inhabitants of Thebais, hold their religious assemblies on the sabbath, but do not participate of the mysteries in the manner usual among Christians in general: for after having eaten and satisfied themselves with food of all kinds, in the evening making their offerings they partake of the mysteries" (Socrates Scholasticus, *Ecclesiastical History* 5.22).

28 b.*Pesachim* 13a.

Give thanks to God, and praise him for those mercies God has bestowed upon you through Messiah, and has delivered you from ignorance, error, and bondage. (Apostolic Constitutions 7.30)

[14.1]
Break bread and give thanks.

Interpreters from sacramental traditions are tempted to view the command "break bread and give thanks" as referring to the Eucharist, but here it simply refers to eating a sacred community meal together and making blessings (*brachot*). "Breaking bread" (*paras lechem*, פרס לחם) is used idiomatically in rabbinic literature to refer to giving thanks before a meal.[29] We see this illustrated in the practice of our Master—"When he was at table with them, he took the bread and blessed and broke it and gave it to them" (Luke 24:30)—and in that of the apostles: "They devoted themselves to the apostles' teaching and the fellowship, to the breaking of bread and the prayers ... And day by day, attending the temple together and breaking bread in their homes, they received their food with glad and generous hearts" (Acts 2:42–46).[30] We also find in the Clementine literature:

Peter came several hours after, and breaking the bread after thanksgiving, and putting salt upon it, he gave it first to our mother, and, after her, to us her sons. And thus we took food along with her and blessed God. (Pseudo-Clementine Homilies 14.1)

In turn, Yeshua's breaking of the bread at the Last Seder does not link this practice specifically to that meal.[31] The Hebrew idiom of breaking bread is removed from the Apostolic Constitutions, which simply has, "Give thanks to God, and praise him" (7.30).

The Greek word "give thanks," *eucharisto* (εὐχαριστῶ), corresponds to the Hebrew word *todah* (תודה) and simply means "to say thanks."[32] "Give thanks" then is the command to recite *Grace after Meals*. Therefore, "breaking bread" and "give thanks" form a type of doublet that refers to giving thanks before and after the meal.

---

29 b.*Pesachim* 46a. See Marcus Jastrow, "פרס I" in *A Dictionary of the Targumim, the Talmud Babli and Yerushalmi, and the Midrashic Literature* (2 vols.; New York, NY, Pardes, 1950), 2:1232.
30 Cf. Acts 20:7–11.
31 Cf. Matthew 26:26; Mark 14:22; Luke 22:19; 1 Corinthians 10:16, 11:24.
32 *Eucharisto* could also correspond to the Hebrew term *barach* (ברך). See Oskar Skarsaune, *In the Shadow of the Temple: Jewish Influences on Early Christianity* (Downers Grove, IL: InterVarsity Press, 2002), 407.

❧ *After having confessed your transgressions.* (DIDACHE 14.1)

Before breaking bread and partaking in the meal, the participants should have confessed their sins. James also urges that confession take place amongst believers—"Confess your sins to one another and pray for one another" (James 5:16)—and the Apostle Paul urges purity of heart before partaking in the Passover Seder: "Let a person examine himself, then, and so eat of the bread and drink of the cup. For anyone who eats and drinks without discerning the body eats and drinks judgment on himself" (1 Corinthians 11:28–29). The instructions concerning confession of sin and reconciliation between individuals disappear from the Apostolic Constitutions version.

The sin in 14.2 refers to interpersonal quarrels, but the "transgressions" (*paraptomata*, παραπτώματα) in verse 1 might also include sins between man and God. Jonathan Draper feels that these are inadvertent minor sins that could be absolved through confession:

> Based on the use of this term in the Septuagint ... the reference is to transgressions against God through minor transgressions of the (ritual?) Law ... the inadvertent everyday transgressions of omission and commission, which do not amount to the kind of deliberate defiance of God's commandments.[33]

Willy Rordorf has suggested that this prayer from 1 Clement might have been used in such a confessional manner:

> [God], pitiful and compassionate, forgive us our iniquities and our unrighteousnesses and our transgressions and shortcomings. Lay not to our account every sin of your servants and your handmaids, but cleanse us with the cleansing of your truth, and guide our steps to walk in holiness and righteousness and singleness of heart and to do such things as are good and well pleasing in your sight. (1 Clement 60.1–2)[34]

In the immediate context, if we interpret the meal referred to in chapter 14 of the Didache as taking place on Saturday night, then in Jewish tradition the *Ma'ariv* (evening) prayers recited right as the Sabbath concluded would be the perfect time to confess any transgressions.

---

33 Draper, "Pure Sacrifice in Didache 14 as Jewish Christian Exegesis," 238.
34 Cf. Community Rule (1QS) I, 21–25. Milavec quoting Rordorf in *The Didache: Faith, Hope, & Life of the Earliest Christian Communities, 50–70 C.E.*, 542.

Alternatively, the term "transgressions" might be used in the general sense to refer to all violations of God's standards, whether inadvertent or intentional, ceremonial or interpersonal. In this case, the command to confess transgression before participating in a ceremonial community meal states a general principle that finds specification in the reconciliation prescribed in 14.2.

[14.1]
After having confessed your transgressions.

⫸ *So that your sacrifice may be pure.* (DIDACHE 14.1)

The Didache is concerned that the meals the community eats together are as a "pure" sacrifice unto the Lord. The Septuagint uses the Greek word *katharos* ("pure," καθαρός) to translate the Hebrew word *tahor* (טהור). The word is also used figuratively to describe something that is morally upright.

The Didache metaphorically refers to the ceremonial community meal and the prayers of the assembly as "your sacrifice." The apostles often used the imagery of the Temple and the sacrifices in a metaphorical sense:

> You yourselves like living stones are being built up as a spiritual house, to be a holy priesthood, to offer spiritual sacrifices acceptable to God through [Messiah Yeshua]. (1 Peter 2:5) [35]

As was pointed out in the overview of this chapter, Judaism views the table as an altar and meals as sacrifices.

In the ancient world, both Jews and Gentiles would have connected sacrifice with a community meal. The Didache did not need to explain what sacrifice was and how purity was connected to it for its non-Jewish readers because these concepts were quite prevalent among all peoples of the ancient world.

The Didache's meal represented the pure sacrifice that Gentiles offered to the God of Israel in anticipation of the coming kingdom:

> [The Didache meals] looked forward to the arrival of the kingdom, wherein perfection of life would be expected of all (10.5, 16.2) ... Gentiles would have found the "confession of failings" to be consistent, helpful, and supportive preparation for offering a "pure sacrifice" to this God whom they now knew as a loving Father preparing his "children" to enter the kingdom he has prepared for them.[36]

---

[35] Romans 12:1; Hebrews 13:10, 15; 1 Clement 44.3–4.
[36] Milavec, *The Didache: Faith, Hope, & Life of the Earliest Christian Communities, 50–70 C.E.*, 540.

[14.1]
So that your sacrifice may be pure.

In this way the sacrificial meal also represented the prophetic future Messianic Kingdom, when the Temple will be rebuilt and all nations will go up to Jerusalem to offer pure sacrifices on the altar (Isaiah 56:6–7).

> ⁞ But do not let anyone who has a quarrel with his fellow come together with you until they have reconciled, so that your sacrifice may not be impure. (DIDACHE 14.2)

After the general principle calling for the confession of sin in verse 1, the Didache now offers a specific example of confession and reconciliation between individuals who have grievances with each other. As in 11.2, "But … anyone who has" (*pas de echon*, πᾶς δὲ ἔχων) here betrays an underlying Semitism and serves as a technical indicator that a more specific principle is being introduced.[37] While the individual was to confess his sins in verse 1, verse 2 states that those sins between him and his fellow needed to be first dealt with by reconciling both parties. "One's fellow human being, however, is the only one who can forgive transgressions against him or her, and they are not nearly so ready to forgive."[38]

The prophets spoke of the abhorrent nature of sacrifices offered by those who failed to repent of sin and transgression and who did wrong to their neighbors:

> What to me is the multitude of your sacrifices? says the LORD; I have had enough of burnt offerings of rams and the fat of well-fed beasts … Wash yourselves; make yourselves clean; remove the evil of your deeds from before my eyes; cease to do evil, learn to do good; seek justice, correct oppression; bring justice to the fatherless, plead the widow's cause. (Isaiah 1:11–17)

Philo of Alexandria addresses the relationship between offering a proper sacrifice and having a clear conscience before God:

> Let the man, therefore, who is adorned with these qualities go forth in cheerful confidence to the temple which most nearly belongs to him,

---

37 Jonathan A. Draper, "Weber, Theissen and 'Wandering Charismatics' in the Didache," *Journal of Early Christian Studies* 6, no. 4 (Winter 1998): 565. Gottfried Schille ["Das Recht der Propheten und Apostel—Gemeinderechtliche Beobachtungen zu Didache Kapitel 11–13," in *Theologische Versuche* I (ed. P. Wätzel and Schille; Berlin, Germany: Evangelische Verlagsanstalt, 1966), 89–90] sees these reflecting the Semitic כל and כי אם.

38 Draper, "Pure Sacrifice in Didache 14 as Jewish Christian Exegesis," 238.

the most excellent of all abodes to offer himself as a sacrifice. But let him in whom covetousness and a desire of unjust things dwell and display themselves, cover his head and be silent, checking his shameless folly and his excessive impudence, in those matters in which caution is profitable; for the temple of the truly living God may not be approached by unholy sacrifices. (*Special Laws* 1:270)[39]

[14.2]
But do not let anyone who has a quarrel with his fellow come together with you until they have reconciled, so that your sacrifice may not be impure.

Didache 14.2 seems to be working from a saying of the Master's similar to this:

If you are offering your gift at the altar and there remember that your brother has something against you, leave your gift there before the altar and go. First be reconciled to your brother, and then come and offer your gift. (Matthew 5:23–24)

The phrase "be reconciled" (*diallassomai*, διαλλάσσομαι) is found in both Matthew 5:24 and Didache 14.2.[40] In a similar manner, the sages stressed that the ceremonies of Yom Kippur can atone for transgressions between God and man but not for transgressions committed between one's fellow and his neighbor. The latter needed to be dealt with personally.[41]

While 14.1 is given in the plural form, verse 2 is in the second-person singular. The responsibility was on the individual within the community to make things right with his brother, whether he had a grievance with him or knew that the individual was upset with him. If reconciliation could not take place, then judges would be brought in to mediate: "Do not crave conflict, but bring those who are quarrelling to peaceful reconciliation. Judge righteously; do not show partiality when rebuking transgressions" (4.3). If either party refused to repent, he was to be shunned: "And if anyone has wronged another person, let no one speak to him nor let him hear from you until he repents" (15.3).

Here the universal word "fellow" is used instead of the more community-specific "brother" found in 4.8. Yeshua used this wider term to indicate a broader sphere than the immediate religious community. This implies that the mandate to resolve wrongs committed against others applies even to wrongs committed against those outside the community. "The norms of the Way of Life applied to all persons,

---

39 Cf. *On the Special Laws* 1.275, 277.
40 Niederwimmer, *The Didache*, 198.
41 m.*Yoma* 8:9. Cf. Didache 4.14 and Barnabas 19.12.

[14.2]
But do not let anyone who has a quarrel with his fellow come together with you until they have reconciled, so that your sacrifice may not be impure.

irrespective of their religious affiliation."[42] Judaism considers it a commandment for a person to reconcile with one who has a grievance against him:

> Rabbi Isaac said: "Whosoever offends his neighbor, and he does it only through words, must pacify him, as it is written: 'My son, if thou art become surety for your neighbor, if you have struck your hands for a stranger—you are snared by the words of your mouth ... do this, now, my son, and deliver yourself, seeing you have come into the hand of your neighbor; go, humble yourself, and urge your neighbor.'" (b.*Yoma* 87a quoting Proverbs 6:1–3)

Practically speaking, the presence of two quarreling members of a community at the same table of fellowship had the real potential to upset the peace and joy of a gathering. Existing tensions were likely to be visible at community gatherings and might have even resulted in verbal arguments.

The Didache uses the negative form "may not be impure." In ritual contexts *koinoo* ("to make impure," κοινόω) is used as the direct opposite of *katharos* ("pure"). The Master speaks of the dangers of spiritual impurity: "It is not what goes into the mouth that defiles a person, but what comes out of the mouth; this defiles a person" (Matthew 15:11).[43]

The Apostolic Constitutions omits any mention of confession of sin or reconciliation and steers the discussion in a different direction. Instead it emphasizes that thanksgiving and praise to God make the offering pure:

> Gather yourselves together, without fail, give thanks to God, and praise him for those mercies God has bestowed upon you through Messiah, and has delivered you from ignorance, error, and bondage, that your sacrifice may be pure, and acceptable to God. (Apostolic Constitutions 7.30)

---

42 Milavec, *The Didache: Faith, Hope, & Life of the Earliest Christian Communities, 50–70 C.E.*, 533.
43 Cf. Mark 7:21–23.

> *For this is what was spoken by the Lord:*
> *"'In every place and time, offer me a pure sacrifice ...*
> *because I am a great king,' says the Lord, 'and my name*
> *is awesome among the Gentiles.'"* (DIDACHE 14.3)

In the last verse of chapter 14, the Didache cites a passage from Malachi to support the idea that community meals conducted by Gentiles in the Diaspora can function as a sacrificial meal unto the Lord. Surprisingly, although the Didache is riddled with biblical language and allusions to Scriptures, this is one of only two direct quotations from the Scriptures by the Didache, the other being Zechariah 14:5 in 16.7.[44]

"Lord" in this context obviously refers to the Lord GOD and not to the Master Yeshua since this is a quotation from Malachi.[45] The Apostolic Constitutions concurs: "God who has said concerning his universal assembly ..." (7.30).

Scholars debate whether the Didache is translating from the Hebrew Bible or borrowing directly from a Greek version. The language does not follow the Septuagint of Malachi.[46] Neither does the Didache's version closely translate the Masoretic text. Interestingly, the version in the Apostolic Constitutions is closer to the Masoretic text.

MALACHI 1:11, 14	DIDACHE 14.3	APOSTOLIC CONSTITUTIONS 7.30
"From the rising of the sun to its setting ... and in every place incense will be offered to my name, and a pure offering ... for I am a great King," says the LORD of hosts, "and my name will be feared among the nations."	"In every place and time, offer me a pure sacrifice ... because I am a great king," says the Lord, "and my name is awesome among the Gentiles."	"In every place will incense and a pure sacrifice be offered to me ... because I am a great king," says the Lord Almighty, "and my name is awesome among the Gentiles."

---

44 Paul quotes the antithesis of this from Isaiah 52:5: "You who boast in the law dishonor God by breaking the law. For, as it is written, 'The name of God is blasphemed among the Gentiles because of you'" (Romans 2:23–24).
45 Niederwimmer, *The Didache*, 198.
46 Ibid., n. 35.

[14.3]
For this is what was spoken by the Lord: "'In every place and time, offer me a pure sacrifice ... because I am a great king,' says the Lord, 'and my name is awesome among the Gentiles.'"

Besides several textual omissions, the most notable differences between the Didache and the Masoretic text is the change "from the rising of the sun until its setting" to "in every place and time." The Didache's phrasing is simply an explanation of the idiom. The sun rises in the east and sets in the west. From east to west indicates "in every place." The sun rises in the morning and sets at night. From morning to night indicates "in every time." Paul might be alluding to the same passage from Malachi when he says, "I desire then that in every place the men should pray" (1 Timothy 2:8).

Oskar Skarsaune argues that the quotation here is a "very free version—perhaps because it was used liturgically already in this period (ca. AD 100). Later this text is quoted again and again by many church fathers."[47] The interpretation method reflects Jewish exegesis and could have been influenced by the Targums, in which the passage is reinterpreted to fit the current situation.[48]

The original verse in Malachi comes in the midst of a rebuke of the priesthood and its nonchalant attitude toward the Temple service. Additionally, it is a reminder that in the coming Messianic Kingdom, all nations will worship the Lord. The verse contains ambiguity. For example, the twice-repeated phrase "My name will be great among the nations" has no verb in the original, so it could be read in the present tense: "My name is great among the nations." In turn, the Jewish sages interpreted this verse as referring to prayer and the study of the Torah by the Jewish people scattered in the Diaspora. In the Targum to Malachi 1:11 we read, "On every occasion when you fulfill my will I hear your prayer and my great name is hallowed because of you, and your prayer is like a pure offering before me." The *Midrash Rabbah* interprets "offerings" as "the evening prayer," and the sages state: "Seeing that you are engaged in the study of Mishnah, it is as if you were offering up sacrifices."[49]

The Didache's interpretation is not far removed from the explanation that was current in Judaism in the first few centuries of the Common Era, in which Malachi 1:11 referred to a sacred fellowship meal conducted in the synagogues of early believers all over the world. Draper observes, "The use of traditional Jewish

---

47 Skarsaune, *In the Shadow of the Temple*, 418. Cf. Clement of Alexandria (*Stromata* 1.14), who quotes the same two verses (Malachi 1:11, 14). Almost all other quotations of these verses in church literature are used to refer to the Eucharist.
48 Draper, "Pure Sacrifice in Didache 14 as Jewish Christian Exegesis," 238.
49 *Leviticus Rabbah* 7:3; *Numbers Rabbah* 13:4.

hermeneutical techniques, themes and traditions does not appear superficial here, but rather an integral part of the thinking and common understanding of the community."⁵⁰

The compiler of the Didache was drawn to the passage's repeated use of the term *goyim* ("Gentiles," גוים), often translated "nations." This served as "a natural link" to the full title of the Didache: *The Teaching of the Lord to the Gentiles through the Twelve Apostles*.⁵¹ Through their fellowship meals, the Gentile believers dispersed throughout the world would be able to offer up sacrifices to the God of Israel just as the priests did in Jerusalem and the Didache finds a proof text for this in Malachi 1:11. The passage was probably chosen also because it contains the term *minchah* ("grain offering"), which the Didache translates with the Septuagint equivalent *thusia* ("sacrifice," θυσία), perhaps emphasizing the sacred role of bread in the place of blood offerings.

Later church literature uses this passage to show that the Eucharist had replaced Temple worship, but we see no such traces of this idea in the Didache.⁵² Milavec points out:

> By lifting out Malachi 1:11 and 1:14b and omitting 1:12–14a, which consists of detailed attacks on the unfitting sacrifices offered by the Jerusalem priests, the framers of the Didache retained the pro-gentile stance of the oracle but entirely suppressed an overt criticism of Israel. The deliberate editing on the part of the framers of the Didache thus reinforces their affirmation of the election of Israel.⁵³

Therefore, the Didache's use of metaphorical sacrificial language was in no way seen as replacing or abolishing the Temple and the priesthood. Instead, it foreshadows the Messianic Era in which all nations, including Gentiles from every tribe and tongue, will go up to Jerusalem and offer sacrifices in the Holy Temple. Solomon's original vision of the foreigner "who is not of your people Israel, [but] comes from a far country for your name's sake,"⁵⁴ will be brought to its fullness when Messiah returns:

[14.3]
For this is what was spoken by the Lord: "'In every place and time, offer me a pure sacrifice ... because I am a great king,' says the Lord, 'and my name is awesome among the Gentiles.'"

---

50   Draper, "Pure Sacrifice in Didache 14 as Jewish Christian Exegesis," 248.
51   Clayton N. Jefford, "Authority and Perspective in the Didache," in *The Didache: A Missing Piece of the Puzzle in Early Jewish Christianity* (eds. Jonathan A. Draper and Clayton N. Jefford; Atlanta, GA: Society of Biblical Literature, 2015), 43.
52   E.g., Justin, *Dialogue with Trypho the Jew* 117.
53   Milavec, *The Didache: Faith, Hope, & Life of the Earliest Christian Communities, 50–70 C.E.*, 556.
54   1 Kings 8:41.

These I will bring to my holy mountain, and make them joyful in my house of prayer; their burnt offerings and their sacrifices will be accepted on my altar; for my house shall be called a house of prayer for all peoples. (Isaiah 56:7)[55]

---

55 Cf. Mark 11:17.

Chapter Fifteen

DIDACHE 15

15.1 Therefore, designate for yourselves overseers and administrators worthy of the Lord—humble men and not lovers of money, and truthful and proven—because they also perform the service of the prophets and teachers.[1]

15.2 Do not then look down on them, for they are your honored ones along with the prophets and teachers.[2]

15.3 Do not rebuke one another in anger but rather in peace, just as you have been taught in the good news.[3] And if anyone has wronged another person, let no one speak to him nor let him hear from you until he repents.

15.4 Carry out your prayers and donations and all your good deeds just as you have been taught in the good news of our Lord.[4]

---

1   1 Timothy 3:1–13.
2   1 Thessalonians 5:12–13; Hebrews 13:7, 17.
3   Matthew 18:15–18.
4   Matthew 6:1–15.

Overview

In previous chapters the Didache introduced the offices of teacher, emissary (apostle), and prophet, but it made no mention of dedicated leadership positions. Now, here in the second to last chapter of the Didache, the organizational structure of a community is finally introduced. A community of believers cannot exist without leaders and organization.

Fledgling communities to whom the Didache author addressed might have been able to function under the leadership of charismatic prophets, teachers, and apostles, but before a group could become an ordered and viable community, it needed to establish a system of authority. In the words of Charles Taylor, "No sooner had the preacher created a congregation than the need of organization arose."[5] Once a traveling teacher or apostle had planted seeds, the need to establish something more structured immediately presented itself. For example, Paul and Barnabas appointed elders over every community in which their efforts for the gospel had taken root:

> When they had preached the gospel to that city and had made many disciples ... they ... appointed elders for them in every church, [and] with prayer and fasting they committed them to the Lord in whom they had believed. (Acts 14:21, 23)

Additionally, the community needed an authority structure under which to discipline members who might stray from the Way of Life. The leadership structure and disciplinary procedures outlined in the Didache offer a simple yet effective way to organize and maintain local communities. This is the same system that was at work in the New Testament and used throughout the early believing communities, as evidenced in early church literature; yet, there is nothing intrinsically Christian or New Testament about the ecclesiastical structure introduced by the Didache. Instead, the early believers adopted the ecclesiastical models and offices already used in synagogues and throughout the Jewish world.

---

5   Charles Taylor, "The Teaching of the Twelve Apostles with Illustrations from the Talmud," in *Didache: The Unknown Teaching of the Apostles* (ed., Brent S. Walters; San Jose, CA: Anti-Nicene Archive, 1991), 187.

Structure

Chapter 15 can be divided into two sections. Verses 1–2 outline the appointment of overseers and administrators. Details are also given about the characteristics necessary for these appointees to qualify for leadership. Emphasis is placed on respecting these leaders in the same manner accorded to prophets and teachers.

Verses 3–4 deal with community discipline and practice. Instructions are given for rebuking those who transgress and for dealing with the sinner who fails to repent. Finally, a general instruction is given to carry out the community services of prayer and charity in accordance with the teachings of our Master.

15.1–2	Appointing overseers and administrators
15.3	Administering community rebuke and discipline
15.4	Conducting all service in accordance with the good news

Appoint Judges

Moses commanded the children of Israel to appoint judges (*shoftim*, שפטים) in every town:[6]

> You shall appoint judges and officers in all your towns that the LORD your God is giving you, according to your tribes, and they shall judge the people with righteous judgment. (Deuteronomy 16:18)

The commandment to "appoint judges" called for the establishment of a judicial system. The Torah's judicial system had three levels of courts: the local court (i.e., the *beit din*, בית דין), the district court, called a small sanhedrin, and the high court, called the Great Sanhedrin. A minimum of three judges presided over each local petite court (*beit din*). Twenty-three judges served on a small sanhedrin. Seventy-one judges served on the Great Sanhedrin.

The apostles specifically enjoined the commandment to appoint judges upon God-fearing Gentile believers by instructing them to appoint overseers/elders and administrators over their communities.[7] Didache 15.1 closely mirrors the language

---

[6] The ensuing introductory discussion appears in D. Thomas Lancaster, *Torah Club: Depths of the Torah* (6 vols.; Marshfield, MO: First Fruits of Zion, 2017), 5:1641–1642.

[7] E.g., 1 Timothy 3:1–13; Titus 1:5–9.

of Deuteronomy 16:18, with the appointment of judges corresponding to overseers and officers to administrators. In fact, one of the seven universal Noachide laws, according to later rabbis, was the injunction to establish courts.[8]

The apostles followed the leadership model of the synagogue. They appointed elders to serve as judges and leaders of each community of believers. One of the elders then functioned as the head elder of the community, like a chief justice in a court of judges (the position of *av beit din*). By the second century, church sources distinguish between elders and overseers (bishops) by identifying the overseer as the head elder over the community. However, in the Didache and the New Testament, the terms seem interchangeable.

The overseer and the elders provided the community with teaching, leadership, and shepherding, but they were also responsible for settling disputes, administering justice, and imposing disciplinary measures. Our Master referred to the judgment of a *beit din* of three judges when he said, "Again I say to you, if two of you agree on earth about anything they ask, it will be done for them by my Father in heaven. For where two or three are gathered in my name, there am I among them" (Matthew 18:19–20). Didache 15.4 has in view this same passage from Matthew, which is often referred to in Christian circles as the "Matthew 18 process."

In his epistles Paul speaks of the appointment of overseers and elders to serve in the capacity of judges and leaders over each community of believers. For example, Paul chastised the Corinthian assembly for failing to appoint three elders for a *beit din*. Without that leadership and governance, the Corinthian assembly ran amok, and believers went to trial against each other in the secular court of law in Corinth.[9] Paul expressed astonishment over believers taking their lawsuits outside the congregation and seeking justice from Roman courts. This was a big taboo in first-century Judaism and still is today because the secular courts do not operate under the Torah's system of jurisprudence. Jewish people sought justice from the *beit din* associated with the local synagogue, and they abided by the decisions reached in those courts.[10] The apostles expected the Gentile believers and the believing communities to adopt the same model.

Likewise, Jewish communities appointed men to the role of administrators (see commentary below), that is, "deacons" (servants) who could carry out the work of the elders, functioning as their hands and feet within the community to

---

8   E.g., t.*Avodah Zarah* 8:4; b.*Sanhedrin* 56a; *Genesis Rabbah* 34:8; cf. *Pesikta of Rav Kahana* 12:1.
9   1 Corinthians 6:1–6.
10 b.*Shabbat* 116a–b.

manage practical affairs and attend to the business of the community. The book of Acts introduces the role of administrator to the ecclesiastical structure with the appointment of the seven deacons in Acts 6:1–6, but this innovation already had precedent within the synagogue and Jewish community.

Appointing Overseers and Administrators

The epistle of 1 Clement contains an important parallel to the injunction to appoint overseers and administrators. The entire epistle of 1 Clement is dedicated to justifying a hierarchical model of congregational authority in which the existing ecclesiastical authority is respected. Clement argued that the original bishops and congregational leaders were appointed by the apostles and that the authority of the office derives from that appointment. One key passage summarizes the thrust of that authority model and even finds a proof text from the Septuagint version of Isaiah to support the hierarchy:

> Preaching through countries and cities, the apostles appointed the first-fruits of their labors, having first proved them by the Spirit, to be overseers and administrators of those who should afterwards believe. Nor was this any new thing, since indeed many ages before us it was already written concerning overseers and administrators. For thus says the Scripture in a certain place, "I will appoint their overseers in righteousness, and their administrators in faith" [Isaiah 60:17 Septuagint]. (1 Clement 42.4–5)

Simplicity

Since the Didache was rediscovered in the late nineteenth century, Catholics and Protestants have sought to demonstrate how the ancient text validates their existing ecclesiastical structures. Both groups felt it necessary to prove how Didache 15 supports their particular organizational system.[11] However, this type of exegesis is anachronistic and distorts the original message of the Didache. For example, in the

---

[11] Aaron Milavec, *The Didache: Faith, Hope, & Life of the Earliest Christian Communities, 50–70 C.E.* (New York, NY: Newman, 2003), 591–594.

Didache "no evidence can be found ... of a three-fold ministry (bishop/presbyter/deacon) that began to emerge in the second century."[12]

The leadership structures of the church that exist today, both Catholic and Protestant, have developed over time, and in some ways are far removed from what we find in the earliest believing communities of the first century. As with everything in the Didache, chapter 15 needs to be approached on its own terms without trying to line it up with current practices. If we want to learn from the Didache, we must examine it within its original context and from a Jewish perspective. Only then can we see the wisdom of early community structure.

The Didache lays out a simple, twofold structure that created a balance of power and ensured that the community ran smoothly. The injunctions of chapter 15 call for humble leaders and respectful congregants to work together toward the larger harmony of the community. Tony Jones writes:

> The ecclesial structure of the Didache community is skeletal, and it's simple: live reconciled lives with one another; confess and forgive one another; appoint some among you to preside over the community and others to serve; and treat those you've appointed with respect.[13]

The injunctions of chapter 15 create a system to solidify and maintain the rules and principles taught in the previous chapters.

Plurality of Leadership

The wisdom of this structure can be seen particularly in the plurality of leadership and in the checks and balances that existed within the believing community. While both prophets and teachers operated within the communities, neither office had exclusive control or final say within the congregation. Instead, the community was to appoint a plurality of overseers and administrators.

This ensured that one person did not possess unlimited power to dictate the direction of the community and that ample checks and balances existed to keep the community from becoming a dictatorship. Churches and ministries fall into corruption when leadership lacks accountability. In the system of organization

---

[12] William Varner, *The Way of the Didache: The First Christian Handbook* (New York, NY: University Press of America, 2007), 88. This is even added to the Apostolic Constitutions' reworking of the Didache in 7.31.

[13] Tony Jones, *The Teaching of the Twelve: Believing & Practicing the Primitive Christianity of the Ancient Didache Community* (Brewster, MA: Paraclete, 2009), 111.

created by the Didache, the lone leader without accountability is not a possibility. Even the head elder, if such a position may be assumed, held only one vote on the council of elders.

A Central Governing Body?

One of the main controversial issues of this chapter has to do with the office of the overseer, or, as it is commonly translated, "bishop." As will be discussed in the commentary, in the Didache the office of the bishop was specific to individual communities, and the bishop exercised authority only within the local congregations. While the Didache concerns itself with the local body and does not give instructions regarding appointing leadership over broader jurisdictions or even over the entire believing community, the New Testament does assume such a central governing body stationed in Jerusalem.

The authority in Jerusalem consisted of a governing body of elders presided over by a head elder. The elders were the legislators responsible for administering the believing community at large. Ranking disciples like Peter and John occupied those offices, as did the brothers and family members of the Master.

Originally, the Master chose twelve core disciples to be the apostles who would spread his message and carry on his leadership after his departure. These men would become the foundation of the sect of the followers of Yeshua. From those twelve the Gospels indicate that the Master had an inner group of three disciples—Peter, James, and John—as is evidenced by Yeshua allowing only them to see the transfiguration.[14] Of these three, the Gospels indicate that Peter was the most prominent. The Master states to Peter:

> Blessed are you, Simon Bar-Jonah! For flesh and blood has not revealed this to you, but my Father who is in heaven. And I tell you, you are Peter, and on this rock I will build my church, and the gates of hell shall not prevail against it. I will give you the keys of the kingdom of heaven, and whatever you bind on earth shall be bound in heaven, and whatever you loose on earth shall be loosed in heaven. (Matthew 16:17–19)

---

14 Matthew 17:1; Mark 9:2; Luke 9:28. Cf. Mark 5:37, 13:3, 14:33. Chrysostom comments on Matthew 17:3: "He took these three as being superior to the rest. Additionally, these three are always mentioned first in the list of disciples along with Andrew who is Peter's brother" (Matthew 10:2; Luke 6:14; Acts 1:13).

These words indicate that the Master bestowed upon Peter a place of honor and precedence. He gave his disciples the authority to make decisions regarding legal rulings for the early Messianic community.[15] Peter's leadership in this process is borne out with Peter often seen as the spokesperson for the believing community in Acts.[16] In fact, Peter's vision of the sheet and his experience with Cornelius, retold throughout the book of Acts, serve as a *ma'aseh* (מעשה, i.e., a legal ruling based on the occurrence of an actual event) that permits a Jewish believer to enter the houses of and eat with the uncircumcised.[17] Only the life experience of those in authority could serve to establish practices of Torah. In Acts 15, Peter occupies a prominent position among the elders within the Jerusalem Council by which he was able to stand up, silence the discussion, and introduce a ruling.[18]

JAMES AND THE JERUSALEM COUNCIL

Peter did not enjoy absolute power, however. He did not wield authority to the exclusion of the other eleven. In Matthew 18:18, Yeshua addressed the twelve disciples in the plural form, saying, "I say to you, whatever you bind on earth shall be bound in heaven, and whatever you loose on earth shall be loosed in heaven" (Matthew 18:18).

Peter served among a council of elders that comprised the Jerusalem Council (Acts 15), and the one who held the position of chief bishop over that body and over all the assemblies was James, the brother of the Master. In Acts 12:17, we read, "Tell these things to James and to the brothers," which indicates James' prominent position. In Acts 15, James summarizes the discussion of the Jerusalem Council and renders the final judgment.[19] Paul indicates that the Master made a special resur-

---

15   David N. Bivin, "'Binding' and 'Loosing' in the Kingdom of Heaven," *Jerusalem Perspective* 23 (November–December 1989): 12–13.
16   Acts 1:15–26, 2:14–41, 3:12–26, 4:8–12.
17   *Ma'aseh* (מעשה) translates as "it once happened." See m.*Brachot* 1:1, 2:5; m.*Sukkah* 2:5; b.*Yevamot* 46b; Menachem Elon, "Ma'aseh," *Encyclopedia Judaica*, CD ROM edition, Judaica Multimedia (1997), and Joseph Shulam and Hilary Le Cornu, *A Commentary on the Jewish Roots of Acts* (2 vols., Jerusalem, Israel: Academon Ltd., 2003), 1:609, 829–830.
18   Acts 15:7–12.
19   Acts 12:17, 15:13–30. See also Acts 21:18.

rection appearance to his brother as well.[20] Although the book of Acts does not record how James came to hold this position of power, Eusebius tells us that after the death of Stephen, "James, whom the ancients surnamed James the Righteous because of his exceeding piety, is recorded to have been the first to be made bishop of the church of Jerusalem."[21] In this way, James became bishop not over a local congregation but over the entire believing sect. This corresponds to the rabbinic title *nasi* (נשיא), which was used for the individual who was in headship over the Sanhedrin. Therefore, James was the *nasi* of the Messianic community. A tradition exists that his appointment was proclaimed by Messiah Yeshua before his death:

> The disciples said to Yeshua, "We know that you will depart from us. Who is to be our leader?" Yeshua said to them, "Wherever you are, you are to go to James the Righteous, for whose sake heaven and earth came into being." (Gospel of Thomas 12)

James was a link to the house of David as the believers waited for the return of the Messiah Yeshua, the ultimate Son of David, to take up his throne. After the death of James, the line of bishops from the Master's family continued in his stead for several generations.

After the death of James the brother of John, it appears that James the brother of the Master took his place in the inner core of Yeshua's disciples. D. Thomas Lancaster writes:

> James the Righteous, Simon Peter, and John the son of Zebedee formed a triumvirate—a high court of three—over the entire assembly. Paul referred to them as the reputed pillars of the assembly of Messiah. Each had a specific role. James represented the family of the Master. Simon Peter ranked as first among the Twelve, head over the Master's school of disciples. John the son of Zebedee, the beloved disciple and an adopted son of the Master's mother, Mary, stood in the unique position of representing the interests of both the family of Yeshua and his school

---

20 1 Corinthians 15:7. Also, Jerome recorded this tradition from the Gospel of the Hebrews in his *Lives of Illustrious Men* (2): "The Master went to James and appeared to him. Now James had sworn that he would not eat bread from the time that he drank the cup of the Master until he would see him risen from among those who sleep … The Master said, "Bring a table and bread." … He took the bread, made a blessing, broke it, and gave it to James the Righteous. He said to him, "My brother, eat your bread, for the son of man has risen from among those who sleep.""

21 Eusebius, *Ecclesiastical History* 2.1.2.

of disciples. As the *nasi* over the assembly, James occupied the highest position in the triumvirate.[22]

All this indicates the existence of strong central leadership located in Jerusalem. The three pillars stood at the head of the assembly of the elders. Working together with Peter, John, and the other elders, James the brother of Yeshua made legal decisions for the Messianic community, as we see in Acts 15. James and the elders in Jerusalem oversaw all believing communities. Paul was commissioned by James and the apostles as an apostle to the Gentiles.

The destruction of Jerusalem and the disastrous Second Jewish Revolt irretrievably diminished this Jewish leadership structure. As the Gentile constituency grew and the church severed itself from Judaism, the authority of the bishop of Rome grew into the institution of papal authority. Originally, this leadership structure was intended to remain with the apostles and the family of Yeshua and to be based within the land of Israel and within the religion of Judaism.

The Didache does not mention this higher ecclesiastical authority structure, but its existence is implied in the document's longer title *The Teaching of the Lord to the Gentiles through the Twelve Apostles*. There was no need for the Didache to mention the Jerusalem leadership because the new Gentile initiates had already accepted their authority by reading and walking out the instructions that the leadership had given them.

Community Discipline

As chapter 15 continues, the need for community leaders becomes clear when the Didache begins to issue instructions regarding rebuke and community discipline. The Didache alludes to the Torah's command to rebuke one's brother and to Yeshua's own instructions on that subject. As in the teachings of Yeshua, the Didache places the legal procedure for community discipline within the context of an established community leadership that can settle disputes and, if necessary, excise community members.

---

[22] D. Thomas Lancaster, *Torah Club: Chronicles of the Apostles* (6 vols.; Marshfield, MO: First Fruits of Zion, 2016), 1:181. Cf. Eusebius, *Ecclesiastical History* 2.1.4, quoting Clement of Alexandria, *Hypotyposes*: "After his resurrection, the Master imparted knowledge to James the Righteous and to John and Peter, and they imparted it to the rest of the [twelve] apostles, the rest of the apostles to the seventy."

Practical Application

The simplicity and efficiency of the Didache's structure of leadership is appropriate for modern congregations to emulate. The plurality of leadership ensures that no single leader ever has too much power or is above accountability and keeps one person from being overwhelmed as was the case with Moses.[23] A congregational leader should govern an assembly in the midst of a leadership team of peers. Those elders of the community should meet the criteria laid out in the Didache and be prepared to issue rebukes, settle disputes, prescribe restitution, and, if necessary, ban community members from fellowship.

The Didache also calls for the active participation of administrators who function under the authority of the elders and carry out the business affairs of the community on behalf of the overseers.

Finally, the Didache calls upon communities to submit to the leadership of the overseers. Those who refuse to submit or to accept the rebuke of the leadership are in danger of excision. All such procedures must be carried out in accordance with the teaching of Yeshua.

---

23 Exodus 18:17–18.

Commentary

Therefore, designate for yourselves overseers and administrators. (DIDACHE 15.1)

Chapter 15 begins with the word "therefore," linking the discussion about the appointment of overseers and administrators to the previous chapter's discussion about settling quarrels and grievances.[24] If the peace of the community was going to be maintained so that the community could break bread and give thanks in peace and thereby present a "pure sacrifice," the community would need ecclesiastical leaders and authorities who could settle disputes and resolve problems.

The command to "designate for yourselves overseers and administrators" is patterned after the injunction in Deuteronomy 16:18, even echoing the Hebrew construction of the command: "You shall appoint for yourself judges and officers in all your gates." This is also related to the Noachide laws where one of the seven injunctions was to establish courts.[25] In Jewish interpretation, the "judges" make rulings and the "officers" ensure that those rulings are enforced.

The brevity and language with which the Didache delivers instructions about designating leaders in the community indicates that it is not introducing something new but rather alluding to an already existing structure. Judaism of the first century had a well-established system of overseers and administrators. The believing communities simply replicated an existing model. The same organizational system that existed in the Jewish synagogue was applied to the Jewish and non-Jewish Messianic communities. William Varner states: "The early Jewish-Christian churches followed the organizational pattern of the Jewish synagogue."[26]

---

[24] Franz Delitzsch in his Hebrew New Testament translates οὖν ("therefore," *oun*) as לכן (*l'chen*). In the Mishnah, *v'chen* ("and likewise") is used by a sage to infer "that the second Halakhah resembles the one proceeding it" (Rabbi Adin Steinsaltz, *The Talmud Steinsaltz Edition: A Reference Guide* [New York, NY: Random, 1989], 92).

[25] E.g., b.*Sanhedrin* 56a; *Genesis Rabbah* 34:8.

[26] Varner, *The Way of the Didache*, 87.

[15.1]
Therefore, designate for yourselves overseers and administrators.

The Greek word *cheirotoneo* (χειροτονέω) simply means to "choose or appoint," but it refers to an ordination ceremony, such as the laying on of hands."[27] The appointment of overseers and administrators was accompanied by the laying on of hands (*smichut*, סמיכות) by the previously elected officers, as we see in the book of Acts: "These [deacons] they set before the apostles, and they prayed and laid their hands on them" (Acts 6:6).[28] To this was added prayer and fasting: "When they had appointed elders for them in every church, with prayer and fasting they committed them to the Lord in whom they had believed" (Acts 14:23). Prayer and fasting almost certainly played a prerequisite role in the designation of overseers and administrators in the Didache community as well.

The office of the overseer/elder is found frequently in the New Testament.[29] At the time of the writing of the Didache, the Greek word *episkopos* (ἐπίσκοπος) was synonymous with *presbus* ("elder," πρέσβυς, mentioned in the Apostolic Constitutions) and corresponded to the synagogue position of *zakan* ("elder," זקן).[30] It was not a monarchial bishop position but rather a localized leader within the community who paralleled the position of judge in the synagogue. By the second century, the terminology had further crystallized, and the title *episkopos* began to indicate the head elder over a community, corresponding to the synagogue position of *av beit din* ("head of the court," אב בית דין).[31] This development defined "the three-fold ministry (bishop/presbyter/deacon) that began to emerge in the second century."[32] The Apostolic Constitutions version of Didache 15.1 also distinguishes between overseers and elders, supporting the threefold hierarchy:

27 The word appears only twice in the New Testament: in Acts 14:23 and 2 Corinthians 8:19. Apostolic Constitutions (8.4–5) uses it in the sense of a formal ordination. The connection between "designate" and the laying on of hands is even clearer in the Georgian version of the Didache: "Through the laying on of hands, you establish for yourself overseers, who are managers of spiritual matters, and administrators, who are servants for the worship of God."

28 Milavec, *The Didache: Faith, Hope, & Life of the Earliest Christian Communities, 50–70 C.E.*, 613. "Laying on of hands" is, after all, one of the elementary principles of faith expressed in Hebrews 6:1–2. For the discussion on the practice of the laying on of hands, see D. Thomas Lancaster, *Elementary Principles: Six Foundational Principles of Ancient Jewish Christianity* (Marshfield, MO: First Fruits of Zion, 2014), 73–84.

29 Acts 11:30, 14:23, 15:2, 4, 22–23, 20:17, 28; 1 Timothy 3:1, 2, 5:19; Titus 1:5, 7; 1 Peter 5:1; James 5:14.

30 Varner speculates as to why the Didache uses the term "overseer" instead of "elder": "This choice was probably due to the fact that congregations with a significant Gentile membership were in view. The word οἰκονόμοι would have a more familiar ring to Gentile readers in describing what basically was the function of this person (oversight) rather than referring to the maturity of the person in view (elder)" (Varner, *The Way of the Didache*, 87).

31 E.g., the epistles of Ignatius and Justin Martyr.

32 Varner, *The Way of the Didache*, 88.

"Designate overseers worthy of the Lord and elders and administrators" (Apostolic Constitutions 7.31).

[15.1] *Therefore, designate for yourselves overseers and administrators.*

Title	Greek Term	Synagogue Equivalent
overseer (bishop)	*episkopos*	*av beit din, (rav)*
elder	*presbus*	*zakan*
administrator (deacon)	*diakonos*	*parnas*

The overseers were in charge of shepherding all aspects of community affairs, including congregational discipline and rebuke.[33] The overseer was required to be able to teach as well.[34] The Apostle Peter adds:

> I exhort the elders among you, as a fellow elder and a witness of the sufferings of [Messiah], as well as a partaker in the glory that is going to be revealed: shepherd the flock of God that is among you, exercising oversight, not under compulsion, but willingly, as God would have you; not for shameful gain, but eagerly; not domineering over those in your charge, but being examples to the flock. And when the chief Shepherd appears, you will receive the unfading crown of glory. (1 Peter 5:1–4)

In Paul's introduction to the Philippians, "administrators" are coupled together with overseers and perform a complementary role as agents of the overseers within the community.[35] In Greek, *diakonos* (διάκονος) literally translates "to wait on people at table"; it refers to a minister, servant, one who helps others, and it is often translated as "deacon." The need for administrators arises first in Acts 6 when the apostles did not have time to teach as well as care for the needs of the community. The apostles, performing in the capacity of overseers, decided, "Therefore, brothers, pick out from among you seven men of good repute, full of the Spirit and of wisdom, whom we will appoint to this duty" (Acts 6:3). The role

---

33 Milavec, *The Didache: Faith, Hope, & Life of the Earliest Christian Communities, 50–70 C.E.*, 599–600.
34 1 Timothy 3:2.
35 Philippians 1:1. Thomas O'Loughlin feels that overseers and administrators are one and the same: "In these latter communities 'the bishops' were not one group and 'the deacons' another, but rather the leaders were known by this double-barreled designation to bring out the twin aspects of their task: to have a watchful eye over the community *and* to be its servants" (O'Loughlin, *The Didache: A Window on the Earliest Christians* [Grand Rapids, MI: Baker, 2010], 125. Also Milavec, *The Didache: Faith, Hope, & Life of the Earliest Christian Communities, 50–70 C.E.*, 590).

[15.1]
Therefore, designate for yourselves overseers and administrators.

of *diakanos* parallels the synagogue position of the *chazzan* (חזן), who arranged the services and maintained the facilities, and the community role of the *parnas* ("provider," פרנס), who was a leader of the people often in charge of distributing charity to the poor.

In the Didache, administrators were "helpers who attend[ed] to the temporal needs of the congregation, especially the care of the poor and the sick."[36] Among other things, they were probably in charge of organizing community meals and prayer services, showing hospitality to visitors, balancing community finances, distributing charity, and burying the dead.[37] Unlike with overseers, who were always men, Paul mentions deaconesses in his letters, indicating that there may have been female deacons in the Didache community as well.[38]

> *Worthy of the Lord—humble men and not lovers of money, and truthful and proven—because they also perform the service of the prophets and teachers.* (DIDACHE 15.1)

Overseers and administrators were designated by the community. However, the Didache stresses that this ordination "was not to be based on popularity or on the personal aspirations of the candidate but upon a discernment process into the character of alternative candidates."[39] They must meet the criteria laid out before they could even be considered for one of these positions.

Clayton Jefford writes, "Even here the formal guidelines of the community, and presumably the authority upon which the redactor makes his/her exhortations, is based upon the Jewish Torah."[40] Robert Grant says similarly, "The sentence echoes the words of Deuteronomy on the appointment of judges, including even the requirement that the judges must not take bribes."[41] This is paralleled in the Talmud:

> Rabbi Yochanan said, "No one may be appointed to the Sanhedrin unless he is a man of stature, wisdom, good appearance, mature age,

---

36 Varner, *The Way of the Didache*, 87.
37 Milavec, *The Didache: Faith, Hope, & Life of the Earliest Christian Communities, 50–70 C.E.*, 602.
38 Romans 16:1; 1 Timothy 3:11. See Milavec, *The Didache: Faith, Hope, & Life of the Earliest Christian Communities, 50–70 C.E.*, 602–605.
39 Milavec, *The Didache: Faith, Hope, & Life of the Earliest Christian Communities, 50–70 C.E.*, 589.
40 Clayton N. Jefford, *The Sayings of Jesus in the Teachings of the Twelve Apostles* (New York, NY: Brill, 1989), 110, n. 47.
41 Robert M. Grant, *Early Christianity and Society: Seven Studies* (San Francisco, CA: Harper & Row, 1977), 41. See Deuteronomy 19:5; Matthew 18:16.

familiar with [the deceits of] sorcery, and fluent in all the seventy languages of man so that the court will not have need of an interpreter." (b.*Sanhedrin* 17a)

The Apostolic Constitutions expands this to:

> Devout men, righteous, humble, not lovers of money, lovers of truth, proven, pious, impartial to one's status—who are able to teach the word of Godliness and preach straightforwardly by means of the ordinances of the Lord.[42] (Apostolic Constitutions 7.31)

[15.1] *Worthy of the Lord—humble men and not lovers of money, and truthful and proven—because they also perform the service of the prophets and teachers.*

The New Testament lays out lists similar to what we find here in the Didache for the qualifications of overseers and administrators. The most detailed version is found in 1 Timothy:

> An overseer must be above reproach, the husband of one wife, sober-minded, self-controlled, respectable, hospitable, able to teach, not a drunkard, not violent but gentle, not quarrelsome, not a lover of money. He must manage his own household well, with all dignity keeping his children submissive, for if someone does not know how to manage his own household, how will he care for God's church? He must not be a recent convert, or he may become puffed up with conceit and fall into the condemnation of the devil. Moreover, he must be well thought of by outsiders, so that he may not fall into disgrace, into a snare of the devil.
>
> Deacons likewise must be dignified, not double-tongued, not addicted to much wine, not greedy for dishonest gain. They must hold the mystery of the faith with a clear conscience. And let them also be tested first; then let them serve as deacons if they prove themselves blameless. Their wives likewise must be dignified, not slanderers, but sober-minded, faithful in all things. Let deacons each be the husband of one wife, managing their children and their own households well." (1 Timothy 3:2–12)[43]

Potential overseers and administrators were to be "worthy of the Lord," an expression used by Paul to describe the godly manner by which all disciples are to

---

42   2 Timothy 2:15; cf. 1 Timothy 3:1–13.
43   Titus 1:5–9. Cf. 1 Clement 42.4–5, 44.2; Polycarp, *To the Philippians* 5.2.

[15.1] *Worthy of the Lord—humble men and not lovers of money, and truthful and proven—because they also perform the service of the prophets and teachers.*

live in imitation of Yeshua and in accordance with his teachings.[44] They were to be "humble," a criterion mentioned by both Paul and Peter.[45] The Didache commands all believers, "Be humble, because the humble will inherit the earth" (3.7).

Candidates who were "lovers of money" were disqualified.[46] Paul, too, lists this criterion for an overseer.[47] This is related to the Torah's injunction for judges: "You shall not accept a bribe, for a bribe blinds the eyes of the wise and subverts the cause of the righteous" (Deuteronomy 16:19). If one loves money he will be more likely to accept bribes. The Didache warns all followers of Messiah against the love of money (3.5).

Overseers and administrators were to be "truthful." The Way of Death is followed by those who "hate the truth" (5.2). The Greek word for "truthful," *alethes* (ἀληθής), literally means "not forgetting" and refers to someone who is dependable, real, and genuine. Aaron Milavec writes:

> While one might be tempted to see this quality as applying to honesty in financial matters, yet most probably this signaled the requirement that an officer has to assess, report, and act upon the expressed needs of the community honestly and accurately.[48]

The Master himself was known as a "true" teacher, and all leaders who follow in his footsteps should share this characteristic.[49]

Finally, like the prophet (11.11), candidates were to be "proven." Before a candidate could be nominated for office, he needed to be a proven member of the community; hence Paul's words on overseers and administrators:

> He must not be a recent convert, or he may become puffed up with conceit and fall into the condemnation of the devil … And let them also be tested first; then let them serve as deacons if they prove themselves blameless. (1 Timothy 3:6, 10)

---

44 Colossians 1:10. "Lord" seems to refer to Yeshua, as that is the sense in Colossians.
45 1 Timothy 3:3; Titus 1:7; 1 Peter 5:3.
46 Jewish ethical teaching connects lack of humility with a love of money: "Woe to the pampered man who has never learned to be patient" (Rabbi Menachem Mendel Levin, *Cheshbon HaNefesh: A Guide to Self-Improvement and Character Refinement* [trans. Rabbi Shraga Silverstein; New York, NY: Feldheim, 1995], 149).
47 1 Timothy 3:3. Cf. 1 Peter 5:2.
48 Milavec, *The Didache: Faith, Hope, & Life of the Earliest Christian Communities, 50–70 C.E.*, 589.
49 Matthew 22:16; Mark 12:14; John 7:18.

A good test of a person's capabilities was how he managed his household: "He must manage his own household well, with all dignity keeping his children submissive, for if someone does not know how to manage his own household, how will he care for God's church?" (1 Timothy 3:4–5). After all, the community became his extended family. We can also imagine that if an overseer or administrator were asked to step down because of a transgression, he must be proven over time before he could return to his position.

Overseers and administrators performed the "service of the prophets and teachers." It was therefore imperative for these men to carry godly characteristics because they were performing a holy service. The Greek word for service is *leitourgia* (λειτουργία), from which we derive the English word "liturgy." It corresponds to the Hebrew word *avodah* (עֲבוֹדָה), which is used often in the Torah to describe the priestly service and in rabbinic literature to refer to the obligation of prayer.[50] *Leitourgia* in the Roman world refers to "unpaid public service."[51] Unlike prophets and teachers, elders and deacons were not paid or reimbursed for their services.[52] Instead, they served the community humbly, operating in the gifts that the Lord had bestowed upon them. Milavec states:

> These bishops and deacons wore no special garb, were addressed with no special titles, and bore no special charisma. They were simply tried and true, older and wiser counselors and unpaid servants, who ensured that the community retained its unity and purpose while leading the most important functions for everyday persons pursuing everyday holiness. This simplicity blessed their lives, and with time, attracted many to their doors.[53]

On the other hand, the elders who also labored in preaching and teaching received the double honor of compensation for their work according to the rule of the Master:

> Let the elders who rule well be considered worthy of double honor, especially those who labor in preaching and teaching. For the Scripture

[15.1]
Worthy of the Lord—humble men and not lovers of money, and truthful and proven—because they also perform the service of the prophets and teachers.

---

50 E.g., Exodus 28–29; Ezekiel 40–46. Cf. Romans 15:27; 2 Corinthians 9:12; Philippians 2:30.
51 Milavec, *The Didache: Faith, Hope, & Life of the Earliest Christian Communities, 50–70 C.E.*, 596.
52 However, some have the opinion that when the Didache states, "For they are your honored ones along with the prophets and teachers," it is making a halachic inclusion that the overseers and administrators are to receive the same provision and gifts that are given to prophets and teachers.
53 Milavec, T*he Didache: Faith, Hope, & Life of the Earliest Christian Communities, 50–70 C.E.*, 608.

says, "You shall not muzzle an ox when it treads out the grain," and, "The laborer deserves his wages." (1 Timothy 5:17–18)

◈ *Do not then look down on them, for they are your honored ones along with the prophets and teachers.* (DIDACHE 15.2)

After providing criteria for the appointment of overseers and administrators, the Didache stresses that, once appointed, these leaders needed to be respected. The Apostolic Constitutions renders this: "Now you are to honor these men as your fathers, as your masters, as your benefactors, as the reasons for your well-being" (Apostolic Constitutions 7.31).

Because "they also perform the service of the prophets and the teachers," they should be honored in the same way. The overseers and the administrators "function alongside and in cooperation with" the prophets and teachers.[54] "Your honored ones along with the prophets and teachers" could be paraphrased as "those among you who are honored by God, to whom God has assigned a special rank."[55] The Didache is reemphasizing and further clarifying the command in 4.1: "Remember night and day the teacher who speaks the word of God to you, and esteem him as the Lord, for where lordship is spoken of, there the Lord is." (See the commentary on 4.1 for the Jewish and biblical background of this commandment.)

The New Testament contains corresponding injunctions to honor and submit to community leadership:

> We ask you, brothers, to respect those who labor among you and are over you in the Lord and admonish you, and to esteem them very highly in love because of their work. Be at peace among yourselves. (1 Thessalonians 5:12–13)

> Remember your leaders, those who spoke to you the word of God. Consider the outcome of their way of life, and imitate their faith ... Obey your leaders and submit to them, for they are keeping watch over your souls, as those who will have to give an account. Let them do this with joy and not with groaning, for that would be of no advantage to you. (Hebrews 13:7, 17)

---

54 Niederwimmer, *The Didache*, 201.
55 Ibid., 202.

◈ *Do not rebuke one another in anger but rather in peace, just as you have been taught in the good news.* (DIDACHE 15.3)

The Didache makes a smooth transition from leadership to community reprimand and discipline, as leaders might naturally need to be involved in such things. The Apostolic Constitutions reads: "Do not rebuke one another in anger but rather in patience, with kindness and peace" (Apostolic Constitutions 7.31).[56]

Rebuke and correction formed an important part of congregational life so that the community would continue walking in the Way of Life. Didache 14.2 stresses that quarreling congregants defiled community meals. Discipline and correction took place internally, within the community. Congregants were not to turn to outside help, as the Master states: "Come to terms quickly with your accuser while you are going with him to court, lest your accuser hand you over to the judge, and the judge to the guard, and you be put in prison" (Matthew 5:25).

The Torah commands a person to rebuke his fellow if he sees him going astray: "You shall reason frankly with your neighbor, lest you incur sin because of him" (Leviticus 19:17).[57] According to Jewish law, the rebuke is to be done gently and in private. Jewish law places no limit on how often someone should be rebuked, even up to a hundred times.[58] To refrain from rebuke when one sees his fellow sinning constitutes a transgression of the Torah, and an individual who fails in this will be punished as if he had committed the same sin.[59] The sages say that lack of rebuke is one of the reasons that Jerusalem was destroyed in 70 CE.[60] Jewish law also requires issuing a warning to an individual who is about to commit a sin, warning him of the consequences and that he will face punishment so that he will not commit the sin out of ignorance.[61]

Our Master Yeshua plainly told his disciples to rebuke: "If your brother sins against you, go and tell him his fault, between you and him alone. If he listens to you, you have gained your brother" (Matthew 18:15). The New Testament contains further admonitions to rebuke transgressors: "As for those who persist in sin,

---

56 Cf. Galatians 5:22.
57 Steinsaltz, *The Talmud Steinsaltz Edition: A Reference Guide*, 271.
58 b.*Bava Metzia* 31a.
59 b.*Shabbat* 55a.
60 b.*Shabbat* 119b.
61 In Qumran literature, the warning is issued after the transgression. See Huub van de Sandt, ed., "Two Windows on a Developing Jewish-Christian Reproof Practice: Matt 18:15–17 and *Did.* 15:3," in *Matthew and the Didache: Two Documents from the Same Jewish-Christian Milieu?* (Minneapolis, MN: Fortress, 2005), 180.

[15.3]
Do not rebuke one another in anger but rather in peace, just as you have been taught in the good news.

rebuke them in the presence of all, so that the rest may stand in fear" (1 Timothy 5:20); "Reprove, rebuke, and exhort, with complete patience and teaching" (2 Timothy 4:2); "He must hold firm to the trustworthy word as taught, so that he may be able to give instruction in sound doctrine and also to rebuke those who contradict it ... Rebuke them sharply, that they may be sound in the faith" (Titus 1:9, 13); "Declare these things; exhort and rebuke with all authority. Let no one disregard you" (Titus 2:15).

The Didache states that rebuke is not to be done in "in anger but rather in peace." The one offering rebuke should not do so in a fit of rage, but instead he should do so dispassionately and without any personal emotional investment. A rebuke should be delivered only in love; a rebuke delivered in love is more likely to be received. Thomas O'Loughlin states: "The concern is that this correction should be a composed affair aimed at showing the Christian who had gone astray the right way, rather than becoming, as is so often the case when someone offers another 'correction,' the occasion for 'tearing a strip off them' in angry denunciation."[62]

The Master states: "Everyone who is angry with his brother will be liable to judgment; whoever insults his brother will be liable to the council; and whoever says, 'You fool!' will be liable to the hell of fire" (Matthew 5:22). The Greek word "peace" here in the Didache is *eirene* (εἰρήνη) and corresponds in the Septuagint to the Hebrew *shalom* (שלום), which means not just "peace" but "completeness." Everything, including rebuking, is to be done in peace, as the psalmist states: "Seek peace and pursue it" (Psalm 34:14).

Similar injunctions are found throughout Jewish literature:

> Love you, therefore, one another from the heart; and if a man sin against you, cast forth the poison of hate and speak peaceably to him, and in your soul hold not guile; and if he confess and repent, forgive him. (Testament of Gad 6:1)

> Question a friend, perhaps he did not do it; but if he did anything, so that he may do it no more. Question a neighbor, perhaps he did not say it; but if he said it, so that he may not say it again. Question a friend, for often it is slander; so do not believe everything you hear. A person may make a slip without intending it. Who has never sinned with his tongue? Question your neighbor before you threaten him; and let the law of the Most High take its course. (Sirach 19:13–17)

---

62 O'Loughlin, *The Didache*, 126.

> They shall rebuke one another in truth, humility, and charity. Let no man address his companion with anger, or ill-temper. (Community Rule [1QS] v, 24–25)

[15.3]
Do not rebuke one another in anger but rather in peace, just as you have been taught in the good news.

The Didache states that the rebuke should be done just as the believers had been "taught in the good news." As we have noted already, "good news" is most likely not a reference to a written gospel but to an oral teaching or to the good news in general, which includes instructions for living in the kingdom of heaven.[63] The specific teaching that the Didache has in view is certainly the instruction regarding community discipline procedures that we find outlined in Matthew 18:

> If your brother sins against you, go and tell him his fault, between you and him alone. If he listens to you, you have gained your brother. But if he does not listen, take one or two others along with you, that every charge may be established by the evidence of two or three witnesses. If he refuses to listen to them, tell it to the church. And if he refuses to listen even to the church, let him be to you as a Gentile and a tax collector. Truly, I say to you, whatever you bind on earth shall be bound in heaven, and whatever you loose on earth shall be loosed in heaven. (Matthew 18:15–18)

The so-called "Matthew 18 process" involves a three-phase legal procedure. It begins with a confidential, person-to-person rebuke. If the offending brother does not accept the rebuke and repent after this conversation, the person conducting the rebuke is to take along one or two additional witnesses in order to prepare for legal procedures. If the offending party still refuses the rebuke, the witnesses are to take the matter "to the church," that is, to present the case before the elders over the assembly (i.e., the *beit din*). If the offending brother refuses the rebuke of the elders, the elders have the authority to dis-fellowship him from the community.[64]

---

[63] "Most scholars agree that this wording refers to some written gospel, but it is difficult to determine whether the text alludes to a canonical or apocryphal gospel" (Van de Sandt and David Flusser, *The Didache: Its Jewish Sources and Its Place in Early Judaism and Christianity* [Minneapolis, MN: Fortress, 2002], 352. "It might be appropriate, therefore, to suggest that Matthew was not used as a source for *Did.* 15:3a. Instead, 'the gospel' which is referred to may be a source which shows a marked correspondence with 1QS 5:24b–25 … The phrase 'Correct one another' in *Did.* 15:3a may even be a verbal of its counterpart 'They shall admonish one another' in 1QS 5:24b–25" (Van de Sandt, "Two Windows on a Developing Jewish-Christian Reproof Practice," 187).

[64] For a fuller explanation of the process from the perspective of Jewish synagogue legal procedure, see D. Thomas Lancaster, *Torah Club: Chronicles of the Messiah* (6 vols.; Marshfield, MO: First Fruits of Zion, 2014), 3:855–861.

> *And if anyone has wronged another person, let no one speak to him nor let him hear from you until he repents.* (DIDACHE 15.3)

Now the text addresses one who transgresses and is rebuked yet refuses to repent. While everyone is given a chance to repent and change, the Way of Life is not a place for hardheartedness. This line is omitted from the Apostolic Constitutions.

The Greek word behind "wronged," *astocheo* (ἀστοχέω), literally means "to miss the mark" and is reminiscent of the Hebrew word *chata* (חטא).[65] The Didache is talking about someone who has transgressed the Torah and sinned against his fellow.

The person who transgresses against a fellow congregant and refuses to repent or to submit to the authority of the leadership is to be shunned until he repents.[66] This is derived from the Master's instruction: "If he refuses to listen even to the church, let him be to you as a Gentile and a tax collector" (Matthew 18:17). Rabbinic procedure prescribed different types of shunning and banning of community members. *Nezifah* (נזיפה) was the mildest form of excommunication and usually lasted only one day outside the land, but seven days within Israel.[67] A *niddui* (נדוי) was a form of excommunication that lasted seven days outside the land but thirty days within Israel. The Talmud records twenty-four offenses that could bring on such a period of shunning.[68] There was also the *cherem* (חרם) ban, which lasted much longer—perhaps permanently—and was the strictest form of excommunication.[69]

The ban in the Didache lasted only until the congregant repented of his sin and made amends with the one he had offended. In Hebrew, "repentance" (*teshuvah*, תשובה) literally means "to turn around." In other words, to truly repent from sin, one must turn from his wrong behavior and begin to walk in righteousness. In some cases monetary restitution might be in order. The overseers determined damages in the same manner as a court of law, issued rulings, and prescribed the path of repentance by which the offender could find his way back to the Way of Life.

---

65   In the New Testament, this word is found in 1 Timothy 1:6, 6:21 and 2 Timothy 2:18.
66   The Georgian version of the Didache renders the ban as, "He should not hear in their midst the teaching of the Lord." This possibly means that the original context was connected to the offender not being allowed to enter the synagogue and listen to the public reading of Scripture.
67   b.*Mo'ed Katan* 16a–17a.
68   b.*Brachot* 19a.
69   For a fuller discussion on the different levels of rabbinic bans see Solomon Schechter and Julius H. Greenstone, "Excommunication," *Jewish Encyclopedia* 5:285–287.

> *Carry out your prayers and donations and all your good deeds just as you have been taught in the good news of our Lord.* (DIDACHE 15.4)

The chapter closes with a general reminder that the congregation should be diligent in its practice of the Way of Life in strict accordance with the instructions of Yeshua. The Apostolic Constitutions truncates this, quoting Acts 10:33: "Keep everything that has been prescribed to you by the Lord" (Apostolic Constitutions 7.31).[70]

Instructions on charity were laid out in 1.5–6, prayers were discussed in chapters 9–11, and the practice of good deeds has been discussed throughout the Didache. Why the repetition here? This simple recap serves to summarize and conclude the Didache's community instructions, pointing the new initiate back to the teaching of Yeshua as the standard for practice.

"Good news of the Lord" is probably not a reference to a written canonical gospel but more likely a general reference to the oral teachings of Yeshua that included instructions for living in the kingdom of heaven—that is, the words of Yeshua. Didache 15.4 seems to be a general reference to the specific type of teaching that we find in the Sermon on the Mount:

> Beware of practicing your righteousness before other people in order to be seen by them, for then you will have no reward from your Father who is in heaven.
>
> Thus, when you give to the needy, sound no trumpet before you, as the hypocrites do in the synagogues and in the streets, that they may be praised by others. Truly, I say to you, they have received their reward. But when you give to the needy, do not let your left hand know what your right hand is doing, so that your giving may be in secret. And your Father who sees in secret will reward you.
>
> And when you pray, you must not be like the hypocrites. For they love to stand and pray in the synagogues and at the street corners, that they may be seen by others. Truly, I say to you, they have received their reward. (Matthew 6:1–5)

---

70 The Georgian version of the Didache renders this as: "Just as you have learned in the good news of our Lord Yeshua the Messiah."

Chapter Sixteen

DIDACHE 16

16.1 Be vigilant[1] for your life—do not let your lamps be snuffed out,[2] and do not let your loins be ungirded[3]—but be ready, for you do not know the hour in which our Lord is coming.[4]

16.2 Gather together often,[5] seeking what is appropriate for your lives, because your entire time of faithfulness will be of no benefit to you if you will not have been made complete at the end of time.

16.3 For in the end of days, false prophets and those who cause corruption will increase in number,[6] and the sheep will be changed into wolves,[7] and love will be changed into hate.[8]

16.4 Because of the increase of lawlessness, those who have fallen away will hate one another;[9] they will also persecute one another, and they will even betray one another.[10] And then the deceiver of the world will appear as a son of God, and he will perform signs and wonders,[11] and the earth will be delivered into his power, and he will commit disgusting acts such as have never taken place since the beginning of time.[12]

---

1 Matthew 24:42–43, 25:13; Luke 21:36; Mark 13:33–37; 1 Corinthians 16:13; 1 Thessalonians 5:6; 1 Peter 5:8.
2 Matthew 25:1–13; Luke 12:35.
3 Luke 12:35; Ephesians 6:14.
4 Matthew 24:36, 42–44, 25:13; Mark 13:32; Luke 12:40.
5 Hebrews 10:25.
6 Matthew 24:4–5, 11, 23–25; Mark 13:5–6, 21–22; Luke 21:8.
7 Matthew 7:15.
8 Matthew 24:12.
9 Matthew 24:10, 12.
10 Matthew 24:10.
11 Matthew 24:24; Mark 13:22; 2 Thessalonians 2:2–4, 9.
12 2 Thessalonians 2:8–12; Revelation 13:1–18.

16.5 Then the entire human race will enter the trial by fire,[13] and many will be caused to stumble[14] and will perish, but those who endure in their faithfulness will be saved[15] by the very one who is cursed.[16]

16.6 And then the signs of the truth will appear: the first sign, an expansion in the heavens;[17] next, the sign of the sound of the trumpet;[18] and the third sign, the resurrection of the dead.[19]

16.7 However, not the resurrection of everyone but rather as it is said:
"The Lord will come, and all the righteous along with him."[20]

16.8 Then the world will behold the Lord coming upon the clouds of heaven.[21]

---

13 1 Peter 4:12.
14 Matthew 24:10.
15 Matthew 10:22, 24:13; Mark 13:13.
16 Galatians 3:13.
17 Matthew 24:30; Mark 13:26; Luke 21:27.
18 Isaiah 27:13; Matthew 24:31; 1 Corinthians 15:52; 1 Thessalonians 4:16.
19 1 Corinthians 15:52; 1 Thessalonians 4:16.
20 Zechariah 14:5; 1 Thessalonians 3:13; Jude 14.
21 Daniel 7:13; Matthew 24:30, 26:64; Mark 13:26, 14:62; Revelation 1:7.

Overview

The Didache ends with an apocalyptic section that maps out prophetic events that culminate in the return of Messiah and the arrival of the Messianic Kingdom. Scholars refer to this chapter as the "little apocalypse."[22] It instructs the faithful to remain steadfast in the Way of Life and warns that many will fall away. It reinforces all the teaching of the previous chapters and provides a fitting conclusion to this introductory work for new Gentile believers.

JEWISH AND ROMAN ESCHATOLOGY

The little apocalypse at the end of the Didache is similar to eschatological sections that appear in other early Christian works of a similar character to the Didache.[23] This was typical of the "tendency to conclude important writings with the promise and threat of an eschatological warning."[24] Speculation about the end of the world was as popular two thousand years ago as it is today. Didache 16 teaches that this end-time period "will be a time of testing that demands endurance, a process of burning that tests and purifies" (16.5). This is a widespread eschatological theme derived from the prophets."[25]

Prophetic literature musing over future calamities appeared frequently in ancient Israel around the time of the destruction of the First Temple, and the popularity of the apocalyptic genre of prophetic literature began to increase significantly around 300 BCE. Like the apocalyptic writings of the New Testament, the Didache's little apocalypse falls within the rich prophetic tradition of Judaism. In the Jewish apocalypse genre, turmoil on earth was merely a symptom of spiritual forces at work behind the scenes. The spiritual forces of darkness and the spiritual forces of light are continually at war, and in the very near future the forces of light will prevail. Although Israel will experience times of trouble, and at times it might

---

22 Clayton N. Jefford, *The Sayings of Jesus in the Teachings of the Twelve Apostles* (New York, NY: Brill, 1989), 87.
23 E.g., *Doctrina Apostolorum* 6; Barnabas 21; Apostolic Constitutions 7.31–32.
24 Jefford, *The Sayings of Jesus*, 114–116.
25 Jonathan A. Draper, "The Holy Vine of David Made Known to the Gentiles through God's Servant Jesus: 'Christian Judaism' in the Didache," in *Jewish Christianity Reconsidered: Rethinking Ancient Groups and Texts* (ed. Matt Jackson-McCabe; Minneapolis, MN: Fortress, 2007), 274.

seem as if evil will prevail, there will always be hope that the future redemption is about to arrive:

> Following its parent Judaism of the Second Temple, Christianity views time as linear. There is a line running from a beginning up to now: this is all our history; and the line continues running through an ever-passing moment we label 'now' into the future. There, in front of us, lies our hope—and, also, the source of our fears.[26]

THE GOSPEL OF THE KINGDOM

The little apocalypse at the conclusion of the Didache offers the new disciple hope for the coming redemption and emphasizes the message of the gospel: "Repent, for the kingdom of heaven is at hand" (Matthew 4:17). The Didache has stressed the need for Gentiles to repent of their former ways and walk in the light of Torah. Now it grants a glimpse into the promise of the arrival of the coming kingdom for which the disciples eagerly wait.

This is not the Didache's first mention of the Parousia—the second coming of Messiah. The Two Ways section makes several allusions to the coming kingdom, and so do the prayers of chapters 8, 9, and 10:[27]

> Be humble, because the humble will inherit the earth. (3.7)

> Do not hesitate to give, and do not complain when giving, for you will find out who is the good payer of wages. (4.7)

> Let your kingdom come; Let your will be done—as in heaven, so on earth. (8.2)

> May your assembly be gathered from the ends of the earth into your kingdom (9.4)

> Gather her, the sanctified, from the four winds to your kingdom that you have prepared for her ... May grace come, and may this world pass away. *Hoshana* to the God of David! ... *Maran etha! Amen.* (10.5–6)

---

26 Thomas O'Loughlin, *The Didache: A Window on the Earliest Christians* (Grand Rapids, MI: Baker, 2010), 129.
27 Cf. Didache 1.5, 4.4, 10, 5.2.

The early followers of Yeshua anticipated the Master's imminent return, even within their own lifetimes. The believers were an eschatological community that today might be characterized as a group of end-times fanatics. They lived in constant anticipation of Yeshua's sudden arrival, and their entire religious expression revolved around their hope for the kingdom.

Thomas O'Loughlin writes:

> The followers of Jesus took as the starting point of their faith that prophecy had just been fulfilled, that God had intervened in history, showing his hand in Jesus. So if God had just intervened, then all that was expected about the end times might now be in train.[28]

Before Yeshua's final ascension, the disciples asked him, "Lord, will you at this time restore the kingdom to Israel?" to which he replied, "It is not for you to know times or seasons that the Father has fixed by his own authority" (Acts 1:6–7).[29] The disciples anticipated that the kingdom could arrive at any moment. The Master warned his disciples, "The days are coming when you will desire to see one of the days of the Son of Man" (Luke 17:22), but he repeatedly stated that "concerning that day and hour no one knows, not even the angels of heaven, nor the Son, but the Father only" (Matthew 24:36).[30]

This Yeshua community's eager anticipation of the Parousia reminds us of the Rambam's twelfth principle of faith:

> I believe with complete faith in the coming of the Messiah, even if he should tarry, I will await his coming.[31]

Maimonides teaches that every Jew is obligated to long for the redemption and the coming of the Messianic Kingdom.

---

28 O'Loughlin, *The Didache*, 142.
29 Cf. Matthew 24:3.
30 Cf. Matthew 24:36; Luke 17:24.
31 Rambam, *Thirteen Principles of Faith*, 12.

Structure

After a general introduction, the chapter lays out a five-stage eschatological vision of events that will precede the Master's return.[32] Each of the last four stages are introduced with "then" (*tote*, τότε), presenting a clear sequential structure.

16.1–2	General Introduction
16.3–4a	Stage 1: False prophets
16.4b	Stage 2: The deceiver comes
16.5	Stage 3: Trial by fire
16.6–7	Stage 4: Signs of truth
16.8	Stage 5: Coming of the Lord

Each of Didache 16's successive stages represents heightening signs that the Master will be returning soon. Because of the almost rhythmic structure of the text from one section to the next, some scholars have speculated that this passage might be based upon a liturgical piece.[33]

The material shares common elements with Paul's warnings about the climactic world events that will culminate in the coming Messianic Kingdom:

> Concerning the coming of our Lord [Yeshua the Messiah] and our being gathered together to him, we ask you, brothers, not to be quickly shaken in mind or alarmed, either by a spirit or a spoken word, or a letter seeming to be from us, to the effect that the day of the Lord has come. Let no one deceive you in any way. For that day will not come, unless the rebellion comes first, and the man of lawlessness is revealed, the son of destruction, who opposes and exalts himself against every so-called god or object of worship, so that he takes his seat in the temple of God, proclaiming himself to be God. (2 Thessalonians 2:1–4)

---

[32] Chart based upon Aaron Milavec, *The Didache: Faith, Hope, & Life of the Earliest Christian Communities, 50–70 C.E.* (New York, NY: Newman, 2003), 633–634.

[33] Marcello del Verme, *Didache and Judaism: Jewish Roots of an Ancient Christian-Jewish Work* (New York, NY: T&T Clark, 2004), 236.

The Didache's eschatology is built upon the same foundation as Paul's, sharing a common source in the words of Yeshua.

Oral Gospel Material

Joseph Verheyden observes that the little apocalypse in Didache 16 "presents itself as the transmitter of a received body of teachings (from the Apostles!) on eschatology."[34] While the Didache does quote and allude to several passages from the Hebrew Scriptures, it primarily transmits eschatological expectations based on the sayings of the Master. For example, it transmits the material from Yeshua's eschatological discourses in the Synoptic Gospels. The following chart correlates the material with the sayings of Yeshua and the prophecies of the Hebrew Scriptures:[35]

Didache 16	Matthew	Mark	Luke	Prophets
1a	24:42, 25:13	13:35		
1b			12:35	
1c	24:42, 44, 25:13		12:40	
2a				
2b				
3	7:15, 24:4–5, 24:11–12, 23–25	13:5–6, 21–22	21:8	
4a	24:10, 12			

---

34 Joseph Verheyden, "Eschatology in the Didache and the Gospel of Matthew," in *Matthew and the Didache: Two Documents from the Same Jewish-Christian Milieu?* (ed. Huub van de Sandt; Minneapolis, MN: Fortress, 2005), 214.

35 Kurt Niederwimmer, *The Didache: Hermeneia—A Critical and Historical Commentary on the Bible* (Minneapolis, MN: Fortress, 1998), 208–213. Added some from Jefford, *The Sayings of Jesus*, 85–87. For a full detailed linguistic analysis of this, see Christopher M. Tuckett, "Synoptic Tradition in the Didache," in *The Didache in Modern Research* (ed. Draper; Leiden, The Netherlands: Brill, 1996), 92–128. George Eldon Ladd writes: "While there are no direct quotations, there are many striking likenesses of language and a number of instances where the Didache follows Matthew over Mark" (Ladd, "The Eschatology of the Didache" [Ph.D. diss., Harvard University, 1949], 22).

Didache 16	Matthew	Mark	Luke	Prophets
4b	24:24	13:22		
4c				
4d	24:21	13:19		Jeremiah 30:7
5a				
5b	24:10			
5c	10:22, 24:13	13:13		
6a	24:30			
6b	24:31	13:27		
7	25:31			Zechariah 14:5
8	24:30, 26:64	13:26, 14:62	21:27, 22:69	Daniel 7:13

As is the case when dealing with other gospel-like material throughout the Didache, scholars debate whether the author of the Didache had a copy of one of the Synoptic Gospels or if he might have been working only from early oral traditions. Some have even proposed that Didache 16 represents a kind of commentary on the apocalyptic sections of the Gospel of Matthew. Others have suggested that it compiles various texts from both the Hebrew Scriptures and the New Testament. What seems most plausible, given the early date of the Didache, is that the writer draws from an "independent pre-gospel tradition."[36] The material sounds similar to Matthew's gospel because both Matthew and the Didache drew on the same source—possibly a Hebrew and/or Aramaic original source that both Matthew and the Didache translated into Greek independently.

The Didache does not ask us to rely upon its own authority but rather that of the Hebrew Scriptures and the words of the Master. The little apocalypse can be read as an aggadic midrash on Scripture that seeks to systematically lay out the signs of the Master's return and exhort his followers to remain steadfast and faithful through the troubled times of persecution ahead.

---

36   Van de Sandt and David Flusser, *The Didache: Its Jewish Sources and Its Place in Early Judaism and Christianity* (Minneapolis, MN: Fortress, 2002), 39.

Remain in the Way of Life

While at first glance this chapter appears to be merely predicting future events surrounding Yeshua's second coming, the material highlights the urgency that disciples must continue daily walking in the Way of Life and avoiding the Way of Death. The little apocalypse makes several allusions to previous material in the Didache. The word "complete" (τελειόω), which appeared in 10.5 and in its adjective form (*teleios*, τέλειος) in 1.4 and 6.2, now shows up again in 16.2, its early and late appearances acting as bookends. We also find a connection to earlier parts of the book with the emphasis on "life" (ζωή) in 16.1, which is a repeated theme of the entire work.[37] Both terms are related to walking in righteous actions. Jonathan Reed writes:

> [Chapter 16] heightens fear of the Way of Death. It also refers back to the section on ritual prescriptions (chapters 7–9) through encouragement of followers to meet frequently (16:2). And the warning in 16:3 about the increase of false prophets in the last days renders the section of the "church order" even more urgent.[38]

The ethics and lifestyle of the Didache's first fifteen chapters are reinforced by the idea that the coming Parousia brings reward for the righteous and punishment for the wicked.

An apocalyptic ending at the conclusion of an ethical treatise is a frequent pattern in Jewish literature, particularly in material addressing new converts.[39] Scholars speculate that "Jewish proselyte catechisms originally ended with such an eschatological warning."[40] For example, we find in the Talmud at the end of instructions for new proselytes:[41]

> He is told, "Be it known to you that the world to come was made only for the righteous, and that Israel at the present time are unable to bear either too much prosperity or too much suffering." (b.*Yevamot* 47a–b)

---

[37] Nancy Pardee, *The Genre and Development of the Didache: A Text-Linguistic Analysis* (Tübingen, Germany: Mohr Siebeck, 2012), 164.
[38] Jonathan Reed, "The Hebrew Epic and the Didache," in *The Didache in Context: Essays on Its Text, History & Transmission* (ed. Jefford; New York, NY: Brill, 1995), 224.
[39] Pardee, *The Genre and Development of the Didache*, 166.
[40] Draper, "The Holy Vine of David Made Known to the Gentiles through God's Servant Jesus," 274.
[41] Cf. Community Rule (1QS) v, 6–14.

> All things we have said unto you we have said only to increase your reward. (*Gerim* 1:5 [60a])

Compare also Jewish universal ethical treatises:

> This is the contest, these are the rewards; these are the prizes; this the gate of life and entrance into immortality, which God in heaven appointed a reward for victory; unto most righteous men and those who will then receive the victor's crown, through this gate will gloriously pass but when this sign will everywhere appear. (Sibylline Oracles 2.149–154)

> We hope that perhaps the remains of the departed will come to the light (again) out of the earth; and afterward they will become gods … These are the mysteries of righteousness; thus living may you complete a good life, to the threshold of old age. (Pseudo-Phocylides 103–104, 229–230)

The rabbis sought to inculcate in the new converts steadfast loyalty and dedication to the Torah on the basis that judgment and recompense were sure to come. The new initiates needed to know that it was not the treasures of this world for which they toiled but life in the kingdom of heaven.

Likewise, new disciples needed to have a clear vision of the kingdom for which they labored and hoped. It was important that new believers gain a balanced perspective on the end times. They needed to understand the calamitous events that were coming so that their faith would not be compromised. They needed to realize the sober responsibility of continuing to walk in the paths of discipleship and according to the revelation of the Torah despite persecution, adversity, and the end of the world. The Apostle Paul writes:

> Concerning the times and the seasons, brothers, you have no need to have anything written to you. For you yourselves are fully aware that the day of the Lord will come like a thief in the night. While people are saying, "There is peace and security," then sudden destruction will come upon them as labor pains come upon a pregnant woman, and they will not escape. (1 Thessalonians 5:1–3)

While believers were to be watchful, ready for the kingdom always, they needed to be warned not to get caught up in worrying about eschatology. Tony Jones writes

that the Didache instructs, "Be watchful. Be ready. But don't obsess."[42] The many itinerant prophets that traveled through the community might indicate a tendency among the early believers to have been swept away in apocalyptic speculation. To counter this, "the framers of the Didache managed to safeguard the values of the community and to counter misleading or dangerous visions of the future by putting forward a step-by-step unfolding of the last days bent on harnessing the enthusiasm of all concerned."[43]

The little apocalypse of Didache 16 was meant to keep the priorities of the community in order. It "served to instill that while Messiah's return was close it was not yet, instill that everyday holiness is what matters, and that one should continually be aware of false prophets."[44]

---

42   Tony Jones, *The Teaching of the Twelve: Believing & Practicing the Primitive Christianity of the Ancient Didache Community* (Brewster, MA: Paraclete, 2009), 118.
43   Milavec, *The Didache: Faith, Hope, & Life of the Earliest Christian Communities, 50–70 C.E.*, 622.
44   Ibid., 624–625.

Commentary

> *Be vigilant for your life—do not let your lamps be snuffed out, and do not let your loins be ungirded— but be ready, for you do not know the hour in which our Lord is coming.*
> (DIDACHE 16.1)

The first two verses of chapter 16 offer up a general introduction before moving into the specific signs preceding the coming kingdom. They exhort the disciple to remain faithful and diligent as the time of Messiah's return draws closer. The Apostolic Constitutions expands and amplifies this to include more words of the Master:

> Be vigilant for your life—"let your loins be girded and your lamps kept burning—and as for you, be like men who are waiting for their Master" [Luke 12:35–36] when he arrives, whether at evening, "or in the morning, or when the rooster crows, or at midnight" [Mark 13:35]. For the Master will come at an hour they do not expect; and when "they open the door to him, praiseworthy are those servants" [Luke 12:37] because they were found vigilant. "For he will gird himself and seat them and go alongside them and serve them" [Luke 12:37]. (Apostolic Constitutions 7.31)[45]

Three mandates are given: "be vigilant," "be ready," and, as we will observe in verse 2, "gather together often."[46] These instructions set up the eschatological timeline of the rest of the chapter. The verse opens with an imperative, the imperative is interpreted with a metaphor, and then the metaphor is finally interpreted.

"Be vigilant" (*gregoreite*, γρηγορεῖτε) was used to introduce apocalyptic sections in the New Testament, especially in the Gospels.[47] It is often used in an eschatological sense in the imperative "be or keep awake," meaning figuratively to "be on the alert, be watchful." It has the sense of warning us to be ready for the unexpected. Disciples needed frequent reminders about the importance of remaining faithful and diligent, never growing lax in their observance and faith.

---

45 Cf. Matthew 24:42–44, 25:1–13; Luke 12:35–37, 40; Mark 13:33, 35.
46 Milavec, *The Didache: Faith, Hope, & Life of the Earliest Christian Communities, 50–70 C.E.*, 634.
47 Matthew 24:42–43, 25:13; Mark 13:33–37; Luke 21:36; 1 Corinthians 16:13; 1 Thessalonians 5:6; 1 Peter 5:8.

[16.1]
Be vigilant for your life—do not let your lamps be snuffed out, and do not let your loins be ungirded—but be ready, for you do not know the hour in which our Lord is coming.

To illustrate the call to vigilance, the Didache uses the metaphors of keeping "lamps" lit and "loins" girded, a semantic repetition such as one might commonly encounter in Hebrew poetry. That is to say, both imperatives mean the same thing.[48] The saying is based directly upon the words of Yeshua: "Let your loins be girded about, and your lamps burning" (Luke 12:35 ERV).[49]

"Lamps" (*luchnoi*, λύχνοι) refers to the common oil lamps with two openings: one for the wick and the other for adding oil. In general, oil lamps burned throughout the night, and therefore "do not let your lamps be snuffed out" means that the believers were to be constantly on alert.[50] These lamps needed regular maintenance to stay lit, and thus the metaphor urges one to continually examine oneself and stay on guard. Similar imagery is found in the Master's parable of the ten virgins.[51] Furthermore, lamps were lit only at night, so the metaphor further alludes to the time of darkness and exile prior to the final redemption.[52] Additionally, lamps and light are often used as metaphors for the Torah and Torah teachers.[53] This may point to the possibility "that the twin admonitions to keep lamps burning and keep loins girt refer to learning and doing Torah (the Way of Life)."[54]

"Do not let your loins be ungirded" was an admonishment to stay ready. "Gird up your loins" is a biblical idiom for preparing for action:

> In the Middle East, one finds non-Westernized men traditionally wearing a cotton, ankle-length tunic without any under-clothing. When preparing for strenuous activity, such men take a band of cloth about two yards in length and wrap it around their waist and between their legs in such a way as to bind their genitals to their body. Alternately, "girding consists in tucking the end of the long loose garment into the

---

48 See "Bicolon" in Wilfred G.E. Watson, *Classical Hebrew Poetry: A Guide to Its Techniques* (Sheffield, England: JSOT, 1986), 12–13. While the Didache simply reads "life," the Georgian version of the Didache reads "the life," i.e., "eternal life," "salvation."

49 "The figures of unquenched lamps and girded loins are found only in the Gospels in an eschatological setting. In 1 Peter 1:13 the figure of girding loins of the mind is used and refers to the coming of Christ, but it is without the eschatological urgency of the passages in the Didache and Luke" (Ladd, "The Eschatology of the Didache," 56).

50 Niederwimmer, *The Didache*, 214–215.

51 Matthew 25:1–13. Also Luke 12:35.

52 Cf. John 9:4; 1 Peter 1:17.

53 E.g., Psalm 119:105; 2 Baruch 17:2, 18:1–2, 46:1–3, 77:13. The Baal Shem Tov is called the "Light of the Seven Days" (Martin Buber, *Tales of the Hasidim* [New York, NY: Knopf Doubleday, 2013], 67). See D. Thomas Lancaster, *Torah Club: Chronicles of the Messiah* (6 vols.; Marshfield, MO: First Fruits of Zion, 2014), 2:467–468.

54 Milavec, *The Didache: Faith, Hope, & Life of the Earliest Christian Communities, 50–70 C.E.*, 636.

girdle, so that the garment did not hinder work or become soiled." (Jeremias 1972: 187, n. 66)[55]

The same idiom appears in Paul's words, "Stand therefore, having girded your loins with truth" (Ephesians 6:14 ERV) and Peter's "Wherefore girding up the loins of your mind (1 Peter 1:13 ERV).[56] Even in death rabbinic literature stresses being prepared for the coming kingdom: "Rabbi Jeremiah gave instructions, 'Shroud me in white shrouds. Dress me in my slippers, and put my sandals on my feet, and place my staff in my hand, and bury me by the side of a road. If the Messiah comes, I shall be ready.'"[57]

The admonition to keep one's loins girded also alludes to the exodus from Egypt ("Eat it ... with your loins girded" [Exodus 12:11 ERV]), and this points to the common Jewish expectation that the final redemption will be like a second exodus:

> Therefore, behold, the days are coming, declares the LORD, when they shall no longer say, "As the LORD lives who brought up the people of Israel out of the land of Egypt," but "As the LORD lives who brought up and led the offspring of the house of Israel out of the north country and out of all the countries where he had driven them." Then they shall dwell in their own land. (Jeremiah 23:7–8)

Draper speculates, "The combination of the two sayings makes the Passover imagery more distinct. The picture is of people at the Passover meal waiting in a vigil through the night, ready for the Lord to bring their deliverance."[58]

The last section of verse 1 stresses that believers need to be prepared because the coming of the Master will be swift. Our Master Yeshua urges us:

> Be like men who are waiting for their master to come home from the wedding feast, so that they may open the door to him at once when he comes and knocks ... But know this, that if the master of the house had known at what hour the thief was coming, he would not have left his house to be broken into. (Luke 12:36, 39)

[16.1]
Be vigilant for your life—do not let your lamps be snuffed out, and do not let your loins be ungirded—but be ready, for you do not know the hour in which our Lord is coming.

---

55 Ibid., 639.
56 Cf. Jeremiah 1:17; Luke 12:35.
57 y.*Kilayim* 9:3.
58 Draper, "The Holy Vine of David Made Known to the Gentiles through God's Servant Jesus," 274. Cf. *Mechilta*, Pischa 7, Exodus 12:11.

The phrase "for you do not know the hour in which our Lord is coming" echoes similar sayings throughout the Gospels.[59] The redemption will arrive "as a thief in the night," a common New Testament image for the coming of the Messiah.[60]

> ◀︎ *Gather together often, seeking what is appropriate for your lives, because your entire time of faithfulness will be of no benefit to you if you will not have been made complete at the end of time.* (DIDACHE 16.2)

In the first verse of the little apocalypse, the Didache urges disciples, "Be vigilant for your life." The Didache now urges the disciples to express that vigilance by gathering together frequently.

In the same manner the writer of the book of Hebrews urges, "Let us consider how to stir up one another to love and good works, not neglecting to meet together, as is the habit of some, but encouraging one another, and all the more as you see the Day drawing near" (Hebrews 10:25). We find this sentiment echoed through early church literature, for example: "It is written: 'Cleave unto the saints, for they that cleave unto them shall be sanctified'" (1 Clement 46.2); "Come together frequently, if it were every hour, especially on the appointed days of meeting. For if you do this, you are within a wall of safety" (Pseudo-Clementine Homilies 3.69).[61] In order to stay strong and committed, the disciples needed to gather together and strengthen one another. Community was not an option but a commandment. If the sect of the followers of Yeshua were to continue and grow, they needed to stick together.

Disciples were to seek after what is good: "Seeking what is appropriate for your lives," literally, what is "good for your souls." This preserves a Hebraism. Biblical Hebrew uses the Hebrew word *nefesh* ("soul," נפש) idiomatically for one's life. The disciples were to follow after that which was appropriate to the Way of Life and the Torah, staying away from that which did not spiritually nourish their souls, that is, the Way of Death. They were to avoid the types of pitfalls mentioned in the Testaments of the Twelve Patriarchs:

---

59   Matthew 24:36, 42–44, 25:13; Mark 13:32; Luke 12:40.
60   Luke 12:39; 1 Thessalonians 5:2, 4; 2 Peter 3:10; Revelation 3:3, 16:15; Gospel of Thomas 21, 103.
61   See further 2 Clement 17.3; Barnabas 4.9–10, 10.11, 19.10; Shepherd of Hermas, Similitude 9.20, 26 (97, 103).

Know you therefore, my children, that in the last times your sons will forsake simplicity, and will cleave unto insatiable desire; and leaving guilelessness, will draw near to malice; and forsaking the commandments of the Lord, they will cleave to Beliar. (Testament of Issachar 6:1)

[16.2]
Gather together often, seeking what is appropriate for your lives, because your entire time of faithfulness will be of no benefit to you if you will not have been made complete at the end of time.

As the Parousia drew near, the disciples would face a time of testing known as the "time of faithfulness," literally "the time of your faith." The testing would last until the "end of time." This phrase introduces the apocalyptic section of Didache 16. Its use here reminds us of the words of Peter; the early believers were, by God's power, "being guarded through faith for a salvation ready to be revealed in the last time" (1 Peter 1:5), and, "He was foreknown before the foundation of the world but was made manifest in the last times for the sake of you" (1 Peter 1:20).[62] The apocryphal epistle of the Epistle of Barnabas echoes the same sentiment:

> We take earnest heed in these last days; for the whole past time of your faith will profit you nothing, unless now in this wicked time we also withstand coming sources of danger, as becomes the sons of God. (Barnabas 4.9)

The Didache has in view the Hebrew concept of faithfulness (*emunah*, אמונה)—not just mental belief in the unseen but faith demonstrated in action and loyalty. Perseverance through fidelity to Torah was closely connected with the end of days:

> The observance of the precepts of the Law does not exclude but corroborates the expectation of the end of time: to wait for the end means to prepare for its arrival by means of a total acceptance of the Law and the precepts God has entrusted to men. The Didache appears to aim at reviving this religious sensitivity, that is a "spirituality of expectation," which associates the operational element (= human action) in accordance with God's will with the attention (= intention) toward the expectation of the latter days.[63]

---

62 Cf. 1 Corinthians 10:11.
63 Del Verme, *Didache and Judaism*, 249. Cf. 2 Clement 6.2–7.2.

[16.2]
Gather together often, seeking what is appropriate for your lives, because your entire time of faithfulness will be of no benefit to you if you will not have been made complete at the end of time.

Through faithfulness to the Way of Life, one became "complete."[64] Righteous action is emphasized in the version of this saying that we find in the Apostolic Constitutions:

> Therefore, be alert and pray[65] that you "do not sleep the sleep of death" [Psalm 13:3 Septuagint]. For your former good deeds will be of no benefit to you if you wander away from the true genuine faithfulness at the last part of your life. (Apostolic Constitutions 7.31)

For in the end of days, false prophets and those who cause corruption will increase in number, and the sheep will be changed into wolves, and love will be changed into hate. (DIDACHE 16.3)

After its initial general introduction, chapter 16 now proceeds to list the specific events that will preclude the return of Messiah and his kingdom. The version in the Apostolic Constitutions is almost identical, only adding "who cause corruption of the word" for the Didache's "who cause corruption."[66]

The phrase "end of days" (*eschatais hemerais*, ἐσχάταις ἡμέραις) links to the previous verse's "end of time" (*eschato kairo*, ἐσχάτῳ καιρῷ), and we find the same terminology ("last days") in the New Testament.[67] The troubles of the end of days begin within the Messianic community. False prophets will rise up from within the community. Believers will become enemies of believers. The danger begins from the inside.

The Didache dedicated an entire chapter (11) to distinguishing between "false prophets" and "true prophets." This is in line with the Torah's warnings against false prophets in Deuteronomy 13:1–5. False prophets posed a real problem to the early believing community. The Master also warned of a coming increase of false prophets: "False christs and false prophets will arise and perform great signs

---

64 See Draper, "Torah and Troublesome Apostles in the Didache Community," *Novum Testamentum* 33, no. 4 (October 1991): 368, who believes that this means that eventually a Gentile would be expected to fully convert. The Georgian version of the Didache renders this: "If you are not completely overcome in the end of time by faith and love."
65 Cf. Mark 13:33 (textual variant): "Be on guard, keep awake and pray."
66 Apostolic Constitutions 7.32.
67 John 6:39–40, 44, 54, 11:24, 12:48; Acts 2:17; 2 Timothy 3:1; Hebrews 1:2; James 5:3; 2 Peter 3:3.

and wonders, so as to lead astray, if possible, even the elect" (Matthew 24:24).[68] In similar language the Apostle Peter states:

> False prophets also arose among the people, just as there will be false teachers among you, who will secretly bring in destructive heresies, even denying the Master who bought them, bringing upon themselves swift destruction. (2 Peter 2:1)[69]

The phrase "those who cause corruption" (*phthoreis*, φθορεῖς) is found in the Septuagint with the sense of "seducer." The same language is used in 5.2: "those who corrupt what God has formed." Aaron Milavec writes:

> One might be on firmer ground to understand "corrupters" as those who seduce the sheep into becoming wolves and acting out all the menacing and frightful forms of conduct named in the Way of Death. As this seduction takes place within the Didache communities, a seduction of another kind is taking place globally under the direction of the "world deceiver."[70]

This corresponds to the Master's warning that in the end "lawlessness will be increased" (Matthew 24:12). Draper feels that the "false prophets" and "those who cause corruption" are the same individuals.[71] Evidence for this can be found in the corresponding saying of the Master, "Many false prophets will arise and lead many astray" (Matthew 24:11).

The Didache presents a reversal on Isaiah's words about the Messianic Kingdom: "The wolf shall dwell with the lamb" (Isaiah 11:6). In the dark times before the Parousia, "the sheep will be changed into wolves." The Master also combines this imagery to warn about false prophets: "Beware of false prophets, who come to you in sheep's clothing but inwardly are ravenous wolves" (Matthew 7:15).[72] Whereas Yeshua warned of wolves disguised in sheep's clothing, the Didache says

[16.3]
For in the end of days, false prophets and those who cause corruption will increase in number, and the sheep will be changed into wolves, and love will be changed into hate.

---

68 Also Matthew 24:4–5, 11, 23–25; Mark 13:5–6, 21–22; Luke 21:8. Cf. 1 Timothy 4:1–4; 2 Peter 3:3–4.
69 Cf. "Near is the ruin when impostors come instead of prophets speaking on the earth" (Sibylline Oracles 2.165–166).
70 Milavec, *The Didache: Faith, Hope, & Life of the Earliest Christian Communities, 50–70 C.E.*, 642.
71 Draper, "Apostles, Teachers, and Evangelists: Stability and Movement of Functionaries in Matthew, James, and the Didache," in *Matthew, James, and Didache: Three Related Documents in Their Jewish and Christian Settings* (ed. Van de Sandt and Jürgen K. Zangenberg; Atlanta, GA: Society of Biblical Literature, 2008), 162. For a study on the use of hendiadys, see Ronald James Williams, *Williams' Hebrew Syntax* (ed. John C. Beckman; Toronto, Canada: University of Toronto Press, 2007), 29–30.
72 Cf. Matthew 7:15, 10:16; Luke 10:3; John 10:12; Acts 20:29.

[16.3] *For in the end of days, false prophets and those who cause corruption will increase in number, and the sheep will be changed into wolves, and love will be changed into hate.*

that the sheep will be turned into wolves. "In a chilling phrase, they are told, 'love will be turned into hate.' They won't be disguised, but they will actually change."[73]

Before the words "love" and "sheep" there is a definite article, but before the words "hate and "wolves" there is none. Milavec comments that "what is meant is not an abstract quality but the particular love of God and neighbor (1.2) that characterizes 'the saints' (4.2) of the community."[74] This is what will be lost as the "sheep" (members of the community) turn into wolves. As the Master tells us, "The love of many will grow cold" (Matthew 24:12). This theme is also touched upon frequently in apocryphal literature.[75]

The end times will begin with a great apostasy. The faithful must be diligent to walk in the Way of Life. Throughout the entire Didache we find warnings against turning aside and walking in the Way of Death. Temptations to turn aside and abandon the path will increase as the end draws near.[76]

> *Because of the increase of lawlessness,*
> *those who have fallen away will hate one another,*
> *they will also persecute one another,*
> *and they will even betray one another.* (DIDACHE 16.4)

This verse continues from the previous one on the theme of the elect falling away. It represents a transition from the internal conflicts within the Messianic community to the worldwide sorrows that are approaching. The Apostolic Constitutions reads, "Because of the increase of lawlessness, 'the love of many will grow cold' [Matthew 24:12]. For human beings will hate one another, they will also persecute one another, and having decided beforehand they will even betray one another" (7.32).[77]

The Master, too, predicts the "increase of lawlessness" (*anomia*, ἀνομία) (Matthew 24:12). In the Didache, those who once followed the Way of Life have now chosen instead the Way of Death. Paul labels the antichrist himself as "the man of lawlessness" and states plainly that "the mystery of lawlessness is already at work" (2 Thessalonians 2:3, 7). Draper suggests:

---

73   Jones, *The Teaching of the Twelve*, 116.
74   Milavec, *The Didache: Faith, Hope, & Life of the Earliest Christian Communities, 50–70 C.E.*, 642.
75   4 Ezra 6:24; 2 Baruch 70:3. Cf. Martyrdom and Ascension of Isaiah 3:21–27.
76   Didache 4.13, 6.1, 11.1–2.
77   Similar content is found in the Jewish universal work Sibylline Oracles (2.167–170, 3.63–68).

It seems the division in the community may revolve around the Torah, since the "betrayal" is characterized by an increase in "lawlessness" (*anomia*), which could refer to wickedness in general, but could also refer to breaches of the Torah.⁷⁸

Hate will increase within the community, and there will be persecution and betrayal. "Betrayal" (*paradosousi*, παραδώσουσι) seems to indicate that members of the community will hand one another over to the authorities, as our Master Yeshua predicted:

> Then many will fall away and betray one another and hate one another … And because lawlessness will be increased, the love of many will grow cold. (Matthew 24:10–12)

Our Master also predicted intense persecution:

> They will lay their hands on you and persecute you, delivering you up to the synagogues and prisons, and you will be brought before kings and governors for my name's sake. (Luke 21:12)⁷⁹

Indeed, many of the apostles and early disciples of Yeshua suffered martyrdom for their faith.⁸⁰ Many were betrayed to the authorities by apostates and fellow believers.

[16.4]
Because of the increase of lawlessness, those who have fallen away will hate one another, they will also persecute one another, and they will even betray one another.

◈ *And then the deceiver of the world will appear as a son of God, and he will perform signs and wonders, and the earth will be delivered into his power, and he will commit disgusting acts such as have never taken place since the beginning of time.* (DIDACHE 16.4)

"And then" introduces a second stage in the events preceding the kingdom of heaven. "The deceiver of the world" is introduced. His deception will be greater than that of the false prophets, for he will deceive both those within the believing community and those without. The Greek word *kosmoplanes* ("deceiver," κοσμοπλανὴς)

---

78 Draper, "The Holy Vine of David Made Known to the Gentiles through God's Servant Jesus," 274.
79 Also Matthew 5:11, 44, 10:23; Luke 21:12; John 15:20.
80 See D. Thomas Lancaster, *Torah Club: Chronicles of the Apostles* (6 vols.; Marshfield, MO: First Fruits of Zion, 2016).

[16.4]
And then the deceiver of the world will appear as a son of God, and he will perform signs and wonders, and the earth will be delivered into his power, and he will commit disgusting acts such as have never taken place since the beginning of time.

is used only here and in the parallel passage in the Apostolic Constitutions (7.32), but it is clear that the antichrist is meant. We find numerous references to such a figure in the Jewish works of the period.[81] The Master teaches, "False christs and false prophets will arise and perform great signs and wonders, so as to lead astray, if possible, even the elect" (Matthew 24:24).[82] Paul describes the antichrist as "the man of lawlessness" who presents himself as a deity, usurps the worship of God within the Temple, and uses satanic power to perform signs and wonders.[83]

The book of Revelation paints a frightening depiction of the rise of this deceiver: "And I saw a beast rising out of the sea, with ten horns and seven heads, with ten diadems on its horns and blasphemous names on its heads" (Revelation 13:1).[84]

The deceiver is able to win many over because he will "appear as a son of God," that is, he will appear to be a divine being.[85] There are a few examples within the history of the Jewish people of these types of wicked individuals, characters such as King Nebuchadnezzar, who took Israel into Babylonian captivity and destroyed the Temple, and Antiochus Epiphanes, who desecrated the Temple and sought to outlaw Torah observance in the time of the Maccabees. In the days of the apostles, the world deceivers in view were, of course, the Roman emperors. They fit the profile of evil worldwide leaders posing as gods while making war against the people of God. In the first century, Gaius Caligula, Nero, and Domitian all vied for the position of antichrist, according to the estimation of the early believers.

Additionally, the deceiver will achieve his influence not through political power but by performing "signs and wonders." What are those signs and wonders? Revelation has the antichrist performing "great signs, even making fire come down from heaven to earth in front of people" (Revelation 13:13). In the Apocalypse of Peter, we find "that this is the deceiver which must come into the world and do signs and wonders to deceive" (Apocalypse of Peter 2). The early Christian writer Lactantius speculates that "power will be given him to do signs and wonders, by the sight of which he may entice men to adore him. He will command fire to come down from heaven, and the sun to stand and leave his course, and an image to speak; and these things shall be done at his word—by which miracles many even of the wise

---

81 1 Enoch 90:22–27, 91:7, 93:9; Jubilees 23:14–16; 4 Ezra 5:1–2; Pesher Habakkuk (1QpHab) II, 1–10. Also known as Beliar; see Jubilees 1:20; Testament of Simeon 2:7; Testament of Levi 3:3; Testament of Issachar 6:1; Testament of Asher 1:8; Testament of Benjamin 6:1.
82 Mark 13:22.
83 2 Thessalonians 2:3–4, 9. See further 2 Thessalonians 2:8–12; Cf. 2 John 1:7.
84 Also Revelation 12:9, 12, 13:1–18.
85 Could possibly be an allusion to or a midrash on Genesis 6:1–2.

shall be enticed by him."[86] We find in Martyrdom and Ascension of Isaiah 4:5–10 that "at his word the sun will rise at night and he will make the moon to appear at the sixth hour ... And there will be the power of his miracles in every city and region." The Greek Apocalypse of Ezra states that he will make "stones bread, and water wine ... He has been exalted to heaven; he shall go down to Hades. At one time he shall become a child; at another, an old man."[87]

In time "the earth will be delivered into his power." "Power" here is literally "hands," which is a Hebrew idiom.[88] The Greek word for "earth" here is *ge* (γῆ), which is used in the Septuagint to translate the Hebrew word *eretz* (ארץ). *Eretz* might refer to the whole earth or, more commonly, to the land of Israel. In turn, the reference here may be to the antichrist taking power of the land of Israel. This seems to be supported by Revelation:

[16.4]
And then the deceiver of the world will appear as a son of God, and he will perform signs and wonders, and the earth will be delivered into his power, and he will commit disgusting acts such as have never taken place since the beginning of time.

> It was allowed to make war on the saints and to conquer them. And authority was given it over every tribe and people and language and nation, and all who dwell on earth will worship it, everyone whose name has not been written before the foundation of the world in the book of life of the Lamb who was slain. (Revelation 13:7–8)

The deceiver "will commit disgusting acts such as have never taken place since the beginning of time." This particular description invokes images of Nero, who was famous, even among the Romans, for committing unprecedented disgusting acts.[89] The description is similar to the language of the prophets:

> Alas! That day is so great; there is none like it; it is a time of distress for Jacob; yet he shall be saved out of it. (Jeremiah 30:7)

> There shall be a time of trouble, such as never has been since there was a nation till that time. (Daniel 12:1)

> A day of darkness and gloom, a day of clouds and thick darkness! Like blackness there is spread upon the mountains a great and powerful people; their like has never been before, nor will be again after them through the years of all generations. (Joel 2:2)

---

86 *Epitome of the Divine Institutions* 7.17.
87 Greek Apocalypse of Ezra 4:27, 32–33.
88 E.g., Judges 3:28. "Small of hand" means "weak," e.g., 2 Kings 19:26 Young's.
89 See the description of Nero as though described by the prophets from Jewish believers in the Martyrdom and Ascension of Isaiah (4:1–13).

[16.4]
And then the deceiver of the world will appear as a son of God, and he will perform signs and wonders, and the earth will be delivered into his power, and he will commit disgusting acts such as have never taken place since the beginning of time.

Although the Didache probably had Nero and Roman emperors like him in mind, Milavec sees an allusion to the sacrileges and persecutions that the Jewish people endured prior to the Hasmonean revolt:

> The Jewish imagination might be inclined to remember the so-called "desolate sacrilege" consisting of a statue of Olympian Zeus which Antiochus IV Epiphanes set up in the Jerusalem temple in 167 CE. The Jewish imagination might also recall the persecution of the saints as in the case wherein Antiochus IV Epiphanes had seven sons subjected to excruciating and prolonged tortures in the sight of their mother, who encouraged them throughout to remain faithful to their God. These things were known to have happened. It is left to the hearer, therefore, to imagine yet worse things.[90]

The Greek behind the description "disgusting acts" can be literally translated as "lawless acts" (*athemita*, ἀθέμιτα). The antichrist and the people of the world who follow after him will demonstrate complete disdain for the Torah. The "disgusting acts" will almost certainly involve idolatrous rites. The Apostle Peter speaks of the lawless idolatries of the nations.[91] Moreover, the "disgusting acts" allude to the shocking persecutions perpetuated against disciples, not unlike the gory games and entertainments of Nero's gardens during the first Neronian persecution.[92]

While the Didache is surprisingly silent on what the fate of the antichrist will be, the Apostolic Constitutions, drawing on 2 Thessalonians 2:8, stresses that this deceiver will ultimately be conquered by Messiah:

> The deceiver of the world will appear—the enemy of the truth, the champion of falsehood whom the Master Yeshua will take away with the breath of his mouth and through his lips he will remove the godless—and many will be caused to stumble over him. (Apostolic Constitutions 7.32)

---

90   Milavec, *The Didache: Faith, Hope, & Life of the Earliest Christian Communities, 50–70 C.E.*, 646.
91   1 Peter 4:3.
92   Cf. Niederwimmer, *The Didache*, 220.

> *Then the entire human race will enter the trial by fire,*
> *and many will be caused to stumble and will perish,*
> *but those who endure in their faithfulness will be saved*
> *by the very one who is cursed.* (DIDACHE 16.5)

Didache 16 begins a third section, again using the adverb "then" (*tote*, τότε). Now, not only will the believers endure a time of testing, but the whole world will enter a fiery ordeal. In the end the righteous will endure, and the wicked will perish. This section is missing almost entirely from the Apostolic Constitutions which simply reads, "But those who endure to the end will be saved" (Apostolic Constitutions 7.32).

The Didache describes the calamitous time before the Parousia as a "trial by fire." The Greek word (*purosin*, πύρωσιν) that is used for "fire" is found only here and in 1 Peter 4:12: "Beloved, do not be surprised at the fiery trial when it comes upon you to test you, as though something strange were happening to you." It describes a process of testing through fire.

The concept of "trial by fire" invokes the common prophetic analogy of a refiner's fire that smelts away dross.[93] A fiery trial can remove impurities: "I will turn my hand against you and will smelt away your dross as with lye and remove all your alloy" (Isaiah 1:25); "The crucible is for silver, and the furnace is for gold, and the LORD tests hearts" (Proverbs 17:3); "In fire gold is tested, and the chosen, in the crucible of humiliation" (Sirach 2:5).[94]

Through these trials the wicked are judged and punished, while the righteous are proven worthy. The trials will come upon all mankind; just as the gospel was to be preached to "the whole creation/all creation under heaven," so now must all people be tested.[95] Some will, even at this stage, appear to be following the Way of Life but will stumble under temptations and fall away. The Master warned us "many will fall away" (Matthew 24:10). The Didache emphasizes the call to remain steadfast.

Those who stumble (go astray from the faith) will be destroyed in contrast to those who endure and are saved. The phrase "caused to stumble and perish" invokes the common prophetic idiom of divine punishment through the placement of stumbling blocks before the people. For example:

---

93   E.g., Isaiah 1:25, 48:10; Zechariah 13:9.
94   Also Jeremiah 6:29; Ezekiel 22:20, 24:11; Zechariah 13:9; Malachi 3:2–3, 4:1.
95   Mark 16:15; Colossians 1:23.

[16.5]
Then the entire human race will enter the trial by fire, and many will be caused to stumble and will perish, but those who endure in their faithfulness will be saved by the very one who is cursed.

Thus says the LORD: "Behold, I will lay before this people stumbling blocks against which they shall stumble; fathers and sons together, neighbor and friend shall perish." (Jeremiah 6:21)

The Master also speaks of those who will endure: "The one who endures to the end will be saved" (Matthew 10:22).[96] The Prophet Daniel writes, "Blessed is he who waits and arrives at the 1,335 days" (Daniel 12:12). We also find in the Sibylline Oracles, "The wise people that are left will have peace, having had trial of evil that later they might rejoice."[97]

The phrase "saved by the very one who is cursed (*katathema*, κατάθεμα)" has puzzled scholars since the Didache's rediscovery. The Greek is enigmatic. Some suggest that this means being saved from the curse of death. They interpret the one who is cursed as the grave.[98]

Assuming that the Greek is not in some way defective, one plausible explanation is that "the one who is cursed" is Messiah.[99] The Torah tells us that "a hanged man is cursed by God" (Deuteronomy 21:23), and Paul quotes this passage when he states in Galatians, "Messiah redeemed us from the curse of the law by becoming a curse for us" (Galatians 3:13).[100] Our Master became a curse on our behalf by dying for our sins in a shameful manner. The Septuagint of Zechariah 12:10 states, "They shall look upon me, because they have mocked me." In this way those who endure and remain faithful disciples are saved by the one who is cursed.

> *And then the signs of the truth will appear:*
> *the first sign, an expansion in the heavens;*
> *next, the sign of the sound of the trumpet;*
> *and the third sign, the resurrection of the dead.* (DIDACHE 16.6)

Again, a new stage is introduced with the adverbial "and then" (*kai tote*, καὶ τότε) in which three "signs of truth" will be revealed. This new stage will begin to bring

---

96   Also Matthew 24:13; Mark 13:13.
97   Sibylline Oracles 5.384–385.
98   Niederwimmer, *The Didache*, 222.
99   The Georgian version of the Didache reads "will be saved even by this terrible curse." Grigol Peradse notes that "The Georgian text reads, probably instead of κατάθεμα – ἀνάθεμα" ("Die Lehre der zwölf Apostel aus der georgischen Überlieferung" *Zeitschrift für die neutestamentliche Wissenschaft und die Kunde der älteren Kirche* 31 (1932): 116).
100 Cf. Zechariah 12:10; 1 Corinthians 12:3; Barnabas 7.9; Odes of Solomon 31:8–13.

hope after the period of trial that the end is drawing near and the Master's kingdom is arriving. The three signs are set up in opposition to the false signs that we are told in 16.4 the deceiver will display.

We find other examples in Jewish literature of three signs that announce the arrival of the kingdom. For example, Paul states, "The Lord himself will descend from heaven with a cry of command, with the voice of an archangel, and with the sound of the trumpet of God. And the dead in [Messiah] will rise first" (1 Thessalonians 4:16).[101] The Sibylline Oracles mentions that Elijah will display three signs.[102] The concept of eschatological signs would not have been unfamiliar to Gentiles coming from the Greco-Roman world as is evidenced by contemporary writings.[103]

In the Didache's little apocalypse, the first sign is "an expansion in the heavens." This is another passage that has puzzled scholars, and numerous interpretations have been proposed. The word *ekpetasis* ("expansion," ἐκπέτασις) is difficult to interpret and can be defined as "expansion," "spread," or "extension." The Apostolic Constitutions 7.32 renders this, "Then the sign of the Son of Man will appear in the heavens," in accordance with the Master's words, "Then will appear in heaven the sign of the Son of Man and then all the tribes of the earth will mourn, and they will see the Son of Man coming on the clouds of heaven with power and great glory" (Matthew 24:30).[104] Marcello del Verme feels that "it is more likely that the text refers to some sort of opening in the sky, a recurring image in apocalyptic texts,"[105] perhaps even "the image of turmoils in heaven that are described in Matthew 24:29, with the darkening of the sun and the moon and the stars falling out of the skies."[106]

A clue may be found in the tenth benediction of the *Amidah*: "Sound a great shofar for our freedom, and lift up a banner for the gathering of our exiles. Blessed

[16.6]
And then the signs of the truth will appear: the first sign, an expansion in the heavens; next, the sign of the sound of the trumpet; and the third sign, the resurrection of the dead.

---

[101] Notice how Paul's three signs line up almost perfectly with the Didache's except that Paul has "with a cry of command" for the Didache's "an expansion in the heavens." Alan Garrow feels that Paul is drawing upon Didache 16 in 1 Thessalonians 4:15–17. He argues that the "word from the Lord" (4:15) was "the tradition preserved in Didache 16." See Alan J.P. Garrow, "The Eschatological Tradition behind 1 Thessalonians: Didache 16," *Journal for the Study of the New Testament* 32, no. 2 (2009): 191–215. More likely, Paul and the Didache share a common eschatological tradition.
[102] Sibylline Oracles 2.188–195.
[103] E.g., Plutarch, *Sulla* 7.2–5; Tacitus, *Histories* 5.13. Josephus expected the same familiarity for his readers when he described great portents and signs during big events in Jewish history (especially the destruction of the Temple), described at length in Josephus, *Jewish War* 6.5.3 §§288–300.
[104] Mark 13:26; Luke 21:27. Cf. Isaiah 6:1–2; Revelation 19:11.
[105] Del Verme, *Didache and Judaism*, 253. Cf. Psalm 104:2.
[106] Verheyden, "Eschatology in the Didache and the Gospel of Matthew," 210. Cf. Revelation 6:14.

[16.6]
And then the signs of the truth will appear: the first sign, an expansion in the heavens; next, the sign of the sound of the trumpet; and the third sign, the resurrection of the dead.

are you, O LORD, who gathers the dispersed among his people Israel."[107] This connects the idea of the blowing of the shofar (the Didache's second sign) with the lifting up of a banner (or sign). In fact, "the raising of the totem usually accompanied the blowing of the shofar."[108] For example, "He will raise a signal for nations far away, and whistle for them from the ends of the earth" (Isaiah 5:26); "Set up a standard on the earth; blow the trumpet among the nations" (Jeremiah 51:27).[109] In turn, the first two signs of the Didache are connected with the ingathering of the exiles, as was already spoken of in 9.4 and 10.5:

> The first sign is the נס פרש בשמים [*nes paras beshamayim*], the totem promised by Isaiah 11:10 which the Messiah would raise to rout the nations and gather the exiles of Israel. This is confirmed by the extensive commentary in the Targum to Isaiah whenever נס [*nes*] appears in the Old Testament.[110]

The *nes* is an actual pole or some type of standard or banner displayed atop a pole.[111] The NASB translates this as "signal." Ultimately, this sign will draw the nations to Jerusalem and to Messiah:

> "To him shall be the obedience of the peoples" [Genesis 49:10] ... that is, to whom the nations of the world will flock as it says [in Isaiah 11:10], "Then in that day the nations will resort to the root of Jesse, who will stand as a signal for the peoples; and his resting place will be glorious." (*Genesis Rabbah* 98:8, 99:8)

The second sign is that of the "trumpet," that is, the *shofar* (שופר). The Apostolic Constitutions 7.32 adds, "Next shall be the sound of the trumpet made by the archangel," in accordance with the Master's words, "He will send out his angels with a loud trumpet call, and they will gather his elect from the four winds, from one

---

107 This version is from the *Genizah Amidah* as found in Rabbi Lawrence A. Hoffman, *The Amidah* (vol. 2 of *My People's Prayer Book: Traditional Prayers, Modern Commentaries*; Woodstock, VT: Jewish Lights, 1998), 40. It is also found in the *Ahavah Rabbah* prayer of Shacharit services and in the *Mussaf* liturgy of Rosh HaShanah and Yom Kippur.
108 Jonathan A. Draper, "The Development of 'the Sign of the Son of Man' in the Jesus Tradition," *New Testament Studies* 39, no. 1 (January 1993): 7.
109 Also Isaiah 11:10–12, 13:2.
110 Jonathan A. Draper, "The Jesus Tradition in the Didache," *The Didache in Modern Research* (ed. Draper; Leiden, The Netherlands: Brill, 1996), 72–91.
111 Some have suggested that this sign was the cross and find support in the early hymnal written by Jewish believers, the Odes of Solomon (27:1–3, 42:1–2).

end of heaven to the other" (Matthew 24:31).[112] This in connection with the signal that announces the ingathering of the exiles: "In that day a great trumpet will be blown, and those who were lost in the land of Assyria and those who were driven out to the land of Egypt will come and worship the LORD on the holy mountain at Jerusalem" (Isaiah 27:13). Zechariah likens that great shofar blast to a "whistle," as a father might call for his lost children.[113] The Apostle Paul writes of this signal happening "in a moment, in the twinkling of an eye, at the last trumpet. For the trumpet will sound, and the dead will be raised imperishable, and we shall be changed" (1 Corinthians 15:52).[114]

Finally, the third sign is the resurrection of the dead.[115] In Judaism the resurrection of the dead is considered to be the highest display of the power of God. This is why the Master told the Sadducees, who did not believe in the resurrection, that they did not know "the power of God."[116] In the second blessing of the *Amidah*, which is called *Gevurot* ("Power," גבורות), we read, "You are mighty ... you support the dead ... and sustain life giving life to the dead ... Blessed are you, O LORD, who gives life to the dead."[117] The Apostolic Constitutions 7.32 reads, "In that interim shall be the revival of those who were asleep." This is not a general resurrection ("not the resurrection of everyone" [16.7]) but only of the righteous, as in the ingathering of Matthew 24:31. The Master states, "I am the resurrection and the life" (John 11:25), and his resurrection was a promise of the great resurrection to come. The Apostle Paul writes, "Each in his own order: [Messiah] the firstfruits, then at his coming those who belong to [Messiah]" (1 Corinthians 15:23). This resurrection will be the last sign that Messiah's arrival is upon us.

[16.6]
And then the signs of the truth will appear: the first sign, an expansion in the heavens; next, the sign of the sound of the trumpet; and the third sign, the resurrection of the dead.

---

112 Alan Garrow argues that Matthew 24:30–31 was derived directly from Didache 16.6, 8. See Garrow, *The Gospel of Matthew's Dependence on the Didache* (New York, NY: Bloomsbury, 2012), 203–207. Far more likely, Matthew 24 and Didache 16 share a common eschatological tradition preserved in the early transmission of Yeshua's teachings.
113 Zechariah 10:8–10.
114 Joel 2:1; Zephaniah 1:16; 4 Ezra 6:23; Sibylline Oracles 8.239; Matthew 24:31; 1 Thessalonians 4:16; Revelation 8–11.
115 The Georgian version of the Didache adds "immediately in joy."
116 Matthew 22:29; Mark 12:24.
117 This version is from the *Genizah Amidah* as found in Rabbi Hoffman, *The Amidah*, 38.

> *However, not the resurrection of everyone but rather as it is said: "The Lord will come, and all the righteous along with him."* (DIDACHE 16.7)

The Didache now clarifies that this is not a general resurrection but rather only of the righteous.[118] As the Apostle Paul states:

> The Lord himself will descend from heaven with a cry of command, with the voice of an archangel, and with the sound of the trumpet of God. And the dead in [Messiah] will rise first. Then we who are alive, who are left, will be caught up together with them in the clouds to meet the Lord in the air, and so we will always be with the Lord. (1 Thessalonians 4:16–17)

> That he may establish your hearts blameless in holiness before our God and Father, at the coming of our Lord [Yeshua] with all his saints. (1 Thessalonians 3:13)[119]

In Matthew 25, the Master states that he will be accompanied by the angels:

> When the Son of Man comes in his glory, and all the angels with him, then he will sit on his glorious throne. (Matthew 25:31)

The word "saints," or "holy ones," is ambiguous and can refer either to angels or the righteous.[120] The theme is found first in a passage in the first century BCE apocalypse 1 Enoch (1:9), which is later quoted in Jude 14, in which "holy ones" can refer to both angels and the righteous: "Behold! He comes with ten thousands of his holy ones to execute judgment upon all."

---

[118] This clarifying note about the resurrection and the accompanying proof text are omitted from the Apostolic Constitutions. Since the Apostolic Constitutions is eager to add scriptural proof texts to bolster the Didache's text, this may indicate that this section was added to the Didache by a secondary editor and that it was not included in the version of the Didache from which the author of the Apostolic Constitutions worked. See Jefford, "Authority and Perspective in the Didache," in *The Didache: A Missing Piece of the Puzzle in Early Jewish Christianity* (eds. Draper and Jefford; Atlanta, GA: Society of Biblical Literature, 2015), 42.

[119] Cf. Jude 14.

[120] We find the combination of the two in Martyrdom and Ascension of Isaiah (4:14, 16): "And after [one thousand] three hundred and thirty-two days the Lord will come with his angels and with the hosts of the saints from the seventh heaven, with the glory of the seventh heaven, and will drag Beliar, and his hosts also, into Gehenna."

The Didache here in verse 7 quotes Zechariah 14:5 as a proof text. This is only one of two direct scriptural citations in the entire work.[121] It employs the common introductory formula "it is said" (*shene'emar*, שנאמר), which was used in rabbinic literature to introduce quotes from the Scriptures.[122] Draper writes:

> This text is used in a number of rabbinic writings to justify the resurrection of the martyrs of Israel (b.*Pesachim* 50a; *Ruth Rabbah* 5; *Ecclesiastes Rabbah* 5). It also lies behind Paul's teaching in 1 Thessalonians 3:13; 2 Thessalonians 1:3–10; and several passages in the Synoptic Gospels, where "saints" is used interchangeably with "angels" (Matthew 25:31; Mark 8:35–38; and parr.) It seems therefore that this text was used widely by early Jewish writers to argue for the resurrection of the martyrs in the eschatological age and that the Didache represents a very early form of the tradition.[123]

[16.7]
However, not the resurrection of everyone but rather as it is said: "The Lord will come, and all the righteous along with him."

In Jewish eschatology "the righteous" usually refers primarily to Israel, and the wicked primarily are the nations.[124] The sages state, "All Israel has a share in the world to come, as it is written, 'Your people shall all be righteous; they shall possess the land forever, the branch of my planting, the work of my hands, that I might be glorified' (Isaiah 60:21)" (m.*Sanhedrin* 10:1). However, elsewhere they add, "There are also righteous people among the nations of the world who have a share in the world to come" (t.*Sanhedrin* 13:2). In the Didache, "the righteous" refers to Israel along with the righteous Gentiles who have been immersed into Messiah.

As with most occurrences of "Lord" in the Didache, scholars debate as to whether this refers to God the Father or to Yeshua. Contextually, it seems that both instances in verses 7 and 8 are intended to refer to Messiah. Even though the

---

121 The quotation follows the Septuagint closely, only differing with *eksei ho kurios* (Ἥξει ὁ κύριος) (Didache 16.7) instead of *eksei kurios ho theos mou* (ἥξει κύριος ὁ θεός μου) (Zechariah 14:5). "The only issue of textual form here is that the Didache quotation agrees with the Septuagint reading 'with Him' instead of the reading 'with you' of the MT. The Didachist evidently sees the 'holy ones' of Zechariah 14:5 as believers, not angels (cf. 1 Thessalonians 3:13). Elsewhere, the New Testament sees angels as also accompanying the Lord at His advent (Matthew 25:31)" (Varner, "The Didache's Use of the Old and New Testaments," *The Master's Seminary Journal* 16, no. 1 [Spring 2005]: 140). This quotation is also found in Matthew 25:31, in which ἄγγελοι is "angels," whereas in the Didache ἅγιοι refers to the resurrected believers.
122 Bruce M. Metzger, "The Formulas Introducing Quotations of Scripture in the NT and the Mishnah," *Journal of Biblical Literature* 70, no. 4 (December 1951): 297–307.
123 Draper, "The Holy Vine of David Made Known to the Gentiles through God's Servant Jesus," 277.
124 Ladd, "The Eschatology of the Didache," 117. The Georgian version of the Didache reads "his holy ones."

[16.7]
However, not the resurrection of everyone but rather as it is said: "The Lord will come, and all the righteous along with him."

verse quoted originally referred to God, by extension it refers to the Master, who comes as the agent of the Father.[125]

Because the fate of the wicked is not mentioned, some have assumed that the wicked remain in eternal death or suggest the possibility of universal salvation. However, the Master teaches that both the righteous and the wicked will be resurrected: "An hour is coming when all who are in the tombs will hear his voice and come out, those who have done good to the resurrection of life, and those who have done evil to the resurrection of judgment" (John 5:29), and the book of Acts indicates this as well: "There will be a resurrection of both the just and the unjust" (Acts 24:15). Jewish tradition bases the idea of the two resurrections on Daniel 12:2: "And many of those who sleep in the dust of the earth shall awake, some to everlasting life, and some to shame and everlasting contempt."[126] Additionally, the early followers of Messiah believed in a literal Messianic Era. In turn, most plausible is the suggestion of another general resurrection and judgment after the Messianic Kingdom.[127] This is in line with Revelation:

> Then I saw thrones, and seated on them were those to whom the authority to judge was committed. Also I saw the souls of those who had been beheaded for the testimony of [Yeshua] and for the word of God, and those who had not worshiped the beast or its image and had not received its mark on their foreheads or their hands. They came to life and reigned with [Messiah] for a thousand years. The rest of the dead did not come to life until the thousand years were ended. This is the first resurrection. Blessed and holy is the one who shares in the first resurrection! Over such the second death has no power, but they will

---

125 For a different opinion, see Milavec, *The Didache: Faith, Hope, & Life of the Earliest Christian Communities, 50–70 C.E.*, 660–663.

126 "Rabbi Saadiah Gaon explained that not all would be resurrected at the Redemption, 'He does not say all ... who sleep ... because all ... would include all of mankind, and He made this promise only to Israel. Therefore he says, many ... And when he says: these for everlasting life and others for shame ... His intent is not that among those who are resurrected some will be rewarded and some punished, for those who deserve punishment will not be resurrected at the time of the redemption. Rather, He means that those who will awaken will have everlasting life, and those who will not awaken will be for shame and for everlasting abhorrence. For all the righteous, [including] those who repented, will live; only the unbelieving and those who died without repentance will remain. All this will happen at the time of the redemption' (*Emunos V'Deos* 7)" (Rabbi Hersh Godlwurm, *Daniel: Artscroll Tanach Series* [Brooklyn, NY: Artscroll, 2000], 320).

127 See Varner, *The Way of the Didache*, 100.

be priests of God and of [Messiah], and they will reign with him for a thousand years. (Revelation 20:4–6)

Some have even suggested, due to the way that the Didache ends so abruptly in verse 16.8, that there may have been a longer ending for chapter 16 that included mention of a general resurrection.[128] The Epistle of Barnabas includes an allusion to two resurrections:

> It is good, then, that one who has been discipled in the Lord's righteous requirements—whichever have been recorded—to walk in accordance with them. For the one who does these things shall be glorified in the kingdom of God; the one who chooses those opposite things shall perish together with his works. For this reason, there is resurrection; for this reason, there is reimbursement. (Barnabas 21.1)

[16.7] *However, not the resurrection of everyone but rather as it is said: "The Lord will come, and all the righteous along with him."*

⫸ *Then the world will behold the Lord coming upon the clouds of heaven.* (DIDACHE 16.8)

The fifth and final stage of eschatological events is now introduced, once again using the adverb "then" (*tote*, τότε). The Didache ends with the arrival of Messiah and the inauguration of the Messianic Era. These events are the fulfillment of the Master's words, "The kingdom of heaven is at hand" (Matthew 4:17). O'Loughlin writes:

> [The Didache] opens with a choice facing every individual: the choice of life as a disciple of the Lord or death; it ends with all the disciples being gathered into eternal life by the Lord.[129]

The verse appears to be a midrashic paraphrase of Daniel 7:13: "I saw in the night visions, and behold, with the clouds of heaven there came one like a son of man, and he came to the Ancient of Days and was presented before him."[130] However, it also adds gospel material: "Then will appear in heaven the sign of the Son of Man, and then all the tribes of the earth will mourn, and they will see the Son of Man coming on the clouds of heaven with power and great glory" (Matthew 24:30), and, "I tell you, from now on you will see the Son of Man seated at

---

128 Ladd, "The Eschatology of the Didache," 154–164.
129 O'Loughlin, *The Didache*, 143.
130 Pardee, *The Genre and Development of the Didache*, 177. Also 4 Ezra 13:3; Sibylline Oracles 2.297–303. Cf. Psalm 68:4.

> [16.8]
> Then the world will behold the Lord coming upon the clouds of heaven.

the right hand of Power and coming on the clouds of heaven" (Matthew 26:64).[131] Kurt Niederwimmer states, "The Didache quotes common apocalyptic material (from Daniel), and agrees with Matthew (against Mark) precisely at those points where both agree with Daniel."[132]

It is fitting that the Master will return on clouds: "When he had said these things, as [the disciples] were looking on, he was lifted up, and a cloud took him out of their sight" (Acts 1:9). Two angels told them, "Men of Galilee, why do you stand looking into heaven? This [Yeshua], who was taken up from you into heaven, will come in the same way as you saw him go into heaven" (Acts 1:11). The Apostle John states, "Behold, he is coming with the clouds, and every eye will see him, even those who pierced him, and all tribes of the earth will wail on account of him. Even so. Amen" (Revelation 1:7).[133] In the same way, "The glory of the LORD appeared in the cloud (Exodus 16:10); "The LORD descended in the cloud and stood with him there, and proclaimed the name of the LORD" (Exodus 34:5); "He makes the clouds his chariot" (Psalm 104:3).[134]

As we stated above, it seems that this was not the original full ending of the Didache, as is also indicated by the Buenos manuscript:

> The scribe placed a period after τοῦ οὐρανοῦ ["of heaven," *tou ouranou*], leaving the rest of the line blank, and the rest of the page as well. Apparently the copyist thus signaled his conviction that the conclusion of the Didache was missing.[135]

This is curious especially in light of the fact that everywhere else the scribe used every usable space writing in small letters frequently employing abbreviations.

Additionally, Didache 16 fails to address important concepts such as the destruction of the antichrist, the destruction of Israel's enemies, the ingathering of the exiles, the arrival of the kingdom in Israel, and a general resurrection followed by the final judgment. Since many of these themes play prominently in the liturgical expressions of chapters 9 and 10, one would expect them to be included here in the little apocalypse. George Eldon Ladd has suggested that the ending that we possess now represents a version that was perhaps edited down sometime around the third century when the concept of a physical earthly kingdom (millennialism)

---

131 Also Matthew 26:64; Mark 13:26, 14:62; Revelation 1:7; Apocalypse of Thomas.
132 Niederwimmer, *The Didache*, 226.
133 Cf. Revelation 14:14, 16.
134 Cf. 2 Samuel 22:10–12.
135 Niederwimmer, *The Didache*, 226.

was no longer a common belief within the church.¹³⁶ It could be that the original ending was too Israel-centric for later redactors. If there was a longer ending originally, it almost certainly would have included a more complete picture of the final redemption and the arrival of the Messianic Era.

[16.8]
Then the world will behold the Lord coming upon the clouds of heaven.

However, O'Loughlin argues, "There is a certain crispness to the ending as we have it that makes the notion of a longer ending unnecessary."¹³⁷ Additionally, if the Didache's source is close to that of Matthew 24, then perhaps the ending is abrupt because the source ends quite abruptly as well.¹³⁸ Matthew 24 also does not include details about the destruction of the antichrist, the kingdom being inaugurated, or a final judgment. However, the Didache adds other material such as that regarding the antichrist and the resurrection that is not explicitly mentioned in Matthew 24.

The Georgian version of the Didache ends with Messiah "coming on the clouds with power and great glory,¹³⁹ so that he might judge every man according to his works, in his righteousness, and before the whole human race and before the angels. Amen." We also have a longer ending in the Apostolic Constitutions, but that appears to have been expanded:¹⁴⁰

> And then "the Lord will come and all of the righteous along with him"¹⁴¹ in the midst of a whirlwind¹⁴² upon the clouds of heaven¹⁴³ along with his powerful angels¹⁴⁴ to sit upon the throne of¹⁴⁵ his kingdom and to condemn the deceiver of the world¹⁴⁶—namely, the Adversary—and to render reward or punishment to each one according to what he has

---

136 Ladd, "The Eschatology of the Didache," 154–164. It is for this same reason that the book of Revelation was rejected by those who opposed an earthly kingdom until Augustine came along and spiritualized the concept of the millennium. However, in regard to the Didache, "there was no possibility of spiritualizing its concept. The only solution for those who valued highly the rest of the work would be to omit the last page" (ibid., 158).
137 O'Loughlin, *The Didache*, 141.
138 Ladd, "The Eschatology of the Didache," 89.
139 Cf. Matthew 24:30; Mark 13:26; Luke 21:27.
140 Robert E. Aldridge argues that the Apostolic Constitutions version represents the original ending of the Didache. He bases this on among other things that both Didache 16 and the Apostolic Constitutions ending have close parallels to Matthew 25–25. See Aldridge, "The Lost Ending of the Didache," *Vigiliae Christianae* 53, no. 1 (February 1999): 1–15.
141 Didache 16.7; Zechariah 14:5.
142 2 Kings 2:1, 11 Septuagint.
143 Didache 16.8. Cf. Daniel 7:13; Matthew 24:30, 26:64; Mark 13:26, 14:62; Revelation 1:7.
144 Matthew 16:27.
145 Matthew 19:28, 25:31. Cf. Revelation 3:21.
146 Didache 16.4. Cf. Matthew 24:24; 2 Thessalonians 2:2–4; 1 John 2:22, 4:3; Revelation 12:9.

[16.8]
Then the world will behold the Lord coming upon the clouds of heaven.

done.[147] Then the wicked will go to an eternal place of torment, but the righteous will go to eternal life,[148] inheriting those things "which no eye saw, and no ear heard, and moreover no man's heart imagined, which God has prepared for those who love him" [1 Corinthians 2:9],[149] and they will rejoice in the kingdom of God, the kingdom ushered in by the Messiah Yeshua. (Apostolic Constitutions 7.32)

William Varner creates his own reconstructed ending:

> ... with the angels of His power, in the throne of His kingdom, to condemn the devil, the deceiver of the world, and to render to everyone according to his deeds. Then shall the wicked go away into everlasting punishment, but the righteous shall enter eternal life. And they shall rejoice in the kingdom of God, which is in Christ Jesus.[150]

In a way it is fitting that we do not know what the original ending of the Didache was. After all, according to the apostles and the Didache the fate and end of every man is ultimately in their own hands and unknown. It is up to us to follow the Way of Life and hold close to our Master until his return.

---

147 Matthew 16:27. Cf. Job 34:11; Psalm 62:12; Proverbs 24:12; Jeremiah 17:10, 32:19; Romans 2:6.
148 Matthew 25:46. Cf. Daniel 12:2; John 3:36, 5:29.
149 Paul here is drawing from Isaiah 64:4, which the sages also use to talk about the World to Come (b.*Brachot* 34b).
150 Varner, *The Way of the Didache*, 100. Garrow speculates to reconstruct: "And all the holy ones with him, on his royal throne, to judge the world deceiver and to reward each according to his deeds. Then shall go away the evil into eternal punishment but the righteous shall enter into life eternal, inheriting those things which eye has not seen and ear has not heard and which has not arisen in the heart of man. Those things which God has prepared for those who love him" (Garrow, "The Eschatological Tradition behind 1 Thessalonians: Didache 16," 202–203).

Conclusion

We have come to the conclusion of one of the greatest biblical textual finds of the modern era. The real value of the Didache's rediscovery lies not in the document itself but in what we choose to do with its message. If we treat it merely as a curiosity for the halls of academia it loses its spiritual significance. Instead, the teachings need to be put back into their Messianic Jewish context and delivered to the laymen in both Messianic Judaism and the broader church. It is my prayer that this commentary will contribute to that endeavor.

The Didache guides the reader through the basics of faith in Yeshua, but on closer examination, those basic principles sketch out the essence of discipleship. Each chapter is based on the Scriptures and in particular the words of our Master. The Didache asks us not to relay its teaching on its own authority but upon the Word of God, with which it is thoroughly infused.

We first learned about the Two Ways, urging us to stay on the Way of Life and avoid the Way of Death. The Way of Life is to love the God who made us and to love our fellow as ourselves. The Two Ways section (chapters 1–6) primarily dealt with instructions for loving our neighbors. The Didache teaches us about our responsibility to give to others, to abide by ethical standards, and to honor our teachers. Most of all, it teaches us to live a life of sacrifice where we lay down our pride, our desires, and sometimes even our lives for our fellow human beings.

Chapter 7 began a halachic section focusing on expressing our love to our Creator. We learned about immersion in Messiah, daily prayer, weekly fasting, liturgy, giving back to HaShem of what he has given to us, fellowship meals, and congregational structure. We saw how the dual theme of love continued to permeate the Didache's chapters, even in the midst of legal material.

Finally, we concluded our study with a "little apocalypse." The Didache gives us a glimpse of Messianic Jewish expectation for the end of days. The little apocalypse calls upon us to remain steadfast in our faith in Messiah and in the practice of the Way of Life. It also urges us to remain in fellowship with others. Through gathering together with like-minded believers, we will be strengthened and be able to withstand the guiles of false prophets and the deceiver. Ultimately the Didache's concern lies not so much with the individual as it does with the spiritual success of the community.

The Didache consistently emphasizes actions over correct doctrine. The Way of Life contains no creeds or theological dissertations, but instead, it focuses only on living a life of sacrificial discipleship on a daily basis. The Master's main message was "Repent for the kingdom of heaven is at hand." Everything else he taught us was about how to live in that kingdom. His instruction was not limited to the future when the Messianic Era arrives; he meant it for his disciples to live in the present age, even for us to live out today. We express our theology—our faith in Messiah Yeshua and the coming kingdom—through our actions and manner of living.

As we discovered, the Didache contains instruction first passed along orally and only later written down. Its teachings originate from the period when the followers of Messiah still identified within the Jewish people and as a sect of Judaism. The Didache does not teach that Gentile believers replace Israel or become Jewish. Instead, it teaches in line with the New Testament that Gentile believers enter the kingdom, brought near to the covenants by way of association with the Messiah, while at the same time retaining their distinct role as members of the kingdom from the nations. The instruction in the Didache assumed that Gentile believers would stand with the Jewish people, under the authority of the Torah and in anticipation of the coming redemption, while respecting God's election of the land and people of Israel.

As we await the return of the Master, may the words of the Didache inspire us and encourage us to work out our faith with fear and trembling, to walk on the narrow path, the path of discipleship, the Way of Life. And may it remind us to hope in the coming redemption, remembering that our kingdom is not of this world. May it be soon and in our days. Amen.

Appendices

Epistle of Barnabas

The Epistle of Barnabas was composed in the early second century but some of the material dates to an earlier period. Sections 18:1–20:2 contain content very similar to the Two Ways material of Didache 1–6 and might very well go back to the Apostolic Era. It is therefore an important textual witness to the Didache and points to an alternate strain of Didache tradition.

18.1 Now let us transition to yet another kind of knowledge and teaching. There are two ways[1] of teaching and authority: one of light and one of darkness;[2] however, there is a great difference between the two ways.[3] For over the one are assigned illuminating angels of God, but over the other are assigned angels of the Adversary.[4]

18.2 Likewise, the one way is that of the Lord who is from everlasting and forever,[5] but the other way is that of the prince of this present time of evil.[6]

19.1 Now the Way of Light[7] is this: if anyone intends to journey to the appointed place, he must hurry to arrive there through his deeds. Therefore, the knowledge given us in which to walk is this:

---

* Shaded text represents where the Greek text matches the *Codex Hierosolymitanus* manuscript of the Didache.

---

1   Didache 1:1.
2   Cf. Didache 1:1.
3   Didache 1:1.
4   Cf. Ephesians 6:12; Revelation 12:7.
5   Cf. 1 Timothy 1:17.
6   Cf. Romans 8:18; 2 Corinthians 4:4.
7   Cf. Didache 1:2; Deuteronomy 30:15; Psalms 16:11; Proverbs 15:24; Jeremiah 21:8; Matthew 7:13–14.

19.2 You shall love[8] the One who made you.[9] You shall revere the One who formed you.[10] You shall give glory to the One who ransomed you from death.[11] Be simple-hearted[12] and rich in spirit.[13] Do not associate with those who go along the Way of Death. You shall hate everything that does not please the Lord.[14] You shall hate every form of hypocrisy.[15] Do not forsake the commandments of the Lord.[16]

19.3 Do not aggrandize yourself,[17] but rather be humble-minded in everything.[18] Do not take credit for yourself. Do not plot evil against your fellow.[19] Do not give overconfidence to yourself.[20]

19.4 Do not commit sexual immorality.[21] Do not commit adultery.[22] Do not practice pederasty.[23] The word of God must not depart from you among those in impurity. Do not show partiality[24] when rebuking anyone's transgressions.[25] Be humble.[26] Be quiet.[27] Be one who trembles at the words that you have heard.[28] Do not hold grudges against your brother.[29]

---

8   Cf. Deuteronomy 6:5, 11:1; Matthew 22:37; Mark 12:30.
9   Didache 1:2.
10 Cf. Jeremiah 1:5; Psalms 139:13–16.
11 Cf. Psalm 56:13, 116:8.
12 Cf. Matthew 6:22; Luke 11:34.
13 Cf. 2 Corinthians 6:10.
14 Didache 4:12.
15 Ibid.
16 Didache 4:13. Cf. Numbers 15:39; Deuteronomy 4:2; Revelation 12:17, 14:12.
17 Didache 3:9.
18 Cf. Proverbs 29:23; Ephesians 4:2; 1 Peter 3:8.
19 Didache 2:6. Cf. Proverbs 3:29; Zechariah 8:17.
20 Didache 3:9.
21 Didache 2:2. Cf. Leviticus 18:6–20, 20:10–14; Matthew 5:27, 15:19; Mark 7:21; John 4:17–18; Acts 15:20, 29, 21:25; Romans 1:29; 1 Corinthians 5:1, 9–11, 6:9, 13, 18, 7:2, 10:8; 2 Corinthians 12:21; Galatians 5:19; Ephesians 5:3, 5; Colossians 3:5; 1 Thessalonians 4:3–5, 7; 1 Timothy 1:10; Hebrews 12:16, 13:4; Jude 7; Revelation 2:14, 20–21, 21:8, 22:15.
22 Didache 2:2; Exodus 20:14; Leviticus 20:10; Deuteronomy 5:18; Matthew 5:27, 15:19, 19:9, 18; Mark 7:21, 10: 11–12, 19; Luke 16:18, 18:20; John 8:3–5; Romans 2:22, 13:9; James 2:11; Revelation 2:22.
23 Didache 2:2; Leviticus 18:22; Romans 1:26–28; 1 Corinthians 6:9–10; Jude 4; Revelation 22:15.
24 Didache 4:3. Cf. Leviticus 19:15; Deuteronomy 16:19.
25 Didache 4:3.
26 Cf. Didache 3:7; Psalm 37:11; Matthew 5:5.
27 Cf. Didache 3:8.
28 Didache 3:8. Cf. Isaiah 66:2, 5.
29 Didache 2:3. Cf. Exodus 23:1; Leviticus 19:18; Deuteronomy 19:16; 1 Peter 2:1.

19.5 Do not be indecisive as to whether or not your judgment is correct.[30] Do not take the Lord's name in vain.[31] You shall love your fellow even more than your own life.[32] Do not murder children through abortion[33] nor —I say again—kill them after they have been born.[34] Do not withhold your hand from your son or daughter, but teach them the fear of God from their youth.[35]

19.6 Do not covet the things that belong to your fellow.[36] Do not be greedy.[37] Do not connect yourself with the lofty, but rather associate with the lowly and righteous.[38] Accept the things that happen to you as being for the good,[39] knowing that nothing happens apart from God.[40]

19.7 Do not be double-minded[41] or double-tongued.[42] Submit yourselves to your masters[43] in humility and fear, as they are an example of the authority of God.[44] Do not harshly give orders to your servant or maid who put their hope in the same God, or else they might lose their fear of God who is over both of you because he did not intend to call anyone according to status; rather, he calls those whom the Spirit has prepared.[45]

19.8 Share all things in common with your fellow.[46] Do not claim ownership, for if you are common partners in what is incorruptible, how much more

---

30 Didache 4:4.
31 Exodus 20:7; Deuteronomy 5:11.
32 Didache 1:2, 2:7. Cf. Leviticus 19:18; Deuteronomy 6:5; Matthew 5:43, 19:19, 22:37–39; Mark 12:31; Luke 10:27; John 15:13; Romans 13:9; Galatians 5:14; James 2:8.
33 Didache 2:2. Cf. Exodus 20:13; Leviticus 18:21, 20:2–5; Deuteronomy 5:17, 18:10.
34 Ibid.
35 Didache 4:9.
36 Didache 2:2; Exodus 20:17; Deuteronomy 5:21; Romans 7:7, 13:9.
37 Didache 2:6; Exodus 20:17; Deuteronomy 5:21; Romans 7:7, 13:9.
38 Didache 3:9. Cf. Romans 12:16.
39 Didache 3:10. Cf. Romans 8:28; James 1:2; 1 Peter 1:6.
40 Didache 3:10.
41 Didache 2:4. Cf. Psalms 119:113; James 1:7–8, 4:8.
42 Didache 2:4. Cf. 1 Timothy 3:8. One manuscript reads instead γλωσσώδης, "overly chatty." Also, one ancient authority adds παγὶς γὰρ θανάτου ἐστιν ἡ διγλωσσία, "for a double tongue is a deadly trap."
43 Cf. Ephesians 6:5; Colossians 3:22.
44 Didache 4:11. Cf. Romans 13:1–7; Ephesians 6:5; Colossians 3:22; Titus 2:9, 3:1; 1 Peter 2:13–18.
45 Didache 4:10.
46 Didache 4:8. Cf. Acts 2:44, 4:32.

so in what is corruptible![47] Do not be hasty-tongued,[48] for the mouth is a deadly trap.[49] Be pure as much as you can for your life's sake.

19.9 Do not be one who stretches out his hands to receive but then pulls them back in regard to giving.[50] You shall love as the apple of your eye[51] all those teachers who speak the word of the Lord to you.[52]

19.10 Remember the Day of Judgment[53] night and day,[54] and every single day[55] seek the presence of the righteous:[56] either by laboring through your words and going out to encourage them as well as by trying to save a life[57] through your words; or work toward a ransom for your sins[58] through your own means.[59]

19.11 Do not hesitate to give, and do not complain when giving, for you will find out who is the good payer of wages.[60] Keep what you have received,[61] neither adding to nor subtracting from it.[62] You shall utterly hate that which is evil.[63] Judge righteously.[64]

19.12 Do not crave conflict, but gather and bring those who are quarrelling to peaceful reconciliation.[65] Confess your transgressions.[66] You will not draw near in prayer with a guilty conscience.[67] This is the Way of Light.[68]

---

47 Didache 4:8. Cf. Romans 15:27.
48 Cf. Proverbs 12:18, 13:3, 15:28, 29:20; Ecclesiastes 5:1, 5; m.*Avot* 1:17.
49 Cf. Didache 2:4; Proverbs 21:6.
50 Didache 4:5.
51 Cf. Deuteronomy 32:10; Zechariah 2:8; Psalms 17:8; Proverbs 7:2.
52 Didache 4:1. Cf. Hebrews 13:7.
53 2 Peter 2:9, 3:7.
54 Didache 4:1; Mark 5:5; 1 Thessalonians 3:10, 2:9; 2 Thessalonians 3:8; 1 Timothy 5:5; 2 Timothy 1:3.
55 Hebrews 3:13.
56 Didache 4:2.
57 Cf. Galatians 6:1; James 5:20; Jude 23.
58 Ibid.
59 Didache 4:6. Cf. 1 Corinthians 4:12.
60 Didache 4:7.
61 Didache 4:13. Cf. 1 Corinthians 11:2, 15:3; 2 Thessalonians 2:15; 2 Timothy 2:2.
62 Didache 4:13. Cf. Deuteronomy 4:2, 12:32; Revelation 22:18–19.
63 Cf. Psalms 97:10, 119:104, 128, 163; Proverbs 8:13; Romans 12:9.
64 Didache 4:3. Cf. Leviticus 19:15; Deuteronomy 1:16–17.
65 Didache 4:3.
66 Didache 4:14. Cf. James 5:16.
67 Didache 4:14. Cf. 1 Corinthians 11:28.
68 Cf. Didache 4:14.

20.1 But the Way of Darkness[69] is perversely twisted[70] and full of curses.[71] For it is the way of eternal death with punishment[72] in which are the things that destroy people's souls: idolatry, overconfidence, loftiness of one's power, hypocrisy, duplicity, adultery, murder, robbery, arrogance, willful transgression, deceit, malice, egocentrism, use of potions, magic, greed—irreverence of God.[73]

20.2 It is the way of those who persecute good; those who hate truth; those who love falsehood; those who are ignorant of the wages of righteousness; those who do not cling to what is good[74] or to righteous judgment; those who are not mindful of the widow and orphan;[75] those who keep watch, not out of fear of God but for wickedness; those who are far, even far-removed, from being considerate and persevering; those who love frivolous things;[76] those who seek repayment; those who are merciless to the poor; those who do not trouble themselves for the oppressed; those who are prone to slander; those who do not recognize the one who made them; those who murder children; those who corrupt what God has formed; those who turn away the needy; those who oppress the greatly distressed; those who are advocates of the wealthy; and those who are lawless judges of the poor—those who are utterly sinful.[77]

---

69 Cf. Didache 5:1.
70 Cf. Isaiah 40:4; Proverbs 21:8, 28:18; Luke 3:5; Acts 2:40; Philippians 2:15.
71 Didache 5:1.
72 Cf. Hebrews 10:29.
73 Cf. Didache 5:1; Leviticus 19:14, 32, 25:17, 36, 43; Deuteronomy 6:24, 10:20, 14:23; Sirach 1:11–30, 7:1–17; Matthew 15:19; Romans 1:29–30; 1 Corinthians 6:9; 1 Timothy 1:10; 1 Peter 2:17; Revelation 14:7, 21:8, 22:15.
74 Cf. Romans 12:9.
75 Cf. Exodus 22:22; Deuteronomy 10:18, 14:29, 27:19; Jeremiah 7:6; Psalm 10:14, 18, 68:5, 82:3, 94:6, 146:9; Proverbs 23:10; Esther 2:7; Lamentations 5:3; Job 6:27, 29:12, 31:16–18; James 1:27.
76 Cf. Philippians 3:19.
77 Didache 5:2.

Oxyrhynchus Papyrus Fragments

In 1922, two Greek fragments containing sections of the Didache were discovered in Oxyrhynchus, Egypt. The nature of the texts (now cataloged as Oxyrhynchus Papyrus 1782) was slightly different and of a more expanded form than the version we have now in the complete Didache. These fragments date back to the late fourth century, making them the oldest Didache manuscripts found to date and some 650 years older than *Codex Hierosolymitanus*. The here has been linked by chapter and verse to the corresponding sections of the Didache.

1.3   Do not even the Gentiles do[1] this? However, you are to feel brotherly affection for those who hate you,[2] and you will not have any enemies. Hear what you need[3] to do to save your spirit.[4] First of all,
1.4   keep away from natural inclinations.
2.7   and some you are to pray for, yet some you are to love even more than your own life.
3.1   My child, flee from every evil thing and its like.
3.2   Do not be an angry person because anger leads to murder.

* Shaded text represents where the Greek text matches the *Codex Hierosolymitanus* manuscript of the Didache.

---

1   Cf. Matthew 5:47; Luke 6:32–33.
2   Cf. Matthew 5:44; Luke 6:27.
3   Acts 9:6.
4   Cf. Ephesians 1:13.

Bibliography

Adair, James R., Jr. "Nash Papyrus." *Eerdmans Dictionary of the Bible*. Edited by David Noel Freedman. Grand Rapids, MI: Eerdmans, 2000: 948.

Aldridge, Robert E. "Peter and the 'Two Ways,'" *Vigiliae Christianae* 53, no. 3 (August 1999): 233–264.

Aldridge, Robert E. "The Lost Ending of the Didache." *Vigiliae Christianae* 53, no. 1 (February 1999): 1–15.

Allen, George Cantrell. *The Didache or the Teaching of the Twelve Apostles*. London, England: Astolat, 1903.

Alon, Gedaliah. "The Halacha in the Teaching of the Apostles." Pages 165–194 in *The Didache in Modern Research*. Edited by Jonathan A. Draper. Leiden, The Netherlands: Brill, 1996.

Bacchiocchi, Samuele. *From Sabbath to Sunday: A Historical Investigation of the Rise of Sunday Observance in Early Christianity*. Rome, Italy: Pontifical Gregorian University, 1977.

Bauckham, Richard. "James and the Jerusalem Council Decision." *Introduction to Messianic Judaism*. Edited by David Rudolph and Joel Willitts. Grand Rapids, MI: Zondervan, 2013, 178–186.

Bauer, Walter. *A Greek-English Lexicon of the New Testament and Other Early Christian Literature*. Edited by William Arndt, Frederick W. Danker, and F. Wilbur Gingrich. Chicago, IL: University of Chicago, 1958.

Bercot, David W., ed. *A Dictionary of Early Christian Beliefs: A Reference Guide to More Than 700 Topics Discussed by the Early Church Fathers*. Peabody, MA: Hendrickson, 1998.

Berkovitz, Jay R. "Changing Conceptions of Gentiles at the Threshold of Modernity: The Napoleonic Sanhedrin." Pages 129–150 in *Formulating Responses in an Egalitarian Age*. Edited by Marc D. Stern. New York, NY: Rowman & Littlefield, 2005.

Betz, Johannes. "The Eucharist in the Didache." Pages 244–275 in *The Didache in Modern Research*. Edited by Jonathan A. Draper. Leiden, The Netherlands: Brill, 1996.

Bivin, David N. and Roy Blizzard, Jr. *Understanding the Difficult Words of Jesus: New Insights from a Hebraic Perspective*. Shippensburg, PA: Destiny Image, 1994.

Bivin, David N. "'Binding' and 'Loosing' in the Kingdom of Heaven," *Jerusalem Perspective* 23 (November–December 1989): 12–13.

Bivin, David N. "'And' or 'In order to' Remarry," *Jerusalem Perspective* 50 (January–March 1996):10–17, 35–38.

Bivin, David N. "The Hem of His Garment." *Jerusalem Perspective* 7 (1988): 2.

Bivin, David N. "The Traveling Teacher." *Jerusalem Perspective* 10 (July 1988): 1, 4.

Blackman, Philip. *Mishnayoth*. 7 vols. Gateshead, England: Judaica, 1983.

Blomberg, Craig L. *Neither Poverty nor Riches: A Biblical Theology of Possessions*. Downers Grove, IL: Intervarsity Press, 1999.

Bonchek, Avigdor. *Studying the Torah: A Guide to In-Depth Interpretation*. Northvale, NJ: Jason Aronson, 1997.

Brannon, Rick. *The Apostolic Fathers: A New Transaction*. Bellingham, WA: Lexham Press, 2017.

Broyde, Michael J. "Jewish Law and American Public Policy: A Principled Jewish View and Some Practical Jewish Observations." Pages 109–129 in *Formulating Responses in an Egalitarian Society*. Edited by Marc Stern. New York, NY: Rowman & Littlefield, 2005.

Buber, Martin. *Tales of the Hasidim*. New York, NY: Knopf Doubleday, 2013.

Burke, Jon. "Then the Devil left: Satan's lack of presence in the Apostolic Fathers" (unpublished, 2015).

Burns, Joshua Ezra, *The Christian Schism in Jewish History and Jewish Memory*. New York, NY: Cambridge University Press, 2016.

Calhoun, Robert Matthew. "The Use and Operation of the Lord's Prayer in Christian Amulets." (annual meeting of SBL, Sand Diego, CA, 24 November 2019

Cohen, Dr. Abraham. *The Minor Tractates of the Talmud*. 2 vols. London, England: Soncino, 1965.

Cohen, Rabbi Simcha Bunim. *Laws of Daily Living*. Brooklyn, NY: ArtScroll, 2007.

Connolly, R.H. "The Didache in Relation to the Epistle of Barnabas," *Journal of Theological Studies* XXXIII (1932): 237–253.

Conybeare, C. "The Eusebian Form of the Text of Matthew 28:19." *Zeitschrift fur Neutestamentlich Wissenschaft* (1901): 275–288.

Cordovaero, Rabbi Moshe. *Sefer Tomer Devorah*. Translated by Rabbi Dov Fink and Rabbi Shimon Finkelman. Jerusalem, Israel: Tomer, 2005.

Del Verme, Marcello. *Didache and Judaism: Jewish Roots of an Ancient Christian-Jewish Work*. New York, NY: T&T Clark, 2004.

Dix, Gregory and Henry Chadwick, eds. *The Treatise on the Apostolic Tradition of St. Hippolytus of Rome, Bishop and Martyr*. New York, NY: Routledge, 1991.

Domb, Cyril, ed. *Maaser Kesafim: Giving a Tenth to Charity*. New York, NY: Feldheim, 1982.

Draper, Jonathan A. "Do the Didache and Matthew Reflect an 'Irrevocable Parting of the Ways' with Judaism?" Pages 217–24 in *Matthew and the Didache: Two Documents from the Same Jewish-Christian Milieu?* Edited by Huub van de Sandt. Minneapolis, MN: Fortress, 2005.

Draper, Jonathan A. "A Continuing Enigma: the 'Yoke of the Lord' in Didache 6:2–3 and Early Jewish-Christian Relations." Pages 106–123 in *The Image of the Judaeo-Christians in Ancient Jewish and Christian Literature*. Edited by Peter J. Tomson and Doris Lambers-Petry. Tübingen, Germany: Mohr Siebeck, 2003.

Draper, Jonathan A. "Apostles, Teachers, and Evangelists: Stability and Movement of Functionaries in Matthew, James, and the Didache." Pages 137–174 in *Matthew, James, and Didache: Three Related Documents in Their Jewish and Christian Settings*. Edited by Huub van de Sandt and Jurgen K. Zangenberg. Atlanta, GA: Society of Biblical Literature, 2008.

Draper, Jonathan A. "Children and Slaves in the Community of the Didache and the Two Ways Tradition." Pages 85–122 in *The Didache: A Missing Piece of the Puzzle in Early Christianity*. Edited by Jonathan A. Draper and Clayton N. Jefford. Atlanta, GA: SBL Press, 2015.

Draper, Jonathan A. "Pure Sacrifice in Didache 14 as Jewish Christian Exegesis." *Neotestamentica* 42, no. 2 (2008): 223–252.

Draper, Jonathan A. "Ritual Process and Ritual Symbol in Didache 7–10." *Vigiliae Christianae* 54, no. 2 (2000): 121–158.

Draper, Jonathan A. "The Development of 'the Sign of the Son of Man' in the Jesus Tradition." *New Testament Studies* 39, no. 1 (January 1993): 1–21.

Draper, Jonathan A. "A Commentary on the Didache in the Light of the Dead Sea Scrolls and Related Documents," Unpublished dissertation, St. John's College September 1983. Phd University of Cambridge.

Draper, Jonathan A. "The Holy Vine of David Made Known to the Gentiles through God's Servant Jesus: 'Christian Judaism' in the Didache." Pages 257–283 in *Jewish Christianity Reconsidered: Rethinking Ancient Groups and Texts*. Edited by Matt Jackson-McCabe. Minneapolis, MN: Fortress, 2007.

Draper, Jonathan A. "The Jesus Tradition in the Didache." Pages 72–91 in *The Didache in Modern Research*. Edited by Jonathan A. Draper. Leiden, The Netherlands: Brill, 1996.

Draper, Jonathan A. "Torah and Troublesome Apostles in the Didache Community" *Novum Testamentum* 33, no. 4 (October 1991): 340–364.

Draper, Jonathan A. "Weber, Theissen and 'Wandering Charismatics' in the Didache." *Journal of Early Christian Studies* 6, no. 4 (Winter 1998): 541–576.

Draper, Jonathan A. "Mission, Ethics, and Identity in the Didache." Pages 462–482 in *Sensitivity towards Outsiders: Exploring Dynamic Relationship between Mission and Ethics in the New Testament and Early Christianity*. Tübingen, Germany: Mohr Siebeck, 2014.

Draper, Jonathan A. "A Commentary on the Didache in Light of the Dead Sea Scrolls and Related Documents." Ph.D. diss., St. John's College, 1983.

Eby, Aaron and Toby Janicki. *Hallowed Be Your Name: Sanctifying God's Sacred Name*. Marshfield, MO: First Fruits of Zion, 2008.

Eby, Aaron. "I Will Give Praise: A Poem Ascribed to Simon Peter," *Messiah Journal* 112 (Winter 2013): 45–50.

Eby, Aaron. *Biblically Kosher: A Messianic Jewish Perspective on Kashrut*. Marshfield, MO: First Fruits of Zion, 2012.

Eby, Aaron. *First Steps in Messianic Jewish Prayer*. Marshfield, MO: First Fruits of Zion, 2014.

Eby, Aaron. *The Sabbath Table*. Marshfield, MO: Vine of David, 2014.

Eby, Aaron, trans. *We Thank You: Blessings of Thanks before and after Meals*. Marshfield, MO: Vine of David, 2008.

Eby, Aaron, trans. *Meal of Messiah: The Wedding Supper of the Lamb*. Marshfield, MO: Vine of David, 2013.

Edelstein, Rabbi Yosef. "Insights into Exodus: Parshat Tetzaveh," n.p. Cited 21 November 2013. Online: http://www.ou.org/torah/savannah/5760/tetzaveh60.htm

Ekenberg, Anders. "Evidence for Jewish Believers in 'Church Orders' and Liturgical Texts." Pages 640–658 in *Jewish Believers in Jesus: The Early Centuries*. Edited by Oskar Skarsaune and Reidar Hvalvik. Peabody, MA: Hendrickson, 2007.

Ellis, E. Earle. *The Old Testament in Early Christianity: Canon and Interpretation in the Light of Modern Research*. Grand Rapids, MI: Baker, 1991.

Elon, Menachem. "Abortion," *Encyclopedia Judaica*, 1:271.

Erhman, Bart D. ed. *Loeb Classical Library: The Apostolic Fathers Volume* I. Translated by Bart D. Ehrman. London, England: Harvard University.

Eubank, Nathan. *Wages of Cross-bearing and Debt of Sin: The Economy of Heaven in Matthew's Gospel*. Berlin, Germany: Walter de Gruyte, 2013.

Filan, Stephen. "Identity in the Didache Community." Pages 17–32 in *The Didache: A Missing Piece of the Puzzle in Early Jewish Christianity*. Edited by Jonathan A. Draper and Clayton N. Jefford. Atlanta, GA: Society of Biblical Literature, 2015.

Flusser, David. "Some Notes on Easter and the Passover Haggadah." *Immanuel* 7 (Spring 1977): 52–60.

Flusser, David. *Judaism and the Origins of Christianity*. Jerusalem, Israel: Magnes, 1988.

Fox, Robin Lane. *Pagans and Christians*. New York, NY: Knopf, 1987.

Frend, W.H.C. *Martyrdom & Persecution in the Early Church: A Study of a Conflict from the Maccabees to Donatus*. Garden City, NY: Anchor, 1967.

Friedrich, Gerhard. "σαββατον, σαββατισμος, παρασκευη." *TDNT*, 7:32.

Gaebelein, Frank E. ed. *The Expositor's Bible Commentary: Matthew, Mark, Luke*. 12 vols. Grand Rapids, MI: Zondervan, 1990.

Garrow, Alan J.P. "An Extant Instance of 'Q.'" *New Testament Studies* 62, no. 3, 2016: 398–417.

Garrow, Alan J.P. "The Eschatological Tradition behind 1 Thessalonians: Didache 16." *Journal for the Study of the New Testament* 32, no. 2 (2009): 191–215.

Garrow, Alan J.P. *The Gospel of Matthew's Dependence on the Didache*. New York, NY: Bloomsbury, 2012.

Gaston, Lloyd. *Paul and the Torah*. Vancouver, BC: University of British Columbia, 1987.

Gerhardsson, Birger. *The Shema in the New Testament: Deuteronomy 6:4–5 in Significant Passages*. Uppsala, Sweden: Almqvist and Wiksell, 1996.

Gifts of the Spirit: Complete Conference Lectures of the 2013 National Shavu'ot Conference. (Compilation). Marshfield, MO: First Fruits of Zion, 2013.

Godlwurm, Rabbi Hersh. *Daniel: Artscroll Tanach Series*. Brooklyn, NY: Artscroll, 2000.

Goodspeed, Edgar J. *The Apostolic Fathers: An American*. London, England: Independent, 1950.

Goodspeed, Edgar J. "The Didache, Barnabas, and the Doctrina." *American Theological Review* 27 (1945): 228–247.

Grant, Dov. "Learning Halachah: Likutei Halachos on Parshas Shoftim." n.p. Cited 6 September 2011. Online: http://www.nanach.org/likutay-halachos/devarim/shoftim.html.

Grant, Robert M. *Early Christianity and Society: Seven Studies*. San Francisco, CA: Harper & Row, 1977.

Greenspan, Mark. "T'rumah and Tz'dakah: How We Define Synagogue Dues." *The Rabbinical Assembly* (Parashat T'rumah). Cited 16 September 2015. Online: http://www.rabbinicalassembly.org/sites/default/files/public/resources-ideas/source-sheets/tol-parashot/t-rumah.pdf.

Greenstone, Julius H., Emil G. Hirsch, and Hartwig Hirschfeld eds. "Fasting and Fast-Days." *Jewish Encyclopedia* (1906). Cited 15 November 2014. Online: http://www.jewishencyclopedia.com/articles/6033-fasting.

Grenfell, Bernard P. and Arthur S. Hunt. *The Oxyrhynchus Papyri: Part XV*. London, England: Oxford University, 1922.

HaKohen, Rabbi Yisrael Meir. *The Concise Book of Mitzvoth: The Commandments Which Can Be Observed Today*. New York, NY: Feldheim, 1990.

"Halacha Highlight: Immersing in a Mikveh before Studying Torah," *Daf Yomi Digest* 22 (August 23, 2012): 2. Cited 8 October 2013. Online: http://www.dafdigest.org/berachos/Berachos%20022.pdf.

Harmon, A.M., trans. *Lucian*. 8 vols. Cambridge, MA: Harvard University Press, 1936.

Harris, J. Rendel. *The Teaching of the Apostles*. London, England: C.J. Clay and Sons, 1887.

Hartin, Patrick J. "Ethics in the Letter of James, the Gospel of Matthew, and the Didache: Their Place in Early Christian Literature." Pages 289–314 in *Matthew, James, and Didache: Three Related Documents in their Jewish and Christian Settings*. Edited

by Huub van de Sandt and Jurgen K. Zangenberg. Atlanta, GA: Society of Biblical Literature, 2008.

Hartman, Lars. "Baptism 'Into the Name of Jesus' and Early Christology." *Studia Theologica* 28 (1974): 21–48.

Hayes, Christine Elizabeth. *Gentile Impurities and Jewish Identities: Intermarriage and Conversion from the Bible to the Talmud*. New York, NY: Oxford University Press, 2002.

Heinemann, Joseph. *Prayer in the Talmud: Forms and Patterns*. Studia Judaica 9. New York, NY: De Gruyter, 1977.

Herczeg, Rabbi Yisrael Isser Zvi. *The Torah: With Rashi's Commentary Translated, Annotated and Elucidated, The Sapirstein Edition*. 5 vols. Brooklyn, NY: Mesorah, 2002.

Hitchcock, Roswell D. and Francis Brown. *Teaching of the Twelve Apostles: Recently Discovered and Published by Philotheos Bryennios, Metropolitan of Nicomedia*. Santa Clara, CA: Church History Publishing, 2001.

Hodge, Caroline Johnson. *If Sons, Then Heirs: A Study of Kinship and Ethnicity in the Letters of Paul*. New York, NY: Oxford University Press, 2007.

Hoffman, Rabbi Lawrence A., ed. *My People's Prayer Book: Traditional Prayers, Modern Commentaries*. 10 vols. Woodstock, VT: Jewish Lights, 2002.

Horner, G.W. "A New Papyrus Fragment of the 'Didache' in Coptic," *Journal of Theological Studies* 25 (1924): 225–231.

Horner, G.W. *The Statutes of the Apostles or Canones Ecclesiastici*. London, England: Williams & Norgate, 1904.

Hubbard, D.A. "Ethiopian Eunuch." Page 346 in *The New Bible Dictionary*. Edited by J.D. Douglas. Westmont, IL: InterVarsity Press, 1962.

Instone-Brewer, David. *Traditions of the Rabbis from the Era of the New Testament*. 2 vols. Grand Rapids, MI: Eerdmans Publishing Company, 2004.

Janicki, Toby and D. Thomas Lancaster. "Paul and Idol Food," *Messiah Journal* 114 (Fall 2013): 15–32.

Janicki, Toby. "Gentiles and the Holy Spirit." Pages 135–159 in *Gifts of the Spirit: Complete Conference Lectures of the 2013 National Shavu'ot Conference*. (Compilation). Marshfield, MO: First Fruits of Zion, 2013.

Janicki, Toby. "Remembering Yeshua's Chief Disciple: The Apostle Peter in Rabbinic Literature." *Messiah Journal* 112 (Winter 2013): 37–44.

Janicki, Toby. "The Apostolic Constitutions: A Christian Sabbath Amidah," *Messiah Journal* 114 (Fall 2013): 76–88.

Janicki, Toby. "The Ger Toshav Residing within Israel," *Messiah Journal* 120 (Summer 2015): 15–22.

Janicki, Toby. *God-Fearers: Gentiles & the God of Israel*. Marshfield, MO: First Fruits of Zion, 2012.

Janicki, Toby. *What about Tithing?* Marshfield, MO: First Fruits of Zion, 2014.

Jastrow, Marcus. *A Dictionary of the Targumim, the Talmud Babli and Yerushalmi, and the Midrashic Literature.* 2 vols. New York, NY: Pardes, 1950.

Jefford, Clayton N. "Authority and Perspective in the Didache." Pages 33–58 in *The Didache: A Missing Piece of the Puzzle in Early Jewish Christianity.* Edited by Jonathan A. Draper and Clayton N. Jefford. Atlanta, GA: Society of Biblical Literature, 2015.

Jefford, Clayton N. *Didache: The Teaching of the Twelve Apostles* (Salem, MA: Polebridge Press, 2013), 8-9

Jefford, Clayton N. *The Sayings of Jesus in the Teaching of the Twelve Apostles.* New York, NY: Brill, 1989.

Johnson, Sherman Elbridge. "A Subsidiary Motive for the Writing of the Didache." Pages 107 –122 in *Munera Studiosa.* Edited by Massey Hamilton Shepherd, Jr. and Sherman Elbridge Johnson. Cambridge, MA: Episcopal Theological School, 1946.

Jones, F. Stanley and Paul A. Mirecki. "Considerations on the Coptic Papyrus of the Didache." Pages 47–87 in *The Didache in Context: Essays on Its Text, History & Transmission.* Edited by Clayton N. Jefford. Leiden, The Netherlands: Brill, 1995.

Jones, Tony. *The Teaching of the Twelve: Believing & Practicing the Primitive Christianity of the Ancient Didache Community.* Brewster, MA: Paraclete, 2009.

Khomych, Taras, 2011 "Perfection in the Didache: Ethical Objective or Eschatological Hope?", StPatr 51: 3-13.

King, Rev. David, D.M., "Pericanonicity as Revealed in the Intellectuality of the Didache," (paper presented at the Early Christian Interpretations of Pauline and Synoptic Traditions, Rome, Italy, 3 July 2019).

Klijn, A.F.J. *Jewish-Christian Gospel Tradition.* Supplements to *Vigiliae Christianae* 17. Leiden, The Netherlands: Brill, 1993.

Kloppenborg, John S. "Poverty and Piety in Matthew, James, and the Didache." Pages 201–232 in *Matthew, James, and Didache: Three Related Documents in Their Jewish and Christian Settings.* Edited by Huub Van de Sandt and Jurgen K. Zangenberg. Atlanta, GA: Society of Biblical Literature, 2008.

Knappenberger, EK, "Enemy-Love and Moral Vision in Didache 1:3," Eastern Mennonite Seminary, 15 October 2016.

Kraemer, David C. "A Developmental Perspective on the Laws of Niddah." Pages 235–243 in *Exploring Judaism: The Collected Essays of David Kraemer.* Edited by David C. Kraemer. Atlanta, GA: Scholars, 1999.

Kraft, Robert. *Barnabas and the Didache.* Vol. 3 of *The Apostolic Fathers: A New and Commentary.* Edited by Robert M. Grant. New York, NY: Thomas Nelson, 1965.

Kramer, Chaim. *Rebbe Nachman's Torah: Genesis.* Edited by Y. Hall. New York, NY: Breslov Research Institute, 2011.

Krupnick, Eliyahu. *The Gateway to Learning: A Systematic Introduction to the Study of Talmud.* New York, NY: Feldheim, 1998.

La Sor, William Sanford. "Discovering What Jewish Miqva'ot Can Tell Us about Christian Baptism." *Biblical Archaeology Review* 13, no. 1 (January–February 1987): 52–59.

Lachs, Samuel Tobias. *A Rabbinic Commentary on the New Testament: The Gospels of Matthew, Mark and Luke.* Jersey City, NJ: KTAV, 1987.

Ladd, George Eldon. "The Eschatology of the Didache." Ph.D. diss., Harvard University, 1949.

Lake, Krisopp. *The Apostolic Fathers.* New York, NY: Macmillan, 1912.

Lake, Krisopp. *The Didache: Teaching of the Twelve Apostles.* Philadelphia, PA: Dalcassian Publishing, 2018.

Lancaster, D. Thomas. "Life of the Party: The Miracle of Changing Water to Wine." *Messiah Journal* 100 (Spring 2009): 21–25.

Lancaster, D. Thomas. "Simeon, Son of Clopas." *Messiah Journal* 112 (Winter 2013): 51–52.

Lancaster, D. Thomas. *Elementary Principles: Six Foundational Principles of Ancient Jewish Christianity.* Marshfield, MO: First Fruits of Zion, 2014.

Lancaster, D. Thomas. *Grafted In: Israel, Gentiles, and the Mystery of the Gospel.* Marshfield, MO: First Fruits of Zion, 2009.

Lancaster, D. Thomas. *The Holy Epistle to the Galatians.* Marshfield, MO: First Fruits of Zion, 2011.

Lancaster, D. Thomas. *Torah Club: Chronicles of the Apostles.* 6 vols. Marshfield, MO: First Fruits of Zion, 2016.

Lancaster, D. Thomas. *Torah Club: Chronicles of the Messiah.* 6 vols. Marshfield, MO: First Fruits of Zion, 2014.

Lancaster, D. Thomas. *Torah Club: Depths of the Torah.* 6 vols. Marshfield, MO: First Fruits of Zion, 2017.

Lancaster, D. Thomas. *Torah Club: Unrolling the Scroll.* 6 vols. Marshfield, MO: First Fruits of Zion, 2014.

Larsen, Matthew and Michael Svigel. "The First Century Two Ways Catechesis and Hebrews 6:1–6." Pages 477–496 in *The Didache: A Missing Piece of the Puzzle in Early Jewish Christianity.* Edited by Jonathan A. Draper and Clayton N. Jefford. Atlanta, GA: Society of Biblical Literature, 2015.

Le Cornu, Hilary and Joseph Shulam. *A Commentary on the Jewish Roots of Acts 1–15.* Jerusalem, Israel: Academon/Netivyah, 2003.

Levertoff, Paul Philip. *Love and the Messianic Age.* Marshfield, MO: Vine of David, 2009.

Levin, Rabbi Menachem Mendel. *Cheshbon HaNefesh: A Guide to Self-Improvement and Character Refinement.* Translated by Rabbi Shraga Silverstein. New York, NY: Feldheim, 1995.

Levine, Baruch A. *JPS Torah Commentary: Leviticus*. New York, NY: Jewish Publication Society, 1989.

Lichtenstein, Rabbi Aaron. *The Seven Laws of Noah*, 3rd edition. New York, NY: Rabbi Jacob Joseph School Press, 1995.

Lichtenstein, Yechiel Tzvi. *Commentary on the New Testament*. Translated by Aaron Eby and Robert Morris. Marshfield, MO: Vine of David, unpublished. of *Bi'ur Lesifrei Brit HaChadashah*. 8 vols. Leipzig, Germany: Professor G. Dahlman, 1891–1904.

Liebes, Yehudah. "Who Makes the Horn of Jesus to Flourish." *Immanuel* 21 (1987): 55–66.

Lietzmann, Hans. *Mass and Lord's Supper: A Study in the History of the Liturgy*. Leiden, The Netherlands: Brill, 1979.

Lightfoot, J.B. *The Apostolic Fathers*. London, England: Macmillan, 1898.

Lumpkin, Joseph. *The Didache: The Teaching of the Twelve Apostles: A Different Faith – A Different Salvation*. Blountsville, AL: Fifth Estate Press, 2012.

Luzzatto, Rabbi Moshe Chaim. *Path of the Just: Mesillas Yesharim*. Translated by Yosef Leibler. Nanuet, NY: Feldheim, 2004.

Majeski, Rabbi Shloma. *A Tzaddik and His Students: The Rebbe-Chassid Relationship*. Brooklyn, NY: Sichos in English, 2008.

Manns, Frederic. *Le Judeochristianisme, memoire ou prophetie*. Paris, France: Beauchesne, 2000.

Manson, T.W. *The Sayings of Jesus*. London, England: SCM, 1971.

Marmorstein, Rabbi A. *The Old Rabbinic Doctrine of God*. New York, NY: KTAV, 1968.

Martindale, Wayne and Jerry Root, eds. *The Quotable Lewis: An Encyclopedic Collection of Quotes from the Complete Published Works of C.S. Lewis*. Carol Stream, IL: Tyndale, 1990.

Mazza, Enrico. "Didache 9–10: Elements of a Eucharistic Interpretation." Pages 276–299 in *The Didache in Modern Research*. Edited by Jonathan A. Draper. Leiden, The Netherlands: Brill, 1996.

Mazza, Enrico. *The Celebration of the Eucharist: The Origin of the Rite and the Development of Its Interpretation*. Collegeville, MN: Liturgical, 1999.

McDonald, James I.H. *Kerygma and Didache: The Articulation and Structure of the Earliest Christian Message*. New York, NY: Cambridge University Press, 1980.

Metzger, Bruce M. "The Formulas Introducing Quotations of Scripture in the NT and the Mishnah." *Journal of Biblical Literature* 70, no. 4 (December 1951): 297–307.

Milavec, Aaron. "Gentile Identity in the Didache Communities as Early Signs of the Parting of the Ways." Paper presented at the annual meeting of the Society of Biblical Literature, San Antonio, TX, 23 November 2004.

Milavec, Aaron. "The Distress Signals of Didache Research." Pages 68–72 in *The Didache: A Missing Piece of the Puzzle in Early Jewish Christianity*. Edited by Jonathan A. Draper and Clayton N. Jefford. Atlanta, GA: Society of Biblical Literature, 2015.

Milavec, Aaron. *The Didache: Faith, Hope, & Life of the Earliest Christian Communities, 50–70 C.E.* New York, NY: Newman, 2003.

Milavec, Aaron. *The Didache: Text, , Analysis, and Commentary*. Collegeville, MN: Liturgical, 2003.

Milgrom, Jacob. *The JPS Torah Commentary: Numbers*. New York, NY: Jewish Publication Society, 1990.

Miller, Chris A. "Did Peter's Vision in Acts 10 Pertain to Men or the Menu?" *Bibliotheca Sacra* 159, no. 635 (2002): 302–317.

Millgram, Abraham. *Jewish Worship*. Philadelphia, PA: Jewish Publication Society, 1971.

Mitchell, Nathan. "Baptism in the Didache." Pages 227–255 in *The Didache in Context: Essays on Its Text, History & Transmission*. Edited by Clayton N. Jefford. Leiden, The Netherlands: Brill, 1995.

Moyes, Gordon. "A Fresh Look at New Testament Baptism." Cited 30 November 2011. Online: http://www.gordonmoyes.com/wp-content/uploads//FreshLookatBaptism.pdf.

Mueller, Joseph G. "The Ancient Church Order Literature: Genre or Tradition?" *Journal of Early Christian Studies* 15, no. 3 (Fall 2007): 337–380.

Murray, Michelle. *Playing A Jewish Game: Gentile Christian Judaizing in the First and Second Centuries CE*. Waterloo, Ontario: Wilfred Laurier University Press, 2004.

Nadler, Allan. "Holy Kugel: The Sanctification of Ashkenazic Ethnic Foods in Hasidism." Pages 193–214 in *Food and Judaism*. Vol. 15 of *Studies in Jewish Civilization*. Edited by Leonard J. Greenspoon, Ronald A. Simkins, and Gerald Shapiro. Omaha, NE: Creighton University Press, 2005.

Nanos, Mark D. *The Irony of Galatians: Paul's Letter in First-Century Context*. Minneapolis, MN: Fortress, 2002.

Nathan of Nemirov. *Rebbe Nachman's Wisdom*. Translated by Rabbi Aryeh Kaplan. Monsey, NY: Breslov Research Institute, 1973.

Nessim, Daniel F.J. "Didache and Trinity: Proto-Trinitarianism in an Early Christian Community." A paper presented at the annual meeting of the ETS. San Antonio, TX, November 16, 2006.

Nessim, Daniel. "Didache, Torah, Gentile and Jew: A Paradigm of Unity and Distinction." Ph.D. diss., University of Exeter, forthcoming.

Nestlebaum, Chana. *Positive Word Power: Building a Better World with the Words You Speak*. Edited by Shaindy Appelbaum. Brooklyn, NY: Mesorah, 2009.

Neustadter, David. "The Universal Nature of *Pru Urvu* and an Analysis of its Implications." *Tradition* 40, no. 4 (2007): 50–67.

Niederwimmer, Kurt. *The Didache: A Commentary*. Minneapolis, MN: Fortress Press, 1998.

O'Loughlin, Thomas. *The Didache: A Window on the Earliest Christians*. Grand Rapids, MI: Baker, 2010.

O'Loughlin, Thomas. "The Didache as a Source for Picturing the Earliest Christian Communities: The Case of the Practice of Fasting." Christian Origins:Worship, Belief and Society. Ed. K O'Mahony. Sheffield: Sheffield Academic Press, 2003. 83-112.

O'Loughlin, Thomas. "The Mission Strategy of the Didache," Transformation: An International Journal of Holisitic Mission Studies 2011 28: 77-92

Pardee, Nancy. *The Genre and Development of the Didache: A Text-Linguistic Analysis*. Tübingen, Germany: Mohr Siebeck, 2012.

Patai, Raphael. *The Messiah Texts: Jewish Legends of Three Thousand Years*. Detroit, MI: Wayne State University, 1988.

Peradse, Grigol. "Die Lehre der zwolf Apostel aus der georgischen Uberlieferung." *Zeitschrift fur die neutestamentliche Wissenschaft und die Kunde der alteren Kirche* 31 (1932): 111–116.

Perrin, Norman. *Rediscovering the Teaching of Jesus*. New York, NY: Harper & Row, 1976.

Pines, Shlomo. *The Jewish Christians of the Early Centuries of Christianity According to a New Source*. Jerusalem, Israel: Central, 1966.

Reed, Jonathan. "The Hebrew Epic and the Didache." Pages 211–225 in *The Didache in Context: Essays on Its Text, History & Transmission*. Edited by Clayton N. Jefford. New York, NY: Brill, 1995.

Rhodes, James N. "The Two Ways Tradition in the Epistle of Barnabas: Revisiting an Old Question." *The Catholic Biblical Quarterly* 73 (2011): 797–816.

Roberts, Alexander and James Donaldson. *Fathers of the Third and Fourth Centuries*. Vol. 7 of *The Ante-Nicene Fathers*. Edited by A Cleveland Cox et al. New York, NY: Christian Literature Publishing, 1886.

Robinson, J.M. *The Sayings of Gospel Q: Collected Essays*. Edited by C. Heil and J. Verheyden. Bibliotheca Ephemeridum Theologicarum Lovaniensium. Leuven, Belgium: Peeters, 2005.

Robinson, John A.T. *Jesus and His Coming*. Second edition. Philadelphia, PA: Westminster, 1979.

Rordorf, Willy and Andre Tuilier. *La Doctrine des Douze Apotres (Didache)*. Paris, France: Cerf, 1978.

Rordorf, Willy. "Baptism According to the Didache." Pages 212–222 in *The Didache in Modern Research*. Edited by Jonathan A. Draper. Leiden, The Netherlands: Brill, 1996.

Rosenberg, Rabbi A.J. *Genesis: A New English* . 3 vols. New York, NY: Judaica, 1993.

Rosenberg, Rabbi A.J. *Shemoth: A New English*. 2 vols. New York, NY: Judaica, 1995.

Rudder, Joshua. *The Two Ways: A Lost Early Christian Manual of Personal and Communal Ethics, Discipline and Morality*. Los Angeles, CA: Native Language, 2009.

Sadan, Tzvi. *The Concealed Light: Names of Messiah in Jewish Sources*. Marshfield, MO: Vine of David, 2012.

Saeki, P.Y. *The Nestorian Documents and Relics in China*. Tokyo, Japan: The Toho Bunka Gakuin, 1951.

Safrai, Shmuel. "Early Testimonies in the New Testament of Laws and Practices Relating to Pilgrimage and Passover." Pages 41–51 in *Jesus' Last Week: Jerusalem Studies in the Synoptic Gospels*. Edited by R. Steven Notley, Marc Turnage, and Brian Becker. Boston, MA: Brill, 2006.

Sandelin, Karl-Gustav. *Wisdom as Nourisher*. Turku, Finland: Abo Akademi, 1986.

Sarna, Nahum M. *JPS Torah Commentary: Exodus*. Philadelphia, PA: Jewish Publication Society, 1991.

Sarna, Nahum M. *The JPS Torah Commentary: Genesis*. New York, NY: Jewish Publication Society, 1989.

"*Savlanut*—Patience 2," 21, n.p. Cited 3 October 2013. Online: http://www.mussarleadership.org/pdfs/Savlanut%202.pdf .

Schaff, Philip. *The Oldest Church Manual Called the Teaching of the Twelve Apostles*. Edinburgh, Scotland: T&T Clark, 1885.

Schechter, Solomon and Kaufman Kohler. "Didache." Pages 4:585–588 in *Jewish Encyclopedia*. New York, NY: KTAV, 1906.

Scheinbaum, Rabbi A.L. *Peninim on the Torah: An Anthology of Thought-Provoking Ideas, Practical Insights, and Review Questions & Answers on the Weekly Parsha Fifth Series*. Cleveland Heights, OH: Peninim, 1998.

Scherman, Rabbi Nosson and Rabbi Meir Lebowitz, eds. *Yad Avraham Mishnah Series: Seder Tohoros*. 10 vols. Brooklyn, NY: Mesorah, 2001.

Scherman, Rabbi Nosson and Rabbi Meir Zlotowitz, eds. *Yad Avraham Mishnah Series: Seder Zeraim*. 8 vols. Brooklyn, NY: Mesorah, 2003.

Scherman, Rabbi Nosson. *The Complete ArtScroll Siddur: Nusach Ashkenaz*. Brooklyn, NY: Mesorah, 2007.

Schille, Gottfried. "Das Recht der Propheten und Apostel—Gemeinderechtliche Beobachtungen zu Didache Kapitel 11–13." *Theologische Versuche* I. Edited by P. Watzel and G. Schille. Berlin, Germany: Evangelische Verlaganstalt, 1966.

Schneerson, Rabbi Menachem Mendel. *HaYom Yom: From Day to Day*. Brooklyn, NY: Otzar Hachassidim Lubavitch, 2006.

Schneerson, Rabbi Menachem Mendel. *Proceeding Together: The Earliest Talks of the Lubavitcher Rebbe Rabbi Menachem M. Schneerson*. Translated by Uri Kaploun. 4 vols. Brooklyn, NY: Sichos in English, 1995.

Schwartz, Rabbi Avraham Tzvi. "Deceit and Truth." Cited 02 October 2013. Online: https://sharings.wordpress.com/2009/05/21/self-growth-keep-smiling-27th-iyar-5769/.

Schwartz, Rabbi Yoel. *Service from the Heart: Renewing the Ancient Path of Biblical Prayer and Service*. Edited by Rabbi Michael Katz et al. Rose, OK: Oklahoma B'nai Noah Society, 2007.

Segal, Philip. "Early Christian and Rabbinic Liturgical Affinities." *New Testament Studies* 30 (1984): 63–90.

Simon, Marcel. "The Apostolic Decree and Its Setting in the Ancient Church." *Bulletin of the John Rylands Library* 52, no. 2 (1969–1970): 437–460.

Skarsaune, Oskar and Reidar Hvalvik. *Jewish Believers in Jesus: The Early Centuries*. Peabody, MA: Hendrickson, 2007.

Skarsaune, Oskar. *In the Shadow of the Temple: Jewish Influences on Early Christianity*. Downers Grove, IL: InterVarsity Press, 2002.

Smith, Murray J. "The Lord Jesus and His Coming in the Didache." Pages 363–407 in *The Didache: A Missing Piece of the Puzzle in Early Christianity*. Edited by Jonathan A. Draper and Clayton N. Jefford. Atlanta, GA: Society of Biblical Literature, 2015.

Spence, Canon. *The Teaching of the Twelve Apostles*. London, England: James Nisbet and Co., 1885.

Sperber, Daniel. *Why Jews Do What They Do: The History of Jewish Customs Throughout the Cycle of the Jewish Year*. Hoboken, NJ: KTAV, 1999.

Spivak, E.J. *A Christian-Jewish School: Didache, Doctrina, Matthew*. PhD dissertation. Department of Divinity and Religious Studies. Aberdeen, Scotland: Aberdeen University, (2007).

Steinsaltz, Rabbi Adin. *The Talmud Steinsaltz Edition: A Reference Guide*. New York, NY: Random, 1989.

Stewart (-Sykes), Alistair. *On the Two Ways: Life or Death, Light or Darkness: Foundational Texts in the Tradition*. Yonkers, NY: St. Vladimir's Seminary Press, 2011.

Stewart, Alistar C., "Didache 14: Eucharistic?" QL 93 (2012), 3–16.

Stokl Ben Ezra, Daniel. *The Impact of Yom Kippur on Early Christianity: The Day of Atonement from Second Temple Judaism to the Fifth Century*. Tübingen, Germany: Mohr Siebeck, 2003.

Stuiber, Alfred. "'Das ganze Joch des Herrn' (Didache 6.2–3)." Pages 323–329 in *Studia Patristica* 4.2. TU 79. Berlin, Germany: Akademie-Verlag, 1961.

Sturcke, Henry. "Branches on the Vine of David: What Can the *Didache* Tell Us about the Sabbath in the Early Jesus Movement?" (unpublished).

Svirsky, Meira. *A Woman's Mitzvah: A Fully Sourced Guide to the Laws of Family Purity.* Jerusalem, Israel: Old City, 2007.

Syreeni, Kari. "The Sermon on the Mount and the Two Ways Teaching of the Didache." Pages 95–96 in *Matthew and the Didache: Two Documents from the Same Jewish-Christian Milieu?* Edited by Huub van de Sandt. Minneapolis, MN: Fortress, 2005.

Taylor, Charles. "The Teaching of the Twelve Apostles with Illustrations from the Talmud." Pages 146–205 in *Didache: The Unknown Teaching of the Twelve Apostles.* Edited by Brent S. Walters. San Jose, CA: Anti-Nicene Archive, 1991.

Taylor, Joan. *The Immerser: John the Baptist within Second Temple Judaism.* Grand Rapids, MI: Eerdmans, 1997.

Teicher, J.L. "Ancient Eucharistic Prayers in Hebrew (Dura-Europos Parchment D. Pg. 25)." *Jewish Quarterly Review* 54, no. 2 (October 1963): 99–109.

Telfer, William. "The Didache and the Apostolic Synod of Antioch." *Journal of Theological Studies* 40 (1939): 133–146, 258–271.

Thayer, Joseph H. *Thayer's Greek-English Lexicon of the New Testament.* Peabody, MA: Hendrickson, 2000.

Tidwell, Neville. "Didache XIV:1 (*Kata Kuriaken de Kuriou*) Revisited." *Vigiliae Christianae* 53, no. 2 (1999): 197–207.

Tigay, Jeffrey. *JPS Torah Commentary: Deuteronomy.* Philadelphia, PA: Jewish Publication Society, 1996.

Tilton, Joshua N. *Jesus' Gospel: Searching for the Core of Jesus' Message.* Joshua N. Tilton, 2013.

Tomson, Peter J. *'If This Be from Heaven ...': Jesus and the New Testament Authors in Their Relationship to Judaism.* Sheffield, England: Sheffield Academic, 2001.

Tomson, Peter J. *Paul and the Jewish Law: Halakha in the Letters of the Apostle to the Gentiles.* Minneapolis, MN: Fortress, 1990.

Tuckett, Christopher M. "The Didache and the Writings That Later Formed the New Testament." Pages 83–127 in *The Reception of the New Testament in the Apostolic Fathers.* Edited by Andrew F. Gregory and Christopher M. Tuckett. New York, NY: Oxford University Press, 2005.

Tuckett, Christopher M. "Synoptic Tradition in the Didache." Pages 92–128 in *The Didache in Modern Research.* Edited by Jonathan A. Draper. Leiden, The Netherlands: Brill, 1996.

Van de Sandt, Huub and David Flusser. *The Didache: Its Jewish Sources and Its Place in Early Judaism and Christianity.* Minneapolis, MN: Fortress, 2002.

Van de Sandt, Huub. "'Do Not Give What Is Holy to the Dogs' (Did 9:5d and Matt 7:6a): The Eucharistic Food of the Didache in Its Jewish Purity Setting." *Vigiliae Christianae* 56, no. 3 (August 2002): 223–246.

Van de Sandt, Huub. "Law and Ethics in Matthew's Antitheses and James's Letter: A Reorientation of Halakah in Line with the Jewish Two Ways 3:1–6." Pages 91–122 in *Matthew, James, and Didache: Three Related Documents in Their Jewish and Christian Settings*. Edited by Huub van de Sandt and Jurgen K. Zangenberg. Atlanta, GA: Society of Biblical Literature, 2008.

Van de Sandt, Huub, ed. "Two Windows on a Developing Jewish-Christian Reproof Practice: Matt 18:15–17 and Did. 15:3." Pages 173–192 in *Matthew and the Didache: Two Documents from the Same Jewish-Christian Milieu?* Minneapolis, MN: Fortress, 2005.

Van der Horst, P.W., ed. *The Sentences of Pseudo-Phocylides*. Leiden, The Netherlands: Brill, 1978.

Van der Meer, Frederick and Christine Mohrmann. *Atlas of the Early Christian World*. London, England: Nelson, 1966.

Varner, William. "The Didache's Use of the Old and New Testaments." *The Master's Seminary Journal* 16, no. 1 (Spring 2005): 127–151.

Varner, William. *The Way of the Didache: The First Christian Handbook*. New York, NY: University Press of America, 2007.

Verheyden, Joseph. "Eschatology in the Didache and the Gospel of Matthew." Pages 193–215 in *Matthew and the Didache: Two Documents from the Same Jewish-Christian Milieu?* Edited by Huub van de Sandt. Minneapolis, MN: Fortress, 2005.

Vermes, Geza. "From Jewish to Gentile: How the Jesus Movement became Christianity." *Biblical Archeology Review* 38, no. 6 (November/December 2012): 53–58, 74.

Voobus, Arthur. *Liturgical Traditions in the Didache*. Wetteren, Belgium: Cultura, 1968.

Wagshul, Rabbi Yitzchok Dovid. "Torah Or: Exodus." New York, NY: Purity Press, unpublished book.

Walker, Joan Hazelden. "A Pre-Marcan Dating for the Didache: Further Thoughts of a Liturgist." *Studia Biblica* 3 (1978): 403–411.

Watson, Wilfred G.E. *Classical Hebrew Poetry: A Guide to Its Techniques*. Sheffield, England: JSOT, 1986.

Weinberger, Rabbi Dovid. *The Artscroll Women's Siddur: Sefard*. Brooklyn, NY: Artscroll, 2005.

Weiner, Rabbi Moshe and Rabbi J. Immanuel Schochet. *Prayers, Blessings, Principles of Faith, and Divine Service for Noahides*. Edited by Dr. Michael Schulman. Pittsburgh, PA: Ask Noah International, 2010.

Weiner, Rabbi Moshe. *The Divine Code*. Second edition. Edited by Dr. Michael Schulman. Pittsburgh, PA: Ask Noah International, 2011.

Weren, Wim J.C. "The 'Ideal Community' according to Matthew, James, and the Didache." Page 186 n.14 in *Matthew, James, and Didache: Three Related Documents in Their*

Jewish and Christian Settings. Edited by Huub van de Sandt and Jurgen K. Zangenberg. Atlanta, GA: Society of Biblical Literature, 2008.

Williams, Ronald James. *Williams' Hebrew Syntax*. Third edition. Edited by John C. Beckman. Toronto, Canada: University of Toronto, 2007.

Willitts, Joel. "The Bride of Messiah and the Israel-ness of the New Heavens and New Earth." Pages 245–254 in *Introduction to Messianic Judaism*. Edited by David Rudolph and Joel Willitts. Grand Rapids, MI: Zondervan, 2013.

Wink, Walter. *Engaging the Powers: Discernment and Resistance in a World of Domination*. Minneapolis, MN: Fortress, 1992.

Yadin, Yigael. *Tefillin from Qumran (XQ Phyl 1–4)*. Jerusalem, Israel: Israel Exploration Society, 1969.

Yitzchak of Berditchev, Rabbi Levi. *Kedushat Levi*. Translated by Eliyahu Munk. Brooklyn, NY: Lambda, 2009.

Young, Brad. *Jesus the Jewish Theologian*. Peabody, MA: Hendrickson, 1995.

Zaloshinsky, Rabbi Gavriel. *The Ways of the Tzaddikim*. Translated by Rabbi Shraga Silverstein. 2 vols. New York, NY: Feldheim, 1996.

Zangenberg, Jurgen K. "Reconstructing the Social and Religious Milieu of the Didache: Methods, Sources, and Possible Results." Pages 43–69 in *Matthew, James, and Didache: Three Related Documents in Their Jewish and Christian Settings*. Edited by Huub van de Sandt and Jurgen K. Zangenberg. Atlanta, GA: Society of Biblical Literature, 2008.

Zetterholm, Magnus. *The Formation of Christianity in Antioch: A Social-Scientific Approach to the Separation between Judaism and Christianity*. London, England: Routledge, 2005.

Zlotowitz, Rabbi Meir. *Shir HaShirim: Song of Songs/A New with a Commentary Anthologized from Talmudic, Midrashic and Rabbinic Sources*. Brooklyn, NY: Mesorah, 2000.

www.ingramcontent.com/pod-product-compliance
Lightning Source LLC
Chambersburg PA
CBHW081426070526
44586CB00020B/2503